Poems of
BYRON, KEATS
and SHELLEY

POEMS OF
BYRON, KEATS
and SHELLEY

Selected and Edited by

ELLIOTT COLEMAN

Illustrations by Barnett I. Plotkin

DOUBLEDAY & COMPANY, Inc.   GARDEN CITY, NEW YORK

To Malcolm C. Moos *and* Charles L. Sherman

All Rights Reserved

CONTENTS

JOHN KEATS
1795–1821

PERCY BYSSHE SHELLEY
1792–1822

CONTENTS

FOREWORD

Byron, Keats, and Shelley were born mature and so could die young and leave behind, in the cases of Byron and Shelley a vast amount of poetry, in the case of Keats, a wealth of it. All were in the vanguard of thinking for their own day, and all remain surprisingly germane today. Though they championed different causes and though their short lives took varying directions, their ideals interacted, bringing a freshness of vision very nearly unsurpassed in English poetry. Their names invariably come to our minds as a literary triumvirate, standing for youthful vigor and lyric beauty, and for depth and maturity at an early age.

All three were social philosophers, though Byron and Shelley had the time, strength, and impulse to make their convictions more explicit than did Keats. They opted for the good and for the light over the dark in their fierce fight against sham, injustice, cruelty, ugliness, ignorance, and cant. In theory and in practice, they invariably end by celebrating truth, beauty, and love. Many of these celebrations in verse are universally known, and they appear in this collection as grand conclusions. In prose, and often in letters, the three authors have been joined in the same communion.

They may differ in matters of taste or technicality. It is interesting to recall Keats's distaste for Alexander Pope; and not so much Byron's extravagant admiration of Pope, but the fact that he based it first of all upon Pope's positive moral influence. A great deal of the work included in this collection is the work of darkness, the reproduction of the dark side of things. Here two of the three have few peers, though they bow to Homer, Sophocles, Dante, and Shakespeare. To Milton? To Goethe? From the other side would they nod to Baudelaire, to Leopardi, to Unamuno, to Joyce, to Proust? In any event, Byron in *Don Juan,* and

Shelley in *The Cenci* and elsewhere make certain twentieth-century *darklingers* look pallid. Besides his underlying sadness, Keats gives a darker sense of what he can do in *La Belle Dame Sans Merci*. For a sober experience of the diabolic, read portions of Shelley. For human savagery that is horrifying to read, see the episode of shipwreck in *Don Juan* that is followed by cannibalism in a jaunty meter.

Shelley was not only a moral philosopher but also an aesthetician, and morality and aesthetics come together in the essay which he called *A Defence of Poetry* but which in spite of the title took the initiative. Accused of being an amoralist or even an immoralist, Shelley first clears poetry of the charge of immorality by showing why by its nature it must be moral:

> The whole objection, however, of the immorality of poetry rests upon a misconception of the manner in which poetry acts to produce the moral improvement of man. Ethical science arranged the elements which poetry had created, and propounds schemes and proposes examples of civil and domestic life: nor is it for want of admirable doctrines that men hate, and despise, and censure, and deceive, and subjugate one another. But poetry acts in another and diviner manner. It awakens and enlarges the mind itself by rendering it the receptacle of a thousand unapprehended combinations of thought. Poetry lifts the veil from the hidden beauty of the world, and makes familiar things be as if they were not familiar; it reproduces all that it represents, and the impersonations clothed in its Elysian light stand thenceforward in the minds of those who have once contemplated them, as memorials of that gentle and exalted content which extends itself over all thoughts and actions in which it coexists. The great secret of morals is love; or a going out of our own nature, and an identification of ourselves with the beautiful which exists in thought, action, or person, not our own. A man, to be greatly good, must imagine intensely and comprehensively; he must put himself in the place of another and of many others. The pains and pleasures of his species must become his own. The great instrument of moral good is the imagination; and poetry administers to

the effect by acting upon the cause. Poetry enlarges the circumference of the imagination by replenishing it with thoughts of ever new delight, which have the power of attracting and assimilating to their own nature all other thoughts, and which form new intervals and interstices whose void forever craves fresh food. Poetry strengthens the faculty which is the organ of the moral nature of man, in the same manner as exercise strengthens a limb.

Poetry reproduces what it represents. How familiar is the example of beauty in *To a Skylark:*

> Higher, still, and higher,
>   From the earth thou springest!
> Like a cloud of fire
>   The blue deep thou wingest!
> And, singing, still dost soar, and soaring ever singest . . .

How true is the identification of the person of the poet with the person and the action of this marvelous creature. But Shelley gives precedence to the higher thought that the great instrument of *moral* good is the imagination. Utterance must be *truly* imaginative to be poetry at all. Yet Shelley sees a danger and issues a warning to poets against too strictly embodying in their expressions concepts of right and wrong. These concepts may be too close to their own time and place. Although the greatest poets do not err in this respect, those whose faculty is less intense—he names Euripides, Lucan, Tasso, and Spenser—"have frequently affected a moral aim, and the effect of their poetry is diminished in exact proportion to the degree in which they compel us to advert to this purpose."

Among the pleasures of reading Shelley's great essay are the good shocks: the statement that the true poetry of a people may live in its institutions, as with Rome; the reminders that when poetic composition begins, inspiration is already on the decline, and that the best poetry is a feeble shadow of the original conception; the observation that poetry, unlike reasoning, is not a power to be exerted according to the will; the assertion that "the abolition of personal slavery is the basis of the highest political hope that it can enter into the mind of man to conceive"; the conclusion that Dante's "apotheosis of Beatrice in

xiv FOREWORD

Paradise, and the gradations of his own love and her loveliness, by which as by steps he feigns himself to have ascended to the throne of the Supreme Cause, is the most glorious imagination of modern poetry."

According to Shelley, "Poetry acts in a divine and unapprehended manner, beyond and above consciousness." Here he is prophetic. And for our epoch, an epoch when many of the poems of the highest intensity were to be written in prose, he is prophetic again but has yet to be heeded: "The distinction between poets and prose writers is a vulgar error."

Not only by the standards of today but by the standards of their day, Byron and Shelley, for men in their twenties, were erudite. Versed in several languages and literatures, they were translators as well as originators. The young Keats had the advantage of a good schooling, including a medical apprenticeship of several years, but due to some early difficulties and to his later very poor health, he was behind the other two in learning, though he was remarkably informed and strove to learn to the end. At the close of his life his most intense creations were the most original of all. He has been conceived as the most really personal and emotional of the three in his love poems,

> Pillow'd upon my fair love's ripening breast,
> To feel for ever its soft fall and swell,
> Awake for ever in a sweet unrest,
> Still, still to hear her tender-taken breath . . .

but the philosophic Keats is a psychologist of art. It is well, particularly in comparison with Shelley's views, to consider what Keats wrote in a letter to Richard Woodhouse in 1818:

As to the poetical Character itself (I mean that sort, of which, if I am anything, I am a member; that sort distinguished from the Wordsworthian, or egotistical Sublime; which is a thing per se, and stands alone,) it is not itself— it has no self— It is everything and nothing— It has no character—it enjoys light and shade; it lives in gusto, be it foul or fair, high or low, rich or poor, mean or elevated— It has as much delight in conceiving an Iago as an Imogen. What shocks the virtuous philosopher delights the chameleon poet. It does no harm from its relish of the dark side of

things, any more than its taste for the bright one, because
they both end in speculation. A poet is the most unpoetical of anything in existence, because he has no Identity—
he is continually in for and filling some other body. The
Sun,—the Moon,—the Sea, and men and women, who are
creatures of impulse, are poetical, and have about them an
unchangeable attribute; the poet has none, no identity—he
is certainly the most unpoetical of all God's creatures . . .
It is a wretched thing to confess; but it is a very fact, that
not one word I ever utter can be taken for granted as an
opinion growing out of my identical Nature—how can it
be when I have no Nature? When I am in a room with people, if I am ever free from speculating on creations of my
own brain, then, not myself goes home to myself, but the
identity of everyone in the room begins to press upon me,
so that I am in a very little time annihilated—not only
among men; it would be the same in a nursery of Children.

Keats's sense of the oppression upon him of other identities and of
his personal annihilation, because of his vocation of unpoetical poet,
counters Shelley's imperative for the poet to identify with others, with
all men at all costs because of his vocation to poethood. The imperative
was profoundly met in his own life. The important thing is that the
art of both poets involves a lessening of the self, a giving of it away to
others. And although this recognition is less explicit in Byron's theory
and practice of poetry, it is implicit in his life and in his art.

There are narratives in Shelley and Keats, especially in their poems
of classical mythology, and even in Byron, which have to be broken up.
They seem interminable, and they are intolerable. Chunks of them,
broken off, make good reading precisely because the story line has disappeared. Poetry tomorrow may have to come in instantaneous sharp
fragments, from the preconscious, surrounded by silences, glowing with
light, swelling, receding in sound, palpitating in space. Much of the
poetry of today plods on in the same old will-directed grind to repeat
a vanished past. Much of the poetry of yesterday, if forced to appear
today, at once does a vanishing act; it simply cannot exist for us. But
great poets survive. They are everlasting. Fed by subterranean forces
and electrified by celestial lights, they are perpetually in orbit. And

debonair poets such as Byron, Keats, and Shelley, great persons that they are, speak to us today directly, in magnificent fragmentations.

One element which leads today's reader to speculation is the solid place of war in things. Byron is the poet of war, and to read Byron is to go to war and to survive and to ask "Why?" The shocking poetry of war in Byron hardly calls for fragmentation. It remains intact, and does the fragmentizing, because despite all the modern inventions, war today remains to a considerable extent the hand-to-hand Byronic war. There is also the spirit of withholding the hand forever in the modern covetousness and the compulsion to power, a spirit which robs humanity of even mortal contact. Still, it seems to be possible to kill or to shake, and the episodes that stun in Byron are at the same time often ironical at horror though never at the horror of the lust for massacre.

Byron, for all his fascination for and involvement with war and conflict, was a social philosopher—a moralist and aesthetician. His prophetic vision of labor and hire was demonstrated when he spoke before the House of Lords in 1811, and a fine example of his moral vision is presented in the drama *Cain*. In any case, rarely would his writings on war or his thoughts on labor and automation be reprinted alongside

> She walks in beauty, like the night
> Of cloudless climes and starry skies . . .

But of course the cloudless climes and starry skies make their reappearances here, often to quite extended lengths, for Byron, Keats, and Shelley are poets of love—outstandingly so. Byron has more love affairs in his poems than the others. He had more love affairs. Is there anyone who in one way or another knew more about the subject? Though Shelley was a kind of self-appointed authority on what true love is, he was more exacting with himself in drawing the lines and in trying to make the world follow: the lines of the unselfish dedication of every lover. In some true sense, Keats died of love, a love far more than that for himself.

So love proceeds in many gradations and forms throughout the poems of the three poets of love, as they hold their youthful, nearly shattered balance: Byron by his humor, Keats by his wit, and Shelley by his magnanimity.

> Maid of Athens, ere we part,
> Give, oh, give me back my heart!

And there shall be for thee all soft delight
That shadowy thought can win,
A bright torch, and a casement ope at night,
To let the warm love in!

And so thy thoughts, when thou art gone,
Love itself shall slumber on.

    It had been the purpose of this marveling reader not to use the word *romantic* in any preface to these selections. Perhaps it must be used this once to call some attention to its not being used. Byron, Keats, and Shelley may have "drunk the milk of Paradise," but too often and for too long one aspect of their inclinations and accomplishments has been used as a label that limits them. Their range is too great for that. And their sources and resources, ancient and modern, are too complex for that.

    Actually, in a deep and abiding sense, all three of these poets are classicists. They were imbued with classical education and disciplined by it all their short lives. Although Greek influence came later upon Keats, both Shelley and Keats were far too full of it. They had to have recourse to Greek mythology because original Christian acts and terms had been debased and would not do for them. In all three, except in their highest moments (fortunately there are plenty of those), old and rigid forms often dominate, and sometimes distort, their poetic thought.

    On the other hand it is true with all alert writers that form can dictate thought and even raise it to a subtlety and a strength otherwise unattainable at that point or maybe any point. Nevertheless a deadening can set in through formality; it occasionally does with these poets. Although we feel it more than some of their contemporaries, the attention of those contemporaries was distracted to what was new in the versification of these bright and willful young men, and mostly they condemned it. What was new was the hope of a future poetry in English. It is the reason for the publication of this book. It is that newness, as Sir Herbert Read has well shown, which repeatedly brings to life the deepest experience of life, an experience which then becomes codified, often brilliantly, for a period. Some of that newness persists as new for some time in the codification till everything dries up and is ready for burning. But another phoenix springs afresh. Paradoxically, it is both brand new and yet recognizable because it has the same lines or the same outlines of the old bird. The colors are different.

With a thorough view of English verse a constant in their minds, Byron, Keats, and Shelley began as boys to versify. Much of what they wrote was verse of no real distinction except for its fidelity to models, but early in the cases of Byron and Shelley, and suddenly in the case of Keats, who started later, they all were poets. It is interesting to see how they took their vocation and how they took each other. Byron was serious about even the most hilarious of his poems, as his voluminous notes on all his poetry show, but he did not take himself too seriously. He could be careless. Keats had to take himself as well as his poetry more seriously because of increasing uncertainties and anxieties that became excruciating, and because of the tuberculosis that turned his attention so much to himself and destroyed him. Byron was moved by the remarkable Gamba family to help the Italians whose cause he favored. He was moved by Greece to help the Greeks toward independence; he died during that effort. Shelley, it is true, was a vehement social reformer in the abstract and very sincerely so, but the wide generosity of his nature most expressed itself in a personal way. He wanted to help everybody, and he helped many. And he thought almost any poet who was good was better than he. He considered Byron a far better poet than himself, and later on, Matthew Arnold, who was born the year Shelley drowned, agreed with him. To a considerable degree, Byron reciprocated Shelley's esteem, and not simply as the result of Shelley's adulation. Keats greatly admired Byron, though he was reserved about Shelley. When not reserved, he could be quite sharply, if justifiably, critical. It is appropriate that Keats's section in this collection begin with a tribute to Byron, that Shelley's section end with a sonnet to Byron; it is splendid that Shelley's section should begin with *Adonais*, the completely selfless elegy to the dead Keats. Byron's tribute to its author was to stand by his pyre on the beach of the Ligurian Sea.

This anthology presents the three poets not *by* alphabetical order, though they are *in* that order, but by compromise in a temporal scheme. Byron was born first and lived to thirty-six, surviving both the others. Shelley was born next and lived to within a month of thirty, surviving Keats. Keats was born last and did not live quite four months past twenty-five.

Born		Died
1788	BYRON	1824
1795	KEATS	1821
1792	SHELLEY	1822

It is safe to say that the best of a good writer is in his works and that the reader does not need to know his life to know his mind. In large part this is true, especially of poets, whether they write in verse or in prose, for the poet wears no mask. Unconsciously, preconsciously, consciously, he expresses his reality. In the instances of these three particular poets, however, an acquaintance with the storms and tragedies of their personal lives assists the understanding of their poetry.

Suffering entered these hearts, and suffering has a way of making some people do more than they otherwise might have done. The deformity, the early griefs, the later ambiguities of George Gordon Noël, Lord Byron (sixth Baron); the short stature, the unreturned love, the sickness of John Keats; the noble, misread turmoil in the destiny of Percy Bysshe Shelley and his underestimation of his own work—these things may actually have brought these three men to that need and desire which stirs the depths to give up to the conscious spirit the means unknown till then of performing actions of the highest significance in life, in art, and through such products as *Stanzas to the Po*, or *Ode on a Grecian Urn*, or *Ode to the West Wind*, to transform the minds of us all.

Life of life! thy lips enkindle . . .

ELLIOTT COLEMAN

GEORGE GORDON, LORD BYRON

(1788–1824)

N THE YEAR 1785 an ex-naval officer and notorious scapegrace named "Mad Jack" Byron arrived in Bath, the mecca of fortune hunters. Captain Byron had previously eloped with the wife of the Marquess of Carmarthen, but having run through that lady's fortune and survived her death in France, he was seeking a replacement. He found a short, unattractive Scots heiress named Kitty Gordon, whom he boldly courted and captured in the face of her family's protests and bore triumphantly to France. Two years later the new Mrs. Byron was back in England, disillusioned and pregnant. The baby was born in a London lodging house on January 22, 1788.

George Gordon Byron arrived in the world with a defective foot, a lameness which troubled him all his life, evidently the product of the clumsy obstetrics of the day. His father saw the child only once. Appearing unexpectedly in London, he asserted his parental rights and carried the infant off, only to bring him back to his mother the next morning, complaining that he had cried all night. Mad Jack returned to France and died soon after.

Oddly, Kitty Gordon Byron romanticized her late husband, especially over her whisky bottle. As soon as he was old enough to listen, the little boy was entertained with tales of his father's family distinction and heroism in the American war. When the lad was six, Kitty abruptly changed her tune and in an alcoholic outburst damned all the Byrons, with special emphasis on Captain Jack.

At seven the lad indicated one direction his life was to take by falling in love with a girl named Mary Duff, to whom he was still so attached nine years later that news of her marriage caused him to fly into a rage. Before that, he had received a very different piece of news while a ten-year-old student at Aberdeen Grammar School. The headmaster summoned him to his study, solemnly informed him that the death of his grandfather had made him Lord Byron, and gave him a slice of cake and a glass of wine. So affected was the lad by his elevation to the nobility that when he was addressed at rollcall as *"Dominum,"* he was unable to make the customary reply of *"Adsum."*

The estate itself proved something of a disappointment. Newstead Abbey was a fine property which the late Lord Byron, a notorious eccentric, had allowed to fall into decay. Hardly habitable, it produced little income. Nevertheless, there was some money, and the glory of the title did not tarnish. Mrs. Gordon liked to introduce her boy as "My son, Lord Byron." Among those to whom she introduced him was Augusta, daughter of Mad Jack by his first wife, who was being raised by her maternal grandmother, Lady Holderness. Byron and Augusta liked each other at sight.

In 1801 the young Lord entered Harrow, where he distinguished himself by many quarrels and fights, including one successful defense of a bust of Napoleon which his schoolfellows wanted to smash. He was popular, and even idolized by the younger boys, and despite his lameness played cricket against Eton. Late in 1804 he entered Cambridge, where he found life thoroughly to his liking and where he at once took to spending extravagantly on wine, women, song, clothes, and furnishings. Very soon he was in financial difficulties, his appointed legal guardian refusing to advance him further sums, and he fell into the hands of moneylenders. By the time he came of age in 1809 his debts had reached £12,000—upwards of $200,000 of modern U.S. currency.

Considerably more galling was the failure of a little book of verses, *Hours of Idleness,* which he had gotten printed, and to which the magisterial Tory *Edinburgh Review* accorded a gratuitous and scathing notice. Byron masked his fury with affected indifference and set to work at once on a satiric revenge titled *English Bards and Scotch Reviewers,* in which he demonstrated a real talent for irony and invective.

Money problems notwithstanding, Byron made plans for a "Grand Tour," not exactly of Europe, at the moment dominated by Napoleon and mostly at war with Great Britain, but of the Mediterranean region. Borrowing recklessly, he set off, accompanied by his closest Cambridge friend, John Cam Hobhouse, three servants, and a sparring partner. At Seville a Spanish lady of mature years invited him to live with her. At Malta he carried on a possibly Platonic affair with the Austrian wife of a British Consul and almost fought a duel. In Albania he was royally entertained by the Turkish governor. In Greece he had an affair with a twelve-year-old beauty named Teresa Macri, and perhaps with her sisters as well. He thought of taking Teresa with him on his travels, but her mother demanded too large a payment and so instead he wrote one of his most famous early poems, *Maid of Athens*. He swam the Hellespont in company with Mr. Ekinhead, a lieutenant of marines, visited Constantinople, re-dallied in Greece, and finally returned to England in the summer of 1811, having been abroad two years.

English Bards had won him a bit of renown in his absence and he now offered to one Robert Dallas, who had been instrumental in getting the previous work printed, a paraphrase of Horace's "Art of Poetry" which he had written as a follow-up. Dallas, disappointed, pressed for something else, and Byron handed over the first two cantos of *Childe Harold*. Dallas recognized the freshness of the work and took it to John Murray, a leading London publisher. The first edition sold out in three days. Just two months earlier Byron had taken his seat in the House of Lords and had seized the occasion of the maiden speech expected of new members to voice a radical and eloquent plea in favor of the "frame-breakers," the workmen who had sabotaged the new textile machinery which threatened their livelihoods. The speech had gained him attention; coming on top of it the poem won him celebrity. In his own often-quoted phrase, "I awoke and found myself famous."

It is difficult to see why the two cantos, which do not measure up to the remainder of the poem from a later period, inspired such enthusiasm, and perhaps it was the poet himself as much as his work which captivated London. At least the combination of the two was irresistible, above all to women. Twenty-four years old, he had a profile which created a new adjective, "Byronic"—auburn curls, casually elegant dress and a disdainful smile. He had the to-the-manor-born air and habit. Despite his chaotic finances he insisted that Dallas take the entire six hundred pounds sterling that Murray paid for a copyright to *Childe Harold*.

Samuel Rogers, a well-known poet, was besieged with requests for introductions to the new sensation. Among the most importunate came from Lady Caroline Lamb, a slender young daughter of the aristocracy who already enjoyed a reputation as a madcap. Lady Caroline's husband, the son of Lord and Lady Melbourne, was the first of several husbands who exhibited a remarkable complacency to his wife's interest in Byron. In Caro Lamb's case interest amounted to absolutely shameless pursuit, to which Byron surrendered with restrained passion, and of which he quickly tired. It ended on a comic-opera note with Lady Caroline running away and Byron collaring her and bringing her back to her mother and mother-in-law, who shipped her off to Ireland. She was promptly succeeded as Byron's mistress by Lady Oxford, an amusing woman sixteen years the poet's senior. Her marital adventures —the Earl of Oxford carried complacency to the point of imperturbability—had already resulted in a family which London nicknamed the "Harleian Miscellany," after a collection of oddly assorted manuscripts from the Earl's library. Lord Oxford stayed in London while Byron lorded it at the family's country home.

In the summer of 1813 Byron, back in London, met his half-sister Augusta for the first time in twelve years. The two had corresponded warmly, and they now hit it off altogether too perfectly. What happened in this situation no one will ever know for certain, but the salons were soon buzzing with a deliciously frightful rumor. Augusta was yet another lady with a complacent husband—hers, a retired army officer named Colonel Leigh, devoted every waking moment to betting on horses and never paid any attention to his wife. Affection between half-brother and half-sister, who of course had been brought up separately and regarded each other more as cousins than siblings, was strong and lifelong, and possibly immoral.

If so, it is likely that there was a psychological connection between Byron's feelings of guilt over Augusta and his decision to marry a prim society belle named Annabella Milbanke with whom he had carried on an arch correspondence. A less guarded than usual hint of marriage brought a passionate acceptance from the lady, which Byron read at the breakfast table and tossed across to Augusta with the sardonic comment, "It never rains but it pours."

From the very first moments the marriage was catastrophic. Annabella was all calm sweetness in the face of Byron's temperament, a posture which goaded him to paroxysms of fury. She may have been sexually unresponsive; in any case he found her boring. Plagued by creditors, he found an excuse to go off to Augusta, who soon returned his visit in London and became part of the household, an arrangement to which Annabella put an end by leaving shortly after the birth of a daughter. The mercurial Byron now begged her to come back, addressing her tenderly as "Bell, dearest Bell." But Annabella got a lawyer and filed separation proceedings.

His endless succession of London liaisons had hardly been interrupted by marriage, but now a particularly determined feminine pursuer drove him out of the country. This young lady was a sister-in-law of Shelley named Claire Clairmont who wrote, cajoled, and forced herself on him in a manner reminiscent of Caroline Lamb. Between Claire and his creditors, Byron felt constrained to leave for Switzerland.

The press had reviled him since the appearance of a poem (*To a Lady Weeping*) reflecting on the Prince Regent, and just before his departure he was subjected to the climax in a growing campaign of ostracism on the part of scandalized respectability. On April 18, 1816, he attended a ball with Hobhouse and Augusta, who was seen to be pregnant. One by one, every lady present swept out of the ballroom, one saucy heiress pausing long enough to address the poet: "This would not have happened if you had married me!"

Byron got out of England a step ahead of his London creditors, who seized his furniture and regretted missing his new coach. The reversal of his popular fortune in the space of four years was complete. At the Hotel d'Angleterre, on Lake Geneva, he wrote down his age in the register as "100," but even this sad jest backfired. The humorless proprietor awoke him to insist on his correct age, which was twenty-eight.

The arrival of the Shelleys cheered him immensely. Byron was one of the few who had recognized the talent in *Queen Mab*, and he was greatly taken with Shelley in person. He also liked Mary Shelley, and their company induced him to put up with Claire Clairmont, who had accompanied them expressly to follow Byron. She soon succeeded in creeping back into his bed, her late night and early morning passages from the Shelley house giving the Swiss peasants amusement. She copied out *The Prisoner of Chillon*, which Byron wrote after an excursion with Shelley, who took the poem back to England along with the fine third canto of *Childe Harold*.

The departure of the Shelleys signaled the departure of Byron, who expressed only impatient and limited interest in the fact that Claire was pregnant. " 'Carry off!' " he wrote. "I should like to know who has been carried off . . . I have been more ravished myself than anybody since the Trojan War." At Shelley's urging, he at length agreed to take care of the child personally as soon as she (as it turned out) was one year old.

When Hobhouse came through Switzerland on his way to Venice, Byron packed up and joined him; Switzerland without Shelley had no further attractions. In Venice he lost no time in setting up a typically Byronic establishment, occupying the upper story of the house of a draper named Segati and taking Signora Segati as his mistress. When Hobhouse returned after an absence he found that Byron had moved to a summer place outside Venice, called La Mira, where Marianna Segati stayed openly, and which her supple husband visited weekends in order to carry on with a mistress of his own. One afternoon while horseback riding, Byron and Hobhouse encountered some peasant women, one of whom was a rangy, black-eyed beauty nicknamed La Fornarina, "the baker's wife." Soon Byron's horse was tethered nightly outside La Fornarina's hut, and when the poet returned to Venice in the fall La Fornarina bullied her husband into buying an oven in the city. She moved into the magnificent palazzo on the Grand Canal which Byron leased, and took over the household, disciplining the servants and managing his domestic economy.

All this time he continued to write poetry which he sent off regularly to John Murray in London. *Manfred,* dealing with the subject of incest, stirred gossip which troubled Augusta Leigh, who sought the advice of Lady Byron. Annabella replied categorically. "You can only speak of *Manfred,*" she wrote, "with the most decided expressions of your disapprobation."

The sale of Newstead Abbey in 1817 at last freed Byron from financial problems. The departure of Hobhouse in the beginning of 1818 removed any other lingering restraint, and he gave full rein to dissipation. La Fornarina did not suffice; soon all the gondoliers in Venice were vying to serve as procurer to the fabulously generous English milord. Late at night a lighted candle on a plank was sometimes discerned moving down the Grand Canal. It was Byron swimming home from a rendezvous, pushing his clothes before him. "He allows fathers and mothers to bargain with him for their daughters," wrote Shelley, who visited him in the role of intermediary for Claire Clairmont, to arrange for Byron to take Claire's daughter Allegra. Byron refused to see the mother, and threatened to quit at once any city Claire entered. The little girl moved into her father's Palazzo Mocenigo, which by now was picturesquely enlivened by a menagerie of monkeys, dogs, and exotic birds. English tourists never failed to include it in their sightseeing, some going so far as to bribe the servants to let them in for a closer look.

Eventually Byron tired of it all, sent the pimps and courtesans packing and even got rid of the redoubtable Fornarina after a scuffle with a carving knife. For several months he devoted himself to a new long poem destined to be his masterpiece, *Don Juan.* Then, in April 1819, he was presented to a lovely 19-year-old Contessa with golden-auburn hair. Teresa Guiccioli, married to a 58-year-old ex-rake, captivated Byron as had no other woman except Augusta. Within a few days she slipped away during her husband's inveterate siesta, boarded a gondola waiting at her door and was taken to Byron's secret casino. She was "strong enough to resist at the first encounter," she recalled later, thereby perhaps further captivating Byron.

Count Guiccioli presently grew suspicious and took Teresa home to Ravenna, but Byron, truly smitten, followed. He found the Count, whom he encountered at the theatre, half-hostile, half-receptive. The truth was, the Count thought Byron might assist him in getting an appointment as British consul at Ravenna, guaranteeing him a secure situation in case of a revolution.

At Ravenna Shelley visited him, and the two poets sat up all night talking. Shelley urged Byron to "come out of the dismal 'wood of error' into the sun and write something new and cheerful." Shortly after, Byron resumed work on Don Juan. He had discovered an old eight-line rhyme scheme in Italian poetry which gave full play to his gift for satire and humor. The poem, on which Byron worked for the next several years, without ever finishing, is in Kenneth Hopkins' words "the most triumphant tour de force in English poetry," with "quotable, memorable lines by the hundred." John Murray published it canto by canto, as Byron forwarded them, and though they repeatedly horrified the prudes they steadily raised Byron's reputation to its pinnacle.

On the pretext of visiting a medical specialist, Teresa returned to Venice with Byron, an arrangement which, if it did not scandalize her husband, scandalized her father. To placate the father, the husband took his wife back to Ravenna. Byron considered returning to England, but at the last moment changed his mind. For one thing, he decided that Allegra should receive a Catholic education because she would never be able to find a husband in England. He put the little girl in a convent and went off to Ravenna, where he moved into the upper floor of Count Guiccioli's palazzo—menagerie and all. Ultimately, the Pope granted Teresa an annulment at the request of her father. But following an easily suppressed revolt in the Romagna, Teresa's father and brother were exiled, and when Byron and Teresa stayed on together the Pope intervened to separate the lovers in the interests of decency. They were reunited in Pisa, where Shelley had invited Byron. There Byron resumed work on Don Juan, momentarily interrupted because Teresa found it shocking.

That spring (1822) was one of tragedy. One morning in April Teresa brought Byron the news that four-year-old Allegra had died of a contagion which had spread through the convent school. Byron sank into a chair, his face gray. He sent word to Shelley to notify Claire, who had expressed apprehensions over the convent school. Unknown to Byron, Claire was actually in Pisa. Shelley, fearing a violent reaction on Claire's part, had her conveyed to a cottage he had rented on the Bay of Lerici, whence Byron presently received a letter beginning, "Murderer . . ."

Byron had Allegra buried in England, at Harrow where, however, the Rector and church wardens ruled that as an illegitimate child she could only be interred outside the church.

A part of the poet's life certainly perished with his daughter. The "Pisan circle" of English expatriates, which for one moment had promised to be amusing and invigorating, turned morose and ominous. Hardly two months later Shelley sailed down from his cottage for his last visit. Five nights after his departure from Byron's house a wild-eyed Mary Shelley burst in with the news that he had never reached home.

From this shock Byron did not recover. The burial scene on the beach was an agony from which he fled by swimming far out to sea. He had apparently considered for some time the possibility of enlisting his name and fortune in the Greek war of independence, and now his resolution began to harden. He had undertaken to support Leigh Hunt's new magazine, *The Liberal,* but he was tired of the project long before it finally failed. For a while his spirits were superficially restored by a visit from Hobhouse, but he remained irritable, even quarreling with Mary Shelley, of whom he was genuinely fond and whom he assisted financially.

In his middle thirties, he had tasted every pleasure and experienced every disillusion. Even Teresa Guiccioli sensed that he was leaving and that nothing would stop him. She made no attempt. He fitted out a ship, the *Hercules,* taking with him all the cash he could realize. He was accompanied by Pietro Gamba, Teresa's brother, and by Edward Trelawny, expert sailor, factotum, and adventurer. As the *Hercules* worked through the Straits of Messina, Trelawny, looking back on Italy, said, "Nature must have intended this for Paradise." Byron replied, "But the Devil has converted it into Hell."

Throughout his last months Byron was intermittently ill and feverish. Nevertheless he contributed significantly to the Greek cause, advancing money to leaders he thought most reliable, subsidizing propaganda and training a fighting force which he intended to command in person. Early in 1824 he surprised his friends with a poem, for he had virtually given up writing. It was the eloquent and touching *On This Day I Complete My Thirty-Sixth Year*. A few weeks later he experienced a severe recurrence of fever; on April 19 he died.

The Greek Provisional Government decreed twenty days of national mourning. The wooden coffin was shipped home to England by Pietro Gamba, who took care to sail separately himself in order to avoid publicity recalling his sister's liaison with Byron. In London Hobhouse arranged for a funeral procession, but once more English respectability ostracized the poet: a long line of noble carriages followed the coffin, but they were empty save for the footmen. The common people lining the streets were more respectful of genius and more tolerant of its faults.

During his Italian sojourn Byron had devoted time to writing his memoirs, which he had entrusted to the poet Tom Moore. Lady Byron and her friends, fearing that they might reflect on her, took steps to have them suppressed, enlisting Augusta Leigh's support. A number of persons had already read the manuscript, and judging from their comments it contained little that would have been offensive even by the standards of the day. But the decision was taken to burn it—a decision in which Byron's publisher John Murray oddly and conspicuously concurred, even though he had not himself read it. Instead of taking the rational course of prudent timidity and locking the memoirs up for a number of years, Murray assisted in casting into the flames of the fireplace irreplaceable leaves, invaluable for an understanding of Byron and of undoubted literary importance in themselves—as one biographer suggested, a book to place on the shelf beside Rousseau's *Confessions*.

From

HEBREW MELODIES

"She Walks in Beauty . . ."

SHE walks in beauty, like the night
  Of cloudless climes and starry skies;
And all that's best of dark and bright
  Meet in her aspect and her eyes:
Thus mellow'd to that tender light
  Which heaven to gaudy day denies.

One shade the more, one ray the less,
  Had half impair'd the nameless grace
Which waves in every raven tress,
  Or softly lightens o'er her face;
Where thoughts serenely sweet express
  How pure, how dear their dwelling-place.

And on that cheek, and o'er that brow,
  So soft, so calm, yet eloquent,
The smiles that win, the tints that glow,
  But tell of days in goodness spent,
A mind at peace with all below,
  A heart whose love is innocent!

1814

"The Harp the Monarch Minstrel Swept"

THE harp the monarch minstrel swept,
  The King of men, the loved of Heaven,
Which Music hallow'd while she wept
  O'er tones her heart of hearts had given.
  Redoubled be her tears, its chords are riven!
It soften'd men of iron mould;
  It gave them virtues not their own;
No ear so dull, no soul so cold,
  That felt not, fired not to the tone,
  Till David's lyre grew mightier than his throne!

It told the triumphs of our King,
  It wafted glory to our God;
It made our gladden'd valleys ring,
  The cedars bow, the mountains nod;
  Its sound aspired to Heaven, and there abode!
Since then, though heard on earth no more,
  Devotion and her daughter Love
Still bid the bursting spirit soar
  To sounds that seem as from above,
  In dreams that day's broad light can not remove.
                                          1814

"If that High World . . ."

IF that high world, which lies beyond
  Our own, surviving Love endears;
If there the cherish'd heart be fond,
  The eye the same, except in tears—
How welcome those untrodden spheres!
  How sweet this very hour to die!
To soar from earth, and find all fears
  Lost in thy light—Eternity!

It must be so: 'tis not for self
  That we so tremble on the brink;
And striving to o'erleap the gulf,
  Yet cling to Being's severing link.
Oh! in that future let us think
  To hold each heart the heart that shares;
With them the immortal waters drink,
  And soul in soul grow deathless theirs!

1814

The Wild Gazelle

THE wild gazelle on Judah's hills
  Exulting yet may bound,
And drink from all the living rills
  That gush on holy ground;
Its airy step and glorious eye
May glance in tameless transport by:—

A step as fleet, and eye more bright,
  Hath Judah witness'd there;
And o'er her scenes of lost delight
  Inhabitants more fair.
The cedars wave on Lebanon,
But Judah's statelier maids are gone!

More blest each palm that shades those plains
  Than Israel's scatter'd race;
For, taking root, it there remains
  In solitary grace:
It cannot quit its place of birth,
It will not live in other earth.

But we must wander witheringly,
  In other lands to die;
And where our fathers' ashes be,
  Our own may never lie:
Our temple hath not left a stone,
And Mockery sits on Salem's throne.

1814

"Oh! Weep for Those . . ."

OH! weep for those that wept by Babel's stream,
Whose shrines are desolate, whose land a dream;
Weep for the harp of Judah's broken shell;
Mourn—where their God hath dwelt, the godless dwell!

And where shall Israel lave her bleeding feet?
And when shall Zion's songs again seem sweet?
And Judah's melody once more rejoice
The hearts that leap'd before its heavenly voice?

Tribes of the wandering foot and weary breast,
How shall ye flee away and be at rest!
The wild-dove hath her nest, the fox his cave,
Mankind their country—Israel but the grave!

1814

"On Jordan's Banks . . ."

On Jordan's banks the Arab's camels stray,
On Sion's hill the False One's votaries pray,
The Baal-adorer bows on Sinai's steep—
Yet there—even there—Oh God! thy thunders sleep:

There—where thy finger scorch'd the tablet stone!
There—where thy shadow to thy people shone!
Thy glory shrouded in its garb of fire:
Thyself—none living see and not expire!

Oh! in the lightning let thy glance appear;
Sweep from his shiver'd hand the oppressor's spear:
How long by tyrants shall thy land be trod!
How long thy temple worshipless, Oh God!

1814

"Oh! Snatch'd Away in Beauty's Bloom"

Oн! snatch'd away in beauty's bloom,
On thee shall press no ponderous tomb;
   But on thy turf shall roses rear
   Their leaves, the earliest of the year;
And the wild cypress wave in tender gloom:

And oft by yon blue gushing stream
   Shall Sorrow lean her drooping head,
And feed deep thought with many a dream,
   And lingering pause, and lightly tread,
   Fond wretch! as if her step disturb'd the dead!

Away! we know that tears are vain,
   That death nor heeds nor hears distress:
Will this unteach us to complain?
   Or make one mourner weep the less?
And thou—who tell'st me to forget,
   Thy looks are wan, thine eyes are wet.

                         1814

Song of Saul Before His Last Battle

WARRIORS and chiefs! should the shaft or the sword
Pierce me in leading the host of the Lord,
Heed not the corse, though a king's, in your path:
Bury your steel in the bosoms of Gath!

Thou who art bearing my buckler and bow,
Should the soldiers of Saul look away from the foe,
Stretch me that moment in blood at thy feet!
Mine be the doom which they dared not to meet.

Farewell to others, but never we part,
Heir to my royalty, son of my heart!
Bright is the diadem, boundless the sway,
Or kingly the death, which awaits us to-day!

                         1815

Vision of Belshazzar

The King was on his throne
   The Satraps throng'd the hall;
A thousand bright lamps shone
   O'er that high festival.
A thousand cups of gold,
   In Judah deem'd divine—
Jehovah's vessels hold
   The godless Heathen's wine!

In that same hour and hall,
   The fingers of a hand
Came forth against the wall,
   And wrote as if on sand:
The fingers of a man,
   A solitary hand
Along the letters ran,
   And traced them like a wand.

The monarch saw, and shook,
   And bade no more rejoice;
All bloodless wax'd his look,
   And tremulous his voice.
"Let the men of lore appear,
   The wisest of the earth,
And expound the words of fear,
   Which mar our royal mirth."

Chaldea's seers are good,
   But here they have no skill;
And the unknown letters stood
   Untold and awful still.
And Babel's men of age
   Are wise and deep in lore;
But now they were not sage,
   They saw—but knew no more.

A captive in the land,
   A stranger and a youth,

He heard the king's command,
　　He saw that writing's truth,
The lamps around were bright,
　　The prophecy in view;
He read it on that night,—
　　The morrow proved it true.

"Belshazzar's grave is made,
　　His kingdom pass'd away,
He, in the balance weigh'd,
　　Is light and worthless clay;
The shroud, his robe of state,
　　His canopy the stone:
The Mede is at his gate!
　　The Persian on his throne!"

　　　　　　　　　　　　　　1815

The Destruction of Sennacherib

THE Assyrian came down like the wolf on the fold,
And his cohorts were gleaming in purple and gold;
And the sheen of their spears was like stars on the sea,
When the blue wave rolls nightly on deep Galilee.

Like the leaves of the forest when Summer is green,
That host with their banners at sunset were seen:
Like the leaves of the forest when Autumn hath blown,
That host on the morrow lay wither'd and strown.

For the Angel of Death spread his wings on the blast,
And breathed in the face of the foe as he pass'd;
And the eyes of the sleepers wax'd deadly and chill,
And their hearts but once heaved, and for ever grew still!

And there lay the steed with his nostril all wide,
But through it there roll'd not the breath of his pride:
And the foam of his gasping lay white on the turf,
And cold as the spray of the rock-beating surf.

And there lay the rider distorted and pale,
With the dew on his brow and the rust on his mail;
And the tents were all silent, the banners alone,
The lances unlifted, the trumpet unblown.

And the widows of Ashur are loud in their wail,
And the idols are broke in the temple of Baal;
And the might of the Gentile, unsmote by the sword,
Hath melted like snow in the glance of the Lord!

1815

"In the Valley of Waters . . ."

A PARAPHRASE OF PSALM CXXXVIII

In the valley of waters we wept o'er the day
When the host of the stranger made Salem his prey,
And our heads on our bosoms all droopingly lay,
And our hearts were so full of the land far away.

The song they demanded in vain—it lay still
In our souls, as the wind that hath died on the hill;
They call'd for the harp—but our blood they shall spill
Ere our right hands shall teach them one tone of our skill.

All stringlessly hung on the willow's sad tree,
As dead as her dead leaf those mute harps must be;
Our hands may be fetter'd—our tears still are free
For our God and our glory—and Sion! oh thee!

1815

Stanzas for Music

THEY say that Hope is happiness;
  But genuine Love must prize the past,
And Memory wakes the thoughts that bless;
  They rose the first—they set the last;

And all that Memory loves the most
  Was once our only Hope to be,
And all that Hope adored and lost
  Hath melted into Memory.

Alas! it is delusion all:
  The future cheats us from afar,
Nor can we be what we recall,
  Nor dare we think on what we are.

                                        1815

OTHER SHORT POEMS

To a Vain Lady

Ah, heedless girl! why thus disclose
    What ne'er was meant for other ears?
Why thus destroy thine own repose
    And dig the source of future tears?

Oh, thou wilt weep, imprudent maid,
    While lurking envious foes will smile,
For all the follies thou hast said
    Of those who spoke but to beguile.

Vain girl! thy ling'ring woes are nigh,
    If thou believ'st what striplings say:
Oh, from the deep temptation fly,
    Nor fall the specious spoiler's prey.

Dost thou repeat, in childish boast,
    The words man utters to deceive?
Thy peace, thy hope, thy all is lost,
    If thou canst venture to believe.

While now amongst thy female peers
    Thou tell'st again the soothing tale;
Canst thou not mark the rising sneers
    Duplicity in vain would veil,

These tales in secret silence hush,
    Nor make thyself the public gaze:
What modest maid without a blush
    Recounts a flattering coxcomb's praise?

Will not the laughing boy despise
 Her who relates each fond conceit—
Who, thinking Heaven is in her eyes,
 Yet cannot see the slight deceit?

For she who takes a soft delight
 These amorous nothings in revealing,
Must credit all we say or write,
 While vanity prevents concealing.

Cease, if you prize your beauty's reign!
 No jealousy bids me reprove:
One, who is thus from nature vain,
 I pity, but I cannot love.

1807

"Bright Be the Place of Thy Soul"

Bright be the place of thy soul!
 No lovelier spirit than thine
E'er burst from its mortal control,
 In the orbs of the blessed to shine.

On earth thou wert all but divine,
 As thy soul shall immortally be;
And our sorrow may cease to repine,
 When we know that thy God is with thee.

Light be the turf of thy tomb!
 May its verdure like emeralds be:
There should not be the shadow of gloom
 In aught that reminds us of thee.

Young flowers and an evergreen tree
 May spring from the spot of thy rest:
But nor cypress nor yew let us see;
 For why should we mourn for the blest?

1808

"When We Two Parted"

WHEN we two parted
　　In silence and tears,
Half broken-hearted
　　To sever for years,
Pale grew thy cheek and cold,
　　Colder thy kiss;
Truly that hour foretold
　　Sorrow to this:

The dew of the morning
　　Sunk chill on my brow—
It felt like the warning
　　Of what I feel now.
Thy vows are all broken,
　　And light is thy fame;
I hear thy name spoken,
　　And share in its shame.

They name thee before me,
　　A knell to mine ear;
A shudder comes o'er me—
　　Why wert thou so dear?
They know not I knew thee,
　　Who knew thee too well:—
Long, long shall I rue thee,
　　Too deeply to tell.

In secret we met—
　　In silence I grieve,
That thy heart could forget,
　　Thy spirit deceive.
If I should meet thee
　　After long years,
How should I greet thee?
　　With silence and tears.

1808

Written After Swimming from Sestos to Abydos

IF, in the month of dark December,
   Leander, who was nightly wont
(What maid will not the tale remember?)
   To cross thy stream, broad Hellespont!

If, when the wintry tempest roar'd,
   He sped to Hero, nothing loth,
And thus of old thy current pour'd,
   Fair Venus! how I pity both!

For *me*, degenerate modern wretch,
   Though in the genial month of May,
My dripping limbs I faintly stretch,
   And think I've done a feat to-day.

But since he cross'd the rapid tide,
   According to the doubtful story,
To woo,—and—Lord knows what beside,
   And swam for Love, as I for Glory!

'Twere hard to say who fared the best:
   Sad mortals! thus the Gods still plague you!
He lost his labour, I my jest:
   For he was drown'd, and I've the ague.

                      1810

"Maid of Athens, Ere We Part"

Ζώη μοῦ, σάς ἀγαπῶ*

MAID of Athens, ere we part,
Give, oh, give me back my heart!
Or, since that has left my breast,
Keep it now, and take the rest!
Hear my vow before I go,
Ζώη μοῦ, σάς ἀγαπῶ.

By those tresses unconfined,
Woo'd by each Aegean wind;
By those lids whose jetty fringe
Kiss thy soft cheeks' blooming tinge;
By those wild eyes like the roe,
Ζώη μοῦ, σάς ἀγαπῶ.

By that lip I long to taste;
By that zone-encircled waist;
By all the token-flowers that tell
What words can never speak so well;
By love's alternate joy and woe,
Ζώη μοῦ, σάς ἀγαπῶ.

Maid of Athens! I am gone:
Think of me, sweet, when alone.
Though I fly to Istambol,
Athens holds my heart and soul:
Can I cease to love thee? No!
Ζώη μοῦ, σάς ἀγαπῶ.

1810

* *My life, I love you*

"Remember Him Whom Passion's Power"

REMEMBER him whom passion's power
Severely, deeply, vainly proved:
Remember thou that dangerous hour
When neither fell, though both were loved.

That yielding breast, that melting eye,
Too much invited to be bless'd:
That gentle prayer, that pleading sigh,
The wilder wish reproved, repress'd.

Oh! let me feel that all I lost,
But saved thee all that conscience fears;
And blush for every pang it cost
To spare the vain remorse of years.

Yet think of this when many a tongue,
Whose busy accents whisper blame,
Would do the heart that loved thee wrong,
And brand a nearly blighted name.

Think that, whate'er to others, thou
Hast seen each selfish thought subdued:
I bless thy purer soul even now,
Even now, in midnight solitude.

Oh, God! that we had met in time,
Our hearts as fond, thy hand more free;
When thou hadst loved without a crime,
And I been less unworthy thee!

Far may thy days, as heretofore,
From this our gaudy world be past!
And, that too bitter moment o'er,
Oh, may such trial be thy last!

This heart, alas! perverted long,
Itself destroy'd might there destroy;
To meet thee in the glittering throng,
Would wake Presumption's hope of joy.

Then to the things whose bliss or woe,
   Like mine, is wild and worthless all,
That world resign—such scenes forego,
   Where those who feel must surely fall.

Thy youth, thy charms, thy tenderness,
   Thy soul from long seclusion pure,
From what even here hath pass'd, may guess,
   What there thy bosom must endure.

Oh! pardon that imploring tear,
   Since not by Virtue shed in vain,
My frenzy drew from eyes so dear;
   For me they shall not weep again.

Though long and mournful must it be,
   The thought that we no more may meet;
Yet I deserve the stern decree,
   And almost deem the sentence sweet.

Still, had I loved thee less, my heart
   Had then less sacrificed to thine;
It felt not half so much to part,
   As if its guilt had made thee mine.

1813

Sonnet, To Genevra

THINE eyes' blue tenderness, thy long fair hair,
   And the wan lustre of thy features—caught
   From contemplation—where serenely wrought,
Seems Sorrow's softness charm'd from its despair—
Have thrown such speaking sadness in thine air,
   That—but I know thy blessed bosom fraught
   With mines of unalloy'd and stainless thought—
I should have deem'd thee doom'd to earthly care.

With such an aspect, by his colours blent,
   When from his beauty-breathing pencil born
(Except that *thou* hast nothing to repent),
   The Magdalen of Guido saw the morn—
Such seem'st thou—but how much more excellent!
   With nought Remorse can claim—nor Virtue scorn.

1813

Sonnet, To the Same

THY cheek is pale with thought, but not from woe,
   And yet so lovely, that if Mirth could flush
   Its rose of whiteness with the brightest blush,
My heart would wish away that ruder glow:
And dazzle not thy deep-blue eyes—but, oh!
   While gazing on them sterner eyes will gush,
   And into mine my mother's weakness rush,
Soft as the last drops round heaven's airy bow.
For, through thy long dark lashes low depending,
   The soul of melancholy Gentleness
Gleams like a seraph from the sky descending,
   Above all pain, yet pitying all distress;
At once such majesty with sweetness blending,
   I worship more, but cannot love thee less.

1813

To Belshazzar

BELSHAZZAR! from the banquet turn,
   Nor in thy sensual fulness fall;
Behold! while yet before thee burn
   The graven words, the glowing wall.
Many a despot men miscall
   Crown'd and anointed from on high;
But thou, the weakest, worst of all—
   Is it not written, thou must die?

Go! dash the roses from thy brow—
  Grey hairs but poorly wreathe with them;
Youth's garlands misbecome thee now,
  More than thy very diadem,
Where thou hast tarnish'd every gem:—
  Then throw the worthless bauble by,
Which, worn by thee, ev'n slaves contemn;
  And learn like better men to die!

Oh! early in the balance weigh'd
  And ever light of word and worth,
Whose soul expired ere youth decay'd,
  And left thee but a mass of earth.
To see thee moves the scorner's mirth:
  But tears in Hope's averted eye
Lament that even thou hadst birth—
  Unfit to govern, live, or die.

1815

Stanzas for Music

THERE be none of Beauty's daughters
  With a magic like thee;
And like music on the waters
  Is thy sweet voice to me:
When, as if its sound were causing
The charm'd ocean's pausing,
The waves lie still and gleaming,
And the lull'd winds seem dreaming.

And the midnight moon is weaving
  Her bright chain o'er the deep;
Whose breast is gently heaving,
  As an infant's asleep:
So the spirit bows before thee,
To listen and adore thee;
With a full but soft emotion,
Like the swell of Summer's ocean.

1816

Stanzas for Music

I SPEAK not, I trace not, I breathe not thy name,
There is grief in the sound, there is guilt in the fame:
But the tear which now burns on my cheek may impart
The deep thoughts that dwell in that silence of heart.

Too brief for our passion, too long for our peace
Were those hours—can their joy or their bitterness cease?
We repent—we abjure—we will break from our chain,—
We will part,—we will fly—to unite it again!

Oh! thine be the gladness, and mine be the guilt!
Forgive me, adored one!—forsake, if thou wilt;—
But the heart which is thine shall expire undebased,
And *man* shall not break it—whatever *thou* mayst.

And stern to the haughty, but humble to thee,
This soul, in its bitterest blackness, shall be;
And our days seem as swift, and our moments more sweet,
With thee by my side, than with worlds at our feet.

One sigh of thy sorrow, one look of thy love,
Shall turn me or fix, shall reward or reprove;
And the heartless may wonder at all I resign—
Thy lip shall reply, not to them, but to *mine*.

1814

Stanzas to Augusta

THOUGH the day of my destiny's over,
    And the star of my fate hath declined,
Thy soft heart refused to discover
    The faults which so many could find;
Though thy soul with my grief was acquainted,
    It shrunk not to share it with me,
And the love which my spirit hath painted.
    It never hath found but in *thee*.

Then when nature around me is smiling,
    The last smile which answers to mine,
I do not believe it beguiling,
    Because it reminds me of thine:
And when winds are at war with the ocean,
    As the breasts I believed in with me,
If their billows excite an emotion,
    It is that they bear me from *thee*.

Though the rock of my last hope is shiver'd,
    And its fragments are sunk in the wave,
Though I feel that my soul is deliver'd
    To pain—it shall not be its slave.
There is many a pang to pursue me:
    They may crush, but they shall not contemn—
They may torture, but shall not subdue me:
    'Tis of *thee* that I think—not of them.

Though human, thou didst not deceive me,
    Though woman, thou didst not forsake,
Though loved, thou forborest to grieve me,
    Though slander'd, thou never couldst shake,—
Though trusted, thou didst not disclaim me,
    Though parted, it was not to fly,
Though watchful, 'twas not to defame me,
    Nor, mute, that the world might belie.

Yet I blame not the world, nor despise it,
    Nor the war of the many with one;
If my soul was not fitted to prize it,
    'Twas folly not sooner to shun.
And if dearly that error hath cost me,
    And more than I once could foresee,
I have found that, whatever it lost me,
    It could not deprive me of *thee*.

From the wreck of the past, which hath perish'd
    Thus much I at least may recall,
It hath taught me that what I most cherish'd
    Deserved to be dearest of all.

In the desert a fountain is springing,
　In the wide waste there still is a tree,
And a bird in the solitude singing,
　Which speaks to my spirit of *thee*.

1816

To Thomas Moore

My boat is on the shore,
　And my bark is on the sea;
But, before I go, Tom Moore,
　Here's a double health to thee!

Here's a sigh to those who love me,
　And a smile to those who hate;
And, whatever sky's above me,
　Here's a heart for every fate.

Though the ocean roar around me,
　Yet it still shall bear me on;
Though a desert should surround me,
　It hath springs that may be won.

Were 't the last drop in the well,
　As I gasp'd upon the brink,
Ere my fainting spirit fell,
　'Tis to thee that I would drink.

With that water, as this wine,
　The libation I would pour
Should be—peace with thine and mine,
　And a health to thee, Tom Moore.

1817

"So We'll Go No More A Roving"

So we'll go no more a roving
   So late into the night,
Though the heart be still as loving,
   And the moon be still as bright.

For the sword outwears its sheath,
   And the soul wears out the breast,
And the heart must pause to breathe,
   And love itself have rest.

Though the night was made for loving,
   And the day returns too soon,
Yet we'll go no more a roving
   By the light of the moon.

1817

On the Bust of Helen by Canova

IN this belovèd marble view,
   Above the works and thoughts of Man,
What Nature *could*, but *would not*, do,
   And Beauty and Canova *can!*
Beyond imagination's power,
   Beyond the Bard's defeated art,
With Immortality her dower,
   Behold the *Helen* of the *heart!*

1816

Stanzas to the Po

RIVER, that rollest by the ancient walls,
    Where dwells the lady of my love, when she
Walks by thy brink, and there perchance recalls
    A faint and fleeting memory of me;

What if thy deep and ample stream should be
    A mirror of my heart, where she may read
The thousand thoughts I now betray to thee,
    Wild as thy wave, and headlong as thy speed!

What do I say—a mirror of my heart?
    Are not thy waters sweeping, dark, and strong?
Such as my feelings were and are, thou art;
    And such as thou art were my passions long.

Time may have somewhat tamed them,—not for ever;
    Thou overflow'st thy banks, and not for aye
Thy bosom overboils, congenial river!
    Thy floods subside, and mine have sunk away.

But left long wrecks behind, and now again,
    Borne in our old unchanged career, we move;
Thou tendest wildly onwards to the main,
    And I—to loving one I should not love.

The current I behold will sweep beneath
    Her native walls and murmur at her feet;
Her eyes will look on thee, when she shall breathe
    The twilight air, unharm'd by summer's heat.

She will look on thee,—I have look'd on thee,
    Full of that thought; and, from that moment, ne'er
Thy waters could I dream of, name, or see,
    Without the inseparable sigh for her!

Her bright eyes will be imaged in thy stream,—
    Yes! they will meet the wave I gaze on now:
Mine cannot witness, even in a dream,
    That happy wave repass me in its flow!

The wave that bears my tears returns no more:
  Will she return by whom that wave shall sweep?—
Both tread thy banks, both wander on thy shore,
  I by thy source, she by the dark-blue deep.

But that which keepeth us apart is not
  Distance, nor depth of wave, nor space of earth,
But the distraction of a various lot,
  As various as the climates of our birth.

A stranger loves the lady of the land,
  Born far beyond the mountains, but his blood
Is all meridian, as if never fann'd
  By the black wind that chills the polar flood.

My blood is all meridian; were it not,
  I had not left my clime, nor should I be,
In spite of tortures, ne'er to be forgot,
  A slave again of love,—at least of thee.

'Tis vain to struggle—let me perish young—
  Live as I lived, and love as I have loved;
To dust if I return, from dust I sprung,
  And then, at least, my heart can ne'er be moved.

1819

Sonnet to George the Fourth

ON THE REPEAL OF LORD EDWARD FITZGERALD'S FORFEITURE

To be the father of the fatherless,
  To stretch the hand from the throne's height, and raise
  His offspring, who expired in other days
To make thy sire's sway by a kingdom less,—
This is to be a monarch, and repress
  Envy into unutterable praise.
  Dismiss thy guard, and trust thee to such traits,
For who would lift a hand, except to bless?

Were it not easy, sir, and is 't not sweet
  To make thyself beloved? and to be
    Omnipotent by mercy's means? for thus
Thy sovereignty would grow but more complete,
  A despot thou, and yet thy people free,
    And by the heart, not hand, enslaving us.

1819

Stanzas

WRITTEN WHEN ABOUT TO JOIN THE ITALIAN CARBONARI

WHEN a man hath no freedom to fight for at home,
  Let him combat for that of his neighbours;
Let him think of the glories of Greece and of Rome,
  And get knock'd on the head for his labours.

To do good to mankind is the chivalrous plan,
  And is always as nobly requited;
Then battle for freedom wherever you can,
  And, if not shot or hang'd you'll get knighted.

1820

On My Thirty-Third Birthday

THROUGH life's dull road, so dim and dirty,
I have dragg'd to three and thirty.
What have these years left to me?
Nothing—except thirty-three.

1821

Stanzas

WRITTEN ON THE ROAD BETWEEN FLORENCE AND PISA

Oh, talk not to me of a name great in story;
The days of our youth are the days of our glory;
And the myrtle and ivy of sweet two-and-twenty
Are worth all your laurels, though ever so plenty.

What are garlands and crowns to the brow that is wrinkled?
'Tis but as a dead flower with May-dew besprinkled.
Then away with all such from the head that is hoary!
What care I for the wreaths that can *only* give glory?

Oh Fame!—if I e'er took delight in thy praises,
'Twas less for the sake of thy high sounding phrases,
Than to see the bright eyes of the dear one discover
She thought that I was not unworthy to love her.

There chiefly I sought thee, *there* only I found thee;
Her glance was the best of the rays that surround thee;
When it sparkled o'er aught that was bright in my story,
I knew it was love, and I felt it was glory.

                                          1821

From

ENGLISH BARDS
AND SCOTCH REVIEWERS

A SATIRE

*   *   *   *   *

A man must serve his time to ev'ry trade
Save censure—critics all are ready made.
Take hackney'd jokes from Miller, got by rote,
With just enough of learning to misquote;
A mind well skill'd to find or forge a fault;
A turn for punning, call it Attic salt;
To Jeffrey go, be silent and discreet,
His pay is just ten sterling pounds per sheet:
Fear not to lie, 'twill seem a sharper hit;
Shrink not from blasphemy, 'twill pass for wit;
Care not for feeling—pass your proper jest,
And stand a critic, hated yet caress'd.

And shall we own such judgment? no—as soon
Seek roses in December—ice in June;
Hope constancy in wind, or corn in chaff;
Believe a woman or an epitaph,
Or any other thing that's false, before
You trust in critics, who themselves are sore;
Or yield one single thought to be misled
By Jeffrey's heart, or Lambe's Boeotian head.
To these young tyrants, by themselves misplaced,
Combined usurpers on the throne of taste;

To these when authors bend in humble awe,
And hail their voice as truth, their word as law—
While these are censors, 'twould be sin to spare;
While such are critics, why should I forbear?
But yet, so near all modern worthies run,
'Tis doubtful whom to seek, or whom to shun;
Nor know we when to spare, or where to strike,
Our bards and censors are so much alike.

Then should you ask me, why I venture o'er
The path which Pope and Gifford trod before;
If not yet sicken'd, you can still proceed:
Go on; my rhyme will tell you as you read.
"But hold!" exclaims a friend, "here's some neglect:
This, that, and t'other line seems incorrect."
What then? the self-same blunder Pope has got,
And careless Dryden—"Ay, but Pye has not:"—
Indeed!—'tis granted, faith!—but what care I?
Better to err with Pope, than shine with Pye.

Time was, ere yet in these degenerate days
Ignoble themes obtain'd mistaken praise,
When sense and wit with poesy allied,
No fabled graces, flourish'd side by side,
From the same fount their inspiration drew,
And rear'd by taste, bloom'd fairer as they grew.
Then, in this happy isle, a Pope's pure strain
Sought the rapt soul to charm, nor sought in vain;
A polish'd nation's praise aspired to claim,
And raised the people's, as the poet's fame.
Like him great Dryden pour'd the tide of song,
In stream less smooth, indeed, yet doubly strong.
Then Congreve's scenes could cheer, or Otway's melt—
For nature then an English audience felt.
But why these names, or greater still, retrace,
When all to feebler bards resign their place?
Yet to such times our lingering looks are cast,
When taste and reason with those times are past.
Now look around, and turn each trifling page,
Survey the precious works that please the age;
This truth at least let satire's self allow,
No dearth of bards can be complained of now.
The loaded press beneath her labour groans,
And printers' devils shake their weary bones;

While Southey's epics cram the creaking shelves,
And Little's lyrics shine in hot-press'd twelves.
Thus saith the preacher: "Nought beneath the sun
Is new;" yet still from change to change we run:
What varied wonders tempt us as they pass!
The cow-pox, tractors, galvanism, and gas,
In turns appear, to make the vulgar stare,
Till the swoln bubble bursts—and all is air!
Nor less new schools of Poetry arise,
Where dull pretenders grapple for the prize:
O'er taste awhile these pseudo-bards prevail;
Each country book-club bows the knee to Baal,
And, hurling lawful genius from the throne,
Erects a shrine and idol of its own;
Some leaden calf—but whom it matters not,
From soaring Southey down to grovelling Stott.

Behold! in various throngs the scribbling crew,
For notice eager, pass in long review;
Each spurs his jaded Pegasus apace,
And rhyme and blank maintain an equal race:
Sonnets on sonnets crowd, and ode on ode;
And tales of terror jostle on the road;
Immeasurable measures move along;
For simpering folly loves a varied song,
To strange mysterious dulness still the friend,
Admires the strain she cannot comprehend.
Thus Lays of Minstrels—may they be the last!—
On half-strung harps whine mournful to the blast,
While mountain spirits prate to river sprites,
That dames may listen to the sound at nights;
And goblin brats, of Gilpin Horner's brood,
Decoy young border-nobles through the wood,
And skip at every step, Lord knows how high,
And frighten foolish babes, the Lord knows why;
While high-born ladies in their magic cell,
Forbidding knights to read who cannot spell,
Despatch a courier to a wizard's grave,
And fight with honest men to shield a knave.

Next view in state, proud prancing on his roan,
The golden-crested haughty Marmion,
Now forging scrolls, now foremost in the fight,
Not quite a felon, yet but half a knight,

The gibbet or the field prepared to grace;
A mighty mixture of the great and base.
And think'st thou, Scott! by vain conceit perchance,
On public taste to foist thy stale romance,
Though Murray with his Miller may combine
To yield thy muse just half-a-crown per line?
No! when the sons of song descend to trade,
Their bays are sear, their former laurels fade.
Let such forego the poet's sacred name,
Who rack their brains for lucre, not for fame:
Still for stern Mammon may they toil in vain!
And sadly gaze on gold they cannot gain!
Such be their meed, such still the just reward
Of prostituted muse and hireling bard!
For this we spurn Apollo's venal son,
And bid a long "good night to Marmion."

These are the themes that claim our plaudits now;
These are the bards to whom the muse must bow;
While Milton, Dryden, Pope, alike forgot,
Resign their hallow'd bays to Walter Scott.

The time has been, when yet the muse was young,
When Homer swept the lyre, and Maro sung,
An epic scarce ten centuries could claim,
While awe-struck nations hail'd the magic name:
The work of each immortal bard appears
The single wonder of a thousand years.
Empires have moulder'd from the face of earth,
Tongues have expired with those who gave them birth,
Without the glory such a strain can give,
As even in ruin bids the language live.
Not so with us, though minor bards content,
On one great work a life of labour spent:
With eagle pinion soaring to the skies,
Behold the ballad-monger Southey rise!
To him let Camoëns, Milton, Tasso yield,
Whose annual strains, like armies, take the field.
First in the ranks see Joan of Arc advance,
The scourge of England and the boast of France!
Though burnt by wicked Bedford for a witch,
Behold her statue placed in glory's niche;

Her fetters burst, and just released from prison,
A virgin phoenix from her ashes risen.
Next see tremendous Thalaba come on,
Arabia's monstrous, wild, and wond'rous son;
Domdaniel's dread destroyer, who o'erthrew
More mad magicians than the world e'er knew.
Immortal hero! all thy foes o'ercome,
For ever reign—the rival of Tom Thumb!
Since startled metre fled before thy face,
Well wert thou doom'd the last of all thy race!
Well might triumphant genii bear thee hence,
Illustrious conqueror of common sense!
Now, last and greatest, Madoc spreads his sails,
Cacique in Mexico, and prince in Wales;
Tells us strange tales, as other travellers do,
More old than Mandeville's, and not so true.
Oh, Southey! Southey! cease thy varied song!
A bard may chant too often and too long:
As thou art strong in verse, in mercy, spare!
A fourth, alas! were more than we could bear.
But if, in spite of all the world can say,
Thou still wilt verseward plod thy weary way;
If still in Berkley ballads most uncivil,
Thou wilt devote old women to the devil,
The babe unborn thy dread intent may rue:
"God help thee," Southey, and thy readers too.

Next comes the dull disciple of thy school,
That mild apostate from poetic rule,
The simple Wordsworth, framer of a lay
As soft as evening in his favourite May,
Who warns his friend "to shake off toil and trouble,
And quit his books, for fear of growing double;"
Who, both by precept and example, shows
That prose is verse, and verse is merely prose;
Convincing all, by demonstration plain,
Poetic souls delight in prose insane;
And Christmas stories tortured into rhyme
Contain the essence of the true sublime.
Thus, when he tells the tale of Betty Foy,
The idiot mother of "an idiot boy;"
A moon-struck, silly lad, who lost his way,
And, like his bard, confounded night with day;

So close on each pathetic part he dwells,
And each adventure so sublimely tells,
That all who view the "idiot in his glory"
Conceive the bard the hero of the story.

Shall gentle Coleridge pass unnoticed here,
To turgid ode and tumid stanza dear?
Though themes of innocence amuse him best,
Yet still obscurity's a welcome guest.
If Inspiration should her aid refuse
To him who takes a pixy for a muse,
Yet none in lofty numbers can surpass
The bard who soars to elegise an ass.
So well the subject suits his noble mind,
He brays, the laureate of the long-ear'd kind.

*   *   *   *   *

Delightful Bowles! still blessing and still blest,
All love thy strain, but children like it best.
'Tis thine, with gentle Little's moral song,
To soothe the mania of the amorous throng!
With thee our nursery damsels shed their tears,
Ere miss as yet completes her infant years:
But in her teens thy whining powers are vain;
She quits poor Bowles for Little's purer strain.
Now to soft themes thou scornest to confine
The lofty numbers of a harp like thine:
"Awake a louder and a loftier strain,"
Such as none heard before, or will again!
Where all Discoveries jumbled from the flood,
Since first the leaky ark reposed in mud,
By more or less, are sung in every book,
From Captain Noah down to Captain Cook.
Nor this alone; but, pausing on the road,
The bard sighs forth a gentle episode;
And gravely tells—attend, each beauteous miss!—
When first Madeira trembled to a kiss.
Bowles! in thy memory let this precept dwell,
Stick to thy sonnets, man!—at least they sell.
But if some new-born whim, or larger bribe,
Prompt thy crude brain, and claim thee for a scribe;
If chance some bard, though once by dunces fear'd,
Now, prone in dust, can only be revered;

If Pope, whose fame and genius, from the first,
Have foil'd the best of critics, needs the worst,
Do thou essay; each fault, each failing scan;
The first of poets was, alas! but man.
Rake from each ancient dunghill ev'ry pearl,
Consult Lord Fanny, and confide in Curll;
Let all the scandals of a former age
Perch on thy pen, and flutter o'er thy page;
Affect a candour which thou canst not feel,
Clothe envy in the garb of honest zeal;
Write, as if St. John's soul could still inspire,
And do from hate what Mallet did for hire.
Oh! hadst thou lived in that congenial time,
To rave with Dennis, and with Ralph to rhyme;
Throng'd with the rest around his living head,
Not raised thy hoof against the lion dead;
A meet reward had crown'd thy glorious gains,
And link'd thee to the Dunciad for thy pains.

* * * * *

Now to the Drama turn—Oh! motley sight!
What precious scenes the wondering eyes invite!
Puns, and a prince within a barrel pent,
And Dibdin's nonsense yield complete content.
Though now, thank Heaven! the Rosciomania's o'er,
And full-grown actors are endured once more;
Yet what avail their vain attempts to please,
While British critics suffer scenes like these;
While Reynolds vents his "dammes!" "poohs!" and "zounds!"
And common-place and common sense confounds?
While Kenney's World—ah! where is Kenney's wit?—
Tires the sad gallery, lulls the listless pit;
And Beaumont's pilfer'd Caratach affords
A tragedy complete in all but words?
Who but must mourn, while these are all the rage,
The degradation of our vaunted stage!
Heavens! is all sense of shame and talent gone?
Have we no living bard of merit?—none!
Awake, George Colman! Cumberland, awake!
Ring the alarum bell! let folly quake!
Oh, Sheridan, if aught can move thy pen,
Let Comedy assume her throne again;

Abjure the mummery of the German schools;
Leave new Pizarros to translating fools;
Give, as thy last memorial to the age,
One classic drama, and reform the stage.
Gods! o'er those boards shall Folly rear her head,
Where Garrick trod, and Siddons lives to tread?
On those shall Farce display Buffoon'ry's mask,
And Hook conceal his heroes in a cask?
Shall sapient managers new scenes produce
From Cherry, Skeffington, and Mother Goose?
While Shakspeare, Otway, Massinger, forgot,
On stalls must moulder, or in closets rot?
Lo! with what pomp the daily prints proclaim
The rival candidates for Attic fame!
In grim array though Lewis' spectres rise,
Still Skeffington and Goose divide the prize.
And sure *great* Skeffington must claim our praise,
For skirtless coats and skeletons of plays
Renown'd alike; whose genius ne'er confines
Her flight to garnish Greenwood's gay designs;
Nor sleeps with *Sleeping Beauties*, but anon
In five facetious acts comes thundering on,
While poor John Bull, bewilder'd with the scene,
Stares, wondering what the devil it can mean;
But as some hands applaud, a venal few!
Rather than sleep, why John applauds it too.

*   *   *   *   *

To the famed throng now paid the tribute due,
Neglected genius! let me turn to you.
Come forth, oh Campbell! give thy talents scope;
Who dares aspire if thou must cease to hope?
And thou, melodious Rogers! rise at last,
Recall the pleasing memory of the past;
Arise! let blest remembrance still inspire,
And strike to wonted tones thy hallow'd lyre;
Restore Apollo to his vacant throne,
Assert thy country's honour and thine own.
What! must deserted Poesy still weep
Where her last hopes with pious Cowper sleep?
Unless, perchance, from his cold bier she turns,
To deck the turf that wraps her minstrel, Burns!

No! though contempt hath mark'd the spurious brood,
The race who rhyme from folly, or for food,
Yet still some genuine sons 'tis hers to boast,
Who, least affecting, still affect the most;
Feel as they write, and write but as they feel—
Bear witness, Gifford, Sotheby, Macneil.

"Why slumbers Gifford?" once was ask'd in vain;
Why slumbers Gifford? let us ask again.
Are there no follies for his pen to purge?
Are there no fools whose backs demand the scourge?
Are there no sins for satire's bard to greet?
Stalks not gigantic Vice in every street?
Shall peers or princes tread pollution's path,
And 'scape alike the law's and muse's wrath?
Nor blaze with guilty glare through future time,
Eternal beacons of consummate crime?
Arouse thee, Gifford! be thy promise claim'd,
Make bad men better, or at least ashamed.

Unhappy White! while life was in its spring,
And thy young muse just waved her joyous wing,
The spoiler swept that soaring lyre away,
Which else had sounded an immortal lay.
Oh! what a noble heart was here undone,
When Science' self destroy'd her favourite son!
Yes, she too much indulged thy fond pursuit,
She sow'd the seeds, but death has reap'd the fruit.
'Twas thine own genius gave the final blow,
And help'd to plant the wound that laid thee low:
So the struck eagle, stretch'd upon the plain,
No more through rolling clouds to soar again,
View'd his own feather on the fatal dart,
And wing'd the shaft that quiver'd in his heart;
Keen were his pangs, but keener far to feel
He nursed the pinion which impell'd the steel;
While the same plumage that had warm'd his nest
Drank the last life-drop of his bleeding breast.

* * * * *

Blest is the man who dares approach the bower
Where dwelt the muses at their natal hour;
Whose steps have press'd, whose eye has mark'd afar,
The clime that nursed the sons of song and war,
The scenes which glory still must hover o'er,
Her place of birth, her own Achaian shore.
But doubly blest is he whose heart expands
With hallow'd feelings for those classic lands;
Who rends the veil of ages long gone by,
And views their remnants with a poet's eye.
Wright! 'twas thy happy lot at once to view
Those shores of glory, and to sing them too;
And sure no common muse inspired thy pen
To hail the land of gods and godlike men.

And you, associate bards! who snatch'd to light
Those gems too long withheld from modern sight;
Whose mingling taste combined to cull the wreath
Where Attic flowers Aonian odours breathe,
And all their renovated fragrance flung,
To grace the beauties of your native tongue;
Now let those minds, that nobly could transfuse
The glorious spirit of the Grecian muse,
Though soft the echo, scorn a borrow'd tone:
Resign Achaia's lyre, and strike your own.

Let these, or such as these, with just applause,
Restore the muse's violated laws;
But not in flimsy Darwin's pompous chime,
That mighty master of unmeaning rhyme,
Whose gilded cymbals, more adorn'd than clear,
The eye delighted, but fatigued the ear;
In show the simple lyre could once surpass,
But now, worn down, appear in native brass,
While all his train of hovering sylphs around
Evaporate in similes and sound.
Him let them shun, with him let tinsel die:
False glare attracts, but more offends the eye.

Yet let them not to vulgar Wordsworth stoop,
The meanest object of the lowly group,
Whose verse, of all but childish prattle void,
Seems blessed harmony to Lamb and Lloyd:

Let them—but hold, my muse, nor dare to teach
A strain far, far beyond thy humble reach:
The native genius with their being given
Will point the path, and peal their notes to heaven.

And thou, too, Scott! resign to minstrels rude
The wilder slogan of a border feud:
Let others spin their meagre lines for hire;
Enough for genius if itself inspire!
Let Southey sing, although his teeming muse,
Prolific every spring, be too profuse;
Let simple Wordsworth chime his childish verse,
And brother Coleridge lull the babe at nurse;
Let spectre-mongering Lewis aim, at most,
To rouse the galleries, or to raise a ghost;
Let Moore still sigh; let Strangford steal from Moore,
And swear that Camoëns sang such notes of yore;
Let Hayley hobble on, Montgomery rave,
And godly Grahame chant a stupid stave;
Let sonneteering Bowles his strains refine,
And whine and whimper to the fourteenth line;
Let Stott, Carlisle, Matilda, and the rest
Of Grub-street and of Grosvenor-place the best,
Scrawl on, 'till death release us from the strain,
Or Common Sense assert her rights again.

*   *   *   *   *

For me, who, thus unask'd, have dared to tell
My country, what her sons should know too well,
Zeal for her honour bade me here engage
The host of idiots that infest her age;
No just applause her honour'd name shall lose,
As first in freedom, dearest to the muse.
Oh! would thy bards but emulate thy fame,
And rise more worthy, Albion, of thy name!
What Athens was in science, Rome in power,
What Tyre appear'd in her meridian hour,
'Tis thine at once, fair Albion! to have been—
Earth's chief dictatress, ocean's lovely queen:
But Rome decay'd, and Athens strew'd the plain,
And Tyre's proud piers lie scatter'd in the main;
Like these, thy strength may sink, in ruin hurl'd
And Britain fall, the bulwark of the world.

But let me cease, and dread Cassandra's fate
With warning ever scoff'd at, till too late;
To themes less lofty still my lay confine,
And urge thy bards to gain a name like thine.

*   *   *   *   *

1809

THE PRISONER OF CHILLON

A FABLE

Sonnet on Chillon

Eternal spirit of the chainless Mind!
   Brightest in dungeons, Liberty! thou art,
   For there thy habitation is the heart—
The heart which love of thee alone can bind;
And when thy sons to fetters are consign'd—
   To fetters, and the damp vault's dayless gloom,
   Their country conquers with their martyrdom,
And Freedom's fame finds wings on every wind.
Chillon! thy prison is a holy place,
   And thy sad floor an altar—for 'twas trod,
Until his very steps have left a trace,
Worn, as if thy cold pavement were a sod,
By Bonnivard!—May none those marks efface!
   For they appeal from tyranny to God.

I

My hair is grey, but not with years,
   Nor grew it white
   In a single night,
As men's have grown from sudden fears:
My limbs are bow'd, though not with toil,
   But rusted with a vile repose,
For they have been a dungeon's spoil,
   And mine has been the fate of those

To whom the goodly earth and air
Are bann'd, and barr'd—forbidden fare;
But this was for my father's faith
I suffer'd chains and courted death;
That father perish'd at the stake
For tenets he would not forsake;
And for the same his lineal race
In darkness found a dwelling-place.
We were seven—who now are one,
   Six in youth, and one in age,
Finish'd as they had begun,
   Proud of Persecution's rage;
One in fire, and two in field,
Their belief with blood have seal'd,
Dying as their father died,
For the God their foes denied:
Three were in a dungeon cast,
Of whom this wreck is left the last.

II

There are seven pillars of Gothic mould
In Chillon's dungeons deep and old;
There are seven columns, massy and grey,
Dim with a dull imprison'd ray,
A sunbeam which hath lost its way,
And through the crevice and the cleft
Of the thick wall is fallen and left,
Creeping o'er the floor so damp,
Like a marsh's meteor lamp:
And in each pillar there is a ring,
   And in each ring there is a chain;
That iron is a cankering thing,
   For in these limbs its teeth remain,
With marks that will not wear away,
Till I have done with this new day,
Which now is painful to these eyes,
Which have not seen the sun so rise
For years—I cannot count them o'er,
I lost their long and heavy score
When my last brother droop'd and died,
And I lay living by his side.

III

They chain'd us each to a column stone,
And we were three—yet, each alone;
We could not move a single pace,
We could not see each other's face,
But with that pale and livid light
That made us strangers in our sight:
And thus together, yet apart,
Fetter'd in hand, but join'd in heart,
'Twas still some solace, in the dearth
Of the pure elements of earth,
To hearken to each other's speech,
And each turn comforter to each,
With some new hope, or legend old,
Or song heroically bold:
But even these at length grew cold.
Our voices took a dreary tone,
An echo of the dungeon-stone,
   A grating sound—not full and free
   As they of yore were wont to be:
   It might be fancy, but to me
They never sounded like our own.

IV

I was the eldest of the three,
   And to uphold and cheer the rest
   I ought to do—and did my best;
And each did well in his degree.
   The youngest, whom my father loved,
Because our mother's brow was given
To him, with eyes as blue as heaven—
   For him my soul was sorely moved:
And truly might it be distress'd
To see such bird in such a nest;
For he was beautiful as day
   (When day was beautiful to me
   As to young eagles, being free)
   A polar day, which will not see
A sunset till its summer's gone,

Its sleepless summer of long light,
The snow-clad offspring of the sun:
  And thus he was as pure and bright,
And in his natural spirit gay,
With tears for nought but others' ills;
And then they flow'd like mountain rills,
Unless he could assuage the woe
Which he abhorr'd to view below.

V

The other was as pure of mind,
But form'd to combat with his kind;
Strong in his frame, and of a mood
Which 'gainst the world in war had stood,
And perish'd in the foremost rank
  With joy:—but not in chains to pine:
His spirit wither'd with their clank,
  I saw it silently decline—
  And so perchance in sooth did mine:
But yet I forced it on to cheer
Those relics of a home so dear.
He was a hunter of the hills,
  Had follow'd there the deer and wolf;
  To him this dungeon was a gulf,
And fetter'd feet the worst of ills.

VI

Lake Leman lies by Chillon's walls:
A thousand feet in depth below
Its massy waters meet and flow;
Thus much the fathom-line was sent
From Chillon's snow-white battlement,
  Which round about the wave inthrals:
A double dungeon wall and wave
Have made—and like a living grave.
Below the surface of the lake
The dark vault lies wherein we lay:
We heard it ripple night and day;
  Sounding o'er our heads it knock'd;

And I have felt the winter's spray
Wash through the bars when winds were high,
And wanton in the happy sky;
   And then the very rock hath rock'd,
   And I have felt it shake, unshock'd,
Because I could have smiled to see
   The death that would have set me free.

VII

I said my nearer brother pined,
I said his mighty heart declined,
He loathed and put away his food;
It was not that 'twas coarse and rude,
For we were used to hunters' fare,
And for the like had little care:
The milk drawn from the mountain goat
Was changed for water from the moat,
Our bread was such as captives' tears
Have moisten'd many a thousand years,
Since man first pent his fellow men
Like brutes within an iron den;
But what were these to us or him?
These wasted not his heart or limb;
My brother's soul was of that mould
Which in a palace had grown cold,
Had his free breathing been denied
The range of the steep mountain's side.
But why delay the truth?—he died.
I saw, and could not hold his head,
Nor reach his dying hand—nor dead,—
Though hard I strove, but strove in vain,
To rend and gnash my bonds in twain.
He died—and they unlock'd his chain,
And scoop'd for him a shallow grave
Even from the cold earth of our cave.
I begg'd them, as a boon, to lay
His corse in dust whereon the day
Might shine—it was a foolish thought,
But then within my brain it wrought,
That even in death his freeborn breast
In such a dungeon could not rest.

I might have spared my idle prayer;
They coldly laugh'd—and laid him there:
The flat and turfless earth above
The being we so much did love;
His empty chain above it leant,
Such murder's fitting monument!

VIII

But he, the favourite and the flower,
Most cherish'd since his natal hour,
His mother's image in fair face,
The infant love of all his race,
His martyr'd father's dearest thought,
My latest care, for whom I sought
To hoard my life, that his might be
Less wretched now, and one day free;
He, too, who yet had held untired
A spirit natural or inspired—
He, too, was struck, and day by day
Was wither'd on the stalk away.
Oh God! it is a fearful thing
To see the human soul take wing
In any shape, in any mood:—
I've seen it rushing forth in blood,
I've seen it on the breaking ocean
Strive with a swoln convulsive motion;
I've seen the sick and ghastly bed
Of Sin delirious with its dread:
But these were horrors—this was woe
Unmix'd with such—but sure and slow:
He faded, and so calm and meek,
So softly worn, so sweetly weak,
So tearless, yet so tender—kind,
And grieved for those he left behind;
With all the while a cheek whose bloom
Was as a mockery of the tomb,
Whose tints as gently sunk away
As a departing rainbow's ray;—
An eye of most transparent light,
That almost made the dungeon bright;
And not a word of murmur, not
A groan o'er his untimely lot,—

A little talk of better days,
A little hope my own to raise,
For I was sunk in silence—lost
In this last loss, of all the most;
And then the sighs he would suppress
Of fainting nature's feebleness,
More slowly drawn, grew less and less:
I listen'd, but I could not hear—
I call'd, for I was wild with fear;
I knew 'twas hopeless, but my dread
Would not be thus admonishèd;
I call'd, and thought I heard a sound—
I burst my chain with one strong bound,
And rush'd to him:—I found him not,
I only stirr'd in this black spot,
I only lived—*I* only drew
The accursèd breath of dungeon-dew;
The last—the sole—the dearest link
Between me and the eternal brink,
Which bound me to my falling race,
Was broken in this fatal place.
One on the earth, and one beneath—
My brothers—both had ceased to breathe:
I took that hand which lay so still,
Alas! my own was full as chill,
I had not strength to stir, or strive,
But felt that I was still alive—
A frantic feeling, when we know
That what we love shall ne'er be so.
    I know not why
    I could not die,
I had no earthly hope—but faith,
And that forbade a selfish death.

IX

What next befell me then and there
    I know not well—I never knew;
First came the loss of light, and air,
    And then of darkness too:
I had no thought, no feeling—none—
Among the stones I stood a stone,

And was, scarce conscious what I wist,
As shrubless crags within the mist;
For all was blank, and bleak, and grey,
It was not night—it was not day,
It was not even the dungeon-light,
So hateful to my heavy sight,
But vacancy absorbing space,
And fixedness—without a place;
There were no stars—no earth—no time—
No check—no change—no good—no crime—
But silence, and a stirless breath
Which neither was of life nor death;
A sea of stagnant idleness,
Blind, boundless, mute, and motionless!

X

A light broke in upon my brain,—
    It was the carol of a bird;
It ceased, and then it came again,
    The sweetest song ear ever heard,
And mine was thankful till my eyes
Ran over with the glad surprise,
And they that moment could not see
I was the mate of misery;
But then by dull degrees came back
My senses to their wonted track;
I saw the dungeon walls and floor
Close slowly round me as before;
I saw the glimmer of the sun
Creeping as it before had done;
But through the crevice where it came
That bird was perch'd, as fond and tame,
    And tamer than upon the tree;
A lovely bird, with azure wings,
And song that said a thousand things,
    And seem'd to say them all for me!
I never saw its like before,
I ne'er shall see its likeness more:
It seem'd like me to want a mate,
But was not half so desolate,
And it was come to love me when
None lived to love me so again,

And cheering from my dungeon's brink,
Had brought me back to feel and think.
I know not if it late were free,
    Or broke its cage to perch on mine,¯
But knowing well captivity,
    Sweet bird! I could not wish for thine!
Or if it were, in wingèd guise,
A visitant from Paradise;
For—Heaven forgive that thought! the while
Which made me both to weep and smile—
I sometimes deem'd that it might be
My brother's soul come down to me;
But then at last away it flew,
And then 'twas mortal—well I knew,
For he would never thus have flown,
And left me twice so doubly lone,—
Lone—as the corse within its shroud,
Lone—as a solitary cloud,
    A single cloud on a sunny day,
While all the rest of heaven is clear,
A frown upon the atmosphere
That hath no business to appear
    When skies are blue and earth is gay.

XI

A kind of change came in my fate,
My keepers grew compassionate;
I know not what had made them so,
They were inured to sights of woe,
But so it was:—my broken chain
With links unfasten'd did remain,
And it was liberty to stride
Along my cell from side to side,
And up and down, and then athwart,
And tread it over every part;
And round the pillars one by one,
Returning where my walk begun,
Avoiding only, as I trod,
My brothers' graves without a sod;
For if I thought with heedless tread
My step profaned their lowly bed,
My breath came gaspingly and thick,
And my crush'd heart fell blind and sick.

XII

I made a footing in the wall,
   It was not therefrom to escape,
For I had buried one and all
   Who loved me in a human shape;
And the whole earth would henceforth be
A wider prison unto me:
No child, no sire, no kin had I,
No partner in my misery;
I thought of this, and I was glad,
For thought of them had made me mad;
But I was curious to ascend
To my barr'd windows, and to bend
Once more upon the mountains high
The quiet of a loving eye.

XIII

I saw them—and they were the same,
They were not changed like me in frame;
I saw their thousand years of snow
On high—their wide long lake below,
And the blue Rhone in fullest flow;
I heard the torrents leap and gush
O'er channell'd rock and broken bush;
I saw the white-wall'd distant town,
And whiter sails go skimming down.
And then there was a little isle,
Which in my very face did smile,
   The only one in view;
A small green isle, it seem'd no more,
Scarce broader than my dungeon floor,
But in it there were three tall trees,
And o'er it blew the mountain breeze,
And by it there were waters flowing,
And on it there were young flowers growing,
   Of gentle breath and hue.
The fish swam by the castle wall,
And they seem'd joyous each and all;

The eagle rode the rising blast,
Methought he never flew so fast
As then to me he seem'd to fly;
And then new tears came in my eye,
And I felt troubled—and would fain
I had not left my recent chain.
And when I did descend again,
The darkness of my dim abode
Fell on me as a heavy load;
It was as is a new-dug grave,
Closing o'er one we sought to save—
And yet my glance, too much oppress'd,
Had almost need of such a rest.

XIV

It might be months, or years, or days—
    I kept no count—I took no note,
I had no hope my eyes to raise
    And clear them of their dreary mote—
At last men came to set me free,
    I ask'd not why, and reck'd not where,
It was at length the same to me,
Fetter'd or fetterless to be,
    I'd learn'd to love despair.
And thus when they appear'd at last,
And all my bonds aside were cast,
These heavy walls to me had grown
A hermitage—and all my own!
And half I felt as they were come
To tear me from a second home:
With spiders I had friendship made,
And watch'd them in their sullen trade,
Had seen the mice by moonlight play,
And why should I feel less than they?
We were all inmates of one place,
And I, the monarch of each race,
Had power to kill—yet, strange to tell!
In quiet we had learn'd to dwell—
My very chains and I grew friends,
So much a long communion tends
To make us what we are:—even I
Regain'd my freedom with a sigh.

1816

From

CHILDE HAROLD'S PILGRIMAGE

CANTO I

*   *   *   *   *

12

The sails were fill'd, and fair the light winds blew,
As glad to waft him from his native home;
And fast the white rocks faded from his view,
And soon were lost in circumambient foam:
And then, it may be, of his wish to roam
Repented he, but in his bosom slept
The silent thought, nor from his lips did come
One word of wail, whilst others sate and wept,
And to the reckless gales unmanly moaning kept.

13

But when the sun was sinking in the sea,
He seized his harp, which he at times could string,
And strike, albeit with untaught melody,
When deem'd he no strange ear was listening:
And now his fingers o'er it did he fling,
And tuned his farewell in the dim twilight.
While flew the vessel on her snowy wing,
And fleeting shores receded from his sight,
Thus to the elements he pour'd his last "Good Night."

"Adieu, adieu! my native shore
  Fades o'er the waters blue;
The night-winds sigh, the breakers roar,
  And shrieks the wild sea-mew.
Yon sun that sets upon the sea
  We follow in his flight;
Farewell awhile to him and thee,
  My native Land—Good Night!

"A few short hours and he will rise
  To give the morrow birth;
And I shall hail the main and skies,
  But not my mother earth.
Deserted is my own good hall,
  Its hearth is desolate;
Wild weeds are gathering on the wall;
  My dog howls at the gate.

"Come hither, hither, my little page!
  Why dost thou weep and wail?
Or dost thou dread the billows' rage,
  Or tremble at the gale?
But dash the tear-drop from thine eye;
  Our ship is swift and strong:
Our fleetest falcon scarce can fly
  More merrily along."

"Let winds be shrill, let waves roll high,
  I fear not wave nor wind;
Yet marvel not, Sir Childe, that I
  Am sorrowful in mind;
For I have from my father gone,
  A mother whom I love,
And have no friend, save these alone,
  But thee—and One above.

"My father bless'd me fervently,
  Yet did not much complain;
But sorely will my mother sigh
  Till I come back again."—
"Enough, enough, my little lad!
  Such tears become thine eye;
If I thy guileless bosom had,
  Mine own would not be dry.

"Come hither, hither, my stanch yeoman,
    Why dost thou look so pale?
Or dost thou dread a French foeman?
    Or shiver at the gale?"—
"Deem'st thou I tremble for my life?
    Sir Childe, I'm not so weak;
But thinking on an absent wife
    Will blanch a faithful cheek.

"My spouse and boys dwell near thy hall,
    Along the bordering lake,
And when they on their father call,
    What answer shall she make?"—
"Enough, enough, my yeoman good,
    Thy grief let none gainsay;
But I, who am of lighter mood,
    Will laugh to flee away.

"For who would trust the seeming sighs
    Of wife or paramour?
Fresh feres will dry the bright blue eyes
    We late saw streaming o'er.
For pleasures past I do not grieve,
    Nor perils gathering near;
My greatest grief is that I leave
    No thing that claims a tear.

"And now I'm in the world alone,
    Upon the wide, wide sea:
But why should I for others groan,
    When none will sigh for me?
Perchance my dog will whine in vain,
    Till fed by stranger hands;
But long ere I come back again,
    He'd tear me where he stands.

"With thee, my bark, I'll swiftly go
    Athwart the foaming brine;
Nor care what land thou bear'st me to,
    So not again to mine.
Welcome, welcome, ye dark blue waves!
    And when you fail my sight,
Welcome, ye deserts, and ye caves!
    My native Land—Good Night!"

14

On, on the vessel flies, the land is gone,
And winds are rude in Biscay's sleepless bay.
Four days are sped, but with the fifth anon,
New shores descried make every bosom gay;
And Cintra's mountain greets them on their way,
And Tagus dashing onward to the deep,
His fabled golden tribute bent to pay;
And soon on board the Lusian pilots leap,
And steer 'twixt fertile shores where yet few rustics reap.

15

Oh, Christ, it is a goodly sight to see
What Heaven hath done for this delicious land!
What fruits of fragrance blush on every tree!
What goodly prospects o'er the hills expand!
But man would mar them with an impious hand:
And when the Almighty lifts his fiercest scourge
'Gainst those who most transgress his high command,
With treble vengeance will his hot shafts urge
Gaul's locust host, and earth from fellest foemen purge.

16

What beauties doth Lisboa first unfold!
Her image floating on that noble tide,
Which poets vainly pave with sands of gold,
But now whereon a thousand keels did ride
Of mighty strength, since Albion was allied,
And to the Lusians did her aid afford:
A nation swoln with ignorance and pride,
Who lick yet loathe the hand that waves the sword
To save them from the wrath of Gaul's unsparing lord.

* * * * *

35

Oh, lovely Spain! renown'd, romantic land!
Where is that standard which Pelagio bore,
When Cava's traitor-sire first called the band
That dyed thy mountain streams with Gothic gore?
Where are those bloody banners which of yore
Waved o'er thy sons, victorious to the gale,
And drove at last the spoilers to their shore?
Red gleam'd the cross, and waned the crescent pale,
While Afric's echoes thrill'd with Moorish matrons' wail.

36

Teems not each ditty with the glorious tale?
Ah! such, alas! the hero's amplest fate!
When granite moulders and when records fail,
A peasant's plaint prolongs his dubious date.
Pride! bend thine eye from heaven to thine estate,
See how the Mighty shrink into a song!
Can Volume, Pillar, Pile preserve thee great?
Or must thou trust Tradition's simple tongue,
When Flattery sleeps with thee, and History does thee wrong?

37

Awake, ye sons of Spain! awake! advance!
Lo! Chivalry, your ancient goddess, cries,
But wields not, as of old, her thirsty lance,
Nor shakes her crimson plumage in the skies:
Now on the smoke of blazing bolts she flies,
And speaks in thunder through yon engine's roar:
In every peal she calls—"Awake! arise!"
Say, is her voice more feeble than of yore,
When her war-song was heard on Andalusia's shore?

*   *   *   *   *

71

All have their fooleries—not alike are thine,
Fair Cadiz, rising o'er the dark blue sea!
Soon as the matin bell proclaimeth nine,
Thy saint adorers count the rosary:
Much is the Virgin teased to shrive them free
(Well do I ween the only virgin there)
From crimes as numerous as her beadsmen be;
Then to the crowded circus forth they fare:
Young, old, high, low, at once the same diversion share.

72

The lists are oped, the spacious area clear'd,
Thousands on thousands piled are seated round;
Long ere the first loud trumpet's note is heard,
Ne vacant space for lated wight is found:
Here dons, grandees, but chiefly dames abound,
Skill'd in the ogle of a roguish eye,
Yet ever well inclined to heal the wound;
None through their cold disdain are doom'd to die,
As moon-struck bards complain, by love's sad archery.

73

Hush'd is the din of tongues; on gallant steeds,
With milk-white crest, gold spur, and light-pois'd lance,
Four cavaliers prepare for venturous deeds,
And lowly bending to the lists advance;
Rich are their scarfs, their chargers featly prance:
If in the dangerous game they shine to-day,
The crowd's loud shout and ladies' lovely glance,
Best prize of better acts, they bear away,
And all that kings or chiefs e'er gain their toils repay.

74

In costly sheen and gaudy cloak array'd,
But all afoot, the light-limb'd Matadore
Stands in the centre, eager to invade
The lord of lowing herds; but not before

The ground with cautious tread is traversed o'er,
Lest aught unseen should lurk to thwart his speed:
His arms a dart, he fights aloof, nor more
Can man achieve without the friendly steed—
Alas! too oft condem'd for him to bear and bleed.

75

Thrice sounds the clarion; lo! the signal falls,
The den expands, and Expectation mute
Gapes round the silent circle's peopled walls.
Bounds with one lashing spring the mighty brute,
And, wildly staring, spurns, with sounding foot,
The sand, nor blindly rushes on his foe:
Here, there, he points his threatening front, to suit
His first attack, wide waving to and fro
His angry tail; red rolls his eye's dilated glow.

76

Sudden he stops; his eye is fix'd; away,
Away, thou heedless boy! prepare the spear:
Now is thy time, to perish, or display
The skill that yet may check his mad career.
With well-timed croupe the nimble coursers veer;
On foams the bull, but not unscathed he goes;
Streams from his flank the crimson torrent clear;
He flies, he wheels, distracted with his throes;
Dart follows dart; lance, lance; loud bellowings speak his woes.

77

Again he comes; nor dart nor lance avail,
Nor the wild plunging of the tortured horse;
Though man and man's avenging arms assail,
Vain are his weapons, vainer is his force.
One gallant steed is stretch'd a mangled corse;
Another, hideous sight! unseam'd appears,
His gory chest unveils life's panting source,
Though death-struck still his feeble frame he rears,
Staggering, but stemming all, his lord unharm'd he bears.

78

Foil'd, bleeding, breathless, furious to the last,
Full in the centre stands the bull at bay,
'Mid wounds, and clinging darts, and lances brast,
And foes disabled in the brutal fray:
And now the Matadores around him play,
Shake the red cloak, and poise the ready brand:
Once more through all he bursts his thundering way—
Vain rage! the mantle quits the conynge hand,
Wraps his fierce eye—'tis past—he sinks upon the sand!

*   *   *   *   *

To Inez

Nay, smile not at my sullen brow,
    Alas! I cannot smile again;
Yet Heaven avert that ever thou
    Shouldst weep, and haply weep in vain.

And dost thou ask, what secret woe
    I bear, corroding joy and youth?
And wilt thou vainly seek to know
    A pang, ev'n thou must fail to soothe?

It is not love, it is not hate,
    Nor low Ambition's honours lost,
That bids me loathe my present state,
    And fly from all I prized the most;

It is that weariness which springs
    From all I meet, or hear, or see;
To me no pleasure Beauty brings;
    Thine eyes have scarce a charm for me.

It is that settled, ceaseless gloom
    The fabled Hebrew wanderer bore;
That will not look beyond the tomb,
    But cannot hope for rest before.

What Exile from himself can flee?
  To zones, though more and more remote,
Still, still pursues, where'er I be,
  The blight of life—the demon Thought.

Yet others rapt in pleasure seem,
  And taste of all that I forsake;
Oh! may they still of transport dream,
  And ne'er, at least like me, awake!

Through many a clime 'tis mine to go,
  With many a retrospection curst,
And all my solace is to know,
  Whate'er betides, I've known the worst.

What is that worst? Nay do not ask—
  In pity from the search forbear:
Smile on—nor venture to unmask
  Man's heart, and view the Hell that's there.

85

Adieu, fair Cadiz! yea, a long adieu!
Who may forget how well thy walls have stood!
When all were changing thou alone wert true,
First to be free, and last to be subdued:
And if amidst a scene, a shock so rude,
Some native blood was seen thy streets to dye;
A traitor only fell beneath the feud:
Here all were noble, save Nobility;
None hugg'd a conqueror's chain, save fallen Chivalry!

*   *   *   *   *

CANTO II

*   *   *   *   *

2

Ancient of days! august Athena! where,
Where are thy men of might? thy grand in soul?
Gone, glimmering thro' the dream of things that were;
First in the race that led to Glory's goal,
They won, and pass'd away—is this the whole?
A schoolboy's tale, the wonder of an hour!
The warrior's weapon and the sophist's stole
Are sought in vain, and o'er each mouldering tower,
Dim with the mist of years, gray flits the shade of power.

3

Son of the Morning, rise! approach you here!
Come—but molest not yon defenceless urn:
Look on this spot—a nation's sepulchre!
Abode of gods, whose shrines no longer burn.
Even gods must yield—religions take their turn:
'Twas Jove's—'tis Mahomet's—and other creeds
Will rise with other years, till man shall learn
Vainly his incense soars, his victim bleeds;
Poor child of Doubt and Death, whose hope is built on reeds.

*   *   *   *   *

9

There, thou!—whose love and life together fled,
Have left me here to love and live in vain—
Twined with my heart, and can I deem thee dead,
When busy Memory flashes on my brain?

Well—I will dream that we may meet again,
And woo the vision to my vacant breast:
If aught of young Remembrance then remain,
Be as it may Futurity's behest,
For me 'twere bliss enough to know thy spirit blest!

*   *   *   *   *

15

Cold is the heart, fair Greece! that looks on thee,
Nor feels as lovers o'er the dust they loved;
Dull is the eye that will not weep to see
Thy walls defaced, thy mouldering shrines removed
By British hands, which it had best behoved
To guard those relics ne'er to be restored.
Curst be the hour when from their isle they roved,
And once again thy hapless bosom gored,
And snatch'd thy shrinking Gods to northern climes abhorr'd!

*   *   *   *   *

22

Through Calpe's straits survey the steepy shore;
Europe and Afric on each other gaze!
Lands of the dark-eyed Maid and dusky Moor
Alike beheld beneath pale Hecate's blaze:
How softly on the Spanish shore she plays,
Disclosing rock, and slope, and forest brown,
Distinct, though darkening with her waning phase;
But Mauritania's giant-shadows frown,
From mountain-cliff to coast descending sombre down.

23

'Tis night, when Meditation bids us feel
We once have loved, though love is at an end:
The heart; lone mourner of its baffled zeal,
Though friendless now, will dream it had a friend.

Who with the weight of years would wish to bend,
When Youth itself survives young Love and Joy?
Alas! when mingling souls forget to blend,
Death hath but little left him to destroy!
Ah! happy years! once more, who would not be a boy?

*   *   *   *   *

26

But 'midst the crowd, the hum, the shock of men,
To hear, to see, to feel, and to possess,
And roam along, the world's tired denizen,
With none who bless us, none whom we can bless;
Minions of splendour shrinking from distress!
None that, with kindred consciousness endued,
If we were not, would seem to smile the less
Of all that flatter'd, follow'd, sought, and sued:
This is to be alone; this, this is solitude!

*   *   *   *   *

73

Fair Greece! sad relic of departed worth!
Immortal, though no more; though fallen, great!
Who now shall lead thy scatter'd children forth,
And long accustom'd bondage uncreate?
Not such thy sons who whilome did await,
The hopeless warriors of a willing doom,
In bleak Thermopylae's sepulchral strait—
Oh! who that gallant spirit shall resume,
Leap from Eurotas' banks, and call thee from the tomb?

74

Spirit of freedom! when on Phyle's brow
Thou sat'st with Thrasybulus and his train,
Couldst thou forebode the dismal hour which now
Dims the green beauties of thine Attic plain?

Not thirty tyrants now enforce the chain,
But every carle can lord it o'er thy land;
Nor rise thy sons, but idly rail in vain,
Trembling beneath the scourge of Turkish hand,
From birth till death enslaved; in word, in deed, unmann'd.

* * * * *

88

Where'er we tread 'tis haunted, holy ground;
No earth of thine is lost in vulgar mould,
But one vast realm of wonder spreads around,
And all the Muse's tales seem truly told,
Till the sense aches with gazing to behold
The scenes our earliest dreams have dwelt upon:
Each hill and dale, each deepening glen and wold
Defies the power which crush'd thy temples gone:
Age shakes Athena's tower, but spares gray Marathon.

* * * * *

96

Oh! ever loving, lovely, and beloved!
How selfish Sorrow ponders on the past,
And clings to thoughts now better far removed!
But Time shall tear thy shadow from me last.
All thou couldst have of mine, stern Death! thou hast;
The parent, friend, and now the more than friend:
Ne'er yet for one thine arrows flew so fast,
And grief with grief continuing still to blend,
Hath snatch'd the little joy that life had yet to lend.

97

Then must I plunge again into the crowd,
And follow all that Peace disdains to seek?
Where Revel calls, and Laughter, vainly loud,
False to the heart, distorts the hollow cheek,

To leave the flagging spirit doubly weak:
Still o'er the features, which perforce they cheer,
To feign the pleasure or conceal the pique;
Smiles form the channel of a future tear,
Or raise the writhing lip with ill-dissembled sneer.

98

What is the worst of woes that wait on age?
What stamps the wrinkle deeper on the brow?
To view each loved one blotted from life's page,
And be alone on earth, as I am now.
Before the Chastener humbly let me bow,
O'er hearts divided and o'er hopes destroy'd:
Roll on, vain days! full reckless may ye flow,
Since Time hath reft whate'er my soul enjoy'd,
And with the ills of Eld mine earlier years alloy'd.

CANTO III

1

Is thy face like thy mother's, my fair child!
Ada! sole daughter of my house and heart?
When last I saw thy young blue eyes they smiled,
And then we parted,—not as now we part,
But with a hope.—
                    Awaking with a start,
The waters heave around me; and on high
The winds lift up their voices: I depart,
Whither I know not; but the hour's gone by,
When Albion's lessening shores could grieve or glad mine eye.

2

Once more upon the waters! yet once more!
And the waves bound beneath me as a steed
That knows his rider. Welcome to their roar!
Swift be their guidance, wheresoe'er it lead!

Though the strain'd mast should quiver as a reed,
And the rent canvass fluttering strew the gale,
Still must I on; for I am as a weed,
Flung from the rock, on Ocean's foam, to sail
Where'er the surge may sweep, the tempest's breath prevail.

3

In my youth's summer I did sing of One,
The wandering outlaw of his own dark mind;
Again I seize the theme then but begun,
And bear it with me, as the rushing wind
Bears the cloud onwards: in that Tale I find
The furrows of long thought, and dried-up tears,
Which, ebbing, leave a sterile track behind,
O'er which all heavily the journeying years
Plod the last sands of life,—where not a flower appears.

4

Since my young days of passion—joy, or pain,
Perchance my heart and harp have lost a string,
And both may jar: it may be that in vain
I would essay as I have sung to sing.
Yet, though a dreary strain, to this I cling;
So that it wean me from the weary dream
Of selfish grief or gladness—so it fling
Forgetfulness around me—it shall seem
To me, though to none else, a not ungrateful theme.

5

He, who grown aged in this world of woe,
In deeds, not years, piercing the depths of life,
So that no wonder waits him; nor below
Can love, or sorrow, fame, ambition, strife,
Cut to his heart again with the keen knife
Of silent, sharp endurance:—he can tell
Why thought seeks refuge in lone caves, yet rife
With airy images, and shapes which dwell
Still unimpair'd, though old, in the soul's haunted cell.

6

'Tis to create, and in creating live
A being more intense, that we endow
With form our fancy, gaining as we give
The life we image, even as I do now.
What am I? Nothing; but not so art thou,
Soul of my thought! with whom I traverse earth,
Invisible but gazing, as I glow
Mix'd with thy spirit, blended with thy birth,
And feeling still with thee in my crush'd feelings' dearth.

7

Yet must I think less wildly:—I *have* thought
Too long and darkly, till my brain became,
In its own eddy boiling and o'erwrought,
A whirling gulf of phantasy and flame:
And thus, untaught in youth my heart to tame,
My springs of life were poison'd. 'Tis too late!
Yet am I changed; though still enough the same
In strength to bear what time can not abate,
And feed on bitter fruits without accusing Fate.

*   *   *   *   *

11

But who can view the ripen'd rose, nor seek
To wear it? who can curiously behold
The smoothness and the sheen of beauty's cheek,
Nor feel the heart can never all grow old?
Who can contemplate Fame through clouds unfold
The star which rises o'er her steep, nor climb?
Harold, once more within the vortex, roll'd
On with the giddy circle, chasing Time,
Yet with a nobler aim than in his youth's fond prime.

12

But soon he knew himself the most unfit
Of men to herd with Man, with whom he held
Little in common; untaught to submit
His thoughts to others, though his soul was quell'd

In youth by his own thoughts; still uncompell'd
He would not yield dominion of his mind
To spirits against whom his own rebell'd;
Proud though in desolation, which could find
A life within itself, to breathe without mankind.

13

Where rose the mountains, there to him were friends;
Where roll'd the ocean, thereon was his home;
Where a blue sky and glowing clime extends,
He had the passion and the power to roam;
The desert, forest, cavern, breaker's foam,
Were unto him companionship; they spake
A mutual language, clearer than the tome
Of his land's tongue, which he would oft forsake
For Nature's pages, glass'd by sunbeams on the lake.

14

Like the Chaldean, he could watch the stars,
Till he had peopled them with beings bright
As their own beams; and earth, and earth-born jars,
And human frailties, were forgotten quite:
Could he have kept his spirit to that flight,
He had been happy; but this clay will sink
Its spark immortal, envying it the light
To which it mounts, as if to break the link
That keeps us from yon heaven which woos us to its brink.

15

But in Man's dwellings he became a thing
Restless and worn, and stern and wearisome,
Droop'd as a wild-born falcon with clipt wing,
To whom the boundless air alone were home:
Then came his fit again, which to o'ercome,
As eagerly the barr'd-up bird will beat
His breast and beak against his wiry dome
Till the blood tinge his plumage, so the heat
Of his impeded soul would through his bosom eat.

* * * * *

17

Stop!—for thy tread is on an Empire's dust!
An Earthquake's spoil is sepulchred below!
Is the spot mark'd with no colossal bust?
Nor column trophied for triumphal show?
None; but the moral's truth tells simpler so,
As the ground was before, thus let it be;—
How that red rain hath made the harvest grow!
And is this all the world has gain'd by thee,
Thou first and last of fields! king-making Victory!

*   *   *   *   *

20

If not, o'er one fallen despot boast no more!
In vain fair cheeks were furrow'd with hot tears
For Europe's flowers, long rooted up before
The trampler of her vineyards; in vain years
Of death, depopulation, bondage, fears,
Have all been borne, and broken by the accord
Of roused-up millions: all that most endears
Glory, is when the myrtle wreathes a sword
Such as Harmodius drew on Athens' tyrant lord.

21

There was a sound of revelry by night,
And Belgium's capital had gather'd then
Her Beauty and her Chivalry, and bright
The lamps shone o'er fair women and brave men;
A thousand hearts beat happily; and when
Music arose with its voluptuous swell,
Soft eyes look'd love to eyes which spake again,
And all went merry as a marriage-bell;
But hush! hark! a deep sound strikes like a rising knell!

22

Did ye not hear it?—No; 'twas but the wind,
Or the car rattling o'er the stony street;
On with the dance! let joy be unconfined;
No sleep till morn, when Youth and Pleasure meet

To chase the glowing Hours with flying feet:—
But, hark!—that heavy sound breaks in once more,
As if the clouds its echo would repeat;
And nearer, clearer, deadlier than before!
Arm! Arm! it is—it is—the cannon's opening roar!

23

Within a window'd niche of that high hall
Sate Brunswick's fated chieftain; he did hear
That sound the first amidst the festival,
And caught its tone with Death's prophetic ear;
And when they smiled because he deem'd it near,
His heart more truly knew that peal too well
Which stretch'd his father on a bloody bier,
And roused the vengeance blood alone could quell:
He rush'd into the field, and, foremost fighting, fell.

24

Ah; then and there was hurrying to and fro,
And gathering tears, and tremblings of distress,
And cheeks all pale, which but an hour ago
Blush'd at the praise of their own loveliness;
And there were sudden partings, such as press
The life from out young hearts, and choking sighs
Which ne'er might be repeated: who could guess
If ever more should meet those mutual eyes,
Since upon night so sweet such awful morn could rise!

25

And there was mounting in hot haste: the steed,
The mustering squadron, and the clattering car,
Went pouring forward with impetuous speed,
And swiftly forming in the ranks of war;
And the deep thunder peal on peal afar;
And near, the beat of the alarming drum
Roused up the soldier ere the morning star;
While throng'd the citizens with terror dumb,
Or whispering, with white lips—"The foe! They come! they come!"

26

And wild and high the "Camerons' gathering" rose!
The war-note of Lochiel, which Albyn's hills
Have heard, and heard too have her Saxon foes:—
How in the noon of night that pibroch thrills,
Savage and shrill! But with the breath which fills
Their mountain-pipe, so fill the mountaineers
With the fierce native daring which instils
The stirring memory of a thousand years,
And Evan's, Donald's fame rings in each clansman's ears!

27

And Ardennes waves above them her green leaves
Dewy with nature's tear-drops, as they pass,
Grieving, if aught inanimate e'er grieves,
Over the unreturning brave,—alas!
Ere evening to be trodden like the grass
Which now beneath them, but above shall grow
In its next verdure, when this fiery mass
Of living valour, rolling on the foe,
And burning with high hope, shall moulder cold and low.

28

Last noon beheld them full of lusty life,
Last eve in Beauty's circle proudly gay,
The midnight brought the signal-sound of strife,
The morn the marshalling in arms,—the day
Battle's magnificently stern array!
The thunder-clouds close o'er it, which when rent,
The earth is cover'd thick with other clay,
Which her own clay shall cover, heap'd and pent,
Rider and horse,—friend, foe—in one red burial blent!

29

Their praise is hymn'd by loftier harps than mine:
Yet one I would select from that proud throng,
Partly because they blend me with his line,
And partly that I did his sire some wrong,

And partly that bright names will hallow song;
And his was of the bravest, and when shower'd
The death-bolts deadliest the thinn'd files along,
Even where the thickest of war's tempest lower'd,
They reach'd no nobler breast than thine, young, gallant Howard!

30

There have been tears and breaking hearts for thee,
And mine were nothing, had I such to give;
But when I stood beneath the fresh green tree,
Which living waves where thou didst cease to live,
And saw around me the wide field revive
With fruits and fertile promise, and the Spring
Come forth her work of gladness to contrive,
With all her reckless birds upon the wing,
I turn'd from all she brought to those she could not bring.

*   *   *   *   *

32

They mourn, but smile at length; and, smiling, mourn.
The tree will wither long before it fall;
The hull drives on, though mast and sail be torn;
The roof-tree sinks, but moulders on the hall
In massy hoariness; the ruin'd wall
Stands when its wind-worn battlements are gone;
The bars survive the captive they enthral;
The day drags through, though storms keep out the sun;
And thus the heart will break, yet brokenly live on:

33

Even as a broken mirror, which the glass
In every fragment multiplies; and makes
A thousand images of one that was,
The same, and still the more, the more it breaks;
And thus the heart will do which not forsakes,
Living in shatter'd guise, and still, and cold,
And bloodless, with its sleepless sorrow aches,
Yet withers on till all without is old,
Showing no visible sign, for such things are untold.

*   *   *   *   *

72

I live not in myself, but I become
Portion of that around me; and to me
High mountains are a feeling, but the hum
Of human cities torture: I can see
Nothing to loathe in nature, save to be
A link reluctant in a fleshly chain,
Class'd among creatures, when the soul can flee,
And with the sky, the peak, the heaving plain
Of ocean, or the stars, mingle, and not in vain.

73

And thus I am absorb'd, and this is life:
I look upon the peopled desert past
As on a place of agony and strife,
Where, for some sin, to sorrow I was cast,
To act and suffer, but remount at last
With a fresh pinion; which I feel to spring,
Though young, yet waxing vigorous as the blast
Which it would cope with, on delighted wing,
Spurning the clay-cold bonds which round our being cling.

74

And when, at length, the mind shall be all free
From what it hates in this degraded form,
Reft of its carnal life, save what shall be
Existent happier in the fly and worm,—
When elements to elements conform,
And dust is as it should be, shall I not
Feel all I see, less dazzling, but more warm?
The bodiless thought? the Spirit of each spot,
Of which, even now, I share at times the immortal lot?

75

Are not the mountains, waves, and skies, a part
Of me and of my soul, as I of them?
Is not the love of these deep in my heart
With a pure passion? should I not contemn

All objects, if compared with these? and stem
A tide of suffering, rather than forego
Such feelings for the hard and worldly phlegm
Of those whose eyes are only turn'd below,
Gazing upon the ground, with thoughts which dare not glow?

*   *   *   *   *

88

Ye stars! which are the poetry of Heaven!
If in your bright leaves we would read the fate
Of men and empires,—'tis to be forgiven,
That in our aspirations to be great,
Our destinies o'erleap their mortal state,
And claim a kindred with you; for ye are
A beauty and a mystery, and create
In us such love and reverence from afar,
That fortune, fame, power, life, have named themselves a star.

89

All heaven and earth are still—though not in sleep,
But breathless, as we grow when feeling most;
And silent, as we stand in thoughts too deep:—
All heaven and earth are still: from the high host
Of stars, to the lull'd lake and mountain-coast,
All is concentred in a life intense,
Where not a beam, nor air, nor leaf is lost,
But hath a part of being, and a sense
Of that which is of all Creator and defence.

90

Then stirs the feeling infinite, so felt
In solitude, where we are *least* alone;
A truth, which through our being then doth melt
And purifies from self: it is a tone,
The soul and source of music, which makes known
Eternal harmony, and sheds a charm,
Like to the fabled Cytherea's zone,
Binding all things with beauty;—'twould disarm
The spectre Death, had he substantial power to harm.

*   *   *   *   *

95

Now, where the quick Rhone thus has cleft his way,
The mightiest of the storms hath ta'en his stand:
For here, not one, but many, make their play,
And fling their thunderbolts from hand to hand,
Flashing and cast around: of all the band,
The brightest through these parted hills hath fork'd
His lightnings,—as if he did understand,
That in such gaps as desolation work'd,
There the hot shaft should blast whatever therein lurk'd.

96

Sky, mountains, river, winds, lake, lightnings! ye,
With night, and clouds, and thunder, and a soul
To make these felt and feeling, well may be
Things that have made me watchful; the far roll
Of your departing voices is the knoll
Of what in me is sleepless,—if I rest.
But where of ye, oh tempests! is the goal?
Are ye like those within the human breast?
Or do ye find, at length, like eagles, some high nest?

97

Could I embody and unbosom now
That which is most within me,—could I wreak
My thoughts upon expression, and thus throw
Soul, heart, mind, passions, feelings, strong or weak,
All that I would have sought, and all I seek,
Bear, know, feel, and yet breathe—into *one* word,
And that one word were Lightning, I would speak;
But as it is, I live and die unheard,
With a most voiceless thought, sheathing it as a sword.

*   *   *   *   *

113

I have not loved the world, nor the world me;
I have not flatter'd its rank breath, nor bow'd
To its idolatries a patient knee,—
Nor coin'd my cheek to smiles,—nor cried aloud
In worship of an echo; in the crowd
They could not deem me one of such; I stood
Among them, but not of them; in a shroud
Of thoughts which were not their thoughts, and still could,
Had I not filed my mind, which thus itself subdued.

114

I have not loved the world, nor the world me,—
But let us part fair foes; I do believe,
Though I have found them not, that there may be
Words which are things,—hopes which will not deceive,
And virtues which are merciful, nor weave
Snares for the failing: I would also deem
O'er others' griefs that some sincerely grieve;
That two, or one, are almost what they seem,—
That goodness is no name, and happiness no dream.

115

My daughter! with thy name this song begun—
My daughter! with thy name thus much shall end—
I see thee not,—I hear thee not,—but none
Can be so wrapt in thee; thou art the friend
To whom the shadows of far years extend:
Albeit my brow thou never shouldst behold,
My voice shall with thy future visions blend,
And reach into thy heart,—when mine is cold,—
A token and a tone, even from thy father's mould.

116

To aid thy mind's development,—to watch
Thy dawn of little joys—to sit and see
Almost thy very growth,—to view thee catch
Knowledge of objects,—wonders yet to thee!

To hold thee lightly on a gentle knee,
And print on thy soft cheek a parent's kiss,—
This, it should seem, was not reserved for me;
Yet this was in my nature:—as it is,
I know not what is there, yet something like to this.

* * * * *

CANTO IV

1

I stood in Venice, on the Bridge of Sighs;
A palace and a prison on each hand:
I saw from out the wave her structures rise
As from the stroke of the enchanter's wand:
A thousand years their cloudy wings expand
Around me, and a dying Glory smiles
O'er the far times, when many a subject land
Look'd to the wingèd Lion's marble piles,
Where Venice sate in state, throned on her hundred isles!

2

She looks a sea Cybele, fresh from ocean,
Rising with her tiara of proud towers
At airy distance with majestic motion,
A ruler of the waters and their powers:
And such she was;—her daughters had their dowers
From spoils of nations, and the exhaustless East
Pour'd in her lap all gems in sparkling showers:
In purple was she robed, and of her feast
Monarchs partook, and deem'd their dignity increased.

3

In Venice Tasso's echoes are no more,
And silent rows the songless gondolier;
Her palaces are crumbling to the shore,
And music meets not always now the ear:

Those days are gone—but Beauty still is here.
States fall, arts fade—but Nature doth not die:
Nor yet forget how Venice once was dear,
The pleasant place of all festivity,
The revel of the earth, the masque of Italy!

* * * * *

5

The beings of the mind are not of clay;
Essentially immortal, they create
And multiply in us a brighter ray
And more beloved existence: that which fate
Prohibits to dull life, in this our state
Of mortal bondage, by these spirits supplied,
First exiles, then replaces what we hate;
Watering the heart whose early flowers have died,
And with a fresher growth replenishing the void.

* * * * *

23

But ever and anon of griefs subdued
There comes a token like a scorpion's sting,
Scarce seen, but with fresh bitterness imbued;
And slight withal may be the things which bring
Back on the heart the weight which it would fling
Aside for ever: it may be a sound—
A tone of music,—summer's eve—or spring,
A flower—the wind—the ocean—which shall wound,
Striking the electric chain wherewith we are darkly bound;

24

And how and why we know not, nor can trace
Home to its cloud this lightning of the mind,
But feel the shock renew'd, nor can efface
The blight and blackening which it leaves behind,

Which out of things familiar, undesign'd,
When least we deem of such, calls up to view
The spectres whom no exorcism can bind,
The cold—the changed—perchance the dead—anew,
The mourn'd, the loved, the lost—too many! yet how few!

*   *   *   *   *

54

In Santa Croce's holy precincts lie
Ashes which make it holier, dust which is
Even in itself an immortality,
Though there were nothing save the past, and this,
The particle of those sublimities
Which have relapsed to chaos:—here repose
Angelo's, Alfieri's bones, and his,
The starry Galileo, with his woes;
Here Machiavelli's earth return'd to whence it rose.

55

These are four minds, which, like the elements,
Might furnish forth creation:—Italy!
Time, which hath wrong'd thee with ten thousand rents
Of thine imperial garment, shall deny,
And hath denied, to every other sky,
Spirits which soar from ruin:—thy decay
Is still impregnate with divinity,
Which gilds it with revivifying ray,
Such as the great of yore, Canova is to-day.

56

But where repose the all Etruscan three—
Dante, and Petrarch, and, scarce less than they,
The Bard of Prose, creative spirit! he
Of the Hundred Tales of love—where did they lay
Their bones, distinguish'd from our common clay
In death as life? Are they resolved to dust,
And have their country's marbles nought to say?
Could not her quarries furnish forth one bust?
Did they not to her breast their filial earth entrust?

57

Ungrateful Florence! Dante sleeps afar,
Like Scipio, buried by the upbraiding shore;
Thy factions, in their worse than civil war,
Proscribed the bard whose name for evermore
Their children's children would in vain adore
With the remorse of ages: and the crown
Which Petrarch's laureate brow supremely wore,
Upon a far and foreign soil had grown,
His life, his fame, his grave, though rifled—not thine own.

58

Boccaccio to his parent earth bequeath'd
His dust,—and lies it not her great among,
With many a sweet and solemn requiem breathed
O'er him who form'd the Tuscan's siren tongue?
That music in itself, whose sounds are song,
The poetry of speech? No;—even his tomb
Uptorn, must bear the hyaena bigot's wrong,
Nor more amidst the meaner dead find room,
Nor claim a passing sigh, because it told for *whom!*

59

And Santa Croce wants their mighty dust;
Yet for this want more noted, as of yore
The Caesar's pageant, shorn of Brutus' bust,
Did but of Rome's best Son remind her more:
Happier Ravenna! on thy hoary shore,
Fortress of falling empire! honour'd sleeps
The immortal exile;—Arqua, too, her store
Of tuneful relics proudly claims and keeps,
While Florence vainly begs her banish'd dead and weeps.

*　　*　　*　　*　　*

78

O Rome! my country! city of the soul!
The orphans of the heart must turn to thee,
Lone mother of dead empires! and control
In their shut breasts their petty misery.

What are our woes and sufferance? Come and see
The cypress, hear the owl, and plod your way
O'er steps of broken thrones and temples, ye
Whose agonies are evils of a day!—
A world is at our feet as fragile as our clay.

*   *   *   *   *

81

The double night of ages, and of her,
Night's daughter, Ignorance, hath wrapt and wrap
All round us; we but feel our way to err:
The ocean hath his chart, the stars their map,
And Knowledge spreads them on her ample lap;
But Rome is as the desert, where we steer
Stumbling o'er recollections; now we clap
Our hands and cry "Eureka!" it is clear—
When but some false mirage of ruin rises near.

*   *   *   *   *

107

Cypress and ivy, weed and wallflower grown
Matted and mass'd together, hillocks heap'd
On what were chambers, arch crush'd, column strown
In fragments, choked-up vaults, and frescos steep'd
In subterranean damps, where the owl peep'd,
Deeming it midnight;—Temples, baths, or halls?
Pronounce who can; for all that Learning reap'd
From her research hath been, that these are walls—
Behold the Imperial Mount! 'tis thus the mighty falls.

108

There is the moral of all human tales;
'Tis but the same rehearsal of the past;
First Freedom, and then Glory—when that fails,
Wealth, vice, corruption,—barbarism at last.

And History, with all her volumes vast,
Hath but *one* page,—'tis better written here,
Where gorgeous Tyranny had thus amass'd
All treasures, all delights, that eye or ear,
Heart, soul, could seek, tongue ask.—Away with words! draw near,

109

Admire, exult—despise—laugh, weep,—for here
There is such matter for all feeling:—Man!
Thou pendulum betwixt a smile and tear,
Ages and realms are crowded in this span;
This mountain, whose obliterated plan
The pyramid of empires pinnacled,
Of Glory's gew-gaws shining in the van,
Till the sun's rays with added flame were fill'd!
Where are its golden roofs! where those who dared to build?

110

Tully was not so eloquent as thou,
Thou nameless column with the buried base!
What are the laurels of the Caesar's brow?
Crown me with ivy from his dwelling-place.
Whose arch or pillar meets me in the face,
Titus' or Trajan's? No—'tis that of Time:
Triumph, arch, pillar, all he doth displace
Scoffing; and apostolic statues climb
To crush the imperial urn, whose ashes slept sublime,

111

Buried in air, the deep blue sky of Rome,
And looking to the stars: they had contain'd
A spirit which with these would find a home,
The last of those who o'er the whole earth reign'd,
The Roman globe, for after none sustain'd
But yielded back his conquests:—he was more
Than a mere Alexander, and, unstain'd
With household blood and wine, serenely wore
His sovereign virtues—still we Trajan's name adore.

112

Where is the rock of Triumph, the high place
Where Rome embraced her heroes? where the steep
Tarpeian? fittest goal of Treason's race,
The promontory whence the Traitor's Leap
Cured all ambition. Did the conquerors heap
Their spoils here? Yes: and in yon field below,
A thousand years of silenced factions sleep—
The Forum, where the immortal accents glow,
And still the eloquent air breathes—burns with Cicero!

*   *   *   *   *

126

Our life is a false nature—'tis not in
The harmony of things,—this hard decree,
This uneradicable taint of sin,
This boundless upas, this all-blasting tree,
Whose root is earth, whose leaves and branches be
The skies which rain their plagues on men like dew—
Disease, death, bondage—all the woes we see—
And worse, the woes we see not—which throb through
The immedicable soul, with heart-aches ever new.

*   *   *   *   *

146

Simple, erect, severe, austere, sublime—
Shrine of all saints, and temple of all gods,
From Jove to Jesus—spared and blest by time;
Looking tranquillity, while falls or nods
Arch, empire, each thing round thee, and man plods
His way through thorns to ashes—glorious dome!
Shalt thou not last? Time's scythe and tyrants' rods
Shiver upon thee—sanctuary and home
Of art and piety—Pantheon! pride of Rome!

147

Relic of nobler days, and noblest arts;
Despoil'd yet perfect, with thy circle spreads
A holiness appealing to all hearts—
To art a model; and to him who treads
Rome for the sake of ages, Glory sheds
Her light through thy sole aperture; to those
Who worship, here are altars for their beads;
And they who feel for genius may repose
Their eyes on honour'd forms, whose busts around them close.

*   *   *   *   *

153

But lo! the dome—the vast and wondrous dome,
To which Diana's marvel was a cell—
Christ's mighty shrine above his martyr's tomb!
I have beheld the Ephesian's miracle—
Its columns strew the wilderness, and dwell
The hyaena and the jackal in their shade;
I have beheld Sophia's bright roofs swell
Their glittering mass i' the sun, and have survey'd
Its sanctuary the while the usurping Moslem pray'd:

154

But thou; of temples old, or altars new,
Standest alone—with nothing like to thee—
Worthiest of God, the holy and the true.
Since Zion's desolation, when that He
Forsook his former city, what could be,
Of earthly structures in his honour piled,
Of a sublimer aspect? Majesty,
Power, Glory, Strength, and Beauty, all are aisled
In this eternal ark of worship undefiled.

155

Enter: its grandeur overwhelms thee not;
And why? it is not lessen'd; but thy mind,
Expanded by the genius of the spot,
Has grown colossal, and can only find

A fit abode, wherein appear enshrined
Thy hopes of immortality; and thou
Shalt one day, if found worthy, so defined,
See thy God face to face, as thou dost now
His Holy of Holies, nor be blasted by his brow.

*   *   *   *   *

160

Or, turning to the Vatican, go see
Laocoön's torture dignifying pain—
A father's love and mortal's agony
With an immortal's patience blending:—vain
The struggle; vain, against the coiling strain
And gripe, and deepening of the dragon's grasp,
The old man's clench; the long envenom'd chain
Rivets the living links,—the enormous asp
Enforces pang on pang, and stifles gasp on gasp.

161

Or view the Lord of the unerring bow,
The God of life, and poesy, and light—
The Sun in human limbs array'd, and brow
All radiant from his triumph in the fight;
The shaft hath just been shot—the arrow bright
With an immortal's vengeance; in his eye
And nostril beautiful disdain, and might,
And majesty, flash their full lightnings by,
Developing in that one glance the Deity.

162

But in his delicate form—a dream of Love,
Shaped by some solitary nymph, whose breast
Long'd for a deathless lover from above,
And madden'd in that vision—are exprest
All that ideal beauty ever bless'd
The mind with in its most unearthly mood,
When each conception was a heavenly guest—
A ray of immortality—and stood,
Star-like, around, until they gather'd to a god!

*   *   *   *   *

173

Lo, Nemi! navell'd in the woody hills
So far, that the uprooting wind, which tears
The oak from his foundation, and which spills
The ocean o'er its boundary, and bears
Its foam against the skies, reluctant spares
The oval mirror of thy glassy lake;
And, calm as cherish'd hate, its surface wears
A deep cold settled aspect nought can shake,
All coil'd into itself and round, as sleeps the snake.

*   *   *   *   *

177

Oh! that the Desert were my dwelling-place,
With one fair Spirit for my minister,
That I might all forget the human race,
And, hating no one, love but only her!
Ye Elements!—in whose ennobling stir
I feel myself exalted—can ye not
Accord me such a being? Do I err
In deeming such inhabit many a spot?
Though with them to converse can rarely be our lot.

178

There is a pleasure in the pathless woods,
There is a rapture on the lonely shore,
There is society, where none intrudes,
By the deep Sea, and music in its roar:
I love not Man the less, but Nature more,
From these our interviews, in which I steal
From all I may be, or have been before,
To mingle with the Universe, and feel
What I can ne'er express, yet can not all conceal.

179

Roll on, thou deep and dark blue Ocean—roll!
Ten thousand fleets sweep over thee in vain;
Man marks the earth with ruin—his control
Stops with the shore;—upon the watery plain

The wrecks are all thy deed, nor doth remain
A shadow of man's ravage, save his own,
When for a moment, like a drop of rain,
He sinks into thy depths with bubbling groan,
Without a grave, unknell'd, uncoffin'd, and unknown.

180

His steps are not upon thy paths,—thy fields
Are not a spoil for him,—thou dost arise
And shake him from thee; the vile strength he wields
For earth's destruction thou dost all despise,
Spurning him from thy bosom to the skies,
And send'st him, shivering in thy playful spray
And howling, to his Gods, where haply lies
His petty hope in some near port or bay,
And dashest him again to earth;—there let him lay.

181

The armaments which thunder-strike the walls
Of rock-built cities, bidding nations quake
And monarchs tremble in their capitals,
The oak leviathans, whose huge ribs make
Their clay creator the vain title take
Of lord of thee, and arbiter of war;
These are thy toys, and, as the snowy flake,
They melt into thy yeast of waves, which mar
Alike the Armada's pride, or spoils of Trafalgar.

182

Thy shores are empires, changed in all save thee—
Assyria, Greece, Rome, Carthage, what are they?
Thy waters wasted them while they were free,
And many a tyrant since; their shores obey
The stranger, slave, or savage; their decay
Has dried up realms to deserts:—not so thou.
Unchangeable save to thy wild waves' play—
Time writes no wrinkle on thine azure brow—
Such as creation's dawn beheld, thou rollest now.

183

Thou glorious mirror, where the Almighty's form
Glasses itself in tempests; in all time,
Calm or convulsed—in breeze, or gale, or storm,
Icing the pole, or in the torrid clime
Dark-heaving;—boundless, endless, and sublime—
The image of Eternity—the throne
Of the Invisible; even from out thy slime
The monsters of the deep are made; each zone
Obeys thee; thou goest forth, dread, fathomless, alone.

184

And I have loved thee, Ocean! and my joy
Of youthful sports was on thy breast to be
Borne, like thy bubbles, onward: from a boy
I wanton'd with thy breakers—they to me
Were a delight; and if the freshening sea
Made them a terror—'twas a pleasing fear,
For I was as it were a child of thee,
And trusted to thy billows far and near,
And laid my hand upon thy mane—as I do here.

*   *   *   *   *

1809–18

From

THE BRIDE OF ABYDOS

A TURKISH TALE

CANTO II

1

THE winds are high on Helle's wave,
 As on that night of stormy water
When Love, who sent, forgot to save
The young, the beautiful, the brave,
 The lonely hope of Sestos' daughter.
Oh! when alone along the sky
Her turret-torch was blazing high,
Though rising gale, and breaking foam,
And shrieking sea-birds warn'd him home;
And clouds aloft and tides below,
With signs and sounds, forbade to go;
He could not see, he would not hear
Or sound or sign foreboding fear;
His eye but saw that light of love,
The only star it hail'd above;
His ear but rang with Hero's song,
"Ye waves, divide not lovers long!"—
That tale is old, but love anew
May nerve young hearts to prove as true.

2

The winds are high, and Helle's tide
    Rolls darkly heaving to the main;
And Night's descending shadows hide
    That field with blood bedew'd in vain,
The desert of old Priam's pride:
    The tombs, sole relics of his reign,
All—save immortal dreams that could beguile
The blind old man of Scio's rocky isle!

3

Oh! yet—for there my steps have been:
    These feet have press'd the sacred shore,
These limbs that buoyant wave hath borne—
Minstrel! with thee to muse, to mourn,
    To trace again those fields of yore,
Believing every hillock green
    Contains no fabled hero's ashes,
And that around the undoubted scene
    Thine own "broad Hellespont" still dashes,
Be long my lot! and cold were he
Who there could gaze denying thee!

4

The night hath closed on Helle's stream,
    Nor yet hath risen on Ida's hill
That moon, which shone on his high theme:
No warrior chides her peaceful beam,
    But conscious shepherds bless it still.
Their flocks are grazing on the mound
    Of him who felt the Dardan's arrow:
That mighty heap of gather'd ground
Which Ammon's son ran proudly round,
By nations raised, by monarchs crown'd,
    Is now a lone and nameless barrow!
    Within—thy dwelling-place how narrow!
Without—can only strangers breathe
The name of him that *was* beneath:
Dust long outlasts the storied stone;
But Thou—thy very dust is gone!

5

Late, late to-night will Dian cheer
The swain, and chase the boatman's fear;
Till then—no beacon on the cliff
May shape the course of struggling skiff;
The scatter'd lights that skirt the bay,
All, one by one, have died away;
The only lamp of this lone hour
Is glimmering in Zuleika's tower.
Yes! there is light in that lone chamber,
    And o'er her silken Ottoman
Are thrown the fragrant beads of amber,
    O'er which her fairy fingers ran;
Near these, with emerald rays beset,
(How could she thus that gem forget?)
Her mother's sainted amulet,
Whereon engraved the Koorsee text,
Could smooth this life, and win the next;
And by her comboloio lies
A Koran of illumined dyes;
And many a bright emblazon'd rhyme
By Persian scribes redeem'd from time,
And o'er those scrolls, not oft so mute,
Reclines her now neglected lute;
And round her lamp of fretted gold
Bloom flowers in urns of China's mould;
The richest work of Iran's loom,
And Sheeraz' tribute of perfume;
All that can eye or sense delight
    Are gather'd in that gorgeous room:
    But yet it hath an air of gloom.
She, of this Peri cell the sprite,
What doth she hence, and on so rude a night?

* * * * *

24

One bound he made, and gain'd the sand:
    Already at his feet hath sunk
The foremost of the prying band,
    A gasping head, a quivering trunk.

Another falls—but round him close
A swarming circle of his foes;
From right to left his path he cleft,
    And almost met the meeting wave:
His boat appears—not five oars' length—
His comrades strain with desperate strength—
    Oh! are they yet in time to save?
His feet the foremost breakers lave;
His band are plunging in the bay,
Their sabres glitter through the spray;
Wet—wild—unwearied to the strand
They struggle—now they touch the land!
They come—'tis but to add to slaughter—
His heart's best blood is on the water!

25

Escaped from shot, unharm'd by steel,
Or scarcely grazed its force to feel,
Had Selim won, betray'd, beset,
To where the strand and billows met;
There, as his last step left the land,
And the last death-blow dealt his hand—
Ah, wherefore did he turn to look
    For her his eye but sought in vain?
That pause, that fatal gaze he took,
    Hath doom'd his death, or fix'd his chain.
Sad proof, in peril and in pain,
How late will lover's hope remain!
His back was to the dashing spray;
Behind, but close, his comrades lay,
When, at the instant, hiss'd the ball—
"So may the foes of Giaffir fall!"
Whose voice is heard? whose carbine rang?
Whose bullet through the night-air sang,
Too nearly, deadly aim'd to err?
'Tis thine—Abdallah's Murderer!
The father slowly rued thy hate,
The son hath found a quicker fate:
Fast from his breast the blood is bubbling,
The whiteness of the sea-foam troubling,—
If aught his lips essay'd to groan,
The rushing billows choked the tone!

*   *   *   *   *

27

By Helle's stream there is a voice of wail!
And woman's eye is wet, man's cheek is pale:
Zuleika! last of Giaffir's race,
   Thy destined lord is come too late:
He sees not—ne'er shall see thy face!
     Can he not hear
The loud Wul-wulleh warn his distant ear?
   Thy handmaids weeping at the gate,
   The Koran-chanters of the hymn of fate,
   The silent slaves with folded arms that wait,
Sighs in the hall, and shrieks upon the gale,
    Tell him thy tale!
Thou didst not view thy Selim fall!
   That fearful moment when he left the cave
    Thy heart grew chill:
He was thy hope—thy joy—thy love—thine all—
   And that last thought on him thou couldst not save
    Sufficed to kill;
Burst forth in one wild cry—and all was still.
   Peace to thy broken heart, and virgin grave!
Ah! happy! but of life to lose the worst!
That grief—though deep—though fatal—was thy first!
Thrice happy! ne'er to feel nor fear the force
Of absence, shame, pride, hate, revenge, remorse!
And, oh! that pang where more than madness lies!
The worm that will not sleep—and never dies;
Thought of the gloomy day and ghastly night,
That dreads the darkness, and yet loathes the light,
That winds around, and tears the quivering heart!
Ah! wherefore not consume it—and depart!
Woe to thee, rash and unrelenting chief!
   Vainly thou heap'st the dust upon thy head,
   Vainly the sackcloth o'er thy limbs dost spread:
   By that same hand Abdallah—Selim bled.
Now let it tear thy beard in idle grief:
Thy pride of heart, thy bride for Osman's bed,
She, whom thy sultan had but seen to wed,
    Thy Daughter's dead!

Hope of thine age, thy twilight's lonely beam,
The Star hath set that shone on Helle's stream.
What quench'd its ray?—the blood that thou hast shed!
Hark! to the hurried question of Despair:
"Where is my child?"—an Echo answers—"Where?"

28

Within the place of thousand tombs
  That shine beneath, while dark above
The sad but living cypress glooms
And withers not, though branch and leaf
Are stamp'd with an eternal grief,
  Like early unrequited love,
One spot exists, which ever blooms,
  Ev'n in that deadly grove—
A single rose is shedding there
  Its lonely lustre, meek and pale:
It looks as planted by Despair—
  So white—so faint—the slightest gale
Might whirl the leaves on high;
  And yet, though storms and blight assail,
And hands more rude than wintry sky
  May wring it from the stem—in vain—
  To-morrow sees it bloom again!
The stalk some spirit gently rears,
And waters with celestial tears;
  For well may maids of Helle deem
That this can be no earthly flower,
Which mocks the tempest's withering hour,
And buds unshelter'd by a bower;
Nor droops, though spring refuse her shower,
  Nor woos the summer beam.
To it the livelong night there sings
  A bird unseen—but not remote:
Invisible his airy wings,
But soft as harp that Houri strings
  His long entrancing note!
It were the Bulbul; but his throat,
  Though mournful, pours not such a strain;
For they who listen cannot leave
The spot, but linger there and grieve
  As if they loved in vain!

And yet so sweet the tears they shed,
'Tis sorrow so unmix'd with dread,
They scarce can bear the morn to break
  That melancholy spell,
And longer yet would weep and wake,
  He sings so wild and well!
But when the day-blush bursts from high
Expires that magic melody.
And some have been who could believe
(So fondly youthful dreams deceive,
  Yet harsh be they that blame)
That note so piercing and profound
Will shape and syllable its sound
  Into Zuleika's name.
'Tis from her cypress summit heard,
That melts in air the liquid word:
'Tis from her lowly virgin earth
That white rose takes its tender birth.
There late was laid a marble stone;
Eve saw it placed—the Morrow gone!

*   *   *   *   *

1813

From

THE GIAOUR

A FRAGMENT OF A TURKISH TALE

ADVERTISEMENT

The Tale which these disjointed fragments present is
founded upon circumstances now less common in the East
than formerly; either because the ladies are more circumspect than in the "olden time;" or because the Christians
have better fortune, or less enterprise. The story, when
entire, contained the adventures of a female slave, who was
thrown, in the Mussulman manner, into the sea for infi-
delity, and avenged by a young Venetian, her lover, at the
time the Seven Islands were possessed by the Republic of
Venice, and soon after the Arnauts were beaten back
from the Morea, which they had ravaged for some time
subsequent to the Russian invasion. The desertion of the
Mainotes, on being refused the plunder of Misitra, led to
the abandonment of that enterprise, and to the desolation
of the Morea, during which the cruelty exercised on all
sides was unparalleled even in the annals of the faithful.

No breath of air to break the wave
That rolls below the Athenian's grave,
That tomb which, gleaming o'er the cliff,
First greets the homeward-veering skiff,
High o'er the land he saved in vain:
When shall such hero live again?

Fair clime! where every season smiles
Benignant o'er those blessed isles,
Which, seen from far Colonna's height,
Make glad the heart that hails the sight,
And lend to loneliness delight.
There, mildly dimpling, Ocean's cheek
Reflects the tints of many a peak
Caught by the laughing tides that lave
These Edens of the eastern wave;
And if, at times, a transient breeze
Break the blue crystal of the seas,
Or sweep one blossom from the trees,
How welcome is each gentle air
That wakes and wafts the odours there!

*   *   *   *   *

He who hath bent him o'er the dead,
Ere the first day of death is fled,
The first dark day of nothingness,
The last of danger and distress
(Before Decay's effacing fingers
Have swept the lines where beauty lingers),
And mark'd the mild angelic air,
The rapture of repose that's there,
The fix'd, yet tender traits that streak
The languor of the placid cheek,
And—but for that sad shrouded eye,
  That fires not, wins not, weeps not, now,
  And but for that chill, changeless brow,
Where cold Obstruction's apathy
Appals the gazing mourner's heart,
As if to him it could impart
  The doom he dreads, yet dwells upon:
  Yes, but for these, and these alone,
  Some moments, ay, one treacherous hour,
  He still might doubt the tyrant's power;
  So fair, so calm, so softly seal'd,
  The first, last look by death reveal'd!
Such is the aspect of this shore:
'Tis Greece, but living Greece no more!
So coldly sweet, so deadly fair,
We start, for soul is wanting there.

Hers is the loveliness in death,
That parts not quite with parting breath;
But beauty with that fearful bloom,
That hue which haunts it to the tomb,
Expression's last receding ray,
A gilded halo hovering round decay,
The farewell beam of Feeling pass'd away!
Spark of that flame, perchance of heavenly birth,
Which gleams, but warms no more its cherish'd earth!

*   *   *   *   *

As rising on its purple wing
The insect-queen of eastern spring,
O'er emerald meadows of Kashmeer
Invites the young pursuer near,
And leads him on from flower to flower
A weary chase and wasted hour,
Then leaves him, as it soars on high,
With panting heart and tearful eye:
So Beauty lures the full-grown child,
With hue as bright, and wing as wild;
A chase of idle hopes and fears,
Begun in folly, closed in tears.
If won, to equal ills betray'd,
Woe waits the insect and the maid;
A life of pain, the loss of peace,
From infant's play, and man's caprice:
The lovely toy so fiercely sought
Hath lost its charm by being caught;
For every touch that wooed its stay
Hath brush'd its brightest hues away,
Till, charm, and hue, and beauty gone,
'Tis left to fly or fall alone.
With wounded wing, or bleeding breast,
Ah! where shall either victim rest?
Can this with faded pinion soar
From rose to tulip as before?
Or Beauty, blighted in an hour,
Find joy within her broken bower?
No: gayer insects fluttering by
Ne'er droop the wing o'er those that die,

And lovelier things have mercy shown
To every failing but their own,
And every woe a tear can claim,
Except an erring sister's shame.

The Mind that broods o'er guilty woes,
  Is like the Scorpion girt by fire;
In circle narrowing as it glows,
The flames around their captive close,
Till, inly search'd by thousand throes,
  And maddening in her ire,
One sad and sole relief she knows,
The sting she nourish'd for her foes,
Whose venom never yet was vain,
Gives but one pang, and cures all pain,
And darts into her desperate brain:
So do the dark in soul expire,
Or live like Scorpion girt by fire;
So writhes the mind Remorse hath riven,
Unfit for earth, undoom'd for heaven,
Darkness above, despair beneath,
Around it flame, within it death!

        *   *   *   *   *

Some o'er their courser's harness leant,
  Half shelter'd by the steed;
Some fly behind the nearest rock,
And there await the coming shock,
  Nor tamely stand to bleed
Beneath the shaft of foes unseen,
Who dare not quit their craggy screen.
Stern Hassan only from his horse
Disdains to light, and keeps his course,
Till fiery flashes in the van
Proclaim too sure the robber clan
Have well secured the only way
Could now avail the promised prey.
Then curl'd his very beard with ire,
And glared his eye with fiercer fire:
"Though far and near the bullets hiss,
I've 'scaped a bloodier hour than this."
And now the foe their covert quit,
And call his vassals to submit:

But Hassan's frown and furious word
Are dreaded more than hostile sword,
Nor of his little band a man
Resign'd carbine or ataghan,
Nor raised the craven cry, Amaun!
In fuller sight, more near and near,
The lately ambush'd foes appear,
And, issuing from the grove, advance
Some who on battle-charger prance.
Who leads them on with foreign brand,
Far flashing in his red right hand?
" 'Tis he! 'tis he! I know him now;
I know him by his pallid brow;
I know him by the evil eye
That aids his envious treachery;
I know him by his jet-black barb:
Though now array'd in Arnaut garb,
Apostate from his own vile faith,
It shall not save him from the death.
'Tis he! well met in any hour!
Lost Leila's love, accursèd Giaour!"

　　As rolls the river into ocean,
In sable torrent wildly streaming;
　　As the sea-tide's opposing motion,
In azure column proudly gleaming,
Beats back the current many a rood,
In curling foam and mingling flood,
While eddying whirl, and breaking wave,
Roused by the blast of winter, rave;
Through sparkling spray, in thundering clash,
The lightnings of the waters flash
In awful whiteness o'er the shore,
That shines and shakes beneath the roar;
Thus—as the stream and ocean greet,
With waves that madden as they meet—
Thus join the bands, whom mutual wrong,
And fate, and fury, drive along.
The bickering sabres' shivering jar;
　　And, pealing wide, or ringing near
　　Its echoes on the throbbing ear,
The death-shot, hissing from afar:
The shock, the shout, the groan of war,

Reverberate along that vale,
More suited to the shepherd's tale:
Though few the numbers—theirs the strife
That neither spares nor speaks for life!
Ah! fondly youthful hearts can press,
To seize and share the dear caress,
But Love itself could never pant
For all that Beauty sighs to grant,
With half the fervour Hate bestows
Upon the last embrace of foes,
When grappling in the fight they fold
Those arms that ne'er shall lose their hold.
Friends meet to part; Love laughs at faith:
True foes, once met, are join'd till death!

*   *   *   *   *

To love the softest hearts are prone,
But such can ne'er be all his own;
Too timid in his woes to share,
Too meek to meet, or brave despair;
And sterner hearts alone may feel
The wound that time can never heal.
The rugged metal of the mine
Must burn before its surface shine,
But plunged within the furnace-flame,
It bends and melts—though still the same;
Then temper'd to thy want, or will,
'Twill serve thee to defend or kill;
A breastplate for thine hour of need,
Or blade to bid thy foeman bleed;
But if a dagger's form it bear,
Let those who shape its edge beware!
Thus passion's fire, and woman's art,
Can turn and tame the sterner heart;
From these its form and tone are ta'en,
And what they make it, must remain,
But break—before it bend again.

If solitude succeed to grief,
Release from pain is slight relief;
The vacant bosom's wilderness
Might thank the pang that made it less.

We loathe what none are left to share:
Even bliss—'twere woe alone to bear;
The heart once left thus desolate
Must fly at last for ease—to hate.
It is as if the dead could feel
The icy worm around them steal,
And shudder, as the reptiles creep
To revel o'er their rotting sleep,
Without the power to scare away
The cold consumers of their clay!

*   *   *   *   *

1813

PARISINA

I

It is the hour when from the boughs
   The nightingale's high note is heard:
It is the hour when lovers' vows
   Seem sweet in every whisper'd word;
And gentle winds, and waters near,
Make music to the lonely ear,
Each flower the dews have lightly wet,
And in the sky the stars are met,
And on the wave is deeper blue,
And on the leaf a browner hue,
And in the heaven that clear obscure,
So softly dark, and darkly pure,
Which follows the decline of day,
As twilight melts beneath the moon away.

II

But it is not to list to the waterfall
That Parisina leaves her hall,
And it is not to gaze on the heavenly light
That the lady walks in the shadow of night:
And if she sits in Este's bower,
'Tis not for the sake of its full-blown flower;
She listens—but not for the nightingale—
Though her ear expects as soft a tale.
There glides a step through the foliage thick,
And her cheek grows pale—and her heart beats quick.

There whispers a voice through the rustling leaves,
And her blush returns, and her bosom heaves:
A moment more—and they shall meet—
'Tis past—her lover's at her feet.

III

And what unto them is the world beside,
With all its change of time and tide?
Its living things—its earth and sky
Are nothing to their mind and eye.
And heedless as the dead are they
    Of aught around, above, beneath;
As if all else had pass'd away,
    They only for each other breathe:
Their very sighs are full of joy
    So deep, that, did it not decay,
That happy madness would destroy
    The hearts which feel its fiery sway.
Of guilt, of peril, do they deem,
In that tumultuous tender dream?
Who, that have felt that passion's power,
Or paused or fear'd in such an hour,
Or thought how brief such moments last?
But yet—they are already past!
Alas! we must awake before
We know such vision comes no more.

IV

With many a lingering look they leave
    The spot of guilty gladness past;
And though they hope and vow, they grieve
    As if that parting were the last.
The frequent sigh—the long embrace—
    The lip that there would cling for ever,
While gleams on Parisina's face
    The Heaven she fears will not forgive her,
As if each calmly conscious star
Beheld her frailty from afar—
The frequent sigh, the long embrace,
Yet binds them to their trysting-place.

But it must come, and they must part
In fearful heaviness of heart,
With all the deep and shuddering chill
Which follows fast the deeds of ill.

V

And Hugo is gone to his lonely bed,
    To covet there another's bride;
But she must lay her conscious head
    A husband's trusting heart beside.
But fever'd in her sleep she seems,
And red her cheek with troubled dreams,
    And mutters she in her unrest
A name she dares not breathe by day,
    And clasps her Lord unto the breast
Which pants for one away:
And he to that embrace awakes,
And, happy in the thought, mistakes
That dreaming sigh, and warm caress,
For such as he was wont to bless;
And could in very fondness weep
O'er her who loves him even in sleep.

VI

He clasp'd her sleeping to his heart,
    And listen'd to each broken word:
He hears—Why doth Prince Azo start,
    As if the Archangel's voice he heard?
And well he may—a deeper doom
Could scarcely thunder o'er his tomb,
When he shall wake to sleep no more,
And stand the eternal throne before.
And well he may—his earthly peace
Upon that sound is doom'd to cease.
That sleeping whisper of a name
Bespeaks her guilt and Azo's shame.
And whose that name? that o'er his pillow
Sounds fearful as the breaking billow

Which rolls the plank upon the shore,
  And dashes on the pointed rock
The wretch who sinks to rise no more;
  So came upon his soul the shock.
And whose that name? 'tis Hugo's,—his—
In sooth he had not deem'd of this!—
'Tis Hugo's,—he, the child of one
He loved—his own all-evil son—
The offspring of his wayward youth,
When he betray'd Bianca's truth;
The maid whose folly could confide
In him who made her not his bride.

VII

He pluck'd his poniard in its sheath,
  But sheathed it ere the point was bare;
Howe'er unworthy now to breathe,
  He could not slay a thing so fair—
  At least, not smiling, sleeping there:
Nay, more:—he did not wake her then,
  But gazed upon her with a glance
  Which, had she roused her from her trance,
Had frozen her sense to sleep again;
And o'er his brow the burning lamp
Gleam'd on the dew-drops big and damp.
She spake no more—but still she slumber'd—
While, in his thought, her days are number'd.

VIII

And with the morn he sought, and found,
In many a tale from those around,
The proof of all he fear'd to know,
Their present guilt, his future woe.
The long-conniving damsels seek
  To save themselves, and would transfer
  The guilt, the shame, the doom, to her:
Concealment is no more; they speak
All circumstance which may compel
Full credence to the tale they tell;
And Azo's tortured heart and ear
Have nothing more to feel or hear.

IX

He was not one who brook'd delay:
　　Within the chamber of his state,
The chief of Este's ancient sway
　　Upon his throne of judgment sate;
His nobles and his guards are there,—
Before him is the sinful pair;
Both young—and *one* how passing fair!
With swordless belt, and fetter'd hand,
Oh, Christ! that thus a son should stand
　　Before a father's face!
Yet thus must Hugo meet his sire,
And hear the sentence of his ire,
　　The tale of his disgrace!
And yet he seems not overcome,
Although, as yet, his voice be dumb.

X

And still, and pale, and silently
　　Did Parisina wait her doom;
How changed since last her speaking eye
　　Glanced gladness round the glittering room,
Where high-born men were proud to wait—
Where Beauty watch'd to imitate
　　Her gentle voice, her lovely mien—
And gather from her air and gait
　　The graces of its queen.
Then,—had her eye in sorrow wept,
A thousand warriors forth had leapt,
A thousand swords had sheathless shone,
And made her quarrel all their own.
Now,—what is she? and what are they?
Can she command, or these obey?
All silent and unheeding now,
With downcast eyes and knitting brow,
And folded arms, and freezing air,
And lips that scarce their scorn forbear,
Her knights and dames, her court—is there;
And he, the chosen one, whose lance
Had yet been couch'd before her glance,

Who—were his arm a moment free—
Had died or gain'd her liberty;
The minion of his father's bride,—
He, too, is fetter'd by her side;
Nor sees her swoln and full eye swim
Less for her own despair than him;
Those lids,—o'er which the violet vein,
Wandering, leaves a tender stain,
Shining through the smoothest white
That e'er did softest kiss invite,—
Now seem'd with hot and livid glow
To press, not shade, the orbs below,
Which glance so heavily, and fill,
As tear on tear grows gathering still.

XI

And he for her had also wept,
    But for the eyes that on him gazed:
His sorrow, if he felt it, slept;
    Stern and erect his brow was raised.
Whate'er the grief his soul avow'd,
He would not shrink before the crowd;
But yet he dared not look on her:
Remembrance of the hours that were—
His guilt, his love, his present state—
His father's wrath, all good men's hate—
His earthly, his eternal fate—
And hers,—oh, hers! he dared not throw
One look upon that death-like brow!
Else had his rising heart betray'd
Remorse for all the wreck it made.

XII

And Azo spake:—"But yesterday
    I gloried in a wife and son;
That dream this morning pass'd away;
    Ere day declines, I shall have none.
My life must linger on alone.
Well,—let that pass,—there breathes not one
Who would not do as I have done:

Those ties are broken—not by me;
   Let that too pass;—the doom's prepared!
Hugo, the priest awaits on thee,
   And then—thy crime's reward!
Away! address thy prayers to Heaven,
   Before its evening stars are met—
Learn if thou there canst be forgiven;
   Its mercy may absolve thee yet.
But here, upon the earth beneath,
   There is no spot where thou and I
Together, for an hour, could breathe:
   Farewell! I will not see thee die—
But thou, frail thing! shalt view his head—
   Away! I cannot speak the rest:
   Go! woman of the wanton breast!
Not I, but thou his blood dost shed;
Go! if that sight thou canst outlive,
And joy thee in the life I give."

XIII

And here stern Azo hid his face,
   For on his brow the swelling vein
   Throbb'd as if back upon his brain
   The hot blood ebb'd and flow'd again;
And therefore bow'd he for a space,
And pass'd his shaking hand along
His eye, to veil it from the throng;
While Hugo raised his chainèd hands,
And for a brief delay demands
His father's ear: the silent sire
Forbids not what his words require.

   "It is not that I dread the death—
For thou hast seen me by thy side
All redly through the battle ride,
And that not once a useless brand
Thy slaves have wrested from my hand,
Hath shed more blood in cause of thine,
Than e'er can stain the axe of mine.
   Thou gav'st, and mayst resume my breath,
A gift for which I thank thee not;
Nor are my mother's wrongs forgot,

Her slighted love and ruin'd name,
Her offspring's heritage of shame;
But she is in the grave, where he,
Her son, thy rival, soon shall be.
Her broken heart—my sever'd head—
Shall witness for thee from the dead
How trusty and how tender were
Thy youthful love—paternal care.
'Tis true, that I have done thee wrong,
    But wrong for wrong:—this, deem'd thy bride,
    The other victim of thy pride,
Thou know'st for me was destined long.
Thou saw'st, and covetedst her charms;
    And with thy very crime—my birth,
    Thou tauntedst me—as little worth;
A match ignoble for her arms,
Because, forsooth, I could not claim
The lawful heirship of thy name,
Nor sit on Este's lineal throne:
    Yet, were a few short summers mine,
    My name should more than Este's shine
With honours all my own.
I had a sword—and have a breast
That should have won as haught a crest
As ever waved along the line
Of all these sovereign sires of thine.
Not always knightly spurs are worn
The brightest by the better born;
And mine have lanced my courser's flank
Before proud chiefs of princely rank,
When charging to the cheering cry
Of 'Este and of Victory!'
I will not plead the cause of crime,
Nor sue thee to redeem from time
A few brief hours or days that must
At length roll o'er my reckless dust;—
Such maddening moments as my past,
They could not, and they did not, last.
Albeit my birth and name be base,
And thy nobility of race
Disdain'd to deck a thing like me—
    Yet in my lineaments they trace
    Some features of my father's face,
And in my spirit—all of thee.

From thee this tamelessness of heart,
From thee—nay, wherefore dost thou start?—
From thee in all their vigour came
My arm of strength, my soul of flame—
Thou didst not give me life alone,
But all that made me more thine own.
See what thy guilty love hath done!
Repaid thee with too like a son!
I am no bastard in my soul,
For that, like thine, abhorr'd control:
And for my breath, that hasty boon
Thou gav'st and wilt resume so soon,
I valued it no more than thou,
When rose thy casque above thy brow,
And we, all side by side, have striven,
And o'er the dead our coursers driven.
The past is nothing—and at last
The future can but be the past;
Yet would I that I then had died:
    For though thou work'dst my mother's ill,
And made thy own my destined bride,
    I feel thou art my father still;
And, harsh as sounds thy hard decree,
'Tis not unjust, although from thee.
Begot in sin, to die in shame,
My life began and ends the same:
As err'd the sire, so err'd the son,
And thou must punish both in one.
My crime seems worst to human view,
But God must judge between us too!"

XIV

He ceased—and stood with folded arms,
    On which the circling fetters sounded;
    And not an ear but felt as wounded,
    Of all the chiefs that there were rank'd,
    When those dull chains in meeting clank'd:
Till Parisina's fatal charms
Again attracted every eye—
Would she thus hear him doom'd to die?
She stood, I said, all pale and still,
The living cause of Hugo's ill:

Her eyes unmoved, but full and wide,
Not once had turn'd to either side;
Nor once did those sweet eyelids close,
Or shade the glance o'er which they rose.
But round their orbs of deepest blue
The circling white dilated grew—
And there with glassy gaze she stood
As ice were in her curdled blood;
But every now and then a tear
   So large and slowly gather'd, slid
   From the long dark fringe of that fair lid,
It was a thing to see, not hear!
And those who saw, it did surprise,
Such drops could fall from human eyes.
To speak she thought—the imperfect note
Was choked within her swelling throat,
Yet seemed in that low hollow groan
Her whole heart gushing in the tone.
It ceased—again she thought to speak,
Then burst her voice in one long shriek,
And to the earth she fell like stone
Or statue from its base o'erthrown,
More like a thing that ne'er had life,—
A monument of Azo's wife—
Than her, that living guilty thing,
Whose every passion was a sting,
Which urged to guilt, but could not bear
That guilt's detection and despair.
But yet she lived—and all too soon
Recovered from that death-like swoon,
But scarce to reason—every sense
Had been o'erstrung by pangs intense;
And each frail fibre of her brain
(As bow-strings, when relax'd by rain,
The erring arrow launch aside)
Sent forth her thoughts all wild and wide—
The past a blank, the future black,
With glimpses of a dreary track,
Like lightning on the desert path,
When midnight storms are mustering wrath.
She fear'd—she felt that something ill
Lay on her soul, so deep and chill;
That there was sin and shame she knew,
That some one was to die—but who?

She had forgotten:—did she breathe?
Could this be still the earth beneath,
The sky above, and men around,
Or were they fiends who now so frown'd
On one, before whose eyes each eye
Till then had smiled in sympathy?
All was confused and undefined
To her all-jarr'd and wandering mind;
A chaos of wild hopes and fears:
And now in laughter, now in tears,
But madly still in each extreme,
She strove with that convulsive dream;
For so it seem'd on her to break—
Oh! vainly must she strive to wake!

XV

The Convent bells are ringing,
  But mournfully and slow;
In the grey square turret swinging,
  With a deep sound, to and fro.
  Heavily to the heart they go!
Hark! the hymn is singing—
  The song for the dead below,
  Or the living who shortly shall be so!
For a departing being's soul
The death-hymn peals and the hollow bells knoll.
He is near his mortal goal;
Kneeling at the friar's knee;
Sad to hear, and piteous to see—
Kneeling on the bare cold ground,
With the block before and the guards around—
And the headsman with his bare arm ready
That the blow may be both swift and steady,
Feels if the axe be sharp and true—
Since he set its edge anew:
While the crowd in a speechless circle gather
To see the Son fall by the doom of the Father.

XVI

It is a lovely hour as yet
Before the summer sun shall set,
Which rose upon that heavy day,
And mock'd it with his steadiest ray;
And his evening beams are shed
Full on Hugo's fated head,
As, his last confession pouring
To the monk his doom deploring
In penitential holiness,
He bends to hear his accents bless
With absolution such as may
Wipe our mortal stains away.
That high sun on his head did glisten
As he there did bow and listen,
And the rings of chestnut hair
Curl'd half down his neck so bare,
But brighter still the beam was thrown
Upon the axe which near him shone
With a clear and ghastly glitter—
Oh! that parting hour was bitter!
Even the stern stood chill'd with awe:
Dark the crime, and just the law—
Yet they shudder'd as they saw.

XVII

The parting prayers are said and over
Of that false son and daring lover!
His beads and sins are all recounted,
His hours to their last minute mounted,
His mantling cloak before was stripp'd,
His bright brown locks must now be clipp'd:
'Tis done—all closely are they shorn.
The vest which till this moment worn,
The scarf which Parisina gave,
Must not adorn him to the grave;
Even that must now be thrown aside,
And o'er his eyes the kerchief tied;
But no—that last indignity
Shall ne'er approach his haughty eye.

All feelings seemingly subdued,
In deep disdain were half renew'd,
When headsman's hands prepared to bind
Those eyes which would not brook such blind;
As if they dared not look on death.
"No—yours my forfeit blood and breath;
These hands are chain'd—but let me die
At least with an unshackled eye—
Strike"—and as the word he said,
Upon the block he bow'd his head.
These the last accents Hugo spoke:
"Strike"—and flashing fell the stroke—
Roll'd the head—and, gushing, sunk
Back the stain'd and heaving trunk,
In the dust, which each deep vein
Slaked with its ensanguined rain.
His eyes and lips a moment quiver,
Convulsed and quick—then fix for ever.
He died, as erring man should die,
　　Without display, without parade;
　　Meekly had he bow'd and pray'd,
　　As not disdaining priestly aid,
Nor desperate of all hope on high.
And while, before the prior kneeling,
His heart was wean'd from earthly feeling,
His wrathful sire, his paramour—
What were they in such an hour?
No more reproach—no more despair;
No thought but heaven, no word but prayer,
Save the few which from him broke,
When bared to meet the headsman's stroke,
He claim'd to die with eyes unbound,
His sole adieu to those around.

XVIII

Still as the lips that closed in death,
Each gazer's bosom held his breath:
But yet, afar, from man to man,
A cold electric shiver ran,
As down the deadly blow descended
On him whose life and love thus ended;
And with a hushing sound compress'd,
A sigh shrunk back on every breast;

But no more thrilling noise rose there,
   Beyond the blow that to the block
   Pierced through with forced and sullen shock,
Save one:—what cleaves the silent air
So madly shrill, so passing wild,
That, as a mother's o'er her child,
Done to death by sudden blow,
To the sky these accents go,
Like a soul's in endless woe?
Through Azo's palace-lattice driven,
That horrid voice ascends to heaven,
And every eye is turn'd thereon;
But sound and sight alike are gone!
It was a woman's shriek—and ne'er
In madlier accents rose despair;
And those who heard it as it past,
In mercy wish'd it were the last.

XIX

Hugo is fallen; and, from that hour,
No more in palace, hall, or bower,
Was Parisina heard or seen.
Her name—as if she ne'er had been—
Was banish'd from each lip and ear,
Like words of wantonness or fear;
And from Prince Azo's voice, by none
Was mention heard of wife or son;
No tomb, no memory had they;
Theirs was unconsecrated clay;
At least the knight's who died that day.
But Parisina's fate lies hid
Like dust beneath the coffin lid:
Whether in convent she abode,
And won to heaven her dreary road,
By blighted and remorseful years
Of scourge, and fast, and sleepless tears;
Or if she fell by bowl or steel,
For that dark love she dared to feel;
Or if, upon the moment smote,
She died by tortures less remote,
Like him she saw upon the block,
With heart that shared the headsman's shock,

In quicken'd brokenness that came,
In pity, o'er her shatter'd frame,
None knew—and none can ever know;
But whatsoe'er its end below,
Her life began and closed in woe!

XX

And Azo found another bride,
And goodly sons grew by his side;
But none so lovely and so brave
As him who wither'd in the grave;
Or, if they were—on his cold eye
Their growth but glanced unheeded by,
Or noticed with a smother'd sigh.
But never tear his cheek descended,
And never smile his brow unbended;
And o'er that fair broad brow were wrought
The intersected lines of thought;
Those furrows which the burning share
Of Sorrow ploughs untimely there;
Scars of the lacerating mind
Which the Soul's war doth leave behind.
He was past all mirth or woe:
Nothing more remain'd below
But sleepless nights and heavy days,
A mind all dead to scorn or praise,
A heart which shunn'd itself—and yet
That would not yield, nor could forget,
Which, when it least appear'd to melt,
Intensely thought, intensely felt:
The deepest ice which ever froze
Can only o'er the surface close;
The living stream lies quick below,
And flows—and cannot cease to flow.
Still was his seal'd-up bosom haunted
By thoughts which Nature hath implanted,
Too deeply rooted thence to vanish:
Howe'er our stifled tears we banish,
When struggling as they rise to start,
We check those waters of the heart,
They are not dried—those tears unshed
But flow back to the fountain head,

And, resting in their spring more pure,
For ever in its depth endure,
Unseen, unwept, but uncongeal'd,
And cherish'd most where least reveal'd.
With inward starts of feeling left,
To throb o'er those of life bereft;
Without the power to fill again
The desert gap which made his pain;
Without the hope to meet them where
United souls shall gladness share;
With all the consciousness that he
Had only pass'd a just decree,
That they had wrought their doom of ill;
Yet Azo's age was wretched still.
The tainted branches of the tree,
    If lopp'd with care, a strength may give,
    By which the rest shall bloom and live
All greenly fresh and wildly free:
But if the lightning, in its wrath,
The waving boughs with fury scathe,
The massy trunk the ruin feels,
And never more a leaf reveals.

1815

From

MANFRED

A DRAMATIC POEM

ACT I—Scene I

* * * * *

Earth, ocean, air, night, mountains, winds, thy star,
    Are at thy beck and bidding, Child of Clay!
Before thee at thy quest their spirits are—
    What wouldst thou with us, son of mortals—say?

Manf.   Forgetfulness—
First Spir.   Of what—of whom—and why?
Manf.   Of that which is within me: read it there—
   Ye know it, and I cannot utter it.
Spir.   We can but give thee that which we possess;
   Ask of us subjects, sovereignty, the power
   O'er earth, the whole, or portion, or a sign
   Which shall control the elements, whereof
   We are the dominators—each and all,
   These shall be thine.
Manf.   Oblivion, self-oblivion—
   Can ye not wring from out the hidden realms
   Ye offer so profusely what I ask?
Spir.   It is not in our essence, in our skill;
   But—thou may'st die.
Manf.   Will death bestow it on me?

Spir.   We are immortal, and do not forget:
  We are eternal, and to us the past
  Is, as the future, present. Art thou answer'd?
Manf.   Ye mock me—but the power which brought ye here
  Hath made you mine. Slaves, scoff not at my will!
  The mind, the spirit, the Promethean spark,
  The lightning of my being, is as bright,
  Pervading, and far darting as your own,
  And shall not yield to yours, though coop'd in clay!
  Answer, or I will teach you what I am.
Spir.   We answer as we answer'd; our reply
  Is even in thine own words.
Manf.   Why say ye so?
Spir.   If, as thou say'st, thine essence be as ours,
  We have replied in telling thee, the thing
  Mortals call death hath nought to do with us.
Manf.   I then have call'd ye from your realms in vain;
  Ye cannot, or ye will not, aid me.
Spir.   Say;
  What we possess we offer; it is thine:
  Bethink ere thou dismiss us, ask again—
  Kingdom, and sway, and strength, and length of days—
Manf.   Accursèd! what have I to do with days?
  They are too long already.—Hence—begone!
Spir.   Yet pause: being here, our will would do thee service;
  Bethink thee, is there then no other gift
  Which we can make not worthless in thine eyes?
Manf.   No, none: yet stay—one moment, ere we part—
  I would behold ye face to face. I hear
  Your voices, sweet and melancholy sounds,
  As music on the waters; and I see
  The steady aspect of a clear large star;
  But nothing more. Approach me as ye are,
  Or one, or all, in your accustom'd forms.
Spir.   We have no forms beyond the elements
  Of which we are the mind and principle:
  But choose a form—in that we will appear.
Manf.   I have no choice; there is no form on earth
  Hideous or beautiful to me. Let him,
  Who is most powerful of ye, take such aspect
  As unto him may seem most fitting—Come!

SEVENTH SPIRIT, *appearing in the shape of a beautiful female figure.*
                    Behold!

Manf.   Oh God! if it be thus, and *thou*
   Art not a madness and a mockery,
   I yet might be most happy.—I will clasp thee,
   And we again will be—   [*The figure vanishes.*
          My heart is crush'd!

               (MANFRED *falls senseless.*)

(*A Voice is heard in the Incantation which follows.*)

   When the moon is on the wave,
     And the glow-worm on the grass,
   And the meteor on the grave,
     And the wisp on the morass;
   When the falling stars are shooting,
   And the answer'd owls are hooting,
   And the silent leaves are still
   In the shadow of the hill,
   Shall my soul be upon thine,
   With a power and with a sign.

   Though thy slumber may be deep,
   Yet thy spirit shall not sleep;
   There are shades which will not vanish,
   There are thoughts thou canst not banish;
   By a power to thee unknown,
   Thou canst never be alone;
   Thou art wrapt as with a shroud,
   Thou art gather'd in a cloud;
   And for ever shalt thou dwell
   In the spirit of this spell.

   Though thou seest me not pass by,
   Thou shalt feel me with thine eye
   As a thing that, though unseen,
   Must be near thee, and hath been;
   And when in that secret dread
   Thou hast turn'd around thy head,
   Thou shalt marvel I am not
   As thy shadow on the spot;
   And the power which thou dost feel
   Shall be what thou must conceal.

And a magic voice and verse
Hath baptized thee with a curse;
And a spirit of the air
Hath begirt thee with a snare;
In the wind there is a voice
Shall forbid thee to rejoice;
And to thee shall Night deny
All the quiet of her sky;
And the day shall have a sun,
Which shall make thee wish it done.

From thy false tears I did distil
An essence which hath strength to kill,
From thy own heart I then did wring
The black blood in its blackest spring;
From thy own smile I snatch'd the snake,
For there it coil'd as in a brake;
From thy own lip I drew the charm
Which gave all these their chiefest harm;
In proving every poison known,
I found the strongest was thine own.

By thy cold breast and serpent smile,
By thy unfathom'd gulfs of guile,
By that most seeming virtuous eye,
By thy shut soul's hypocrisy;
By the perfection of thine art,
Which pass'd for human thine own heart;
By thy delight in others' pain,
And by thy brotherhood of Cain,
I call upon thee! and compel
Thyself to be thy proper Hell!

And on thy head I pour the vial
Which does devote thee to this trial;
Nor to slumber, nor to die,
Shall be in thy destiny;
Though thy death shall still seem near
To thy wish, but as a fear;
Lo! the spell now works around thee,
And the clankless chain hath bound thee;
O'er thy heart and brain together
Hath the word been pass'd—now wither!

Scene II—*The Mountain of the Jungfrau.
—Time, Morning.*

MANFRED *alone upon the cliffs.*

The spirits I have raised abandon me—
The spells which I have studied baffle me—
The remedy I reck'd of tortured me;
I lean no more on super-human aid,
It hath no power upon the past, and for
The future, till the past be gulf'd in darkness,
It is not of my search.—My mother Earth!
And thou, fresh breaking Day, and you, ye Mountains,
Why are ye beautiful? I cannot love ye.
And thou, the bright eye of the universe,
That openest over all, and unto all
Art a delight—thou shin'st not on my heart.
And you, ye crags, upon whose extreme edge
I stand, and on the torrent's brink beneath
Behold the tall pines dwindled as to shrubs
In dizziness of distance; when a leap,
A stir, a motion, even a breath, would bring
My breast upon its rocky bosom's bed
To rest for ever—wherefore do I pause?
I feel the impulse—yet I do not plunge;
I see the peril—yet do not recede;
And my brain reels—and yet my foot is firm:
There is a power upon me which withholds,
And makes it my fatality to live;
If it be life to wear within myself
This barrenness of spirit, and to be
My own soul's sepulchre, for I have ceased
To justify my deeds unto myself—
The last infirmity of evil. Ay,
Thou wingèd and cloud-cleaving minister,   [*An eagle passes.*
Whose happy flight is highest into heaven,
Well mayst thou swoop so near me—I should be
Thy prey, and gorge thine eaglets; thou art gone
Where the eye cannot follow thee; but thine
Yet pierces downward, onward, or above,
With a pervading vision.—Beautiful!

How beautiful is all this visible world!
How glorious in its action and itself!
But we, who name ourselves its sovereigns, we,
Half dust, half deity, alike unfit
To sink or soar, with our mix'd essence make
A conflict of its elements, and breathe
The breath of degradation and of pride,
Contending with low wants and lofty will,
Till our mortality predominates,
And men are—what they name not to themselves,
And trust not to each other. Hark! the note,

[*The Shepherd's pipe in the distance is heard.*

The natural music of the mountain reed—
For here the patriarchal days are not
A pastoral fable—pipes in the liberal air,
Mix'd with the sweet bells of the sauntering herd;
My soul would drink those echoes.—Oh, that I were
The viewless spirit of a lovely sound,
A living voice, a breathing harmony,
A bodiless enjoyment—born and dying
With the blest tone which made me!

Enter from below a CHAMOIS HUNTER.

Hunt.   Even so,
This way the chamois leapt: her nimble feet
Have baffled me; my gains to-day will scarce
Repay my break-neck travail.—What is here?
Who seems not of my trade, and yet hath reach'd
A height which none even of our mountaineers,
Save our best hunters, may attain: his garb
Is goodly, his mien manly, and his air
Proud as a free-born peasant's, at this distance.—
I will approach him nearer.

Manf. (*not perceiving the other*).   To be thus—
Grey-hair'd with anguish, like these blasted pines,
Wrecks of a single winter, barkless, branchless,
A blighted trunk upon a cursèd root,
Which but supplies a feeling to decay—
And to be thus, eternally but thus,
Having been otherwise! Now furrow'd o'er
With wrinkles, plough'd by moments, not by years
And hours—all tortured into ages—hours
Which I outlive!—Ye toppling crags of ice!

Ye avalanches, whom a breath draws down
In mountainous o'erwhelming, come and crush me!
I hear ye momently above, beneath,
Crash with a frequent conflict; but ye pass,
And only fall on things that still would live;
On the young flourishing forest, or the hut
And hamlet of the harmless villager.

Hunt.   The mists begin to rise from up the valley;
I'll warn him to descend, or he may chance
To lose at once his way and life together.

Manf.   The mists boil up around the glaciers; clouds
Rise curling fast beneath me, white and sulphury,
Like foam from the roused ocean of deep Hell,
Whose every wave breaks on a living shore,
Heap'd with the damn'd like pebbles.—I am giddy.

Hunt.   I must approach him cautiously; if near,
A sudden step will startle him, and he
Seems tottering already.

Manf.   Mountains have fallen,
Leaving a gap in the clouds, and with the shock
Rocking their Alpine brethren; filling up
The ripe green valleys with destruction's splinters,
Damming the rivers with a sudden dash,
Which crush'd the waters into mist, and made
Their fountains find another channel—thus,
Thus, in its old age, did Mount Rosenberg—
Why stood I not beneath it?

Hunt.   Friend! have a care,
Your next step may be fatal!—for the love
Of him who made you, stand not on that brink!

Manf. (*not hearing him*).   Such would have been for me a fitting tomb;
My bones had then been quiet in their depth;
They had not then been strewn upon the rocks
For the wind's pastime—as thus—thus they shall be—
In this one plunge.—Farewell, ye opening heavens!
Look not upon me thus reproachfully—
Ye were not meant for me—Earth! take these atoms!

   [As MANFRED *is in act to spring from the cliff, the* CHAMOIS
      HUNTER *seizes and retains him with a sudden grasp.*

Hunt.   Hold, madman!—though aweary of thy life,
Stain not our pure vales with thy guilty blood.—
Away with me—I will not quit my hold.

Manf.   I am most sick at heart—nay, grasp me not—

I am all feebleness—the mountains whirl
Spinning around me—I grow blind.—What art thou?
Hunt.   I'll answer that anon.—Away with me—
   The clouds grow thicker—there—now lean on me—
   Place your foot here—here, take this staff, and cling
   A moment to that shrub—now give me your hand,
   And hold fast by my girdle—softly—well—
   The chalet will be gain'd within an hour.
   Come on, we'll quickly find a surer footing,
   And something like a pathway, which the torrent
   Hath wash'd since winter.—Come, 'tis bravely done—
   You should have been a hunter.—Follow me.
   [*As they descend the rocks with difficulty, the scene closes.*

* * * * *

1816–17

From

CAIN

A MYSTERY

ACT II

Scene I—*The Abyss of Space*

Cain. I tread on air, and sink not; yet I fear
  To sink.
Lucifer. Have faith in me, and thou shalt be
  Borne on the air, of which I am the prince.
Cain. Can I do so without impiety?
Lucifer. Believe—and sink not! doubt—and perish! thus
  Would run the edict of the other God,
  Who names me demon to his angels; they
  Echo the sound to miserable things,
  Which, knowing nought beyond their shallow senses,
  Worship the word which strikes their ear, and deem
  Evil or good what is proclaim'd to them
  In their abasement. I will have none such:
  Worship or worship not, thou shalt behold
  The worlds beyond thy little world, nor be
  Amerced for doubts beyond thy little life,
  With torture of *my* dooming. There will come
  An hour, when, toss'd upon some water-drops,
  A man shall say to a man, "Believe in me,
  And walk the waters;" and the man shall walk
  The billows and be safe. *I* will not say
  Believe in *me*, as a conditional creed
  To save thee; but fly with me o'er the gulf

> Of space an equal flight, and I will show
> What thou darest not deny, the history
> Of past, and present, and of future worlds.

Cain. Oh, god, or demon, or whate'er thou art,
> Is yon our earth?

Lucifer.   Dost thou not recognize
> The dust which form'd your father?

Cain.   Can it be?
> Yon small blue circle, swinging in far ether,
> With an inferior circlet near it still,
> Which looks like that which lit our earthly night?
> Is this our Paradise? Where are its walls,
> And they who guard them?

Lucifer.   Point me out the site
> Of Paradise.

Cain.   How should I? As we move
> Like sunbeams onward, it grows small and smaller,
> And as it waxes little, and then less,
> Gathers a halo round it, like the light
> Which shone the roundest of the stars, when I
> Beheld them from the skirts of Paradise:
> Methinks they both, as we recede from them,
> Appear to join the innumerable stars
> Which are around us; and, as we move on,
> Increase their myriads.

Lucifer.   And if there should be
> Worlds greater than thine own, inhabited
> By greater things, and they themselves far more
> In number than the dust of thy dull earth,
> Though multiplied to animated atoms,
> All living, and all doom'd to death, and wretched,
> What wouldst thou think?

Cain.   I should be proud of thought
> Which knew such things.

Lucifer.   But if that high thought were
> Link'd to a servile mass of matter, and,
> Knowing such things, aspiring to such things,
> And science still beyond them, were chain'd down
> To the most gross and petty paltry wants,
> All foul and fulsome, and the very best
> Of thine enjoyments a sweet degradation,
> A most enervating and filthy cheat,
> To lure thee on to the renewal of

Fresh souls and bodies, all foredoom'd to be
As frail, and few so happy—
Cain.   Spirit! I
Know nought of death, save as a dreadful thing
Of which I have heard my parents speak, as of
A hideous heritage I owe to them
No less than life; a heritage not happy,
If I may judge till now. But, spirit, if
It be as thou hast said (and I within
Feel the prophetic torture of its truth)
Here let me die: for to give birth to those
Who can but suffer many years and die,
Methinks, is merely propagating death,
And multiplying murder.
Lucifer.   Thou canst not
All die—there is what must survive.
Cain.   The Other
Spake not of this unto my father, when
He shut him forth from Paradise, with death
Written upon his forehead. But at least
Let what is mortal of me perish, that
I may be in the rest as angels are.
Lucifer.   I am angelic; wouldst thou be as I am?
Cain.   I know not what thou art: I see thy power,
And see thou show'st me things beyond my power,
Beyond all power of my born faculties,
Although inferior still to my desires
And my conceptions.
Lucifer.   What are they, which dwell
So humbly in their pride, as to sojourn
With worms in clay?
Cain.   And what art thou, who dwellest
So haughtily in spirit, and canst range
Nature and immortality, and yet
Seem'st sorrowful?
Lucifer.   I seem that which I am;
And therefore do I ask of thee, if thou
Wouldst be immortal?
Cain.   Thou hast said, I must be
Immortal in despite of me. I knew not
This until lately—but, since it must be,
Let me, or happy or unhappy, learn
To anticipate my immortality.
Lucifer.   Thou didst before I came upon thee.

Cain.   How?
Lucifer.   By suffering.
Cain.   And must torture be immortal?
Lucifer.   We and thy sons will try. But now, behold!
   Is it not glorious?
Cain.   Oh, thou beautiful
   And unimaginable ether! and
   Ye multiplying masses of increased
   And still-increasing lights! what are ye? what
   Is this blue wilderness of interminable
   Air, where ye roll along, as I have seen
   The leaves along the limpid streams of Eden?
   Is your course measured for ye? Or do ye
   Sweep on in your unbounded revelry
   Through an aërial universe of endless
   Expansion, at which my soul aches to think,
   Intoxicated with eternity?
   Oh God! Oh Gods! or whatsoe'er ye are!
   How beautiful ye are! how beautiful
   Your works, or accidents, or whatsoe'er
   They may be! Let me die, as atoms die
   (If that they die), or know ye in your might
   And knowledge! My thoughts are not in this hour
   Unworthy what I see, though my dust is:
   Spirit! let me expire, or see them nearer.
Lucifer.   Art thou not nearer? look back to thine earth!
Cain.   Where is it? I see nothing save a mass
   Of most innumerable lights.
Lucifer.   Look there!
Cain.   I cannot see it.
Lucifer.   Yet it sparkles still.
Cain.   That!—yonder!
Lucifer.   Yea.
Cain.   And wilt thou tell me so?
   Why, I have seen the fire-flies and fire-worms
   Sprinkle the dusky groves and the green banks
   In the dim twilight, brighter than yon world
   Which bears them.
Lucifer.   Thou hast seen both worms and worlds,
   Each bright and sparkling,—what dost think of them?
Cain.   That they are beautiful in their own sphere,
   And that the night, which makes both beautiful
   The little shining fire-fly in its flight,

And the immortal star in its great course,
Must both be guided.
Lucifer.   But by whom or what?
Cain.   Show me.
Lucifer.   Dar'st thou behold?
Cain.   How know I what
I *dare* behold? As yet, thou hast shown nought
I dare not gaze on further.
Lucifer.   On, then, with me.
Wouldst thou behold things mortal or immortal?
Cain.   Why, what are things?
Lucifer.   *Both* partly: but what doth
Sit next thy heart?
Cain.   The things I see.
Lucifer.   But what
Sate nearest it?
Cain.   The things I have not seen,
Nor ever shall—the mysteries of death.
Lucifer.   What if I show to thee things which have died,
As I have shown thee much which cannot die?
Cain.   Do so.
Lucifer.   Away, then! on our mighty wings.
Cain.   Oh! how we cleave the blue! The stars fade from us!
The earth! where is my earth? let me look on it,
For I was made of it.
Lucifer.   'Tis now beyond thee,
Less in the universe than thou in it;
Yet deem not that thou canst escape it; thou
Shalt soon return to earth, and all its dust;
'Tis part of thy eternity, and mine.
Cain.   Where dost thou lead me?
Lucifer.   To what was before thee!
The phantasm of the world; of which thy world
Is but the wreck.
Cain.   What! is it not then new?
Lucifer.   No more than life is; and that was ere thou
Or *I* were, or the things which seem to us
Greater than either: many things will have
No end; and some, which would pretend to have
Had no beginning, have had one as mean
As thou; and mightier things have been extinct
To make way for much meaner than we can
Surmise; for *moments* only and the *space*

Have been and must be all *unchangeable*.
But changes make not death, except to clay;
But thou art clay—and canst but comprehend
That which was clay, and such thou shalt behold.
Cain.   Clay, spirit! What thou wilt, I can survey.
Lucifer.   Away, then!
Cain.   But the lights fade from me fast,
   And some till now grew larger as we approach'd,
   And wore the look of worlds.
Lucifer.   And such they are.
Cain.   And Edens in them?
Lucifer.   It may be.
Cain.   And men?
Lucifer.   Yea, or things higher.
Cain.   Ay! and serpents too?
Lucifer.   Wouldst thou have men without them? must no reptiles
   Breathe, save the erect ones?
Cain.   How the lights recede!
   Where fly we?
Lucifer.   To the world of phantoms, which
   Are beings past, and shadows still to come.
Cain.   But it grows dark, and dark—the stars are gone!
Lucifer.   And yet thou seest.
Cain.   'Tis a fearful light!
   No sun, no moon, no lights innumerable.
   The very blue of the empurpled night
   Fades to a dreary twilight; yet I see
   Huge dusky masses, but unlike the worlds
   We were approaching, which, begirt with light,
   Seem'd full of life even when their atmosphere
   Of light gave way, and show'd them taking shapes
   Unequal, of deep valleys and vast mountains;
   And some emitting sparks, and some displaying
   Enormous liquid plains, and some begirt
   With luminous belts, and floating moons, which took
   Like them the features of fair earth:—instead,
   All here seems dark and dreadful.
Lucifer.   But distinct.
   Thou seekest to behold death, and dead things?
Cain.   I seek it not; but as I know there are
   Such, and that my sire's sin makes him and me,
   And all that we inherit, liable

To such, I would behold at once what I
Must one day see perforce.
Lucifer.   Behold!
Cain.   'Tis darkness.
Lucifer.   And so it shall be ever; but we will
Unfold its gates!
Cain.   Enormous vapours roll
Apart—what's this?
Lucifer.   Enter!
Cain.   Can I return?
Lucifer.   Return! be sure: how else should death be peopled?
Its present realm is thin to what it will be,
Through thee and thine.
Cain.   The clouds still open wide
And wider, and make widening circles round us.
Lucifer.   Advance!
Cain.   And thou!
Lucifer.   Fear not—without me thou
Couldst not have gone beyond thy world. On! on!
                    [*They disappear through the clouds.*

*   *   *   *   *

1821

From

THE PROPHECY OF DANTE

CANTO II

THE Spirit of the fervent days of Old,
  When words were things that came to pass, and thought
  Flash'd o'er the future, bidding men behold
Their children's children's doom already brought
  Forth from the abyss of time which is to be,
  The chaos of events, where lie half-wrought
Shapes that must undergo mortality;
  What the great Seers of Israel wore within,
  That spirit was on them, and is on me.
And if, Cassandra-like, amidst the din
  Of conflict none will hear, or hearing heed
  This voice from out the Wilderness, the sin
Be theirs, and my own feelings be my meed,
  The only guerdon I have ever known.
  Hast thou not bled? and hast thou still to bleed,
Italia? Ah, to me such things, foreshown
  With dim sepulchral light, bid me forget
  In thine irreparable wrongs my own.
We can have but one country, and even yet
  Thou'rt mine—my bones shall be within thy breast,
  My soul within thy language, which once set
With our old Roman sway in the wide West;
  But I will make another tongue arise
  As lofty and more sweet, in which express'd

The hero's ardour, or the lover's sighs,
  Shall find alike such sounds for every theme,
  That every word, as brilliant as thy skies,
Shall realise a poet's proudest dream,
  And make thee Europe's nightingale of song;
  So that all present speech to thine shall seem
The note of meaner birds, and every tongue
  Confess its barbarism when compared with thine.
  This shalt thou owe to him thou didst so wrong,
Thy Tuscan bard, the banish'd Ghibelline.

Woe! woe! the veil of coming centuries
  Is rent,—a thousand years, which yet supine
Lie like the ocean waves ere winds arise,
  Heaving in dark and sullen undulation,
  Float from eternity into these eyes;
The storms yet sleep, the clouds still keep their station,
  The unborn earthquake yet is in the womb,
  The bloody chaos yet expects creation,
But all things are disposing for thy doom;
  The elements await but for the word,
  "Let there be darkness!" and thou grow'st a tomb!
Yes! thou, so beautiful, shalt feel the sword,
  Thou, Italy! so fair that Paradise,
  Revived in thee, blooms forth to man restored:
Ah! must the sons of Adam lose it twice?
  Thou, Italy! whose ever golden fields,
  Plough'd by the sunbeams solely, would suffice
For the world's granary; thou, whose sky heaven gilds
  With brighter stars, and robes with deeper blue;
  Thou, in whose pleasant places Summer builds
Her palace, in whose cradle Empire grew,
  And form'd the Eternal City's ornaments
  From spoils of kings whom freemen overthrew;
Birthplace of heroes, sanctuary of saints,
  Where earthly first, then heavenly glory made
  Her home; thou, all which fondest fancy paints,
And finds her prior vision but portray'd
  In feeble colours, when the eye—from the Alp
  Of horrid snow, and rock, and shaggy shade
Of desert-loving pine, whose emerald scalp
  Nods to the storm—dilates and dotes o'er thee,
  And wistfully implores, as 'twere, for help
To see thy sunny fields, my Italy,

Nearer and nearer yet, and dearer still
The more approach'd, and dearest were they free;
Thou—thou must wither to each tyrant's will:
  The Goth hath been,—the German, Frank, and Hun,
  Are yet to come,—and on the imperial hill
Ruin, already proud of the deeds done
  By the old barbarians, there awaits the new,
  Throned on the Palatine, while, lost and won,
Rome at her feet lies bleeding; and the hue
  Of human sacrifice and Roman slaughter
  Troubles the clotted air, of late so blue,
And deepens into red the saffron water
  Of Tiber, thick with dead; the helpless priest,
  And still more helpless nor less holy daughter,
Vow'd to their God, have shrieking fled, and ceased
  Their ministry: the nations take their prey,
  Iberian, Almain, Lombard, and the beast
And bird, wolf, vulture, more humane than they
  Are; these but gorge the flesh and lap the gore
  Of the departed, and then go their way;
But those, the human savages, explore
  All paths of torture, and insatiate yet
  With Ugolino hunger prowl for more.
Nine moons shall rise o'er scenes like this and set;
  The chiefless army of the dead, which late
  Beneath the traitor Prince's banner met,
Hath left its leader's ashes at the gate;
  Had but the royal Rebel lived, perchance
  Thou hadst been spared, but his involved thy fate.
Oh! Rome, the spoiler or the spoil of France,
  From Brennus to the Bourbon, never, never
  Shall foreign standard to thy walls advance,
But Tiber shall become a mournful river.
  Oh! when the strangers pass the Alps and Po,
  Crush them, ye rocks! floods, whelm them, and for ever!
Why sleep the idle avalanches so,
  To topple on the lonely pilgrim's head?
  Why doth Eridanus but overflow
The peasant's harvest from his turbid bed?
  Were not each barbarous horde a nobler prey?
  Over Cambyses' host the desert spread
Her sandy ocean, and the sea-waves' sway
  Roll'd over Pharaoh and his thousands,—why,
  Mountains and waters, do ye not as they?

And you, ye men! Romans, who dare not die,
   Sons of the conquerors who overthrew
   Those who o'erthrew proud Xerxes, where yet lie
The dead whose tomb Oblivion never knew,
   Are the Alps weaker than Thermopylae?
   Their passes more alluring to the view
Of an invader? is it they, or ye
   That to each host the mountain-gate unbar,
   And leave the march in peace, the passage free?
Why, Nature's self detains the victor's car,
   And makes your land impregnable, if earth
   Could be so; but alone she will not war,
Yet aids the warrior worthy of his birth,
   In a soil where the mothers bring forth men:
   Not so with those whose souls are little worth;
For them no fortress can avail,—the den
   Of the poor reptile which preserves its sting
   Is more secure than walls of adamant, when
The hearts of those within are quivering.
   Are ye not brave? Yes, yet the Ausonian soil
   Hath hearts, and hands, and arms, and hosts to bring
Against Oppression; but how vain the toil,
   While still Division sows the seeds of woe
   And weakness, till the stranger reaps the spoil.
Oh! my own beauteous land! so long laid low,
   So long the grave of thy own children's hopes,
   When there is but required a single blow
To break the chain, yet—yet the Avenger stops,
   And Doubt and Discord step 'twixt thine and thee,
   And join their strength to that which with thee copes;
What is there wanting then to set thee free,
   And show thy beauty in its fullest light?
   To make the Alps impassable; and we,
Her sons, may do this with *one* deed—Unite!

               1819

From

DON JUAN

CANTO I

1

I WANT a hero: an uncommon want,
  When every year and month sends forth a new one,
Till, after cloying the gazettes with cant,
  The age discovers he is not the true one;
Of such as these I should not care to vaunt,
  I'll therefore take our ancient friend Don Juan—
We all have seen him, in the pantomime,
Sent to the devil somewhat ere his time.

*   *   *   *   *   *

6

Most epic poets plunge "in medias res"
  (Horace makes this the heroic turnpike road),
And then your hero tells, whene'er you please,
  What went before—by way of episode,
While seated after dinner at his ease,
  Beside his mistress in some soft abode,
Palace or garden, paradise, or cavern,
Which serves the happy couple for a tavern.

7

That is the usual method, but not mine—
  My way is to begin with the beginning;
The regularity of my design
  Forbids all wandering as the worst of sinning,
And therefore I shall open with a line
  (Although it cost me half an hour in spinning)
Narrating somewhat of Don Juan's father,
And also of his mother, if you'd rather.

8

In Seville was he born, a pleasant city,
  Famous for oranges and women—he
Who has not seen it will be much to pity,
  So says the proverb—and I quite agree;
Of all the Spanish towns is none more pretty,
  Cadiz perhaps—but that you soon may see;
Don Juan's parents lived beside the river,
A noble stream, and call'd the Guadalquivir.

9

His father's name was José—Don, of course;
  A true Hidalgo, free from every stain
Of Moor or Hebrew blood, he traced his source
  Through the most Gothic gentlemen of Spain.
A better cavalier ne'er mounted horse,
  Or, being mounted, e'er got down again,
Than José, who begot our hero, who
Begot—but that's to come—Well, to renew:

10

His mother was a learned lady, famed
  For every branch of every science known—
In every Christian language ever named,
  With virtues equall'd by her wit alone;
She made the cleverest people quite ashamed,
  And even the good with inward envy groan,
Finding themselves so very much exceeded
In their own way by all the things that she did.

11

Her memory was a mine: she knew by heart
    All Calderon and greater part of Lopé,
So that if any actor miss'd his part,
    She could have served him for the prompter's copy;
For her Feinagle's were an useless art,
    And he himself obliged to shut up shop—he
Could never make a memory so fine as
That which adorn'd the brain of Donna Inez.

12

Her favourite science was the mathematical,
    Her noblest virtue was her magnanimity,
Her wit (she sometimes tried at wit) was Attic all,
    Her serious sayings darken'd to sublimity;
In short, in all things she was fairly what I call
    A prodigy—her morning dress was dimity,
Her evening silk, or, in the summer, muslin,
And other stuffs, with which I won't stay puzzling.

13

She knew the Latin—that is, "the Lord's prayer,"
    And Greek—the alphabet—I'm nearly sure:
She read some French romances here and there,
    Although her mode of speaking was not pure;
For native Spanish she had no great care,
    At least her conversation was obscure;
Her thoughts were theorems, her words a problem,
As if she deem'd that mystery would ennoble 'em.

14

She liked the English and the Hebrew tongue,
    And said there was analogy between 'em;
She proved it somehow out of sacred song,
    But I must leave the proofs to those who've seen 'em;
But this I heard her say, and can't be wrong,
    And all may think which way their judgments lean 'em,
" 'Tis strange—the Hebrew noun which means 'I am,'
The English always use to govern d—n."

15

Some women use their tongues—she *look'd* a lecture,
    Each eye a sermon, and her brow a homily,
An all-in-all sufficient self-director,
    Like the lamented late Sir Samuel Romilly,
The Law's expounder, and the State's corrector,
    Whose suicide was almost an anomaly—
One sad example more, that "All is vanity,"
(The jury brought their verdict in "Insanity.")

*   *   *   *   *

18

Perfect she was, but as perfection is
    Insipid in this naughty world of ours,
Where our first parents never learn'd to kiss,
    Till they were exiled from their earlier bowers,
Where all was peace, and innocence, and bliss
    (I wonder how they got through the twelve hours),
Don José, like a lineal son of Eve,
Went plucking various fruit without her leave.

19

He was a mortal of the careless kind,
    With no great love for learning, or the learn'd,
Who chose to go where'er he had a mind,
    And never dream'd his lady was concern'd;
The world, as usual, wickedly inclined
    To see a kingdom or a house o'erturn'd,
Whisper'd he had a mistress, some said *two*—
But for domestic quarrels *one* will do.

20

Now Donna Inez had, with all her merit,
    A great opinion of her own good qualities;
Neglect, indeed, requires a saint to bear it,
    And such, indeed, she was in her moralities;

But then she had a devil of a spirit,
  And sometimes mix'd up fancies with realities,
And let few opportunities escape
Of getting her liege lord into a scrape.

21

This was an easy matter with a man
  Oft in the wrong, and never on his guard;
And even the wisest, do the best they can,
  Have moments, hours, and days, so unprepared,
That you might "brain them with their lady's fan;"
  And sometimes ladies hit exceeding hard,
And fans turn into falchions in fair hands,
And why and wherefore no one understands.

22

'Tis pity learned virgins ever wed
  With persons of no sort of education,
Or gentlemen who, though well-born and bred,
  Grow tired of scientific conversation:
I don't choose to say much upon this head,
  I'm a plain man, and in a single station,
But—Oh! ye lords of ladies intellectual,
Inform us truly, have they not hen-peck'd you all?

23

Don José and his lady quarrell'd—*why,*
  Not any of the many could divine,
Though several thousand people chose to try,
  'Twas surely no concern of theirs nor mine:
I loathe that low vice—curiosity;
  But if there's anything in which I shine,
'Tis in arranging all my friends' affairs,
Not having, of my own, domestic cares.

24

And so I interfered, and with the best
  Intentions, but their treatment was not kind;
I think the foolish people were possess'd,
  For neither of them could I ever find,

Although their porter afterwards confess'd—
  But that's no matter, and the worst's behind,
For little Juan o'er me threw, down stairs,
A pail of housemaid's water unawares.

25

A little curly-headed, good-for-nothing,
  And mischief-making monkey from his birth;
His parents ne'er agreed, except in doting
  Upon the most unquiet imp on earth;
Instead of quarrelling, had they been but both in
  Their senses, they'd have sent young master forth
To school, or had him soundly whipp'd at home,
To teach him manners for the time to come.

26

Don José and the Donna Inez led
  For some time an unhappy sort of life,
Wishing each other, not divorced, but dead;
  They lived respectably as man and wife,
Their conduct was exceedingly well-bred,
  And gave no outward signs of inward strife,
Until at length the smother'd fire broke out,
And put the business past all kind of doubt.

27

For Inez call'd some druggists and physicians,
  And tried to prove her loving lord was *mad*,
But as he had some lucid intermissions,
  She next decided he was only *bad*;
Yet when they ask'd her for her depositions,
  No sort of explanation could be had,
Save that her duty both to man and God
Required this conduct—which seem'd very odd.

28

She kept a journal, where his faults were noted,
  And open'd certain trunks of books and letters,
All which might, if occasion served, be quoted;
  And then she had all Seville for abettors,

Besides her good old grandmother (who doted);
   The hearers of her case became repeaters,
Then advocates, inquisitors, and judges,
   Some for amusement, others for old grudges.

29

And then this best and meekest woman bore
   With such serenity her husband's woes,
Just as the Spartan ladies did of yore,
   Who saw their spouses kill'd, and nobly chose
Never to say a word about them more—
   Calmly she heard each calumny that rose,
And saw *his* agonies with such sublimity,
That all the world exclaim'd, "What magnanimity!"

30

No doubt this patience, when the world is damning us,
   Is philosophic in our former friends,
'Tis also pleasant to be deem'd magnanimous,
   The more so in obtaining our own ends;
And what the lawyers call a *"malus animus"*
   Conduct like this by no means comprehends:
Revenge in person's certainly no virtue,
But then 'tis not *my* fault if *others* hurt you.

31

And if our quarrels should rip up old stories,
   And help them with a lie or two additional,
I'm not to blame, as you well know—no more is
   Any one else—they were become traditional;
Besides, their resurrection aids our glories
   By contrast, which is what we just were wishing all:
And science profits by this resurrection—
Dead scandals form good subjects for dissection.

32

Their friends had tried at reconciliation,
   Then their relations, who made matters worse,
('Twere hard to tell upon a like occasion
   To whom it may be best to have recourse—

I can't say much for friend or yet relation) :
   The lawyers did their utmost for divorce,
But scarce a fee was paid on either side
Before, unluckily, Don José died.

*   *   *   *   *

37

Dying intestate, Juan was sole heir
   To a chancery suit, and messuages, and lands,
Which, with a long minority and care,
   Promised to turn out well in proper hands:
Inez became sole guardian, which was fair,
   And answer'd but to nature's just demands;
An only son left with an only mother
Is brought up much more wisely than another.

38

Sagest of women, even of widows, she
   Resolved that Juan should be quite a paragon,
And worthy of the noblest pedigree
   (His sire was of Castile, his dam from Aragon):
Then for accomplishments of chivalry,
   In case our lord the king should go to war again,
He learn'd the arts of riding, fencing, gunnery,
And how to scale a fortress—or a nunnery.

39

But that which Donna Inez most desired,
   And saw into herself each day before all
The learned tutors whom for him she hired,
   Was that his breeding should be strictly moral:
Much into all his studies she inquired,
   And so they were submitted first to her, all,
Arts, sciences, no branch was made a mystery
To Juan's eyes, excepting natural history.

40

The languages, especially the dead,
    The sciences, and most of all the abstruse;
The arts, at least all such as could be said
    To be the most remote from common use,
In all these he was much and deeply read;
    But not a page of anything that's loose,
Or hints continuation of the species,
Was ever suffer'd, lest he should grow vicious.

41

His classic studies made a little puzzle,
    Because of filthy loves of gods and goddesses,
Who in the earlier ages raised a bustle,
    But never put on pantaloons or bodices;
His reverend tutors had at times a tussle,
    And for their Aeneids, Iliads, and Odysseys,
Were forced to make an odd sort of apology,
For Donna Inez dreaded the Mythology.

42

Ovid's a rake, as half his verses show him,
    Anacreon's morals are a still worse sample,
Catullus scarcely has a decent poem,
    I don't think Sappho's Ode a good example,
Although Longinus tells us there is no hymn
    Where the sublime soars forth on wings more ample;
But Virgil's songs are pure, except that horrid one
Beginning with "Formosum Pastor Corydon."

43

Lucretius' irreligion is too strong
    For early stomachs, to prove wholesome food;
I can't help thinking Juvenal was wrong,
    Although no doubt his real intent was good,
For speaking out so plainly in his song,
    So much indeed as to be downright rude;
And then what proper person can be partial
To all those nauseous epigrams of Martial?

44

Juan was taught from out the best edition,
 Expurgated by learned men, who place,
Judiciously, from out the schoolboy's vision,
 The grosser parts; but fearful to deface
Too much their modest bard by this omission,
 And pitying sore his mutilated case,
They only add them all in an appendix,
Which saves, in fact, the trouble of an index;

45

For there we have them all "at one fell swoop,"
 Instead of being scatter'd through the pages;
They stand forth marshall'd in a handsome troop,
 To meet the ingenuous youth of future ages,
Till some less rigid editor shall stoop
 To call them back into their separate cages,
Instead of standing staring all together,
Like garden gods—and not so decent either.

46

The Missal too (it was the family Missal)
 Was ornamented in a sort of way
Which ancient mass-books often are, and this all
 Kinds of grotesques illumined; and how they
Who saw those figures on the margin kiss all,
 Could turn their optics to the text and pray,
Is more than I know—but Don Juan's mother
Kept this herself, and gave her son another.

47

Sermons he read, and lectures he endured,
 And homilies, and lives of all the saints;
To Jerome and to Chrysostom inured,
 He did not take such studies for restraints;
But how faith is acquired, and then ensured,
 So well not one of the aforesaid paints
As Saint Augustine in his fine Confessions,
Which make the reader envy his trangressions.

48

This, too, was a seal'd book to little Juan—
    I can't but say that his mamma was right,
If such an education was the true one.
    She scarcely trusted him from out her sight;
Her maids were old, and if she took a new one,
    You might be sure she was a perfect fright;
She did this during even her husband's life—
I recommend as much to every wife.

49

Young Juan wax'd in goodliness and grace;
    At six a charming child, and at eleven
With all the promise of as fine a face
    As e'er to man's maturer growth was given:
He studied steadily and grew apace,
    And seem'd, at least, in the right road to heaven;
For half his days were pass'd at church, the other
Between his tutors, confessor, and mother.

50

At six, I said, he was a charming child,
    At twelve he was a fine, but quiet boy;
Although in infancy a little wild,
    They tamed him down amongst them: to destroy
His natural spirit not in vain they toil'd,
    At least it seem'd so; and his mother's joy
Was to declare how sage, and still, and steady,
Her young philosopher was grown already.

*   *   *   *   *

55

Amongst her numerous acquaintance, all
    Selected for discretion and devotion,
There was the Donna Julia, whom to call
    Pretty were but to give a feeble notion

Of many charms in her as natural
    As sweetness to the flower, or salt to ocean,
Her zone to Venus, or his bow to Cupid
(But this last simile is trite and stupid).

56

The darkness of her Oriental eye
    Accorded with her Moorish origin
(Her blood was not all Spanish, by the by;
    In Spain, you know, this is a sort of sin).
When proud Granada fell, and, forced to fly,
    Boabdil wept, of Donna Julia's kin
Some went to Africa, some stay'd in Spain,
Her great great grandmamma chose to remain.

*   *   *   *   *

60

Her eye (I'm very fond of handsome eyes)
    Was large and dark, suppressing half its fire
Until she spoke; then through its soft disguise
    Flash'd an expression more of pride than ire,
And love than either; and there would arise
    A something in them which was not desire,
But would have been, perhaps, but for the soul
Which struggled through and chasten'd down the whole.

61

Her glossy hair was cluster'd o'er a brow
    Bright with intelligence, and fair and smooth;
Her eyebrow's shape was like the aërial bow;
    Her cheek all purple with the beam of youth,
Mounting, at times, to a transparent glow,
    As if her veins ran lightning; she, in sooth,
Possess'd an air and grace by no means common;
Her stature tall—I hate a dumpy woman.

62

Wedded she was some years, and to a man
    Of fifty; and such husbands are in plenty;
And yet, I think, instead of such a ONE,
    'Twere better to have TWO of five-and-twenty,
Especially in countries near the sun:
    And now I think on't, "mi vien in mente,"
Ladies even of the most uneasy virtue
Prefer a spouse whose age is short of thirty.

63

'Tis a sad thing, I cannot choose but say,
    And all the fault of that indecent sun,
Who cannot leave alone our helpless clay,
    But will keep baking, broiling, burning on,
That, howsoever people fast and pray,
    The flesh is frail, and so the soul undone:
What men call gallantry, and gods adultery,
Is much more common where the climate's sultry.

64

Happy the nations of the moral North!
    Where all is virtue, and the winter season
Sends sin, without a rag on, shivering forth
    ('Twas snow that brought Saint Anthony to reason);
Where juries cast up what a wife is worth,
    By laying whate'er sum, in mulct, they please on
The lover, who must pay a handsome price,
Because it is a marketable vice.

*   *   *   *   *

69

Juan she saw, and, as a pretty child,
    Caress'd him often—such a thing might be
Quite innocently done, and harmless styled,
    When she had twenty years, and thirteen he;

But I am not so sure I should have smiled
    When he was sixteen, Julia twenty-three;
These few short years make wondrous alterations,
Particularly amongst sun-burnt nations.

70

Whate'er the cause might be, they had become
    Changed; for the dame grew distant, the youth shy,
Their looks cast down, their greetings almost dumb,
    And much embarrassment in either eye;
There surely will be little doubt with some
    That Donna Julia knew the reason why,
But as for Juan, he had no more notion
Than he who never saw the sea of ocean.

71

Yet Julia's very coldness still was kind,
    And tremulously gentle her small hand
Withdrew itself from his, but left behind
    A little pressure, thrilling, and so bland
And slight, so very slight, that to the mind
    'Twas but a doubt; but ne'er magician's wand
Wrought change with all Armida's fairy art,
Like what this light touch left on Juan's heart.

72

And if she met him, though she smiled no more,
    She look'd a sadness sweeter than her smile,
As if her heart had deeper thoughts in store
    She must not own, but cherish'd more the while,
For that compression in its burning core;
    Even innocence itself has many a wile,
And will not dare to trust itself with truth,
And love is taught hypocrisy from youth.

*   *   *   *   *

90

Young Juan wander'd by the glassy brooks,
  Thinking unutterable things; he threw
Himself at length within the leafy nooks,
  Where the wild branch of the cork forest grew;
There poets find materials for their books,
  And every now and then we read them through,
So that their plan and prosody are eligible,
Unless, like Wordsworth, they prove unintelligible.

91

He, Juan (and not Wordsworth), so pursued
  His self-communion with his own high soul,
Until his mighty heart, in its great mood,
  Had mitigated part, though not the whole
Of its disease; he did the best he could
  With things not very subject to control,
And turn'd, without perceiving his condition,
Like Coleridge, into a metaphysician.

92

He thought about himself, and the whole earth,
  Of man the wonderful, and of the stars,
And how the deuce they ever could have birth;
  And then he thought of earthquakes, and of wars,
How many miles the moon might have in girth;
  Of air-balloons, and of the many bars
To perfect knowledge of the boundless skies;—
And then he thought of Donna Julia's eyes.

*   *   *   *   *

96

Thus would he while his lonely hours away
  Dissatisfied, not knowing what he wanted;
Nor glowing reverie, nor poet's lay,
  Could yield his spirit that for which it panted,

A bosom whereon he his head might lay,
  And hear the heart beat with the love it granted,
With—several other things which I forget,
Or which, at least, I need not mention yet.

*   *   *   *   *

103

'Twas on a summer's day—the sixth of June:—
  I like to be particular in dates,
Not only of the age, and year, but moon;
  They are a sort of post-house, where the Fates
Change horses, making history change its tune,
  Then spur away o'er empires and o'er states,
Leaving at last not much besides chronology,
Excepting the post-obits of theology.

104

'Twas on the sixth of June, about the hour
  Of half-past six—perhaps still nearer seven—
When Julia sate within as pretty a bower
  As e'er held houri in that heathenish heaven
Described by Mahomet, and Anacreon Moore,
  To whom the lyre and laurels have been given,
With all the trophies of triumphant song—
He won them well, and may he wear them long!

*   *   *   *   *

106

How beautiful she look'd! her conscious heart
  Glow'd in her cheek, and yet she felt no wrong.
Oh Love! how perfect is thy mystic art,
  Strengthening the weak, and trampling on the strong!
How self-deceitful is the sagest part
  Of mortals whom thy lure hath led along!—
The precipice she stood on was immense,
So was her creed in her own innocence.

*   *   *   *   *

111

The hand which still held Juan's, by degrees
    Gently, but palpably, confirm'd its grasp,
As if it said, "Detain me, if you please;"
    Yet there's no doubt she only meant to clasp
His fingers with a pure Platonic squeeze:
    She would have shrunk as from a toad or asp,
Had she imagined such a thing could rouse
A feeling dangerous to a prudent spouse.

112

I cannot know what Juan thought of this,
    But what he did is much what you would do;
His young lip thank'd it with a grateful kiss,
    And then, abash'd at his own joy, withdrew
In deep despair, lest he had done amiss,—
    Love is so very timid when 'tis new:
She blush'd, and frown'd not, but she strove to speak,
And held her tongue, her voice was grown so weak.

113

The sun set, and up rose the yellow moon:
    The devil's in the moon for mischief; they
Who call'd her CHASTE, methinks, began too soon
    Their nomenclature; there is not a day,
The longest, not the twenty-first of June,
    Sees half the business in a wicked way
On which three single hours of moonshine smile—
And then she looks so modest all the while.

114

There is a dangerous silence in that hour,
    A stillness, which leaves room for the full soul
To open all itself, without the power
    Of calling wholly back its self-control;
The silver light which, hallowing tree and tower,
    Sheds beauty and deep softness o'er the whole,
Breathes also to the heart, and o'er it throws
A loving languor, which is not repose.

115

And Julia sate with Juan, half embraced,
    And half retiring from the glowing arm,
Which trembled like the bosom where 'twas placed;
    Yet still she must have thought there was no harm,
Or else 'twere easy to withdraw her waist;
    But then the situation had its charm,
And then—God knows what next—I can't go on;
I'm almost sorry that I e'er begun.

116

Oh Plato! Plato! you have paved the way,
    With your confounded fantasies, to more
Immoral conduct by the fancied sway
    Your system feigns o'er the controlless core
Of human hearts, than all the long array
    Of poets and romancers:—You're a bore,
A charlatan, a coxcomb—and have been,
At best, no better than a go-between.

*   *   *   *   *

123

'Tis sweet to hear the watch-dog's honest bark
    Bay deep-mouth'd welcome as we draw near home;
'Tis sweet to know there is an eye will mark
    Our coming, and look brighter when we come;
'Tis sweet to be awaken'd by the lark,
    Or lull'd by falling waters; sweet the hum
Of bees, the voice of girls, the song of birds,
The lisp of children, and their earliest words.

124

Sweet is the vintage, when the showering grapes
    In Bacchanal profusion reel to earth
Purple and gushing: sweet are our escapes
    From civic revelry to rural mirth;

Sweet to the miser are his glittering heaps,
    Sweet to the father is his first-born's birth,
Sweet is revenge—especially to women,
Pillage to soldiers, prize-money to seamen.

*   *   *   *   *

126

'Tis sweet to win, no matter how, one's laurels,
    By blood or ink; 'tis sweet to put an end
To strife; 'tis sometimes sweet to have our quarrels,
    Particularly with a tiresome friend:
Sweet is old wine in bottles, ale in barrels;
    Dear is the helpless creature we defend
Against the world; and dear the schoolboy spot
We ne'er forget, though there we are forgot.

127

But sweeter still than this, than these, than all,
    Is first and passionate love—it stands alone,
Like Adam's recollection of his fall;
    The tree of knowledge has been pluck'd—all's known—
And life yields nothing further to recall,
    Worthy of this ambrosial sin, so shown,
No doubt in fable, as the unforgiven
Fire which Prometheus filch'd for us from heaven.

*   *   *   *   *

133

Man's a phenomenon, one knows not what,
    And wonderful beyond all wondrous measure;
'Tis pity though, in this sublime world, that
    Pleasure's a sin, and sometimes sin's a pleasure;
Few mortals know what end they would be at,
    But whether glory, power, or love, or treasure,
The path is through perplexing ways, and when
The goal is gain'd, we die, you know—and then—

134

What then?—I do not know, no more do you—
　And so good night.—Return we to our story:
'Twas in November, when fine days are few,
　And the far mountains wax a little hoary,
And clap a white cape on their mantles blue;
　And the sea dashes round the promontory,
And the loud breaker boils against the rock,
And sober suns must set at five o'clock.

＊　＊　＊　＊　＊

136

'Twas midnight—Donna Julia was in bed,
　Sleeping, most probably,—when at her door
Arose a clatter might awake the dead,
　If they had never been awoke before—
And that they have been so we all have read,
　And are to be so, at the least, once more;—
The door was fasten'd, but, with voice and fist,
First knocks were heard, then "Madam—Madam—hist!

137

"For God's sake, Madam—Madam—here's my master,
　With more than half the city at his back—
Was ever heard of such a curst disaster?
　'Tis not my fault—I kept good watch—Alack!
Do pray undo the bolt a little faster—
　They're on the stair just now, and in a crack
Will all be here; perhaps he yet may fly—
Surely the window's not so *very* high!"

＊　＊　＊　＊　＊

140

Poor Donna Julia! starting as from sleep
　(Mind—that I do not say—she had not slept),
Began at once to scream, and yawn, and weep;
　Her maid Antonia, who was an adept,

Contrived to fling the bed-clothes in a heap,
  As if she had just now from out them crept:
I can't tell why she should take all this trouble
To prove her mistress had been sleeping double.

*   *   *   *   *

143

He search'd, *they* search'd, and rummaged everywhere,
  Closet and clothes' press, chest and window-seat,
And found much linen, lace, and several pair
  Of stockings, slippers, brushes, combs, complete,
With other articles of ladies fair,
  To keep them beautiful, or leave them neat:
Arras they prick'd and curtains with their swords,
And wounded several shutters, and some boards.

144

Under the bed they search'd, and there they found—
  No matter what—it was not that they sought;
They open'd windows, gazing if the ground
  Had signs or foot-marks, but the earth said nought;
And then they stared each others' faces round:
  'Tis odd, not one of all these seekers thought,
And seems to me almost a sort of blunder,
Of looking *in* the bed as well as under.

*   *   *   *   *

200

My poem's epic, and is meant to be
  Divided in twelve books; each book containing,
With love, and war, a heavy gale at sea,
  A list of ships, and captains, and kings reigning,
New characters; the episodes are three:
  A panoramic view of hell's in training,
After the style of Virgil and of Homer,
So that my name of Epic's no misnomer.

201

All these things will be specified in time,
  With strict regard to Aristotle's Rules,
The Vade Mecum of the true sublime,
  Which makes so many poets, and some fools.
Prose poets like blank verse, I'm fond of rhyme,
  Good workmen never quarrel with their tools;
I've got new mythological machinery,
And very handsome supernatural scenery.

202

There's only one slight difference between
  Me and my epic brethren gone before,
And here the advantage is my own, I ween
  (Not that I have not several merits more;
But this will more peculiarly be seen);
  They so embellish, that 'tis quite a bore
Their labyrinth of fables to thread through,
Whereas this story's actually true.

203

If any person doubt it, I appeal
  To history, tradition, and to facts,
To newspapers, whose truth all know and feel,
  To plays in five, and operas in three acts:
All these confirm my statement a good deal,
  But that which more completely faith exacts
Is that myself, and several now in Seville,
Saw Juan's last elopement with the devil.

204

If ever I should condescend to prose,
  I'll write poetical commandments, which
Shall supersede beyond all doubt all those
  That went before; in these I shall enrich
My text with many things that no one knows,
  And carry precept to the highest pitch:
I'll call the work "Longinus o'er a Bottle,
Or, Every poet his own Aristotle."

205

Thou shalt believe in Milton, Dryden, Pope:
   Thou shalt not set up Wordsworth, Coleridge, Southey;
Because the first is crazed beyond all hope,
   The second drunk, the third so quaint and mouthy:
With Crabbe it may be difficult to cope,
   And Campbell's Hippocrene is somewhat drouthy:
Thou shalt not steal from Samuel Rogers, nor
Commit—flirtation with the Muse of Moore.

206

Thou shalt not covet Mr. Sotheby's Muse,
   His Pegasus, nor anything that's his:
Thou shalt not bear false witness, like "the Blues"
   (There's one, at least, is very fond of this);
Thou shalt not write, in short, but what I choose:
   This is true criticism, and you may kiss—
Exactly as you please, or not—the rod,
But if you don't, I'll lay it on, by G—d!

*　　*　　*　　*　　*

213

But now at thirty years my hair is grey
   (I wonder what it will be like at forty?
I thought of a peruke the other day)—
   My heart is not much greener; and, in short, I
Have squander'd my whole summer while 'twas May,
   And feel no more the spirit to retort; I
Have spent my life, both interest and principal,
And deem not, what I deem'd, my soul invincible.

214

No more—no more—Oh! never more on me
   The freshness of the heart can fall like dew,
Which out of all the lovely things we see
   Extracts emotions beautiful and new,

Hived in our bosoms like the bag o' the bee:
  Think'st thou the honey with those objects grew?
Alas! 'twas not in them, but in thy power,
To double even the sweetness of a flower.

215

No more—no more—Oh! never more, my heart,
  Canst thou be my sole world, my universe!
Once all in all, but now a thing apart,
  Thou canst not be my blessing or my curse;
The illusion's gone for ever, and thou art
  Insensible, I trust, but none the worse,
And in thy stead I've got a deal of judgment,
Though Heaven knows how it ever found a lodgment.

216

My days of love are over; me no more
  The charms of maid, wife, and still less of widow,
Can make the fool of which they made before,—
  In short, I must not lead the life I did do;
The credulous hope of mutual minds is o'er,
  The copious use of claret is forbid too;
So, for a good old-gentlemanly vice,
I think I must take up with avarice.

*   *   *   *   *

218

What is the end of Fame? 'tis but to fill
  A certain portion of uncertain paper:
Some liken it to climbing up a hill,
  Whose summit, like all hills, is lost in vapour;
For this men write, speak, preach, and heroes kill,
  And bards burn what they call their "midnight taper,"
To have, when the original is dust,
A name, a wretched picture, and worse bust.

*   *   *   *   *

CANTO II

*   *   *   *   *

14

Don Juan stood, and, gazing from the stern,
   Beheld his native Spain receding far:
First partings form a lesson hard to learn,
   Even nations feel this when they go to war;
There is a sort of unexpress'd concern,
   A kind of shock that sets one's heart ajar:
At leaving even the most unpleasant people
And places, one keeps looking at the steeple.

15

But Juan had got many things to leave—
   His mother, and a mistress, and no wife,
So that he had much better cause to grieve
   Than many persons more advanced in life;
And, if we now and then a sigh must heave
   At quitting even those we quit in strife,
No doubt we weep for those the heart endears—
That is, till deeper griefs congeal our tears.

16

So Juan wept, as wept the captive Jews
   By Babel's waters, still remembering Sion:
I'd weep,—but mine is not a weeping Muse,
   And such light griefs are not a thing to die on;
Young men should travel, if but to amuse
   Themselves; and the next time their servants tie on
Behind their carriages their new portmanteau,
Perhaps it may be lined with this my canto.

17

And Juan wept, and much he sigh'd, and thought,
   While his salt tears dropp'd into the salt sea,
"Sweets to the sweet;" (I like so much to quote;
   You must excuse this extract, 'tis where she,
The Queen of Denmark, for Ophelia brought
   Flowers to the grave); and sobbing often, he
Reflected on his present situation,
And seriously resolved on reformation.

18

"Farewell, my Spain! a long farewell!" he cried,
   "Perhaps I may revisit thee no more,
But die, as many an exiled heart hath died,
   Of its own thirst to see again thy shore:
Farewell, where Guadalquivir's waters glide!
   Farewell, my mother! and, since all is o'er,
Farewell, too, dearest Julia!—(here he drew
Her letter out again, and read it through.)

19

"And oh! if e'er I should forget, I swear—
   But that's impossible, and cannot be—
Sooner shall this blue ocean melt to air,
   Sooner shall earth resolve itself to sea,
Than I resign thine image, oh! my fair!
   Or think of anything, excepting thee;
A mind diseased no remedy can physic—
(Here the ship gave a lurch, and he grew sea-sick.)

20

"Sooner shall heaven kiss earth (here he fell sicker),
   Oh, Julia! what is every other woe?
(For God's sake, let me have a glass of liquor;
   Pedro! Battista! help me down below.)

Julia! my love! (you rascal, Pedro, quicker)—
Oh Julia! (this cursed vessel pitches so)—
Beloved Julia! hear me still beseeching!"
(Here he grew inarticulate with retching.)

*   *   *   *   *

22

Love's a capricious power: I've known it hold
    Out through a fever caused by its own heat,
But be much puzzled by a cough and cold,
    And find a quinsy very hard to treat;
Against all noble maladies he's bold,
    But vulgar illnesses don't like to meet,
Nor that a sneeze should interrupt his sigh,
Nor inflammations redden his blind eye.

23

But worst of all is nausea, or a pain
    About the lower region of the bowels;
Love, who heroically breathes a vein,
    Shrinks from the application of hot towels,
And purgatives are dangerous to his reign,
    Sea-sickness death: his love was perfect, how else
Could Juan's passion, while the billows roar,
Resist his stomach, ne'er at sea before?

*   *   *   *   *

27

At one o'clock the wind with sudden shift
    Threw the ship right into the trough of the sea,
Which struck her aft, and made an awkward rift,
    Started the stern-post, also shatter'd the
Whole of her stern-frame, and ere she could lift
    Herself from out her present jeopardy,
The rudder tore away: 'twas time to sound
The pumps, and there were four feet water found.

28

One gang of people instantly was put
   Upon the pumps, and the remainder set
To get up part of the cargo, and what not;
   But they could not come at the leak as yet;
At last they did get at it really, but
   Still their salvation was an even bet:
The water rush'd through in a way quite puzzling,
While they thrust sheets, shirts, jackets, bales of muslin,

29

Into the opening; but all such ingredients
   Would have been vain, and they must have gone down,
Despite of all their efforts and expedients,
   But for the pumps: I'm glad to make them known
To all the brother tars who may have need hence,
   For fifty tons of water were upthrown
By them per hour, and they had all been undone,
But for the maker, Mr. Mann, of London.

30

As day advanced, the weather seem'd to abate,
   And then the leak they reckon'd to reduce,
And keep the ship afloat, though three feet yet
   Kept two hand and one chain-pump still in use.
The wind blew fresh again: as it grew late
   A squall came on, and, while some guns broke loose,
A gust—which all descriptive power transcends—
Laid with one blast the ship on her beam ends.

31

There she lay motionless, and seem'd upset;
   The water left the hold, and wash'd the decks,
And made a scene men do not soon forget;
   For they remember battles, fires, and wrecks,
Or any other thing that brings regret,
   Or breaks their hopes, or hearts, or heads, or necks:
Thus drownings are much talk'd of by the divers
And swimmers who may chance to be survivors.

32

Immediately the masts were cut away,
  Both main and mizen; first the mizen went,
The main-mast follow'd: but the ship still lay
  Like a mere log, and baffled our intent.
Foremast and bowsprit were cut down, and they
  Eased her at last (although we never meant
To part with all till every hope was blighted),
And then with violence the old ship righted.

33

It may be easily supposed, while this
  Was going on, some people were unquiet,
That passengers would find it much amiss
  To lose their lives, as well as spoil their diet;
That even the able seaman, deeming his
  Days nearly o'er, might be disposed to riot,
As upon such occasions tars will ask
For grog, and sometimes drink rum from the cask.

34

There's nought, no doubt, so much the spirit calms
  As rum and true religion: thus it was,
Some plunder'd, some drank spirits, some sung psalms,
  The high wind made the treble, and as bass
The hoarse harsh waves kept time; fright cured the qualms
  Of all the luckless landmen's sea-sick maws:
Strange sounds of wailing, blasphemy, devotion,
Clamour'd in chorus to the roaring ocean.

35

Perhaps more mischief had been done, but for
  Our Juan, who, with sense beyond his years,
Got to the spirit-room, and stood before
  It with a pair of pistols; and their fears,
As if Death were more dreadful by his door
  Of fire than water, spite of oaths and tears,
Kept still aloof the crew, who, ere they sunk,
Thought it would be becoming to die drunk.

36

"Give us more grog," they cried, "for it will be
  All one an hour hence." Juan answer'd "No!
'Tis true that death awaits both you and me,
  But let us die like men, not sink below
Like brutes;"—and thus his dangerous post kept he,
  And none liked to anticipate the blow;
And even Pedrillo, his most reverend tutor,
Was for some rum a disappointed suitor.

37

The good old gentleman was quite aghast,
  And made a loud and pious lamentation;
Repented all his sins, and made a last
  Irrevocable vow of reformation;
Nothing should tempt him more (this peril past)
  To quit his academic occupation,
In cloisters of the classic Salamanca,
To follow Juan's wake like Sancho Panca.

38

But now there came a flash of hope once more;
  Day broke, and the wind lull'd: the masts were gone,
The leak increased; shoals round her, but no shore,
  The vessel swam, yet still she held her own.
They tried the pumps again, and though before
  Their desperate efforts seem'd all useless grown,
A glimpse of sunshine set some hands to bale—
The stronger pump'd, the weaker thrumm'd a sail.

39

Under the vessel's keel the sail was pass'd,
  And for the moment it had some effect,
But with a leak, and not a stick of mast,
  Nor rag of canvass, what could they expect?
But still 'tis best to struggle to the last,
  'Tis never too late to be wholly wreck'd:
And though 'tis true that man can only die once,
'Tis not so pleasant in the Gulf of Lyons.

40

There winds and waves had hurl'd them, and from thence,
  Without their will, they carried them away;
For they were forced with steering to dispense,
  And never had, as yet, a quiet day
On which they might repose, or even commence
  A jurymast or rudder, or could say
The ship would swim an hour, which, by good luck,
Still swam—though not exactly like a duck.

41

The wind, in fact, perhaps was rather less,
  But the ship labour'd so, they scarce could hope
To weather out much longer; the distress
  Was also great with which they had to cope
For want of water, and their solid mess
  Was scant enough: in vain the telescope
Was used—nor sail nor shore appear'd in sight,
Nought but the heavy sea, and coming night.

42

Again the weather threaten'd,—again blew
  A gale, and in the fore and after hold
Water appear'd; yet, though the people knew
  All this, the most were patient, and some bold,
Until the chains and leathers were worn through
  Of all our pumps:—a wreck complete she roll'd,
At mercy of the waves, whose mercies are
Like human beings during civil war.

43

Then came the carpenter, at last, with tears
  In his rough eyes, and told the captain he
Could do no more: he was a man in years,
  And long had voyaged through many a stormy sea,
And if he wept at length, they were not fears
  That made his eyelids as a woman's be,
But he, poor fellow, had a wife and children—
Two things for dying people quite bewildering.

44

The ship was evidently settling now
   Fast by the head; and, all distinction gone,
Some went to prayers again, and made a vow
   Of candles to their saints—but there were none
To pay them with; and some look'd o'er the bow;
   Some hoisted out the boats; and there was one
That begg'd Pedrillo for an absolution,
Who told him to be damn'd—in his confusion.

45

Some lash'd them in their hammocks, some put on
   Their best clothes as if going to a fair;
Some cursed the day on which they saw the sun,
   And gnash'd their teeth, and, howling, tore their hair;
And others went on as they had begun,
   Getting the boats out, being well aware
That a tight boat will live in a rough sea,
Unless with breakers close beneath her lee.

46

The worst of all was, that in their condition,
   Having been several days in great distress,
'Twas difficult to get out such provision
   As now might render their long suffering less:
Men, even when dying, dislike inanition;
   Their stock was damaged by the weather's stress:
Two casks of biscuit and a keg of butter
Were all that could be thrown into the cutter.

47

But in the long-boat they contrived to stow
   Some pounds of bread, though injured by the wet;
Water, a twenty-gallon cask or so;
   Six flasks of wine; and they contrived to get
A portion of their beef up from below,
   And with a piece of pork, moreover, met,
But scarce enough to serve them for a luncheon—
Then there was rum, eight gallons in a puncheon.

48

The other boats, the yawl and pinnace, had
  Been stove in the beginning of the gale;
And the long-boat's condition was but bad,
  As there were but two blankets for a sail,
And one oar for a mast, which a young lad
  Threw in by good luck over the ship's rail;
And two boats could not hold, far less be stored,
To save one half the people then on board.

49

'Twas twilight, for the sunless day went down
  Over the waste of waters; like a veil,
Which, if withdrawn, would but disclose the frown
  Of one whose hate is mask'd but to assail,
Thus to their hopeless eyes the night was shown,
  And grimly darkled o'er the faces pale,
And the dim desolate deep: twelve days had Fear
Been their familiar, and now Death was here.

50

Some trial had been making at a raft,
  With little hope in such a rolling sea,
A sort of thing at which one would have laugh'd,
  If any laughter at such times could be,
Unless with people who too much have quaff'd,
  And have a kind of wild and horrid glee,
Half epileptical and half hysterical:—
Their preservation would have been a miracle.

51

At half-past eight o'clock, booms, hencoops, spars,
  And all things, for a chance, had been cast loose,
That still could keep afloat the struggling tars,
  For yet they strove, although of no great use:
There was no light in heaven but a few stars,
  The boats put off o'ercrowded with their crews;
She gave a heel, and then a lurch to port,
And, going down head foremost—sunk, in short.

52

Then rose from sea to sky the wild farewell—
    Then shriek'd the timid, and stood still the brave,
Then some leap'd overboard with dreadful yell,
    As eager to anticipate their grave;
And the sea yawn'd around her like a hell,
    And down she suck'd with her the whirling wave,
Like one who grapples with his enemy,
And strives to strangle him before he die.

53

And first one universal shriek there rush'd,
    Louder than the loud ocean, like a crash
Of echoing thunder; and then all was hush'd,
    Save the wild wind and the remorseless dash
Of billows; but at intervals there gush'd,
    Accompanied with a convulsive splash,
A solitary shriek, the bubbling cry
Of some strong swimmer in his agony.

54

The boats, as stated, had got off before,
    And in them crowded several of the crew;
And yet their present hope was hardly more
    Than what it had been, for so strong it blew
There was slight chance of reaching any shore;
    And then they were too many, though so few—
Nine in the cutter, thirty in the boat,
Were counted in them when they got afloat.

55

All the rest perish'd; near two hundred souls
    Had left their bodies; and, what's worse, alas!
When over Catholics the ocean rolls,
    They must wait several weeks before a mass
Takes off one peck of purgatorial coals,
    Because, till people know what's come to pass,
They won't lay out their money on the dead—
It costs three francs for every mass that's said.

56

Juan got into the long-boat, and there
  Contrived to help Pedrillo to a place;
It seem'd as if they had exchanged their care,
  For Juan wore the magisterial face
Which courage gives, while poor Pedrillo's pair
  Of eyes were crying for their owner's case:
Battista, though (a name call'd shortly Tita),
Was lost by getting at some aqua-vitae.

57

Pedro, his valet, too, he tried to save,
  But the same cause, conducive to his loss,
Left him so drunk, he jump'd into the wave
  As o'er the cutter's edge he tried to cross,
And so he found a wine-and-watery grave;
  They could not rescue him, although so close,
Because the sea ran higher every minute,
And for the boat—the crew kept crowding in it.

58

A small old spaniel,—which had been Don José's,
  His father's, whom he loved, as ye may think,
For on such things the memory reposes
  With tenderness—stood howling on the brink,
Knowing (dogs have such intellectual noses!),
  No doubt, the vessel was about to sink;
And Juan caught him up, and ere he stepp'd
Off, threw him in, then after him he leap'd.

59

He also stuff'd his money where he could
  About his person, and Pedrillo's too,
Who let him do, in fact, whate'er he would,
  Not knowing what himself to say or do,
As every rising wave his dread renew'd;
  But Juan, trusting they might still get through,
And deeming there were remedies for any ill,
Thus re-embark'd his tutor and his spaniel.

60

'Twas a rough night, and blew so stiffly yet,
  That the sail was becalm'd between the seas,
Though on the wave's high top too much to set,
  They dared not take it in for all the breeze;
Each sea curl'd o'er the stern, and kept them wet,
  And made them bale without a moment's ease,
So that themselves as well as hopes were damp'd,
And the poor little cutter quickly swamp'd.

61

Nine souls more went in her: the long-boat still
  Kept above water, with an oar for mast,
Two blankets stitch'd together, answering ill
  Instead of sail, were to the oar made fast:
Though every wave roll'd menacing to fill,
  And present peril all before surpass'd,
They grieved for those who perish'd with the cutter,
And also for the biscuit-casks and butter.

62

The sun rose red and fiery, a sure sign
  Of the continuance of the gale: to run
Before the sea, until it should grow fine,
  Was all that for the present could be done:
A few tea-spoonfuls of their rum and wine
  Were served out to the people, who begun
To faint, and damaged bread wet through the bags,
And most of them had little clothes but rags.

63

They counted thirty, crowded in a space
  Which left scarce room for motion or exertion;
They did their best to modify their case,
  One half sate up, though numb'd with the immersion,
While t'other half were laid down in their place,
  At watch and watch; thus, shivering like the tertian
Ague in its cold fit, they fill'd their boat,
With nothing but the sky for a great coat.

64

'Tis very certain the desire of life
  Prolongs it: this is obvious to physicians,
When patients, neither plagued with friends nor wife,
  Survive through very desperate conditions,
Because they still can hope, nor shines the knife
  Nor shears of Atropos before their visions:
Despair of all recovery spoils longevity,
And makes men's miseries of alarming brevity.

65

'Tis said that persons living on annuities
  Are longer lived than others,—God knows why,
Unless to plague the grantors,—yet so true it is,
  That some, I really think, do never die;
Of any creditors the worst a Jew it is,
  And that's their mode of furnishing supply:
In my young days they lent me cash that way,
Which I found very troublesome to pay.

66

'Tis thus with people in an open boat,
  They live upon the love of life, and bear
More than can be believed, or even thought,
  And stand, like rocks, the tempest's wear and tear;
And hardship still has been the sailor's lot,
  Since Noah's ark went cruising here and there;
She had a curious crew as well as cargo,
Like the first old Greek privateer, the Argo.

67

But man is a carnivorous production,
  And must have meals, at least one meal a day;
He cannot live, like woodcocks, upon suction,
  But, like the shark and tiger, must have prey;
Although his anatomical construction
  Bears vegetables, in a grumbling way,
Your labouring people think beyond all question,
Beef, veal, and mutton, better for digestion.

68

And thus it was with this our hapless crew;
  For on the third day there came on a calm,
And though at first their strength it might renew,
  And lying on their weariness like balm,
Lull'd them like turtles sleeping on the blue
  Of ocean, when they woke they felt a qualm,
And fell all ravenously on their provision,
Instead of hoarding it with due precision.

      *   *   *   *   *

72

The seventh day, and no wind—the burning sun
  Blister'd and scorch'd, and, stagnant on the sea,
They lay like carcasses; and hope was none,
  Save in the breeze that came not; savagely
They glared upon each other—all was done,
  Water, and wine, and food,—and you might see
The longings of the cannibal arise
(Although they spoke not) in their wolfish eyes.

73

At length one whisper'd his companion, who
  Whisper'd another, and thus it went round,
And then into a hoarser murmur grew,
  An ominous, and wild, and desperate sound;
And when his comrade's thought each sufferer knew,
  'Twas but his own, suppress'd till now, he found:
And out they spoke of lots for flesh and blood,
And who should die to be his fellow's food.

74

But ere they came to this, they that day shared
  Some leathern caps, and what remain'd of shoes;
And then they look'd around them, and despair'd,
  And none to be the sacrifice would choose;

At length the lots were torn up, and prepared,
  But of materials that much shock the Muse—
Having no paper, for the want of better,
They took by force from Juan, Julia's letter.

75

The lots were made, and mark'd, and mix'd and handed
  In silent horror, and their distribution
Lull'd even the savage hunger which demanded,
  Like the Promethean vulture, this pollution;
None in particular had sought or plann'd it,
  'Twas nature gnaw'd them to this resolution,
By which none were permitted to be neuter—
And the lot fell on Juan's luckless tutor.

76

He but requested to be bled to death:
  The surgeon had his instruments and bled
Pedrillo; and so gently ebb'd his breath,
  You hardly could perceive when he was dead.
He died as born, a Catholic in faith,
  Like most in the belief in which they're bred,
And first a little crucifix he kiss'd,
And then held out his jugular and wrist.

77

The surgeon, as there was no other fee,
  Had his first choice of morsels for his pains;
But, being thirstiest at the moment, he
  Preferr'd a draught from the fast-flowing veins:
Part was divided, part thrown in the sea,
  And such things as the entrails and the brains
Regaled two sharks, who follow'd o'er the billow—
The sailors ate the rest of poor Pedrillo.

78

The sailors ate him, all save three or four,
  Who were not quite so fond of animal food;
To these was added Juan, who, before
  Refusing his own spaniel, hardly could

Feel now his appetite increased much more;
    'Twas not to be expected that he should,
Even in extremity of their disaster,
Dine with them on his pastor and his master.

79

'Twas better that he did not; for, in fact,
    The consequence was awful in the extreme,
For they, who were most ravenous in the act,
    Went raging mad—Lord! how they did blaspheme!
And foam and roll, with strange convulsions rack'd,
    Drinking salt-water like a mountain-stream,
Tearing, and grinning, howling, screeching, swearing,
And, with hyaena-laughter, died despairing.

80

Their numbers were much thinn'd by this infliction,
    And all the rest were thin enough, Heaven knows;
And some of them had lost their recollection,
    Happier than they who still perceived their woes;
But others ponder'd on a new dissection,
    As if not warn'd sufficiently by those
Who had already perish'd, suffering madly,
For having used their appetites so sadly.

81

And next they thought upon the master's mate,
    As fattest; but he saved himself, because,
Besides being much averse from such a fate,
    There were some other reasons: the first was,
He had been rather indisposed of late;
    And that which chiefly proved his saving clause,
Was a small present made to him at Cadiz,
By general subscription of the ladies.

82

Of poor Pedrillo something still remain'd,
    But it was used sparingly,—some were afraid,
And others still their appetites constrain'd,
    Or but at times a little supper made;

All except Juan, who throughout abstain'd,
   Chewing a piece of bamboo, and some lead:
At length they caught two boobies and a noddy,
And then they left off eating the dead body.

83

And if Pedrillo's fate should shocking be,
   Remember Ugolino condescends
To eat the head of his arch-enemy
   The moment after he politely ends
His tale: if foes be food in hell, at sea
   'Tis surely fair to dine upon our friends,
When shipwreck's short allowance grows too scanty,
Without being much more horrible than Dante.

84

And the same night there fell a shower of rain,
   For which their mouths gaped, like the cracks of earth,
When dried to summer dust; till taught by pain,
   Men really know not what good water's worth;
If you had been in Turkey or in Spain,
   Or with a famish'd boat's-crew had your berth,
Or in the desert heard the camel's bell,
You'd wish yourself where Truth is—in a well.

85

It pour'd down torrents, but they were no richer
   Until they found a ragged piece of sheet,
Which served them as a sort of spongy pitcher,
   And when they deem'd its moisture was complete,
They wrung it out, and, though a thirsty ditcher
   Might not have thought the scanty draught so sweet
As a full pot of porter, to their thinking
They ne'er till now had known the joys of drinking.

86

And their baked lips, with many a bloody crack,
   Suck'd in the moisture, which like nectar stream'd;
Their throats were ovens, their swoln tongues were black,
   As the rich man's in hell, who vainly scream'd

To beg the beggar, who could not rain back
   A drop of dew, when every drop had seem'd
To taste of heaven—If this be true, indeed,
Some Christians have a comfortable creed.

87

There were two fathers in this ghastly crew,
   And with them their two sons, of whom the one
Was more robust and hardy to the view,
   But he died early; and when he was gone,
His nearest messmate told his sire, who threw
   One glance on him, and said, "Heaven's will be done!
I can do nothing," and he saw him thrown
Into the deep, without a tear or groan.

88

The other father had a weaklier child,
   Of a soft cheek, and aspect delicate;
But the boy bore up long, and with a mild
   And patient spirit, held aloof his fate;
Little he said, and now and then he smiled,
   As if to win a part from off the weight
He saw increasing on his father's heart,
With the deep deadly thought, that they must part.

89

And o'er him bent his sire, and never raised
   His eyes from off his face, but wiped the foam,
From his pale lips, and ever on him gazed,
   And when the wish'd-for shower at length was come,
And the boy's eyes, which the dull film half glazed,
   Brighten'd, and for a moment seem'd to roam,
He squeezed from out a rag some drops of rain
Into his dying child's mouth—but in vain.

90

The boy expired—the father held the clay,
   And look'd upon it long, and when at last
Death left no doubt, and the dead burthen lay
   Stiff on his heart, and pulse and hope were past,

He watch'd it wistfully, until away
   'Twas borne by the rude wave wherein 'twas cast;
Then he himself sunk down, all dumb and shivering,
And gave no signs of life, save his limbs quivering.

91

Now overhead a rainbow, bursting through
   The scattering clouds, shone, spanning the dark sea,
Resting its bright base on the quivering blue;
   And all within its arch appear'd to be
Clearer than that without, and its wide hue
   Wax'd broad and waving, like a banner free,
Then changed like to a bow that's bent, and then
Forsook the dim eyes of these shipwreck'd men.

92

It changed, of course; a heavenly chameleon,
   The airy child of vapour and the sun,
Brought forth in purple, cradled in vermilion,
   Baptized in molten gold, and swathed in dun,
Glittering like crescents o'er a Turk's pavilion,
   And blending every colour into one,
Just like a black eye in a recent scuffle
(For sometimes we must box without the muffle).

93

Our shipwreck'd seamen thought it a good omen—
   It is as well to think so now and then;
'Twas an old custom of the Greek and Roman,
   And may become of great advantage when
Folks are discouraged; and most surely no men
   Had greater need to nerve themselves again
Than these; and so this rainbow look'd like hope—
Quite a celestial kaleidoscope.

94

About this time a beautiful white bird,
   Web-footed, not unlike a dove in size
And plumage (probably it might have err'd
   Upon its course), pass'd oft before their eyes,

And tried to perch, although it saw and heard
   The men within the boat, and in this guise
It came and went, and flutter'd round them, till
Night fell:—this seem'd a better omen still.

95

But in this case I also must remark,
   'Twas well this bird of promise did not perch,
Because the tackle of our shatter'd bark
   Was not so safe for roosting as a church;
And had it been the dove from Noah's ark,
   Returning there from her successful search,
Which in their way that moment chanced to fall,
They would have eat her, olive-branch and all.

96

With twilight it again came on to blow,
   But not with violence; the stars shone out,
The boat made way; yet now they were so low,
   They knew not where nor what they were about;
Some fancied they saw land, and some said "No!"
   The frequent fog-banks gave them cause to doubt—
Some swore that they heard breakers, others guns,
And all mistook about the latter once.

97

As morning broke, the light wind died away,
   When he who had the watch sung out, and swore,
If 'twas not land that rose with the sun's ray,
   He wish'd that land he never might see more;
And the rest rubb'd their eyes, and saw a bay,
   Or thought they saw, and shaped their course for shore;
For shore it was, and gradually grew
Distinct, and high, and palpable to view.

98

And then of these some part burst into tears,
   And others, looking with a stupid stare,
Could not yet separate their hopes from fears,
   And seem'd as if they had no further care;

While a few pray'd—(the first time for some years)—
 And at the bottom of the boat three were
Asleep: they shook them by the hand and head,
And tried to awaken them, but found them dead.

99

The day before, fast sleeping on the water,
 They found a turtle of the hawk's-bill kind,
And by good fortune, gliding softly, caught her,
 Which yielded a day's life, and to their mind
Proved even still a more nutritious matter,
 Because it left encouragement behind:
They thought that in such perils, more than chance
Had sent them this for their deliverance.

100

The land appear'd, a high and rocky coast,
 And higher grew the mountains as they drew,
Set by a current, towards it: they were lost
 In various conjectures, for none knew
To what part of the earth they had been toss'd,
 So changeable had been the winds that blew;
Some thought it was Mount Aetna, some the highlands
Of Candia, Cyprus, Rhodes, or other islands.

101

Meantime the current, with a rising gale,
 Still set them onwards to the welcome shore,
Like Charon's bark of spectres, dull and pale,
 Their living freight was now reduced to four;
And three dead, whom their strength could not avail
 To heave into the deep with those before,
Though the two sharks still follow'd them, and dash'd
The spray into their faces as they splash'd.

102

Famine, despair, cold, thirst, and heat had done
 Their work on them by turns, and thinn'd them to
Such things, a mother had not known her son
 Amidst the skeletons of that gaunt crew;

By night chill'd, by day scorch'd, thus one by one
  They perish'd, until wither'd to these few,
But chiefly by a species of self-slaughter,
In washing down Pedrillo with salt water.

103

As they drew nigh the land, which now was seen
  Unequal in its aspect here and there,
They felt the freshness of its growing green,
  That waved in forest-tops, and smooth'd the air,
And fell upon their glazed eyes like a screen
  From glistening waves, and skies so hot and bare—
Lovely seem'd any object that should sweep
Away the vast, salt, dread, eternal deep.

104

The shore look'd wild, without a trace of man,
  And girt by formidable waves; but they
Were mad for land, and thus their course they ran,
  Though right ahead the roaring breakers lay:
A reef between them also now began
  To shew its boiling surf and bounding spray,
But finding no place for their landing better,
They ran the boat for shore,—and overset her.

105

But in his native stream, the Guadalquivir,
  Juan to lave his youthful limbs was wont;
And having learn'd to swim in that sweet river,
  Had often turn'd the art to some account:
A better swimmer you could scarce see ever,
  He could, perhaps, have pass'd the Hellespont,
As once (a feat on which ourselves we prided)
Leander, Mr. Ekenhead, and I did.

106

So, here, though faint, emaciated, and stark,
  He buoy'd his boyish limbs, and strove to ply
With the quick wave, and gain, ere it was dark,
  The beach which lay before him, high and dry:

The greatest danger here was from a shark,
    That carried off his neighbour by the thigh;
As for the other two, they could not swim,
So nobody arrived on shore but him.

107

Nor yet had he arrived but for the oar,
    Which, providentially for him, was wash'd
Just as his feeble arms could strike no more,
    And the hard wave o'erwhelm'd him as 'twas dash'd
Within his grasp; he clung to it, and sore
    The waters beat while he thereto was lash'd;
At last, with swimming, wading, scrambling, he
Roll'd on the beach, half senseless, from the sea:

108

There, breathless, with his digging nails he clung
    Fast to the sand, lest the returning wave,
From whose reluctant roar his life he wrung,
    Should suck him back to her insatiate grave:
And there he lay, full length, where he was flung,
    Before the entrance of a cliff-worn cave,
With just enough of life to feel its pain,
And deem that it was saved, perhaps in vain.

109

With slow and staggering effort he arose,
    But sunk again upon his bleeding knee
And quivering hand; and then he look'd for those
    Who long had been his mates upon the sea;
But none of them appear'd to share his woes,
    Save one, a corpse from out the famish'd three,
Who died two days before, and now had found
An unknown barren beach for burial ground.

110

And, as he gazed, his dizzy brain spun fast,
    And down he sunk; and as he sunk, the sand
Swam round and round, and all his senses pass'd:
    He fell upon his side, and his stretch'd hand

Droop'd dripping on the oar (their jurymast),
    And, like a wither'd lily, on the land
His slender frame and pallid aspect lay,
As fair a thing as e'er was form'd of clay.

111

How long in his damp trance young Juan lay
    He knew not, for the earth was gone for him,
And time had nothing more of night nor day
    For his congealing blood, and senses dim;
And how this heavy faintness pass'd away
    He knew not, till each painful pulse and limb,
And tingling vein seem'd throbbing back to life,
For Death, though vanquish'd, still retired with strife.

112

His eyes he open'd, shut, again unclosed,
    For all was doubt and dizziness; he thought
He still was in the boat, and had but dozed,
    And felt again with his despair o'erwrought,
And wish'd it death in which he had reposed;
    And then once more his feelings back were brought,
And slowly by his swimming eyes was seen
A lovely female face of seventeen.

113

'Twas bending close o'er his, and the small mouth
    Seem'd almost prying into his for breath;
And chafing him, the soft warm hand of youth
    Recall'd his answering spirits back from death;
And, bathing his chill temples, tried to soothe
    Each pulse to animation, till beneath
Its gentle touch and trembling care, a sigh
To these kind efforts made a low reply.

114

Then was the cordial pour'd and mantle flung
    Around his scarce-clad limbs; and the fair arm
Raised higher the faint head which o'er it hung;
    And her transparent cheek, all pure and warm,

Pillow'd his death-like forehead; then she wrung
   His dewy curls, long drench'd by every storm;
And watch'd with eagerness each throb that drew
A sigh from his heaved bosom—and hers, too.

115

And lifting him with care into the cave,
   The gentle girl, and her attendant,—one
Young, yet her elder, and of brow less grave,
   And more robust of figure—then begun
To kindle fire, and as the new flames gave
   Light to the rocks that roof'd them, which the sun
Had never seen, the maid, or whatsoe'er
She was, appear'd distinct, and tall, and fair.

116

Her brow was overhung with coins of gold,
   That sparkled o'er the auburn of her hair,
Her clustering hair, whose longer locks were roll'd
   In braids behind, and, though her stature were
Even of the highest for a female mould,
   They nearly reach'd her heel; and in her air
There was a something which bespoke command,
As one who was a lady in the land.

117

Her hair, I said, was auburn; but her eyes
   Were black as death, their lashes the same hue,
Of downcast length, in whose silk shadow lies
   Deepest attraction; for when to the view
Forth from its raven fringe the full glance flies,
   Ne'er with such force the swiftest arrow flew;
'Tis as the snake late coil'd, who pours his length,
And hurls at once his venom and his strength.

118

Her brow was white and low, her cheeks' pure dye
   Like twilight rosy still with the set sun;
Short upper lip! sweet lips! that make us sigh
   Ever to have seen such; for she was one

Fit for the model of a statuary
    (A race of mere impostors, when all's done—
I've seen much finer women, ripe and real,
Than all the nonsense of their stone ideal).

119

I'll tell you why I say so, for 'tis just
    One should not rail without a decent cause:
There was an Irish lady, to whose bust
    I ne'er saw justice done, and yet she was
A frequent model; and if e'er she must
    Yield to stern Time and Nature's wrinkling laws,
They will destroy a face which mortal thought
Ne'er compass'd, nor less mortal chisel wrought.

120

And such was she, the lady of the cave:
    Her dress was very different from the Spanish,
Simpler, and yet of colours not so grave;
    For, as you know, the Spanish women banish
Bright hues when out of doors, and yet, while wave
    Around them (what I hope will never vanish)
The basquina and the mantilla, they
Seem at the same time mystical and gay.

121

But with our damsel this was not the case:
    Her dress was many-colour'd, finely spun;
Her locks curl'd negligently round her face,
    But through them gold and gems profusely shone,
Her girdle sparkled, and the richest lace
    Flow'd in her veil, and many a precious stone
Flash'd on her little hand; but, what was shocking,
Her small snow feet had slippers, but no stocking.

122

The other female's dress was not unlike,
    But of inferior materials: she
Had not so many ornaments to strike,
    Her hair had silver only, bound to be

Her dowry; and her veil, in form alike,
    Was coarser; and her air, though firm, less free;
Her hair was thicker, but less long; her eyes
    As black, but quicker, and of smaller size.

123

And these two tended him, and cheer'd him both
    With food and raiment, and those soft attentions,
Which are (as I must own) of female growth,
    And have ten thousand delicate inventions:
They made a most superior mess of broth,
    A thing which poesy but seldom mentions,
But the best dish that e'er was cook'd since Homer's
Achilles order'd dinner for new comers.

124

I'll tell you who they were, this female pair,
    Lest they should seem princesses in disguise;
Besides, I hate all mystery, and that air
    Of clap-trap, which your recent poets prize;
And so, in short, the girls they really were
    They shall appear before your curious eyes,
Mistress and maid; the first was only daughter
Of an old man who lived upon the water.

125

A fisherman he had been in his youth,
    And still a sort of fisherman was he;
But other speculations were, in sooth,
    Added to his connection with the sea,
Perhaps, not so respectable, in truth:
    A little smuggling, and some piracy,
Left him, at last, the sole of many masters
Of an ill-gotten million of piastres.

126

A fisher, therefore, was he,—though of men,
    Like Peter the Apostle,—and he fish'd
For wandering merchant-vessels, now and then,
    And sometimes caught as many as he wish'd;

The cargoes he confiscated, and gain
   He sought in the slave-market too, and dish'd
Full many a morsel for that Turkish trade,
By which, no doubt, a good deal may be made.

127

He was a Greek, and on his isle had built
   (One of the wild and smaller Cyclades)
A very handsome house from out his guilt,
   And there he lived exceedingly at ease;
Heaven knows what cash he got, or blood he spilt,
   A sad old fellow was he, if you please;
But this I know, it was a spacious building,
Full of barbaric carving, paint, and gilding.

128

He had an only daughter call'd Haidée,
   The greatest heiress of the Eastern Isles;
Besides, so very beautiful was she,
   Her dowry was as nothing to her smiles:
Still in her teens, and like a lovely tree
   She grew to womanhood, and between whiles
Rejected several suitors, just to learn
How to accept a better in his turn.

129

And walking out upon the beach, below
   The cliff, towards sunset, on that day she found,
Insensible,—not dead, but nearly so,—
   Don Juan, almost famish'd, and half drown'd;
But, being naked, she was shock'd, you know,
   Yet deem'd herself in common pity bound,
As far as in her lay, "to take him in,
A stranger," dying, with so white a skin.

130

But taking him into her father's house
   Was not exactly the best way to save,
But like conveying to the cat the mouse,
   Or people in a trance, into their grave;

Because the good old man had so much "νοῦς,"
   Unlike the honest Arab thieves so brave,
He would have hospitably cured the stranger,
And sold him instantly when out of danger.

131

And therefore, with her maid, she thought it best
   (A virgin always on her maid relies)
To place him in the cave for present rest:
   And when, at last, he open'd his black eyes,
Their charity increased about their guest;
   And their compassion grew to such a size,
It open'd half the turnpike-gates to heaven—
(Saint Paul says 'tis the toll which must be given).

132

They made a fire,—but such a fire as they
   Upon the moment could contrive with such
Materials as were cast up round the bay,—
   Some broken planks and oars, that to the touch
Were nearly tinder, since so long they lay,
   A mast was almost crumbled to a crutch;
But, by God's grace, here wrecks were in such plenty,
That there was fuel to have furnish'd twenty.

133

He had a bed of furs, and a pelisse,
   For Haidée stripp'd her sables off to make
His couch; and that he might be more at ease,
   And warm, in case by chance he should awake,
They also gave a petticoat a-piece,
   She and her maid,—and promised by day-break
To pay him a fresh visit, with a dish
For breakfast, of eggs, coffee, bread, and fish.

*   *   *   *   *

156

For we all know that English people are
    Fed upon beef—I won't say much of beer,
Because 'tis liquor only, and being far
    From this my subject, has no business here;
We know, too, they are very fond of war,
    A pleasure—like all pleasures—rather dear;
So were the Cretans—from which I infer
That beef and battles both were owing to her.

157

But to resume. The languid Juan raised
    His head upon his elbow, and he saw
A sight on which he had not lately gazed,
    As all his latter meals had been quite raw,
Three or four things for which the Lord he praised,
    And feeling still the famish'd vulture gnaw,
He fell upon whate'er was offer'd, like
A priest, a shark, an alderman, or pike.

158

He ate, and he was well supplied: and she,
    Who watch'd him like a mother, would have fed
Him past all bounds, because she smiled to see
    Such appetite in one she had deem'd dead;
But Zoe, being older than Haidée,
    Knew (by tradition, for she ne'er had read)
That famish'd people must be slowly nursed,
And fed by spoonfuls, else they always burst.

159

And so she took the liberty to state,
    Rather by deeds than words, because the case
Was urgent, that the gentleman, whose fate
    Had made her mistress quit her bed to trace
The sea-shore at this hour, must leave his plate,
    Unless he wish'd to die upon the place—
She snatch'd it, and refused another morsel,
Saying, he had gorged enough to make a horse ill.

160

Next they—he being naked, save a tatter'd
    Pair of scarce decent trowsers—went to work,
And in the fire his recent rags they scatter'd,
    And dress'd him, for the present, like a Turk,
Or Greek—that is, although it not much matter'd,
    Omitting turban, slippers, pistols, dirk,—
They furnish'd him, entire, except some stitches,
With a clean shirt, and very spacious breeches.

161

And then fair Haidée tried her tongue at speaking,
    But not a word could Juan comprehend,
Although he listen'd so that the young Greek in
    Her earnestness would ne'er have made an end;
And, as he interrupted not, went eking
    Her speech out to her *protégé* and friend,
Till pausing at the last her breath to take,
She saw he did not understand Romaic.

162

And then she had recourse to nods, and signs,
    And smiles, and sparkles of the speaking eye,
And read (the only book she could) the lines
    Of his fair face, and found, by sympathy,
The answer eloquent, where the soul shines
    And darts in one quick glance a long reply;
And thus in every look she saw express'd
A world of words, and things at which she guess'd.

163

And now, by dint of fingers and of eyes,
    And words repeated after her, he took
A lesson in her tongue; but by surmise,
    No doubt, less of her language than her look,
As he who studies fervently the skies
    Turns oftener to the stars than to his book,
Thus Juan learn'd his alpha beta better
From Haidée's glance than any graven letter.

164

'Tis pleasing to be school'd in a strange tongue
   By female lips and eyes—that is, I mean,
When both the teacher and the taught are young,
   As was the case, at least, where I have been;
They smile so when one's right, and when one's wrong
   They smile still more, and then there intervene
Pressure of hands, perhaps even a chaste kiss;—
I learn'd the little that I know by this:

165

That is, some words of Spanish, Turk, and Greek,
   Italian not at all, having no teachers;
Much English I cannot pretend to speak,
   Learning that language chiefly from its preachers,
Barrow, South, Tillotson, whom every week
   I study, also Blair, the highest reachers
Of eloquence in piety and prose—
I hate your poets, so read none of those.

166

As for the ladies, I have nought to say,
   A wanderer from the British world of fashion,
Where I, like other "dogs, have had my day,"
   Like other men too, may have had my passion—
But that, like other things, has pass'd away,
   And all her fools whom I *could* lay the lash on:
Foes, friends, men, women, now are nought to me
But dreams of what has been, no more to be.

167

Return we to Don Juan. He begun
   To hear new words, and to repeat them; but
Some feelings, universal as the sun,
   Were such as could not in his breast be shut
More than within the bosom of a nun:
   He was in love—as you would be, no doubt,
With a young benefactress,—so was she
Just in the way we very often see.

168

And every day by daybreak—rather early
    For Juan, who was somewhat fond of rest—
She came into the cave, but it was merely
    To see her bird reposing in his nest;
And she would softly stir his locks so curly,
    Without disturbing her yet slumbering guest,
Breathing all gently o'er his cheek and mouth,
As o'er a bed of roses the sweet south.

169

And every morn his colour freshlier came,
    And every day help'd on his convalescence;
'Twas well, because health in the human frame
    Is pleasant, besides being true love's essence,
For health and idleness to passion's flame
    Are oil and gunpowder; and some good lessons
Are also learnt from Ceres and from Bacchus,
Without whom Venus will not long attack us.

170

While Venus fills the heart (without heart really
    Love, though good always, is not quite so good),
Ceres presents a plate of vermicelli,—
    For love must be sustain'd like flesh and blood,—
While Bacchus pours out wine, or hands a jelly:
    Eggs, oysters too, are amatory food;
But who is their purveyor from above
Heaven knows,—it may be Neptune, Pan, or Jove.

171

When Juan woke, he found some good things ready,
    A bath, a breakfast, and the finest eyes
That ever made a youthful heart less steady,
    Besides her maid's, as pretty for their size;
But I have spoken of all this already—
    And repetition's tiresome and unwise,—
Well—Juan, after bathing in the sea,
Came always back to coffee and Haidée.

172

Both were so young, and one so innocent,
    That bathing pass'd for nothing; Juan seem'd
To her, as 'twere the kind of being sent
    Of whom these two years she had nightly dream'd,
A something to be loved, a creature meant
    To be her happiness, and whom she deem'd
To render happy; all who joy would win
Must share it,—Happiness was born a twin.

173

It was such pleasure to behold him, such
    Enlargement of existence to partake
Nature with him, to thrill beneath his touch,
    To watch his slumbering, and to see him wake:
To live with him forever were too much;
    But then the thought of parting made her quake;
He was her own, her ocean-treasure, cast
Like a rich wreck—her first love, and her last.

174

And thus a moon roll'd on, and fair Haidée
    Paid daily visits to her boy, and took
Such plentiful precautions, that still he
    Remain'd unknown within his craggy nook;
At last her father's prows put out to sea
    For certain merchantmen upon the look,
Not as of yore to carry off an Io,
But three Ragusan vessels, bound for Scio.

175

Then came her freedom, for she had no mother,
    So that, her father being at sea, she was
Free as a married woman, or such other
    Female, as where she likes may freely pass,
Without even the incumbrance of a brother,
    The freest she that ever gazed on glass;
I speak of Christian lands in this comparison,
Where wives, at least, are seldom kept in garrison.

176

Now she prolong'd her visits and her talk
  (For they must talk), and he had learnt to say
So much as to propose to take a walk,—
  For little had he wander'd since the day
On which, like a young flower snapp'd from the stalk,
  Drooping and dewy on the beach he lay,—
And thus they walk'd out in the afternoon,
And saw the sun set opposite the moon.

*   *   *   *   *

179

Man, being reasonable, must get drunk;
  The best of life is but intoxication:
Glory, the grape, love, gold, in these are sunk
  The hopes of all men, and of every nation;
Without their sap, how branchless were the trunk
  Of life's strange tree, so fruitful on occasion:
But to return,—Get very drunk; and when
You wake with headache, you shall see what then.

180

Ring for your valet—bid him quickly bring
  Some hock and soda-water, then you'll know
A pleasure worthy Xerxes the great king;
  For not the bless'd sherbet, sublimed with snow,
Not the first sparkle of the desert-spring,
  Nor Burgundy in all its sunset glow,
After long travel, ennui, love, or slaughter,
Vie with that draught of hock and soda-water.

*   *   *   *   *

183

It was the cooling hour, just when the rounded
  Red sun sinks down behind the azure hill,
Which then seems as if the whole earth it bounded,
  Circling all nature, hush'd, and dim, and still,

With the far mountain-crescent half surrounded
  On one side, and the deep sea calm and chill
Upon the other, and the rosy sky,
  With one star sparkling through it like an eye.

184

And thus they wander'd forth, and hand in hand,
  Over the shining pebbles and the shells,
Glided along the smooth and harden'd sand,
  And in the worn and wild receptacles
Work'd by the storms, yet work'd as it were plann'd,
  In hollow halls, with sparry roofs and cells,
They turn'd to rest; and, each clasp'd by an arm,
Yielded to the deep twilight's purple charm.

185

They look'd up to the sky, whose floating glow
  Spread like a rosy ocean, vast and bright;
They gazed upon the glittering sea below,
  Whence the broad moon rose circling into sight;
They heard the waves splash, and the wind so low,
  And saw each other's dark eyes darting light
Into each other—and, beholding this,
Their lips drew near, and clung into a kiss;

186

A long, long kiss, a kiss of youth, and love,
  And beauty, all concentrating like rays
Into one focus kindled from above;
  Such kisses as belong to early days,
Where heart, and soul, and sense, in concert move,
  And the blood's lava, and the pulse a blaze,
Each kiss a heart-quake,—for a kiss's strength,
I think, it must be reckon'd by its length.

187

By length I mean duration; theirs endured
  Heaven knows how long—no doubt they never reckon'd;
And if they had, they could not have secured
  The sum of their sensations to a second:

They had not spoken; but they felt allured,
　　As if their souls and lips each other beckon'd,
Which, being join'd, like swarming bees they clung—
Their hearts the flowers from whence the honey sprung.

188

They were alone, yet not alone as they
　　Who shut in chambers, think it loneliness;
The silent ocean, and the star-light bay,
　　The twilight glow which momently grew less,
The voiceless sands and dropping caves, that lay
　　Around them, made them to each other press,
As if there were no life beneath the sky
Save theirs, and that their life could never die.

*　　*　　*　　*　　*

196

An infant when it gazes on a light,
　　A child the moment when it drains the breast,
A devotee when soars the Host in sight,
　　An Arab with a stranger for a guest,
A sailor when the prize has struck in fight,
　　A miser filling his most hoarded chest,
Feel rapture; but not such true joy are reaping
As they who watch o'er what they love while sleeping.

197

For there it lies so tranquil, so beloved,
　　All that it hath of life with us is living;
So gentle, stirless, helpless, and unmoved,
　　And all unconscious of the joy 'tis giving,
All it hath felt, inflicted, pass'd, and proved,
　　Hush'd into depths beyond the watcher's diving:
There lies the thing we love with all its errors,
And all its charms, like death without its terrors.

*　　*　　*　　*　　*

199

Alas! the love of women! it is known
  To be a lovely and a fearful thing;
For all of theirs upon that die is thrown,
  And if 'tis lost, life hath no more to bring
To them but mockeries of the past alone,
  And their revenge is as the tiger's spring,
Deadly, and quick, and crushing; yet as real
Torture is theirs, what they inflict they feel.

200

They are right; for man, to man so oft unjust,
  Is always so to women; one sole bond
Awaits them, treachery is all their trust;
  Taught to conceal, their bursting hearts despond
Over their idol, till some wealthier lust
  Buys them in marriage—and what rests beyond?
A thankless husband, next a faithless lover,
Then dressing, nursing, praying, and all's over.

201

Some take a lover, some take drams or prayers,
  Some mind their household, others dissipation,
Some run away, and but exchange their cares,
  Losing the advantage of a virtuous station;
Few changes e'er can better their affairs,
  Theirs being an unnatural situation,
From the dull palace to the dirty hovel:
Some play the devil, and then write a novel.

*   *   *   *   *

205

Oh Love! of whom great Caesar was the suitor
  Titus the master, Antony the slave,
Horace, Catullus scholars, Ovid tutor,
  Sappho the sage blue-stocking, in whose grave

All those may leap who rather would be neuter
   (Leucadia's rock still overlooks the wave)—
Oh Love! thou art the very god of evil,
For, after all, we cannot call thee devil.

206

Thou mak'st the chaste connubial state precarious,
   And jestest with the brows of mightiest men:
Caesar and Pompey, Mahomet, Belisarius,
   Have much employ'd the Muse of history's pen;
Their lives and fortunes were extremely various,
   Such worthies Time will never see again;
Yet to these four in three things the same luck holds,
They all were heroes, conquerors, and cuckolds.

207

Thou mak'st philosophers: there's Epicurus
   And Aristippus, a material crew!
Who to immoral courses would allure us
   By theories quite practicable too;
If only from the devil they would insure us,
   How pleasant were the maxim (not quite new),
"Eat, drink, and love, what can the rest avail us?"
So said the royal sage Sardanapalus.

*   *   *   *   *

213

Yet 'tis a painful feeling, and unwilling,
   For surely, if we always could perceive
In the same object graces quite as killing
   As when she rose upon us like an Eve,
'Twould save us many a heart-ache, many a shilling
   (For we must get them any how, or grieve);
Whereas, if one sole lady pleased for ever,
How pleasant for the heart, as well as liver!

214

The heart is like the sky, a part of heaven,
  But changes night and day, too, like the sky;
Now o'er it clouds and thunder must be driven,
  And darkness and destruction as on high:
But when it hath been scorch'd, and pierced, and riven,
  Its storms expire in water-drops; the eye
Pours forth at last the heart's blood turn'd to tears,
Which make the English climate of our years.

215

The liver is the lazaret of bile,
  But very rarely executes its function,
For the first passion stays there such a while
  That all the rest creep in and form a junction
Like knots of vipers on a dunghill's soil,—
  Rage, fear, hate, jealousy, revenge, compunction,—
So that all mischiefs spring up from this entrail,
Like earthquakes from the hidden fire call'd "central."

216

In the mean time, without proceeding more
  In this anatomy, I've finish'd now
Two hundred and odd stanzas as before,
  That being about the number I'll allow
Each canto of the twelve, or twenty-four;
  And, laying down my pen, I make my bow,
Leaving Don Juan and Haidée to plead
For them and theirs, with all who deign to read.

CANTO III

*　　*　　*　　*　　*

2

Oh, Love! what is it in this world of ours
　　Which makes it fatal to be loved? Ah, why
With cypress branches hast thou wreathed thy bowers,
　　And made thy best interpreter a sigh?
As those who dote on odours pluck the flowers,
　　And place them on their breast—but place to die—
Thus the frail beings we would fondly cherish
Are laid within our bosoms but to perish.

3

In her first passion woman loves her lover,
　　In all the others all she loves is love,
Which grows a habit she can ne'er get over,
　　And fits her loosely—like an easy glove,
As you may find, whene'er you like to prove her:
　　One man alone at first her heart can move;
She then prefers him in the plural number,
Not finding that the additions much encumber.

4

I know not if the fault be men's or theirs;
　　But one thing's pretty sure; a woman planted
(Unless at once she plunge for life in prayers)
　　After a decent time must be gallanted;
Although, no doubt, her first of love affairs
　　Is that to which her heart is wholly granted;
Yet there are some, they say, who have had *none*,
But those who have ne'er end with only *one*.

5

'Tis melancholy, and a fearful sign
  Of human frailty, folly, also crime,
That love and marriage rarely can combine,
  Although they both are born in the same clime;
Marriage from love, like vinegar from wine—
  A sad, sour, sober beverage—by time
Is sharpen'd from its high celestial flavour
Down to a very homely household savour.

6

There's something of antipathy, as 'twere,
  Between their present and their future state;
A kind of flattery that's hardly fair
  Is used, until the truth arrives too late—
Yet what can people do, except despair?
  The same things change their names at such a rate;
For instance—passion in a lover's glorious,
But in a husband is pronounced uxorious.

7

Men grow ashamed of being so very fond,
  They sometimes also get a little tired
(But that, of course, is rare), and then despond:
  The same things cannot always be admired,
Yet 'tis "so nominated in the bond,"
  That both are tied till one shall have expired.
Sad thought! to lose the spouse that was adorning
Our days, and put one's servants into mourning.

8

There's doubtless something in domestic doings
  Which forms, in fact, true love's antithesis;
Romances paint at full length people's wooings,
  But only give a bust of marriages;
For no one cares for matrimonial cooings,
  There's nothing wrong in a connubial kiss:
Think you, if Laura had been Petrarch's wife,
He would have written sonnets all his life?

9

All tragedies are finish'd by a death,
    All comedies are ended by a marriage;
The future states of both are left to faith,
    For authors fear description might disparage
The worlds to come of both, or fall beneath,
    And then both worlds would punish their miscarriage;
So leaving each their priest and prayer-book ready,
They say no more of Death or of the Lady.

10

The only two that in my recollection
    Have sung of heaven and hell, or marriage, are
Dante and Milton, and of both the affection
    Was hapless in their nuptials, for some bar
Of fault or temper ruin'd the connection
    (Such things, in fact, it don't ask much to mar):
But Dante's Beatrice and Milton's Eve
Were not drawn from their spouses, you conceive.

11

Some persons say that Dante meant theology
    By Beatrice, and not a mistress—I,
Although my opinion may require apology,
    Deem this a commentator's fantasy,
Unless indeed it was from his own knowledge he
    Decided thus, and show'd good reason why;
I think that Dante's more abstruse ecstatics
Meant to personify the mathematics.

12

Haidée and Juan were not married, but
    The fault was theirs, not mine; it is not fair,
Chaste reader, then, in any way to put
    The blame on me, unless you wish they were;
Then, if you'd have them wedded, please to shut
    The book which treats of this erroneous pair,
Before the consequences grow too awful—
'Tis dangerous to read of loves unlawful.

13

Yet they were happy,—happy in the illicit
    Indulgence of their innocent desires;
But more imprudent grown with every visit,
    Haidée forgot the island was her sire's.
When we have what we like, 'tis hard to miss it,
    At least in the beginning, ere one tires;
Thus she came often, not a moment losing,
Whilst her piratical papa was cruising.

14

Let not his mode of raising cash seem strange,
    Although he fleeced the flags of every nation,
For into a prime minister but change
    His title, and 'tis nothing but taxation;
But he, more modest, took an humbler range
    Of life, and in an honester vocation
Pursued o'er the high seas his watery journey,
And merely practised as a sea-attorney.

15

The good old gentleman had been detain'd
    By winds and waves, and some important captures;
And, in the hope of more, at sea remain'd,
    Although a squall or two had damp'd his raptures
By swamping one of the prizes; he had chain'd
    His prisoners, dividing them like chapters,
In number'd lots; they all had cuffs and collars,
And averaged each from ten to a hundred dollars.

16

Some he disposed of off Cape Matapan,
    Among his friends the Mainots; some he sold
To his Tunis correspondents, save one man
    Toss'd overboard unsaleable (being old);
The rest—save here and there some richer one,
    Reserved for future ransom—in the hold
Were link'd alike, as for the common people he
Had a large order from the Dey of Tripoli.

17

The merchandise was served in the same way,
   Pieced out for different marts in the Levant;
Except some certain portions of the prey,
   Light classic articles of female want,
French stuffs, lace, tweezers, toothpicks, teapot, tray,
   Guitars and castanets from Alicant,
All which selected from the spoil he gathers,
Robb'd for his daughter by the best of fathers.

18

A monkey, a Dutch mastiff, a mackaw,
   Two parrots, with a Persian cat and kittens,
He chose from several animals he saw—
   A terrier, too, which once had been a Briton's,
Who dying on the coast of Ithaca,
   The peasants gave the poor dumb thing a pittance:
These to secure in this strong blowing weather,
He caged in one huge hamper altogether.

19

Then having settled his marine affairs,
   Despatching single cruisers here and there,
His vessel having need of some repairs,
   He shaped his course to where his daughter fair
Continued still her hospitable cares;
   But that part of the coast being shoal and bare,
And rough with reefs, which ran out many a mile,
His port lay on the other side o' the isle.

20

And there he went ashore without delay,
   Having no custom-house or quarantine
To ask him awkward questions on the way
   About the time and place where he had been:
He left his ship to be hove down next day,
   With orders to the people to careen;
So that all hands were busy beyond measure,
In getting out goods, ballast, guns, and treasure.

21

Arriving at the summit of a hill
  Which overlook'd the white walls of his home,
He stopp'd.—What singular emotions fill
  Their bosoms who have been induced to roam!
With fluttering doubts if all be well or ill—
  With love for many, and with fears for some;
All feelings which o'erleap the years long lost,
And bring our hearts back to their starting-post.

22

The approach of home to husbands and to sires,
  After long travelling by land or water,
Most naturally some small doubt inspires—
  A female family's a serious matter
(None trusts the sex more, or so much admires—
  But they hate flattery, so I never flatter);
Wives in their husbands' absences grow subtler,
And daughters sometimes run off with the butler.

23

An honest gentleman at his return
  May not have the good fortune of Ulysses;
Not all lone matrons for their husbands mourn,
  Or show the same dislike to suitors' kisses;
The odds are that he finds a handsome urn
  To his memory—and two or three young misses
Born to some friend, who holds his wife and riches,—
And that *his* Argus—bites him by the breeches.

24

If single, probably his plighted fair
  Has in his absence wedded some rich miser;
But all the better, for the happy pair
  May quarrel, and the lady growing wiser,
He may resume his amatory care
  As cavalier servente, or despise her;
And that his sorrow may not be a dumb one,
Write odes on the Inconstancy of Woman.

25

And oh! ye gentlemen who have already
  Some chaste *liaison* of the kind—I mean
An honest friendship with a married lady—
  The only thing of this sort ever seen
To last—of all connections the most steady,
  And the true Hymen (the first's but a screen)—
Yet for all that keep not too long away,
I've known the absent wrong'd four times a day.

26

Lambro, our sea-solicitor, who had
  Much less experience of dry land than ocean,
On seeing his own chimney-smoke, felt glad;
  But not knowing metaphysics, had no notion
Of the true reason of his not being sad,
  Or that of any other strong emotion;
He loved his child, and would have wept the loss of her,
But knew the cause no more than a philosopher.

27

He saw his white walls shining in the sun,
  His garden trees all shadowy and green;
He heard his rivulet's light bubbling run,
  The distant dog-bark; and perceived between
The umbrage of the wood so cool and dun
  The moving figures and the sparkling sheen
Of arms (in the East all arm)—and various dyes
Of colour'd garbs, as bright as butterflies.

28

And as the spot where they appear he nears,
  Surprised at these unwonted signs of idling,
He hears—alas! no music of the spheres,
  But an unhallow'd, earthly sound of fiddling!
A melody which made him doubt his ears,
  The cause being past his guessing or unriddling;
A pipe, too, and a drum, and, shortly after,
A most unoriental roar of laughter.

29

And still more nearly to the place advancing,
    Descending rather quickly the declivity,
Through the waved branches, o'er the greensward glancing,
    'Midst other indications of festivity,
Seeing a troop of his domestics dancing
    Like dervises, who turn as on a pivot, he
Perceived it was the Pyrrhic dance so martial,
To which the Levantines are very partial.

30

And further on a group of Grecian girls,
    The first and tallest her white kerchief waving,
Were strung together like a row of pearls,
    Link'd hand in hand, and dancing; each too having
Down her white neck long floating auburn curls
    (The least of which would set ten poets raving);
Their leader sang—and bounded to her song,
With choral step and voice, the virgin throng.

31

And here assembled cross-legg'd round their trays,
    Small social parties just begun to dine;
Pilaus and meats of all sorts met the gaze,
    And flasks of Samian and of Chian wine,
And sherbet cooling in the porous vase;
    Above them their dessert grew on its vine,
The orange and pomegranate, nodding o'er,
Dropp'd in their laps, scarce pluck'd, their mellow store.

32

A band of children, round a snow-white ram,
    There wreathe his venerable horns with flowers;
While peaceful as if still an unwean'd lamb,
    The patriarch of the flock all gently cowers
His sober head, majestically tame,
    Or eats from out the palm, or playful lowers
His brow as if in act to butt, and then,
Yielding to their small hands, draws back again.

33

Their classical profiles, and glittering dresses,
    Their large black eyes, and soft seraphic cheeks,
Crimson as cleft pomegranates, their long tresses,
    The gesture which enchants, the eye that speaks,
The innocence which happy childhood blesses,
    Made quite a picture of these little Greeks;
So that the philosophical beholder
Sigh'd for their sakes—that they should e'er grow older.

34

Afar a dwarf buffoon stood telling tales
    To a sedate grey circle of old smokers,
Of secret treasures found in hidden vales,
    Of wonderful replies from Arab jokers,
Of charms to make good gold and cure bad ails,
    Of rocks bewitch'd that open to the knockers,
Of magic ladies who, by one sole act,
Transform'd their lords to beasts (but that's a fact).

35

Here was no lack of innocent diversion
    For the imagination or the senses,
Song, dance, wine, music, stories from the Persian,
    All pretty pastimes in which no offence is;
But Lambro saw all these things with aversion,
    Perceiving in his absence such expenses,
Dreading that climax of all human ills,
The inflammation of his weekly bills.

36

Ah! what is man? what perils still environ
    The happiest mortals even after dinner—
A day of gold from out an age of iron
    Is all that life allows the luckiest sinner;
Pleasure (whene'er she sings, at least) 's a siren,
    That lures, to flay alive the young beginner;
Lambro's reception at his people's banquet
Was such as fire accords to a wet blanket.

37

He—being a man who seldom used a word
    Too much, and wishing gladly to surprise
(In general he surprised men with the sword)
    His daughter—had not sent before to advise
Of his arrival, so that no one stirr'd;
    And long he paused to re-assure his eyes,
In fact much more astonish'd than delighted
To find so much good company invited.

38

He did not know (alas! how men will lie)
    That a report (especially the Greeks)
Avouch'd his death (such people never die),
    And put his house in mourning several weeks,—
But now their eyes and also lips were dry;
    The bloom, too, had return'd to Haidée's cheeks.
Her tears, too, being return'd into their fount,
She now kept house upon her own account.

39

Hence all this rice, meat, dancing, wine, and fiddling,
    Which turn'd the isle into a place of pleasure;
The servants all were getting drunk or idling,
    A life which made them happy beyond measure.
Her father's hospitality seem'd middling,
    Compared with what Haidée did with his treasure;
'Twas wonderful how things went on improving,
While she had not one hour to spare from loving.

40

Perhaps you think, in stumbling on this feast,
    He flew into a passion, and in fact
There was no mighty reason to be pleased;
    Perhaps you prophesy some sudden act,
The whip, the rack, or dungeon at the least,
    To teach his people to be more exact,
And that, proceeding at a very high rate,
He show'd the royal *penchants* of a pirate.

41

You're wrong.—He was the mildest manner'd man
    That ever scuttled ship or cut a throat:
With such true breeding of a gentleman,
    You never could divine his real thought;
No courtier could, and scarcely woman can
    Gird more deceit within a petticoat;
Pity he loved adventurous life's variety,
He was so great a loss to good society.

42

Advancing to the nearest dinner tray,
    Tapping the shoulder of the nighest guest,
With a peculiar smile, which by the way,
    Boded no good, whatever it express'd,
He ask'd the meaning of this holiday;
    The vinous Greek to whom he had address'd
His question, much too merry to divine
The questioner, fill'd up a glass of wine,

43

And, without turning his facetious head,
    Over his shoulder, with a Bacchant air,
Presented the o'erflowing cup, and said,
    "Talking's dry work, I have no time to spare."
A second hiccup'd, "Our old master's dead,
    You'd better ask our mistress who's his heir."
"Our mistress!" quoth a third: "Our mistress!—pooh!—
You mean our master—not the old, but new."

44

These rascals, being new comers, knew not whom
    They thus address'd—and Lambro's visage fell—
And o'er his eye a momentary gloom
    Pass'd but he strove quite courteously to quell
The expression, and, endeavouring to resume
    His smile, requested one of them to tell
The name and quality of his new patron,
Who seem'd to have turn'd Haidée into a matron.

45

"I know not," quoth the fellow, "who or what
  He is, nor whence he came—and little care;
But this I know, that this roast capon's fat,
  And that good wine ne'er wash'd down better fare;
And if you are not satisfied with that,
  Direct your questions to my neighbour there;
He'll answer all for better or for worse,
For none likes more to hear himself converse."

46

I said that Lambro was a man of patience,
  And certainly he show'd the best of breeding,
Which scarce even France, the paragon of nations,
  E'er saw her most polite of sons exceeding:
He bore these sneers against his near relations,
  His own anxiety, his heart, too, bleeding,
The insults, too, of every servile glutton,
Who all the time was eating up his mutton.

47

Now in a person used to much command—
  To bid men come, and go, and come again—
To see his orders done, too, out of hand—
  Whether the word was death, or but the chain—
It may seem strange to find his manners bland;
  Yet such things are, which I cannot explain,
Though doubtless he who can command himself
Is good to govern—almost as a Guelf.

48

Not that he was not sometimes rash or so,
  But never in his real and serious mood;
Then calm, concentrated, and still, and slow,
  He lay coil'd like the boa in the wood.
With him it never was a word and blow,
  His angry word once o'er, he shed no blood,
But in his silence there was much to rue,
And his *one* blow left little work for *two*.

49

He ask'd no further questions, and proceeded
   On to the house, but by a private way,
So that the few who met him hardly heeded,
   So little they expected him that day;
If love paternal in his bosom pleaded
   For Haidée's sake, is more than I can say,
But certainly to one deem'd dead, returning,
This revel seem'd a curious mode of mourning.

50

If all the dead could now return to life,
   (Which God forbid!) or some, or a great many,
For instance, if a husband or his wife
   (Nuptial examples are as good as any),
No doubt whate'er might be their former strife,
   The present weather would be much more rainy—
Tears shed into the grave of the connection
Would share most probably its resurrection.

51

He enter'd in the house no more his home,
   A thing to human feelings the most trying,
And harder for the heart to overcome,
   Perhaps, than even the mental pangs of dying;
To find our hearthstone turn'd into a tomb,
   And round its once warm precincts palely lying
The ashes of our hopes, is a deep grief,
Beyond a single gentleman's belief.

52

He enter'd in the house—his home no more,
   For without hearts there is no home—and felt
The solitude of passing his own door
   Without a welcome; there he long had dwelt,
There his few peaceful days Time had swept o'er,
   There his worn bosom and keen eye would melt
Over the innocence of that sweet child,
His only shrine of feelings undefiled.

53

He was a man of a strange temperament,
  Of mild demeanour though of savage mood;
Moderate in all his habits, and content
  With temperance in pleasure as in food,
Quick to perceive, and strong to bear, and meant
  For something better, if not wholly good:
His country's wrongs and his despair to save her
Had stung him from a slave to an enslaver.

54

The love of power, and rapid gain of gold,
  The hardness by long habitude produced,
The dangerous life in which he had grown old,
  The mercy he had granted oft abused,
The sights he was accustom'd to behold,
  The wild seas, and wild men with whom he cruised,
Had cost his enemies a long repentance,
And made him a good friend, but bad acquaintance.

55

But something of the spirit of old Greece
  Flash'd o'er his soul a few heroic rays,
Such as lit onward to the Golden Fleece
  His predecessors in the Colchian days;
'Tis true he had no ardent love for peace—
  Alas! his country show'd no path to praise:
Hate to the world and war with every nation
He waged, in vengeance of her degradation.

56

Still o'er his mind the influence of the clime
  Shed its Ionian elegance, which show'd
Its power unconsciously full many a time,—
  A taste seen in the choice of his abode,
A love of music and of scenes sublime,
  A pleasure in the gentle stream that flow'd
Past him in crystal, and a joy in flowers,
Bedew'd his spirit in his calmer hours.

57

But whatsoe'er he had of love reposed
    On that belovèd daughter; she had been
The only thing which kept his heart unclosed
    Amidst the savage deeds he'd done and seen,
A lonely pure affection unopposed:
    There wanted but the loss of this to wean
His feelings from all milk of human kindness,
And turn him, like the Cyclops, mad with blindness.

58

The cubless tigress in her jungle raging
    Is dreadful to the shepherd and the flock;
The ocean when its yeasty war is waging
    Is awful to the vessel near the rock;
But violent things will sooner bear assuaging,
    Their fury being spent by its own shock,
Than the stern, single, deep, and wordless ire
Of a strong human heart, and in a sire.

59

It is a hard, although a common case,
    To find our children running restive—they
In whom our brightest days we would retrace,
    Our little selves re-form'd in finer clay,
Just as old age is creeping on apace,
    And clouds come o'er the sunset of our day,
They kindly leave us, though not quite alone,
But in good company—the gout or stone.

*   *   *   *   *

62

The dinner made about a hundred dishes;
    Lamb and pistachio nuts—in short, all meats,
And saffron soups, and sweetbreads; and the fishes
    Were of the finest that e'er flounced in nets,
Dress'd to a Sybarite's most pamper'd wishes;
    The beverage was various sherbets
Of raisin, orange, and pomegranate juice,
Squeezed through the rind, which makes it best for use.

63

These were ranged round, each in its crystal ewer,
    And fruits and date-bread loaves closed the repast,
And Mocha's berry, from Arabia pure,
    In small fine China cups, came in at last—
Gold cups of filigree, made to secure
    The hand from burning, underneath them placed,
Cloves, cinnamon, and saffron too, were boil'd
Up with the coffee, which (I think) they spoil'd.

64

The hangings of the room were tapestry, made
    Of velvet panels, each of different hue,
And thick with damask flowers of silk inlaid;
    And round them ran a yellow border too;
The upper border, richly wrought, display'd,
    Embroider'd delicately o'er with blue,
Soft Persian sentences, in lilac letters,
From poets, or the moralists their betters.

65

These Oriental writings on the wall,
    Quite common in those countries, are a kind
Of monitors adapted to recall,
    Like skulls at Memphian banquets, to the mind
The words which shook Belshazzar in his hall,
    And took his kingdom from him: You will find,
Though sages may pour out their wisdom's treasure,
There is no sterner moralist than Pleasure.

66

A beauty at the season's close grown hectic,
    A genius who has drunk himself to death,
A rake turn'd methodistic, or Eclectic—
    (For that's the name they like to pray beneath)—
But most, an alderman struck apoplectic,
    Are things that really take away the breath,—
And show that late hours, wine, and love, are able
To do not much less damage than the table.

67

Haidée and Juan carpeted their feet
    On crimson satin, border'd with pale blue;
Their sofa occupied three parts complete
    Of the apartment—and appear'd quite new;
The velvet cushions (for a throne more meet)
    Were scarlet, from whose glowing centre grew
A sun emboss'd in gold, whose rays of tissue,
Meridian-like, were seen all light to issue.

68

Crystal and marble, plate and porcelain,
    Had done their work of splendour; Indian mats
And Persian carpets, which the heart bled to stain,
    Over the floors were spread; gazelles and cats,
And dwarfs and blacks, and such like things, that gain
    Their bread as ministers and favourites (that's
To say, by degradation) mingled there,
As plentiful as in a court, or fair.

69

There was no want of lofty mirrors, and
    The tables, most of ebony inlaid
With mother of pearl or ivory, stood at hand,
    Or were of tortoise-shell or rare woods made,
Fretted with gold or silver:—by command,
    The greater part of these were ready spread
With viands and sherbets in ice—and wine—
Kept for all comers, at all hours to dine.

70

Of all the dresses I select Haidée's:
    She wore two jelicks—one was of pale yellow;
Of azure, pink, and white, was her chemise—
    'Neath which her breast heaved like a little billow;
With buttons form'd of pearls as large as peas,
    All gold and crimson shone her jelick's fellow,
And the striped white gauze baracan that bound her,
Like fleecy clouds about the moon, flow'd round her.

71

One large gold bracelet clasp'd each lovely arm,
    Lockless—so pliable from the pure gold
That the hand stretch'd and shut it without harm,
    The limb which it adorn'd its only mould;
So beautiful—its very shape would charm;
    And clinging as if loth to lose its hold,
The purest ore inclosed the whitest skin
That e'er by precious metal was held in.

72

Around, as princess of her father's land,
    A like gold bar above her instep roll'd,
Announced her rank; twelve rings were on her hand;
    Her hair was starr'd with gems; her veil's fine fold
Below her breast was fasten'd with a band
    Of lavish pearls, whose worth could scarce be told;
Her orange silk full Turkish trowsers furl'd
About the prettiest ankle in the world.

73

Her hair's long auburn waves down to her heel
    Flow'd like an Alpine torrent which the sun
Dyes with his morning light, and would conceal
    Her person if allow'd at large to run,
And still they seem'd resentfully to feel
    The silken fillet's curb, and sought to shun
Their bonds whene'er some zephyr caught began
To offer his young pinion as her fan.

74

Round her she made an atmosphere of life,
    The very air seem'd lighter from her eyes,
They were so soft and beautiful, and rife
    With all we can imagine of the skies,
And pure as Psyche ere she grew a wife—
    Too pure even for the purest human ties;
Her overpowering presence made you feel
It would not be idolatry to kneel.

75

Her eyelashes, though dark as night, were tinged
    (It is the country's custom), but in vain;
For those large black eyes were so blackly fringed,
    The glossy rebels mock'd the jetty stain,
And in their native beauty stood avenged:
    Her nails were touch'd with henna; but again
The power of art was turn'd to nothing, for
They could not look more rosy than before.

76

The henna should be deeply dyed to make
    The skin relieved appear more fairly fair;
She had no need of this, day ne'er will break
    On mountain tops more heavenly white than her:
The eye might doubt if it were well awake,
    She was so like a vision; I might err,
But Shakspeare also says 'tis very silly
"To gild refined gold, or paint the lily."

77

Juan had on a shawl of black and gold,
    But a white baracan, and so transparent,
The sparkling gems beneath you might behold,
    Like small stars through the milky way apparent;
His turban, furl'd in many a graceful fold,
    An emerald aigrette with Haidée's hair in 't
Surmounted as its clasp—a glowing crescent,
Whose rays shone ever trembling, but incessant.

78

And now they were diverted by their suite,
    Dwarfs, dancing girls, black eunuchs, and a poet,
Which made their new establishment complete;
    The last was of great fame, and liked to show it:
His verses rarely wanted their due feet;
    And for his theme—he seldom sung below it,
He being paid to satirize or flatter,
As the psalm says, "inditing a good matter."

79

He praised the present, and abused the past,
  Reversing the good custom of old days,
An eastern anti-jacobin at last
  He turn'd, preferring pudding to *no* praise—
For some few years his lot had been o'ercast
  By his seeming independent in his lays,
But now he sung the Sultan and the Pacha,
With truth like Southey, and with verse like Crashaw.

80

He was a man who had seen many changes,
  And always changed as true as any needle;
His polar star being one which rather ranges,
  And not the fix'd—he knew the way to wheedle;
So vile he 'scaped the doom which oft avenges;
  And being fluent (save indeed when fee'd ill),
He lied with such a fervour of intention—
There was no doubt he earn'd his laureate pension.

81

But he had genius,—when a turncoat has it,
  The "Vates irritabilis" takes care
That without notice few full moons shall pass it;
  Even good men like to make the public stare:—
But to my subject—let me see—what was it?—
  Oh!—the third canto—and the pretty pair—
Their loves, and feasts, and house, and dress, and mode
Of living in their insular abode.

82

Their poet, a sad trimmer, but no less
  In company a very pleasant fellow,
Had been the favourite of full many a mess
  Of men, and made them speeches when half mellow;
And though his meaning they could rarely guess,
  Yet still they deign'd to hiccup or to bellow
The glorious meed of popular applause,
Of which the first ne'er knows the second cause.

83

But now being lifted into high society,
   And having pick'd up several odds and ends
Of free thoughts in his travels, for variety,
   He deem'd, being in a lone isle among friends,
That, without any danger of a riot, he
   Might for long lying make himself amends;
And, singing as he sung in his warm youth,
Agree to a short armistice with truth.

       *   *   *   *   *

    The isles of Greece! the isles of Greece!
      Where burning Sappho loved and sung,
    Where grew the arts of war and peace,
      Where Delos rose and Phoebus sprung!
    Eternal summer gilds them yet,
    But all, except their sun, is set.

    The Scian and the Teian muse,
      The hero's harp, the lover's lute,
    Have found the fame your shores refuse;
      Their place of birth alone is mute
    To sounds which echo further west
    Than your sires' "Islands of the Blest."

    The mountains look on Marathon—
      And Marathon looks on the sea;
    And musing there an hour alone,
      I dream'd that Greece might still be free;
    For standing on the Persians' grave,
    I could not deem myself a slave.

    A king sate on the rocky brow
      Which looks o'er sea-born Salamis;
    And ships, by thousands, lay below,
      And men in nations;—all were his!
    He counted them at break of day—
    And when the sun set where were they?

And where are they? and where art thou,
    My country? On thy voiceless shore
The heroic lay is tuneless now—
    The heroic bosom beats no more!
And must thy lyre, so long divine,
Degenerate into hands like mine?

'Tis something, in the dearth of fame,
    Though link'd among a fetter'd race,
To feel at least a patriot's shame,
    Even as I sing, suffuse my face;
For what is left the poet here?
For Greeks a blush—for Greece a tear.

Must *we* but weep o'er days more bless'd?
    Must *we* but blush?—Our fathers bled.
Earth! render back from out thy breast
    A remnant of our Spartan dead!
Of the three hundred grant but three,
To make a new Thermopylae!

What! silent still? and silent all?
    Ah! no;—the voices of the dead
Sound like a distant torrent's fall,
    And answer, "Let one living head,
But one arise,—we come, we come!"
'Tis but the living who are dumb.

In vain—in vain: strike other chords;
    Fill high the cup with Samian wine!
Leave battles to the Turkish hordes,
    And shed the blood of Scio's vine!
Hark! rising to the ignoble call—
How answers each bold Bacchanal!

You have the Pyrrhic dance as yet,
    Where is the Pyrrhic phalanx gone?
Of two such lessons, why forget
    The nobler and the manlier one?
You have the letters Cadmus gave—
Think ye he meant them for a slave?

Fill high the bowl with Samian wine!
　　We will not think of themes like these!
It made Anacreon's song divine:
　　He served—but served Polycrates—
A tyrant; but our masters then
Were still, at least, our countrymen.

The tyrant of the Chersonese
　　Was freedom's best and bravest friend;
That tyrant was Miltiades!
　　Oh! that the present hour would lend
Another despot of the kind!
Such chains as his were sure to bind.

Fill high the bowl with Samian wine!
　　On Suli's rock, and Parga's shore,
Exists the remnant of a line
　　Such as the Doric mothers bore;
And there, perhaps, some seed is sown,
The Heracleidan blood might own.

Trust not for freedom to the Franks—
　　They have a king who buys and sells:
In native swords, and native ranks,
　　The only hope of courage dwells;
But Turkish force, and Latin fraud,
Would break your shield, however broad.

Fill high the bowl with Samian wine!
　　Our virgins dance beneath the shade—
I see their glorious black eyes shine;
　　But gazing on each glowing maid,
My own the burning tear-drop laves,
To think such breasts must suckle slaves.

Place me on Sunium's marbled steep,
　　Where nothing, save the waves and I,
May hear our mutual murmurs sweep;
　　There, swan-like, let me sing and die:
A land of slaves shall ne'er be mine—
Dash down yon cup of Samian wine!

87

Thus sung, or would, or could, or should have sung,
  The modern Greek, in tolerable verse;
If not like Orpheus quite, when Greece was young,
  Yet in these times he might have done much worse:
His strain display'd some feeling—right or wrong;
  And feeling in a poet is the source
Of others' feeling; but they are such liars,
And take all colours—like the hands of dyers.

88

But words are things, and a small drop of ink,
  Falling like dew, upon a thought, produces
That which makes thousands, perhaps millions, think.
  'Tis strange, the shortest letter which man uses,
Instead of speech, may form a lasting link
  Of ages: to what straits old Time reduces
Frail man, when paper—even a rag like this,
Survives himself, his tomb, and all that's his.

89

And when his bones are dust, his grave a blank,
  His station, generation, even his nation,
Become a thing, or nothing, save to rank
  In chronological commemoration,
Some dull MS. oblivion long has sank,
  Or graven stone found in a barrack's station,
In digging the foundation of a closet,
May turn his name up, as a rare deposit.

90

And glory long has made the sages smile;
  'Tis something, nothing, words, illusion, wind—
Depending more upon the historian's style
  Than on the name a person leaves behind:
Troy owes to Homer what whist owes to Hoyle:
  The present century was growing blind
To the great Marlborough's skill in giving knocks,
Until his late Life by Archdeacon Coxe.

91

Milton's the prince of poets—so we say;
 A little heavy, but no less divine:
An independent being in his day—
 Learn'd, pious, temperate in love and wine;
But, his life falling into Johnson's way,
 We're told this great high priest of all the Nine
Was whipt at college—a harsh sire—odd spouse,
For the first Mrs. Milton left his house.

92

All these are, *certes*, entertaining facts,
 Like Shakspeare's stealing deer, Lord Bacon's bribes;
Like Titus' youth, and Caesar's earliest acts;
 Like Burns (whom Doctor Currie well describes);
Like Cromwell's pranks;—but although truth exacts
 These amiable descriptions from the scribes,
As most essential to their hero's story,
They do not much contribute to his glory.

93

All are not moralists like Southey, when
 He prated to the world of "Pantisocracy;"
Or Wordsworth unexcised, unhired, who then
 Season'd his pedlar poems with democracy;
Or Coleridge, long before his flighty pen
 Let to the *Morning Post* its aristocracy;
When he and Southey, following the same path,
Espoused two partners (milliners of Bath).

94

Such names at present cut a convict figure,
 The very Botany Bay in moral geography;
Their loyal treason, renegado rigour,
 Are good manure for their more bare biography.
Wordsworth's last quarto, by the way, is bigger
 Than any since the birthday of typography;
A drowsy frowzy poem, call'd the "Excursion,"
Writ in a manner which is my aversion.

95

He there builds up a formidable dyke
  Between his own and others' intellect;
But Wordsworth's poem, and his followers, like
  Joanna Southcote's Shiloh and her sect,
Are things which in this century don't strike
  The public mind, so few are the elect;
And the new births of both their stale virginities
Have proved but dropsies, taken for divinities.

96

But let me to my story: I must own,
  If I have any fault, it is digression—
Leaving my people to proceed alone,
  While I soliloquize beyond expression;
But these are my addresses from the throne,
  Which put off business to the ensuing session:
Forgetting each omission is a loss to
The world, not quite so great as Ariosto.

97

I know that what our neighbours call *"longueurs"*
  (We've not so good a *word*, but have the *thing*
In that complete perfection which ensures
  An epic from Bob Southey every spring),
Form not the true temptation which allures
  The reader; but 'twould not be hard to bring
Some fine examples of the *epopée*,
To prove its grand ingredient is *ennui*.

98

We learn from Horace, "Homer sometimes sleeps;"
  We feel without him, Wordsworth sometimes wakes,—
To show with what complacency he creeps,
  With his dear *"Waggoners,"* around his lakes;
He wishes for "a boat" to sail the deeps—
  Of ocean?—No, of air; and then he makes
Another outcry for "a little boat,"
And drivels seas to set it well afloat.

99

If he must fain sweep o'er the ethereal plain,
  And Pegasus runs restive in his "Waggon,"
Could he not beg the loan of Charles's Wain?
  Or pray Medea for a single dragon?
Or if, too classic for his vulgar brain,
  He fear'd his neck to venture such a nag on,
And he must needs mount nearer to the moon,
Could not the blockhead ask for a balloon?

100

"Pedlars," and "Boats," and "Waggons!" Oh! ye shades
  Of Pope and Dryden, are we come to this?
That trash of such sort not alone evades
  Contempt, but from the bathos' vast abyss
Floats scum-like uppermost, and these Jack Cades
  Of sense and song above your graves may hiss—
The "little boatman" and his "Peter Bell"
Can sneer at him who drew "Achitophel"!

101

T' our tale.—The feast was over, the slaves gone,
  The dwarfs and dancing girls had all retired;
The Arab lore and poet's song were done,
  And every sound of revelry expired;
The lady and her lover, left alone,
  The rosy flood of twilight's sky admired;—
Ave Maria! o'er the earth and sea,
That heavenliest hour of Heaven is worthiest thee!

102

Ave Maria! blessèd be the hour!
  The time, the clime, the spot, where I so oft
Have felt that moment in its fullest power
  Sink o'er the earth so beautiful and soft,
While swung the deep bell in the distant tower,
  Or the faint dying day-hymn stole aloft,
And not a breath crept through the rosy air,
And yet the forest leaves seem'd stirr'd with prayer.

103

Ave Maria! 'tis the hour of prayer!
  Ave Maria! 'tis the hour of love!
Ave Maria! may our spirits dare
  Look up to thine and to thy Son's above!
Ave Maria! oh that face so fair!
  Those downcast eyes beneath the Almighty dove—
What though 'tis but a pictured image?—strike—
That painting is no idol,—'tis too like.

  *   *   *   *   *

106

The shrill cicalas, people of the pine,
  Making their summer lives one ceaseless song,
Were the sole echoes, save my steed's and mine,
  And vesper bell's that rose the boughs along;
The spectre huntsman of Onesti's line,
  His hell-dogs, and their chase, and the fair throng
Which learn'd from this example not to fly
From a true lover,—shadow'd my mind's eye.

  *   *   *   *   *

110

But I'm digressing; what on earth has Nero,
  Or any such like sovereign buffoons,
To do with the transactions of my hero,
  More than such madmen's fellow man—the moon's?
Sure my invention must be down at zero,
  And I grown one of many "wooden spoons"
Of verse (the name with which we Cantabs please
To dub the last of honours in degrees).

111

I feel this tediousness will never do—
  'Tis being *too* epic, and I must cut down
(In copying) this long canto into two;
  They'll never find it out, unless I own
The fact, excepting some experienced few;
  And then as an improvement 'twill be shown:
I'll prove that such the opinion of the critic is
From Aristotle *passim*.—See Ποιητιχης.

CANTO IV

1

NOTHING so difficult as a beginning
  In poesy, unless perhaps the end;
For oftentimes, when Pegasus seems winning
  The race, he sprains a wing, and down we tend,
Like Lucifer when hurl'd from heaven for sinning;
  Our sin the same, and hard as his to mend,
Being pride, which leads the mind to soar too far,
Till our own weakness shows us what we are.

*   *   *   *   *

11

The heart—which may be broken: happy they!
  Thrice fortunate! who, of that fragile mould,
The precious porcelain of human clay,
  Break with the first fall: they can ne'er behold
The long year link'd with heavy day on day,
  And all which must be borne, and never told;
While life's strange principle will often lie
Deepest in those who long the most to die.

12

"Whom the gods love die young," was said of yore,
  And many deaths do they escape by this:
The death of friends, and that which slays even more—
  The death of friendship, love, youth, all that is,
Except mere breath; and since the silent shore
  Awaits at last even those who longest miss
The old archer's shafts, perhaps the early grave
Which men weep over may be meant to save.

13

Haidée and Juan thought not of the dead—
  The heavens, and earth, and air, seem'd made for them:
They found no fault with Time, save that he fled;
  They saw not in themselves aught to condemn:
Each was the other's mirror, and but read
  Joy sparkling in their dark eyes like a gem,
And knew such brightness was but the reflection
Of their exchanging glances of affection.

14

The gentle pressure and the thrilling touch,
  The least glance better understood than words,
Which still said all, and ne'er could say too much;
  A language, too, but like to that of birds,
Known but to them, at least appearing such
  As but to lovers a true sense affords;
Sweet playful phrases, which would seem absurd
To those who've ceased to hear such, or ne'er heard:

15

All these were theirs, for they were children still,
  And children still they should have ever been;
They were not made in the real world to fill
  A busy character in the dull scene,
But like two beings born from out a rill,
  A nymph and her belovèd, all unseen
To pass their lives in fountains and on flowers,
And never know the weight of human hours.

16

Moons changing had roll'd on, and changeless found
  Those their bright rise had lighted to such joys
As rarely they beheld throughout their round;
  And these were not of the vain kind which cloys,
For theirs were buoyant spirits never bound
  By the mere senses; and that which destroys
Most love, possession, unto them appear'd
A thing which each endearment more endear'd.

17

Oh beautiful! and rare as beautiful!
    But theirs was love in which the mind delights
To lose itself, when the old world grows dull,
    And we are sick of its hack sounds and sights,
Intrigues, adventures of the common school,
    Its petty passions, marriages, and flights,
Where Hymen's torch but brands one strumpet more,
Whose husband only knows her not a wh—re.

18

Hard words; harsh truth; a truth which many know.
    Enough.—The faithful and the fairy pair,
Who never found a single hour too slow,
    What was it made them thus exempt from care?
Young innate feelings all have felt below,
    Which perish in the rest, but in them were
Inherent—what we mortals call romantic,
And always envy, though we deem it frantic.

19

This is in others a factitious state,
    An opium dream of too much youth and reading,
But was in them their nature or their fate:
    No novels e'er had set their young hearts bleeding,
For Haidée's knowledge was by no means great,
    And Juan was a boy of saintly breeding;
So that there was no reason for their loves
More than for those of nightingales or doves.

20

They gazed upon the sunset; 'tis an hour
    Dear unto all, but dearest to *their* eyes,
For it had made them what they were: the power
    Of love had first o'erwhelm'd them from such skies,
When happiness had been their only dower,
    And twilight saw them link'd in passion's ties;
Charm'd with each other, all things charm'd that brought
The past still welcome as the present thought.

21

I know not why, but in that hour to-night,
  Even as they gazed, a sudden tremor came,
And swept, as 'twere, across their hearts' delight,
  Like the wind o'er a harp-string, or a flame,
When one is shook in sound, and one in sight;
  And thus some boding flash'd through either frame,
And call'd from Juan's breast a faint low sigh,
While one new tear arose in Haidée's eye.

22

That large black prophet eye seem'd to dilate
  And follow far the disappearing sun,
As if their last day of a happy date
  With his broad, bright, and dropping orb were gone;
Juan gazed on her as to ask his fate—
  He felt a grief, but knowing cause for none,
His glance inquired of hers for some excuse
For feelings causeless, or at least abstruse.

23

She turn'd to him, and smiled, but in that sort
  Which makes not others smile; then turn'd aside:
Whatever feeling shook her, it seem'd short,
  And master'd by her wisdom or her pride;
When Juan spoke, too—it might be in sport—
  Of this their mutual feeling, she replied—
"If it should be so,—but—it cannot be—
Or I at least shall not survive to see."

24

Juan would question further, but she press'd
  His lips to hers, and silenced him with this,
And then dismiss'd the omen from her breast,
  Defying augury with that fond kiss;
And no doubt of all methods 'tis the best:
  Some people prefer wine—'tis not amiss;
I have tried both; so those who would a part take
May choose between the headache and the heartache.

25

One of the two, according to your choice,
    Women or wine, you'll have to undergo;
Both maladies are taxes on our joys:
    But which to choose, I really hardly know;
And if I had to give a casting voice,
    For both sides I could many reasons show,
And then decide, without great wrong to either,
It were much better to have both than neither.

26

Juan and Haidée gazed upon each other
    With swimming looks of speechless tenderness,
Which mix'd all feelings, friend, child, lover, brother,
    All that the best can mingle and express,
When two pure hearts are pour'd in one another,
    And love too much, and yet can not love less;
But almost sanctify the sweet excess
By the immortal wish and power to bless.

27

Mix'd in each other's arms, and heart in heart,
    Why did they not then die?—they had lived too long,
Should an hour come to bid them breathe apart;
    Years could but bring them cruel things or wrong;
The world was not for them, nor the world's art
    For beings passionate as Sappho's song;
Love was born with them, in them, so intense,
It was their very spirit—not a sense.

28

They should have lived together deep in woods,
    Unseen as sings the nightingale; they were
Unfit to mix in these thick solitudes
    Call'd social, haunts of Hate, and Vice, and Care:
How lonely every freeborn creature broods!
    The sweetest song-birds nestle in a pair;
The eagle soars alone; the gull and crow
Flock o'er their carrion, just like men below.

29

Now pillow'd, cheek to cheek, in loving sleep,
   Haidée and Juan their siesta took;
A gentle slumber, but it was not deep,
   For ever and anon a something shook
Juan, and shuddering o'er his frame would creep;
   And Haidée's sweet lips murmur'd like a brook
A wordless music, and her face so fair
Stirr'd with her dream, as rose-leaves with the air.

30

Or as the stirring of a deep clear stream
   Within an Alpine hollow, when the wind
Walks o'er it, was she shaken by the dream,
   The mystical usurper of the mind—
O'erpowering us to be whate'er may seem
   Good to the soul which we no more can bind;
Strange state of being! (for 'tis still to be)
Senseless to feel, and with seal'd eyes to see.

31

She dream'd of being alone on the sea-shore,
   Chain'd to a rock; she knew not how, but stir
She could not from the spot, and the loud roar
   Grew, and each wave rose roughly, threatening her;
And o'er her upper lip they seem'd to pour,
   Until she sobb'd for breath, and soon they were
Foaming o'er her lone head, so fierce and high—
Each broke to drown her, yet she could not die.

32

Anon—she was released, and then she stray'd
   O'er the sharp shingles with her bleeding feet,
And stumbled almost every step she made;
   And something roll'd before her in a sheet,
Which she must still pursue howe'er afraid;
   'Twas white and indistinct, nor stoop'd to meet
Her glance nor grasp, for still she gazed and grasp'd,
And ran, but it escaped her as she clasp'd.

33

The dream changed:—in a cave she stood, its walls
    Were hung with marble icicles, the work
Of ages on its water-fretted halls,
    Where waves might wash, and seals might breed and lurk;
Her hair was dripping, and the very balls
    Of her black eyes seem'd turn'd to tears, and mirk
The sharp rocks look'd below each drop they caught,
Which froze to marble as it fell, she thought.

34

And wet, and cold, and lifeless at her feet,
    Pale as the foam that froth'd on his dead brow,
Which she essay'd in vain to clear (how sweet
    Were once her cares, how idle seem'd they now!)
Lay Juan, nor could aught renew the beat
    Of his quench'd heart; and the sea dirges low
Rang in her sad ears like a mermaid's song,
And that brief dream appear'd a life too long.

35

And gazing on the dead, she thought his face
    Faded, or alter'd into something new—
Like to her father's features, till each trace
    More like and like to Lambro's aspect grew—
With all his keen worn look and Grecian grace;
    And starting, she awoke, and what to view?
Oh! Powers of Heaven! what dark eye meets she there?
'Tis—'tis her father's—fix'd upon the pair!

36

Then shrieking, she arose, and shrieking fell,
    With joy and sorrow, hope and fear to see
Him whom she deem'd a habitant where dwell
    The ocean-buried, risen from death, to be
Perchance the death of one she loved too well:
    Dear as her father had been to Haidée,
It was a moment of that awful kind—
I have seen such—but must not call to mind.

37

Up Juan sprung to Haidée's bitter shriek,
  And caught her falling, and from off the wall
Snatch'd down his sabre, in hot haste to wreak
  Vengeance on him who was the cause of all:
Then Lambro, who till now forbore to speak,
  Smil'd scornfully, and said, "Within my call
A thousand scimitars await the word;
Put up, young man, put up your silly sword."

38

And Haidée clung around him: "Juan, 'tis—
  'Tis Lambro—'tis my father! Kneel with me—
He will forgive us—yes—it must be—yes.
  Oh! dearest father in this agony
Of pleasure and of pain—even while I kiss
  Thy garment's hem with transport, can it be
That doubt should mingle with my filial joy?
Deal with me as thou wilt, but spare this boy."

39

High and inscrutable the old man stood,
  Calm in his voice, and calm within his eye—
Not always signs with him of calmest mood:
  He look'd upon her, but gave no reply;
Then turn'd to Juan, in whose cheek the blood
  Oft came and went, as there resolved to die;
In arms, at least, he stood, in act to spring
On the first foe whom Lambro's call might bring.

40

"Young man, your sword;" so Lambro once more said:
  Juan replied, "Not while this arm is free."
The old man's cheek grew pale, but not with dread,
  And drawing from his belt a pistol, he
Replied, "Your blood be then on your own head!"
  Then look'd close at the flint, as if to see
'Twas fresh—for he had lately used the lock—
And next proceeded quietly to cock.

41

It has a strange quick jar upon the ear,
    That cocking of a pistol, when you know
A moment more will bring the sight to bear
    Upon your person, twelve yards off, or so;
A gentlemanly distance, not too near,
    If you have got a former friend for foe;
But after having been fired at once or twice,
The ear becomes more Irish and less nice.

42

Lambro presented, and one instant more
    Had stopp'd this canto, and Don Juan's breath,
When Haidée threw herself her boy before;
    Stern as her sire: "On me," she cried, "let death
Descend—the fault is mine; this fatal shore
    He found—but sought not. I have pledg'd my faith;
I love him—I will die with him: I knew
Your nature's firmness—know your daughter's too."

43

A minute past, and she had been all tears,
    And tenderness, and infancy: but now
She stood as one who champion'd human fears—
    Pale, statue-like, and stern, she woo'd the blow;
And tall beyond her sex and their compeers,
    She drew up to her height, as if to show
A fairer mark; and with a fix'd eye scann'd
Her father's face—but never stopp'd his hand.

44

He gazed on her, and she on him; 'twas strange
    How like they look'd! the expression was the same;
Serenely savage, with a little change
    In the large dark eyes' mutual-darted flame;
For she too was as one who could avenge,
    If cause should be—a lioness, though tame:
Her father's blood before her father's face
Boil'd up, and proved her truly of his race.

45

I said they were alike, their features and
   Their stature differing but in sex and years;
Even to the delicacy of their hand
   There was resemblance, such as true blood wears;
And now to see them, thus divided, stand
   In fix'd ferocity, when joyous tears,
And sweet sensations, should have welcomed both,
Show what the passions are in their full growth.

46

The father paused a moment, then withdrew
   His weapon, and replaced it; but stood still,
And looking on her, as to look her through,
   "Not I," he said, "have sought this stranger's ill;
Not I have made this desolation: few
   Would bear such outrage, and forbear to kill;
But I must do my duty—how thou hast
Done thine, the present vouches for the past.

47

"Let him disarm; or, by my father's head,
   His own shall roll before you like a ball!"
He raised his whistle, as the word he said,
   And blew; another answer'd to the call,
And rushing in disorderly, though led,
   And arm'd from boot to turban, one and all,
Some twenty of his train came, rank on rank;
He gave the word, "Arrest or slay the Frank."

48

Then, with a sudden movement, he withdrew
   His daughter; while compress'd within his clasp,
'Twixt her and Juan interposed the crew;
   In vain she struggled in her father's grasp—
His arms were like a serpent's coil: then flew
   Upon their prey, as darts an angry asp,
The file of pirates; save the foremost, who
Had fallen, with his right shoulder half cut through.

49

The second had his cheek laid open; but
    The third, a wary cool old sworder, took
The blows upon his cutlass, and then put
    His own well in; so well, ere you could look,
His man was floor'd, and helpless at his foot,
    With the blood running like a little brook
From two smart sabre gashes, deep and red—
One on the arm, the other on the head.

50

And then they bound him where he fell, and bore
    Juan from the apartment: with a sign
Old Lambro bade them take him to the shore,
    Where lay some ships which were to sail at nine.
They laid him in a boat, and plied the oar
    Until they reach'd some galliots, placed in line;
On board of one of these, and under hatches,
They stow'd him, with strict orders to the watches.

51

The world is full of strange vicissitudes,
    And here was one exceedingly unpleasant:
A gentleman so rich in the world's goods,
    Handsome and young, enjoying all the present,
Just at the very time when he least broods
    On such a thing, is suddenly to sea sent,
Wounded and chain'd, so that he cannot move,
And all because a lady fell in love.

52

Here I must leave him, for I grow pathetic,
    Moved by the Chinese nymph of tears, green tea!
Than whom Cassandra was not more prophetic;
    For if my pure libations exceed three,
I feel my heart become so sympathetic,
    That I must have recourse to black Bohea:
'Tis pity wine should be so deleterious,
For tea and coffee leave us much more serious,

53

Unless when qualified with thee, Cogniac!
  Sweet Naiad of the Phlegethontic rill!
Ah! why the liver wilt thou thus attack,
  And make, like other nymphs, thy lovers ill?
I would take refuge in weak punch, but *rack*
  (In each sense of the word), whene'er I fill
My mind and midnight beakers to the brim,
Wakes me next morning with its synonym.

54

I leave Don Juan for the present, safe—
  Not sound, poor fellow, but severely wounded;
Yet could his corporal pangs amount to half
  Of those with which his Haidée's bosom bounded?
She was not one to weep, and rave, and chafe,
  And then give way, subdued because surrounded;
Her mother was a Moorish maid, from Fez,
Where all is Eden, or a wilderness.

55

There the large olive rains its amber store
  In marble fonts; there grain, and flower, and fruit,
Gush from the earth until the land runs o'er;
  But there, too, many a poison-tree has root,
And midnight listens to the lion's roar,
  And long, long deserts scorch the camel's foot,
Or heaving whelm the helpless caravan;
And as the soil is, so the heart of man.

56

Afric is all the sun's, and as her earth
  Her human clay is kindled; full of power
For good or evil, burning from its birth,
  The Moorish blood partakes the planet's hour,
And like the soil beneath it will bring forth:
  Beauty and love were Haidée's mother's dower;
But her large dark eye show'd deep Passion's force,
Though sleeping like a lion near a source.

57

Her daughter, temper'd with a milder ray,
   Like summer clouds all silvery, smooth, and fair,
Till slowly charged with thunder they display
   Terror to earth, and tempest to the air,
Had held till now her soft and milky way;
   But, overwrought with passion and despair,
The fire burst forth from her Numidian veins,
Even as the Simoom sweeps the blasted plains.

58

The last sight which she saw was Juan's gore,
   And he himself o'ermaster'd and cut down;
His blood was running on the very floor
   Where late he trod, her beautiful, her own;
Thus much she view'd an instant and no more,—
   Her struggles ceased with one convulsive groan;
On her sire's arm, which until now scarce held
Her writhing, fell she like a cedar fell'd.

59

A vein had burst, and her sweet lips' pure dyes
   Were dabbled with the deep blood which ran o'er;
And her head droop'd as when the lily lies
   O'ercharged with rain: her summon'd handmaids bore
Their lady to her couch with gushing eyes;
   Of herbs and cordials they produced their store,
But she defied all means they could employ,
Like one life could not hold, nor death destroy.

60

Days lay she in that state unchanged, though chill—
   With nothing livid, still her lips were red;
She had no pulse, but death seem'd absent still;
   No hideous sign proclaim'd her surely dead;
Corruption came not in each mind to kill
   All hope; to look upon her sweet face bred
New thoughts of life, for it seem'd full of soul—
She had so much, earth could not claim the whole.

61

The ruling passion, such as marble shows
   When exquisitely chisell'd, still lay there,
But fix'd as marble's unchanged aspect throws
   O'er the fair Venus, but for ever fair;
O'er the Laocoön's all eternal throes,
   And ever-dying Gladiator's air,
Their energy like life forms all their fame,
Yet looks not life, for they are still the same.

62

She woke at length, but not as sleepers wake,
   Rather the dead, for life seem'd something new,
A strange sensation which she must partake
   Perforce, since whatsoever met her view
Struck not on memory, though a heavy ache
   Lay at her heart, whose earliest beat still true
Brought back the sense of pain without the cause,
For, for a while, the furies made a pause.

63

She look'd on many a face with vacant eye,
   On many a token without knowing what;
She saw them watch her without asking why,
   And reck'd not who around her pillow sat;
Not speechless, though she spoke not; not a sigh
   Relieved her thoughts; dull silence and quick chat
Were tried in vain by those who served; she gave
No sign, save breath, of having left the grave.

64

Her handmaids tended, but she heeded not;
   Her father watch'd, she turn'd her eyes away;
She recognised no being, and no spot,
   However dear or cherish'd in their day;
They changed from room to room—but all forgot—
   Gentle, but without memory she lay;
At length those eyes, which they would fain be weaning
Back to old thoughts, wax'd full of fearful meaning.

65

And then a slave bethought her of a harp;
   The harper came, and tuned his instrument;
At the first notes, irregular and sharp,
   On him her flashing eyes a moment bent,
Then to the wall she turn'd, as if to warp
   Her thoughts from sorrow through her heart re-sent;
And he began a long low island song
Of ancient days, ere tyranny grew strong.

66

Anon her thin wan fingers beat the wall
   In time to his old tune; he changed the theme,
And sung of love, the fierce name struck through all
   Her recollection, on her flash'd the dream
Of what she was, and is, if ye could call
   To be so being; in a gushing stream
The tears rush'd forth from her o'erclouded brain,
Like mountain mists at length dissolved in rain.

67

Short solace, vain relief!—thought came too quick,
   And whirl'd her brain to madness; she arose
As one who ne'er had dwelt among the sick,
   And flew at all she met, as on her foes;
But no one ever heard her speak or shriek,
   Although her paroxysm drew towards its close;—
Hers was a frenzy which disdain'd to rave,
Even when they smote her, in the hope to save.

68

Yet she betray'd at times a gleam of sense;
   Nothing could make her meet her father's face,
Though on all other things with looks intense
   She gazed, but none she ever could retrace;
Food she refused, and raiment: no pretence
   Avail'd for either; neither change of place,
Nor time, nor skill, nor remedy, could give her
Senses to sleep—the power seem'd gone for ever.

69

Twelve days and nights she wither'd thus; at last,
  Without a groan, or sigh, or glance, to show
A parting pang, the spirit from her pass'd:
  And they who watch'd her nearest could not know
The very instant, till the change that cast
  Her sweet face into shadow, dull and slow,
Glazed o'er her eyes—the beautiful, the black—
Oh! to possess such lustre—and then lack!

70

She died, but not alone; she held within
  A second principle of life, which might
Have dawn'd a fair and sinless child of sin,
  But closed its little being without light,
And went down to the grave unborn, wherein
  Blossom and bough lie wither'd with one blight;
In vain the dews of Heaven descend above
The bleeding flower and blasted fruit of love.

71

Thus lived—thus died she; never more on her
  Shall sorrow light, or shame. She was not made
Through years or moons the inner weight to bear,
  Which colder hearts endure, till they are laid
By age in earth; her days and pleasures were
  Brief, but delightful—such as had not stay'd
Long with her destiny; but she sleeps well
By the sea-shore, whereon she loved to dwell.

72

That isle is now all desolate and bare,
  Its dwellings down, its tenants pass'd away;
None but her own and father's grave is there,
  And nothing outward tells of human clay:

Ye could not know where lies a thing so fair—
　No stone is there to show, no tongue to say
What was; no dirge, except the hollow sea's,
Mourns o'er the beauty of the Cyclades.

*　　*　　*　　*　　*

104

I pass each day where Dante's bones are laid:
　A little cupola, more neat than solemn,
Protects his dust, but reverence here is paid
　To the bard's tomb, and not the warrior's column.
The time must come, when both alike decay'd,
　The chieftain's trophy, and the poet's volume,
Will sink where lie the songs and wars of earth,
Before Pelides' death or Homer's birth.

105

With human blood that column was cemented,
　With human filth that column is defiled,
As if the peasant's coarse contempt were vented,
　To show his loathing of the spot he soil'd:
Thus is the trophy used, and thus lamented
　Should ever be those blood-hounds, from whose wild
Instinct of gore and glory earth has known
Those sufferings Dante saw in hell alone.

106

Yet there will still be bards: though fame is smoke,
　Its fumes are frankincense to human thought;
And the unquiet feelings, which first woke
　Song in the world, will seek what then they sought;
As on the beach the waves at last are broke,
　Thus to their extreme verge the passions brought,
Dash into poetry, which is but passion,
Or at least was so ere it grew a fashion.

107

If in the course of such a life as was
  At once adventurous and contemplative,
Men, who partake all passions as they pass,
  Acquire the deep and bitter power to give
Their images again as in a glass,
  And in such colours that they seem to live;
You may do right forbidding them to show 'em,
But spoil (I think) a very pretty poem.

*   *   *   *   *

CANTO V

*   *   *   *   *

10

Like a backgammon board the place was dotted
  With whites and blacks, in groups on show for sale
Though rather more irregularly spotted:
  Some bought the jet, while others chose the pale.
It chanced, amongst the other people lotted,
  A man of thirty, rather stout and hale,
With resolution in his dark grey eye,
Next Juan stood, till some might choose to buy.

*   *   *   *   *

32

I think with Alexander, that the act
  Of eating, with another act or two,
Makes us feel our mortality in fact
  Redoubled; when a roast and a ragout,

And fish, and soup, by some side dishes back'd,
    Can give us either pain or pleasure, who
Would pique himself on intellects, whose use
Depends so much upon the gastric juice?

            *   *   *   *   *

                    40

The purchaser of Juan and acquaintance
    Bore off his bargains to a gilded boat,
Embark'd himself and them, and off they went thence
    As fast as oars could pull and water float;
They look'd like persons being led to sentence,
    Wondering what next, till the caique was brought
Up in a little creek below a wall
O'ertopp'd with cypresses dark-green and tall.

                    41

Here their conductor tapping at the wicket
    Of a small iron door, 'twas open'd, and
He led them onward, first through a low thicket
    Flank'd by large groves which tower'd on either hand:
They almost lost their way, and had to pick it—
    For night was closing ere they came to land.
The eunuch made a sign to those on board,
Who row'd off, leaving them without a word.

            *   *   *   *   *

                    46

It was indeed a wide extensive building
    Which open'd on their view, and o'er the front
There seem'd to be besprent a deal of gilding
    And various hues, as is the Turkish wont,—
A gaudy taste; for they are little skill'd in
    The arts of which these lands were once the font:
Each villa on the Bosphorus looks a screen
New painted, or a pretty opera-scene.

47

And nearer as they came, a genial savour
  Of certain stews, and roast-meats, and pilaus,
Things which in hungry mortals' eyes find favour,
  Made Juan in his harsh intentions pause,
And put himself upon his good behaviour:
  His friend, too, adding a new saving clause,
Said, "In Heaven's name let's get some supper now,
And then I'm with you, if you're for a row."

*   *   *   *   *

50

Turkey contains no bells, and yet men dine:
  And Juan and his friend, albeit they heard
No Christian knoll to table, saw no line
  Of lackeys usher to the feast prepared,
Yet smelt roast-meat, beheld a huge fire shine,
  And cooks in motion with their clean arms bared,
And gazed around them to the left and right
With the prophetic eye of appetite.

*   *   *   *   *

54

As the black eunuch enter'd with his brace
  Of purchased infidels, some raised their eyes
A moment without slackening from their pace;
  But those who sate ne'er stirr'd in any wise:
One or two stared the captives in the face,
  Just as one views a horse to guess his price;
Some nodded to the negro from their station,
But no one troubled him with conversation.

*   *   *   *   *

56

Some faint lamps gleaming from the lofty walls
　Gave light enough to hint their farther way,
But not enough to show the imperial halls
　In all the flashing of their full array;
Perhaps there's nothing—I'll not say appals,
　But saddens more by night as well as day,
Than an enormous room without a soul
To break the lifeless splendour of the whole.

*　　*　　*　　*　　*

64

At last they reach'd a quarter most retired,
　Where echo woke as if from a long slumber;
Though full of all things which could be desired,
　One wonder'd what to do with such a number
Of articles which nobody required;
　Here wealth had done its utmost to encumber
With furniture an exquisite apartment,
Which puzzled Nature much to know what Art meant.

65

It seem'd, however, but to open on
　A range or suite of further chambers, which
Might lead to Heaven knows where; but in this one
　The moveables were prodigally rich:
Sofas 'twas half a sin to sit upon,
　So costly were they; carpets, every stitch
Of workmanship so rare, that made you wish
You could glide o'er them like a golden fish.

*　　*　　*　　*　　*

68

The suit he thought most suitable to each
　Was, for the elder and the stouter, first
A Candiote cloak, which to the knee might reach,
　And trowsers not so tight that they would burst,

But such as fit an Asiatic breech;
  A shawl, whose folds in Cashmire had been nurst,
Slippers of saffron, dagger rich and handy;
In short, all things which form a Turkish Dandy.

*   *   *   *   *

73

Baba eyed Juan, and said, "Be so good
  As dress yourself—" and pointed out a suit
In which a Princess with great pleasure would
  Array her limbs; but Juan standing mute,
As not being in a masquerading mood,
  Gave it a slight kick with his Christian foot;
And when the old negro told him to "Get ready,"
Replied, "Old gentleman, I'm not a lady."

74

"What you may be, I neither know nor care,"
  Said Baba, "but pray do as I desire;
I've no more time nor many words to spare."
  "At least," said Juan, "sure I may enquire
The cause of this odd travesty?"—"Forbear,"
  Said Baba, "to be curious: 'twill transpire,
No doubt, in proper place, and time, and season:
I've no authority to tell the reason."

75

"Then if I do," said Juan, "I'll be——"—"Hold!"
  Rejoin'd the negro, "pray be not provoking;
This spirit's well, but it may wax too bold,
  And you will find us not too fond of joking."
"What, sir!" said Juan, "shall it e'er be told
  That I unsex'd my dress?" But Baba, stroking
The things down, said, "Incense me, and I call
Those who will leave you of no sex at all.

76

"I offer you a handsome suit of clothes:
    A woman's, true, but then there is a cause
Why you should wear them."—"What, though my soul loathes
    The effeminate garb?"—thus, after a short pause,
Sigh'd Juan, muttering also some slight oaths,
    "What the devil shall I do with all this gauze?"
Thus he profanely term'd the finest lace
Which e'er set off a marriage-morning face.

77

And then he swore; and, sighing, on he slipp'd
    A pair of trowsers of flesh-colour'd silk;
Next with a virgin zone he was equipp'd,
    Which girt a slight chemise as white as milk;
But, tugging on his petticoat, he tripp'd,
    Which—as we say—or as the Scotch say, *whilk,*
(The rhyme obliges me to this; sometimes
Monarchs are less imperative than rhymes)—

78

Whilk, which (or what you please), was owing to
    His garment's novelty, and his being awkward;
And yet at last he managed to get through
    His toilet, though no doubt a little backward:
The negro Baba help'd a little too,
    When some untoward part of raiment stuck hard;
And, wrestling both his arms into a gown,
He paused, and took a survey up and down.

79

One difficulty still remain'd—his hair
    Was hardly long enough; but Baba found
So many false long tresses all to spare,
    That soon his head was most completely crown'd,
After the manner then in fashion there;
    And this addition with such gems was bound
As suited the *ensemble* of his toilet,
While Baba made him comb his head and oil it.

80

And now being femininely all array'd,
  With some small aid from scissors, paint, and tweezers,
He look'd in almost all respects a maid,
  And Baba smilingly exclaim'd, "You see, sirs,
A perfect transformation here display'd;
  And now, then, you must come along with me, sirs,
That is—the Lady:" clapping his hands twice,
Four blacks were at his elbow in a trice.

81

"You, sir," said Baba, nodding to the one,
  "Will please to accompany those gentlemen
To supper; but you, worthy Christian nun,
  Will follow me: no trifling, sir, for when
I say a thing, it must at once be done.
  What fear you? think you this a lion's den?
Why, 'tis a palace; where the truly wise
Anticipate the Prophet's paradise.

*   *   *   *   *

91

Before they entered, Baba paused to hint
  To Juan some slight lessons as his guide:
"If you could just contrive," he said, "to stint
  That somewhat manly majesty of stride,
'Twould be as well, and (though there's not much in 't)
  To swing a little less from side to side,
Which has at times an aspect of the oddest;—
And also could you look a little modest,

92

" 'Twould be convenient; for these mutes have eyes
  Like needles, which might pierce those petticoats;
And if they should discover your disguise,
  You know how near us the deep Bosphorus floats;

And you and I may chance, ere morning rise,
   To find our way to Marmora without boats,
Stitch'd up in sacks—a mode of navigation
A good deal practised here upon occasion."

*   *   *   *   *

96

The lady rising up with such an air
   As Venus rose with from the wave, on them
Bent like an antelope a Paphian pair
   Of eyes, which put out each surrounding gem;
And raising up an arm as moonlight fair,
   She sign'd to Baba, who first kiss'd the hem
Of her deep purple robe, and speaking low,
Pointed to Juan, who remain'd below.

*   *   *   *   *

106

And he advanced, though with but a bad grace,
   Though on more *thorough-bred* or fairer fingers
No lips e'er left their transitory trace;
   On such as these the lip too fondly lingers,
And for one kiss would fain imprint a brace,
   As you will see, if she you love will bring hers
In contact; and sometimes even a fair stranger's
An almost twelvemonth's constancy endangers.

107

The lady eyed him o'er and o'er, and bade
   Baba retire, which he obey'd in style,
As if well used to the retreating trade;
   And taking hints in good part all the while,
He whisper'd Juan not to be afraid,
   And looking on him with a sort of smile,
Took leave with such a face of satisfaction,
As good men wear who have done a virtuous action.

*   *   *   *   *

114

Juan, the latest of her whims, had caught
   Her eye in passing on his way to sale;
She order'd him directly to be bought,
   And Baba, who had ne'er been known to fail
In any kind of mischief to be wrought,
   At all such auctions knew how to prevail:
She had no prudence, but he had; and this
Explains the garb which Juan took amiss.

115

His youth and features favour'd the disguise,
   And should you ask how she, a sultan's bride,
Could risk or compass such strange phantasies,
   This I must leave sultanas to decide:
Emperors are only husbands in wives' eyes,
   And kings and consorts oft are mystified,
As we may ascertain with due precision,
Some by experience, others by tradition.

116

But to the main point, where we have been tending:—
   She now conceived all difficulties past,
And deem'd herself extremely condescending
   When, being made her property at last,
Without more preface, in her blue eyes blending
   Passion and power, a glance on him she cast,
And merely saying, "Christian, canst thou love?"
Conceived that phrase was quite enough to move.

117

And so it was, in proper time and place;
   But Juan, who had still his mind o'erflowing
With Haidée's isle and soft Ionian face,
   Felt the warm blood, which in his face was glowing,
Rush back upon his heart, which fill'd apace,
   And left his cheeks as pale as snow-drops blowing;
These words went through his soul like Arab-spears,
So that he spoke not, but burst into tears.

*   *   *   *   *

121

But tears must stop like all things else; and soon
   Juan, who for an instant had been moved
To such a sorrow by the intrusive tone
   Of one who dared to ask if "he *had* loved,"
Call'd back the stoic to his eyes, which shone
   Bright with the very weakness he reproved;
And although sensitive to beauty, he
Felt most indignant still at not being free.

122

Gulbeyaz, for the first time in her days,
   Was much embarrass'd, never having met
In all her life with aught save prayers and praise;
   And as she also risk'd her life to get
Him whom she meant to tutor in love's ways
   Into a comfortable tête-à-tête,
To lose the hour would make her quite a martyr,
And they had wasted now almost a quarter.

       *   *   *   *   *

127

"Thou ask'st if I can love? be this the proof
   How much I *have* loved—that I love not *thee!*
In this vile garb, the distaff, web, and woof,
   Were fitter for me: Love is for the free!
I am not dazzled by this splendid roof,
   Whate'er thy power, and great it seems to be;
Heads bow, knees bend, eyes watch around a throne,
And hands obey—our hearts are still our own."

       *   *   *   *   *

139

Her first thought was to cut off Juan's head;
   Her second, to cut only his—acquaintance;
Her third, to ask him where he had been bred;
   Her fourth, to rally him into repentance;

Her fifth, to call her maids and go to bed;
　　Her sixth, to stab herself; her seventh, to sentence
The lash to Baba—but her grand resource
Was to sit down again, and cry of course.

140

She thought to stab herself, but then she had
　　The dagger close at hand, which made it awkward;
For Eastern stays are little made to pad,
　　So that a poniard pierces if 'tis struck hard:
She thought of killing Juan—but, poor lad!
　　Though he deserved it well for being so backward,
The cutting off his head was not the art
Most likely to attain her aim—his heart.

141

Juan was moved; he had made up his mind
　　To be impaled, or quarter'd as a dish
For dogs, or to be slain with pangs refined,
　　Or thrown to lions, or made baits for fish,
And thus heroically stood resign'd,
　　Rather than sin—except to his own wish;
But all his great preparatives for dying
Dissolved like snow before a woman crying.

142

As through his palms Bob Acres' valour oozed,
　　So Juan's virtue ebb'd, I know not how;
And first he wonder'd why he had refused;
　　And then, if matters could be made up now;
And next his savage virtue he accused,
　　Just as a friar may accuse his vow,
Or as a dame repents her of her oath,
Which mostly ends in some small breach of both.

143

So he began to stammer some excuses;
　　But words are not enough in such a matter,
Although you borrow'd all that e'er the Muses
　　Have sung, or even a dandy's dandiest chatter,

Or all the figures Castlereagh abuses;
  Just as a languid smile began to flatter
His peace was making, but before he ventured
Further, old Baba rather briskly enter'd.

* * * * *

157

The Turks do well to shut—at least, sometimes—
  The women up, because, in sad reality,
Their chastity in these unhappy climes
  Is not a thing of that astringent quality,
Which in the North prevents precarious crimes,
  And makes our snow less pure than our morality:
The sun, which yearly melts the polar ice,
Has quite the contrary effect on vice.

* * * * *

From Preface to Cantos VI, VII, and VIII

THE DETAILS of the siege of Ismail in two of the following cantos (i.e. the seventh and eighth) are taken from a French Work, entitled *Histoire de la Nouvelle Russie*. Some of the incidents attributed to Don Juan really occurred, particularly the circumstance of his saving the infant, which was the actual case of the late Duc de Richelieu, then a young volunteer in the Russian service, and afterward the founder and benefactor of Odessa, where his name and memory can never cease to be regarded with reverence. . . .

With regard to the objections which have been made . . . to the already published cantos of this poem, I shall content myself with two quotations from Voltaire:—"La pudeur s'est enfuite des coeurs, et s'est refugiée sur les lèvres." [Modesty has fled from hearts and taken refuge on lips.] . . . "Plus les moeurs sont dépravés, plus les expressions deviennent mesurées; on croit regagner en langage ce qu'on a perdu en vertu." [The more depraved morals become, the more prudish the expressions; one hopes to recover in language what has been lost in virtue.]

This is the real fact, as applicable to the degraded and hypocritical mass which leavens the present English generation, and is the only answer they deserve. The hackneyed and lavished title of Blasphemer—which, with Radical, Liberal, Jacobin, Reformer, &c., are the changes which the hirelings are daily ringing in the ears of those who will listen—should be welcome to all who recollect on *whom* it was originally bestowed. Socrates and Jesus Christ were put to death publicly as *blasphemers,* and so have been and may be many who dare to oppose the most notorious abuses of the name of God and the mind of man. But persecution is not refutation, nor even triumph: the "wretched infidel," as he is called, is probably happier in his prison than the proudest of his assailants. With his opinions I have nothing to do—they may be right or wrong—but he has suffered for them, and that very suffering for conscience' sake will make more proselytes to deism than the example of heterodox prelates to Christianity, suicide statesmen to oppression, or overpensioned homicides to the impious alliance which insults the world with the name of "Holy!" I have no wish to trample on the dishonoured or the dead; but it would be well if the adherents to the classes from whence those persons sprung should abate a little of the *cant* which is the crying sin of this double-dealing and false-speaking time of selfish spoilers, and—but enough for the present.

Pisa, July, 1822

CANTO VI

* * * * *

51

It was a spacious chamber (Oda is
  The Turkish title), and ranged round the wall
Were couches, toilets—and much more than this
  I might describe, as I have seen it all,
But it suffices—little was amiss;
  'Twas on the whole a nobly furnish'd hall,
With all things ladies want, save one or two,
And even those were nearer than they knew.

52

Dudù, as has been said, was a sweet creature,
　　Not very dashing, but extremely winning,
With the most regulated charms of feature,
　　Which painters cannot catch like faces sinning
Against proportion—the wild strokes of nature
　　Which they hit off at once in the beginning,
Full of expression, right or wrong, that strike,
And, pleasing or unpleasing, still are like.

53

But she was a soft landscape of mild earth,
　　Where all was harmony and calm, and quiet,
Luxuriant, budding; cheerful without mirth,
　　Which, if not happiness, is much more nigh it
Than are your mighty passions and so forth,
　　Which some call "the sublime:" I wish they'd try it:
I've seen your stormy seas and stormy women,
And pity lovers rather more than seamen.

54

But she was pensive more than melancholy,
　　And serious more than pensive, and serene,
It may be, more than either—not unholy
　　Her thoughts, at least till now, appear to have been.
The strangest thing was, beauteous, she was wholly
　　Unconscious, albeit turn'd of quick seventeen,
That she was fair, or dark, or short, or tall;
She never thought about herself at all.

55

And therefore was she kind and gentle as
　　The Age of Gold (when gold was yet unknown,
By which its nomenclature came to pass;
　　Thus most appropriately has been shown
"Lucus à non lucendo," not what was,
　　But what was not; a sort of style that's grown
Extremely common in this age, whose metal
The devil may decompose, but never settle:

56

I think it may be of "Corinthian Brass,"
  Which was a mixture of all metals, but
The brazen uppermost). Kind reader! pass
  This long parenthesis: I could not shut
It sooner for the soul of me, and class
  My faults even with your own! which meaneth, Put
A kind construction upon them and me;
But *that* you won't—then don't—I am not less free.

57

'Tis time we should return to plain narration,
  And thus my narrative proceeds:—Dudù,
With every kindness short of ostentation,
  Show'd Juan, or Juanna, through and through
This labyrinth of females, and each station
  Described—what's strange—in words extremely few:
I have but one simile, and that's a blunder,
For wordless woman, which is *silent* thunder.

58

And next she gave her (I say *her*, because
  The gender still was epicene, at least
In outward show, which is a saving clause)
  An outline of the customs of the East,
With all their chaste integrity of laws,
  By which the more a haram is increased,
The stricter doubtless grow the vestal duties
Of any supernumerary beauties.

59

And then she gave Juanna a chaste kiss:
  Dudù was fond of kissing—which I'm sure
That nobody can ever take amiss,
  Because 'tis pleasant, so that it be pure,
And between females means no more than this—
  That they have nothing better near or newer.
"Kiss" rhymes to "bliss" in fact as well as verse—
I wish it never led to something worse.

*   *   *   *   *

64

There was deep silence in the chamber: dim
    And distant from each other burn'd the lights,
And slumber hover'd o'er each lovely limb
    Of the fair occupants: if there be sprites,
They should have walk'd there in their sprightliest trim,
    By way of change from their sepulchral sites,
And shown themselves as ghosts of better taste
Than haunting some old ruin or wild waste.

65

Many and beautiful lay those around,
    Like flowers of different hue, and clime, and root,
In some exotic garden sometimes found,
    With cost, and care, and warmth induced to shoot.
One, with her auburn tresses lightly bound,
    And fair brows gently drooping, as the fruit
Nods from the tree, was slumbering with soft breath
And lips apart, which show'd the pearls beneath.

66

One with her flush'd cheek laid on her white arm,
    And raven ringlets gather'd in dark crowd
Above her brow, lay dreaming soft and warm;
    And smiling through her dream, as through a cloud
The moon breaks, half unveil'd each further charm,
    As, slightly stirring in her snowy shroud,
Her beauties seized the unconscious hour of night
All bashfully to struggle into light.

67

This is no bull, although it sounds so; for
    'Twas night, but there were lamps, as hath been said.
A third's all-pallid aspect offer'd more
    The traits of sleeping sorrow, and betray'd
Through the heaved breast the dream of some far shore
    Beloved and deplored; while slowly stray'd
(As night-dew, on a cypress glittering, tinges
The black bough) tear-drops through her eyes' dark fringes.

68

A fourth, as marble, statue-like and still,
    Lay in a breathless, hush'd, and stony sleep;
White, cold, and pure, as looks a frozen rill,
    Or the snow minaret on an Alpine steep,
Or Lot's wife done in salt,—or what you will;—
    My similes are gather'd in a heap,
So pick and choose—perhaps you'll be content
With a carved lady on a monument.

69

And lo! a fifth appears;—and what is she?
    A lady of a "certain age," which means
Certainly agèd—what her years might be
    I know not, never counting past their teens;
But there she slept, not quite so fair to see,
    As ere that awful period intervenes
Which lays both men and women on the shelf,
To meditate upon their sins and self.

70

But all this time how slept, or dream'd, Dudù?
    With strict inquiry I could ne'er discover,
And scorn to add a syllable untrue;
    But ere the middle watch was hardly over,
Just when the fading lamps waned dim and blue,
    And phantoms hover'd or might seem to hover,
To those who like their company, about
The apartment, on a sudden she scream'd out:

71

And that so loudly, that upstarted all
    The Oda, in a general commotion:
Matron and maids, and those whom you may call
    Neither, came crowding like the waves of ocean,
One on the other, throughout the whole hall,
    All trembling, wondering, without the least notion
More than I have myself of what could make
The calm Dudù so turbulently wake.

72

But wide awake she was, and round her bed,
　With floating draperies and with flying hair,
With eager eyes, and light but hurried tread,
　And bosoms, arms, and ankles glancing bare,
And bright as any meteor ever bred
　By the North Pole,—they sought her cause of care,
For she seem'd agitated, flush'd, and frighten'd,
Her eye dilated and her colour heighten'd.

73

But what is strange—and a strong proof how great
　A blessing is sound sleep—Juanna lay
As fast as ever husband by his mate
　In holy matrimony snores away.
Not all the clamour broke her happy state
　Of slumber, ere they shook her,—so they say
At least,—and then she too unclosed her eyes,
And yawn'd a good deal with discreet surprise.

74

And now commenced a strict investigation,
　Which, as all spoke at once, and more than once,
Conjecturing, wondering, asking a narration,
　Alike might puzzle either wit or dunce
To answer in a very clear oration.
　Dudù had never pass'd for wanting sense,
But, being "no orator, as Brutus is,"
Could not at first expound what was amiss.

75

At length she said, that, in a slumber sound
　She dream'd a dream of walking in a wood—
A "wood obscure" like that where Dante found
　Himself in at the age when all grow good;
Life's half-way house, where dames with virtue crown'd
　Run much less risk of lovers turning rude;—
And that this wood was full of pleasant fruits,
And trees of goodly growth and spreading roots;

76

And in the midst a golden apple grew,—
    A most prodigious pippin,—but it hung
Rather too high and distant, that she threw
    Her glances on it, and then, longing, flung
Stones, and whatever, she could pick up, to
    Bring down the fruit, which still perversely clung
To its own bough, and dangled yet in sight,
But always at a most provoking height;—

77

That on a sudden, when she least had hope,
    It fell down of its own accord, before
Her feet; that her first movement was to stoop
    And pick it up, and bite it to the core;
That just as her young lip began to ope
    Upon the golden fruit the vision bore,
A bee flew out and stung her to the heart,
And so—she awoke with a great scream and start.

78

All this she told with some confusion and
    Dismay, the usual consequence of dreams
Of the unpleasant kind, with none at hand
    To expound their vain and visionary gleams.
I've known some odd ones which seem'd really plann'd
    Prophetically, or that which one deems
"A strange coincidence," to use a phrase
By which such things are settled now-a-days.

79

The damsels, who had thoughts of some great harm,
    Began, as is the consequence of fear,
To scold a little at the false alarm
    That broke for nothing on their sleeping ear.
The matron too was wroth to leave her warm
    Bed for the dream she'd been obliged to hear,
And chafed at poor Dudù, who only sigh'd,
And said that she was sorry she had cried.

80

"I've heard of stories of a cock and bull;
  But visions of an apple and a bee,
To take us from our natural rest, and pull
  The whole Oda from their beds at half-past three,
Would make us think the moon is at its full.
  You surely are unwell, child! we must see,
To-morrow, what his Highness's physician
Will say to this hysteric of a vision.

81

"And poor Juanna too—the child's first night
  Within these walls to be broke in upon
With such a clamour! I had thought it right
  That the young stranger should not lie alone,
And, as the quietest of all, she might
  With you, Dudù, a good night's rest have known;
But now I must transfer her to the charge
Of Lolah—though her couch is not so large."

82

Lolah's eyes sparkled at the proposition;
  But poor Dudù, with large drops in her own,
Resulting from the scolding or the vision,
  Implored that present pardon might be shown
For this first fault, and that on no condition
  (She added in a soft and piteous tone)
Juanna should be taken from her, and
Her future dreams should all be kept in hand.

83

She promised never more to have a dream,
  At least to dream so loudly as just now;
She wonder'd at herself how she could scream—
  'Twas foolish, nervous, as she must allow,
A fond hallucination, and a theme
  For laughter—but she felt her spirits low,
And begg'd they would excuse her; she'd get over
This weakness in a few hours, and recover.

84

And here Juanna kindly interposed,
    And said she felt herself extremely well
Where she then was, as her sound sleep disclosed
    When all around rang like a tocsin-bell:
She did not find herself the least disposed
    To quit her gentle partner, and to dwell
Apart from one who had no sin to show,
Save that of dreaming once "mal-à-propos."

85

As thus Juanna spoke, Dudù turn'd round,
    And hid her face within Juanna's breast:
Her neck alone was seen, but that was found
    The colour of a budding rose's crest.
I can't tell why she blush'd, nor can expound
    The mystery of this rupture of their rest;
All that I know is, that the facts I state
Are true as truth has ever been of late.

86

And so good night to them,—or, if you will,
    Good morrow—for the cock had crown, and light
Began to clothe each Asiatic hill,
    And the mosque crescent struggled into sight
Of the long caravan, which in the chill
    Of dewy dawn wound slowly round each height
That stretches to the stony belt which girds
Asia, where Kaff looks down upon the Kurds.

*   *   *   *   *

CANTO VIII

* * * * *

61

Of all men, saving Sylla the man-slayer,
   Who passes for in life and death most lucky,
Of the great names which in our faces stare,
   The General Boon, back-woodsman of Kentucky,
Was happiest amongst mortals anywhere:
   For, killing nothing but a bear or buck, he
Enjoy'd the lonely, vigorous, harmless days
Of his old age in wilds of deepest maze.

62

Crime came not near him—she is not the child
   Of solitude; Health shrank not from him—for
Her home is in the rarely trodden wild,
   Where if men seek her not, and death be more
Their choice than life, forgive them, as beguiled
   By habit to what their own hearts abhor—
In cities caged. The present case in point I
Cite is, that Boon lived hunting up to ninety;

63

And what's still stranger, left behind a name
   For which men vainly decimate the throng,
Not only famous, but of that *good* fame,
   Without which glory's but a tavern song—
Simple, serene, the antipodes of shame,
   Which hate nor envy e'er could tinge with wrong;
An active hermit, even in age the child
Of Nature, or the Man of Ross run wild.

64

'Tis true he shrank from men, even of his nation;
  When they built up unto his darling trees,—
He moved some hundred miles off, for a station
  Where there were fewer houses and more ease;
The inconvenience of civilisation
  Is, that you neither can be pleased nor please;
But where he met the individual man,
He show'd himself as kind as mortal can.

65

He was not all alone: around him grew
  A sylvan tribe of children of the chase,
Whose young, unwaken'd world was ever new,
  Nor sword nor sorrow yet had left a trace
On her unwrinkled brow, nor could you view
  A frown on nature's or on human face;
The free-born forest found and kept them free,
And fresh as is a torrent or a tree.

66

And tall and strong and swift of foot were they,
  Beyond the dwarfing city's pale abortions,
Because their thoughts had never been the prey
  Of care or gain: the green woods were their portions;
No sinking spirits told them they grew grey;
  No fashion made them apes of her distortions;
Simple they were, not savage; and their rifles,
Though very true, were not yet used for trifles.

67

Motion was in their days, rest in their slumbers,
  And cheerfulness the handmaid of their toil;
Nor yet too many nor too few their numbers;
  Corruption could not make their hearts her soil;
The lust which stings, the splendour which encumbers,
  With the free foresters divide no spoil;
Serene, not sullen, were the solitudes
Of this unsighing people of the woods.

68

So much for Nature:—by way of variety,
  Now back to thy great joys, Civilisation!
And the sweet consequence of large society,
  War, pestilence, the despot's desolation,
The kingly scourge, the lust of notoriety,
  The millions slain by soldiers for their ration,
The scenes like Catherine's boudoir at threescore,
With Ismail's storm to soften it the more.

69

The town was enter'd: first one column made
  Its sanguinary way good—then another;
The reeking bayonet and the flashing blade
  Clash'd 'gainst the scimitar, and babe and mother
With distant shrieks were heard heaven to upbraid:
  Still closer sulphury clouds began to smother
The breath of morn and man, where, foot by foot,
The madden'd Turks their city still dispute.

70

Koutousow, he who afterwards beat back
  (With some assistance from the frost and snow)
Napoleon on his bold and bloody track,
  It happen'd was himself beat back just now.
He was a jolly fellow, and could crack
  His jest alike in face of friend or foe,
Though life, and death, and victory were at stake;
But here it seem'd his jokes had ceased to take.

71

For having thrown himself into a ditch,
  Follow'd in haste by various grenadiers,
Whose blood the puddle greatly did enrich,
  He climb'd to where the parapet appears;
But there his project reach'd its utmost pitch—
  ('Mongst other deaths the General Ribaupierre's
Was much regretted), for the Moslem men
Threw them all down into the ditch again.

72

And had it not been for some stray troops, landing
    They knew not where, being carried by the stream
To some spot, where they lost their understanding,
    And wander'd up and down as in a dream,
Until they reach'd, as day-break was expanding,
    That which a portal to their eyes did seem,—
The great and gay Koutousow might have lain
Where three parts of his column yet remain.

* * * * *

86

But then the fact's a fact—and 'tis the part
    Of a true poet to escape from fiction
Whene'er he can; for there is little art
    In leaving verse more free from the restriction
Of truth than prose, unless to suit the mart
    For what is sometimes call'd poetic diction,
And that outrageous appetite for lies
Which Satan angles with for souls like flies.

* * * * *

90

And one good action in the midst of crimes
    Is "quite refreshing," in the affected phrase
Of these ambrosial Pharisaic times,
    With all their pretty milk-and-water ways,
And may serve therefore to bedew these rhymes,
    A little scorch'd at present with the blaze
Of conquest and its consequences, which
Make epic poesy so rare and rich.

91

Upon a taken bastion, where there lay
    Thousands of slaughter'd men, a yet warm group
Of murder'd women, who had found their way
    To this vain refuge, made the good heart droop

And shudder;—while, as beautiful as May,
  A female child of ten years tried to stoop
And hide her little palpitating breast
Amidst the bodies lull'd in bloody rest.

92

Two villanous Cossacks pursued the child
  With flashing eyes and weapons: match'd with them,
The rudest brute that roams Siberia's wild,
  Has feelings pure and polish'd as a gem,—
The bear is civilised, the wolf is mild;
  And whom for this at last must we condemn?
Their natures, or their sovereigns, who employ
All arts to teach their subjects to destroy?

93

Their sabres glitter'd o'er her little head,
  Whence her fair hair rose twining with affright,
Her hidden face was plunged amidst the dead:
  When Juan caught a glimpse of this sad sight,
I shall not say exactly what he *said*,
  Because it might not solace "ears polite;"
But what he *did*, was to lay on their backs,—
The readiest way of reasoning with Cossacks.

94

One's hip he slash'd, and split the other's shoulder,
  And drove them with their brutal yells to seek
If there might be chirurgeons who could solder
  The wounds they richly merited, and shriek
Their baffled rage and pain; while waxing colder
  As he turn'd o'er each pale and gory cheek,
Don Juan raised his little captive from
The heap a moment more had made her tomb.

95

And she was chill as they, and on her face
  A slender streak of blood announced how near
Her fate had been to that of all her race;
  For the same blow which laid her mother here,

Had scarr'd her brow, and left its crimson trace
  As the last link with all she had held dear;
But else unhurt, she open'd her large eyes,
And gazed on Juan with a wild surprise.

96

Just at this instant, while their eyes were fix'd
  Upon each other, with dilated glance,
In Juan's look, pain, pleasure, hope, fear, mix'd
  With joy to save, and dread of some mischance
Unto his protégée; while hers, transfix'd
  With infant terrors, glared as from a trance,
A pure, transparent, pale, yet radiant face,
Like to a lighted alabaster vase;—

97

Up came John Johnson—(I will not say "*Jack*,"
  For that were vulgar, cold, and commonplace
On great occasions, such as an attack
  On cities, as hath been the present case),
Up Johnson came, with hundreds at his back,
  Exclaiming:—"Juan! Juan! On, boy! brace
Your arm, and I'll bet Moscow to a dollar,
That you and I will win Saint George's collar.

98

"The Seraskier is knock'd upon the head,
  But the stone bastion still remains, wherein
The old Pacha sits among some hundreds dead,
  Smoking his pipe quite calmly 'midst the din
Of our artillery and his own: 'tis said
  Our kill'd, already piled up to the chin,
Lie round the battery; but still it batters,
And grape in volleys, like a vineyard, scatters.

99

"Then up with me!"—But Juan answer'd, "Look
  Upon this child—I saved her—must not leave
Her life to chance; but point me out some nook
  Of safety, where she less may shrink and grieve,

And I am with you."—Whereon Johnson took
    A glance around—and shrugg'd—and twitch'd his sleeve
And black silk neckcloth—and replied, "You're right;
    Poor thing! what's to be done? I'm puzzled quite."

100

Said Juan: "Whatsoever is to be
    Done, I'll not quit her till she seems secure
Of present life a good deal more than we."
    Quoth Johnson: "*Neither* will I quite ensure;
But at the least *you* may die gloriously."
    Juan replied: "At least I will endure
Whate'er is to be borne—but not resign
This child, who is parentless, and therefore mine."

101

Johnson said: "Juan, we've no time to lose;
    The child's a pretty child—a very pretty—
I never saw such eyes—but hark! now choose
    Between your fame and feelings, pride and pity;—
Hark! how the roar increases!—no excuse
    Will serve when there is plunder in a city;—
I should be loth to march without you, but,
By God! we'll be too late for the first cut."

102

But Juan was immovable; until
    Johnson, who really loved him in his way,
Pick'd out amongst his followers with some skill
    Such as he thought the least given up to prey;
And swearing if the infant came to ill
    That they should all be shot on the next day,
But if she were deliver'd safe and sound,
They should at least have fifty rubles round,

103

And all allowances besides of plunder
    In fair proportion with their comrades;—then
Juan consented to march on through thunder,
    Which thinn'd at every step their ranks of men:

And yet the rest rush'd eagerly—no wonder,
  For they were heated by the hope of gain,
A thing which happens everywhere each day—
No hero trusteth wholly to half pay.

*   *   *   *   *

127

But let me put an end unto my theme:
  There was an end of Ismail—hapless town!
Far flash'd her burning towers o'er Danube's stream,
  And redly ran his blushing waters down.
The horrid war-whoop and the shriller scream
  Rose still; but fainter were the thunders grown:
Of forty thousand who had mann'd the wall,
Some hundreds breathed—the rest were silent all!

128

In one thing ne'ertheless 'tis fit to praise
  The Russian army upon this occasion,
A virtue much in fashion now-a-days,
  And therefore worthy of commemoration:
The topic's tender, so shall be my phrase—
  Perhaps the season's chill, and their long station
In winter's depth, or want of rest and victual,
Had made them chaste—they ravish'd very little.

129

Much did they slay, more plunder, and no less
  Might here and there occur some violation
In the other line;—but not to such excess
  As when the French, that dissipated nation,
Take towns by storm: no causes can I guess,
  Except cold weather and commiseration;
But all the ladies, save some twenty score,
Were almost as much virgins as before.

130

Some odd mistakes too happen'd in the dark,
  Which show'd a want of lanterns, or of taste—
Indeed the smoke was such they scarce could mark
  Their friends from foes,—besides such things from haste
Occur, though rarely, when there is a spark
  Of light to save the venerably chaste:—
But six old damsels, each of seventy years,
Were all deflower'd by different grenadiers.

131

But on the whole their continence was great;
  So that some disappointment there ensued
To those who had felt the inconvenient state
  Of "single blessedness," and thought it good
(Since it was not their fault, but only fate,
  To bear these crosses) for each waning prude
To make a Roman sort of Sabine wedding,
Without the expense and the suspense of bedding.

132

Some voices of the buxom middle-aged
  Were also heard to wonder in the din
(Widows of forty were these birds long caged)
  "Wherefore the ravishing did not begin!"
But, while the thirst for gore and plunder raged,
  There was small leisure for superfluous sin;
But whether they escaped or no, lies hid
In darkness—I can only hope they did.

*   *   *   *   *

CANTO IX

*   *   *   *   *

8

Great men have always scorn'd great recompenses:
  Epaminondas saved his Thebes, and died,
Not leaving even his funeral expenses:
  George Washington had thanks and nought beside,
Except the all-cloudless glory (which few men's is)
  To free his country: Pitt too had his pride,
And, as a high-soul'd minister of state, is
Renown'd for ruining Great Britain gratis.

*   *   *   *   *

51

An English lady ask'd of an Italian,
  What were the actual and official duties
Of the strange thing some women set a value on,
  Which hovers oft about some married beauties,
Call'd "Cavalier Servente?"—a Pygmalion,
  Whose statues warm (I fear, alas! too true 'tis)
Beneath his art. The dame, press'd to disclose them,
Said—"Lady, I beseech you to *suppose them*."

52

And thus I supplicate your supposition,
  And mildest, matron-like interpretation
Of the imperial favourite's condition
  'Twas a high place, the highest in the nation,
In fact, if not in rank; and the suspicion
  Of any one's attaining to his station,
No doubt gave pain, where each new pair of shoulders,
If rather broad, made stocks rise and their holders.

53

Juan, I said, was a most beauteous boy,
    And had retain'd his boyish look beyond
The usual hirsute seasons which destroy,
    With beards and whiskers and the like, the fond
Parisian aspect which upset old Troy
    And founded Doctors' Commons:—I have conn'd
The history of divorces, which, though chequer'd,
Calls Ilion's the first damages on record.

54

And Catherine, who loved all things (save her lord,
    Who was gone to his place), and pass'd for much,
Admiring those (by dainty dames abhorr'd)
    Gigantic gentlemen, yet had a touch
Of sentiment; and he she most adored
    Was the lamented Lanskoi, who was such
A lover as had cost her many a tear,
And yet but made a middling grenadier.

*   *   *   *   *

57

Catherine, who was the grand epitome
    Of that great cause of war, or peace, or what
You please (it causes all the things which be,
    So you may take your choice of this or that)—
Catherine, I say, was very glad to see
    The handsome herald, on whose plumage sat
Victory; and, pausing as she saw him kneel
With his dispatch, forgot to break the seal.

58

Then recollecting the whole empress, nor
    Forgetting quite the woman (which composed
At least three parts of this great whole), she tore
    The letter open with an air which posed

The court, that watch'd each look her visage wore
   Until a royal smile at length disclosed
Fair weather for the day. Though rather spacious,
Her face was noble, her eyes fine, mouth gracious.

59

Great joy was hers, or rather joys; the first
   Was a ta'en city, thirty thousand slain.
Glory and triumph o'er her aspect burst,
   As an East-Indian sunrise on the main.
These quench'd a moment her ambition's thirst—
   So Arab deserts drink in summer's rain:
In vain!—As fall the dews on quenchless sands,
Blood only serves to wash Ambition's bands!

*   *   *   *   *

62

Though somewhat large, exuberant, and truculent,
   When *wroth*—while *pleased*, she was as fine a figure
As those who like things rosy, ripe, and succulent,
   Would wish to look on, while they are in vigour.
She could repay each amatory look you lent
   With interest, and in turn was wont with rigour
To exact of Cupid's bills the full amount
At sight, nor would permit you to discount.

*   *   *   *   *

66

Shakspeare talks of "the herald Mercury
   New lighted on a heaven-kissing hill:"
And some such visions cross'd her majesty,
   While her young herald knelt before her still.
'Tis very true the hill seem'd rather high
   For a lieutenant to climb up; but skill
Smooth'd even the Simplon's steep, and, by God's blessing,
With youth and health all kisses are "heaven-kissing."

67

Her majesty look'd down, the youth look'd up—
    And so they fell in love;—she with his face,
His grace, his God-knows-what: for Cupid's cup
    With the first draught intoxicates apace,
A quintessential laudanum or "black drop,"
    Which makes one drunk at once, without the base
Expedient of full bumpers; for the eye
In love drinks all life's fountains (save tears) dry.

68

He, on the other hand, if not in love,
    Fell into that no less imperious passion,
Self-love—which, when some sort of thing above
    Ourselves a singer, dancer, much in fashion,
Or duchess, princess, empress, "deigns to prove"
    ('Tis Pope's phrase) a great longing, though a rash one,
For one especial person out of many,
Makes us believe ourselves as good as any.

69

Besides, he was of that delighted age
    Which makes all females' ages equal—when
We don't much care with whom we may engage,
    As bold as Daniel in the lions' den,
So that we can our native sun assuage
    In the next ocean, which may flow just then,
To make a twilight in, just as Sol's heat is
Quench'd in the lap of the salt sea, or Thetis.

70

And Catherine (we must say thus much for Catherine),
    Though bold and bloody, was the kind of thing
Whose temporary passion was quite flattering,
    Because each lover look'd a sort of king,
Made up upon an amatory pattern—
    A royal husband in all save the *ring*—
Which, being the damn'dest part of matrimony,
Seem'd taking out the sting to leave the honey.

71

And when you add to this, her womanhood
    In its meridian, her blue eyes, or gray
(The last, if they have soul, are quite as good,
    Or better, as the best examples say:
Napoleon's, Mary's (Queen of Scotland) should
    Lend to that colour a transcendent ray;
And Pallas also sanctions the same hue,
Too wise to look through optics black or blue)—

72

Her sweet smile, and her then majestic figure,
    Her plumpness, her imperial condescension,
Her preference of a boy to men much bigger
    (Fellows whom Messalina's self would pension),
Her prime of life, just now in juicy vigour,
    With other *extras* which we need not mention,—
All these, or any one of these, explain
Enough to make a stripling very vain.

*   *   *   *   *

76

The noblest kind of love is love Platonical,
    To end or to begin with; the next grand
Is that which may be christen'd love canonical,
    Because the clergy take the thing in hand;
The third sort to be noted in our chronicle
    As flourishing in every Christian land,
Is, when chaste matrons to their other ties
Add what may be call'd *marriage in disguise.*

77

Well, we won't analyse—our story must
    Tell for itself: the sovereign was smitten,
Juan much flatter'd by her love, or lust;—
    I cannot stop to alter words once written,

And the two are so mix'd with human dust,
　　That he who *names one*, both perchance may hit on;
But in such matters Russia's mighty empress
Behaved no better than a common sempstress.

78

The whole court melted into one wide whisper,
　　And all lips were applied unto all ears!
The elder ladies' wrinkles curl'd much crisper
　　As they beheld; the younger cast some leers
On one another, and each lovely lisper
　　Smiled as she talk'd the matter o'er; but tears
Of rivalship rose in each clouded eye
Of all the standing army who stood by.

79

All the ambassadors of all the powers
　　Inquired, Who was this very new young man,
Who promised to be great in some few hours?
　　Which is full soon—though life is but a span.
Already they beheld the silver showers
　　Of rubles rain, as fast as specie can,
Upon his cabinet, besides the presents
Of several ribands and some thousand peasants.

80

Catherine was generous,—all such ladies are:
　　Love, that great opener of the heart and all
The ways that lead there, be they near or far,
　　Above, below, by turnpikes great or small,—
Love (though she had a cursed taste for war,
　　And was not the best wife, unless we call
Such Clytemnestra; though perhaps 'tis better
That one should die, than two drag on the fetter)—

81

Love had made Catherine make each lover's fortune,
　　Unlike our own half-chaste Elizabeth,
Whose avarice all disbursemerts did importune,
　　If history, the grand liar, ever saith

The truth; and though grief her old age might shorten,
  Because she put a favourite to death,
Her vile, ambiguous method of flirtation,
And stinginess, disgrace her sex and station.

82

But when the levee rose, and all was bustle
  In the dissolving circle, all the nations'
Ambassadors began as 'twere to bustle
  Round the young man with their congratulations;
Also the softer silks were heard to rustle
  Of gentle dames, among whose recreations
It is to speculate on handsome faces,
Especially when such lead to high places.

83

Juan, who found himself, he knew not how,
  A general object of attention, made
His answers with a very graceful bow,
  As if born for the ministerial trade.
Though modest, on his unembarrass'd brow
  Nature had written "gentleman." He said
Little, but to the purpose; and his manner
Flung hovering graces o'er him like a banner.

*   *   *   *   *

CANTO X

*   *   *   *   *

69

Don Juan now saw Albion's earliest beauties—
  Thy cliffs, *dear* Dover! harbour, and hotel;
Thy custom-house with all its delicate duties;
  Thy waiters running mucks at every bell;
Thy packets, all whose passengers are booties
  To those who upon land or water dwell;
And last, not least, to strangers uninstructed,
Thy long, long bills, whence nothing is deducted.

70

Juan, though careless, young, and magnifique,
  And rich in rubles, diamonds, cash, and credit,
Who did not limit much his bills per week,
  Yet stared at this a little, though he paid it
(His *Maggior Duomo*, a smart subtle Greek,
  Before him summ'd the awful scroll and read it):
But doubtless as the air, though seldom sunny,
Is free, the respiration's worth the money.

71

On with the horses! Off to Canterbury!
  Tramp, tramp o'er pebble, and splash, splash through puddle,
Hurrah! how swiftly speeds the post so merry!
  Not like slow Germany, wherein they muddle
Along the road, as if they went to bury
  Their fare; and also pause, besides, to fuddle
With "schnapps"—sad dogs! whom "Hundsfot," or "Verflucter"
Affect no more than lightning a conductor.

72

Now there is nothing gives a man such spirits,
  Leavening his blood as Cayenne doth a curry,
As going at full speed—no matter where its
  Direction be, so 'tis but in a hurry,
And merely for the sake of its own merits:
  For the less cause there is for all this flurry,
The greater is the pleasure in arriving
At the great *end* of travel—which is driving.

73

They saw at Canterbury the cathedral;
  Black Edward's helm, and Becket's bloody stone,
Were pointed out as usual by the bedral,
  In the same quaint, uninterested tone:—
There's glory again for you, gentle reader! All
  Ends in a rusty casque and dubious bone,
Half-solved into those sodas or magnesias,
Which form that bitter draught, the human species.

74

The effect on Juan was of course sublime.
  He breathed a thousand Cressys, as he saw
That casque, which never stoop'd, except to Time.
  Even the bold churchman's tomb excited awe,
Who died in the then great attempt to climb
  O'er kings, who *now* at least *must talk* of law,
Before they butcher. Little Leila gazed,
And ask'd why such a structure had been raised.

* * * * *

CANTO XI

* * * * *

8

Don Juan had got out on Shooter's Hill;
  Sunset the time, the place the same declivity
Which looks along that vale of good and ill,
  Where London streets ferment in full activity;
While every thing around was calm and still,
  Except the creak of wheels, which on their pivot he
Heard,—and that bee-like, bubbling, busy hum
Of cities, that boil over with their scum:—

9

I say, Don Juan, rapt in contemplation,
  Walk'd on behind his carriage, o'er the summit,
And lost in wonder of so great a nation,
  Gave way to 't, since he could not overcome it.
"And here," he cried, "is Freedom's chosen station;
  Here peals the people's voice, nor can entomb it
Racks, prisons, inquisitions; resurrection
Awaits it, each new meeting or election.

10

"Here are chaste wives, pure lives; here people pay
    But what they please; and if that things be dear,
'Tis only that they love to throw away
    Their cash, to show how much they have a-year:
Here laws are all inviolate; none lay
    Traps for the traveller; every highway's clear:
Here—" he was interrupted by a knife,
With "Damn your eyes! your money or your life."

11

These freeborn sounds proceeded from four pads,
    In ambush laid, who had perceived him loiter
Behind his carriage; and, like handy lads,
    Had seized the lucky hour to reconnoitre,
In which the heedless gentleman who gads
    Upon the road, unless he prove a fighter,
May find himself, within that isle of riches,
Exposed to lose his life as well as breeches.

12

Juan, who did not understand a word
    Of English, save their shibboleth, "God damn!"
And even that he had so rarely heard,
    He sometimes thought 'twas only their "Salām,"
Or "God be with you!"—and 'tis not absurd
    To think so; for, half English as I am
(To my misfortune), never can I say
I heard them wish "God with you," save that way;—

13

Juan yet quickly understood their gesture,
    And, being somewhat choleric and sudden,
Drew forth a pocket-pistol from his vesture,
    And fired it into one assailant's pudding—
Who fell, as rolls an ox o'er in his pasture,
    And roar'd out, as he writhed his native mud in,
Unto his nearest follower or henchman,
"Oh Jack! I'm floor'd by that 'ere bloody Frenchman!"

14

On which Jack and his train set off at speed,
    And Juan's suite, late scatter'd at a distance,
Came up, all marvelling at such a deed,
    And offering, as usual, late assistance.
Juan, who saw the moon's late minion bleed
    As if his veins would pour out his existence,
Stood calling out for bandages and lint,
And wish'd he'd been less hasty with his flint.

15

"Perhaps," thought he, "it is the country's wont
    To welcome foreigners in this way: now
I recollect some innkeepers who don't
    Differ, except in robbing with a bow,
In lieu of a bare blade and brazen front.
    But what is to be done? I can't allow
The fellow to lie groaning on the road:
So take him up; I'll help you with the load."

16

But, ere they could perform this pious duty,
    The dying man cried, "Hold! I've got my gruel!
Oh! for a glass of *max!* We've miss'd our booty;
    Let me die where I am!" And, as the fuel
Of life shrunk in his heart, and thick and sooty
    The drops fell from his death-wound, and he drew ill
His breath, he from his swelling throat untied
A kerchief, crying "Give Sal that!"—and died.

17

The cravat stain'd with bloody drops fell down
    Before Don Juan's feet: he could not tell
Exactly why it was before him thrown,
    Nor what the meaning of the man's farewell.
Poor Tom was once a kiddy upon town,
    A thorough varmint, and a *real* swell
Full flash, all fancy, until fairly diddled—
His pockets first, and then his body riddled.

18

Don Juan, having done the best he could
    In all the circumstances of the case,
As soon as "Crowner's quest" allow'd, pursued
    His travels to the capital apace;—
Esteeming it a little hard he should
    In twelve hours' time, and very little space,
Have been obliged to slay a freeborn native
In self-defence: this made him meditative.

*   *   *   *   *

57

Sir Walter reign'd before me; Moore and Campbell
    Before and after; but now grown more holy,
The Muses upon Sion's hill must ramble
    With poets almost clergymen, or wholly;
And Pegasus hath a psalmodic amble
    Beneath the very Reverend Rowley Powley,
Who shoes the glorious animal with stilts,
A modern Ancient Pistol—by the hilts!

*   *   *   *   *

59

Then there's my gentle Euphues, who, they say
    Sets up for being a sort of *moral me*;
He'll find it rather difficult some day
    To turn out both, or either, it may be
Some persons think that Coleridge hath the sway;
    And Wordsworth has supporters, two or three;
And that deep-mouth'd Boeotian, "Savage Landor,"
Has taken for a swan, rogue Southey's gander.

60

John Keats—who was kill'd off by one critique
    Just as he really promised something great,
If not intelligible, without Greek
    Contrived to talk about the gods of late,

Much as they might have been supposed to speak.
    Poor fellow! His was an untoward fate:
'Tis strange the mind, that fiery particle,
Should let itself be snuff'd out by an article.

61

The list grows long of live and dead pretenders
    To that which none will gain—or none will know
The conqueror at least; who ere Time renders
    His last award, will have the long grass grow
Above his burnt-out brain and sapless cinders.
    If I might augur, I should rate but low
Their chances; they're too numerous, like the thirty
Mock tyrants, when Rome's annals wax'd but dirty.

62

This is the literary *lower* empire,
    Where the praetorian bands take up the matter;—
A "dreadful trade" like his who "gathers samphire,"
    The insolent soldiery to soothe and flatter,
With the same feelings as you'd coax a vampire.
    Now, were I once at home, and in good satire,
I'd try conclusions with those Janizaries,
And show them *what* an intellectual war is.

63

I think I know a trick or two would turn
    Their flanks;—but it is hardly worth my while
With such small gear to give myself concern:
    Indeed I've not the necessary bile;
My natural temper's really aught but stern,
    And even my Muse's worst reproof's a smile;
And then she drops a brief and modest curtsy,
And glides away, assured she never hurts ye.

64

My Juan, whom I left in deadly peril
    Amongst live poets and blue ladies, pass'd
With some small profit through that field so sterile.
    Being tired in time, and neither least nor last,

Left it before he had been treated very ill;
  And henceforth found himself more gaily class'd
Amongst the higher spirits of the day,
The sun's true son, no vapour, but a ray.

*   *   *   *   *

CANTO XII

1

OF all the barbarous middle ages, that
  Which is most barbarous is the middle age
Of man; it is—I really scarce know what;
  But when we hover between fool and sage,
  A period something like a printed page,
Black letter upon foolscap, while our hair
Grows grizzled, and we are not what we were;—

2

Too old for youth—too young, at thirty-five,
  To herd with boys, or hoard with good threescore,—
I wonder people should be left alive;
  But since they are, that epoch is a bore:
Love lingers still, although 'twere late to wive;
  And as for other love, the illusion's o'er;
And money, that most pure imagination,
Gleams only through the dawn of its creation.

3

Oh Gold! why call we misers miserable?
  Theirs is the pleasure that can never pall;
Theirs is the best bower anchor, the chain cable
  Which holds fast other pleasures great and small.
Ye who but see the saving man at table,
  And scorn his temperate board, as none at all,
And wonder how the wealthy can be sparing,
Know not what visions spring from each cheese-paring.

4

Love or lust makes man sick, and wine much sicker;
    Ambition rends, and gaming gains a loss;
But making money, slowly first, then quicker,
    And adding still a little through each cross
(Which *will* come over things), beats love or liquor,
    The gamester's counter, or the statesman's *dross.*
Oh Gold! I still prefer thee unto paper,
Which makes bank credit like a bark of vapour.

5

Who hold the balance of the world? Who reign
    O'er congress, whether royalist or liberal?
Who rouse the shirtless patriots of Spain?
    (That make old Europe's journals squeak and gibber all.)
Who keep the world, both old and new, in pain
    Or pleasure? Who make politics run glibber all?
The shade of Buonaparte's noble daring?—
Jew Rothschild, and his fellow-Christian Baring.

6

Those, and the truly liberal Lafitte,
    Are the true lords of Europe. Every loan
Is not a merely speculative hit,
    But seats a nation or upsets a throne.
Republics also get involved a bit;
    Columbia's stock hath holders not unknown
On 'Change; and even thy silver soil, Peru,
Must get itself discounted by a Jew.

7

Why call the miser miserable? as
    I said before: the frugal life is his,
Which in a saint or cynic ever was
    The theme of praise: a hermit would not miss
Canonization for the self-same cause,
    And wherefore blame gaunt wealth's austerities?
Because, you'll say, nought calls for such a trial;—
Then there's more merit in his self-denial.

8

He is your only poet;—passion, pure
    And sparkling on from heap to heap, displays,
Possess'd, the ore, of which *mere hopes* allure
    Nations athwart the deep: the golden rays
Flash up in ingots from the mine obscure;
    On him the diamond pours its brilliant blaze,
While the mild emerald's beam shades down the dies
Of other stones, to soothe the miser's eyes.

9

The lands on either side are his; the ship
    From Ceylon, Inde, or far Cathay, unloads
For him the fragrant produce of each trip;
    Beneath his cars of Ceres groan the roads,
And the vine blushes like Aurora's lip;
    His very cellars might be kings' abodes,
While he, despising every sensual call,
Commands—the intellectual lord of all.

10

Perhaps he hath great projects in his mind,
    To build a college, or to found a race,
A hospital, a church,—and leave behind
    Some dome surmounted by his meagre face:
Perhaps he fain would liberate mankind
    Even with the very ore which makes them base;
Perhaps he would be wealthiest of his nation,
Or revel in the joys of calculation.

11

But whether all, or each, or none of these,
    May be the hoarder's principle of action,
The fool will call such mania a disease:—
    What is his *own?* Go—look at each transaction,
Wars, revels, loves—do these bring men more ease
    Than the mere plodding through each "vulgar fraction?"
Or do they benefit mankind? Lean miser!
Let spendthrifts' heirs inquire of yours—who's wiser?

12

How beauteous are rouleaus! how charming chests
　Containing ingots, bags of dollars, coins,
Not of old victors (all whose heads and crests
　Weigh not the thin ore where their visage shines,
But) of fine unclipp'd gold, where dully rests
　Some likeness which the glittering cirque confines,
Of modern, reigning, sterling, stupid stamp:—
Yes! ready money *is* Aladdin's lamp.

13

"Love rules the camp, the court, the grove,"—"for love
　Is heaven, and heaven is love:"—so sings the bard;
Which it were rather difficult to prove
　(A thing with poetry in general hard).
Perhaps there may be something in "the grove,"
　At least it rhymes to "love;" but I'm prepared
To doubt (no less than landlords of their rental)
If "courts" and "camps" be quite so sentimental.

14

But if Love don't, *Cash* does, and Cash alone:
　Cash rules the grove, and fells it too besides;
Without cash, camps were thin, and courts were none;
　Without cash, Malthus tells you—"take no brides."
So Cash rules Love the ruler, on his own
　High ground, as Virgin Cynthia sways the tides;
And, as for "Heaven being Love," why not say honey
Is wax? Heaven is not Love, 'tis Matrimony.

15

Is not all love prohibited whatever,
　Excepting marriage? which is love, no doubt,
After a sort; but somehow people never
　With the same thought the two words have help'd out:

Love may exist *with* marriage, and *should* ever,
   And marriage also may exist without;
But love *sans* bans is both a sin and shame,
And ought to go by quite another name.

*   *   *   *   *

CANTO XIV

*   *   *   *   *

4

A sleep without dreams, after a rough day
   Of toil, is what we covet most; and yet
How clay shrinks back from more quiescent clay!
   The very Suicide that pays his debt
At once without instalments (an old way
   Of paying debts, which creditors regret)
Lets out impatiently his rushing breath,
Less from disgust of life than dread of death.

5

'Tis round him, near him, here, there, everywhere;
   And there's a courage which grows out of fear,
Perhaps of all most desperate, which will dare
   The worst to *know* it:—when the mountains rear
Their peaks beneath your human foot, and there
   You look down o'er the precipice, and drear
The gulf of rock yawns,—you can't gaze a minute
Without an awful wish to plunge within it.

6

'Tis true, you don't—but, pale and struck with terror,
   Retire: but look into your past impression!
And you will find, though shuddering at the mirror
   Of your own thoughts, in all their self-confession,

The lurking bias, be it truth or error,
  To the *unknown*; a secret prepossession,
To plunge with all your fears—but where? You know not,
And that's the reason why you do—or do not.

*   *   *   *   *

12

I think that were I *certain* of success,
  I hardly could compose another line:
So long I've battled either more or less,
  That no defeat can drive me from the Nine.
This feeling 'tis not easy to express,
  And yet 'tis not affected, I opine.
In play, there are two pleasures for your choosing—
The one is winning, and the other losing.

13

Besides, my Muse by no means deals in fiction:
  She gathers a repertory of facts,
Of course with some reserve and slight restriction,
  But mostly sings of human things and acts—
And that's one cause she meets with contradiction;
  For too much truth, at first sight, ne'er attracts;
And were her object only what's call'd glory,
With more ease too, she'd tell a different story.

14

Love, war, a tempest—surely there's variety;
  Also a seasoning slight of lucubration;
A bird's-eye view too of that wild, Society;
  A slight glance thrown on men of every station.
If you have nought else, here's at least satiety
  Both in performance and in preparation;
And though these lines should only line portmanteaus
Trade will be all the better for these Cantos.

15

The portion of this world which I at present
  Have taken up to fill the following sermon,
Is one of which there's no description recent.
  The reason why, is easy to determine:
Although it seems both prominent and pleasant,
  There is a sameness in its gems and ermine,
A dull and family likeness through all ages,
Of no great promise for poetic pages.

16

With much to excite, there's little to exalt;
  Nothing that speaks to all men and all times;
A sort of varnish over every fault;
  A kind of common-place, even in their crimes;
Factitious passions, wit without much salt,
  A want of that true nature which sublimes
Whate'er it shows with truth; a smooth monotony
Of character, in those at least who have got any.

17

Sometimes, indeed, like soldiers off parade,
  They break their ranks and gladly leave the drill;
But then the roll-call draws them back afraid,
  And they must be or seem what they were: still
Doubtless it is a brilliant masquerade;
  But when of the first sight you've had your fill,
It palls—at least it did so upon me,
This paradise of pleasure and *ennui*.

18

When we have made our love, and gamed our gaming,
  Dress'd, voted, shone, and, may be, something more;
With dandies dined; heard senators declaiming;
  Seen beauties brought to market by the score;
Sad rakes to sadder husbands chastely taming;
  There's little left but to be bored or bore.
Witness those *"ci-devant jeunes hommes"* who stem
The stream, nor leave the world which leaveth them.

19

'Tis said—indeed a general complaint—
    That no one has succeeded in describing
The monde exactly as they ought to paint:
    Some say, that authors only snatch, by bribing
The porter, some slight scandals strange and quaint
    To furnish matter for their moral gibing;
And that their books have but one style in common—
My lady's prattle, filter'd through her woman.

20

But this can't well be true, just now; for writers
    Are grown of the beau monde a part potential:
I've seen them balance even the scale with fighters,
    Especially when young, for that's essential.
Why do their sketches fail them as inditers
    Of what they deem themselves most consequential,
The *real* portrait of the highest tribe?
'Tis that, in fact, there's little to describe.

*   *   *   *   *

80

I do declare, upon an affidavit,
    Romances I ne'er read like those I've seen;
Nor, if unto the world I ever gave it,
    Would some believe that such a tale had been:
But such intent I never had, nor have it;
    Some truths are better kept behind a screen,
Especially when they would look like lies;
I therefore deal in generalities.

*   *   *   *   *

94

Love bears within its breast the very germ
    Of change; and how should this be otherwise?
That violent things more quickly find a term
    Is shown through nature's whole analogies;

And how should the most fierce of all be firm?
    Would you have endless lightning in the skies?
Methinks Love's very title says enough:
How should "the *tender* passion" e'er be *tough?*

95

Alas! by all experience, seldom yet
    (I merely quote what I have heard from many)
Had lovers not some reason to regret
    The passion which made Solomon a zany.
I've also seen some wives (not to forget
    The marriage state, the best or worst of any)
Who were the very paragons of wives,
Yet made the misery of at least two lives.

96

I've also seen some female *friends* ('tis odd,
    But true—as, if expedient, I could prove)
That faithful were, through thick and thin, abroad,
    At home, far more than ever yet was Love—
Who did not quit me when Oppression trod
    Upon me; whom no scandal could remove;
Who fought, and fight, in absence too, my battles,
Despite the snake Society's loud rattles.

*   *   *   *   *

101

'Tis strange—but true; for truth is always strange,
    Stranger than fiction: if it could be told,
How much would novels gain by the exchange!
    How differently the world would men behold!
How oft would vice and virtue places change!
    The new world would be nothing to the old,
If some Columbus of the moral seas
Would show mankind their souls' antipodes.

102

What "antres vast and deserts idle" then
  Would be discover'd in the human soul!
What icebergs in the hearts of mighty men,
  With self-love in the centre as their pole!
What Anthropophagi are nine of ten
  Of those who hold the kingdoms in control!
Were things but only call'd by their right name,
Caesar himself would be ashamed of fame.

CANTO XV

*   *   *   *   *

10

Fair Adeline, the more ingenuous
  Where she was interested (as was said),
Because she was not apt, like some of us,
  To like too readily, or too high bred
To show it (points we need not now discuss)
  Would give up artlessly both heart and head
Unto such feelings as seem'd innocent
For objects worthy of the sentiment.

11

Some parts of Juan's history, which Rumour,
  That live gazette, had scatter'd to disfigure,
She had heard; but women hear with more good humour
  Such aberrations than we men of rigour.
Besides, his conduct, since in England, grew more
  Strict, and his mind assumed a manlier vigour;
Because he had, like Alcibiades,
The art of living in all climes with ease.

12

His manner was perhaps the more seductive,
  Because he ne'er seem'd anxious to seduce;
Nothing affected, studied, or constructive
  Of coxcombry or conquest: no abuse
Of his attractions marr'd the fair perspective,
  To indicate a Cupidon broke loose,
And seem to say, "Resist us if you can"—
Which makes a dandy while it spoils a man.

13

They are wrong—that's not the way to set about it;
  As, if they told the truth, could well be shown.
But, right or wrong, Don Juan was without it;
  In fact, his manner was his own alone:
Sincere he was—at least you could not doubt it,
  In listening merely to his voice's tone.
The devil hath not in all his quiver's choice
An arrow for the heart like a sweet voice.

14

By nature soft, his whole address held off
  Suspicion: though not timid, his regard
Was such as rather seem'd to keep aloof,
  To shield himself, than put you on your guard:
Perhaps, 'twas hardly quite assured enough,
  But modesty's at times its own reward,
Like virtue; and the absence of pretension
Will go much farther than there's need to mention.

15

Serene, accomplish'd, cheerful, but not loud;
  Insinuating without insinuation;
Observant of the foibles of the crowd,
  Yet ne'er betraying this in conversation!
Proud with the proud, yet courteously proud,
  So as to make them feel he knew his station
And theirs:—without a struggle for priority,
He neither brook'd nor claim'd superiority.

16

That is, with men: with women he was what
    They pleased to make or take him for; and their
Imagination's quite enough for that;
    So that the outline's tolerably fair.
They fill the canvass up—and "verbum sat."
    If once their phantasies be brought to bear
Upon an object, whether sad or playful,
They can transfigure brighter than a Raphael.

17

Adeline, no deep judge of character,
    Was apt to add a colouring from her own:
'Tis thus the good will amiably err,
    And eke the wise, as has been often shown.
Experience is the chief philosopher,
    But saddest when his science is well known:
And persecuted sages teach the schools
Their folly in forgetting there are fools.

*   *   *   *   *

28

When Adeline, in all her growing sense
    Of Juan's merits and his situation,
Felt on the whole an interest intense—
    Partly perhaps because a fresh sensation,
Or that he had an air of innocence,
    Which is for innocence a sad temptation,—
As women hate half measures, on the whole,
She 'gan to ponder how to save his soul.

*   *   *   *   *

30

Juan replied, with all becoming deference,
    He had a predilection for that *tie;*
But that at present, with immediate reference
    To his own circumstances, there might lie

Some difficulties, as in his own preference,
    Or that of her to whom he might apply;
That still he'd wed with such or such a lady,
If that they were not married all already.

*   *   *   *   *

48

Now it so happen'd, in the catalogue
    Of Adeline, Aurora was omitted,
Although her birth and wealth had given her vogue
    Beyond the charmers we've already cited:
Her beauty also seem'd to form no clog
    Against her being mention'd as well fitted,
By many virtues, to be worth the trouble
Of single gentlemen who would be double.

49

And this omission, like that of the bust
    Of Brutus at the pageant of Tiberius,
Made Juan wonder, as no doubt he must.
    This he express'd half smiling and half serious;
When Adeline replied, with some disgust,
    And with an air, to say the least, imperious,
She marvell'd "what he saw in such a baby
As that prim, silent, cold Aurora Raby!"

50

Juan rejoin'd—"She was a Catholic,
    And therefore fittest, as of his persuasion;
Since he was sure his mother would fall sick
    And the Pope thunder excommunication,
If—" But here Adeline, who seem'd to pique
    Herself extremely on the inoculation
Of others with her own opinions, stated—
As usual—the same reason which she late did.

51

And wherefore not? A reasonable reason,
  If good, is none the worse for repetition;
If bad, the best way's certainly to tease on
  And amplify; you lose much by concision;
Whereas insisting in or out of season
  Convinces all men, even a politician,
Or—what is just the same—it wearies out.
So the end's gain'd, what signifies the route?

52

Why Adeline had this slight prejudice—
  For prejudice it was—against a creature
As pure as sanctity itself from vice,
  With all the added charm of form and feature,
For me appears a question far too nice,
  Since Adeline was liberal by nature;
But nature's nature, and has more caprices
Than I have time, or will, to take to pieces.

53

Perhaps she did not like the quiet way
  With which Aurora on those baubles look'd,
Which charm most people in their earlier day:
  For there are few things by mankind less brook'd,
And womankind too, if we so may say,
  Than finding thus their genius stand rebuked,
Like "Anthony's by Caesar," by the few
Who look upon them as they ought to do.

54

It was not envy—Adeline had none;
  Her place was far beyond it, and her mind.
It was not scorn—which could not light on one
  Whose greatest fault was leaving few to find.
It was not jealousy, I think: but shun
  Following the "ignes fatui" of mankind.
It was not—but 'tis easier far, alas!
To say what it was not, than what it was.

55

Little Aurora deem'd she was the theme
    Of such discussion. She was there a guest;
A beauteous ripple of the brilliant stream
    Of rank and youth, though purer than the rest,
Which flow'd on for a moment in the beam
    Time sheds a moment o'er each sparkling crest.
Had she known this, she would have calmly smiled—
She had so much, or little, of the child.

56

The dashing and proud air of Adeline
    Imposed not upon her: she saw her blaze
Much as she would have seen a glow-worm shine,
    Then turn'd unto the stars for loftier rays.
Juan was something she could not divine,
    Being no sibyl in the new world's ways;
Yet she was nothing dazzled by the meteor,
Because she did not pin her faith on feature.

57

His fame too,—for he had that kind of fame
    Which sometimes plays the deuce with womankind,
A heterogenous mass of glorious blame,
    Half virtues and whole vices being combined;
Faults which attract because they are not tame;
    Follies trick'd out so brightly that they blind:—
These seals upon her wax made no impression,
Such was her coldness or her self-possession.

58

Juan knew nought of such a character—
    High, yet resembling not his lost Haidée;
Yet each was radiant in her proper sphere:
    The island girl, bred up by the lone sea,

More warm, as lovely, and not less sincere,
  Was Nature's all: Aurora could not be,
Nor would be thus;—the difference in them
Was such as lies between a flower and gem.

*   *   *   *   *

61

The conference or congress (for it ended
  As congresses of late do) of the Lady
Adeline and Don Juan rather blended
  Some acids with the sweets—for she was heady;
But, ere the matter could be marr'd or mended,
  The silvery bell rung, not for "dinner ready,"
But for that hour, call'd *half-hour*, given to dress,
Though ladies' robes seem scant enough for less.

62

Great things were now to be achieved at table,
  With massy plate for armour, knives and forks
For weapons; but what Muse since Homer's able
  (His feasts are not the worst part of his works)
To draw up in array a single day-bill
  Of modern dinners? where more mystery lurks
In soups or sauces, or a sole ragoût,
Than witches, b—ches, or physicians, brew.

63

There was a goodly "soupe à la *bonne femme*,"
  Though God knows whence it came from; there was too
A turbot for relief of those who cram,
  Relieved with "dindon à la Périgueux;"
There also was——the sinner that I am!
  How shall I get this gourmand stanza through?
"Soupe à la Beauveau," whose relief was dory,
Relieved itself by pork, for greater glory.

64

But I must crowd all into one grand mess
    Or mass; for should I stretch into detail,
My Muse would run much more into excess,
    Than when some squeamish people deem her frail.
But, though a "bonne vivante," I must confess
    Her stomach's not her peccant part; this tale
However doth require some slight refection,
Just to relieve her spirits from dejection.

65

Fowls "à la Condé," slices eke of salmon,
    With "sauces Génévoises," and haunch of venison;
Wines too, which might again have slain young Ammon—
    A man like whom I hope we shan't see many soon;
They also set a glazed Westphalian ham on,
    Whereon Apicius would bestow his benison;
And then there was champagne with foaming whirls,
As white as Cleopatra's melted pearls.

66

Then there was God knows what "à l'Allemande,"
    "A l'Espagnole," "timballe," and "salpicon"—
With things I can't withstand or understand,
    Though swallow'd with much zest upon the whole;
And "entremets" to piddle with at hand,
    Gently to lull down the subsiding soul;
While great Lucullus' *Rome triumphal* muffles
(*There's fame*) young partridge fillets, deck'd with truffles.

67

What are the *fillets* on the victor's brow
    To these? They are rags or dust. Where is the arch
Which nodded to the nation's spoils below?
    Where the triumphal chariot's haughty march?
Gone to where victories must like dinners go.
    Further I shall not follow the research:
But oh! ye modern heroes with your cartridges,
When will your names lend lustre e'en to partridges?

68

Those truffles too are no bad accessaries,
　Follow'd by "petits puits d'amour"—a dish
Of which perhaps the cookery rather varies,
　So every one may dress it to his wish,
According to the best of dictionaries,
　Which encyclopedise both flesh and fish;
But even sans "confitures," it no less true is,
There's pretty picking in those "petits puits."

69

The mind is lost in mighty contemplation
　Of intellect expanded on two courses;
And indigestion's grand multiplication
　Requires arithmetic beyond my forces.
Who would suppose, from Adam's simple ration,
　That cookery could have call'd forth such resources,
As form a science and a nomenclature
From out the commonest demands of nature?

70

The glasses jingled, and the palates tingled;
　The diners of celebrity dined well;
The ladies with more moderation mingled
　In the feast, pecking less than I can tell;
Also the younger men too; for a springald
　Can't, like ripe age, in gormandise excel,
But thinks less of good eating than the whisper
(When seated next him) of some pretty lisper.

71

Alas! I must leave undescribed the gibier,
　The salmi, the consommé, the purée,
All which I use to make my rhymes run glibber
　Than could roast beef in our rough John Bull way:
I must not introduce even a spare rib here,
　"Bubble and squeak" would spoil my liquid lay;
But I have dined, and must forego, alas!
The chaste description e'en of a "bécasse."

72

And fruits, and ice, and all that art refines
　　From nature for the service of the *goût*—
Taste or the *gout*,—pronounce it as inclines
　　Your stomach. Ere you dine, the French will do;
But *after*, there are sometimes certain signs
　　Which prove plain English truer of the two.
Hast ever *had* the gout? I have not had it—
But I may have, and you too, reader, dread it.

73

The simple olives, best allies of wine,
　　Must I pass over in my bill of fare?
I must, although a favourite "plat" of mine
　　In Spain, and Lucca, Athens, everywhere:
On them and bread 'twas oft my luck to dine,
　　The grass my table-cloth, in open air,
On Sunium or Hymettus, like Diogenes,
Of whom half my philosophy the progeny is.

74

Amidst this tumult of fish, flesh, and fowl,
　　And vegetables, all in masquerade,
The guests were placed according to their roll,
　　But various as the various meats display'd:
Don Juan sate next an "à l'Espagnole"—
　　No damsel, but a dish, as hath been said;
But so far like a lady, that 'twas drest
Superbly, and contain'd a world of zest.

75

By some odd chance too, he was placed between
　　Aurora and the Lady Adeline—
A situation difficult, I ween,
　　For man therein, with eyes and heart, to dine.
Also the conference which we have seen
　　Was not such as to encourage him to shine;
For Adeline, addressing few words to him,
With two transcendent eyes seem'd to look through him.

76

I sometimes almost think that eyes have ears:
    This much is sure, that, out of earshot, things
Are somehow echoed to the pretty dears,
    Of which I can't tell whence their knowledge springs.
Like that same mystic music of the spheres,
    Which no one hears so loudly though it rings.
'Tis wonderful how oft the sex have heard
Long dialogues which pass'd without a word!

77

Aurora sat with that indifference
    Which piques a preux chevalier—as it ought:
Of all offences that's the worst offence,
    Which seems to hint you are not worth a thought.
Now Juan, though no coxcomb in pretence,
    Was not exactly pleased to be so caught;
Like a good ship entangled among ice,
And after so much excellent advice.

78

To his gay nothings, nothing was replied,
    Or something which was nothing, as urbanity
Required. Aurora scarcely look'd aside,
    Nor even smiled enough for any vanity.
The devil was in the girl! Could it be pride,
    Or modesty, or absence, or inanity?
Heaven knows! But Adeline's malicious eyes
Sparkled with her successful prophecies,

79

And look'd as much as if to say, "I said it;"
    A kind of triumph I'll not recommend,
Because it sometimes, as I've seen or read it,
    Both in the case of lover and of friend,
Will pique a gentleman, for his own credit,
    To bring what was a jest to a serious end;
For all men prophesy what *is* or *was*,
And hate those who won't let them come to pass.

80

Juan was drawn thus into some attentions,
    Slight but select, and just enough to express,
To females of perspicuous comprehensions,
    That he would rather make them more than less.
Aurora at the last (so history mentions,
    Though probably much less a fact than guess)
So far relax'd her thoughts from their sweet prison,
As once or twice to smile, if not to listen.

81

From answering, she began to question; this
    With her was rare: and Adeline, who as yet
Thought her predictions went not much amiss,
    Began to dread she'd thaw to a coquette—
So very difficult, they say, it is
    To keep extremes from meeting, when once set
In motion; but she here too much refined—
Aurora's spirit was not of that kind.

82

But Juan had a sort of winning way,
    A proud humility, if such there be,
Which show'd such deference to what females say,
    As if each charming word were a decree.
His tact too temper'd him from grave to gay,
    And taught him when to be reserved or free:
He had the art of drawing people out,
Without their seeing what he was about.

83

Aurora, who in her indifference
    Confounded him in common with the crowd
Of flutterers, though she deem'd he had more sense
    Than whispering foplings, or than witlings loud,—

Commenced (from such slight things will great commence)
  To feel that flattery which attracts the proud
Rather by deference than compliment,
  And wins even by a delicate dissent.

*　　*　　*　　*　　*

85

Aurora, who look'd more on books than faces,
  Was very young, although so very sage,
Admiring more Minerva than the Graces,
  Especially upon a printed page.
But Virtue's self, with all her tightest laces,
  Has not the natural stays of strict old age;
And Socrates, that model of all duty,
Own'd to a penchant, though discreet, for beauty.

86

And girls of sixteen are thus far Socratic,
  But innocently so, as Socrates;
And really, if the sage sublime and Attic
  At seventy years had phantasies like these,
Which Plato in his dialogues dramatic
  Has shown, I know not why they should displease
In virgins—always in a modest way,
Observe; for that with me's a "sine quâ."

*　　*　　*　　*　　*

99

Between two worlds life hovers like a star,
  'Twixt night and morn, upon the horizon's verge.
How little do we know that which we are!
  How less what we may be! The eternal surge
Of time and tide rolls on, and bears afar
  Our bubbles; as the old burst, new emerge,
Lash'd from the foam of ages; while the graves
Of empires heave but like some passing waves.

CANTO XVI

*   *   *   *   *

7

I merely mean to say what Johnson said,
    That in the course of some six thousand years,
All nations have believed that from the dead
    A visitant at intervals appears;
And what is strangest upon this strange head,
    Is, that whatever bar the reason rears
'Gainst such belief, there's something stronger still
In its behalf, let those deny who will.

*   *   *   *   *

48

Aurora—since we are touching upon taste,
    Which now-a-days is the thermometer
By whose degrees all characters are class'd—
    Was more Shakspearian, if I do not err.
The worlds beyond this world's perplexing waste
    Had more of her existence, for in her
There was a depth of feeling to embrace
Thoughts, boundless, deep, but silent too as Space.

49

Not so her gracious, graceful, graceless Grace,
    The full-grown Hebe of Fitz-Fulke, whose mind,
If she had any, was upon her face,
    And that was of a fascinating kind.
A little turn for mischief you might trace
    Also thereon,—but that's not much; we find
Few females without some such gentle leaven,
For fear we should suppose us quite in heaven.

50

I have not heard she was at all poetic,
    Though once she was seen reading the "Bath Guide,"
And "Hayley's Triumphs," which she deem'd pathetic,
    Because, she said, *her temper* had been tried
So much, the bard had really been prophetic
    Of what she had gone through with—since a bride.
But of all verse, what most insured her praise
Were sonnets to herself, or "bouts rimés."

51

'Twere difficult to say what was the object
    Of Adeline, in bringing this same lay
To bear on what appear'd to her the subject
    Of Juan's nervous feelings on that day.
Perhaps she merely had the simple project
    To laugh him out of his supposed dismay;
Perhaps she might wish to confirm him in it,
Though why I cannot say—at least this minute.

52

But so far the immediate effect
    Was to restore him to his self-propriety,
A thing quite necessary to the elect,
    Who wish to take the tone of their society:
In which you cannot be too circumspect,
    Whether the mode be persiflage or piety,
But wear the newest mantle of hypocrisy,
On pain of much displeasing the gynocracy.

53

And therefore Juan now began to rally
    His spirits, and, without more explanation,
To jest upon such themes in many a sally.
    Her Grace, too, also seized the same occasion,
With various similar remarks to tally,
    But wish'd for a still more detail'd narration
Of this same mystic friar's curious doings,
About the present family's deaths and wooings.

54

Of these few could say more than has been said;
    They pass'd, as such things do, for superstition
With some, while others, who had more in dread
    The theme, half credited the strange tradition;
And much was talk'd on all sides on that head:
    But Juan, when cross-question'd on the vision,
Which some supposed (though he had not avow'd it)
Had stirr'd him, answer'd in a way to cloud it.

55

And then, the mid-day having worn to one,
    The company prepared to separate;
Some to their several pastimes, or to none,
    Some wondering 'twas so early, some so late.
There was a goodly match, too, to be run
    Between some greyhounds on my lord's estate,
And a young race-horse of old pedigree,
Match'd for the spring, whom several went to see.

56

There was a picture-dealer who had brought
    A special Titian, warranted original,
So precious that it was not to be bought,
    Though princes the possessor were besieging all.
The king himself had cheapen'd it, but thought
    The civil list he deigns to accept (obliging all
His subjects by his gracious acceptation)—
Too scanty, in these times of low taxation.

57

But as Lord Henry was a connoisseur,—
    The friend of artists, if not arts,—the owner,
With motives the most classical and pure,
    So that he would have been the very donor,
Rather than seller, had his wants been fewer,
    So much he deem'd his patronage an honour,
Had brought the *capo d'opera*, not for sale,
But for his judgment—never known to fail.

58

There was a modern Goth, I mean a Gothic
   Bricklayer of Babel, call'd an architect,
Brought to survey these grey walls, which though so thick
   Might have from time acquired some slight defect;
Who, after rummaging the abbey through thick
   And thin, produced a plan, whereby to erect
New buildings of correctest conformation,
And throw down old, which he call'd *restoration*.

59

The cost would be a trifle—an "old song."
   Set to some thousands ('tis the usual burden
Of that same tune, when people hum it long)—
   The price would speedily repay its worth in
An edifice no less sublime than strong,
   By which Lord Henry's good taste would go forth in
Its glory, through all ages shining sunny,
For Gothic daring shown in English money.

60

There were two lawyers busy on a mortgage
   Lord Henry wish'd to raise for a new purchase;
Also a lawsuit upon tenures burgage,
   And one on tithes which sure are Discord's torches,
Kindling Religion till she throws down *her* gage,
   "Untying" squires "to fight against the churches;"
There was a prize ox, a prize pig, and ploughman,
For Henry was a sort of Sabine showman.

61

There were two poachers caught in a steel trap,
   Ready for gaol, their place of convalescence;
There was a country girl in a close cap
   And scarlet cloak (I hate the sight to see, since—
Since—since—in youth I had the sad mishap—
   But luckily I've paid few parish fees since):
That scarlet cloak, alas! unclosed with rigour,
Presents the problem of a double figure.

62

A reel within a bottle is a mystery,
  One can't tell how it e'er got in or out,
Therefore the present piece of natural history
  I leave to those who are fond of solving doubt,
And merely state, though not for the consistory,
  Lord Henry was a justice, and that Scout
The constable, beneath a warrant's banner,
Had bagg'd this poacher upon Nature's manor.

*   *   *   *   *

78

But I'm too late, and therefore must make play,
  'Twas a great banquet, such as Albion old
Was wont to boast—as if a glutton's tray
  Were something very glorious to behold.
But 'twas a public feast and public day,—
  Quite full, right dull, guests hot, and dishes cold,
Great plenty, much formality, small cheer,
And everybody out of their own sphere.

79

The squires familiarly formal, and
  My lords and ladies proudly condescending;
The very servants, puzzling how to hand
  Their plates—without it might be too much bending
From their high places by the sideboard's stand—
  Yet, like their masters, fearful of offending.
For any deviation from the graces
Might cost both man and master too—their *places*.

80

There were some hunters bold, and coursers keen,
  Whose hounds ne'er err'd, nor greyhounds deign'd to lurch;
Some deadly shots too, Septembrizers, seen
  Earliest to rise, and last to quit the search

Of the poor partridge through his stubble screen.
    There were some massy members of the church,
Takers of tithes, and makers of good matches,
And several who sung fewer psalms than catches.

81

There were some country wags too—and alas!
    Some exiles from the town, who had been driven
To gaze, instead of pavement, upon grass,
    And rise at nine in lieu of long eleven.
And lo! upon that day it came to pass,
    I sate next that o'erwhelming son of Heaven,
The very powerful parson, Peter Pith,
The loudest wit I e'er was deafen'd with.

82

I knew him in his livelier London days,
    A brilliant diner out, though but a curate;
And not a joke he cut but earn'd its praise,
    Until preferment, coming at a sure rate,
(Oh, Providence! how wondrous are thy ways,
    Who would suppose thy gifts sometimes obdurate?)
Gave him, to lay the devil who looks o'er Lincoln,
A fat fen vicarage, and nought to think on.

83

His jokes were sermons, and his sermons jokes;
    But both were thrown away amongst the fens;
For wit hath no great friend in aguish folks.
    No longer ready ears and short-hand pens
Imbibed the gay bon mot, or happy hoax:
    The poor priest was reduced to common sense,
Or to coarse efforts very loud and long,
To hammer a hoarse laugh from the thick throng.

84

There *is* a difference, says the song, "between
    A beggar and a queen," or *was* (of late
The latter worse used of the two we've seen—
    But we'll say nothing of affairs of state);

A difference " 'twixt a bishop and a dean,"
  A difference between crockery-ware and plate,
As between English beef and Spartan broth—
  And yet great heroes have been bred by both.

85

But of all nature's discrepancies, none
  Upon the whole is greater than the difference
Beheld between the country and the town,
  Of which the latter merits every preference
From those who've few resources of their own,
  And only think, or act, or feel, with reference
To some small plan of interest or ambition—
But which are limited to no condition.

*   *   *   *   *

100

While Adeline dispensed her airs and graces,
  The fair Fitz-Fulke seem'd very much at ease;
Though too well-bred to quiz men to their faces,
  Her laughing blue eyes with a glance could seize
The ridicules of people in all places—
  That honey of your fashionable bees—
And store it up for mischievous enjoyment;
And this at present was her kind employment.

*   *   *   *   *

110

And full of sentiments, sublime as billows
  Heaving between this world and worlds beyond,
Don Juan, when the midnight hour of pillows
  Arrived, retired to his; but to despond
Rather than rest. Instead of poppies, willows
  Waved o'er his couch; he meditated, fond
Of those sweet bitter thoughts which banish sleep,
And make the worldling sneer, the youngling weep.

111

The night was as before: he was undrest,
    Saving his night-gown, which is an undress;
Completely "sans culotte," and without vest;
    In short, he hardly could be clothed with less;
But apprehensive of his spectral guest,
    He sate, with feelings awkward to express
(By those who have not had such visitations),
Expectant of the ghost's fresh operations.

112

And not in vain he listen'd;—Hush! what's that?
    I see—I see—Ah, no!—'tis not—yet 'tis—
Ye powers! it is the—the—the—Pooh! the cat!
    The devil may take that stealthy pace of his!
So like a spiritual pit-a-pat,
    Or tiptoe of an amatory Miss,
Gliding the first time to a rendezvous,
And dreading the chaste echoes of her shoe.

113

Again—what is 't? The wind? No, no,—this time
    It is the sable Friar as before,
With awful footsteps, regular as rhyme,
    Or (as rhymes may be in these days) much more.
Again through shadows of the night sublime,
    When deep sleep fell on men, and the world wore
The starry darkness round her like a girdle
Spangled with gems—the monk made his blood curdle.

114

A noise like to wet fingers drawn on glass,
    Which sets the teeth on edge; and a slight clatter,
Like showers which on the midnight gusts will pass,
    Sounding like very supernatural water,
Came over Juan's ear, which throbb'd, alas!
    For immaterialism's a serious matter;
So that even those whose faith is the most great
In souls immortal, shun them tête-à-tête.

115

Were his eyes open?—Yes! and his mouth too.
    Surprise has this effect—to make one dumb,
Yet leave the gate which eloquence slips through
    As wide as if a long speech were to come.
Nigh and more nigh the awful echoes drew,
    Tremendous to a mortal tympanum:
His eyes were open, and (as was before
Stated) his mouth. What open'd next?—the door.

116

It open'd with a most infernal creak,
    Like that of hell. "Lasciate ogni speranza,
Voi che entrate!" The hinge seem'd to speak,
    Dreadful as Dante's *rima*, or this stanza;
Or—but all words upon such themes are weak:
    A single shade's sufficient to entrance a
Hero—for what is substance to a spirit?
Or how is 't *matter* trembles to come near it?

117

The door flew wide,—not swiftly, but, as fly
    The sea-gulls, with a steady, sober flight—
And then swung back; nor close—but stood awry,
    Half letting in long shadows on the light,
Which still in Juan's candlesticks burn'd high,
    For he had two, both tolerably bright,—
And in the door-way, darkening darkness, stood
The sable Friar in his solemn hood.

118

Don Juan shook, as erst he had been shaken
    The night before; but, being sick of shaking,
He first inclined to think he had been mistaken;
    And then to be ashamed of such mistaking;
His own internal ghost began to awaken
    Within him, and to quell his corporal quaking—
Hinting that soul and body on the whole
Were odds against a disembodied soul.

119

And then his dread grew wrath, and his wrath fierce;
    And he arose, advanced—the shade retreated;
But Juan, eager now the truth to pierce,
    Follow'd, his veins no longer cold, but heated,
Resolved to thrust the mystery *carte* and *tierce*,
    At whatsoever risk of being defeated:
The ghost stopp'd, menaced, then retired, until
He reach'd the ancient wall, then stood stone still.

120

Juan put forth one arm—Eternal powers!
    It touch'd no soul, nor body, but the wall,
On which the moonbeams fell in silvery showers,
    Chequer'd with all the tracery of the hall;
He shudder'd, as no doubt the bravest cowers
    When he can't tell what 'tis that doth appal.
How odd, a single hobgoblin's non-entity
Should cause more fear than a whole host's identity!

121

But still the shade remain'd: the blue eyes glared,
    And rather variably for stony death:
Yet one thing rather good the grave had spared,
    The ghost had a remarkably sweet breath.
A straggling curl show'd he had been fair-hair'd;
    A red lip, with two rows of pearl beneath,
Gleam'd forth, as through the casement's ivy shroud
The moon peep'd, just escaped from a grey cloud.

122

And Juan, puzzled, but still curious, thrust
    His other arm forth—Wonder upon wonder!
It press'd upon a hard but glowing bust,
    Which beat as if there was a warm heart under.
He found, as people on most trials must,
    That he had made at first a silly blunder,
And that in his confusion he had caught
Only the wall instead of what he sought.

123

The ghost, if ghost it were, seem'd a sweet soul,
　　As ever lurk'd beneath a holy hood:
A dimpled chin, a neck of ivory, stole
　　Forth into something much like flesh and blood;
Back fell the sable frock and dreary cowl,
　　And they reveal'd—alas! that e'er they should!
In full, voluptuous, but *not o'er*grown bulk,
The phantom of her frolic Grace—Fitz-Fulke!

(The manuscript ends unfinished at this point.)

1818–24

ON THIS DAY I COMPLETE
MY THIRTY-SIXTH YEAR

'Tis time this heart should be unmoved,
    Since others it hath ceased to move:
Yet, though I cannot be beloved,
       Still let me love!

My days are in the yellow leaf;
    The flowers and fruits of love are gone;
The worm, the canker, and the grief
       Are mine alone!

The fire that on my bosom preys
    Is lone as some volcanic isle;
No torch is kindled at its blaze—
       A funeral pile!

The hope, the fear, the jealous care,
    The exalted portion of the pain
And power of love, I cannot share,
       But wear the chain.

But 'tis not *thus*—and 'tis not *here*—
    Such thoughts should shake my soul, nor *now*,
Where glory decks the hero's bier,
       Or binds his brow.

The sword, the banner, and the field,
  Glory and Greece, around me see!
The Spartan, borne upon his shield,
    Was not more free.

Awake! (not Greece—she *is* awake!)
  Awake, my spirit! Think through *whom*
Thy life-blood tracks its parent lake,
    And then strike home!

Tread those reviving passions down,
  Unworthy manhood! unto thee
Indifferent should the smile or frown
    Of beauty be.

If thou regret'st thy youth, *why live?*
  The land of honourable death
Is here:—up to the field, and give
    Away thy breath!

Seek out—less often sought than found—
  A soldier's grave, for thee the best,
Then look around, and choose thy ground,
    And take thy rest.
              Missolonghi, January 22, 1824

JOHN KEATS

(1795–1821)

N OCTOBER 29 or 31, 1795, in a room over the stable of the Swan and Hoop inn and livery establishment in London, a son was born to Thomas and Frances Keats. Thomas Keats, a sturdy, ambitious young fellow from the West Country, had come to London to make his fortune. Frances Jennings Keats was the handsome daughter of the proprietor of the inn, where Tom had won the job of head ostler. Three brothers and a sister followed firstborn John, named after his maternal grandfather, the innkeeper. In 1800 the growing family moved out of the stable loft to a house nearby. When John Jennings retired as head of the Swan and Hoop, he turned the establishment over to his son-in-law, and the Keats family seemed destined for settled, happy, and prosperous lives. In 1803 John Keats, going on eight years old, was enrolled at Mr. Clarke's school at Enfield, twelve miles north of London.

Less than a year later the first of a succession of disasters struck when Thomas Keats was killed by a fall from a horse. The second followed when headstrong Frances Keats remarried only two months after her first husband's death. Soon after, she left her new husband, who was apparently more interested in acquiring the Swan and Hoop than in his bride. Instead of returning to her family Frances disappeared, evidently with another man, leaving the children in the care of her parents.

The effect of his father's death on John Keats must have been serious; probably even more severe was the effect of his mother's astonishing conduct. Overnight he turned into a rebellious lad. Despite his small size, or possibly partly because of it, he won a schoolyard reputation as a fist fighter. "He would fight anyone, morning, noon or night," recalled a classmate later.

Although grandfather Jennings left a tidy estate of £13,000 at his death in 1805, plans for John Keats's further education at Harrow and perhaps a university were canceled by the loss of the inn. He was fourteen, still attending Mr. Clarke's school, when his mother dramatically reappeared—dying of tuberculosis. John Keats nursed her through the agonizing last weeks of the disease, a frightful experience that left him once more profoundly altered. No more fighting, no more sports. Instead he plunged into reading, and into intermittent fits of moody despair.

Grandmother Jennings, a practical and intelligent woman, enlisted a London tea merchant named Richard Abbey as a guardian of the children. George Keats entered Abbey's business house; John chose the profession of medicine and was apprenticed to Mr. Thomas Hammond of Edmonton, in the near neighborhood. Despite his sincere if not enthusiastic adoption of a profession, he continued to be enthralled by his discovery of books—Bacon, Addison, Swift, Locke, Shakespeare, Milton, Pope, Fielding, Smollett, Sterne, and a number of histories. Often he slipped away from Edmonton to trudge four miles across the fields for long talks with Cowden Clarke, son of his old headmaster. In 1813 Clarke introduced him to Spenser. Keats borrowed the first book of *The Faerie Queene* and read it through in a night. He also discovered the poetry of two young contemporaries, Byron and Chatterton, and essayed a few verses of his own.

The hero of the young liberal intellectuals of the day was Leigh Hunt, poet and editor, whose *Examiner* was a gadfly to the Tories in power and who in consequence of a daring article was serving two years in prison. Cowden Clarke knew Hunt personally. When Hunt's sentence was up in February of 1815 Clarke planned to walk into London to greet him. Keats met Clarke in the fields, walked part way, and at the last gate gave him a sonnet he had written in Hunt's honor. Clarke later introduced the young man to the older, a service which brought immediate satisfaction to Keats but eventually was to have some disastrous effects.

Through the winter of 1815–16 Keats worked as a "dresser," a sort of surgical intern, at Guy's Hospital in Southwark, while continuing to dally with poetry. By spring he was expressing open disillusionment with medicine and asserting that poetry was "the only thing worthy the attention of superior minds." He took up Bohemian dress, wearing an open shirt collar à la Byron, and letting his hair grow long. On May 5 he had the immense satisfaction of seeing his first poem, *To Solitude*, published in Leigh Hunt's *Examiner*. But when his poetic distraction threatened his prospects in an examination for a medical certificate in July, he crammed intensively and rather to his friends' surprise, passed.

In the fall the first shadow of another major tragedy appeared—his younger brother Tom showed signs of "consumption," and Keats took him off to Margate on the Kentish coast north of Dover. In the winter the two moved into new London lodgings with George Keats, over an archway of Bird-in-Hand Court, Cheapside, a few steps from Mermaid Tavern and Bow Church.

When Leigh Hunt published an article, "Young Poets," singling him out for particular praise, Keats was encouraged to bring out a book of his poetry, though he was fully aware that his talent was not yet mature. One night when he stayed over at Hunt's and could not sleep, he rose and composed the remarkable *Sleep and Poetry*. His father had died at thirty; his mother at thirty-six. In the poem Keats asked,

> O for ten years, that I may overwhelm
> Myself in poesy; so I may do the deed
> That my own soul has to itself decreed . . .

Shortly after, in the middle of an operation at the hospital, he suddenly felt overwhelmed. He resolved to quit surgery.

The decision to abandon medicine found no favor with the young man's guardian, who put obstacles in the way of his touching the rest of his inheritance. But Keats stuck to his resolution, going off to the Isle of Wight in the summer to work on *Endymion*. This long poem he had begun as the result of a friendly challenge from Shelley, whom he had met at Hunt's. Each of the poets was to undertake a 4,000-line poem and finish in six months. Even before the poem was finished, Keats was lionized by the young liberal element in London, dining out nearly every evening and enjoying it thoroughly. Keats liked food and drink, loved company and good conversation. His only disillusionment among the many persons he met that fall and winter was Wordsworth, once a flaming young liberal but now a pompous middle-aged bore. When Keats started to say something in reply to something of Wordsworth's, Mrs. Wordsworth put her hand on his arm and whispered: "Mr. Wordsworth is never interrupted."

In the spring of 1818 George Keats, newly married, suddenly decided to quit the tea-brokerage business and go to America. John Keats and a friend, Charles Brown, accompanied the couple by stagecoach to Liverpool, then set off on a walking tour of the North Country. A sonnet to Burns, written at Burns's birthplace, with its reference to "This mortal body of a thousand days," is one of a number of premonitions of early death which Keats voiced at this time. Besides the slow tragedy of his brother Tom, he had reasons for concern about his own health. Nevertheless, he and Brown covered twenty miles a day walking, spending their evenings studying maps and reading Milton aloud.

He returned to London to find Tom dying. On top of this shock came another: *Blackwood's,* one of the leading Tory reviews, a bitter adversary of Leigh Hunt and his "school," gave *Endymion* a scathing, vicious review, terming it "drivelling idiocy," dwelling sarcastically on the author's plebeian origins and recommending that he return to his apothecary's trade and leave poetry to his betters. The reviewer, one John Gibson Lockhart, evidently lacked the nerve to sign his review except with the letter "Z." He was later unmasked by a libel suit filed by William Hazlitt, a liberal critic whom he had abused. Worse in effect than the *Blackwood's* article, if not so personally offensive, was the harsh treatment given *Endymion* by the *Quarterly,* the most influential review in Britain. Damning the poem as another effusion of "Cockney" verse, the *Quarterly* defined it as "the most incongruous ideas in the most uncouth language." The undisguised class animosity in the attacks on Keats is hard to credit, even allowing for the virulent atmosphere of Tory-dominated England in these post-Waterloo years. Keats's friends came to his defense in their publications, but the *Quarterly* review effectively killed sales of *Endymion.* In the meantime he nursed Tom to the end, as he had his mother, and touchingly wrote his brother George in America: "His last moments were not so painful, and his very last was without a pang."

One brilliant ray lighted the dark winter. Despite a certain self-consciousness induced by his short stature, Keats had enjoyed the favor of women, but had never fallen in love until he met pretty nineteen-year-old Fanny Brawne, daughter of a neighbor of one of his friends. Under the influence of this new sensation he rose above tragedy and insult to compose the brilliant and flawless *Eve of St. Agnes,* one of the enduring masterpieces of English poetry. With it he moved into full artistic maturity, though he was barely twenty-three years old.

Over the next few months of 1819 Keats worked at an astounding pace on a variety of poems, heroically separating himself from Fanny Brawne to permit concentration. He was in financial difficulties, not improved by news from America that brother George, who had gone into partnership with the brilliant painter but ill-starred businessman John James Audubon, was also in straits and needed help. But above all Keats needed money to marry Fanny Brawne. He wrote a verse drama, *Otho the Great*, for which a friend supplied a poor plot framework and which failed to attract a producer. He started a more promising play, *King Stephen*, working entirely on his own. But far more important to his ultimate reputation were the series of odes—*To Psyche, To a Nightingale, On a Grecian Urn*—the narrative poem *Lamia*, the mystical *La Belle Dame Sans Merci*, the sonnet *Bright Star*, and several other short poems. Though Keats himself did not realize it, when the specter of disease which had hovered over him at last revealed itself unmistakably one February day in 1820, he had already achieved triumphant immortality.

In the last months of his life, in a pathetic attempt to thwart the tuberculosis that had killed his mother and brother Tom (and a few years later would kill George Keats in America), he said a last farewell to Fanny Brawne, and journeyed to Rome in company with his artist friend Joseph Severn. Four months after settling in a house neighboring the Spanish Steps, Keats was dead.

The publication of his poems of 1819 made little impression at first. It took a new Victorian generation, Browning and Tennyson and Matthew Arnold, to appreciate the rich and complex legacy of Keats. In Arnold's words, "He is with Shakespeare."

EARLY POEMS

To Byron

Byron! how sweetly sad thy melody!
  Attuning still the soul to tenderness,
  As if soft Pity, with unusual stress,
Had touch'd her plaintive lute, and thou, being by,
Hadst caught the tones, nor suffer'd them to die.
  O'ershadowing sorrow doth not make thee less
  Delightful: thou thy griefs dost dress
With a bright halo, shining beamily,
As when a cloud the golden moon doth veil,
  Its sides are ting'd with a resplendent glow,
Through the dark robe oft amber rays prevail,
  And like fair veins in sable marble flow;
Still warble, dying swan! still tell the tale,
  The enchanting tale, the tale of pleasing woe.
                                    December 1814

Ode to Apollo

In thy western halls of gold
  When thou sittest in thy state,
Bards, that erst sublimely told
  Heroic deeds, and sang of fate,
With fervour seize their adamantine lyres,
Whose chords are solid rays, and twinkle radiant fires.

Here Homer with his nervous arms
   Strikes the twanging harp of war,
And even the western splendour warms,
   While the trumpets sound afar:
But, what creates the most intense surprise,
His soul looks out through renovated eyes.

Then, through thy Temple wide, melodious swells
   The sweet majestic tone of Maro's lyre:
The soul delighted on each accent dwells,—
   Enraptur'd dwells,—not daring to respire,
The while he tells of grief around a funeral pyre.

'Tis awful silence then again;
   Expectant stand the spheres;
   Breathless the laurell'd peers,
Nor move, till ends the lofty strain,
Nor move till Milton's tuneful thunders cease,
And leave once more the ravish'd heavens in peace.

Thou biddest Shakspeare wave his hand,
   And quickly forward spring
The Passions—a terrific band—
   And each vibrates the string
That with its tyrant temper best accords,
While from their Master's lips pour forth the inspiring words.

A silver trumpet Spenser blows,
   And, as its martial notes to silence flee,
From a virgin chorus flows
   A hymn in praise of spotless Chastity.
'Tis still! Wild warblings from the Aeolian lyre
Enchantment softly breathe, and tremblingly expire.

Next thy Tasso's ardent numbers
   Float along the pleasèd air,
Calling youth from idle slumbers,
   Rousing them from Pleasure's lair:—
Then o'er the strings his fingers gently move,
And melt the soul to pity and to love.

But when *Thou* joinest with the Nine,
And all the powers of song combine,
   We listen here on earth:

The dying tones that fill the air,
And charm the ear of evening fair,
From thee, Great God of Bards, receive their heavenly birth.
February 1815

Sonnet: "Keen, Fitful Gusts . . ."

KEEN, fitful gusts are whisp'ring here and there
   Among the bushes half leafless, and dry;
   The stars look very cold about the sky,
And I have many miles on foot to fare.
Yet feel I little of the cool bleak air,
   Or of the dead leaves rustling drearily,
   Or of those silver lamps that burn on high,
Or of the distance from home's pleasant lair:
For I am brimful of the friendliness
   That in a little cottage I have found;
Of fair-hair'd Milton's eloquent distress,
   And all his love for gentle Lycid drown'd;
Of lovely Laura in her light green dress,
   And faithful Petrarch gloriously crown'd.
1816

On First Looking into Chapman's Homer

MUCH have I travell'd in the realms of gold,
   And many goodly states and kingdoms seen;
   Round many western islands have I been
Which bards in fealty to Apollo hold.
Oft of one wide expanse had I been told
   That deep-brow'd Homer ruled as his demesne:
   Yet did I never breathe its pure serene
Till I heard Chapman speak out loud and bold:
Then felt I like some watcher of the skies
   When a new planet swims into his ken;
Or like stout Cortez when with eagle eyes
   He star'd at the Pacific—and all his men
Look'd at each other with a wild surmise—
   Silent, upon a peak in Darien.
October 1816

Sleep and Poetry

As I lay in my bed slepe full unmete
Was unto me, but why that I ne might
Rest I ne wist, for there n'as erthly wight
(As I suppose) had more of hertis ese
Than I, for I n'ad sicknesse nor disese.
CHAUCER

WHAT is more gentle than a wind in summer?
What is more soothing than the pretty hummer
That stays one moment in an open flower,
And buzzes cheerily from bower to bower?
What is more tranquil than a musk-rose blowing
In a green island, far from all men's knowing?
More healthful than the leafiness of dales?
More secret than a nest of nightingales?
More serene than Cordelia's countenance?
More full of visions than a high romance?
What, but thee, Sleep? Soft closer of our eyes!
Low murmurer of tender lullabies!
Light hoverer around our happy pillows!
Wreather of poppy buds, and weeping willows!
Silent entangler of a beauty's tresses!
Most happy listener! when the morning blesses
Thee for enlivening all the cheerful eyes
That glance so brightly at the new sun-rise.

But what is higher beyond thought than thee?
Fresher than berries of a mountain-tree?
More strange, more beautiful, more smooth, more regal,
Than wings of swans, than doves, than dim-seen eagle?
What is it? And to what shall I compare it?
It has a glory, and nought else can share it:
The thought thereof is awful, sweet, and holy,
Chasing away all worldliness and folly:
Coming sometimes like fearful claps of thunder,
Or the low rumblings earth's regions under;
And sometimes like a gentle whispering
Of all the secrets of some wond'rous thing

That breathes about us in the vacant air;
So that we look around with prying stare,
Perhaps to see shapes of light, aerial limning;
And catch soft floatings from a faint-heard hymning;
To see the laurel wreath, on high suspended,
That is to crown our name when life is ended.
Sometimes it gives a glory to the voice,
And from the heart up-springs, rejoice! rejoice!
Sounds which will reach the Framer of all things,
And die away in ardent mutterings.

No one who once the glorious sun has seen,
And all the clouds, and felt his bosom clean
For his great Maker's presence, but must know
What 'tis I mean, and feel his being glow:
Therefore no insult will I give his spirit,
By telling what he sees from native merit.

O Poesy! for thee I hold my pen,
That am not yet a glorious denizen
Of thy wide heaven—should I rather kneel
Upon some mountain-top until I feel
A growing splendour round about me hung,
And echo back the voice of thine own tongue?
O Poesy! for thee I grasp my pen,
That am not yet a glorious denizen
Of thy wide heaven; yet, to my ardent prayer,
Yield from thy sanctuary some clear air,
Smoothed for intoxication by the breath
Of flowering bays, that I may die a death
Of luxury, and my young spirit follow
The morning sunbeams to the great Apollo
Like a fresh sacrifice; or, if I can bear
The o'erwhelming sweets, 'twill bring to me the fair
Visions of all places: a bowery nook
Will be elysium—an eternal book
Whence I may copy many a lovely saying
About the leaves, and flowers—about the playing
Of nymphs in woods, and fountains; and the shade
Keeping a silence round a sleeping maid;
And many a verse from so strange influence
That we must ever wonder how, and whence
It came. Also imaginings will hover
Round my fire-side, and haply there discover

Vistas of solemn beauty, where I'd wander
In happy silence, like the clear Meander
Through its lone vales; and where I found a spot
Of awfuller shade, or an enchanted grot,
Or a green hill o'erspread with chequer'd dress
Of flowers, and fearful from its loveliness,
Write on my tablets all that was permitted,
All that was for our human senses fitted.
Then the events of this wide world I'd seize
Like a strong giant, and my spirit tease
Till at its shoulders it should proudly see
Wings to find out an immortality.

Stop and consider! life is but a day;
A fragile dewdrop on its perilous way
From a tree's summit; a poor Indian's sleep
While his boat hastens to the monstrous steep
Of Montmorenci. Why so sad a moan?
Life is the rose's hope while yet unblown;
The reading of an ever-changing tale;
The light uplifting of a maiden's veil;
A pigeon tumbling in clear summer air;
A laughing school-boy, without grief or care,
Riding the springy branches of an elm.

O for ten years, that I may overwhelm
Myself in poesy; so I may do the deed
That my own soul has to itself decreed.
Then I will pass the countries that I see
In long perspective, and continually
Taste their pure fountains. First the realm I'll pass
Of Flora, and old Pan: sleep in the grass,
Feed upon apples red, and strawberries,
And choose each pleasure that my fancy sees;
Catch the white-handed nymphs in shady places,
To woo sweet kisses from averted faces,—
Play with their fingers, touch their shoulders white
Into a pretty shrinking with a bite
As hard as lips can make it: till agreed,
A lovely tale of human life we'll read.
And one will teach a tame dove how it best
May fan the cool air gently o'er my rest;

Another, bending o'er her nimble tread,
Will set a green robe floating round her head,
And still will dance with ever-varied ease,
Smiling upon the flowers and the trees:
Another will entice me on, and on
Through almond blossoms and rich cinnamon;
Till in the bosom of a leafy world
We rest in silence, like two gems upcurl'd
In the recesses of a pearly shell.

And can I ever bid these joys farewell?
Yes, I must pass them for a nobler life,
Where I may find the agonies, the strife
Of human hearts: for lo! I see afar,
O'er-sailing the blue cragginess, a car
And steeds with streamy manes—the charioteer
Looks out upon the winds with glorious fear:
And now the numerous tramplings quiver lightly
Along a huge cloud's ridge; and now with sprightly
Wheel downward come they into fresher skies,
Tipt round with silver from the sun's bright eyes.
Still downward with capacious whirl they glide;
And now I see them on a green-hill's side
In breezy rest among the nodding stalks.
The charioteer with wond'rous gesture talks
To the trees and mountains; and there soon appear
Shapes of delight, of mystery, and fear,
Passing along before a dusky space
Made by some mighty oaks: as they would chase
Some ever-fleeting music, on they sweep.
Lo! how they murmur, laugh, and smile, and weep:
Some with upholden hand and mouth severe;
Some with their faces muffled to the ear
Between their arms; some, clear in youthful bloom,
Go glad and smilingly athwart the gloom;
Some looking back, and some with upward gaze;
Yes, thousands in a thousand different ways
Flit onward—now a lovely wreath of girls
Dancing their sleek hair into tangled curls;
And now broad wings. Most awfully intent
The driver of those steeds is forward bent,
And seems to listen: O that I might know
All that he writes with such a hurrying glow.

The visions all are fled—the car is fled
Into the light of heaven, and in their stead
A sense of real things comes doubly strong,
And, like a muddy stream, would bear along
My soul to nothingness: but I will strive
Against all doubtings, and will keep alive
The thought of that same chariot, and the strange
Journey it went.

Is there so small a range
In the present strength of manhood, that the high
Imagination cannot freely fly
As she was wont of old? prepare her steeds,
Paw up against the light, and do strange deeds
Upon the clouds? Has she not shewn us all?
From the clear space of ether, to the small
Breath of new buds unfolding? From the meaning
Of Jove's large eyebrow, to the tender greening
Of April meadows? here her altar shone,
E'en in this isle; and who could paragon
The fervid choir that lifted up a noise
Of harmony, to where it aye will poise
Its mighty self of convoluting sound,
Huge as a planet, and like that roll round,
Eternally around a dizzy void?
Ay, in those days the Muses were nigh cloy'd
With honours; nor had any other care
Than to sing out and soothe their wavy hair.

Could all this be forgotten? Yes, a schism
Nurtured by foppery and barbarism,
Made great Apollo blush for this his land.
Men were thought wise who could not understand
His glories: with a puling infant's force
They sway'd about upon a rocking-horse,
And thought it Pegasus. Ah, dismal-soul'd!
The winds of heaven blew, the ocean roll'd
Its gathering waves—ye felt it not. The blue
Bared its eternal bosom, and the dew
Of summer nights collected still to make
The morning precious: beauty was awake!
Why were ye not awake? But ye were dead
To things ye knew not of,—were closely wed

To musty laws lined out with wretched rule
And compass vile: so that ye taught a school
Of dolts to smooth, inlay, and clip, and fit,
Till, like the certain wands of Jacob's wit,
Their verses tallied. Easy was the task:
A thousand handicraftsmen wore the mask
Of Poesy. Ill-fated, impious race!
That blasphem'd the bright Lyrist to his face,
And did not know it,—no, they went about,
Holding a poor, decrepid standard out,
Mark'd with most flimsy mottoes, and in large
The name of one Boileau!

                      O ye whose charge
It is to hover round our pleasant hills!
Whose congregated majesty so fills
My boundly reverence, that I cannot trace
Your hallowed names, in this unholy place,
So near those common folk; did not their shames
Affright you? Did our old lamenting Thames
Delight you? did ye never cluster round
Delicious Avon, with a mournful sound,
And weep? Or did ye wholly bid adieu
To regions where no more the laurel grew?
Or did ye stay to give a welcoming
To some lone spirits who could proudly sing
Their youth away, and die? 'Twas even so:
But let me think away those times of woe:
Now 'tis a fairer season; ye have breathed
Rich benedictions o'er us; ye have wreathed
Fresh garlands: for sweet music has been heard
In many places;—some has been upstirr'd
From out its crystal dwelling in a lake,
By a swan's ebon bill; from a thick brake,
Nested and quiet in a valley mild,
Bubbles a pipe; fine sounds are floating wild
About the earth: happy are ye and glad.

These things are, doubtless; yet in truth we've had
Strange thunders from the potency of song;
Mingled indeed with what is sweet and strong
From majesty: but in clear truth the themes
Are ugly clubs, the Poets Polyphemes

Disturbing the grand sea. A drainless shower
Of light is Poesy; 'tis the supreme of power;
'Tis might half slumb'ring on its own right arm.
The very archings of her eyelids charm
A thousand willing agents to obey,
And still she governs with the mildest sway:
But strength alone though of the Muses born
Is like a fallen angel: trees uptorn,
Darkness, and worms, and shrouds, and sepulchres
Delight it; for it feeds upon the burrs
And thorns of life; forgetting the great end
Of Poesy, that it should be a friend
To soothe the cares, and lift the thoughts of man.

Yet I rejoice: a myrtle fairer than
E'er grew in Paphos, from the bitter weeds
Lifts its sweet head into the air, and feeds
A silent space with ever sprouting green.
All tenderest birds there find a pleasant screen,
Creep through the shade with jaunty fluttering,
Nibble the little cuppèd flowers and sing.
Then let us clear away the choking thorns
From round its gentle stem; let the young fawns,
Yeanèd in after-times, when we are flown,
Find a fresh sward beneath it, overgrown
With simple flowers: let there nothing be
More boisterous than a lover's bended knee;
Nought more ungentle than the placid look
Of one who leans upon a closèd book;
Nought more untranquil than the grassy slopes
Between two hills. All hail, delightful hopes!
As she was wont, th' imagination
Into most lovely labyrinths will be gone,
And they shall be accounted poet kings
Who simply tell the most heart-easing things.
O may these joys be ripe before I die.

Will not some say that I presumptuously
Have spoken? that from hastening disgrace
'Twere better far to hide my foolish face?
That whining boyhood should with reverence bow
Ere the dread thunderbolt could reach? How!
If I do hide myself, it sure shall be
In the very fane, the light of Poesy:

If I do fall, at least I will be laid
Beneath the silence of a poplar shade;
And over me the grass shall be smooth shaven;
And there shall be a kind memorial graven.
But off, Despondence! miserable bane!
They should not know thee, who athirst to gain
A noble end, are thirsty every hour.
What though I am not wealthy in the dower
Of spanning wisdom; though I do not know
The shiftings of the mighty winds that blow
Hither and thither all the changing thoughts
Of man: though no great minist'ring reason sorts
Out the dark mysteries of human souls
To clear conceiving: yet there ever rolls
A vast idea before me, and I glean
Therefrom my liberty; thence too I've seen
The end and aim of Poesy. 'Tis clear
As anything most true; as that the year
Is made of the four seasons—manifest
As a large cross, some old cathedral's crest,
Lifted to the white clouds. Therefore should I
Be but the essence of deformity,
A coward, did my very eyelids wink
At speaking out what I have dared to think.
Ah! rather let me like a madman run
Over some precipice; let the hot sun
Melt my Daedalian wings, and drive me down
Convuls'd and headlong! Stay! an inward frown
Of conscience bids me be more calm awhile.
An ocean dim, sprinkled with many an isle,
Spreads awfully before me. How much toil!
How many days! what desperate turmoil!
Ere I can have explored its widenesses.
Ah, what a task! upon my bended knees,
I could unsay those—no, impossible!
Impossible!

       For sweet relief I'll dwell
On humbler thoughts, and let this strange assay
Begun in gentleness die so away.
E'en now all tumult from my bosom fades:
I turn full-hearted to the friendly aids
That smooth the path of honour; brotherhood,
And friendliness the nurse of mutual good.

The hearty grasp that sends a pleasant sonnet
Into the brain ere one can think upon it;
The silence when some rhymes are coming out;
And when they're come, the very pleasant rout:
The message certain to be done to-morrow.
'Tis perhaps as well that it should be to borrow
Some precious book from out its snug retreat,
To cluster round it when we next shall meet.
Scarce can I scribble on; for lovely airs
Are fluttering round the room like doves in pairs;
Many delights of that glad day recalling,
When first my senses caught their tender falling.
And with these airs come forms of elegance
Stooping their shoulders o'er a horse's prance,
Careless, and grand—fingers soft and round
Parting luxuriant curls;—and the swift bound
Of Bacchus from his chariot, when his eye
Made Ariadne's cheek look blushingly.
Thus I remember all the pleasant flow
Of words at opening a portfolio.

      Things such as these are ever harbingers
To trains of peaceful images: the stirs
Of a swan's neck unseen among the rushes:
A linnet starting all about the bushes:
A butterfly, with golden wings broad parted,
Nestling a rose, convuls'd as though it smarted
With over pleasure—many, many more,
Might I indulge at large in all my store
Of luxuries: yet I must not forget
Sleep, quiet with his poppy coronet:
For what there may be worthy in these rhymes
I partly owe to him: and thus, the chimes
Of friendly voices had just given place
To as sweet a silence, when I 'gan retrace
The pleasant day, upon a couch at ease.
It was a poet's house who keeps the keys
Of pleasure's temple. Round about were hung
The glorious features of the bards who sung
In other ages—cold and sacred busts
Smiled at each other. Happy he who trusts
To clear Futurity his darling fame!
Then there were fauns and satyrs taking aim

At swelling apples with a frisky leap
And reaching fingers, 'mid a luscious heap
Of vine leaves. Then there rose to view a fane
Of liny marble, and thereto a train
Of nymphs approaching fairly o'er the sward:
One, loveliest, holding her white hand toward
The dazzling sunrise: two sisters sweet
Bending their graceful figures till they meet
Over the trippings of a little child:
And some are hearing, eagerly, the wild
Thrilling liquidity of dewy piping.
See, in another picture, nymphs are wiping
Cherishingly Diana's timorous limbs;—
A fold of lawny mantle dabbling swims
At the bath's edge, and keeps a gentle motion
With the subsiding crystal: as when ocean
Heaves calmly its broad swelling smoothiness o'er
Its rocky marge, and balances once more
The patient weeds; that now unshent by foam
Feel all about their undulating home.

Sappho's meek head was there half smiling down
At nothing; just as though the earnest frown
Of over-thinking had that moment gone
From off her brow, and left her all alone.

Great Alfred's too, with anxious, pitying eyes,
As if he always listened to the sighs
Of the goaded world; and Kosciusko's, worn
By horrid suffrance—mightily forlorn.

Petrarch, outstepping from the shady green,
Starts at the sight of Laura; nor can wean
His eyes from her sweet face. Most happy they!
For over them was seen a free display
Of outspread wings, and from between them shone
The face of Poesy: from off her throne
She overlook'd things that I scarce could tell.
The very sense of where I was might well
Keep Sleep aloof: but more than that there came
Thought after thought to nourish up the flame
Within my breast; so that the morning light
Surprised me even from a sleepless night;

And up I rose refresh'd, and glad, and gay,
Resolving to begin that very day
These lines; and howsoever they be done,
I leave them as a father does his son.

November-December 1816

Calidore

A FRAGMENT

Young Calidore is paddling o'er the lake;
His healthful spirit eager and awake
To feel the beauty of a silent eve,
Which seem'd full loth this happy world to leave;
The light dwelt o'er the scene so lingeringly.
He bares his forehead to the cool blue sky,
And smiles at the far clearness all around,
Until his heart is well nigh over wound,
And turns for calmness to the pleasant green
Of easy slopes, and shadowy trees that lean
So elegantly o'er the waters' brim
And show their blossoms trim.
Scarce can his clear and nimble eyesight follow
The freaks and dartings of the black-wing'd swallow,
Delighting much, to see it half at rest,
Dip so refreshingly its wings, and breast
'Gainst the smooth surface, and to mark anon,
The widening circles into nothing gone.

And now the sharp keel of his little boat
Comes up with ripple, and with easy float,
And glides into a bed of water-lilies:
Broad-leav'd are they, and their white canopies
Are upward turn'd to catch the heavens' dew.
Near to a little island's point they grew;
Whence Calidore might have the goodliest view
Of this sweet spot of earth. The bowery shore
Went off in gentle windings to the hoar
And light blue mountains: but no breathing man
With a warm heart, and eye prepared to scan

Nature's clear beauty, could pass lightly by
Objects that look'd out so invitingly
On either side. These, gentle Calidore
Greeted, as he had known them long before.

The sidelong view of swelling leafiness,
Which the glad setting sun in gold doth dress;
Whence, ever and anon, the jay outsprings,
And scales upon the beauty of its wings.

The lonely turret, shatter'd, and outworn,
Stands venerably proud; too proud to mourn
Its long lost grandeur: fir-trees grow around,
Aye dropping their hard fruit upon the ground.

The little chapel, with the cross above,
Upholding wreaths of ivy; the white dove,
That on the windows spreads his feathers light,
And seems from purple clouds to wing its flight.

Green tufted islands casting their soft shades
Across the lake; sequester'd leafy glades,
That through the dimness of their twilight show
Large dock-leaves, spiral foxgloves, or the glow
Of the wild cat's-eyes, or the silvery stems
Of delicate birch-trees, or long grass which hems
A little brook. The youth had long been viewing
These pleasant things, and heaven was bedewing
The mountain flowers, when his glad senses caught
A trumpet's silver voice. Ah! it was fraught
With many joys for him: the warder's ken
Had found white coursers prancing in the glen:
Friends very dear to him he soon will see;
So pushes off his boat most eagerly,
And soon upon the lake he skims along,
Deaf to the nightingale's first under-song;
Nor minds he the white swans that dream so sweetly:
His spirit flies before him so completely.

And now he turns a jutting point of land,
Whence may be seen the castle gloomy, and grand:
Nor will a bee buzz round two swelling peaches,
Before the point of his light shallop reaches

Those marble steps that through the water dip:
Now over them he goes with hasty trip,
And scarcely stays to ope the folding doors:
Anon he leaps along the oaken floors
Of halls and corridors.

   Delicious sounds! those little bright-eyed things
That float about the air on azure wings,
Had been less heartfelt by him than the clang
Of clattering hoofs; into the court he sprang,
Just as two noble steeds, and palfreys twain,
Were slanting out their necks with loosen'd rein;
While from beneath the threat'ning port cullis
They brought their happy burthens. What a kiss,
What gentle squeeze he gave each lady's hand!
How tremblingly their delicate ankles spann'd!
Into how sweet a trance his soul was gone,
While whisperings of affection
Made him delay to let their tender feet
Come to the earth; with an incline so sweet
From their low palfreys o'er his neck they bent:
And whether there were tears of languishment,
Or that the evening dew had pearl'd their tresses,
He feels a moisture on his cheek, and blesses
With lips that tremble, and with glistening eye,
All the soft luxury
That nestled in his arms. A dimpled hand,
Fair as some wonder out of fairy land,
Hung from his shoulder like the drooping flowers
Of whitest Cassia, fresh from summer showers:
And this he fondled with his happy cheek,
As if for joy he would no further seek;
When the kind voice of good Sir Clerimond
Came to his ear, like something from beyond
His present being: so he gently drew
His warm arms, thrilling now with pulses new,
From their sweet thrall, and forward gently bending,
Thank'd Heaven that his joy was never ending;
While 'gainst his forehead he devoutly press'd
A hand Heaven made to succour the distress'd;
A hand that from the world's bleak promontory
Had lifted Calidore for deeds of glory.

Amid the pages, and the torches' glare,
There stood a knight, patting the flowing hair
Of his proud horse's mane: he was withal
A man of elegance, and stature tall:
So that the waving of his plumes would be
High as the berries of a wild ash-tree,
Or as the wingèd cap of Mercury.
His armour was so dexterously wrought
In shape, that sure no living man had thought
It hard, and heavy steel: but that indeed
It was some glorious form, some splendid weed,
In which a spirit new come from the skies
Might live, and show itself to human eyes.
'Tis the far-fam'd, the brave Sir Gondibert,
Said the good man to Calidore alert;
While the young warrior with a step of grace
Came up,—a courtly smile upon his face,
And mailèd hand held out, ready to greet
The large-eyed wonder, and ambitious heat
Of the aspiring boy; who as he led
Those smiling ladies, often turned his head
To admire the visor arched so gracefully
Over a knightly brow; while they went by
The lamps that from the high-roof'd hall were pendent,
And gave the steel a shining quite transcendent.

Soon in a pleasant chamber they are seated;
The sweet-lipp'd ladies have already greeted
All the green leaves that round the window clamber,
To show their purple stars, and bells of amber.
Sir Gondibert has doff'd his shining steel,
Gladdening in the free, and airy feel
Of a light mantle; and while Clerimond
Is looking round about him with a fond
And placid eye, young Calidore is burning
To hear of knightly deeds, and gallant spurning
Of all unworthiness; and how the strong of arm
Kept off dismay, and terror, and alarm
From lovely woman: while brimful of this,
He gave each damsel's hand so warm a kiss,
And had such manly ardour in his eye,
That each at other look'd half-staringly;
And then their features started into smiles,
Sweet as blue heavens o'er enchanted isles.

Softly the breezes from the forest came,
Softly they blew aside the taper's flame;
Clear was the song from Philomel's far bower;
Grateful the incense from the lime-tree flower;
Mysterious, wild, the far heard trumpet's tone;
Lovely the moon in ether, all alone:
Sweet too the converse of these happy mortals,
As that of busy spirits when the portals
Are closing in the west; or that soft humming
We hear around when Hesperus is coming.
Sweet be their sleep. . . .

1816

To Kosciusko

Good Kosciusko, thy great name alone
   Is a full harvest whence to reap high feeling;
   It comes upon us like the glorious pealing
Of the wide spheres—an everlasting tone.
And now it tells me, that in worlds unknown,
   The names of heroes, burst from clouds concealing,
   Are changed to harmonies, for ever stealing
Through cloudless blue, and round each silver throne.
It tells me too, that on a happy day,
   When some good spirit walks upon the earth,
     Thy name with Alfred's, and the great of yore,
Gently commingling, gives tremendous birth
To a loud hymn, that sounds far, far away
     To where the great God lives for evermore.

December 1816

Written in Disgust of Vulgar Superstition

The church bells toll a melancholy round,
   Calling the people to some other prayers,
   Some other gloominess, more dreadful cares,
More hearkening to the sermon's horrid sound.
Surely the mind of man is closely bound

In some black spell; seeing that each one tears
Himself from fireside joys, and Lydian airs,
And converse high of those with glory crown'd.
Still, still they toll, and I should feel a damp,—
  A chill as from a tomb, did I not know
That they are dying like an outburnt lamp;
  That 'tis their sighing, wailing ere they go
Into oblivion;—that fresh flowers will grow,
And many glories of immortal stamp.

                              December 1816

Sonnet: "Happy Is England . . ."

HAPPY is England! I could be content
  To see no other verdure than its own;
  To feel no other breezes than are blown
Through its tall woods with high romances blent:
Yet do I sometimes feel a languishment
  For skies Italian, and an inward groan
  To sit upon an Alp as on a throne,
And half forget what world or worldling meant.
Happy is England, sweet her artless daughters;
  Enough their simple loveliness for me,
    Enough their whitest arms in silence clinging:
  Yet do I often warmly burn to see
    Beauties of deeper glance, and hear their singing,
And float with them about the summer waters.

                              December 1816

Sonnet: "After Dark Vapours . . ."

AFTER dark vapours have oppress'd our plains
  For a long dreary season, comes a day
  Born of the gentle South, and clears away
From the sick heavens all unseemly stains.
The anxious month, relieved its pains,
  Takes as a long-lost right the feel of May;
  The eyelids with the passing coolness play,
Like rose leaves with the drip of summer rains.

And calmest thoughts come round us; as, of leaves
   Budding,—fruit ripening in stillness,—Autumn suns
Smiling at eve upon the quiet sheaves,—
Sweet Sappho's cheek,—a sleeping infant's breath,—
   The gradual sand that through an hour-glass runs,—
A woodland rivulet,—a Poet's death.

January 1817

On Seeing the Elgin Marbles

My spirit is too weak—mortality
   Weighs heavily on me like unwilling sleep,
   And each imagin'd pinnacle and steep
Of godlike hardship tells me I must die
Like a sick Eagle looking at the sky.
   Yet 'tis a gentle luxury to weep
   That I have not the cloudy winds to keep,
Fresh for the opening of the morning's eye.
Such dim-conceivèd glories of the brain
   Bring round the heart an indescribable feud;
So do these wonders a most dizzy pain,
   That mingles Grecian grandeur with the rude
Wasting of old Time—with a billowy main—
   A sun—a shadow of a magnitude.

March 1817

On the Sea

It keeps eternal whisperings around
   Desolate shores, and with its mighty swell
   Gluts twice ten thousand caverns, till the spell
Of Hecate leaves them their old shadowy sound.
Often 'tis in such gentle temper found,
   That scarcely will the very smallest shell
   Be mov'd for days from where it sometime fell,
When last the winds of Heaven were unbound.
O ye! who have your eyeballs vex'd and tir'd,
   Feast them upon the wideness of the Sea;

O ye! whose ears are dinn'd with uproar rude,
Or fed too much with cloying melody,—
    Sit ye near some old cavern's mouth, and brood
Until ye start, as if the sea-nymphs quired!

April 1817

Sonnet: "When I Have Fears . . ."

WHEN I have fears that I may cease to be
    Before my pen has glean'd my teeming brain,
Before high pilèd books, in charactry,
    Hold like rich garners the full-ripen'd grain;
When I behold, upon the night's starr'd face,
    Huge cloudy symbols of a high romance,
And think that I may never live to trace
    Their shadows, with the magic hand of chance;
And when I feel, fair creature of an hour!
    That I shall never look upon thee more,
Never have relish in the faery power
    Of unreflecting love;—then on the shore
Of the wide world I stand alone, and think
Till Love and Fame to nothingness do sink.

1817

Lines on the Mermaid Tavern

SOULS of Poets dead and gone,
What Elysium have ye known,
Happy field or mossy cavern,
Choicer than the Mermaid Tavern?
Have ye tippled drink more fine
Than mine host's Canary wine?
Or are fruits of Paradise
Sweeter than those dainty pies
Of venison? O generous food!
Drest as though bold Robin Hood
Would, with his maid Marian,
Sup and bowse from horn and can.

I have heard that on a day
Mine host's sign-board flew away,
Nobody knew whither, till
An astrologer's old quill
To a sheepskin gave the story,
Said he saw you in your glory,
Underneath a new-old sign
Sipping beverage divine,
And pledging with contented smack
The Mermaid in the Zodiac.

Souls of Poets dead and gone,
What Elysium have ye known,
Happy field or mossy cavern,
Choicer than the Mermaid Tavern?
                                    February 1818

From

ENDYMION

A ROMANCE

BOOK I

A THING of beauty is a joy for ever:
Its loveliness increases; it will never
Pass into nothingness; but still will keep
A bower quiet for us, and a sleep
Full of sweet dreams, and health, and quiet breathing.
Therefore, on every morrow, are we wreathing
A flowery band to bind us to the earth,
Spite of despondence, of the inhuman dearth
Of noble natures, of the gloomy days,
Of all the unhealthy and o'er-darken'd ways
Made for our searching: yes, in spite of all,
Some shape of beauty moves away the pall
From our dark spirits. Such the sun, the moon,
Trees old and young, sprouting a shady boon
For simple sheep; and such are daffodils
With the green world they live in; and clear rills
That for themselves a cooling covert make
'Gainst the hot season; the mid-forest brake,
Rich with a sprinkling of fair musk-rose blooms:
And such too is the grandeur of the dooms
We have imagined for the mighty dead;
All lovely tales that we have heard or read:
An endless fountain of immortal drink,
Pouring unto us from the heaven's brink.

Nor do we merely feel these essences
For one short hour; no, even as the trees
That whisper round a temple become soon
Dear as the temple's self, so does the moon,
The passion poesy, glories infinite,
Haunt us till they become a cheering light
Unto our souls, and bound to us so fast,
That, whether there be shine, or gloom o'ercast,
They alway must be with us, or we die.

*   *   *   *   *

Leading the way, young damsels danced along,
Bearing the burden of a shepherd song;
Each having a white wicker, overbrimm'd
With April's tender younglings: next, well trimm'd,
A crowd of shepherds with as sunburnt looks
As may be read of in Arcadian books;
Such as sat listening round Apollo's pipe,
When the great deity, for earth too ripe,
Let his divinity o'erflowing die
In music, through the vales of Thessaly:
Some idly trail'd their sheep-hooks on the ground,
And some kept up a shrilly mellow sound
With ebon-tipped flutes: close after these,
Now coming from beneath the forest trees,
A venerable priest full soberly,
Begirt with minist'ring looks: alway his eye
Steadfast upon the matted turf he kept,
And after him his sacred vestments swept.
From his right hand there swung a vase, milk-white,
Of mingled wine, out-sparkling generous light;
And in his left he held a basket full
Of all sweet herbs that searching eye could cull:
Wild thyme, and valley-lilies whiter still
Than Leda's love, and cresses from the rill.
His aged head, crowned with beechen wreath,
Seem'd like a poll of ivy in the teeth
Of winter hoar. Then came another crowd
Of shepherds, lifting in due time aloud
Their share of the ditty. After them appear'd,
Up-follow'd by a multitude that rear'd
Their voices to the clouds, a fair-wrought car,
Easily rolling so as scarce to mar

The freedom of three steeds of dapple brown:
Who stood therein did seem of great renown
Among the throng. His youth was fully blown,
Showing like Ganymede to manhood grown;
And, for those simple times, his garments were
A chieftain king's; beneath his breast, half bare,
Was hung a silver bugle, and between
His nervy knees there lay a boar-spear keen.
A smile was on his countenance; he seem'd
To common lookers-on, like one who dream'd
Of idleness in groves Elysian:
But there were some who feelingly could scan
A lurking trouble in his nether lip,
And see that oftentimes the reins would slip
Through his forgotten hands: then would they sigh,
And think of yellow leaves, of owlets' cry,
Of logs piled solemnly.—Ah, well-a-day,
Why should our young Endymion pine away!

*   *   *   *   *

Even while they brought the burden to a close,
A shout from the whole multitude arose,
That linger'd in the air like dying rolls
Of abrupt thunder, when Ionian shoals
Of dolphins bob their noses through the brine.
Meantime, on shady levels, mossy fine,
Young companies nimbly began dancing
To the swift treble pipe, and humming string.
Aye, those fair living forms swam heavenly
To tunes forgotten—out of memory:
Fair creatures! whose young children's children bred
Thermopylae its heroes—not yet dead,
But in old marbles ever beautiful.
High genitors, unconscious did they cull
Time's sweet first-fruits—they danced to weariness,
And then in quiet circles did they press
The hillock turf, and caught the latter end
Of some strange history, potent to send
A young mind from its bodily tenement.
Or they might watch the quoit-pitchers, intent
On either side; pitying the sad death
Of Hyacinthus, when the cruel breath

Of Zephyr slew him,—Zephyr penitent,
Who now, ere Phoebus mounts the firmament,
Fondles the flower amid the sobbing rain.
The archers too, upon a wider plain,
Beside the feathery whizzing of the shaft,
And the dull twanging bowstring, and the raft
Branch down sweeping from a tall ash top,
Call'd up a thousand thoughts to envelope
Those who would watch. Perhaps, the trembling knee
And frantic gape of lonely Niobe,
Poor, lonely Niobe! when her lovely young
Were dead and gone, and her caressing tongue
Lay a lost thing upon her paly lip,
And very, very deadliness did nip
Her motherly cheeks. Aroused from this sad mood
By one, who at a distance loud halloo'd,
Uplifting his strong bow into the air,
Many might after brighter visions stare:
After the Argonauts, in blind amaze
Tossing about on Neptune's restless ways,
Until, from the horizon's vaulted side,
There shot a golden splendour far and wide,
Spangling those million poutings of the brine
With quivering ore: 'twas even an awful shine
From the exaltation of Apollo's bow;
A heavenly beacon in their dreary woe.
Who thus were ripe for high contemplating,
Might turn their steps towards the sober ring
Where sat Endymion and the aged priest
'Mong shepherds gone in eld, whose looks increased
The silvery setting of their mortal star.
There they discoursed upon the fragile bar
That keeps us from our homes ethereal;
And what our duties there: to nightly call
Vesper, the beauty-crest of summer weather;
To summon all the downiest clouds together
For the sun's purple couch; to emulate
In minist'ring the potent rule of fate
With speed of fire-tail'd exhalations;
To tint her pallid cheek with bloom, who cons
Sweet poesy by moonlight: besides these,
A world of other unguess'd offices.
Anon they wander'd, by divine converse,
Into Elysium; vying to rehearse

Each one his own anticipated bliss.
One felt heart-certain that he could not miss
His quick-gone love, among fair blossom'd boughs,
Where every zephyr-sigh pouts, and endows
Her lips with music for the welcoming.
Another wish'd, 'mid that eternal spring,
To meet his rosy child, with feathery sails,
Sweeping, eye-earnestly, through almond vales:
Who, suddenly, should stoop through the smooth wind,
And with the balmiest leaves his temples bind;
And, ever after, through those regions be
His messenger, his little Mercury.
Some were athirst in soul to see again
Their fellow-huntsmen o'er the wide champaign
In times long past; to sit with them, and talk
Of all the chances in their earthly walk;
Comparing, joyfully, their plenteous stores
Of happiness, to when upon the moors,
Benighted, close they huddled from the cold,
And shared their famish'd scrips. Thus all out-told
Their fond imaginations,—saving him
Whose eyelids curtain'd up their jewels dim,
Endymion: yet hourly had he striven
To hide the cankering venom, that had riven
His fainting recollections. Now indeed
His senses had swoon'd off: he did not heed
The sudden silence, or the whispers low,
Or the old eyes dissolving at his woe,
Or anxious calls, or close of trembling palms,
Or maiden's sigh, that grief itself embalms:
But in the self-same fixed trance he kept,
Like one who on the earth had never stept.
Aye, even as dead-still as a marble man,
Frozen in that old tale Arabian.

*   *   *   *   *

O magic sleep! O comfortable bird,
That broodest o'er the troubled sea of the mind
Till it is hush'd and smooth! O unconfined
Restraint! imprison'd liberty! great key
To golden palaces, strange minstrelsy,
Fountains grotesque, new trees, bespangled caves,
Echoing grottoes, full of tumbling waves

And moonlight; aye, to all the mazy world
Of silvery enchantment!—who, upfurl'd
Beneath thy drowsy wing a triple hour,
But renovates and lives?—Thus, in the bower,
Endymion was calm'd to life again.

               *   *   *   *   *

"Whence that completed form of all completeness?
Whence came that high perfection of all sweetness?
Speak, stubborn earth, and tell me where, O where
Hast thou a symbol of her golden hair?
Not oat-sheaves drooping in the western sun;
Not—thy soft hand, fair sister! let me shun
Such follying before thee—yet she had,
Indeed, locks bright enough to make me mad;
And they were simply gordian'd up and braided,
Leaving, in naked comeliness, unshaded,
Her pearl round ears, white neck, and orbed brow;
The which were blended in, I know not how,
With such a paradise of lips and eyes,
Blush-tinted cheeks, half smiles, and faintest sighs,
That, when I think thereon, my spirit clings
And plays about its fancy, till the stings
Of human neighbourhood envenom all.
Unto what awful power shall I call?
To what high fane?—Ah! see her hovering feet,
More bluely vein'd, more soft, more whitely sweet
Than those of sea-born Venus, when she rose
From out her cradle shell. The wind out-blows
Her scarf into a fluttering pavilion;
'Tis blue, and over-spangled with a million
Of little eyes, as though thou wert to shed,
Over the darkest, lushest bluebell bed,
Handfuls of daisies."—"Endymion, how strange!
Dream within dream!"—"She took an airy range,
And then, towards me, like a very maid,
Came blushing, waning, willing, and afraid,
And press'd me by the hand: Ah! 'twas too much;
Methought I fainted at the charmed touch,
Yet held my recollection, even as one
Who dives three fathoms where the waters run
Gurgling in beds of coral: for anon,
I felt upmounted in that region

Where falling stars dart their artillery forth,
And eagles struggle with the buffeting north
That balances the heavy meteor-stone;—
Felt too, I was not fearful, nor alone,
But lapp'd and lull'd along the dangerous sky.
Soon, as it seem'd, we left our journeying high,
And straightway into frightful eddies swoop'd;
Such as ay muster where gray time has scoop'd
Huge dens and caverns in a mountain's side:
There hollow sounds aroused me, and I sigh'd
To faint once more by looking on my bliss—
I was distracted; madly did I kiss
The wooing arms which held me, and did give
My eyes at once to death: but 'twas to live,
To take in draughts of life from the gold fount
Of kind and passionate looks; to count, and count
The moments, by some greedy help that seem'd
A second self, that each might be redeem'd
And plunder'd of its load of blessedness.
Ah, desperate mortal! I ev'n dared to press
Her very cheek against my crowned lip,
And, at that moment, felt my body dip
Into a warmer air: a moment more,
Our feet were soft in flowers. There was store
Of newest joys upon that alp. Sometimes
A scent of violets, and blossoming limes,
Loiter'd around us; then of honey cells,
Made delicate from all white-flower bells;
And once, above the edges of our nest,
An arch face peep'd,—an Oread as I guess'd.

"Why did I dream that sleep o'erpower'd me
In midst of all this heaven? Why not see,
Far off, the shadows of his pinions dark,
And stare them from me? But no, like a spark
That needs must die, although its little beam
Reflects upon a diamond, my sweet dream
Fell into nothing—into stupid sleep.
And so it was, until a gentle creep,
A careful moving caught my waking ears,
And up I started: Ah! my sighs, my tears,
My clenched hands;—for lo! the poppies hung
Dew-dabbled on their stalks, the ouzel sung

A heavy ditty, and the sullen day
Had chidden herald Hesperus away,
With leaden looks: the solitary breeze
Bluster'd, and slept, and its wild self did tease
With wayward melancholy; and I thought,
Mark me, Peona! that sometimes it brought
Faint fare-thee-wells, and sigh-shrilled adieus!—
Away I wander'd—all the pleasant hues
Of heaven and earth had faded: deepest shades
Were deepest dungeons; heaths and sunny glades
Were full of pestilent light; our taintless rills
Seem'd sooty, and o'erspread with upturn'd gills
Of dying fish; the vermeil rose had blown
In frightful scarlet, and its thorns outgrown
Like spiked aloe. If an innocent bird
Before my heedless footsteps stirr'd, and stirr'd
In little journeys, I beheld in it
A disguised demon, missioned to knit
My soul with under darkness; to entice
My stumblings down some monstrous precipice:
Therefore I eager follow'd, and did curse
The disappointment. Time, that aged nurse,
Rock'd me to patience. Now, thank gentle heaven!
These things, with all their comfortings, are given
To my down-sunken hours, and with thee,
Sweet sister, help to stem the ebbing sea
Of weary life."

          *   *   *   *   *

                    "But there are
Richer entanglements, enthralments far
More self-destroying, leading, by degrees,
To the chief intensity: the crown of these
Is made of love and friendship, and sits high
Upon the forehead of humanity.
All its more ponderous and bulky worth
Is friendship, whence there ever issues forth
A steady splendour; but at the tip-top,
There hangs by unseen film, an orbed drop
Of light, and that is love: its influence
Thrown in our eyes genders a novel sense,
At which we start and fret: till in the end,
Melting into its radiance, we blend,

Mingle, and so become a part of it,—
Nor with aught else can our souls interknit
So wingedly: when we combine therewith,
Life's self is nourish'd by its proper pith,
And we are nurtured like a pelican brood.
Aye, so delicious is the unsating food,
That men, who might have tower'd in the van
Of all the congregated world, to fan
And winnow from the coming step of time
All chaff of custom, wipe away all slime
Left by men-slugs and human serpentry,
Have been content to let occasion die,
Whilst they did sleep in love's Elysium.
And, truly, I would rather be struck dumb,
Than speak against this ardent listlessness:
For I have ever thought that it might bless
The world with benefits unknowingly;
As does the nightingale, up-perched high,
And cloister'd among cool and bunched leaves—
She sings but to her love, nor e'er conceives
How tiptoe Night holds back her dark-gray hood.
Just so may love, although 'tis understood
The mere commingling of passionate breath,
Produce more than our searching witnesseth:
What I know not: but who, of men, can tell
That flowers would bloom, or that green fruit would swell
To melting pulp, that fish would have bright mail,
The earth its dower of river, wood, and vale,
The meadows runnels, runnels pebble-stones,
The seed its harvest, or the lute its tones,
Tones ravishment, or ravishment its sweet,
If human souls did never kiss and greet?"

* * * * *

BOOK II

O SOVEREIGN power of love! O grief! O balm!
All records, saving thine, come cool, and calm,
And shadowy, through the mist of passed years:
For others, good or bad, hatred and tears
Have become indolent; but touching thine,
One sigh doth echo, one poor sob doth pine,

One kiss brings honey-dew from buried days.
The woes of Troy, towers smothering o'er their blaze,
Stiff-holden shields, far-piercing spears, keen blades,
Struggling, and blood, and shrieks—all dimly fades
Into some backward corner of the brain;
Yet, in our very souls, we feel amain
The close of Troïlus and Cressid sweet.
Hence, pageant history! hence, gilded cheat!
Swart planet in the universe of deeds!
Wide sea, that one continuous murmur breeds
Along the pebbled shore of memory!
Many old rotten-timber'd boats there be
Upon thy vaporous bosom, magnified
To goodly vessels; many a sail of pride,
And golden-keel'd, is left unlaunch'd and dry.
But wherefore this? What care, though owl did fly
About the great Athenian admiral's mast?
What care, though striding Alexander past
The Indus with his Macedonian numbers?
Though old Ulysses tortured from his slumbers
The glutted Cyclops, what care?—Juliet leaning
Amid her window-flowers,—sighing,—weaning
Tenderly her fancy from its maiden snow,
Doth more avail than these: the silver flow
Of Hero's tears, the swoon of Imogen,
Fair Pastorella in the bandit's den,
Are things to brood on with more ardency
Than the death-day of empires. Fearfully
Must such conviction come upon his head,
Who, thus far, discontent, has dared to tread,
Without one muse's smile, or kind behest,
The path of love and poesy. But rest,
In chafing restlessness, is yet more drear
Than to be crush'd, in striving to uprear
Love's standard on the battlements of song.
So once more days and nights aid me along,
Like legion'd soldiers.

                *   *   *   *   *

                            "Whoso encamps
To take a fancied city of delight,
O what a wretch is he! and when 'tis his,
After long toil and travelling, to miss

The kernel of his hopes, how more than vile:
Yet, for him there's refreshment even in toil:
Another city doth he set about,
Free from the smallest pebble-bead of doubt
That he will seize on trickling honey-combs:
Alas, he finds them dry; and then he foams,
And onward to another city speeds.
But this is human life: the war, the deeds,
The disappointment, the anxiety,
Imagination's struggles, far and nigh,
All human; bearing in themselves this good,
That they are still the air, the subtle food,
To make us feel existence, and to show
How quiet death is. Where soil is, men grow,
Whether to weeds or flowers; but for me,
There is no depth to strike in: I can see
Naught earthly worth my compassing; so stand
Upon a misty, jutting head of land—
Alone? No, no; and by the Orphean lute,
When mad Eurydice is listening to 't,
I'd rather stand upon this misty peak,
With not a thing to sigh for, or to seek,
But the soft shadow of my thrice seen love,
Than be—I care not what."

*   *   *   *   *

After a thousand mazes overgone,
At last, with sudden step, he came upon
A chamber, myrtle-wall'd, embower'd high,
Full of light, incense, tender minstrelsy,
And more of beautiful and strange beside:
For on a silken couch of rosy pride,
In midst of all, there lay a sleeping youth
Of fondest beauty; fonder, in fair sooth,
Than sighs could fathom, or contentment reach:
And coverlids gold-tinted like the peach,
Or ripe October's faded marigolds,
Fell sleek about him in a thousand folds—
Not hiding up an Apollonian curve
Of neck and shoulder, nor the tenting swerve
Of knee from knee, nor ankles pointing light;
But rather, giving them to the fill'd sight

Officiously. Sideway his face reposed
On one white arm, and tenderly unclosed,
By tenderest pressure, a faint damask mouth
To slumbery pout; just as the morning south
Disparts a dew-lipp'd rose. Above his head,
Four lily stalks did their white honours wed
To make a coronal; and round him grew
All tendrils green, of every bloom and hue,
Together intertwined and trammell'd fresh:
The vine of glossy sprout; the ivy mesh,
Shading its Ethiop berries; and woodbine,
Of velvet-leaves and bugle-blooms divine;
Convolvulus in streaked vases flush;
The creeper, mellowing for an autumn blush;
And virgin's bower, trailing airily;
With others of the sisterhood. Hard by,
Stood serene Cupids watching silently.
One, kneeling to a lyre, touch'd the strings,
Muffling to death the pathos with his wings;
And, ever and anon, uprose to look
At the youth's slumber; while another took
A willow bough, distilling odorous dew,
And shook it on his hair; another flew
In through the woven roof, and fluttering-wise
Rain'd violets upon his sleeping eyes.

At these enchantments, and yet many more,
The breathless Latmian wonder'd o'er and o'er;
Until impatient in embarrassment,
He forthright pass'd, and lightly treading went
To that same feather'd lyrist, who straightway,
Smiling, thus whisper'd: "Though from upper day
Thou art a wanderer, and thy presence here
Might seem unholy, be of happy cheer!
For 'tis the nicest touch of human honour,
When some ethereal and high-favouring donor
Presents immortal bowers to mortal sense;
As now 'tis done to thee, Endymion. Hence
Was I in no wise startled. So recline
Upon these living flowers. Here is wine,
Alive with sparkles—never, I aver,
Since Ariadne was a vintager,
So cool a purple: taste these juicy pears,
Sent me by sad Vertumnus, when his fears

Were high about Pomona: here is cream,
Deepening to richness from a snowy gleam;
Sweeter than that nurse Amalthea skimm'd
For the boy Jupiter: and here, undimm'd
By any touch, a bunch of blooming plums
Ready to melt between an infant's gums:
And here is manna pick'd from Syrian trees,
In starlight, by the three Hesperides.
Feast on, and meanwhile I will let thee know
Of all these things around us." He did so,
Still brooding o'er the cadence of his lyre;
And thus: "I need not any hearing tire
By telling how the sea-born goddess pined
For a mortal youth, and how she strove to bind
Him all in all unto her doting self.
Who would not be so prison'd? but, fond elf,
He was content to let her amorous plea
Faint through his careless arms; content to see
An unseized heaven dying at his feet;
Content, O fool! to make a cold retreat,
When on the pleasant grass such love, lovelorn,
Lay sorrowing; when every tear was born
Of diverse passion; when her lips and eyes
Were closed in sullen moisture, and quick sighs
Came vex'd and pettish through her nostrils small.
Hush! no exclaim—yet, justly might'st thou call
Curses upon his head.—I was half glad,
But my poor mistress went distract and mad,
When the boar tusk'd him: so away she flew
To Jove's high throne, and by her plainings drew
Immortal tear-drops down the thunderer's beard;
Whereon, it was decreed he should be rear'd
Each summer-time to life. Lo! this is he,
That same Adonis, safe in the privacy
Of this still region all his winter-sleep.
Aye, sleep; for when our love-sick queen did weep
Over his waned corse, the tremulous shower
Heal'd up the wound, and, with a balmy power,
Medicined death to a lengthened drowsiness:
The which she fills with visions, and doth dress
In all this quiet luxury; and hath set
Us young immortals, without any let,
To watch his slumber through. 'Tis well nigh pass'd,
Even to a moment's filling up, and fast

She scuds with summer breezes, to pant through
The first long kiss, warm firstling, to renew
Embower'd sports in Cytherea's isle.
Look! how those winged listeners all this while
Stand anxious: see! behold!"—This clamant word
Broke through the careful silence; for they heard
A rustling noise of leaves, and out there flutter'd
Pigeons and doves: Adonis something mutter'd,
The while one hand, that erst upon his thigh
Lay dormant, moved convulsed and gradually
Up to his forehead. Then there was a hum
Of sudden voices, echoing, "Come! come!
Arise! awake! Clear summer has forth walk'd
Unto the clover-sward, and she has talk'd
Full soothingly to every nested finch:
Rise, Cupids! or we'll give the bluebell pinch
To your dimpled arms. Once more sweet life begin!"
At this, from every side they hurried in,
Rubbing their sleepy eyes with lazy wrists,
And doubling overhead their little fists
In backward yawns. But all were soon alive:
For, as delicious wine doth, sparkling, dive
In nectar'd clouds and curls through water fair,
So from the arbour roof down swell'd an air
Odorous and enlivening; making all
To laugh, and play, and sing, and loudly call
For their sweet queen: when lo! the wreathed green
Disparted, and far upward could be seen
Blue heaven, and a silver car, air-borne,
Whose silent wheels, fresh wet from clouds of morn,
Spun off a drizzling dew,—which falling chill
On soft Adonis' shoulders, made him still
Nestle and turn uneasily about.
Soon were the white doves plain, with necks stretch'd out,
And silken traces lighten'd in descent;
And soon, returning from love's banishment,
Queen Venus leaning downward open-arm'd:
Her shadow fell upon his breast, and charm'd
A tumult to his heart, and a new life
Into his eyes. Ah, miserable strife,
But for her comforting! unhappy sight,
But meeting her blue orbs! Who, who can write
Of these first minutes?

*   *   *   *   *

Thus spake he, and that moment felt endued
With power to dream deliciously; so wound
Through a dim passage, searching till he found
The smoothest mossy bed and deepest, where
He threw himself, and just into the air
Stretching his indolent arms, he took, O bliss!
A naked waist: "Fair Cupid, whence is this?"
A well-known voice sigh'd, "Sweetest, here am I!"
At which soft ravishment, with doting cry
They trembled to each other.—Helicon!
O fountain'd hill! Old Homer's Helicon!
That thou wouldst spout a little streamlet o'er
These sorry pages; then the verse would soar
And sing above this gentle pair, like lark
Over his nested young: but all is dark
Around thine aged top, and thy clear fount
Exhales in mists to heaven. Aye, the count
Of mighty Poets is made up; the scroll
Is folded by the Muses; the bright roll
Is in Apollo's hand: our dazed eyes
Have seen a new tinge in the western skies:
The world has done its duty. Yet, oh yet,
Although the sun of poesy is set,
These lovers did embrace, and we must weep
That there is no old power left to steep
A quill immortal in their joyous tears.
Long time in silence did their anxious fears
Question that thus it was; long time they lay
Fondling and kissing every doubt away;
Long time ere soft caressing sobs began
To mellow into words, and then there ran
Two bubbling springs of talk from their sweet lips.
"O known Unknown! from whom my being sips
Such darling essence, wherefore may I not
Be ever in these arms? in this sweet spot
Pillow my chin for ever? ever press
These toying hands and kiss their smooth excess?
Why not for ever and for ever feel
That breath about my eyes? Ah, thou wilt steal
Away from me again, indeed, indeed—
Thou wilt be gone away, and wilt not heed
My lonely madness. Speak, delicious fair
Is—is it to be so? No! Who will dare

To pluck thee from me? And, of thine own will,
Full well I feel thou wouldst not leave me. Still
Let me entwine thee surer, surer—now
How can we part? Elysium! Who art thou?
Who, that thou canst not be for ever here,
Or lift me with thee to some starry sphere?
Enchantress! tell me by this soft embrace,
By the most soft completion of thy face,
Those lips, O slippery blisses, twinkling eyes,
And by these tenderest, milky sovereignties—
These tenderest, and by the nectar-wine,
The passion"——"O doved Ida the divine!
Endymion! dearest! Ah, unhappy me!
His soul will 'scape us—O felicity!
How he does love me! His poor temples beat
To the very tune of love—how sweet, sweet, sweet.
Revive, dear youth, or I shall faint and die;
Revive, or these soft hours will hurry by
In tranced dullness; speak, and let that spell
Affright this lethargy! I cannot quell
Its heavy pressure, and will press at least
My lips to thine, that they may richly feast
Until we taste the life of love again.
What! dost thou move? dost kiss? O bliss! O pain!
I love thee, youth, more than I can conceive;
And so long absence from thee doth bereave
My soul of any rest: yet must I hence:
Yet, can I not to starry eminence
Uplift thee; nor for very shame can own
Myself to thee. Ah, dearest, do not groan
Or thou wilt force me from this secrecy,
And I must blush in heaven."

*   *   *   *   *

BOOK III

THERE are who lord it o'er their fellow-men
With most prevailing tinsel: who unpen
Their baaing vanities, to browse away
The comfortable green and juicy hay
From human pastures; or, O torturing fact!
Who, through an idiot blink, will see unpack'd

Fire-branded foxes to sear up and singe
Our gold and ripe-ear'd hopes. With not one tinge
Of sanctuary splendour, not a sight
Able to face an owl's, they still are dight
By the blear-eyed nations in empurpled vests,
And crowns, and turbans. With unladen breasts,
Save of blown self-applause, they proudly mount
To their spirit's perch, their being's high account,
Their tiptop nothings, their dull skies, their thrones—
Amid the fierce intoxicating tones
Of trumpets, shoutings, and belabour'd drums,
And sudden cannon. Ah! how all this hums,
In wakeful ears, like uproar past and gone—
Like thunder-clouds that spake to Babylon,
And set those old Chaldeans to their tasks.—
Are then regalities all gilded masks?
No, there are throned seats unscalable
But by a patient wing, a constant spell,
Or by ethereal things that, unconfined,
Can make a ladder of the eternal wind,
And poise about in cloudy thunder-tents
To watch the abysm-birth of elements.
Aye, 'bove the withering of old-lipp'd Fate
A thousand Powers keep religious state,
In water, fiery realm, and airy bourne;
And, silent as a consecrated urn,
Hold spherey sessions for a season due.
Yet few of these far majesties, ah, few!
Have bared their operations to this globe—
Few, who with gorgeous pageantry enrobe
Our piece of heaven—whose benevolence
Shakes hand with our own Ceres; every sense
Filling with spiritual sweets to plenitude,
As bees gorge full their cells. And, by the feud
'Twixt Nothing and Creation, I here swear,
Eterne Apollo! that thy Sister fair
Is of all these the gentlier-mightiest.
When thy gold breath is misting in the west,
She unobserved steals unto her throne,
And there she sits most meek and most alone;
As if she had not pomp subservient;
As if thine eye, high Poet! was not bent
Towards her with the Muses in thine heart;
As if the minist'ring stars kept not apart,

Waiting for silver-footed messages.
O Moon! the oldest shades 'mong oldest trees
Feel palpitations when thou lookest in:
O Moon! old boughs lisp forth a holier din
The while they feel thine airy fellowship.
Thou dost bless everywhere, with silver lip
Kissing dead things to life. The sleeping kine,
Couch'd in thy brightness, dream of fields divine:
Innumerable mountains rise, and rise,
Ambitious for the hallowing of thine eyes;
And yet thy benediction passeth not
One obscure hiding-place, one little spot
Where pleasure may be sent: the nested wren
Has thy fair face within its tranquil ken,
And from beneath a sheltering ivy leaf
Takes glimpses of thee; thou art a relief
To the poor patient oyster, where it sleeps
Within its pearly house.—The mighty deeps,
The monstrous sea is thine—the myriad sea!
O Moon! far-spooming Ocean bows to thee,
And Tellus feels his forehead's cumbrous load.

　　Cynthia! where art thou now? What far abode
Of green or silvery bower doth enshrine
Such utmost beauty? Alas, thou dost pine
For one as sorrowful: thy cheek is pale
For one whose cheek is pale: thou dost bewail
His tears, who weeps for thee. Where dost thou sigh?
Ah! surely that light peeps from Vesper's eye,
Or what a thing is love! 'Tis She, but lo!
How changed, how full of ache, how gone in woe!
She dies at the thinnest cloud; her loveliness
Is wan on Neptune's blue: yet there's a stress
Of love-spangles, just off yon cape of trees,
Dancing upon the waves, as if to please
The curly foam with amorous influence.
O, not so idle: for down-glancing thence,
She fathoms eddies, and runs wild about
O'erwhelming water-courses; scaring out
The thorny sharks from hiding-holes, and fright'ning
Their savage eyes with unaccustom'd lightning.
Where will the splendour be content to reach?
O love! how potent hast thou been to teach

Strange journeyings! Wherever beauty dwells,
In gulf or aerie, mountains or deep dells,
In light, in gloom, in star or blazing sun,
Thou pointest out the way, and straight 'tis won.
Amid his toil thou gavest Leander breath;
Thou leddest Orpheus through the gleams of death;
Thou madest Pluto bear thin element;
And now, O winged Chieftain! thou hast sent
A moonbeam to the deep, deep water-world,
To find Endymion.

              On gold sand impearl'd
With lily shells, and pebbles milky white,
Poor Cynthia greeted him, and soothed her light
Against his pallid face: he felt the charm
To breathlessness, and suddenly a warm
Of his heart's blood: 'twas very sweet; he stay'd
His wandering steps, and half-entranced laid
His head upon a tuft of straggling weeds,
To taste the gentle moon, and freshening beads,
Lash'd from the crystal roof by fishes' tails.
And so he kept, until the rosy veils
Mantling the east, by Aurora's peering hand
Were lifted from the water's breast, and fann'd
Into sweet air; and sober'd morning came
Meekly through billows:—when like taper-flame
Left sudden by a dallying breath of air,
He rose in silence, and once more 'gan fare
Along his fated way.

              Far had he roam'd,
With nothing save the hollow vast, that foam'd
Above, around, and at his feet; save things
More dead than Morpheus' imaginings:
Old rusted anchors, helmets, breastplates large
Of gone sea-warriors; brazen beaks and targe;
Rudders that for a hundred years had lost
The sway of human hand; gold vase emboss'd
With long-forgotten story, and wherein
No reveller had ever dipp'd a chin
But those of Saturn's vintage; mouldering scrolls,
Writ in the tongue of heaven, by those souls
Who first were on the earth; and sculptures rude
In ponderous stone, developing the mood

Of ancient Nox;—then skeletons of man,
Of beast, behemoth, and leviathan,
And elephant, and eagle, and huge jaw
Of nameless monster. A cold leaden awe
These secrets struck into him; and unless
Dian had chased away that heaviness,
He might have died: but now, with cheered feel,
He onward kept; wooing these thoughts to steal
About the labyrinth in his soul of love.

*   *   *   *   *

                    "Now let me borrow,
For moments few, a temperament as stern
As Pluto's sceptre, that my words not burn
These uttering lips, while I in calm speech tell
How specious heaven was changed to real hell.

    "One morn she left me sleeping: half awake
I sought for her smooth arms and lips, to slake
My greedy thirst with nectarous camel-draughts;
But she was gone. Whereat the barbed shafts
Of disappointment stuck in me so sore,
That out I ran and search'd the forest o'er.
Wandering about in pine and cedar gloom
Damp awe assail'd me; for there 'gan to boom
A sound of moan, an agony of sound,
Sepulchral from the distance all around.
Then came a conquering earth-thunder, and rumbled
That fierce complain to silence: while I stumbled
Down a precipitous path, as if impell'd.
I came to a dark valley.—Groanings swell'd
Poisonous about my ears, and louder grew,
The nearer I approach'd a flame's gaunt blue,
That glared before me through a thorny brake.
This fire, like the eye of gordian snake,
Bewitch'd me towards; and I soon was near
A sight too fearful for the feel of fear:
In thicket hid I cursed the haggard scene—
The banquet of my arms, my arbour queen,
Seated upon an uptorn forest root;
And all around her shapes, wizard and brute,
Laughing, and wailing, grovelling, serpenting,
Showing tooth, tusk, and venom-bag, and sting!

O such deformities! old Charon's self,
Should he give up awhile his penny pelf,
And take a dream 'mong rushes Stygian,
It could not be so fantasied. Fierce, wan,
And tyrannizing was the lady's look,
As over them a gnarled staff she shook.
Ofttimes upon the sudden she laugh'd out,
And from a basket emptied to the rout
Clusters of grapes, the which they raven'd quick
And roar'd for more; with many a hungry lick
About their shaggy jaws. Avenging, slow,
Anon she took a branch of mistletoe,
And emptied on 't a black dull-gurgling phial:
Groan'd one and all, as if some piercing trial
Was sharpening for their pitiable bones.
She lifted up the charm: appealing groans
From their poor breasts went sueing to her ear
In vain; remorseless as an infant's bier
She whisk'd against their eyes the sooty oil.
Whereat was heard a noise of painful toil,
Increasing gradual to a tempest rage,
Shrieks, yells, and groans of torture-pilgrimage;
Until their grieved bodies 'gan to bloat
And puff from the tail's end to stifled throat:
Then was appalling silence: then a sight
More wildering than all that hoarse affright;
For the whole herd, as by a whirlwind writhen,
Went though the dismal air like one huge Python
Antagonizing Boreas,—and so vanish'd.
Yet there was not a breath of wind: she banish'd
These phantoms with a nod. Lo! from the dark
Came waggish fauns, and nymphs, and satyrs stark,
With dancing and loud revelry,—and went
Swifter than centaurs after rapine bent.—
Sighing an elephant appear'd and bow'd
Before the fierce witch, speaking thus aloud
In human accent: 'Potent goddess! chief
Of pains resistless! make my being brief,
Or let me from this heavy prison fly:
Or give me to the air, or let me die!
I sue not for my happy crown again;
I sue not for my phalanx on the plain;
I sue not for my lone, my widow'd wife:
I sue not for my ruddy drops of life,

My children fair, my lovely girls and boys!
I will forget them; I will pass these joys;
Ask nought so heavenward, so too—too high:
Only I pray, as fairest boon, to die,
Or be deliver'd from this cumbrous flesh,
From this gross, detestable, filthy mesh,
And merely given to the cold bleak air.
Have mercy, Goddess! Circe, feel my prayer!'

"That curst magician's name fell icy numb
Upon my wild conjecturing: truth had come
Naked and sabre-like against my heart.
I saw a fury whetting a death-dart;
And my slain spirit, overwrought with fright,
Fainted away in that dark lair of night.
Think, my deliverer, how desolate
My waking must have been! disgust, and hate,
And terrors manifold divided me
A spoil amongst them."

*   *   *   *   *

"On a day,
Sitting upon a rock above the spray,
I saw grow up from the horizon's brink
A gallant vessel: soon she seem'd to sink
Away from me again, as though her course
Had been resumed in spite of hindering force—
So vanish'd: and not long, before arose
Dark clouds, and muttering of winds morose.
Old Aeolus would stifle his mad spleen,
But could not; therefore, all the billows green
Toss'd up the silver spume against the clouds.
The tempest came: I saw that vessel's shrouds
In perilous bustle; while upon the deck
Stood trembling creatures. I beheld the wreck;
The final gulfing; the poor struggling souls;
I heard their cries amid loud thunder-rolls.
O they had all been saved but crazed eld
Annull'd my vigorous cravings; and thus quell'd
And curb'd, think on 't, O Latmian! did I sit
Writhing with pity, and a cursing fit
Against that hell-born Circe. The crew had gone,
By one and one, to pale oblivion;

And I was gazing on the surges prone,
With many a scalding tear, and many a groan,
When at my feet emerged an old man's hand,
Grasping this scroll, and this same slender wand.
I knelt with pain—reach'd out my hand—had grasp'd
These treasures—touch'd the knuckles—they unclasp'd—
I caught a finger: but the downward weight
O'erpower'd me—it sank. Then 'gan abate
The storm, and through chill aguish gloom outburst
The comfortable sun. I was athirst
To search the book, and in the warming air
Parted its dripping leaves with eager care.
Strange matters did it treat of, and drew on
My soul page after page, till well nigh won
Into forgetfulness; when, stupefied,
I read these words, and read again, and tried
My eyes against the heavens, and read again.
O what a load of misery and pain
Each Atlas-line bore off!—a shine of hope
Came gold around me, cheering me to cope
Strenuous with hellish tyranny. Attend!
For thou hast brought their promise to an end."

In the wide sea there lives a forlorn wretch,
Doom'd with enfeebled carcase to outstretch
His loath'd existence through ten centuries,
And then to die alone. Who can devise
A total opposition? No one. So
One million times ocean must ebb and flow,
And he oppressed. Yet he shall not die,
These things accomplish'd:—If he utterly
Scans all the depths of magic, and expounds
The meanings of all motions, shapes, and sounds;
If he explores all forms and substances
Straight homeward to their symbol-essences;
He shall not die. Moreover, and in chief,
He must pursue this task of joy and grief
Most piously;—all lovers tempest-tost,
And in the savage overwhelming lost,
He shall deposit side by side, until
Time's creeping shall the dreary space fulfil:
Which done, and all these labours ripened,
A youth, by heavenly power loved and led,

Shall stand before him; whom he shall direct
How to consummate all. The youth elect
Must do the thing, or both will be destroy'd.—

"Then," cried the young Endymion, overjoy'd,
"We are twin brothers in this destiny!"

*   *   *   *   *

BOOK IV

MUSE of my native land! loftiest Muse!
O first-born on the mountains! by the hues
Of heaven on the spiritual air begot:
Long didst thou sit alone in northern grot,
While yet our England was a wolfish den;
Before our forests heard the talk of men;
Before the first of Druids was a child;—
Long didst thou sit amid our regions wild,
Rapt in a deep prophetic solitude.
There came an eastern voice of solemn mood:—
Yet wast thou patient. Then sang forth the Nine,
Apollo's garland:—yet didst thou divine
Such home-bred glory, that they cried in vain,
"Come hither, Sister of the Island!" Plain
Spake fair Ausonia; and once more she spake
A higher summons:—still didst thou betake
Thee to thy native hopes. O thou hast won
A full accomplishment! The thing is done,
Which undone, these our latter days had risen
On barren souls. Great Muse, thou know'st what prison
Of flesh and bone, curbs, and confines, and frets
Our spirits' wings: despondency besets
Our pillows; and the fresh to-morrow morn
Seems to give forth its light in very scorn
Of our dull, uninspired, snail-paced lives.
Long have I said, how happy he who shrives
To thee! But then I thought on poets gone,
And could not pray:—nor can I now—so on
I move to the end in lowliness of heart.—

"Ah, woe is me! that I should fondly part
From my dear native land! Ah, foolish maid!
Glad was the hour, when, with thee, myriads bade
Adieu to Ganges and their pleasant fields!
To one so friendless the clear freshet yields
A bitter coolness; the ripe grape is sour:
Yet I would have, great gods! but one short hour
Of native air—let me but die at home."

* * * * *

"O Sorrow,
   Why dost borrow
The natural hue of health, from vermeil lips?—
    To give maiden blushes
    To the white rose bushes?
Or is 't thy dewy hand the daisy tips?

"O Sorrow,
   Why dost borrow
The lustrous passion from a falcon-eye?—
    To give the glowworm light?
    Or, on a moonless night,
To tinge, on siren shores, the salt sea-spry?

"O Sorrow,
   Why dost borrow
The mellow ditties from a mourning tongue?—
    To give at evening pale
    Unto the nightingale,
That thou mayst listen the cold dews among?

"O Sorrow,
   Why dost borrow
Heart's lightness from the merriment of May?—
    A lover would not tread
    A cowslip on the head,
Though he should dance from eve till peep of day—
    Nor any drooping flower
    Held sacred for thy bower,
Wherever he may sport himself and play.

"To Sorrow,
    I bade good morrow,
And thought to leave her far away behind;
    But cheerly, cheerly,
    She loves me dearly;
She is so constant to me, and so kind:
    I would deceive her,
    And so leave her,
But ah! she is so constant and so kind."

*   *   *   *   *

    Endymion! unhappy! it nigh grieves
Me to behold thee thus in last extreme:
Enskied ere this, but truly that I deem
Truth the best music in a first-born song.
Thy lute-voiced brother will I sing ere long,
And thou shalt aid—hast thou not aided me?
Yes, moonlight Emperor! felicity
Has been thy meed for many thousand years;
Yet often have I, on the brink of tears,
Mourn'd as if yet thou wert a forester;—
Forgetting the old tale.

              He did not stir
His eyes from the dead leaves, or one small pulse
Of joy he might have felt. The spirit culls
Unfaded amaranth, when wild it strays
Through the old garden-ground of boyish days.
A little onward ran the very stream
By which he took his first soft poppy dream;
And on the very bark 'gainst which he leant
A crescent he had carved, and round it spent
His skill in little stars. The teeming tree
Had swollen and green'd the pious charactery,
But not ta'en out. Why, there was not a slope
Up which he had not fear'd the antelope;
And not a tree, beneath whose rooty shade
He had not with his tamed leopards play'd;
Nor could an arrow light, or javelin,
Fly in the air where his had never been—
And yet he knew it not.

*   *   *   *   *

          So he inwardly began
On things for which no wording can be found;
Deeper and deeper sinking, until drown'd
Beyond the reach of music: for the choir
Of Cynthia he heard not, though rough brier
Nor muffling thicket interposed to dull
The vesper hymn, far swollen, soft and full,
Through the dark pillars of those sylvan aisles.
He saw not the two maidens, nor their smiles,
Wan as primroses gather'd at midnight
By chilly-finger'd spring. "Unhappy wight!
Endymion!" said Peona, "we are here!
What wouldst thou ere we all are laid on bier?"
Then he embraced her, and his lady's hand
Press'd, saying: "Sister, I would have command,
If it were heaven's will, on our sad fate."
At which that dark-eyed stranger stood elate
And said, in a new voice, but sweet as love,
To Endymion's amaze: "By Cupid's dove,
And so thou shalt! and by the lily truth
Of my own breast thou shalt, beloved youth!"
And as she spake, into her face there came
Light, as reflected from a silver flame:
Her long black hair swell'd ampler, in display
Full golden; in her eyes a brighter day
Dawn'd blue, and full of love. Aye, he beheld
Phoebe, his passion! joyous she upheld
Her lucid bow, continuing thus: "Drear, drear
Has our delaying been; but foolish fear
Withheld me first; and then decrees of fate;
And then 'twas fit that from this mortal state
Thou shouldst, my love, by some unlook'd-for change
Be spiritualized. Peona, we shall range
These forests, and to thee they safe shall be
As was thy cradle; hither shalt thou flee
To meet us many a time." Next Cynthia bright
Peona kiss'd, and bless'd with fair good night:
Her brother kiss'd her too, and knelt adown
Before his goddess, in a blissful swoon.
She gave her fair hands to him, and behold,
Before three swiftest kisses he had told,
They vanish'd far away!—Peona went
Home through the gloomy wood in wonderment.

                 1817–18

POEMS OF 1818–19

Written in Answer to a Sonnet Ending Thus:—

"Dark eyes are dearer far
Than those that mock the hyacinthine bell."

J. H. REYNOLDS

BLUE! 'Tis the life of heaven,—the domain
    Of Cynthia,—the wide palace of the sun,—
The tent of Hesperus, and all his train,—
    The bosomer of clouds, gold, gray, and dun.
Blue! 'Tis the life of waters—ocean
    And all its vassal streams, pools numberless,
May rage, and foam, and fret, but never can
    Subside, if not to dark blue nativeness.
Blue! Gentle cousin of the forest-green,
    Married to green in all the sweetest flowers,—
Forget-me-not,—the blue bell,—and, that queen
    Of secrecy, the violet: what strange powers
Hast thou, as a mere shadow! But how great,
When in an Eye thou art, alive with fate!

                            February 1818

Fancy

EVER let the Fancy roam,
Pleasure never is at home:
At a touch sweet Pleasure melteth,
Like to bubbles when rain pelteth;

Then let winged Fancy wander
Through the thought still spread beyond her:
Open wide the mind's cage-door,
She'll dart forth, and cloudward soar.
O sweet Fancy! let her loose;
Summer's joys are spoilt by use,
And the enjoying of the Spring
Fades as does its blossoming;
Autumn's red-lipp'd fruitage too,
Blushing through the mist and dew,
Cloys with tasting: What do then?
Sit thee by the ingle, when
The sear faggot blazes bright,
Spirit of a winter's night;
When the soundless earth is muffled,
And the caked snow is shuffled
From the ploughboy's heavy shoon;
When the Night doth meet the Noon
In a dark conspiracy
To banish Even from her sky.
Sit thee there, and send abroad,
With a mind self-overawed,
Fancy, high-commission'd:—send her!
She has vassals to attend her:
She will bring, in spite of frost,
Beauties that the earth hath lost;
She will bring thee, all together,
All delights of summer weather;
All the buds and bells of May,
From dewy sward or thorny spray;
All the heaped Autumn's wealth,
With a still, mysterious stealth:
She will mix these pleasures up
Like three fit wines in a cup,
And thou shalt quaff it:—thou shalt hear
Distant harvest-carols clear;
Rustle of the reaped corn;
Sweet birds antheming the morn:
And, in the same moment—hark!
'Tis the early April lark,
Or the rooks, with busy caw,
Foraging for sticks and straw.
Thou shalt, at one glance, behold
The daisy and the marigold;

White-plumed lilies, and the first
Hedge-grown primrose that hath burst;
Shaded hyacinth, alway
Sapphire queen of the mid-May;
And every leaf, and every flower
Pearled with the self-same shower.
Thou shalt see the field-mouse peep
Meagre from its celled sleep;
And the snake all winter-thin
Cast on sunny bank its skin;
Freckled nest-eggs thou shalt see
Hatching in the hawthorn-tree,
When the hen-bird's wing doth rest
Quiet on her mossy nest;
Then the hurry and alarm
When the bee-hive casts its swarm;
Acorns ripe down-pattering
While the autumn breezes sing.

Oh, sweet Fancy! let her loose;
Every thing is spoilt by use;
Where's the cheek that doth not fade,
Too much gazed at? Where's the maid
Whose lip mature is ever new?
Where's the eye, however blue,
Doth not weary? Where's the face
One would meet in every place?
Where's the voice, however soft,
One would hear so very oft?
At a touch sweet Pleasure melteth
Like to bubbles when rain pelteth.
Let, then, winged Fancy find
Thee a mistress to thy mind:
Dulcet-eyed as Ceres' daughter
Ere the God of Torment taught her
How to frown and how to chide;
With a waist and with a side
White as Hebe's, when her zone
Slipt its golden clasp, and down
Fell her kirtle to her feet,
While she held the goblet sweet,
And Jove grew languid.—Break the mesh
Of the Fancy's silken leash;

Quickly break her prison-string,
And such joys as these she'll bring.—
Let the winged Fancy roam,
Pleasure never is at home.

                              December 1818

Ode

Written on the blank page before Beaumont and
Fletcher's tragi-comedy, *The Fair Maid of the Inn*.

BARDS of Passion and of Mirth,
Ye have left your souls on earth!
Have ye souls in heaven too,
Double-lived in regions new?
Yes, and those of heaven commune
With the spheres of sun and moon;
With the noise of fountains wond'rous
And the parle of voices thund'rous;
With the whisper of heaven's trees
And one another, in soft ease
Seated on Elysian lawns
Browsed by none but Dian's fawns;
Underneath large blue-bells tented,
Where the daisies are rose-scented,
And the rose herself has got
Perfume which on earth is not;
Where the nightingale doth sing
Not a senseless, tranced thing,
But divine melodious truth;
Philosophic numbers smooth;
Tales and golden histories
Of heaven and its mysteries.

    Thus ye live on high, and then
On the earth ye live again;
And the souls ye left behind you
Teach us, here, the way to find you,
Where your other souls are joying,
Never slumber'd, never cloying.
Here, your earth-born souls still speak
To mortals, of their little week;

Of their sorrows and delights;
Of their passions and their spites;
Of their glory and their shame;
What doth strengthen and what maim.
Thus ye teach us, every day,
Wisdom, though fled far away.

Bards of Passion and of Mirth,
Ye have left your souls on earth!
Ye have souls in heaven too,
Double-lived in regions new!

December 1818

Ode on Melancholy

I

No, no! go not to Lethe, neither twist
 Wolf's-bane, tight-rooted, for its poisonous wine;
Nor suffer thy pale forehead to be kiss'd
 By nightshade, ruby grape of Proserpine;
Make not your rosary of yew-berries,
 Nor let the beetle, or the death-moth be
  Your mournful Psyche, nor the downy owl
A partner in your sorrow's mysteries;
 For shade to shade will come too drowsily,
  And drown the wakeful anguish of the soul.

II

But when the melancholy fit shall fall
 Sudden from heaven like a weeping cloud,
That fosters the droop-headed flowers all,
 And hides the green hills in an April shroud;
Then glut thy sorrow on a morning rose,
 Or on the rainbow of the salt-sand wave,
  Or on the wealth of globed peonies;
Or if thy mistress some rich anger shows,
 Emprison her soft hand, and let her rave,
  And feed deep, deep upon her peerless eyes.

III

She dwells with Beauty—Beauty that must die;
    And Joy, whose hand is ever at his lips
Bidding adieu; and aching Pleasure nigh,
    Turning to poison while the bee-mouth sips:
Aye, in the very temple of Delight
    Veil'd Melancholy has her sovran shrine,
        Though seen of none save him whose strenuous tongue
    Can burst Joy's grape against his palate fine;
His soul shall taste the sadness of her might,
    And be among her cloudy trophies hung.

1819

The Eve of St. Agnes

I

St. Agnes' Eve—Ah, bitter chill it was!
The owl, for all his feathers, was a-cold;
The hare limp'd trembling through the frozen grass,
And silent was the flock in woolly fold:
Numb were the Beadsman's fingers, while he told
His rosary, and while his frosted breath,
Like pious incense from a censer old,
Seem'd taking flight for heaven, without a death,
Past the sweet Virgin's picture, while his prayer he saith.

II

His prayer he saith, this patient, holy man;
Then takes his lamp, and riseth from his knees,
And back returneth, meagre, barefoot, wan,
Along the chapel aisle by slow degrees:
The sculptured dead, on each side, seem to freeze,

Emprison'd in black, purgatorial rails:
Knights, ladies, praying in dumb orat'ries,
He passeth by; and his weak spirit fails
To think how they may ache in icy hoods and mails.

III

Northward he turneth through a little door,
And scarce three steps, ere Music's golden tongue
Flatter'd to tears this aged man and poor;
But no—already had his death-bell rung;
The joys of all his life were said and sung:
His was harsh penance on St. Agnes' Eve:
Another way he went, and soon among
Rough ashes sat he for his soul's reprieve,
And all night kept awake, for sinners' sake to grieve.

IV

That ancient Beadsman heard the prelude soft;
And so it chanced, for many a door was wide,
From hurry to and fro. Soon, up aloft,
The silver, snarling trumpets 'gan to chide:
The level chambers, ready with their pride,
Were glowing to receive a thousand guests:
The carved angels, ever eager-eyed,
Stared, where upon their heads the cornice rests,
With hair blown back, and wings put cross-wise on their breasts.

V

At length burst in the argent revelry,
With plume, tiara, and all rich array,
Numerous as shadows haunting fairily
The brain, new-stuff'd, in youth, with triumphs gay
Of old romance. These let us wish away,
And turn, sole-thoughted, to one Lady there,
Whose heart had brooded, all that wintry day,
On love, and wing'd St. Agnes' saintly care,
As she had heard old dames full many times declare.

VI

They told her how, upon St. Agnes' Eve,
Young virgins might have visions of delight,
And soft adorings from their loves receive
Upon the honey'd middle of the night,
If ceremonies due they did aright;
As, supperless to bed they must retire,
And couch supine their beauties, lily white;
Nor look behind, nor sideways, but require
Of Heaven with upward eyes for all that they desire.

VII

Full of this whim was thoughtful Madeline:
The music, yearning like a God in pain,
She scarcely heard: her maiden eyes divine,
Fix'd on the floor, saw many a sweeping train
Pass by—she heeded not at all: in vain
Came many a tiptoe, amorous cavalier,
And back retired; not cool'd by high disdain,
But she saw not: her heart was otherwhere;
She sigh'd for Agnes' dreams, the sweetest of the year.

VIII

She danced along with vague, regardless eyes,
Anxious her lips, her breathing quick and short:
The hallow'd hour was near at hand: she sighs
Amid the timbrels, and the throng'd resort
Of whisperers in anger, or in sport;
'Mid looks of love, defiance, hate, and scorn,
Hoodwink'd with faery fancy; all amort,
Save to St. Agnes and her lambs unshorn,
And all the bliss to be before to-morrow morn.

IX

So, purposing each moment to retire,
She linger'd still. Meantime, across the moors,
Had come young Porphyro, with heart on fire
For Madeline. Beside the portal doors,
Buttress'd from moonlight, stands he, and implores
All saints to give him sight of Madeline,
But for one moment in the tedious hours,
That he might gaze and worship all unseen;
Perchance speak, kneel, touch, kiss—in sooth such things have been.

X

He ventures in: let no buzz'd whisper tell:
All eyes be muffled, or a hundred swords
Will storm his heart, Love's fev'rous citadel:
For him, those chambers held barbarian hordes,
Hyena foemen, and hot-blooded lords,
Whose very dogs would execrations howl
Against his lineage: not one breast affords
Him any mercy, in that mansion foul,
Save one old beldame, weak in body and in soul.

XI

Ah, happy chance! the aged creature came,
Shuffling along with ivory-headed wand,
To where he stood, hid from the torch's flame,
Behind a broad hall-pillar, far beyond
The sound of merriment and chorus bland:
He startled her; but soon she knew his face,
And grasp'd his fingers in her palsied hand,
Saying, "Mercy, Porphyro! hie thee from this place;
They are all here to-night, the whole bloodthirsty race!

XII

Get hence! get hence! there's dwarfish Hildebrand;
He had a fever late, and in the fit
He cursed thee and thine, both house and land:
Then there's that old Lord Maurice, not a whit
More tame for his gray hairs—Alas me! flit!
Flit like a ghost away."—"Ah, Gossip dear,
We're safe enough; here in this arm-chair sit,
And tell me how"—"Good Saints! not here, not here;
Follow me, child, or else these stones will be thy bier."

XIII

He follow'd through a lowly arched way,
Brushing the cobwebs with his lofty plume;
And as she mutter'd "Well-a—well-a-day!"
He found him in a little moonlight room,
Pale, latticed, chill, and silent as a tomb.
"Now tell me where is Madeline," said he,
"O tell me, Angela, by the holy loom
Which none but secret sisterhood may see,
When they St. Agnes' wool are weaving piously."

XIV

"St. Agnes! Ah! it is St. Agnes' Eve—
Yet men will murder upon holy days:
Thou must hold water in a witch's sieve,
And be liege-lord of all the Elves and Fays,
To venture so: it fills me with amaze
To see thee, Porphyro!—St. Agnes' Eve!
God's help! my lady fair the conjuror plays
This very night: good angels her deceive!
But let me laugh awhile, I've mickle time to grieve."

XV

Feebly she laugheth in the languid moon,
While Porphyro upon her face doth look,
Like puzzled urchin on an aged crone
Who keepeth closed a wond'rous riddle-book,
As spectacled she sits in chimney nook.
But soon his eyes grew brilliant, when she told
His lady's purpose; and he scarce could brook
Tears, at the thought of those enchantments cold,
And Madeline asleep in lap of legends old.

XVI

Sudden a thought came like a full-blown rose,
Flushing his brow, and in his pained heart
Made purple riot: then doth he propose
A stratagem, that makes the beldame start:
"A cruel man and impious thou art:
Sweet lady, let her pray, and sleep, and dream
Alone with her good angels, far apart
From wicked men like thee. Go, go! I deem
Thou canst not surely be the same that thou didst seem."

XVII

"I will not harm her, by all saints I swear,"
Quoth Porphyro: "O may I ne'er find grace
When my weak voice shall whisper its last prayer,
If one of her soft ringlets I displace,
Or look with ruffian passion in her face:
Good Angela, believe me by these tears;
Or I will, even in a moment's space,
Awake, with horrid shout, my foemen's ears,
And beard them, though they be more fang'd than wolves and bears."

XVIII

"Ah! why wilt thou affright a feeble soul?
A poor, weak, palsy-stricken, church-yard thing,
Whose passing-bell may ere the midnight toll;
Whose prayers for thee, each morn and evening,
Were never miss'd." Thus plaining, doth she bring
A gentler speech from burning Porphyro;
So woful, and of such deep sorrowing,
That Angela gives promise she will do
Whatever he shall wish, betide her weal or woe.

XIX

Which was, to lead him, in close secrecy,
Even to Madeline's chamber, and there hide
Him in a closet, of such privacy
That he might see her beauty unespied,
And win perhaps that night a peerless bride,
While legion'd fairies paced the coverlet,
And pale enchantment held her sleepy-eyed.
Never on such a night have lovers met,
Since Merlin paid his Demon all the monstrous debt.

XX

"It shall be as thou wishest," said the Dame:
"All cates and dainties shall be stored there
Quickly on this feast-night: by the tambour frame
Her own lute thou wilt see: no time to spare,
For I am slow and feeble, and scarce dare
On such a catering trust my dizzy head.
Wait here, my child, with patience; kneel in prayer
The while: Ah! thou must needs the lady wed,
Or may I never leave my grave among the dead."

XXI

So saying she hobbled off with busy fear.
The lover's endless minutes slowly pass'd;
The Dame return'd, and whisper'd in his ear
To follow her; with aged eyes aghast
From fright of dim espial. Safe at last,
Through many a dusky gallery, they gain
The maiden's chamber, silken, hush'd and chaste;
Where Porphyro took covert, pleased amain.
His poor guide hurried back with agues in her brain.

XXII

Her falt'ring hand upon the balustrade,
Old Angela was feeling for the stair,
When Madeline, St. Agnes' charmed maid,
Rose, like a mission'd spirit, unaware:
With silver taper's light, and pious care,
She turn'd, and down the aged gossip led
To a safe level matting. Now prepare,
Young Porphyro, for gazing on that bed;
She comes, she comes again, like ring-dove fray'd and fled.

XXIII

Out went the taper as she hurried in;
Its little smoke, in pallid moonshine, died:
She closed the door, she panted, all akin
To spirits of the air, and visions wide:
No uttered syllable, or, woe betide!
But to her heart, her heart was voluble,
Paining with eloquence her balmy side;
As though a tongueless nightingale should swell
Her throat in vain, and die, heart-stifled in her dell.

XXIV

A casement high and triple arch'd there was,
All garlanded with carven imag'ries
Of fruits, and flowers, and bunches of knot-grass,
And diamonded with panes of quaint device,
Innumerable of stains and splendid dyes,
As are the tiger-moth's deep-damask'd wings;
And in the midst, 'mong thousand heraldries,
And twilight saints, and dim emblazonings,
A shielded scutcheon blush'd with blood of queens and kings.

XXV

Full on this casement shone the wintry moon,
And threw warm gules on Madeline's fair breast,
As down she knelt for heaven's grace and boon;
Rose-bloom fell on her hands, together prest,
And on her silver cross soft amethyst,
And on her hair a glory, like a saint:
She seem'd a splendid angel, newly drest,
Save wings, for heaven:—Porphyro grew faint;
She knelt, so pure a thing, so free from mortal taint.

XXVI

Anon his heart revives: her vespers done,
Of all its wreathed pearls her hair she frees;
Unclasps her warmed jewels one by one;
Loosens her fragrant bodice; by degrees
Her rich attire creeps rustling to her knees:
Half-hidden, like a mermaid in sea-weed,
Pensive awhile she dreams awake, and sees,
In fancy, fair St. Agnes in her bed,
But dares not look behind, or all the charm is fled.

XXVII

Soon, trembling in her soft and chilly nest,
In sort of wakeful swoon, perplex'd she lay,
Until the poppied warmth of sleep oppress'd
Her soothed limbs, and soul fatigued away;
Flown, like a thought, until the morrow-day;
Blissfully haven'd both from joy and pain;
Clasp'd like a missal where swart Paynims pray;
Blinded alike from sunshine and from rain,
As though a rose should shut, and be a bud again.

XXVIII

Stol'n to this paradise, and so entranced,
Porphyro gazed upon her empty dress,
And listen'd to her breathing, if it chanced
To wake into a slumberous tenderness;
Which when he heard, that minute did he bless,
And breathed himself: then from the closet crept,
Noiseless as fear in a wide wilderness,
And over the hush'd carpet, silent, stept,
And 'tween the curtains peep'd, where, lo!—how fast she slept.

XXIX

Then by the bed-side, where the faded moon
Made a dim, silver twilight, soft he set
A table, and, half anguish'd, threw thereon
A cloth of woven crimson, gold, and jet:—
O for some drowsy Morphean amulet!
The boisterous, midnight, festive clarion,
The kettle-drum, and far-heard clarionet,
Affray his ears, though but in dying tone:—
The hall-door shuts again, and all the noise is gone.

XXX

And still she slept an azure-lidded sleep,
In blanched linen, smooth, and lavender'd,
While he from forth the closet brought a heap
Of candied apple, quince, and plum, and gourd;
With jellies soother than the creamy curd,
And lucent syrops, tinct with cinnamon;
Manna and dates, in argosy transferr'd
From Fez; and spiced dainties, every one,
From silken Samarcand to cedar'd Lebanon.

XXXI

These delicates he heap'd with glowing hand
On golden dishes and in baskets bright
Of wreathed silver: sumptuous they stand
In the retired quiet of the night,
Filling the chilly room with perfume light.—
"And now, my love, my seraph fair, awake!
Thou art my heaven, and I thine eremite:
Open thine eyes, for meek St. Agnes' sake,
Or I shall drowse beside thee, so my soul doth ache."

XXXII

Thus whispering, his warm, unnerved arm
Sank in her pillow. Shaded was her dream
By the dusk curtains:—'twas a midnight charm
Impossible to melt as iced stream:
The lustrous salvers in the moonlight gleam;
Broad golden fringe upon the carpet lies:
It seem'd he never, never could redeem
From such a steadfast spell his lady's eyes;
So mused awhile, entoil'd in woofed phantasies.

XXXIII

Awakening up, he took her hollow lute,—
Tumultuous,—and, in chords that tenderest be,
He play'd an ancient ditty, long since mute,
In Provence call'd "La belle dame sans mercy:"
Close to her ear touching the melody;—
Wherewith disturb'd, she utter'd a soft moan:
He ceased—she panted quick—and suddenly
Her blue affrayed eyes wide open shone:
Upon his knees he sank, pale as smooth-sculptured stone.

XXXIV

Her eyes were open, but she still beheld,
Now wide awake, the vision of her sleep:
There was a painful change, that nigh expell'd
The blisses of her dream so pure and deep
At which fair Madeline began to weep,
And moan forth witless words with many a sigh;
While still her gaze on Porphyro would keep;
Who knelt, with joined hands and piteous eye,
Fearing to move or speak, she look'd so dreamingly.

XXXV

"Ah, Porphyro!" said she, "but even now
Thy voice was at sweet tremble in mine ear,
Made tuneable with every sweetest vow;
And those sad eyes were spiritual and clear:
How changed thou art! how pallid, chill, and drear!
Give me that voice again, my Porphyro,
Those looks immortal, those complainings dear!
Oh leave me not in this eternal woe,
For if thou diest, my Love, I know not where to go."

XXXVI

Beyond a mortal man impassion'd far
At these voluptuous accents, he arose,
Ethereal, flush'd, and like a throbbing star
Seen mid the sapphire heaven's deep repose;
Into her dream he melted, as the rose
Blendeth its odour with the violet,—
Solution sweet: meantime the frost-wind blows
Like Love's alarum pattering the sharp sleet
Against the window-panes; St. Agnes' moon hath set.

XXXVII

'Tis dark: quick pattereth the flaw-blown sleet:
"This is no dream, my bride, my Madeline!"
'Tis dark: the iced gusts still rave and beat:
"No dream, alas! alas! and woe is mine!
Porphyro will leave me here to fade and pine.—
Cruel! what traitor could thee hither bring?
I curse not, for my heart is lost in thine,
Though thou forsakest a deceived thing;—
A dove forlorn and lost with sick unpruned wing."

XXXVIII

"My Madeline! sweet dreamer! lovely bride!
Say, may I be for aye thy vassal blest?
Thy beauty's shield, heart-shaped and vermeil dyed?
Ah, silver shrine, here will I take my rest
After so many hours of toil and quest,
A famish'd pilgrim,—saved by miracle.
Though I have found, I will not rob thy nest
Saving of thy sweet self; if thou think'st well
To trust, fair Madeline, to no rude infidel.

XXXIX

"Hark! 'tis an elfin storm from faery land,
　　Of haggard seeming, but a boon indeed:
　　Arise—arise! the morning is at hand:—
　　The bloated wassailers will never heed:—
　　Let us away, my love, with happy speed;
　　There are no ears to hear, or eyes to see,—
　　Drown'd all in Rhenish and the sleepy mead:
　　Awake! arise! my love, and fearless be,
For o'er the southern moors I have a home for thee."

XL

She hurried at his words, beset with fears,
　　For there were sleeping dragons all around,
　　At glaring watch, perhaps, with ready spears—
　　Down the wide stairs a darkling way they found.—
　　In all the house was heard no human sound.
　　A chain-droop'd lamp was flickering by each door;
　　The arras, rich with horseman, hawk, and hound,
　　Flutter'd in the besieging wind's uproar;
And the long carpets rose along the gusty floor.

XLI

They glide, like phantoms, into the wide hall;
　　Like phantoms to the iron porch they glide,
　　Where lay the Porter, in uneasy sprawl,
　　With a huge empty flagon by his side:
　　The wakeful bloodhound rose, and shook his hide,
　　But his sagacious eye an inmate owns:
　　By one, and one, the bolts full easy slide:—
　　The chains lie silent on the footworn stones;—
The key turns, and the door upon its hinges groans.

XLII

And they are gone: aye, ages long ago
These lovers fled away into the storm.
That night the Baron dreamt of many a woe,
And all his warrior-guests, with shade and form
Of witch, and demon, and large coffin-worm,
Were long be-nightmared. Angela the old
Died palsy-twitch'd, with meagre face deform;
The Beadsman, after thousand aves told,
For aye unsought-for slept among his ashes cold.

1819

Ode on a Grecian Urn

I

THOU still unravish'd bride of quietness,
    Thou foster-child of Silence and slow Time,
Sylvan historian, who canst thus express
    A flowery tale more sweetly than our rhyme:
What leaf-fringed legend haunts about thy shape
    Of deities or mortals, or of both,
        In Tempe or the dales of Arcady?
    What men or gods are these? what maidens loth?
What mad pursuit? What struggle to escape?
        What pipes and timbrels? What wild ecstasy?

II

Heard melodies are sweet, but those unheard
    Are sweeter; therefore, ye soft pipes, play on;
Not to the sensual ear, but, more endear'd
    Pipe to the spirit ditties of no tone:

Fair youth, beneath the trees, thou canst not leave
   Thy song, nor ever can those trees be bare;
      Bold Lover, never, never canst thou kiss,
Though winning near the goal—yet, do not grieve;
      She cannot fade, though thou hast not thy bliss,
   For ever wilt thou love, and she be fair!

III

Ah, happy, happy boughs! that cannot shed
   Your leaves, nor ever bid the Spring adieu;
And, happy melodist, unwearied,
   For ever piping songs for ever new;
More happy love! more happy, happy love!
   For ever warm and still to be enjoy'd,
      For ever panting, and for ever young;
All breathing human passion far above,
   That leaves a heart high-sorrowful and cloy'd,
      A burning forehead, and a parching tongue.

IV

Who are these coming to the sacrifice?
   To what green altar, O mysterious priest,
Lead'st thou that heifer lowing at the skies,
   And all her silken flanks with garlands drest?
What little town by river or sea shore,
   Or mountain-built with peaceful citadel,
      Is emptied of this folk, this pious morn?
And, little town, thy streets for evermore
   Will silent be; and not a soul to tell
      Why thou art desolate, can e'er return.

V

O Attic shape! Fair attitude! with brede
   Of marble men and maidens overwrought,
With forest branches and the trodden weed;
   Thou, silent form, dost tease us out of thought
As doth eternity: Cold Pastoral!

When old age shall this generation waste,
   Thou shalt remain, in midst of other woe
Than ours, a friend to man, to whom thou say'st,
"Beauty is truth, truth beauty,"—that is all
   Ye know on earth, and all ye need to know.

May 1819

A Dream, After Reading Dante's Episode of Paolo and Francesca

As Hermes once took to his feathers light,
   When lulled Argus, baffled, swoon'd and slept
So on a Delphic reed, my idle spright
   So play'd, so charm'd, so conquer'd, so bereft
The dragon-world of all its hundred eyes;
   And, seeing it asleep, so fled away—
Not to pure Ida with its snow-cold skies,
   Nor unto Tempe where Jove grieved a day;
But to that second circle of sad hell,
   Where 'mid the gust, the whirlwind, and the flaw
Of rain and hail-stones, lovers need not tell
   Their sorrows. Pale were the sweet lips I saw,
Pale were the lips I kiss'd, and fair the form
I floated with, about that melancholy storm.

April 1819

La Belle Dame Sans Merci

(First Version)

O what can ail thee, Knight at arms,
   Alone and palely loitering?
The sedge has withered from the Lake
   And no birds sing!

O what can ail thee, Knight at arms,
   So haggard, and so woe begone?
The Squirrel's granary is full
   And the harvest's done.

I see a lily on thy brow
  With anguish moist and fever dew,
And on thy cheeks a fading rose
  Fast withereth too—

I met a Lady in the Meads,
  Full beautiful, a faery's child
Her hair was long, her foot was light
  And her eyes were wild—

I made a Garland for her head,
  And bracelets too, and fragrant Zone
She look'd at me as she did love
  And made sweet moan—

I set her on my pacing steed
  And nothing else saw all day long
For sidelong would she bend and sing
  A faery's song—

She found me roots of relish sweet
  And honey wild and manna dew
And sure in language strange she said
  I love thee true—

She took me to her elfin grot
  And there she wept and sigh'd full sore,
And there I shut her wild wild eyes
  With kisses four.

And there she lulled me asleep
  And there I dream'd, Ah Woe betide!
The latest dream I ever dreamt
  On the cold hill side.

I saw pale Kings, and Princes too
  Pale warriors, death pale were they all;
They cried, La belle dame sans merci
  Thee hath in thrall.

I saw their starv'd lips in the gloam
  With horrid warning gaped wide,
And I awoke, and found me here
  On the cold hill's side.

And this is why I sojourn here
  Alone and palely loitering;
Though the sedge is withered from the Lake
  And no birds sing—

          1819

La Belle Dame Sans Merci

(Revised Version)

Ah, what can ail thee, wretched wight,
  Alone and palely loitering?
The sedge is wither'd from the lake,
  And no birds sing.

Ah, what can ail thee, wretched wight,
  So haggard and so woe-begone?
The squirrel's granary is full,
  And the harvest's done.

I see a lily on thy brow,
  With anguish moist and fever dew;
And on thy cheek a fading rose
  Fast withereth too.

I met a lady in the meads,
  Full beautiful—a faery's child;
Her hair was long, her foot was light,
  And her eyes were wild.

I set her on my pacing steed,
  And nothing else saw all day long,
For sideways would she lean, and sing
  A faery's song.

I made a garland for her head,
  And bracelets too, and fragrant zone;
She look'd at me as she did love,
  And made sweet moan.

She found me roots of relish sweet,
   And honey wild, and manna dew;
And sure in language strange she said—
   "I love thee true."

She took me to her elfin grot,
   And there she gazed, and sighed deep,
And there I shut her wild wild eyes
   So kiss'd to sleep.

And there we slumber'd on the moss,
   And there I dream'd—Ah! woe betide!
The latest dream I ever dream'd
   On the cold hill side.

I saw pale kings, and princes too,
   Pale warriors, death-pale were they all;
They cried— "La Belle Dame sans Merci
   Hath thee in thrall!"

I saw their starved lips in the gloam,
   With horrid warning gaped wide,
And I awoke, and found me here
   On the cold hill side.

And this is why I sojourn here,
   Alone and palely loitering,
Though the sedge is wither'd from the lake,
   And no birds sing.

                    1819

To Sleep

O soft embalmer of the still midnight,
   Shutting, with careful fingers and benign,
Our gloom-pleased eyes, embower'd from the light,
   Enshaded in forgetfulness divine:
O soothest Sleep! if so it please thee, close,
   In midst of this thine hymn, my willing eyes,
Or wait the amen, ere thy poppy throws
   Around my bed its dewy charities;

Then save me, or the passed day will shine
Upon my pillow, breeding many woes;
   Save me from curious conscience, that still lords
Its strength for darkness, burrowing like a mole;
   Turn the key deftly in the oiled wards,
And seal the hushed casket of my soul.

April 1819

On the Sonnet

IF by dull rhymes our English must be chain'd,
   And, like Andromeda, the Sonnet sweet
Fetter'd, in spite of pained loveliness;
Let us find out, if we must be constrain'd,
   Sandals more interwoven and complete
To fit the naked foot of poesy;
Let us inspect the lyre, and weigh the stress
Of every chord, and see what may be gain'd
   By ear industrious, and attention meet;
Misers of sound and syllable, no less
Than Midas of his coinage, let us be
   Jealous of dead leaves in the bay-wreath crown:
So, if we may not let the Muse be free,
   She will be bound with garlands of her own.

April 1819

Ode to a Nightingale

I

MY heart aches, and a drowsy numbness pains
   My sense, as though of hemlock I had drunk,
Or emptied some dull opiate to the drains
   One minute past, and Lethe-wards had sunk:
'Tis not through envy of thy happy lot,
   But being too happy in thine happiness,—
      That thou, light-winged Dryad of the trees,
         In some melodious plot
Of beechen green, and shadows numberless,
   Singest of summer in full-throated ease.

II

O for a draught of vintage! that hath been
   Cool'd a long age in the deep-delved earth,
Tasting of Flora and the country-green,
   Dance, and Provençal song, and sunburnt mirth!
O for a beaker full of the warm South,
   Full of the true, the blushful Hippocrene,
      With beaded bubbles winking at the brim,
        And purple-stained mouth;
   That I might drink, and leave the world unseen,
      And with thee fade away into the forest dim:

III

Fade far away, dissolve, and quite forget
   What thou among the leaves hast never known,
The weariness, the fever, and the fret
   Here, where men sit and hear each other groan;
Where palsy shakes a few, sad, last gray hairs,
   Where youth grows pale, and spectre-thin, and dies;
      Where but to think is to be full of sorrow
        And leaden-eyed despairs,
   Where Beauty cannot keep her lustrous eyes,
      Or new Love pine at them beyond tomorrow.

IV

Away! away! for I will fly to thee,
   Not charioted by Bacchus and his pards,
But on the viewless wings of Poesy,
   Though the dull brain perplexes and retards:
Already with thee! tender is the night,
   And haply the Queen-Moon is on her throne,
      Cluster'd around by all her starry Fays;
        But here there is no light,
   Save what from heaven is with the breezes blown
      Through verdurous glooms and winding mossy ways.

V

I cannot see what flowers are at my feet,
　　Nor what soft incense hangs upon the boughs,
But, in embalmed darkness, guess each sweet
　　Wherewith the seasonable month endows
The grass, the thicket, and the fruit-tree wild;
　　White hawthorn, and the pastoral eglantine;
　　　　Fast fading violets cover'd up in leaves;
　　　　　　And mid-May's eldest child,
　　The coming musk-rose, full of dewy wine,
　　　　The murmurous haunt of flies on summer eves.

VI

Darkling I listen; and, for many a time
　　I have been half in love with easeful Death,
Call'd him soft names in many a mused rhyme,
　　To take into the air my quiet breath;
Now more than ever seems it rich to die,
　　To cease upon the midnight with no pain,
　　　　While thou art pouring forth thy soul abroad
　　　　　　In such an ecstasy!
　　Still wouldst thou sing, and I have ears in vain—
　　　　To thy high requiem become a sod.

VII

Thou wast not born for death, immortal Bird!
　　No hungry generations tread thee down;
The voice I hear this passing night was heard
　　In ancient days by emperor and clown:
Perhaps the self-same song that found a path
　　Through the sad heart of Ruth, when, sick for home,
　　　　She stood in tears amid the alien corn;
　　　　　　The same that oft-times hath
　　Charm'd magic casements, opening on the foam
　　　　Of perilous seas, in faery lands forlorn.

VIII

Forlorn! the very word is like a bell
  To toll me back from thee to my sole self!
Adieu! the fancy cannot cheat so well
  As she is famed to do, deceiving elf.
Adieu! adieu! thy plaintive anthem fades
  Past the near meadows, over the still stream,
    Up the hill-side; and now 'tis buried deep
      In the next valley-glades:
  Was it a vision, or a waking dream?
  Fled is that music:—do I wake or sleep?

                    May 1819

To Autumn

I

SEASON of mists and mellow fruitfulness,
  Close bosom-friend of the maturing sun;
Conspiring with him how to load and bless
  With fruit the vines that round the thatch-eaves run;
To bend with apples the moss'd cottage-trees,
  And fill all fruit with ripeness to the core;
    To swell the gourd, and plump the hazel shells
With a sweet kernel; to set budding more,
And still more, later flowers for the bees,
Until they think warm days will never cease,
    For Summer has o'er-brimm'd their clammy cells.

II

Who hath not seen thee oft amid thy store?
  Sometimes whoever seeks abroad may find
Thee sitting careless on a granary floor,
  Thy hair soft-lifted by the winnowing wind;
Or on a half-reap'd furrow sound asleep,

Drowsed with the fume of poppies, while thy hook
   Spares the next swath and all its twined flowers:
And sometimes like a gleaner thou dost keep
   Steady thy laden head across a brook;
   Or by a cider-press, with patient look,
     Thou watchest the last oozings, hours by hours.

III

Where are the songs of Spring? Ay, where are they?
   Think not of them, thou hast thy music too,—
While barred clouds bloom the soft-dying day,
   And touch the stubble-plains with rosy hue;
Then in a wailful choir the small gnats mourn
   Among the river sallows, borne aloft
   Or sinking as the light wind lives or dies;
And full-grown lambs loud bleat from hilly bourn;
   Hedge-crickets sing; and now with treble soft
   The redbreast whistles from a garden-croft,
     And gathering swallows twitter in the skies.
               September 1819

A Song about Myself

THERE was a naughty Boy,
  A naughty boy was he,
He would not stop at home,
  He could not quiet be—
    He took
    In his Knapsack
    A Book
    Full of vowels;
    And a shirt
    With some towels—
    A slight cap
    For night cap—
    A hair brush,
    Comb ditto,
    New Stockings,
    For old ones
    Would split O!

This Knapsack,
Tight at 's back,
He rivetted close
And follow'd his Nose
  To the North,
  To the North,
And follow'd his nose
  To the North.

There was a naughty boy
  And a naughty boy was he,
For nothing would he do
  But scribble poetry—
    He took
    An inkstand
    In his hand,
    And a Pen
    Big as ten
    In the other,
    And away
    In a Pother
    He ran
    To the mountains,
    And fountains
    And ghostes,
    And Postes,
    And witches,
    And ditches,
    And wrote
    In his coat,
    When the weather
    Was cool,
    Fear of gout,
    And without
    When the weather
    Was Warm—
    Och the charm
    When we choose
  To follow one's nose
    To the north,
    To the north,
  To follow one's nose
    To the north.

There was a naughty boy
    And a naughty boy was he,
He kept little fishes
    In washing tubs three
        In spite
        Of the might
        Of the Maid,
        Nor afraid
        Of his Granny—good—
        He often would,
        Hurly burly,
        Get up early,
        And go
        By hook or crook
        To the brook,
        And bring home
        Miller's thumb,
        Tittlebat
        Not over fat,
        Minnows small
        As the stall
        Of a glove,
        Not above
        The size
        Of a nice
        Little Baby's
        Little fingers—
        O, he made,
        'Twas his trade,
    Of Fish a pretty Kettle
        A Kettle—
        A Kettle
    Of Fish, a pretty Kettle,
        A Kettle!

There was a naughty Boy,
    And a naughty Boy was he,
He ran away to Scotland
    The people for to see—
        Then he found
        That the ground
        Was as hard,
        That a yard

Was as long,
That a song
Was as merry,
That a cherry
Was as red—
That lead
Was as weighty,
That fourscore
Was as eighty,
That a door
Was as wooden
As in England—
So he stood in his shoes
And he wonder'd,
He wonder'd,
He stood in his shoes
And he wonder'd.

1818

"Two or Three Posies"

Two or three Posies
With two or three simples—
Two or three Noses
With two or three pimples—
Two or three wise men
And two or three ninny's—
Two or three purses
And two or three guineas—
Two or three raps
At two or three doors—
Two or three naps
Of two or three hours—
Two or three Cats
And two or three mice—
Two or three sprats
At a very great price—
Two or three sandies
And two or three tabbies—
Two or three dandies
And two Mrs. ——— mum!

Two or three Smiles
And two or three frowns—
Two or three Miles
To two or three towns—
Two or three pegs
For two or three bonnets—
Two or three dove eggs
To hatch into sonnets—

                                        1818

On Oxford

THE Gothic looks solemn,
The plain Doric column
Supports an old Bishop and Crozier;
The mouldering arch,
Shaded o'er by a larch,
Stands next door to Wilson the Hosier.

Vice,—that is, by turns,—
O'er pale faces mourns
The black tassell'd trencher and common hat;
The charity boy sings,
The Steeple-bell rings
And as for the Chancellor—*dominat.*

There are plenty of trees,
And plenty of ease,
And plenty of fat deer for Parsons;
And when it is venison,
Short is the benison,—
Then each on a leg or thigh fastens.

                                Before 1820

To a Cat

CAT! who has[t] pass'd thy grand clima[c]teric,
  How many mice and rats hast in thy days
  Destroy'd?—How many tit-bits stolen? Gaze
With those bright languid segments green, and prick

Those velvet ears—but pr'ythee do not stick
  Thy latent talons in me—and upraise
  Thy gentle mew—and tell me all thy frays
Of fish and mice, and rats and tender chick:
Nay, look not down, nor lick thy dainty wrists
  For all the wheezy asthma,—and for all
Thy tail's tip is nick'd off—and though the fists
  Of many a maid has given thee many a maul,
Still is that fur as soft as when the lists
  In youth thou enter'dst on glass-bottled wall.

1818

From

LAMIA

PART I

*   *   *   *   *

From vale to vale, from wood to wood, he flew,
Breathing upon the flowers his passion new,
And wound with many a river to its head,
To find where this sweet nymph prepared her secret bed:
In vain; the sweet nymph might nowhere be found,
And so he rested, on the lonely ground,
Pensive, and full of painful jealousies
Of the Wood-Gods, and even the very trees.
There as he stood, he heard a mournful voice,
Such as once heard, in gentle heart, destroys
All pain but pity: thus the lone voice spake:
"When from this wreathed tomb shall I awake!
When move in a sweet body fit for life,
And love, and pleasure, and the ruddy strife
Of hearts and lips! Ah, miserable me!"
The God, dove-footed, glided silently
Round bush and tree, soft-brushing, in his speed,
The taller grasses and full-flowering weed,
Until he found a palpitating snake,
Bright, and cirque-couchant in a dusky brake.

She was a gordian shape of dazzling hue,
Vermilion-spotted, golden, green, and blue;
Striped like a zebra, freckled like a pard,
Eyed like a peacock, and all crimson barr'd;

And full of silver moons, that, as she breathed,
Dissolved, or brighter shone, or interwreathed
Their lustres with the gloomier tapestries—
So rainbow-sided, touch'd with miseries,
She seem'd, at once, some penanced lady elf,
Some demon's mistress, or the demon's self.
Upon her crest she wore a wannish fire
Sprinkled with stars, like Ariadne's tiar:
Her head was serpent, but ah, bitter-sweet!
She had a woman's mouth with all its pearls complete:
And for her eyes—what could such eyes do there
But weep, and weep, that they were born so fair?
As Proserpine still weeps for her Sicilian air.
Her throat was serpent, but the words she spake
Came, as through bubbling honey, for Love's sake,
And thus; while Hermes on his pinions lay,
Like a stoop'd falcon ere he takes his prey:

"Fair Hermes! crown'd with feathers, fluttering light,
I had a splendid dream of thee last night:
I saw thee sitting, on a throne of gold,
Among the Gods, upon Olympus old,
The only sad one; for thou didst not hear
The soft, lute-finger'd Muses chanting clear,
Nor even Apollo when he sang alone,
Deaf to his throbbing throat's long, long melodious moan.
I dreamt I saw thee, robed in purple flakes,
Break amorous through the clouds, as morning breaks,
And, swiftly as a bright Phoebean dart,
Strike for the Cretan isle; and here thou art!
Too gentle Hermes, hast thou found the maid?"
Whereat the star of Lethe not delay'd
His rosy eloquence, and thus inquired:
"Thou smooth-lipp'd serpent, surely high-inspired!
Thou beauteous wreath, with melancholy eyes,
Possess whatever bliss thou canst devise,
Telling me only where my nymph is fled,—
Where she doth breathe!" "Bright planet, thou hast said,"
Return'd the snake, "but seal with oaths, fair God!"
"I swear," said Hermes, "by my serpent rod,
And by thine eyes, and by thy starry crown!"
Light flew his earnest words, among the blossoms blown.
Then thus again the brilliance feminine:
"Too frail of heart! for this lost nymph of thine,

Free as the air, invisibly, she strays
About these thornless wilds; her pleasant days
She tastes unseen; unseen her nimble feet
Leave traces in the grass and flowers sweet;
From weary tendrils, and bow'd branches green,
She plucks the fruit unseen, she bathes unseen:
And by my power is her beauty veil'd
To keep it unaffronted, unassail'd
By the love-glances of unlovely eyes,
Of Satyrs, Fauns, and blear'd Silenus' sighs.
Pale grew her immortality, for woe
Of all these lovers, and she grieved so
I took compassion on her, bade her steep
Her hair in weïrd syrops, that would keep
Her loveliness invisible, yet free
To wander as she loves, in liberty.
Thou shalt behold her, Hermes, thou alone,
If thou wilt, as thou swearest, grant my boon!"
Then, once again, the charmed God began
An oath, and through the serpent's ears it ran
Warm, tremulous, devout, psalterian.
Ravish'd she lifted her Circean head,
Blush'd a live damask, and swift-lisping said,
"I was a woman, let me have once more
A woman's shape, and charming as before.
I love a youth of Corinth—O the bliss!
Give me my woman's form, and place me where he is.
Stoop, Hermes, let me breathe upon thy brow,
And thou shalt see thy sweet nymph even now."
The God on half-shut feathers sank serene,
She breathed upon his eyes, and swift was seen
Of both the guarded nymph near-smiling on the green.
It was no dream; or say a dream it was,
Real are the dreams of Gods, and smoothly pass
Their pleasures in a long immortal dream.
One warm, flush'd moment, hovering, it might seem
Dash'd by the wood-nymph's beauty, so he burn'd;
Then, lighting on the printless verdure, turn'd
To the swoon'd serpent, and with languid arm,
Delicate, put to proof the lithe Caducean charm.
So done, upon the nymph his eyes he bent
Full of adoring tears and blandishment,
And towards her stept: she, like a moon in wane,
Faded before him, cower'd, nor could restrain

Her fearful sobs, self-folding like a flower
That faints into itself at evening hour:
But the God fostering her chilled hand,
She felt the warmth, her eyelids open'd bland,
And, like new flowers at morning song of bees,
Bloom'd, and gave up her honey to the lees.
Into the green-recessed woods they flew;
Nor grew they pale, as mortal lovers do.

    Left to herself, the serpent now began
To change; her elfin blood in madness ran,
Her mouth foam'd, and the grass, therewith besprent,
Wither'd at dew so sweet and virulent;
Her eyes in torture fix'd, and anguish drear,
Hot, glazed, and wide, with lid-lashes all sear,
Flash'd phosphor and sharp sparks, without one cooling tear.
The colours all inflamed throughout her train,
She writhed about, convulsed with scarlet pain:
A deep volcanian yellow took the place
Of all her milder-mooned body's grace;
And, as the lava ravishes the mead,
Spoilt all her silver mail, and golden brede:
Made gloom of all her frecklings, streaks and bars,
Eclipsed her crescents, and lick'd up her stars:
So that, in moments few, she was undrest
Of all her sapphires, greens, and amethyst,
And rubious-argent: of all these bereft,
Nothing but pain and ugliness were left.
Still shone her crown; that vanish'd, also she
Melted and disappear'd as suddenly;
And in the air, her new voice luting soft,
Cried, "Lycius! gentle Lycius!"—Borne aloft
With the bright mists about the mountains hoar
These words dissolved: Crete's forests heard no more.

*   *   *   *   *

PART II

Love in a hut, with water and a crust,
Is—Love, forgive us!—cinders, ashes, dust;
Love in a palace is perhaps at last
More grievous torment than a hermit's fast:—

That is a doubtful tale from faery land,
Hard for the non-elect to understand.
Had Lycius lived to hand his story down,
He might have given the moral a fresh frown,
Or clench'd it quite: but too short was their bliss
To breed distrust and hate, that make the soft voice hiss.
Besides, there, nightly, with terrific glare,
Love, jealous grown of so complete a pair,
Hover'd and buzz'd his wings, with fearful roar,
Above the lintel of their chamber door,
And down the passage cast a glow upon the floor.

　　For all this came a ruin: side by side
They were enthroned, in the even tide,
Upon a couch, near to a curtaining
Whose airy texture, from a golden string,
Floated into the room, and let appear
Unveil'd the summer heaven, blue and clear,
Betwixt two marble shafts:—there they reposed,
Where use had made it sweet, with eyelids closed,
Saving a tithe which love still open kept,
That they might see each other while they almost slept;
When from the slope side of a suburb hill,
Deafening the swallow's twitter, came a thrill
Of trumpets—Lycius started—the sounds fled,
But left a thought, a buzzing in his head.
For the first time, since first he harbour'd in
That purple-lined palace of sweet sin,
His spirit pass'd beyond its golden bourn
Into the noisy world almost forsworn.
The lady, ever watchful, penetrant,
Saw this with pain, so arguing a want
Of something more, more than her empery
Of joys; and she began to moan and sigh
Because he mused beyond her, knowing well
That but a moment's thought is passion's passing bell.
"Why do you sigh, fair creature?" whisper'd he:
"Why do you think?" return'd she tenderly:
"You have deserted me;—where am I now?
Not in your heart while care weighs on your brow:
No, no, you have dismiss'd me; and I go
From your breast houseless: aye, it must be so."
He answer'd, bending to her open eyes,
Where he was mirror'd small in paradise,

"My silver planet, both of eve and morn!
Why will you plead yourself so sad forlorn,
While I am striving how to fill my heart
With deeper crimson, and a double smart?
How to entangle, trammel up and snare
Your soul in mine, and labyrinth you there,
Like the hid scent in an unbudded rose?
Aye, a sweet kiss—you see your mighty woes.
My thoughts! shall I unveil them? Listen then!
What mortal hath a prize, that other men
May be confounded and abash'd withal,
But lets it sometimes pace abroad majestical,
And triumph, as in thee I should rejoice
Amid the hoarse alarm of Corinth's voice.
Let my foes choke, and my friends shout afar,
While through the thronged streets your bridal car
Wheels round its dazzling spokes."—The lady's cheek
Trembled; she nothing said, but, pale and meek,
Arose and knelt before him, wept a rain
Of sorrows at his words; at last with pain
Beseeching him, the while his hand she wrung,
To change his purpose. He thereat was stung,
Perverse, with stronger fancy to reclaim
Her wild and timid nature to his aim;
Besides, for all his love, in self despite,
Against his better self, he took delight
Luxurious in her sorrows, soft and new.
His passion, cruel grown, took on a hue
Fierce and sanguineous as 'twas possible
In one whose brow had no dark veins to swell.
Fine was the mitigated fury, like
Apollo's presence when in act to strike
The serpent—Ha! the serpent! certes, she
Was none. She burnt, she loved the tyranny,
And, all subdued, consented to the hour
When to the bridal he should lead his paramour.
Whispering in midnight silence, said the youth,
"Sure some sweet name thou hast, though, by my truth,
I have not ask'd it, ever thinking thee
Not mortal, but of heavenly progeny,
As still I do. Hast any mortal name,
Fit appellation for this dazzling frame?
Or friends or kinsfolk on the citied earth,
To share our marriage feast and nuptial mirth?"

"I have no friends," said Lamia, "no, not one;
My presence in wide Corinth hardly known:
My parents' bones are in their dusty urns
Sepulchred, where no kindled incense burns,
Seeing all their luckless race are dead, save me,
And I neglect the holy rite for thee.
Even as you list invite your many guests;
But if, as now it seems, your vision rests
With any pleasure on me, do not bid
Old Apollonius—from him keep me hid."
Lycius, perplex'd at words so blind and blank,
Made close inquiry; from whose touch she shrank,
Feigning a sleep; and he to the dull shade
Of deep sleep in a moment was betray'd.

   It was the custom then to bring away
The bride from home at blushing shut of day,
Veil'd, in a chariot, heralded along
By strewn flowers, torches, and a marriage song,
With other pageants: but this fair unknown
Had not a friend. So being left alone,
(Lycius was gone to summon all his kin,)
And knowing surely she could never win
His foolish heart from its mad pompousness,
She set herself, high-thoughted, how to dress
The misery in fit magnificence.
She did so, but 'tis doubtful how and whence
Came, and who were her subtle servitors.
About the halls, and to and from the doors,
There was a noise of wings, till in short space
The glowing banquet-room shone with wide-arched grace.
A haunting music, sole perhaps and lone
Supportress of the faery-roof, made moan
Throughout, as fearful the whole charm might fade.
Fresh carved cedar, mimicking a glade
Of palm and plantain, met from either side,
High in the midst, in honour of the bride:
Two palms and then two plantains, and so on,
From either side their stems branch'd one to one
All down the aisled place; and beneath all
There ran a stream of lamps straight on from wall to wall.
So canopied, lay an untasted feast
Teeming with odours. Lamia, regal drest,

Silently paced about, and as she went,
In pale contented sort of discontent,
Mission'd her viewless servants to enrich
The fretted splendour of each nook and niche.
Between the tree-stems, marbled plain at first,
Came jasper panels; then, anon, there burst
Forth creeping imagery of slighter trees,
And with the larger wove in small intricacies.
Approving all, she faded at self-will,
And shut the chamber up, close, hush'd and still,
Complete and ready for the revels rude,
When dreadful guests would come to spoil her solitude.

     *   *   *   *   *

Soft went the music the soft air along,
While fluent Greek a vowel'd under-song
Kept up among the guests, discoursing low
At first, for scarcely was the wine at flow;
But when the happy vintage touch'd their brains,
Louder they talk, and louder come the strains
Of powerful instruments:—the gorgeous dyes,
The space, the splendour of the draperies,
The roof of awful richness, nectarous cheer,
Beautiful slaves, and Lamia's self, appear,
Now, when the wine has done its rosy deed,
And every soul from human trammels freed,
No more so strange; for merry wine, sweet wine,
Will make Elysian shades not too fair, too divine.
Soon was God Bacchus at meridian height;
Flush'd were their cheeks, and bright eyes double bright:
Garlands of every green, and every scent
From vales deflower'd, or forest-trees branch-rent,
In baskets of bright osier'd gold were brought
High as the handles heap'd, to suit the thought
Of every guest: that each, as he did please,
Might fancy-fit his brows, silk-pillow'd at his ease.

     *   *   *   *   *

1819

From

OTHO THE GREAT

ACT IV

SCENE I—AURANTHE'S *Apartment*

AURANTHE *and* CONRAD *discovered.*

Conrad.   Well, well, I know what ugly jeopardy
  We are caged in; you need not pester that
  Into my ears. Pr'ythee, let me be spared
  A foolish tongue, that I may bethink me
  Of remedies with some deliberation.
  You cannot doubt but 'tis in Albert's power
  To crush or save us?
Auranthe.   No, I cannot doubt.
  He has, assure yourself, by some strange means,
  My secret; which I ever hid from him,
  Knowing his mawkish honesty.
Conrad.   Cursed slave!
Auranthe.   Ay, I could almost curse him now myself.
  Wretched impediment! Evil genius!
  A glue upon my wings, that cannot spread,
  When they should span the provinces! A snake,
  A scorpion, sprawling on the first gold step,
  Conducting to the throne, high canopied.
Conrad.   You would not hear my counsel, when his life
  Might have been trodden out, all sure and hush'd;
  Now the dull animal forsooth must be
  Intreated, managed! When can you contrive
  The interview he demands?

Auranthe.   As speedily
   It must be done as my bribed woman can
   Unseen conduct him to me; but I fear
   'Twill be impossible, while the broad day
   Comes through the panes with persecuting glare.
   Methinks, if 't now were night I could intrigue
   With darkness, bring the stars to second me,
   And settle all this trouble.
Conrad.   Nonsense! Child!
   See him immediately; why not now?
Auranthe.   Do you forget that even the senseless door-posts
   Are on the watch and gape through all the house?
   How many whisperers there are about,
   Hungry for evidence to ruin me:
   Men I have spurn'd, and women I have taunted?
   Besides, the foolish prince sends, minute whiles,
   His pages—so they tell me—to inquire
   After my health, intreating, if I please,
   To see me.
Conrad.   Well, suppose this Albert here;
   What is your power with him?
Auranthe.   He should be
   My echo, my taught parrot! but I fear
   He will be cur enough to bark at me;
   Have his own say; read me some silly creed
   'Bout shame and pity.
Conrad.   What will you do then?
Auranthe.   What I shall do, I know not; what I would
   Cannot be done; for see, this chamber-floor
   Will not yield to the pick-axe and the spade,—
   Here is no quiet depth of hollow ground.
Conrad.   Sister, you have grown sensible and wise,
   Seconding, ere I speak it, what is now,
   I hope, resolved between us.
Auranthe.   Say, what is 't?
Conrad.   You need not be his sexton too; a man
   May carry that with him shall make him die
   Elsewhere,—give that to him; pretend the while
   You will to-morrow succumb to his wishes,
   Be what they may, and send him from the Castle
   On some fool's errand: let his latest groan
   Frighten the wolves!
Auranthe.   Alas! he must not die!

Conrad.   Would you were both hearsed up in stifling lead!
  Detested—
Auranthe.   Conrad, hold! I would not bear
  The little thunder of your fretful tongue,
  Tho' I alone were taken in these toils,
  And you could free me; but remember, sir,
  You live alone in my security:
  So keep your wits at work, for your own sake,
  Not mine, and be more mannerly.
Conrad.   Thou wasp!
  If my domains were emptied of these folk,
  And I had thee to starve—
Auranthe.   O, marvellous!
  But Conrad, now be gone; the Host is look'd for;
  Cringe to the Emperor, entertain the Lords,
  And, do ye mind, above all things, proclaim
  My sickness, with a brother's sadden'd eye,
  Condoling with Prince Ludolph. In fit time
  Return to me.
Conrad.   I leave you to your thoughts.

                                            [*Exit.*

Auranthe (*sola*).   Down, down, proud temper! down, Auranthe's pride!
  Why do I anger him when I should kneel?
  Conrad! Albert! help! help! What can I do?
  O wretched woman! lost, wreck'd, swallow'd up,
  Accursed, blasted! O, thou golden Crown,
  Orbing along the serene firmament
  Of a wide empire, like a glowing moon;
  And thou, bright sceptre! lustrous in my eyes,—
  There—as the fabled fair Hesperian tree,
  Bearing a fruit more precious! graceful thing,
  Delicate, godlike, magic! must I leave
  Thee to melt in the visionary air,
  Ere, by one grasp, this common hand is made
  Imperial? I do not know the time
  When I have wept for sorrow; but methinks
  I could now sit upon the ground, and shed
  Tears, tears of misery! O, the heavy day!
  How shall I bear my life till Albert comes?
  Ludolph! Erminia! Proofs! O heavy day!
  Bring me some mourning weeds, that I may 'tire
  Myself, as fits one wailing her own death:
  Cut off these curls, and brand this lily hand,
  And throw these jewels from my loathing sight,—

Fetch me a missal, and a string of beads,—
A cup of bitter'd water, and a crust,—
I will confess, O holy Abbot!—How!
What is this? Auranthe! thou fool, dolt,
Whimpering idiot! up! up! and quell!
I am safe! Coward! why am I in fear?
Albert! he cannot stickle, chew the cud
In such a fine extreme,—impossible!
Who knocks?

[*Goes to the door, listens, and opens it.*

Enter ALBERT.

Albert, I have been waiting for you here
With such an aching heart, such swooning throbs
On my poor brain, such cruel—cruel sorrow,
That I should claim your pity! Art not well?
Albert. Yes, lady, well.
Auranthe.   You look not so, alas!
But pale, as if you brought some heavy news.
Albert. You know full well what makes me look so pale.
Auranthe. No! Do I? Surely I am still to learn
Some horror; all I know, this present, is
I am near hustled to a dangerous gulf,
Which you can save me from,—and therefore safe,
So trusting in thy love; that should not make
Thee pale, my Albert.
Albert.   It doth make me freeze.
Auranthe. Why should it, love?
Albert.   You should not ask me that,
But make your own heart monitor, and save
Me the great pain of telling. You must know.
Auranthe. Something has vext you, Albert. There are times
When simplest things put on a sombre cast;
A melancholy mood will haunt a man,
Until most easy matters take the shape
Of unachievable tasks; small rivulets
Then seem impassable.
Albert.   Do not cheat yourself
With hope that gloss of words, or suppliant action,
Or tears, or ravings, or self-threaten'd death,
Can alter my resolve.
Auranthe.   You make me tremble;
Not so much at your threats, as at your voice,
Untuned, and harsh, and barren of all love.

Albert.   You suffocate me! Stop this devil's parley,
 And listen to me; know me once for all.
Auranthe.   I thought I did. Alas! I am deceived.
Albert.   No, you are not deceived. You took me for
 A man detesting all inhuman crime;
 And therefore kept from me your demon's plot
 Against Erminia. Silent? Be so still;
 For ever! Speak no more; but hear my words,
 Thy fate. Your safety I have bought to-day
 By blazoning a lie, which in the dawn
 I'll expiate with truth.
Auranthe.   O cruel traitor!
Albert.   For I would not set eyes upon thy shame;
 I would not see thee dragg'd to death by the hair,
 Penanced, and taunted on a scaffolding!
 To-night, upon the skirts of the blind wood
 That blackens northward of these horrid towers,
 I wait for you with horses. Choose your fate.
 Farewell!
Auranthe.   Albert, you jest; I'm sure you must.
 You, an ambitious Soldier! I, a Queen,
 One who could say,—here, rule these Provinces!
 Take tribute from those cities for thyself!
 Empty these armouries, these treasuries,
 Muster thy warlike thousands at a nod!
 Go! Conquer Italy!
Albert.   Auranthe, you have made
 The whole world chaff to me. Your doom is fix'd.
Auranthe.   Out, villain! dastard!
Albert.   Look there to the door!
 Who is it?
Auranthe.   Conrad, traitor!
Albert.   Let him in.

Enter CONRAD.

 Do not affect amazement, hypocrite,
 At seeing me in this chamber.
Conrad.   Auranthe?
Albert.   Talk not with eyes, but speak your curses out
 Against me, who would sooner crush and grind
 A brace of toads, than league with them t' oppress
 An innocent lady, gull an Emperor,

More generous to me than autumn sun
To ripening harvests.
Auranthe.   No more insult, sir!
Albert.   Ay, clutch your scabbard; but, for prudence sake,
Draw not the sword; 'twould make an uproar, Duke,
You would not hear the end of. At nightfall
Your lady sister, if I guess aright,
Will leave this busy castle. You had best
Take farewell too of worldly vanities.
Conrad. Vassal!
Albert. To-morrow, when the Emperor sends
For loving Conrad, see you fawn on him.
Good even!
Auranthe. You'll be seen!
Albert.   See the coast clear then.
Auranthe (as he goes). Remorseless Albert! Cruel, cruel wretch!
                                                    [*She lets him out.*

Conrad. So, we must lick the dust?
Auranthe.   I follow him.
Conrad. How? Where? The plan of your escape?
Auranthe.   He waits
For me with horses by the forest-side,
Northward.
Conrad. Good, good! he dies. You go, say you?
Auranthe. Perforce.
Conrad. Be speedy, darkness! Till that comes,
Fiends keep you company!

                                                    [*Exit.*

Auranthe.   And you! And you!
And all men! Vanish!

                            [*Retires to an inner apartment.*

*   *   *   *   *

1819

THE EVE OF ST. MARK

A FRAGMENT

Upon a Sabbath-day it fell;
Twice holy was the Sabbath-bell,
That call'd the folk to evening prayer;
The city streets were clean and fair
From wholesome drench of April rains;
And, on the western window panes,
The chilly sunset faintly told
Of unmatured green valleys cold,
Of the green thorny bloomless hedge,
Of rivers new with spring-tide sedge,
Of primroses by shelter'd rills,
And daisies on the aguish hills.
Twice holy was the Sabbath-bell:
The silent streets were crowded well
With staid and pious companies,
Warm from their fireside orat'ries;
And moving, with demurest air,
To even-song, and vesper prayer.
Each arched porch, and entry low,
Was fill'd with patient folk and slow,
With whispers hush, and shuffling feet,
While play'd the organ loud and sweet.

The bells had ceased, the prayers begun,
And Bertha had not yet half done
A curious volume, patch'd and torn,
That all day long, from earliest morn,

Had taken captive her two eyes,
Among its golden broideries;
Perplex'd her with a thousand things,—
The stars of Heaven, and angels' wings,
Martyrs in a fiery blaze,
Azure saints and silver rays,
Moses' breastplate, and the seven
Candlesticks John saw in Heaven,
The winged Lion of Saint Mark,
And the Covenantal Ark,
With its many mysteries,
Cherubim and golden mice.

Bertha was a maiden fair,
Dwelling in th' old Minster-square;
From her fireside she could see,
Sidelong, its rich antiquity,
Far as the Bishop's garden-wall;
Where sycamores and elm-trees tall,
Full-leaved, the forest had outstript,
By no sharp north-wind ever nipt,
So shelter'd by the mighty pile.
Bertha arose, and read awhile,
With forehead 'gainst the window-pane.
Again she tried, and then again,
Until the dusk eve left her dark
Upon the legend of St. Mark.
From plaited lawn-frill, fine and thin,
She lifted up her soft warm chin,
With aching neck and swimming eyes,
And dazed with saintly imag'ries.

All was gloom, and silent all,
Save now and then the still foot-fall
Of one returning homewards late,
Past the echoing minster-gate.
The clamorous daws, that all the day
Above tree-tops and towers play,
Pair by pair had gone to rest,
Each in its ancient belfry-nest,
Where asleep they fall betimes,
To music and the drowsy chimes.

All was silent, all was gloom,
Abroad and in the homely room:
Down she sat, poor cheated soul!
And struck a lamp from the dismal coal;
Lean'd forward, with bright drooping hair
And slant book, full against the glare.
Her shadow, in uneasy guise,
Hover'd about, a giant size,
On ceiling-beam and old oak chair,
The parrot's cage, and panel-square;
And the warm angled winter-screen,
On which were many monsters seen,
Call'd doves of Siam, Lima mice,
And legless birds of Paradise,
Macaw, and tender Avadavat,
And silken-furr'd Angora cat.
Untired she read, her shadow still
Glower'd about, as it would fill
The room with wildest forms and shades,
As though some ghostly queen of spades
Had come to mock behind her back,
And dance, and ruffle her garments black.
Untired she read the legend page,
Of holy Mark, from youth to age,
On land, on sea, in pagan chains,
Rejoicing for his many pains.
Sometimes the learned eremite,
With golden star, or dagger bright,
Referr'd to pious poesies
Written in smallest crow-quill size
Beneath the text; and thus the rhyme
Was parcell'd out from time to time:
——"Als writith he of swevenis,
Men han beforne they wake in bliss,
Whanne that hir friendes thinke him bound
In crimped shroude farre under grounde;
And how a litling child mote be
A saint er its nativitie,
Gif that the modre (God her blesse!)
Kepen in solitarinesse,
And kissen devoute the holy croce,
Of Goddes love, and Sathan's force,—
He writith; and thinges many mo
Of swiche thinges I may not show.

Bot I must tellen verilie
Somdel of Saintè Cicilie,
And chieflie what he auctorethe
Of Saintè Markis life and dethe:"

At lcngth her constant eyelids come
Upon the fervent martyrdom;
Then lastly to his holy shrine,
Exalt amid the tapers' shine
At Venice,—

(Unfinished)

1819

From

HYPERION

BOOK II

*   *   *   *   *

                "Great Saturn, thou
Hast sifted well the atom-universe;
But for this reason, that thou art the King,
And only blind from sheer supremacy,
One avenue was shaded from thine eyes,
Through which I wander'd to eternal truth.
And first, as thou wast not the first of powers,
So art thou not the last; it cannot be;
Thou art not the beginning nor the end.
From chaos and parental darkness came
Light, the first fruits of that intestine broil,
That sullen ferment, which for wondrous ends
Was ripening in itself. The ripe hour came,
And with it light, and light engendering
Upon its own producer, forthwith touch'd
The whole enormous matter into life.
Upon that very hour, our parentage,
The Heavens and the Earth, were manifest:
Then thou first-born, and we the giant-race,
Found ourselves ruling new and beauteous realms.
Now comes the pain of truth, to whom 'tis pain;
O folly! for to bear all naked truths,
And to envisage circumstance, all calm,
That is the top of sovereignty. Mark well!
As Heaven and Earth are fairer, fairer far
Than Chaos and blank Darkness, though once chiefs;

And as we show beyond that Heaven and Earth
In form and shape compact and beautiful,
In will, in action free, companionship,
And thousand other signs of purer life;
So on our heels a fresh perfection treads,
A power more strong in beauty, born of us
And fated to excel us, as we pass
In glory that old Darkness: nor are we
Thereby more conquer'd, than by us the rule
Of shapeless Chaos. Say, doth the dull soil
Quarrel with the proud forests it hath fed,
And feedeth still, more comely than itself?
Can it deny the chiefdom of green groves?
Or shall the tree be envious of the dove
Because it cooeth, and hath snowy wings
To wander wherewithal and find its joys?
We are such forest-trees, and our fair boughs
Have bred forth, not pale solitary doves,
But eagles golden-feather'd, who do tower
Above us in their beauty, and must reign
In right thereof; for 'tis the eternal law
That first in beauty should be first in might:
Yea, by that law, another race may drive
Our conquerors to mourn as we do now.
Have ye beheld the young God of the Seas,
My dispossessor? Have ye seen his face?
Have ye beheld his chariot, foam'd along
By noble winged creatures he hath made?
I saw him on the calmed waters scud,
With such a glow of beauty in his eyes,
That it enforced me to bid sad farewell
To all my empire; farewell sad I took,
And hither came, to see how dolorous fate
Had wrought upon ye; and how I might best
Give consolation in this woe extreme.
Receive the truth, and let it be your balm."

    *   *   *   *   *

It was Hyperion:—a granite peak
His bright feet touch'd, and there he stay'd to view
The misery his brilliance had betray'd
To the most hateful seeing of itself.
Golden his hair of short Numidian curl,

Regal his shape majestic, a vast shade
In midst of his own brightness, like the bulk
Of Memnon's image at the set of sun
To one who travels from the dusking East:
Sighs, too, as mournful as that Memnon's harp,
He utter'd, while his hands contemplative
He press'd together, and in silence stood.
Despondence seized again the fallen Gods
At sight of the dejected King of Day,
And many hid their faces from the light:
But fierce Enceladus sent forth his eyes
Among the brotherhood; and, at their glare,
Uprose Iäpetus, and Creüs too,
And Phorcus, sea-born, and together strode
To where he tower'd on his eminence.
There those four shouted forth old Saturn's name;
Hyperion from the peak loud answered "Saturn!"
Saturn sat near the Mother of the Gods,
In whose face was no joy, though all the Gods
Gave from their hollow throats the name of "Saturn!"

BOOK III

* * * * *

"Goddess! I have beheld those eyes before,
And their eternal calm, and all that face,
Or I have dream'd."—"Yes," said the supreme shape,
"Thou hast dream'd of me; and awaking up
Didst find a lyre all golden by thy side,
Whose strings touch'd by thy fingers, all the vast
Unwearied ear of the whole universe
Listen'd in pain and pleasure at the birth
Of such new tuneful wonder. Is 't not strange
That thou shouldst weep, so gifted? Tell me, youth,
What sorrow thou canst feel; for I am sad
When thou dost shed a tear: explain thy griefs
To one who in this lonely isle hath been
The watcher of thy sleep and hours of life,
From the young day when first thy infant hand
Pluck'd witless the weak flowers, till thine arm
Could bend that bow heroic to all times.

Show thy heart's secret to an ancient Power
Who hath forsaken old and sacred thrones
For prophecies of thee, and for the sake
Of loveliness new-born."—Apollo then,
With sudden scrutiny and gloomless eyes,
Thus answer'd, while his white melodious throat
Throbb'd with the syllables:—"Mnemosyne!
Thy name is on my tongue, I know not how;
Why should I tell thee what thou so well seest?
Why should I strive to show what from thy lips
Would come no mystery? For me, dark, dark,
And painful vile oblivion seals my eyes:
I strive to search wherefore I am so sad,
Until a melancholy numbs my limbs;
And then upon the grass I sit, and moan,
Like one who once had wings.—O why should I
Feel cursed and thwarted, when the liegeless air
Yields to my step aspirant? why should I
Spurn the green turf as hateful to my feet?
Goddess benign, point forth some unknown thing:
Are there not other regions than this isle?
What are the stars? There is the sun, the sun!
And the most patient brilliance of the moon!
And stars by thousands! Point me out the way
To any one particular beauteous star,
And I will flit into it with my lyre,
And make its silvery splendour pant with bliss.
I have heard the cloudy thunder: Where is power?
Whose hand, whose essence, what divinity
Makes this alarum in the elements,
While I here idle listen on the shores
In fearless yet in aching ignorance?
O tell me, lonely Goddess, by thy harp,
That waileth every morn and eventide,
Tell me why thus I rave, about these groves!
Mute thou remainest—Mute! yet I can read
A wondrous lesson in thy silent face:
Knowledge enormous makes a God of me.
Names, deeds, gray legends, dire events, rebellions,
Majesties, sovran voices, agonies,
Creations and destroyings, all at once
Pour into the wide hollows of my brain,
And deify me, as if some blithe wine
Or bright elixir peerless I had drunk,

And so become immortal."—Thus the God,
While his enkindled eyes, with level glance
Beneath his white soft temples, steadfast kept
Trembling with light upon Mnemosyne.
Soon wild commotions shook him, and made flush
All the immortal fairness of his limbs:
Most like the struggle at the gate of death;
Or liker still to one who should take leave
Of pale immortal death, and with a pang
As hot as death's is chill, with fierce convulse
Die into life: so young Apollo anguish'd:
His very hair, his golden tresses famed
Kept undulation round his eager neck.
During the pain Mnemosyne upheld
Her arms as one who prophesied.—At length
Apollo shriek'd;—and lo! from all his limbs
Celestial   .   .   .   .   .   .
                    (Unfinished)
                                        1818–19

THE LAST SONNET

BRIGHT star, would I were steadfast as thou art!
   Not in lone splendour hung aloft the night,
And watching, with eternal lids apart,
   Like Nature's patient sleepless Eremite,
The moving waters at their priestlike task
   Of pure ablution round earth's human shores
Or gazing on the new soft fallen mask
   Of snow upon the mountains and the moors:
No—yet still steadfast, still unchangeable,
   Pillow'd upon my fair love's ripening breast,
To feel for ever its soft fall and swell,
   Awake for ever in a sweet unrest,
Still, still to hear her tender-taken breath,
And so live ever—or else swoon to death.

1820

PERCY BYSSHE SHELLEY

(1792–1822)

HE Shelleys were an old Sussex family composed of two branches, the older of which had attained aristocratic rank. The poet belonged to the younger branch. His grandfather, Bysshe Shelley, was an energetic businessman with interests in America as well as England, who with the help of a good marriage succeeded in making a fortune and in 1806, at the age of seventy-five, received the satisfaction of a baronetcy. His son Timothy, the poet's father, was a country squire and Whig Member of Parliament who balanced his political liberalism with extremely prudent religious convictions.

Percy Bysshe Shelley, born at his father's estate of Field Place, near Horsham, on August 4, 1792, grew into a slender, attractive, rather feminine-looking boy with bright blue eyes and long curling hair, the very picture of a budding poet. However his earliest intellectual bent was more scientific than literary. His face and hands were habitually smudged with combustible chemicals, which he mixed to a cheerful intonation of Shakespeare:

"Double, double, toil and trouble;
Fire burn and cauldron bubble!"

Entering Eton at twelve he launched his first rebellion against the Establishment, when he ran afoul of the school's fag system, by which the younger boys were made to perform menial tasks for the older boys. He suffered a good bit of baiting and bullying, but his violent temper gave him a measure of security. Even his masters had to maintain some respect for his scientific experiments, one incautious tutor receiving a

454 PERCY BYSSHE SHELLEY

powerful electric shock when he picked up a mysterious looking apparatus in the boy's room.

But at Eton "philosophy" began to replace chemistry as Shelley's concern. The philosophy was that of the French Revolution, especially as expounded in England by William Godwin in a notorious book called *Political Justice*. Godwin became Shelley's god, and he wanted no other. An indefatigable proselytizer, he spent his holidays converting his two sisters and his favorite girl cousin to the new doctrine. The girls listened entranced to his impassioned exposition, but were dismayed by the young philosopher's contempt for marriage. The group also dabbled in literary production. *Original Poetry by Victor and Cazire*, written in 1810, was a collaboration of Percy and his sister Elizabeth.

In the autumn of 1810 Shelley enrolled at Oxford, his father's alma mater, where he met a young man named Thomas Jefferson Hogg. The two became friends at once, gibing in common at religion and respectability. Timothy Shelley had been unwary enough to request that his son's literary inclination be permitted scope, and early in the spring the local bookseller displayed in his window copies of a pamphlet entitled *The Necessity of Atheism*, signed by "Jeremiah Stukely." The college authorities, shocked beyond measure, apparently had no difficulty in penetrating the pseudonym; Shelley and Hogg were summoned at once, and upon their refusal to deny authorship were expelled.

The two young revolutionaries were crestfallen, for they had enjoyed Oxford immensely. Shelley proposed that they should take lodgings in London and continue their life of study and discussion, a plan which encountered immediate opposition from their fathers. Hogg, Sr., packed his son off to study law in York while Timothy Shelley ordered his own prodigal to return to Field Place and be put under the care of a strict guardian. But the son was no less stubborn than the father, and remained at his lodging house in London. For funds he turned to his sisters, whose girls' school was at nearby Clapham Common. They contributed their pocket money, sometimes sending it in care of a pretty schoolmate named Harriet Westbrook, who lost no time falling under Shelley's proselytizing spell.

The money question soon required a more substantial solution. Shelley achieved it through the intercession of an uncle, Captain Pilfold, a sea dog who had fought under Nelson, and who not only sympathized with his nephew's financial plight but even with his subversive ideology. Captain Pilfold induced Timothy Shelley to agree to an allowance of £400 a year to his wayward son.

Shelley set off for a holiday in Wales in high spirits, which were soon troubled by a letter from Harriet Westbrook. Her father, a tavern-keeper, was as difficult as Shelley's and Hogg's. He insisted that she finish her education at the girls' school even though thanks to Shelley's philosophy she found its sanctimonious atmosphere stifling. Shelley advised Harriet to resist her parents, and penned her father a letter of dissuasion. The innkeeper, who suspected the young nobleman of dishonorable designs on his daughter, paid no attention. Harriet's despair mounted; so did Shelley's sympathy. Returning to London, he found her ill, and hinting of suicide. But she offered another suggestion—if he wished, she would fly with him.

Shelley did not leap at the opportunity. He had had a serious disappointment in love when his cousin Harriet Grove had opted in favor of conventional marriage with another young man instead of Godwinian freedom with Shelley, and he was less smitten by the new Harriet than he had been by the old. Also, he was somewhat entangled, in a purely Platonic way, with a bluestocking spinster named Miss Hitchener who tutored Captain Pilfold's daughters.

The young exponent of atheism and free love prudently advised patience on the part of his eager disciple. But he tentatively agreed to her plan of flight, should it prove necessary as a last resort against a father's tyranny. Harriet lost no time in cashing this blank check. Shelley had scarcely settled at Miss Hitchener's side when a letter from London implored rescue. He returned at once, borrowed a few pounds from a friend, and next morning the two young lovers eloped in the Edinburgh Mail Coach. He was nineteen, Harriet sixteen.

Hogg had been consulted by letter on a delicate point: should Shelley marry Harriet? Hogg threw his influence on the side of convention, and Shelley reluctantly decided to compromise his principles. The decision did not please Timothy Shelley, pillar of respectability. "I'd have willingly supported any number of illegitimate children," the elder Shelley angrily wrote Captain Pilfold. "But that he should have *married* her!" Meantime Hogg, who had counseled marriage, arrived in Edinburgh and in Shelley's momentary absence attempted to seduce Harriet. Harriet indignantly informed her husband, who gently remonstrated with his friend.

Shortly after, another visitor appeared—Harriet's much older sister Eliza. Dark, sour, and protective, Eliza fastened herself on the Shelley household, which presently made the first of an endless series of moves. Visiting the Lake country, Shelley called on Robert Southey, discovering to his disappointment that this former rebel was now a resolute opponent of all reforms, especially Catholic Emancipation, in which Shelley particularly interested himself. A few weeks later, early in 1812, accompanied by Harriet and Eliza, he invaded Ireland in the interest of this cause. In the streets of Dublin he and Harriet played a game, slipping his new pamphlet, *Address to the Irish People*, into the pockets or umbrellas of passersby, and showering them from the balcony of their hotel. At a meeting where a throng had assembled to hear Daniel O'Connell, popular leader of the Irish cause, the young English sympathizer was introduced and delivered a lengthy speech. It was received with only moderate enthusiasm, for in indorsing liberty for Catholics, Shelley stated his conviction that all religious opinion should be tolerated since all religions were equally valid, a notion which struck some of his hearers as extreme.

On their return the Shelleys settled in London and at last made the acquaintance of Shelley's idol, William Godwin. The Godwin household was a curious one, with children from both spouses' previous marriages as well as of their own, and even one daughter of Godwin's first wife by an American lover. Though Godwin had considerably moderated his political stance since publication of *Political Justice*, he welcomed his young disciple as a promising source of financial support to the "Juvenile Library" he was launching.

Acquaintance with Godwin in fact put a fresh strain on Shelley's already burdened and cramped revenues. Miss Hitchener had come to visit and had stayed so long he had been constrained to get rid of her by bestowing £100 of his £400 income on her. At the same time his purse was always open to impoverished writers who fell afoul of Tory persecution. Harriet, seconded or prompted by Eliza, urged him to make peace with his father in the interests of a larger allowance. But when Timothy Shelley demanded a public recantation of atheism the young rebel indignantly refused. To silence Eliza and Harriet, who was in an advanced state of pregnancy, he bought a carriage on credit and refused to ride in it. Perhaps his latest bout with parental authority provoked him to write the atheistic *Queen Mab*, published in 1813, of which a clerical reviewer later declared, "Compared with this, *Don Juan* is a moral tale."

To meet the importunities of Godwin and those of Harriet, Shelley employed the expedient of post-obit bonds, by which he promised to pay £100 when his grandfather died for every £40 of ready cash obtained. But after the birth of their daughter, whom Shelley named "Ianthe," the rift with Harriet deepened. She dropped her pretense of being an intellectual companion, and frankly turned to shopping as the source of pleasure.

The couple were well on the road to estrangement by the time Shelley met Mary Wollstonecraft, Godwin's daughter by his first marriage, who had been away from London. Mary was what Harriet had momentarily seemed; a woman of Shelley's own mold and intellectual stature. Shelley frankly informed both Harriet and Godwin that he had fallen in love with Mary; they expressed equal outrage. Once more Shelley found himself planning an elopement, and once more a helpful sister seconded the enterprise. Claire Clairmont, daughter of Godwin's second wife and therefore actually no relation of Mary's, accompanied the wayward pair. This time they took the Dover coach. Claire's mother energetically pursued, and found they had left by boat for Calais. There she overtook them, but was unable even to persuade Claire herself to return home.

The elopement was brief. After walking, partly aided by a mule, across France to Switzerland—at Troyes, Shelley wrote Harriet asking her to join them—the party about-faced and made their way back to London. There they had to go round to Harriet's lodgings to borrow money for the cab fare. Harriet, imagining that her husband was returning to her, was chagrined, but paid.

Lack of money forced the lovers to separate, meeting occasionally in restaurants and hotels until the death of old Sir Bysshe in January 1815. Because so much of the estate was entailed, Shelley received less than he had been led to expect, but succeeded in arranging an income of £1000, of which he immediately settled £200 on Harriet. He and Mary set up housekeeping, with Claire Clairmont almost as irritating a third party as Eliza Westbrook had been.

Within three months Shelley had two more children, a boy by Harriet in November 1814, and a girl by Mary in February 1815. But Mary's daughter died after a week, and Shelley may have doubted that Harriet's son was his. In January 1816, Mary had a son, William. A few months later the whole menage, including Claire, left to rendezvous with Byron in Switzerland.

Shelley was a warm admirer of Byron's poetry—he listened to a reading of the third canto of *Childe Harold* and despaired of equaling it— and the two men enjoyed each other's company. They toured the lake region by boat, from Rousseau's Meillerie to the castle of Chillon. One stormy night at Byron's lakeside villa the party entertained themselves by reading ghost stories. Byron proposed that they try their hands at writing such tales. All commenced with enthusiasm except Mary, who remained lost in thought. But while none of the others produced anything of value, Mary, after a delayed start, completed *Frankenstein*.

The Shelleys returned to England in the fall, accompanied by Claire, melancholy and pregnant. They had no sooner settled at Bath than they received a piece of tragic news: Fannie Imlay, Mary's half-sister, had committed suicide. Worse quickly followed. The *Times* of London reported: "On Thursday a respectable female far advanced in pregnancy was taken out of the Serpentine river . . . want of honour in her own conduct is supposed to have led to this fatal catastrophe, her husband being abroad." It was Harriet Shelley. She apparently had been living with an army officer recently sent to India.

Shelley sought to recover his two children, but Harriet's parents took legal measures to block the attempt, largely on the ground that his atheism, as expressed in *Queen Mab*, made him an unfit mentor for the young. To Shelley's bitter disappointment the Lord Chancellor placed the children in the custody of a guardian.

In a vain attempt to aid his custody fight, Shelley went through a marriage ceremony with Mary on December 30, 1816. This at least healed the breach which had developed with Godwin. The philosopher had been outraged at the spectacle of his disciple and his daughter jointly putting into practice his own principles, though his vexation did not prevent him from continuing to borrow money from Shelley.

In the winter of 1817–18 Shelley suffered from poor health, and the decision was made to move bag and baggage to Italy. By now the Shelleys had two small children, the second a daughter named Clara. Claire Clairmont was with the party, taking her own child, Allegra, to Byron in Venice.

Italy was a harrowing succession of tragedies. First the baby Clara caught a fever on a journey from Lucca to Este, where Byron had lent the Shelleys a villa, and died in her mother's arms. The following year their two-year-old son William fell ill in Rome and succumbed after an agonizing bedside vigil by his father.

Despite sorrow, perhaps partly because of it, Shelley wrote much of his best poetry in Italy, including *The Cenci, Ode to Liberty, Prometheus Unbound,* and many shorter poems. The eloquent, socialistic

Mask of Anarchy was composed after receipt of news of the "Peterloo Massacre," a labor disturbance back home in England. Late in 1819 Mary Shelley's fourth child was born, a fine boy destined to a long life, whom they baptized Percy. A few months later the Shelleys left Florence, where they had been staying, for Pisa, where Byron and Countess Guiccioli presently joined them and where the "Pisan circle," made up largely of English expatriates, formed.

One member of the circle, an Italian, told Shelley an affecting story. It seemed that a beautiful girl named Emilia was sighing her heart out in a convent near Pisa, imprisoned there by her tyrannical father to appease her jealous stepmother. Shelley grew interested, visited the girl, entered into a correspondence with her, and wrote her a long poem, working up so Shelleyesque a spiritual communion as to irritate Mary. Then Emilia's father offered her a husband, sight unseen, a middle-aged noble who lived in a castle surrounded by a swamp. To Shelley's mortification Emilia accepted at once, went off to the castle and presently, as Mary wrote with satisfaction, was reported leading her husband "a devil of a life."

"The error," Shelley confessed, "consists in seeking in a mortal image the likeness of what is, perhaps, eternal."

Hearing of Keats's arrival in Italy, Shelley wrote a mutual friend that he would "take care to bestow every possible attention on him. I consider his a most valuable life . . . I am aware that I am nourishing a rival who will far surpass me; and this is an additional motive, and will be an added pleasure." When he learned of Keats's death in Rome, he composed *Adonais,* one of the finest tributes written by one poet for another, and which had the effect of persuading Byron of Keats's genius.

In the summer of 1822 the Shelleys rented a cottage on the Bay of Lerici, the "Casa Magni." They shared it with another English couple, the Williamses, with whom they had become fast friends. The Williamses introduced the Shelleys to Trelawny, a mustachioed adventurer who had sailed on British men-of-war and French privateers, and who was thrilled at the opportunity to mingle with poets and intellectuals. It was agreed that the Shelleys and Williamses needed a boat, and Trelawny designed and ordered a light craft which Shelley named the *Ariel.* At the same time Trelawny provided Byron with the sturdier *Bolivar.*

Throughout the spring of 1822 shadows seemed to gather. Shelley, still in intermittently bad health, asked Trelawny to procure some poison for him to have handy. He experienced nightmares and hallucinations. Shortly after the death of Byron's daughter Allegra, he suddenly grasped Williams' arm and pointed out to sea: "There it is again!" he exclaimed. What he saw, he explained, was Allegra rising from the sea and clapping her hands.

In June, Mary Shelley experienced a miscarriage, owing her life to the effective intervention of Shelley, who applied ice to stop the hemorrhage.

The news of the arrival of Leigh Hunt and his family in Genoa renewed Shelley's spirits, and as soon as he knew Hunt to be in Leghorn he set off in *Ariel* with Williams.

They reached Leghorn that night too late to get port clearance, so anchoring alongside Byron's *Bolivar*, they borrowed cushions from the yacht and stretched out to sleep under the stars.

For a week Shelley was occupied in conciliating Byron and Hunt, and persuading Byron to promise his financial support for Hunt's new magazine. Sunday, July 7, Shelley spent roaming Pisa with Hunt. Next morning he had some errands to perform and was not ready to leave until early afternoon. Trelawny weighed anchor on *Bolivar* with the intention of accompanying *Ariel* out to sea. But he had neglected to get a harbor clearance and was forced to remain inside. There was a sea mist, and the air was heavy. The last Trelawny saw of Shelley, the poet was reclining on the tiny quarter deck reading his copy of Keats's latest poems.

A few minutes later the wind rose. Very soon a number of fishing craft came scurrying back to harbor. Trelawny's eyes sought *Ariel* among them, but in vain. The storm struck. It was violent, but over in twenty minutes. He asked some of the fishermen if they had seen *Ariel*; none had.

Not knowing when or whether their husbands had sailed, Mary Shelley and Jane Williams waited in growing anxiety at Casa Magni. Friday the mail arrived—and a letter from Leigh Hunt to Shelley. Mary ripped it open and read the fatal words, "Tell us how you arrived home, for we heard you encountered bad weather when you left Monday."

For a few days Mary clung to the wisp of hope that *Ariel* might have been blown to Elba or Corsica. But Trelawny, reconnoitering the coast, learned of two bodies being washed ashore. Both had been partly eaten by fish, but Trelawny identified Shelley's without difficulty: in the pocket, doubled back as if thrust there in haste, was the copy of Keats.

When Trelawny appeared at the Casa Magni, the expression on his face conveyed his message. "Is there no hope?" Mary whispered. The ex-corsair turned away, unable to speak.

Mary wanted Shelley buried in Rome, where their dead child William lay, but to satisfy the Tuscan quarantine requirements, the bodies had to be cremated.

Trelawny, who had originally come to Pisa in the hope of meeting Shelley, took charge of the grim task. First the body of Williams was burned, the following night that of Shelley, in the presence of a few friends of the Pisan circle, the local health officer, a file of soldiers and a number of awed but curious villagers. Shelley's heart refused to burn; Trelawny thrust his hand into the flames and recovered it.

In Rome, Joseph Severn, the artist who had nursed Keats in his last illness, helped make burial arrangements for Shelley. On the tombstone were inscribed lines from *The Tempest*:

> Nothing of him that doth fade
> But hath suffered a sea-change
> Into something rich and strange.

Two summers later, in London, Mary Shelley wrote in her journal: "What should I have said to a Cassandra who three years ago should have prophesied that Jane and I—Edward and Shelley gone—should watch the funeral procession of Lord Byron up Highgate Hill?"

ADONAIS

AN ELEGY ON THE DEATH
OF JOHN KEATS

'Αστὴρ πρὶν μὲν ἔλαμπες ἐνὶ ζώοισιν ἑῷος.
Νῦν δὲ θανὼν λάμπεις ἕσπερος ἐν φθιμένοις.
PLATO.

I

I WEEP for Adonais—he is dead!
    Oh! weep for Adonais, though our tears
Thaw not the frost which binds so dear a head!
    And thou, sad Hour selected from all years
    To mourn our loss, rouse thy obscure compeers,
And teach them thine own sorrow! Say: "With me
    Died Adonais! Till the Future dares
Forget the Past, his fate and fame shall be
An echo and a light unto eternity."

II

Where wert thou, mighty Mother, when he lay,
    When thy Son lay, pierced by the shaft which flies
In darkness? Where was lorn Urania
    When Adonais died? With veilèd eyes,
    'Mid listening Echoes, in her Paradise
She sate, while one, with soft enamoured breath,
    Rekindled all the fading melodies
With which, like flowers that mock the corse beneath,
He had adorned and hid the coming bulk of Death.

III

Oh! weep for Adonais—he is dead!
    Wake, melancholy Mother, wake and weep!
  Yet wherefore? Quench within their burning bed
    Thy fiery tears, and let thy loud heart keep,
    Like his, a mute and uncomplaining sleep;
  For he is gone where all things wise and fair
    Descend. Oh! dream not that the amorous Deep
  Will yet restore him to the vital air;
Death feeds on his mute voice, and laughs at our despair.

IV

Most musical of mourners, weep again!
    Lament anew, Urania!—He died
Who was the sire of an immortal strain,
    Blind, old, and lonely, when his country's pride
    The priest, the slave, and the liberticide,
  Trampled and mocked with many a loathèd rite
    Of lust and blood. He went unterrified
  Into the gulf of death; but his clear Sprite
Yet reigns o'er earth, the third among the sons of light.

V

Most musical of mourners, weep anew!
    Not all to that bright station dared to climb:
And happier they their happiness who knew,
    Whose tapers yet burn through that night of time
    In which suns perished. Others more sublime,
  Struck by the envious wrath of man or God,
    Have sunk, extinct in their refulgent prime;
  And some yet live, treading the thorny road
Which leads, through toil and hate, to Fame's serene abode.

VI

But now thy youngest, dearest one has perished,
    The nursling of thy widowhood, who grew,
Like a pale flower by some sad maiden cherished,
    And fed with true-love tears instead of dew.
    Most musical of mourners, weep anew!
Thy extreme hope, the loveliest and the last,
    The bloom whose petals, nipped before they blew,
Died on the promise of the fruit, is waste;
The broken lily lies—the storm is overpast.

VII

To that high Capital where kingly Death
    Keeps his pale court in beauty and decay
He came; and bought, with price of purest breath,
    A grave among the eternal.—Come away!
    Haste, while the vault of blue Italian day
Is yet his fitting charnel-roof, while still
    He lies as if in dewy sleep he lay.
Awake him not! surely he takes his fill
Of deep and liquid rest, forgetful of all ill.

VIII

He will awake no more, oh never more!
    Within the twilight chamber spreads apace
The shadow of white Death, and at the door
    Invisible Corruption waits to trace
    His extreme way to her dim dwelling-place;
The eternal Hunger sits, but pity and awe
    Soothe her pale rage, nor dares she to deface
So fair a prey, till darkness and the law
Of change shall o'er his sleep the mortal curtain draw.

IX

Oh weep for Adonais!—The quick Dreams,
    The passion-wingèd Ministers of thought,
Who were his flocks, whom near the living streams
    Of his young spirit he fed, and whom he taught
    The love which was its music, wander not—
Wander no more from kindling brain to brain,
    But droop there whence they sprung; and mourn their lot
Round the cold heart where, after their sweet pain,
They ne'er will gather strength or find a home again.

X

And one with trembling hand clasps his cold head,
    And fans him with her moonlight wings, and cries,
"Our love, our hope, our sorrow, is not dead!
    See, on the silken fringe of his faint eyes,
    Like dew upon a sleeping flower, there lies
A tear some Dream has loosened from his brain."
    Lost Angel of a ruined Paradise!
She knew not 'twas her own,—as with no stain
She faded, like a cloud which had outwept its rain.

XI

One from a lucid urn of starry dew
    Washed his light limbs, as if embalming them;
Another clipped her profuse locks, and threw
    The wreath upon him, like an anadem
    Which frozen tears instead of pearls begem;
Another in her wilful grief would break
    Her bow and wingèd reeds, as if to stem
A greater loss with one which was more weak,
And dull the barbèd fire against his frozen cheek.

XII

Another Splendour on his mouth alit,
    That mouth whence it was wont to draw the breath
  Which gave it strength to pierce the guarded wit,
    And pass into the panting heart beneath
    With lightning and with music: the damp death
Quenched its caress upon his icy lips;
    And, as a dying meteor stains a wreath
Of moonlight vapour which the cold night clips,
It flushed through his pale limbs, and passed to its eclipse.

XIII

And others came,—Desires and Adorations,
    Wingèd Persuasions, and veiled Destinies,
  Splendours, and Glooms, and glimmering Incarnations
    Of hopes and fears, and twilight Fantasies.
    And Sorrow, with her family of Sighs,
And Pleasure, blind with tears, led by the gleam
    Of her own dying smile instead of eyes,
Came in slow pomp;—the moving pomp might seem
Like pageantry of mist on an autumnal stream.

XIV

All he had loved, and moulded into thought
    From shape and hue and odour and sweet sound,
  Lamented Adonais. Morning sought
    Her eastern watch-tower, and her hair unbound,
    Wet with the tears which should adorn the ground,
Dimmed the aërial eyes that kindle day;
    Afar the melancholy thunder moaned,
Pale Ocean in unquiet slumber lay,
And the wild Winds flew round, sobbing in their dismay.

XV

Lost Echo sits amid the voiceless mountains,
    And feeds her grief with his remembered lay,
  And will no more reply to winds or fountains,
    Or amorous birds perched on the young green spray,
    Or herdsman's horn, or bell at closing day;
  Since she can mimic not his lips, more dear
    Than those for whose disdain she pined away
Into a shadow of all sounds:—a drear
Murmur, between their songs, is all the woodmen hear.

XVI

Grief made the young Spring wild, and she threw down
    Her kindling buds, as if she Autumn were,
  Or they dead leaves; since her delight is flown,
    For whom should she have waked the sullen year?
    To Phoebus was not Hyacinth so dear,
  Nor to himself Narcissus, as to both
    Thou, Adonais; wan they stand and sere
Amid the faint companions of their youth,
With dew all turned to tears,—odour, to sighing ruth.

XVII

Thy spirit's sister, the lorn nightingale,
    Mourns not her mate with such melodious pain;
  Not so the eagle, who like thee could scale
    Heaven, and could nourish in the sun's domain
    Her mighty youth with morning, doth complain,
  Soaring and screaming round her empty nest,
    As Albion wails for thee: the curse of Cain
Light on his head who pierced thy innocent breast,
And scared the angel soul that was its earthly guest!

XVIII

Ah woe is me! Winter is come and gone,
    But grief returns with the revolving year.
The airs and streams renew their joyous tone;
    The ants, the bees, the swallows, re-appear;
    Fresh leaves and flowers deck the dead Seasons' bier;
The amorous birds now pair in every brake,
    And build their mossy homes in field and brere;
And the green lizard and the golden snake,
Like unimprisoned flames, out of their trance awake.

XIX

Through wood and stream and field and hill and Ocean,
    A quickening life from the Earth's heart has burst,
As it has ever done, with change and motion,
    From the great morning of the world when first
    God dawned on Chaos. In its steam immersed,
The lamps of Heaven flash with a softer light;
    All baser things pant with life's sacred thirst,
Diffuse themselves, and spend in love's delight
The beauty and the joy of their renewèd might.

XX

The leprous corpse, touched by this spirit tender,
    Exhales itself in flowers of gentle breath;
Like incarnations of the stars, when splendour
    Is changed to fragrance, they illumine death,
    And mock the merry worm that wakes beneath.
Nought we know dies: shall that alone which knows
    Be as a sword consumed before the sheath
By sightless lightning? The intense atom glows
A moment, then is quenched in a most cold repose.

XXI

Alas! that all we loved of him should be,
    But for our grief, as if it had not been,
And grief itself be mortal! Woe is me!
    Whence are we, and why are we? of what scene
    The actors or spectators? Great and mean
Meet massed in death, who lends what life must borrow.
    As long as skies are blue and fields are green,
Evening must usher night, night urge the morrow,
Month follow month with woe, and year wake year to sorrow.

XXII

He will awake no more, oh never more!
    "Wake thou," cried Misery, "childless Mother, rise
Out of thy sleep, and slake in thy heart's core
    A wound more fierce than his, with tears and sighs."
    And all the Dreams that watched Urania's eyes,
And all the Echoes whom their sister's song
    Had held in holy silence, cried "Arise!"
Swift as a Thought by the snake Memory stung,
From her ambrosial rest the fading Splendour sprung.

XXIII

She rose like an autumnal Night that springs
    Out of the East, and follows wild and drear
The golden Day, which, on eternal wings,
    Even as a ghost abandoning a bier,
    Had left the Earth a corpse. Sorrow and fear
So struck, so roused, so rapt Urania;
    So saddened round her like an atmosphere
Of stormy mist; so swept her on her way,
Even to the mournful place where Adonais lay.

XXIV

Out of her secret Paradise she sped,
    Through camps and cities rough with stone and steel
And human hearts, which, to her aery tread
    Yielding not, wounded the invisible
    Palms of her tender feet where'er they fell.
And barbèd tongues, and thoughts more sharp than they,
    Rent the soft Form they never could repel,
    Whose sacred blood, like the young tears of May,
Paved with eternal flowers that undeserving way.

XXV

In the death-chamber for a moment Death,
    Shamed by the presence of that living Might,
Blushed to annihilation, and the breath
    Revisited those lips, and life's pale light
    Flashed through those limbs so late her dear delight.
"Leave me not wild and drear and comfortless,
    As silent lightning leaves the starless night!
Leave me not!" cried Urania. Her distress
Roused Death: Death rose and smiled, and met her vain caress.

XXVI

"Stay yet awhile! speak to me once again!
    Kiss me, so long but as a kiss may live!
And in my heartless breast and burning brain
    That word, that kiss, shall all thoughts else survive,
    With food of saddest memory kept alive,
Now thou art dead, as if it were a part
    Of thee, my Adonais! I would give
All that I am, to be as thou now art:—
But I am chained to Time, and cannot thence depart.

XXVII

"O gentle child, beautiful as thou wert,
 Why didst thou leave the trodden paths of men
Too soon, and with weak hands though mighty heart
 Dare the unpastured dragon in his den?
 Defenceless as thou wert, oh! where was then
Wisdom the mirrored shield, or scorn the spear?—
 Or, hadst thou waited the full cycle, when
Thy spirit should have filled its crescent sphere,
The monsters of life's waste had fled from thee like deer.

XXVIII

"The herded wolves bold only to pursue,
 The obscene ravens clamorous o'er the dead,
The vultures to the conqueror's banner true,
 Who feed where Desolation first has fed,
 And whose wings rain contagion,—how they fled,
When, like Apollo from his golden bow,
 The Pythian of the age one arrow sped,
And smiled!—The spoilers tempt no second blow,
They fawn on the proud feet that spurn them lying low.

XXIX

"The sun comes forth, and many reptiles spawn;
 He sets, and each ephemeral insect then
Is gathered into death without a dawn,
 And the immortal stars awake again.
 So is it in the world of living men:
A godlike mind soars forth, in its delight
 Making earth bare and veiling heaven; and, when
It sinks, the swarms that dimmed or shared its light
Leave to its kindred lamps the spirit's awful night."

XXX

Thus ceased she: and the mountain shepherds came,
   Their garlands sere, their magic mantles rent.
The Pilgrim of Eternity, whose fame
   Over his living head like Heaven is bent,
   An early but enduring monument,
Came, veiling all the lightnings of his song
   In sorrow. From her wilds Ierne sent
The sweetest lyrist of her saddest wrong,
And Love taught Grief to fall like music from his tongue.

XXXI

'Midst others of less note came one frail Form,
   A phantom among men, companionless
As the last cloud of an expiring storm
   Whose thunder is its knell. He, as I guess,
   Had gazed on Nature's naked loveliness
Actaeon-like; and now he fled astray
   With feeble steps o'er the world's wilderness,
And his own thoughts along that rugged way
Pursued like raging hounds their father and their prey.

XXXII

A pard-like Spirit beautiful and swift—
   A love in desolation masked—a Power
Girt round with weakness; it can scarce uplift
   The weight of the superincumbent hour.
   It is a dying lamp, a falling shower,
A breaking billow;—even whilst we speak
   Is it not broken? On the withering flower
The killing sun smiles brightly: on a cheek
The life can burn in blood even while the heart may break.

XXXIII

His head was bound with pansies overblown,
    And faded violets, white and pied and blue;
And a light spear topped with a cypress cone,
    Round whose rude shaft dark ivy-tresses grew
    Yet dripping with the forest's noonday dew,
Vibrated, as the ever-beating heart
    Shook the weak hand that grasped it; of that crew
He came the last, neglected and apart;
A herd-abandoned deer struck by the hunter's dart.

XXXIV

All stood aloof, and at his partial moan
    Smiled through their tears. Well knew that gentle band
Who in another's fate now wept his own.
    As in the accents of an unknown land
    He sung new sorrow, sad Urania scanned
The Stranger's mien, and murmured: "Who art thou?"
    He answered not, but with a sudden hand
Made bare his branded and ensanguined brow,
Which was like Cain's or Christ's—oh! that it should be so!

XXXV

What softer voice is hushed over the dead?
    Athwart what brow is that dark mantle thrown?
What form leans sadly o'er the white death-bed,
    In mockery of monumental stone,
    The heavy heart heaving without a moan?
If it be He who, gentlest of the wise,
    Taught, soothed, loved, honoured, the departed one,
Let me not vex with inharmonious sighs
The silence of that heart's accepted sacrifice.

XXXVI

Our Adonais has drunk poison—oh!
    What deaf and viperous murderer could crown
    Life's early cup with such a draught of woe?
      The nameless worm would now itself disown;
      It felt, yet could escape, the magic tone
Whose prelude held all envy, hate, and wrong,
    But what was howling in one breast alone,
Silent with expectation of the song
Whose master's hand is cold, whose silver lyre unstrung.

XXXVII

Live thou, whose infamy is not thy fame!
    Live! fear no heavier chastisement from me,
    Thou noteless blot on a remembered name!
      But be thyself, and know thyself to be!
      And ever at thy season be thou free
To spill the venom when thy fangs o'erflow:
    Remorse and Self-contempt shall cling to thee;
Hot Shame shall burn upon thy secret brow,
And like a beaten hound tremble thou shalt—as now.

XXXVIII

Nor let us weep that our delight is fled
    Far from these carrion kites that scream below.
    He wakes or sleeps with the enduring dead;
      Thou canst not soar where he is sitting now.
      Dust to the dust: but the pure spirit shall flow
Back to the burning fountain whence it came,
    A portion of the Eternal, which must glow
Through time and change, unquenchably the same,
Whilst thy cold embers choke the sordid hearth of shame.

XXXIX

Peace, peace! he is not dead, he doth not sleep!
  He hath awakened from the dream of life.
'Tis we who, lost in stormy visions, keep
  With phantoms an unprofitable strife,
  And in mad trance strike with our spirit's knife
Invulnerable nothings. We decay
  Like corpses in a charnel; fear and grief
Convulse us and consume us day by day,
And cold hopes swarm like worms within our living clay.

XL

He has outsoared the shadow of our night.
  Envy and calumny and hate and pain,
And that unrest which men miscall delight,
  Can touch him not and torture not again.
  From the contagion of the world's slow stain
He is secure; and now can never mourn
  A heart grown cold, a head grown grey, in vain—
Nor, when the spirit's self has ceased to burn,
With sparkless ashes load an unlamented urn.

XLI

He lives, he wakes—'tis Death is dead, not he;
  Mourn not for Adonais.—Thou young Dawn,
Turn all thy dew to splendour, for from thee
  The spirit thou lamentest is not gone!
  Ye caverns and ye forests, cease to moan!
Cease, ye faint flowers and fountains! and, thou Air,
  Which like a mourning veil thy scarf hadst thrown
O'er the abandoned Earth, now leave it bare
Even to the joyous stars which smile on its despair!

XLII

He is made one with Nature. There is heard
   His voice in all her music, from the moan
Of thunder to the song of night's sweet bird.
   He is a presence to be felt and known
   In darkness and in light, from herb and stone;
Spreading itself where'er that Power may move
   Which has withdrawn his being to its own,
Which wields the world with never-wearied love,
Sustains it from beneath, and kindles it above.

XLIII

He is a portion of the loveliness
   Which once he made more lovely. He doth bear
His part, while the one Spirit's plastic stress
   Sweeps through the dull dense world; compelling there
   All new successions to the forms they wear;
Torturing the unwilling dross that checks its flight
   To its own likeness, as each mass may bear;
And bursting in its beauty and its might
From trees and beasts and men into the Heaven's light.

XLIV

The splendours of the firmament of time
   May be eclipsed, but are extinguished not;
Like stars to their appointed height they climb,
   And death is a low mist which cannot blot
   The brightness it may veil. When lofty thought
Lifts a young heart above its mortal lair,
   And love and life contend in it for what
Shall be its earthly doom, the dead live there,
And move like winds of light on dark and stormy air.

XLV

The inheritors of unfulfilled renown
        Rose from their thrones, built beyond mortal thought
Far in the Unapparent. Chatterton
        Rose pale, his solemn agony had not
        Yet faded from him; Sidney, as he fought,
And as he fell, and as he lived and loved,
        Sublimely mild, a spirit without spot,
    Arose; and Lucan, by his death approved;—
Oblivion as they rose shrank like a thing reproved.

XLVI

And many more, whose names on earth are dark,
        But whose transmitted effluence cannot die
So long as fire outlives the parent spark,
        Rose, robed in dazzling immortality.
        "Thou art become as one of us," they cry;
"It was for thee yon kingless sphere has long
        Swung blind in unascended majesty,
    Silent alone amid an Heaven of song.
Assume thy wingèd throne, thou Vesper of our throng!"

XLVII

Who mourns for Adonais? Oh! come forth,
        Fond wretch, and know thyself and him aright.
    Clasp with thy panting soul the pendulous earth;
        As from a centre, dart thy spirit's light
        Beyond all worlds, until its spacious might
Satiate the void circumference: then shrink
        Even to a point within our day and night;
    And keep thy heart light, lest it make thee sink,
When hope has kindled hope, and lured thee to the brink.

XLVIII

Or go to Rome, which is the sepulchre,
    Oh not of him, but of our joy. 'Tis nought
That ages, empires, and religions, there
    Lie buried in the ravage they have wrought;
    For such as he can lend—they borrow not
Glory from those who made the world their prey;
    And he is gathered to the kings of thought
Who waged contention with their time's decay,
And of the past are all that cannot pass away.

XLIX

Go thou to Rome,—at once the Paradise,
    The grave, the city, and the wilderness;
And where its wrecks like shattered mountains rise,
    And flowering weeds and fragrant copses dress
    The bones of Desolation's nakedness,
Pass, till the Spirit of the spot shall lead
    Thy footsteps to a slope of green access,
Where, like an infant's smile, over the dead
A light of laughing flowers along the grass is spread.

L

And grey walls moulder round, on which dull Time
    Feeds, like slow fire upon a hoary brand;
And one keen pyramid with wedge sublime,
    Pavilioning the dust of him who planned
    This refuge for his memory, doth stand
Like flame transformed to marble; and beneath
    A field is spread, on which a newer band
Have pitched in Heaven's smile their camp of death,
Welcoming him we lose with scarce extinguished breath.

LI

Here pause: these graves are all too young as yet
    To have outgrown the sorrow which consigned
Its charge to each; and, if the seal is set
    Here on one fountain of a mourning mind,
    Break it not thou! too surely shalt thou find
Thine own well full, if thou returnest home,
    Of tears and gall. From the world's bitter wind
Seek shelter in the shadow of the tomb.
What Adonais is why fear we to become?

LII

The One remains, the many change and pass;
    Heaven's light for ever shines, Earth's shadows fly;
Life, like a dome of many-coloured glass,
    Stains the white radiance of Eternity,
    Until Death tramples it to fragments.—Die,
If thou wouldst be with that which thou dost seek!
    Follow where all is fled!—Rome's azure sky,
Flowers, ruins, statues, music,—words are weak
The glory they transfuse with fitting truth to speak.

LIII

Why linger, why turn back, why shrink, my Heart?
    Thy hopes are gone before: from all things here
They have departed; thou shouldst now depart!
    A light is passed from the revolving year,
    And man and woman; and what still is dear
Attracts to crush, repels to make thee wither.
    The soft sky smiles, the low wind whispers near:
'Tis Adonais calls! oh! hasten thither!
No more let Life divide what Death can join together.

LIV

That Light whose smile kindles the Universe,
    That Beauty in which all things work and move,
That Benediction which the eclipsing Curse
    Of birth can quench not, that sustaining Love
Which, through the web of being blindly wove
By man and beast and earth and air and sea,
    Burns bright or dim, as each are mirrors of
The fire for which all thirst, now beams on me,
Consuming the last clouds of cold mortality.

LV

The breath whose might I have invoked in song
    Descends on me; my spirit's bark is driven
Far from the shore, far from the trembling throng
    Whose sails were never to the tempest given.
The massy earth and spherèd skies are riven!
I am borne darkly, fearfully, afar!
    Whilst, burning through the inmost veil of Heaven,
The soul of Adonais, like a star,
Beacons from the abode where the Eternal are.

1821

SHORT POEMS

To Coleridge

ΔΑΚΡΥΣΙ ΔΙΟΙΣΩ ΠΟΤΜΟΝ 'ΑΠΟΤΜΟΝ.

Oʜ! there are spirits of the air,
    And genii of the evening breeze,
And gentle ghosts with eyes as fair
    As starbeams among twilight trees:—
Such lovely ministers to meet
Oft hast thou turned from men thy lonely feet.

With mountain winds, and babbling springs,
    And moonlight seas, that are the voice
Of these inexplicable things,
    Thou didst hold commune, and rejoice
When they did answer thee. But they
Cast like a worthless boon thy love away.

And thou hast sought in starry eyes
    Beams that were never meant for thine,
Another's wealth;—tame sacrifice
    To a fond faith! Still dost thou pine?
Still dost thou hope that greeting hands,
Voice, looks, or lips, may answer thy demands?

Ah! wherefore didst thou build thine hope
    On the false earth's inconstancy?
Did thine own mind afford no scope
    Of love or moving thoughts to thee—
That natural scenes or human smiles
Could steal the power to wind thee in their wiles?

Yes, all the faithless smiles are fled
   Whose falsehood left thee broken-hearted;
   The glory of the moon is dead;
   Night's ghosts and dreams have now departed:
   Thine own soul still is true to thee,
But changed to a foul fiend through misery.

This fiend, whose ghastly presence ever
   Beside thee like thy shadow hangs,
   Dream not to chase;—the mad endeavour
   Would scourge thee to severer pangs.
   Be as thou art. Thy settled fate,
Dark as it is, all change would aggravate.

                        1815

To Wordsworth

POET of Nature, thou hast wept to know
   That things depart which never may return;
Childhood and youth, friendship, and love's first glow,
   Have fled like sweet dreams, leaving thee to mourn.
These common woes I feel. One loss is mine,
   Which thou too feel'st, yet I alone deplore.
Thou wert as a lone star whose light did shine
   On some frail bark in winter's midnight roar:
Thou hast like to a rock-built refuge stood
Above the blind and battling multitude:
In honoured poverty thy voice did weave
   Songs consecrate to truth and liberty.
Deserting these, thou leavest me to grieve,
   Thus, having been, that thou shouldst cease to be.

                        1815

Feelings of a Republican
on the Fall of Bonaparte

I HATED thee, fallen tyrant! I did groan
  To think that a most unambitious slave,
  Like thou, should dance and revel on the grave
Of Liberty. Thou mightst have built thy throne
Where it had stood even now: thou didst prefer
  A frail and bloody pomp, which Time has swept
In fragments towards oblivion. Massacre,
  For this, I prayed, would on thy sleep have crept,
Treason and Slavery, Rapine, Fear, and Lust,
  And stifled thee their minister. I know
Too late, since thou and France are in the dust,
  That Virtue owns a more eternal foe
Than Force or Fraud: old Custom, Legal Crime,
And bloody Faith, the foulest birth of Time.

                                        1815

Hymn to Intellectual Beauty

I

THE awful shadow of some unseen Power
    Floats, though unseen, among us; visiting
    This various world with as inconstant wing
As summer winds that creep from flower to flower.
Like moonbeams that behind some piny mountain shower,
    It visits with inconstant glance
    Each human heart and countenance;
    Like hues and harmonies of evening,
    Like clouds in starlight widely spread,
    Like memory of music fled,
    Like aught that for its grace may be
Dear, and yet dearer for its mystery.

II

Spirit of Beauty, that dost consecrate
    With thine own hues all thou dost shine upon
    Of human thought or form, where art thou gone?
Why dost thou pass away, and leave our state,
This dim vast vale of tears, vacant and desolate?—
      Ask why the sunlight not for ever
      Weaves rainbows o'er yon mountain river;
    Why aught should fail and fade that once is shown;
      Why fear and dream and death and birth
      Cast on the daylight of this earth
    Such gloom; why man has such a scope
For love and hate, despondency and hope!

III

No voice from some sublimer world hath ever
    To sage or poet these responses given:
    Therefore the names of Demon, Ghost, and Heaven,
Remain the records of their vain endeavour;
Frail spells, whose uttered charm might not avail to sever,
      From all we hear and all we see,
      Doubt, chance, and mutability.
    Thy light alone, like mist o'er mountains driven,
      Or music by the night-wind sent
      Through strings of some still instrument,
    Or moonlight on a midnight stream,
Gives grace and truth to life's unquiet dream.

IV

Love, Hope, and Self-esteem, like clouds depart
    And come, for some uncertain moments lent.
    Man were immortal and omnipotent,

Didst thou, unknown and awful as thou art,
Keep with thy glorious train firm state within his heart.
Thou messenger of sympathies
That wax and wane in lovers' eyes—
Thou—that to human thought art nourishment,
Like darkness to a dying flame!
Depart not as thy shadow came:
Depart not, lest the grave should be,
Like life and fear, a dark reality!

V

While yet a boy, I sought for ghosts, and sped
Through many a listening chamber, cave, and ruin,
And starlight wood, with fearful steps pursuing
Hopes of high talk with the departed dead.
I called on poisonous names with which our youth is fed.
I was not heard, I saw them not;
When, musing deeply on the lot
Of life, at that sweet time when winds are wooing
All vital things that wake to bring
News of birds and blossoming,
Sudden thy shadow fell on me:—
I shrieked, and clasped my hands in ecstasy!

VI

I vowed that I would dedicate my powers
To thee and thine: have I not kept the vow?
With beating heart and streaming eyes, even now
I call the phantoms of a thousand hours
Each from its voiceless grave. They have in visioned bowers
Of studious zeal or love's delight
Outwatched with me the envious night:
They know that never joy illumed my brow,
Unlinked with hope that thou wouldst free
This world from its dark slavery;
That thou, O awful Loveliness,
Wouldst give whate'er these words cannot express.

VII

The day becomes more solemn and serene
  When noon is past: there is a harmony
  In autumn, and a lustre in its sky,
Which through the summer is not heard or seen,
As if it could not be, as if it had not been.
    Thus let thy power, which like the truth
    Of nature on my passive youth
  Descended, to my onward life supply
    Its calm,—to one who worships thee,
    And every form containing thee,
  Whom, Spirit fair, thy spells did bind
To fear himself, and love all humankind.

                                        1816

Mont Blanc

LINES WRITTEN IN THE VALE OF CHAMOUNI

I

THE everlasting universe of things
  Flows through the mind, and rolls its rapid waves,
    Now dark—now glittering—now reflecting gloom—
Now lending splendour, where from secret springs
The source of human thought its tribute brings
Of waters,—with a sound but half its own,
    Such as a feeble brook will oft assume
In the wild woods, among the mountains lone,
Where waterfalls around it leap for ever,
Where woods and winds contend, and a vast river
    Over its rocks ceaselessly bursts and raves.

II

Thus thou, Ravine of Arve—dark, deep Ravine—
Thou many-coloured many-voicèd vale,
Over whose pines and crags and caverns sail
Fast cloud-shadows and sunbeams; awful scene,
Where Power in likeness of the Arve comes down
From the ice-gulfs that gird his secret throne,
Bursting through these dark mountains like the flame
Of lightning through the tempest;—thou dost lie,—
Thy giant brood of pines around thee clinging,
Children of elder time, in whose devotion
The chainless winds still come and ever came
To drink their odours, and their mighty swinging
To hear—an old and solemn harmony;
Thine earthly rainbows stretched across the sweep
Of the aethereal waterfall, whose veil
Robes some unsculptured image; the strange sleep
Which, when the voices of the desert fail,
Wraps all in its own deep eternity;
Thy caverns echoing to the Arve's commotion,
A loud lone sound no other sound can tame.
Thou art pervaded with that ceaseless motion,
Thou art the path of that unresting sound,
Dizzy Ravine! And, when I gaze on thee,
I seem, as in a trance sublime and strange,
To muse on my own separate fantasy,
My own, my human mind, which passively
Now renders and receives fast influencings,
Holding an unremitting interchange
With the clear universe of things around;
One legion of wild thoughts, whose wandering wings
Now float above thy darkness, and now rest
Where that or thou art no unbidden guest,
In the still cave of the witch Poesy,—
Seeking—among the shadows that pass by,
Ghosts of all things that are—some shade of thee,
Some phantom, some faint image; till the breast
From which they fled recalls them, thou art there!

III

Some say that gleams of a remoter world
  Visit the soul in sleep,—that death is slumber,
  And that its shapes the busy thoughts outnumber
Of those who wake and live. I look on high;
Has some unknown omnipotence unfurled
  The veil of life and death? Or do I lie
In dream, and does the mightier world of sleep
  Spread far around and inaccessibly
    Its circles? for the very spirit fails,
Driven like a homeless cloud from steep to steep
    That vanishes among the viewless gales!
  Far, far above, piercing the infinite sky,
Mont Blanc appears—still, snowy, and serene.
  Its subject mountains their unearthly forms
Pile around it, ice and rock; broad vales between
  Of frozen floods, unfathomable deeps,
    Blue as the overhanging heaven, that spread
And wind among the accumulated steeps;
  A desert peopled by the storms alone,
  Save when the eagle brings some hunter's bone,
  And the wolf tracks her there. How hideously
Its shapes are heaped around—rude, bare, and high,
Ghastly and scarred and riven!—Is this the scene
Where the old Earthquake-daemon taught her young
  Ruin? Were these their toys? or did a sea
    Of fire envelop once this silent snow?
    None can reply—all seems eternal now.
The wilderness has a mysterious tongue
    Which teaches awful doubt,—or faith so mild,
  So solemn, so serene, that man may be,
    But for such faith, with Nature reconciled.
Thou hast a voice, great Mountain, to repeal
  Large codes of fraud and woe; not understood
  By all, but which the wise and great and good
Interpret, or make felt, or deeply feel.

IV

The fields, the lakes, the forests, and the streams,
  Ocean, and all the living things that dwell
    Within the daedal earth, lightning and rain,
    Earthquake and fiery flood and hurricane,
The torpor of the year when feeble dreams
Visit the hidden buds, or dreamless sleep
    Holds every future leaf and flower, the bound
With which from that detested trance they leap,
    The works and ways of man, their death and birth,
    And that of him, and all that his may be,
  All things that move and breathe, with toil and sound
Are born and die, revolve, subside, and swell.
    Power dwells apart in its tranquillity,
Remote, serene, and inaccessible:
    And *this* the naked countenance of earth
    On which I gaze, even these primaeval mountains
Teach the adverting mind. The glaciers creep
    Like snakes that watch their prey, from their far fountains,
Slow rolling on; there, many a precipice,
    Frost and the Sun in scorn of mortal power
    Have piled—dome, pyramid, and pinnacle,
    A city of death, distinct with many a tower
And wall impregnable of beaming ice.
  Yet not a city, but a flood of ruin,
Is there, that from the boundary of the skies
  Rolls its perpetual stream; vast pines are strewing
Its destined path, or in the mangled soil
    Branchless and shattered stand; the rocks, drawn down
    From yon remotest waste, have overthrown
    The limits of the dead and living world,
    Never to be reclaimed. The dwelling-place
Of insects, beasts, and birds, becomes its spoil;
    Their food and their retreat for ever gone,
    So much of life and joy is lost. The race
Of man flies far in dread; his work and dwelling
    Vanish like smoke before the tempest's stream,
    And their place is not known. Below, vast caves
Shine in the rushing torrents' restless gleam,

Which, from those secret chasms in tumult welling,
Meet in the Vale; and one majestic River,
The breath and blood of distant lands, for ever
    Rolls its loud waters to the ocean waves,
Breathes its swift vapours to the circling air.

V

Mont Blanc yet gleams on high: the power is there,
    The still and solemn power, of many sights
    And many sounds, and much of life and death.
In the calm darkness of the moonless nights,
In the lone glare of day, the snows descend
Upon that Mountain; none beholds them there,
Nor when the flakes burn in the sinking sun,
    Or the star-beams dart through them. Winds contend
    Silently there, and heap the snow, with breath
Rapid and strong, but silently. Its home
    The voiceless lightning in these solitudes
Keeps innocently, and like vapour broods
    Over the snow. The secret Strength of things,
Which governs thought, and to the infinite dome
Of Heaven is as a law, inhabits thee.
And what were thou and earth and stars and sea,
    If to the human mind's imaginings
Silence and solitude were vacancy?

                                1816

Ozymandias

I MET a traveller from an antique land
    Who said: "Two vast and trunkless legs of stone
Stand in the desert. Near them on the sand,
    Half sunk, a shattered visage lies, whose frown
And wrinkled lip and sneer of cold command
Tell that its sculptor well those passions read
    Which yet survive, stamped on these lifeless things,
The hand that mocked them and the heart that fed.

And on the pedestal these words appear:
  'My name is Ozymandias, king of kings:
Look on my works, ye Mighty, and despair!'
  Nothing beside remains. Round the decay
Of that colossal wreck, boundless and bare,
  The lone and level sands stretch far away."

                                        1817

Lines to a Critic

HONEY from silkworms who can gather,
  Or silk from the yellow bee?
The grass may grow in winter weather
  As soon as hate in me.

Hate men who cant, and men who pray,
  And men who rail, like thee;
An equal passion to repay
  They are not coy like me.

Or seek some slave of power and gold
  To be thy dear heart's mate;
Thy love will move that bigot cold
  Sooner than me thy hate.

A passion like the one I prove
  Cannot divided be;
I hate thy want of truth and love—
  How should I then hate thee?

                                        1817

On a Faded Violet

THE odour from the flower is gone
  Which like thy kisses breathed on me;
The colour from the flower is flown
  Which glowed of thee and only thee!

A shrivelled, lifeless, vacant form,
   It lies on my abandoned breast;
And mocks the heart, which yet is warm
   With cold and silent rest.

I weep—my tears revive it not;
   I sigh—it breathes no more on me:
Its mute and uncomplaining lot
   Is such as mine should be.

1818

FROM *Lines Written Among the Euganean Hills*

*   *   *   *   *

Noon descends around me now.
'Tis the noon of autumn's glow;
When a soft and purple mist,
Like a vaporous amethyst,
Or an air-dissolvèd star
Mingling light and fragrance, far
From the curved horizon's bound
To the point of Heaven's profound
Fills the overflowing sky.
And the plains that silent lie
Underneath; the leaves unsodden
Where the infant Frost has trodden
With his morning-wingèd feet
Whose bright print is gleaming yet;
And the red and golden vines,
Piercing with their trellised lines
The rough dark-skirted wilderness;
The dun and bladed grass no less,
Pointing from this hoary tower
In the windless air; the flower
Glimmering at my feet; the line
Of the olive-sandalled Apennine
In the south dimly islanded;
And the Alps, whose snows are spread

High between the clouds and sun;
And of living things each one;
And my spirit, which so long
Darkened this swift stream of song,—
Interpenetrated lie
By the glory of the sky:
Be it love, light, harmony,
Odour, or the soul of all
Which from Heaven like dew doth fall,
Or the mind which feeds this verse
Peopling the lone universe.

Noon descends; and after noon
Autumn's evening meets me soon,
Leading the infantine moon,
And that one star which to her
Almost seems to minister
Half the crimson light she brings
From the sunset's radiant springs.
And the soft dreams of the morn
(Which like wingèd winds had borne,
To that silent isle which lies
'Mid remembered agonies,
The frail bark of this lone being)
Pass, to other sufferers fleeing;
And its ancient pilot, Pain,
Sits beside the helm again.

*   *   *   *   *

1818

Stanzas

WRITTEN IN DEJECTION NEAR NAPLES

I

THE sun is warm, the sky is clear,
    The waves are dancing fast and bright;
Blue isles and snowy mountains wear
    The purple noon's transparent might;
    The breath of the moist earth is light

Around its unexpanded buds;
     Like many a voice of one delight,
The winds, the birds, the ocean floods,
The City's voice itself, is soft like Solitude's.

II

I see the Deep's untrampled floor
     With green and purple sea-weeds strown;
I see the waves upon the shore,
     Like light dissolved, in star-showers thrown.
     I sit upon the sands alone.
The lightning of the noontide ocean
     Is flashing round me, and a tone
Arises from its measured motion,—
How sweet, did any heart now share in my emotion!

III

Alas! I have nor hope nor health,
     Nor peace within nor calm around;
Nor that content, surpassing wealth,
     The sage in meditation found,
     And walked with inward glory crowned;
Nor fame nor power nor love nor leisure.
     Others I see whom these surround—
Smiling they live, and call life pleasure;—
To me that cup has been dealt in another measure.

IV

Yet now despair itself is mild,
     Even as the winds and waters are;
I could lie down like a tired child,
     And weep away the life of care
     Which I have borne and yet must bear,—
Till death like sleep might steal on me,
     And I might feel in the warm air
My cheek grow cold, and hear the sea
Breathe o'er my dying brain its last monotony.

V

Some might lament that I were cold,
  As I when this sweet day is gone,
Which my lost heart, too soon grown old,
  Insults with this untimely moan.
  They might lament—for I am one
Whom men love not, and yet regret;
  Unlike this day, which, when the sun
Shall on its stainless glory set,
Will linger, though enjoyed, like joy in memory yet.

1818

Lines

WRITTEN DURING THE CASTLEREAGH ADMINISTRATION

I

CORPSES are cold in the tomb;
  Stones on the pavement are dumb;
  Abortions are dead in the womb,
And their mothers look pale—like the white shore
  Of Albion, free no more.

II

Her sons are as stones in the way—
  They are masses of senseless clay—
  They are trodden, and move not away;
The abortion with which *she* travaileth
  Is Liberty, smitten to death.

III

Then trample and dance, thou Oppressor,
    For thy victim is no redressor!
    Thou art sole lord and possessor
Of her corpses and clods and abortions—they pave
    Thy path to the grave.

IV

Hearest thou the festival din
    Of Death and Destruction and Sin
    And Wealth crying *Havoc!* within?
'Tis the Bacchanal triumph which makes Truth dumb,
    Thine Epithalamium.

V

Ay, marry thy ghastly wife!
    Let Fear and Disquiet and Strife
    Spread thy couch in the chamber of Life!
Marry Ruin, thou Tyrant! and Hell be thy guide
    To the bed of the bride!

                                        1819

Song to the Men of England

I

MEN of England, wherefore plough
For the lords who lay ye low?
Wherefore weave with toil and care
The rich robes your tyrants wear?

II

Wherefore feed and clothe and save,
From the cradle to the grave,
Those ungrateful drones who would
Drain your sweat—nay, drink your blood?

III

Wherefore, Bees of England, forge
Many a weapon, chain, and scourge,
That these stingless drones may spoil
The forced produce of your toil?

IV

Have ye leisure, comfort, calm,
Shelter, food, love's gentle balm?
Or what is it ye buy so dear
With your pain and with your fear?

V

The seed ye sow another reaps;
The wealth ye find another keeps;
The robes ye weave another wears;
The arms ye forge another bears.

VI

Sow seed,—but let no tyrant reap;
Find wealth,—let no impostor heap;
Weave robes,—let not the idle wear;
Forge arms, in your defence to bear.

VII

Shrink to your cellars, holes, and cells;
In halls ye deck another dwells.
Why shake the chains ye wrought? Ye see
The steel ye tempered glance on ye.

VIII

With plough and spade and hoe and loom,
Trace your grave, and build your tomb,
And weave your winding-sheet, till fair
England be your sepulchre!

1819

England in 1819

An old, mad, blind, despised, and dying king,—
Princes, the dregs of their dull race, who flow
Through public scorn, mud from a muddy spring,—
Rulers who neither see, nor feel, nor know,
But leech-like to their fainting country cling,
Till they drop, blind in blood, without a blow,—
A people starved and stabbed in the untilled field,—
An army which liberticide and prey
Makes as a two-edged sword to all who wield,—
Golden and sanguine laws which tempt and slay;
Religion Christless, Godless, a book sealed,—
A Senate—Time's worst statute unrepealed,—
Are graves from which a glorious Phantom may
Burst to illumine our tempestuous day.

1819

Ode to the West Wind

I

O wild West Wind, thou breath of Autumn's being,
  Thou from whose unseen presence the leaves dead
Are driven like ghosts from an enchanter fleeing,

  Yellow, and black, and pale, and hectic red,
Pestilence-stricken multitudes! O thou
  Who chariotest to their dark wintry bed

The wingèd seeds, where they lie cold and low,
  Each like a corpse within its grave, until
Thine azure sister of the Spring shall blow

  Her clarion o'er the dreaming earth, and fill
(Driving sweet buds like flocks to feed in air)
  With living hues and odours plain and hill;

Wild Spirit, which art moving everywhere;
Destroyer and preserver; hear, oh hear!

II

Thou on whose stream, mid the steep sky's commotion,
  Loose clouds like earth's decaying leaves are shed,
Shook from the tangled boughs of Heaven and Ocean,

  Angels of rain and lightning! there are spread
On the blue surface of thine aëry surge,
  Like the bright hair uplifted from the head

Of some fierce Maenad, even from the dim verge
  Of the horizon to the zenith's height,
The locks of the approaching storm. Thou dirge

Of the dying year, to which this closing night
Will be the dome of a vast sepulchre,
  Vaulted with all thy congregated might

Of vapours, from whose solid atmosphere
Black rain, and fire, and hail, will burst: Oh hear!

III

Thou who didst waken from his summer dreams
  The blue Mediterranean, where he lay,
Lulled by the coil of his crystalline streams,

  Beside a pumice isle in Baiae's bay,
And saw in sleep old palaces and towers
  Quivering within the wave's intenser day,

All overgrown with azure moss, and flowers
  So sweet the sense faints picturing them! Thou
For whose path the Atlantic's level powers

  Cleave themselves into chasms, while far below
The sea-blooms and the oozy woods which wear
  The sapless foliage of the ocean know

Thy voice, and suddenly grow grey with fear,
And tremble and despoil themselves: Oh hear!

IV

If I were a dead leaf thou mightest bear;
  If I were a swift cloud to fly with thee;
A wave to pant beneath thy power, and share

  The impulse of thy strength, only less free
Than thou, O uncontrollable! If even
  I were as in my boyhood, and could be

The comrade of thy wanderings over heaven,
  As then, when to outstrip thy skiey speed
Scarce seemed a vision,—I would ne'er have striven

As thus with thee in prayer in my sore need.
Oh! lift me as a wave, a leaf, a cloud!
   I fall upon the thorns of life! I bleed!

A heavy weight of hours has chained and bowed
One too like thee—tameless, and swift, and proud.

V

Make me thy lyre, even as the forest is:
   What if my leaves are falling like its own?
The tumult of thy mighty harmonies

   Will take from both a deep autumnal tone,
Sweet though in sadness. Be thou, Spirit fierce,
   My spirit! Be thou me, impetuous one!

Drive my dead thoughts over the universe,
   Like withered leaves, to quicken a new birth;
And, by the incantation of this verse,

   Scatter, as from an unextinguished hearth
Ashes and sparks, my words among mankind!
   Be through my lips to unawakened earth

The trumpet of a prophecy! O Wind,
If Winter comes, can Spring be far behind?

                                            1819

An Exhortation

CHAMELEONS feed on light and air:
   Poets' food is love and fame.
If in this wide world of care
   Poets could but find the same
With as little toil as they,
   Would they ever change their hue
   As the light chameleons do,
Suiting it to every ray
         Twenty times a-day?

Poets are on this cold earth
  As chameleons might be
Hidden from their early birth
  In a cave beneath the sea.
Where light is, chameleons change;
  Where love is not, poets do.
Fame is love disguised: if few
Find either, never think it strange
      That poets range.

Yet dare not stain with wealth or power
  A poet's free and heavenly mind.
If bright chameleons should devour
  Any food but beams and wind,
They would grow as earthly soon
  As their brother lizards are.
Children of a sunnier star,
Spirits from beyond the moon,
      Oh! refuse the boon!

                              1819

The Indian Serenade

I ARISE from dreams of thee
  In the first sweet sleep of night,
  When the winds are breathing low,
And the stars are shining bright:
I arise from dreams of thee,
  And a spirit in my feet
Hath led me—who knows how?
  To thy chamber window, Sweet!

The wandering airs they faint
  On the dark, the silent stream—
    The Champak odours fail
  Like sweet thoughts in a dream;
The nightingale's complaint
  It dies upon her heart,
    As I must die on thine,
Oh, belovèd as thou art!

Oh lift me from the grass!
  I die, I faint, I fail!
Let thy love in kisses rain
  On my lips and eyelids pale.
My cheek is cold and white, alas!
  My heart beats loud and fast:
Oh! press it close to thine again,
  Where it will break at last.

1819

On the Medusa
of Leonardo Da Vinci

IN THE FLORENTINE GALLERY

I

IT lieth, gazing on the midnight sky,
  Upon the cloudy mountain peak supine;
Below, far lands are seen tremblingly;
  Its horror and its beauty are divine.
Upon its lips and eyelids seems to lie
  Loveliness like a shadow, from which shine,
Fiery and lurid, struggling underneath,
The agonies of anguish and of death.

II

Yet it is less the horror than the grace
  Which turns the gazer's spirit into stone,
Whereon the lineaments of that dead face
  Are graven, till the characters be grown
Into itself, and thought no more can trace;
  'Tis the melodious hues of beauty, thrown
Athwart the darkness and the glare of pain,
Which humanize and harmonize the strain.

III

And from its head as from one body grow,
   As . . . grass out of a watery rock,
Hairs which are vipers; and they curl and flow,
   And their long tangles in each other lock,
And with unending involutions show
   Their mailèd radiance, as it were to mock
The torture and the death within, and saw
The solid air with many a ragged jaw.

IV

And, from a stone beside, a poisonous eft
   Peeps idly into these Gorgonian eyes;
Whilst in the air a ghastly bat, bereft
   Of sense, has flitted with a mad surprise
Out of the cave this hideous light had cleft,
   And he comes hastening like a moth that hies
After a taper; and the midnight sky
Flares, a light more dread than obscurity.

V

'Tis the tempestuous loveliness of terror;
   For from the serpents gleams a brazen glare
Kindled by that inextricable error,
   Which makes a thrilling vapour of the air
Become a . . . and ever-shifting mirror
   Of all the beauty and the terror there—
A woman's countenance, with serpent locks,
Gazing in death on Heaven from those wet rocks.

1819

Ode to Liberty

Yet, Freedom, yet, thy banner, torn but flying,
Streams like a thunder-storm against the wind.—BYRON

I

A GLORIOUS people vibrated again
  The lightning of the nations: Liberty,
From heart to heart, from tower to tower, o'er Spain,
  Scattering contagious fire into the sky,
Gleamed. My soul spurned the chains of its dismay,
        And in the rapid plumes of song
        Clothed itself, sublime and strong,—
As a young eagle soars the morning clouds among,
    Hovering inverse o'er its accustomed prey:
      Till from its station in the Heaven of fame
    The Spirit's whirlwind rapt it; and the ray
    Of the remotest sphere of living flame
  Which paves the void was from behind it flung,
      As foam from a ship's swiftness, when there came
A voice out of the deep; I will record the same.

II

The Sun and the serenest Moon sprang forth;
    The burning stars of the abyss were hurled
Into the depths of Heaven; the daedal earth,
    That island in the ocean of the world,
Hung in its cloud of all-sustaining air.
        But this divinest universe
        Was yet a chaos and a curse,
For thou wert not: but, power from worst producing worse,
    The spirit of the beasts was kindled there,
      And of the birds, and of the watery forms,—
    And there was war among them, and despair
      Within them, raging without truce or terms.
  The bosom of their violated nurse
      Groaned, for beasts warred on beasts, and worms on worms,
And men on men; each heart was as a hell of storms.

III

Man, the imperial shape, then multiplied
  His generations under the pavilion
Of the Sun's throne: palace and pyramid,
  Temple and prison, to many a swarming million
Were as to mountain-wolves their raggèd caves.
    This human living multitude
    Was savage, cunning, blind, and rude,—
For Thou wert not; but o'er the populous solitude,
  Like one fierce cloud over a waste of waves,
    Hung Tyranny; beneath sate deified
    The sister-pest, congregator of slaves
    Into the shadow of her pinions wide.
Anarchs and priests, who feed on gold and blood
    Till with the stain their inmost souls are dyed,
Drove the astonished herds of men from every side.

IV

The nodding promontories and blue isles
  And cloud-like mountains and dividuous waves
Of Greece basked glorious in the open smiles
  Of favouring Heaven: from their enchanted caves
Prophetic echoes flung dim melody
    On the unapprehensive wild.
    The vine, the corn, the olive mild,
Grew, savage yet, to human use unreconciled;
  And, like unfolded flowers beneath the sea,
    Like the man's thought dark in the infant's brain,
    Like aught that is which wraps what is to be,
    Art's deathless dreams lay veiled by many a vein
Of Parian stone: and, yet a speechless child,
    Verse murmured, and Philosophy did strain
Her lidless eyes for Thee;—when o'er the Aegean main

V

Athens arose: a city such as vision
  Builds from the purple crags and silver towers
Of battlemented cloud, as in derision
  Of kingliest masonry: the ocean floors
Pave it; the evening sky pavilions it;
      Its portals are inhabited
      By thunder-zonèd winds, each head
Within its cloudy wings with sun-fire garlanded,
  A divine work! Athens diviner yet
    Gleamed with its crest of columns, on the will
Of man as on a mount of diamond set;
    For Thou wert, and thine all-creative skill
Peopled, with forms that mock the eternal dead
    In marble immortality, that hill
Which was thine earliest throne and latest oracle.

VI

Within the surface of Time's fleeting river
  Its wrinkled image lies, as then it lay,
Immovably unquiet, and for ever
  It trembles, but it cannot pass away.
The voices of thy bards and sages thunder
      With an earth-awakening blast
      Through the caverns of the past;
Religion veils her eyes, Oppression shrinks aghast:
  A wingèd sound of joy and love and wonder,
    Which soars where Expectation never flew,
Rending the veil of space and time asunder.
    One ocean feeds the clouds and streams and dew,
One Sun illumines Heaven; one Spirit vast
    With life and love makes chaos ever new;—
As Athens doth the world with thy delight renew.

VII

Then Rome was, and from thy deep bosom fairest,
   Like a wolf-cub from a Cadmean Maenad,
She drew the milk of greatness, though thy dearest
   From that Elysian food was yet unweanèd;
And many a deed of terrible uprightness
      By thy sweet love was sanctified;
      And in thy smile and by thy side
Saintly Camillus lived, and firm Atilius died.
   But, when tears stained thy robe of vestal whiteness,
      And gold profaned thy Capitolian throne,
   Thou didst desert, with spirit-wingèd lightness,
      The senate of the tyrants: they sunk prone,
   Slaves of one tyrant. Palatinus sighed
      Faint echoes of Ionian song; that tone
Thou didst delay to hear, lamenting to disown.

VIII

From what Hyreanian glen or frozen hill,
   Or piny promontory of the Arctic main,
Or utmost islet inaccessible,
   Didst thou lament the ruin of thy reign,
Teaching the woods and waves, and desert rocks,
      And every Naiad's ice-cold urn
      To talk in echoes sad and stern,
Of that sublimest law which man had dared unlearn?
   For neither didst thou watch the wizard flocks
      Of the Scald's dreams, nor haunt the Druid's sleep,
   What if the tears rained through thy shattered locks
      Were quickly dried? for thou didst groan, not weep,
   When from its sea of death, to kill and burn,
      The Galilean serpent forth did creep,
And made thy world an undistinguishable heap.

IX

A thousand years the Earth cried, "Where art thou?"
And then the shadow of thy coming fell
On Saxon Alfred's olive-cinctured brow:
And many a warrior-peopled citadel,
Like rocks which fire lifts out of the flat deep,
    Arose in sacred Italy,
    Frowning o'er the tempestuous sea
Of kings and priests and slaves, in tower-crowned majesty.
    That multitudinous anarchy did sweep
    And burst around their walls like idle foam,
Whilst from the human spirit's deepest deep
    Strange melody with love and awe struck dumb
Dissonant arms; and Art, which cannot die,
    With divine wand traced on our earthly home
Fit imagery to pave Heaven's everlasting dome.

X

Thou huntress swifter than the Moon! thou terror
Of the world's wolves! thou bearer of the quiver
Whose sunlike shafts pierce tempest-wingèd Error,
    As light may pierce the clouds when they dissever
In the calm regions of the orient day!
    Luther caught thy wakening glance:
    Like lightning from his leaden lance
Reflected, it dissolved the visions of the trance
    In which, as in a tomb, the nations lay;
    And England's prophets hailed thee as their queen,
In songs whose music cannot pass away
    Though it must flow for ever. Not unseen,
Before the spirit-sighted countenance
    Of Milton, didst thou pass from the sad scene
Beyond whose night he saw, with a dejected mien.

XI

The eager hours and unreluctant years
  As on a dawn-illumined mountain stood,
Trampling to silence their loud hopes and fears,
  Darkening each other with their multitude,—
And cried aloud, "Liberty!" Indignation
    Answered Pity from her cave;
    Death grew pale within the grave,
And Desolation howled to the destroyer, "Save!"
  When, like Heaven's Sun girt by the exhalation
    Of its own glorious light, thou didst arise,
  Chasing thy foes from nation unto nation
    Like shadows: as if day had cloven the skies
  At dreaming midnight o'er the western wave,
    Men started, staggering with a glad surprise,
Under the lightnings of thine unfamiliar eyes.

XII

Thou Heaven of earth! what spells could pall thee then
  In ominous eclipse? A thousand years
Bred from the slime of deep Oppression's den
  Dyed all thy liquid light with blood and tears,
Till thy sweet stars could weep the stain away.
    How, like Bacchanals of blood,
    Round France, the ghastly vintage, stood
Destruction's sceptred slaves, and Folly's mitred brood!
  When one, like them, but mightier far than they,
    The Anarch of thine own bewildered powers,
  Rose: armies mingled in obscure array,
    Like clouds with clouds darkening the sacred bowers
  Of serene Heaven. He, by the past pursued,
    Rests with those dead but unforgotten hours
Whose ghosts scare victor kings in their ancestral towers.

XIII

England yet sleeps: was she not called of old?
    Spain calls her now,—as with its thrilling thunder
Vesuvius wakens Aetna, and the cold
    Snow-crags by its reply are cloven in sunder:
O'er the lit waves every Aeolian isle
        From Pithecusa to Pelorus
        Howls and leaps and glares in chorus:
They cry, "Be dim ye lamps of Heaven suspended o'er us!"
    Her chains are threads of gold,—she need but smile,
      And they dissolve; but Spain's were links of steel,
      Till bit to dust by virtue's keenest file.
      Twins of a single destiny! appeal
    To the eternal years enthroned before us
      In the dim West! Impress us from a seal,
All ye have thought and done! Time cannot dare conceal.

XIV

Tomb of Arminius! render up thy dead,—
    Till, like a standard from a watch-tower's staff,
His soul may stream over the tyrant's head!
    Thy victory shall be his epitaph!
Wild Bacchanal of truth's mysterious wine,
        King-deluded Germany,
        His dead spirit lives in thee!
Why do we fear or hope? Thou art already free!—
    And thou, lost Paradise of this divine
      And glorious world! thou flowery wilderness!
    Thou island of eternity! thou shrine
      Where Desolation, clothed with loveliness,
    Worships the thing thou wert! O Italy,
      Gather thy blood into thy heart; repress
The beasts who make their dens thy sacred palaces!

XV

Oh that the free would stamp the impious name
  Of King into the dust; or write it there,
So that this blot upon the page of fame
  Were as a serpent's path which the light air
Erases, and the flat sands close behind!
      Ye the oracle have heard:
      Lift the victory-flashing sword,
And cut the snaky knots of this foul gordian word,
    Which, weak itself as stubble, yet can bind
    Into a mass irrefragably firm
    The axes and the rods which awe mankind.
    The sound has poison in it; 'tis the sperm
  Of what makes life foul, cankerous, and abhorred.
    Disdain not Thou, at thine appointed term,
To set thine armèd heel on this reluctant worm.

XVI

Oh that the wise from their bright minds would kindle
  Such lamps within the dome of this dim world
That the pale name of Priest might shrink and dwindle
  Into the hell from which it first was hurled,
A scoff of impious pride from fiends impure!
      Till human thoughts might kneel alone,
      Each before the judgment-throne
Of its own aweless soul, or of the Power unknown.
    Oh that the words which make the thoughts obscure
    From which they spring, as clouds of glimmering dew
  From a white lake blot Heaven's blue portraiture,
    Were stripped of their thin masks and various hue,
    And frowns and smiles and splendours not their own,
    Till in the nakedness of false and true
They stand before their Lord, each to receive its due!

XVII

He who taught man to vanquish whatsoever
   Can be between the cradle and the grave
Crowned him the King of Life. Oh vain endeavour.
   If on his own high will, a willing slave,
He has enthroned the oppression and the oppressor!
      What if earth can clothe and feed
      Amplest millions at their need,
And power in thought be as the tree within the seed,—
   Or what if Art, an ardent intercessor,
      Driving on fiery wings to Nature's throne,
   Checks the great Mother stooping to caress her,
      And cries, "Give me, thy child, dominion
   Over all height and depth"—if Life can breed
      New wants, and Wealth, from those who toil and groan
Rend, of thy gifts and hers, a thousandfold for one?

XVIII

Come thou! But lead out of the inmost cave
   Of man's deep spirit—as the morning star
Beckons the Sun from the Eoan wave—
   Wisdom. I hear the pennons of her car,
Self-moving, like cloud chariotted by flame!
      Comes she not? And come ye not,
      Rulers of eternal thought,
To judge with solemn truth Life's ill-apportioned lot,—
   Blind Love, and equal Justice, and the Fame
      Of what has been, the Hope of what will be?
   O Liberty—(if such could be thy name
      Wert thou disjoined from these, or they from thee)—
   If thine or theirs were treasures to be bought
      By blood or tears, have not the wise and free
Wept tears, and blood like tears?—The solemn harmony

XIX

Paused, and the Spirit of that mighty singing
  To its abyss was suddenly withdrawn.
Then, as a wild swan, when sublimely winging
  Its path athwart the thunder-smoke of dawn,
Sinks headlong through the aërial golden light
    On the heavy-sounding plain,
    When the bolt has pierced its brain;
As summer clouds dissolve unburthened of their rain;
  As a far taper fades with fading night;
    As a brief insect dies with dying day;
My song, its pinions disarrayed of might,
  Drooped. O'er it closed the echoes far away
Of the great voice which did its flight sustain,—
  As waves which lately paved his watery way
Hiss round a drowner's head in their tempestuous play.
                           1820

Hymn of Pan

FROM the forests and highlands
  We come, we come;
From the river-girt islands,
  Where loud waves are dumb
Listening to my sweet pipings.
    The wind in the reeds and the rushes,
      The bees on the bells of thyme,
    The birds on the myrtle bushes,
      The cicale above in the lime,
    And the lizards below in the grass,
Were as silent as ever old Tmolus was,
  Listening to my sweet pipings.

Liquid Peneus was flowing,
  And all dark Tempe lay
In Pelion's shadow, outgrowing
  The light of the dying day,

Speeded by my sweet pipings.
  The Sileni and Sylvans and Fauns,
    And the Nymphs of the woods and waves,
  To the edge of the moist river-lawns,
    And the brink of the dewy caves,
And all that did then attend and follow,
Were silent with love,—as you now, Apollo,
  With envy of my sweet pipings.

I sang of the dancing stars,
  I sang of the daedal Earth,
And of Heaven, and the Giant wars,
  And Love, and Death, and Birth.
And then I changed my pipings,—
Singing how down the vale of Maenalus
  I pursued a maiden, and clasped a reed:
Gods and men, we are all deluded thus;
  It breaks in our bosom, and then we bleed.
All wept—as I think both ye now would,
If envy or age had not frozen your blood—
  At the sorrow of my sweet pipings.

1820

The Cloud

I

I BRING fresh showers for the thirsting flowers
  From the seas and the streams;
I bear light shade for the leaves when laid
  In their noonday dreams.
From my wings are shaken the dews that waken
  The sweet buds every one,
When rocked to rest on their Mother's breast,
  As she dances about the sun.
I wield the flail of the lashing hail,
  And whiten the green plains under;
And then again I dissolve it in rain,
  And laugh as I pass in thunder.

II

I sift the snow on the mountains below,
  And their great pines groan aghast;
And all the night 'tis my pillow white,
  While I sleep in the arms of the Blast.
Sublime on the towers of my skiey bowers
  Lightning my pilot sits;
In a cavern under is fettered the Thunder,
  It struggles and howls at fits.
Over earth and ocean with gentle motion
  This pilot is guiding me,
Lured by the love of the Genii that move
  In the depths of the purple sea;
Over the rills and the crags and the hills,
  Over the lakes and the plains,
Wherever he dream under mountain or stream
  The Spirit he loves remains;
And I all the while bask in heaven's blue smile,
  Whilst he is dissolving in rains.

III

The sanguine Sunrise, with his meteor eyes,
  And his burning plumes outspread,
Leaps on the back of my sailing rack,
  When the morning star shines dead:
As on the jag of a mountain crag
  Which an earthquake rocks and swings
An eagle alit one moment may sit
  In the light of its golden wings.
And, when Sunset may breathe, from the lit sea beneath,
  Its ardours of rest and of love,
And the crimson pall of eve may fall
  From the depth of heaven above,
With wings folded I rest on mine airy nest,
  As still as a brooding dove.

IV

That orbèd maiden with white fire laden
    Whom mortals call the Moon
Glides glimmering o'er my fleece-like floor
    By the midnight breezes strewn;
And wherever the beat of her unseen feet,
    Which only the angels hear,
May have broken the woof of my tent's thin roof,
    The stars peep behind her and peer.
And I laugh to see them whirl and flee
    Like a swarm of golden bees,
When I widen the rent in my wind-built tent,—
    Till the calm rivers, lakes, and seas,
Like strips of the sky fallen through me on high,
    Are each paved with the moon and these.

V

I bind the Sun's throne with a burning zone,
    And the Moon's with a girdle of pearl;
The Volcanoes are dim, and the Stars reel and swim,
    When the Whirlwinds my banner unfurl.
From cape to cape, with a bridge-like shape
    Over a torrent sea,
Sunbeam-proof, I hang like a roof;
    The mountains its columns be.
The triumphal arch through which I march,
    With hurricane, fire, and snow,
When the powers of the air are chained to my chair,
    Is the millioned-coloured bow;
The Sphere-fire above its soft colours wove,
    While the moist Earth was laughing below.

VI

I am the daughter of Earth and Water,
    And the nursling of the Sky:
I pass through the pores of the ocean and shores;
    I change, but I cannot die.

For after the rain, when with never a stain
   The pavilion of heaven is bare,
And the winds and sunbeams with their convex gleams
   Build up the blue dome of air,
I silently laugh at my own cenotaph,—
   And out of the caverns of rain,
Like a child from the womb, like a ghost from the tomb,
   I arise, and unbuild it again.

1820

The Question

I

I DREAMED that, as I wandered by the way,
   Bare Winter suddenly was changed to Spring;
And gentle odours led my steps astray,
   Mixed with a sound of waters murmuring
Along a shelving bank of turf, which lay
   Under a copse, and hardly dared to fling
Its green arms round the bosom of the stream,
But kissed it and then fled, as thou mightest in dream.

II

There grew pied wind-flowers and violets;
   Daisies, those pearled Arcturi of the earth,
The constellated flower that never sets;
   Faint oxlips; tender bluebells, at whose birth
The sod scarce heaved; and that tall flower that wets—
   Like a child, half in tenderness and mirth—
Its mother's face with Heaven-collected tears
When the low wind its playmate's voice it hears.

III

And in the warm hedge grew lush eglantine,
   Green cow-bind and the moonlight-coloured may,
And cherry-blossoms, and white cups whose wine
   Was the bright dew yet drained not by the day;

And wild roses, and ivy serpentine,
    With its dark buds and leaves wandering astray;
And flowers, azure, black, and streaked with gold,
Fairer than any wakened eyes behold.

IV

And nearer to the river's trembling edge
    There grew broad flag-flowers, purple pranked with white,
And starry river-buds among the sedge,
    And floating water-lilies, broad and bright,
Which lit the oak that overhung the hedge
    With moonlight beams of their own watery light;
And bulrushes, and reeds of such deep green
As soothed the dazzled eye with sober sheen.

V

Methought that of these visionary flowers
    I made a nosegay, bound in such a way
That the same hues which in their natural bowers
    Were mingled or opposed, the like array
Kept these imprisoned children of the Hours
    Within my hand; and then, elate and gay,
I hastened to the spot whence I had come,
That I might there present it—Oh! to whom?

               1820

To a Skylark

Hail to thee, blithe Spirit!
    Bird thou never wert,
That from Heaven or near it,
    Pourest thy full heart
In profuse strains of unpremeditated art.

Higher, still, and higher,
    From the earth thou springest!
Like a cloud of fire
    The blue deep thou wingest!
And, singing, still dost soar, and soaring ever singest.

In the golden lightning
    Of the sunken sun,
O'er which clouds are bright'ning,
    Thou dost float and run,
Like an unbodied joy whose race is just begun.

    The pale purple even
        Melts around thy flight;
    Like a star of Heaven
        In the broad daylight
Thou art unseen,—but yet I hear thy shrill delight,

    Keen as are the arrows
        Of that silver sphere,
    Whose intense lamp narrows
        In the white dawn clear
Until we hardly see—we feel that it is there.

    All the earth and air
        With thy voice is loud,
    As, when night is bare,
        From one lonely cloud
The moon rains out her beams, and Heaven is overflowed.

    What thou art we know not;
        What is most like thee?
    From rainbow clouds there flow not
        Drop so bright to see
As from thy presence showers a rain of melody:—

    Like a poet hidden
        In the light of thought,
    Singing hymns unbidden,
        Till the world is wrought
To sympathy with hopes and fears it heeded not:

    Like a high-born maiden
        In a palace tower,
    Soothing her love-laden
        Soul in secret hour
With music sweet as love which overflows her bower:

Like a glow-worm golden
In a dell of dew,
Scattering unbeholden
Its aërial hue
Among the flowers and grass which screen it from the view:

Like a rose embowered
In its own green leaves,
By warm winds deflowered,
Till the scent it gives
Makes faint with too much sweet these heavy-wingèd thieves.

Sound of vernal showers
On the twinkling grass,
Rain-awakened flowers,—
All that ever was,
Joyous and clear and fresh,—thy music doth surpass.

Teach us, Sprite or Bird,
What sweet thoughts are thine:
I have never heard
Praise of love or wine
That panted forth a flood of rapture so divine.

Chorus Hymeneal
Or triumphal chant,
Matched with thine, would be all
But an empty vaunt—
A thing wherein we feel there is some hidden want.

What objects are the fountains
Of thy happy strain?
What fields, or waves, or mountains?
What shapes of sky or plain?
What love of thine own kind? what ignorance of pain?

With thy clear keen joyance
Languor cannot be:
Shadow of annoyance
Never came near thee:
Thou lovest, but ne'er knew love's sad satiety.

Waking or asleep,
  Thou of death must deem
Things more true and deep
  Than we mortals dream,
Or how could thy notes flow in such a crystal stream?

We look before and after,
  And pine for what is not:
Our sincerest laughter
  With some pain is fraught;
Our sweetest songs are those that tell of saddest thought.

Yet, if we could scorn
  Hate and pride and fear,
If we were things born
  Not to shed a tear,
I know not how thy joy we ever should come near.

Better than all measures
  Of delightful sound,
Better than all treasures
  That in books are found,
Thy skill to poet were, thou scorner of the ground!

Teach me half the gladness
  That thy brain must know,
Such harmonious madness
  From my lips would flow
The world should listen then—as I am listening now.

1820

Song of Proserpine

WHILE GATHERING FLOWERS ON THE PLAIN OF ENNA

SACRED Goddess, Mother Earth,
  Thou from whose immortal bosom
Gods and men and beasts have birth,
  Leaf and blade, and bud and blossom,
Breathe thine influence most divine
On thine own child, Proserpine.

If with mists of evening dew
   Thou dost nourish these young flowers
Till they grow in scent and hue
   Fairest children of the Hours,
Breathe thine influence most divine
On thine own child, Proserpine.

1820

Letter to Maria Gisborne

LEGHORN, July 1, 1820

THE spider spreads her webs, whether she be
In poet's tower, cellar, or barn, or tree;
The silkworm in the dark-green mulberry leaves
His winding-sheet and cradle ever weaves:
So I, a thing whom moralists call worm,
Sit spinning still round this decaying form,
From the fine threads of rare and subtle thought—
No net of words in garish colours wrought
To catch the idle buzzers of the day—
But a soft cell where, when that fades away,
Memory may clothe in wings my living name,
And feed it with the asphodels of fame
Which in those hearts which must remember me
Grow, making love an immortality.

   Whoever should behold me now, I wist,
Would think I were a mighty mechanist,
Bent with sublime Archimedean art
To breathe a soul into the iron heart
Of some machine portentous, or strange gin,
Which by the force of figured spells might win
Its way over the sea, and sport therein;—
For round the walls are hung dread engines, such
As Vulcan never wrought for Jove to clutch
Ixion or the Titan; or the quick
Wit of that man of God, Saint Dominic,
To convince atheist, Turk, or heretic;
Or those in philanthropic council met
Who thought to pay some interest for the debt

They owed to Jesus Christ for their salvation
By giving a faint foretaste of damnation
To Shakespeare, Sydney, Spenser, and the rest
Who made our land an island of the blessed,
When lamp-like Spain, who now relumes her fire
On Freedom's hearth, grew dim with Empire,
With thumbscrews, wheels with tooth and spike and jag,
Which fishers found under the utmost crag
Of Cornwall, and the storm encompassed isles
Where to the sky the rude sea rarely smiles
Unless in treacherous wrath, as on the morn
When the exulting elements in scorn,
Satiated with destroyed destruction, lay
Sleeping in beauty on their mangled prey,
As panthers sleep. And other strange and dread
Magical forms the brick floor overspread.
Proteus transformed to metal did not make
More figures, or more strange; nor did he take
Such shapes of unintelligible brass,
Or heap himself in such a horrid mass
Of tin and iron not to be understood,
And forms of unimaginable wood,
To puzzle Tubal Cain and all his brood:
Great screws, and cones, and wheels, and groovèd blocks,
The elements of what will stand the shocks
Of wave and wind and time.—Upon the table
More knacks and quips there be than I am able
To catalogize in this verse of mine:
A pretty bowl of wood—not full of wine,
But quicksilver; that dew which the gnomes drink
When at their subterranean toil they swink,
Pledging the demons of the earthquake, who
Reply to them in lava—cry halloo!—
And call out to the cities o'er their head.
Roofs, towns, and shrines, the dying and the dead,
Crash through the chinks of earth: and then all quaff
Another rouse, and hold their sides and laugh.
This quicksilver no gnome has drunk: within
The walnut bowl it lies, veinèd and thin,
In colour like the wake of light that stains
The Tuscan deep when from the moist moon rains
The inmost shower of its white fire—the breeze
Is still—blue Heaven smiles over the pale seas.

And in this bowl of quicksilver—for I
Yield to the impulse of an infancy
Outlasting manhood—I have made to float
A rude idealism of a paper boat,
A hollow screw with cogs: Henry will know
The thing I mean, and laugh at me. If so,
He fears not I should do more mischief.—Next
Lie bills and calculations much perplexed
With steam-boats, frigates, and machinery quaint,
Traced over them in blue and yellow paint.
Then comes a range of mathematical
Instruments, for plans nautical and statical;
A heap of rosin; a queer broken glass
With ink in it; a china cup that was
What it will never be again, I think,—
A thing from which sweet lips were wont to drink
The liquor doctors rail at—and which I
Will quaff in spite of them; and, when we die,
We'll toss up who died first of drinking tea,
And cry out, "heads or tails!" where'er we be.
Near that, a dusty paint-box, some old hooks,
A half-burnt match, an ivory block, three books,
Where conic sections, spherics, logarithms,
To great Laplace from Saunderson and Sims,
Lie heaped in their harmonious disarray
Of figures,—disentangle them who may.
Baron de Tott's Memoirs beside them lie,
And some odd volumes of old chemistry.
Near them a most inexplicable thing,
With lead in the middle—I'm conjecturing
How to make Henry understand; but no!
I'll leave, as Spenser says, with many mo,
This secret in the pregnant womb of time,
Too vast a matter for so weak a rhyme.

And here like some weird Archimage sit I,
Plotting dark spells and devilish enginery,—
The self-impelling steam-wheels of the mind,
Which pump up oaths from clergymen, and grind
The gentle spirit of our meek reviews
Into a powdery foam of salt abuse,
Ruffling the ocean of their self-content.
I sit, and smile,—or sigh, as is my bent,

But not for them. Libeccio rushes round
With an inconstant and an idle sound;
I heed him more than them. The thunder-smoke
Is gathering on the mountains, like a cloak
Folded athwart their shoulders broad and bare;
The ripe corn under the undulating air
Undulates like an ocean; and the vines
Are trembling wide in all their trellised lines;
The murmur of the awakening sea doth fill
The empty pauses of the blast; the hill
Looks hoary through the white electric rain;
And from the glens beyond, in sullen strain,
The interrupted thunder howls; above
One chasm of Heaven smiles, like the eye of Love
On the unquiet world;—while such things are,
How could one worth your friendship heed the war
Of worms? the shriek of the world's carrion jays,
Their censure, or their wonder, or their praise?

  You are not here! The quaint witch Memory sees
In vacant chairs your absent images,
And points where once you sat, and now should be,
But are not.—I demand if ever we
Shall meet as then we met;—and she replies,
Veiling in awe her second-sighted eyes,
"I know the past alone: but summon home
My sister Hope—she speaks of all to come."
But I, an old diviner who knew well
Every false verse of that sweet oracle,
Turned to the sad enchantress once again,
And sought a respite from my gentle pain
In citing every passage o'er and o'er
Of our communion:—How on the sea shore
We watched the ocean and the sky together,
Under the roof of blue Italian weather;
How I ran home through last year's thunder-storm,
And felt the transverse lightning linger warm
Upon my cheek; and how we often made
Feasts for each other where good-will outweighed
The frugal luxury of our country cheer,
As it well might, were it *less* firm and clear
Than ours must ever be;—and how we spun
A shroud of talk to hide us from the sun

Of this familiar life, which seems to be
But is not,—or is but quaint mockery
Of all we would believe; and sadly blame
The jarring and inexplicable frame
Of this wrong world, and then anatomize
The purposes and thoughts of men whose eyes
Were closed in distant years; or widely guess
The issue of the earth's great business,
When we shall be as we no longer are,—
Like babbling gossips safe, who hear the war
Of winds, and sigh, but tremble not;—or how
You listened to some interrupted flow
Of visionary rhyme, in joy and pain
Struck from the inmost fountains of my brain,
With little skill perhaps; or how we sought
Those deepest wells of passion or of thought
Wrought by wise poets in the waste of years,
Staining the sacred waters with our tears,
Quenching a thirst ever to be renewed;
Or how I, wisest lady! then indued
The language of a land which now is free,
And, winged with thoughts of truth and majesty,
Flits round the tyrant's sceptre like a cloud,
And bursts the peopled prisons, and cries aloud,
"My name is Legion!"—that majestic tongue
Which Calderon over the desert flung
Of ages and of nations, and which found
An echo in our hearts, and with the sound
Startled Oblivion. Thou wert then to me
As is a nurse when inarticulately
A child would talk as its grown parents do.
If living winds the rapid clouds pursue,
If hawks chase doves through the aethereal way,
Huntsmen the innocent deer, and beasts their prey,
Why should not we rouse with the spirit's blast
Out of the forest of the pathless past
These recollected pleasures?
                                    You are now
In London; that great sea whose ebb and flow
At once is deaf and loud, and on the shore
Vomits its wrecks, and still howls on for more.
Yet in its depth what treasures! You will see
That which was Godwin,—greater none than he;

Though fallen, and fallen on evil times, to stand,
Among the spirits of our age and land,
Before the dread tribunal of To-come
The foremost,—whilst Rebuke cowers pale and dumb.
You will see Coleridge—he who sits obscure
In the exceeding lustre and the pure
Intense irradiation of a mind
Which, with its own internal lightning blind,
Flags wearily through darkness and despair—
A cloud-encircled meteor of the air,
A hooded eagle among blinking owls.
You will see Hunt—one of those happy souls
Which are the salt of the earth, and without whom
This world would smell like what it is—a tomb;
Who is what others seem. His room no doubt
Is still adorned by many a cast from Shout;
With graceful flowers tastefully placed about,
And coronals of bay from ribbons hung,
And brighter wreaths in neat disorder flung,
The gifts of the most learned among some dozens
Of female friends, sisters-in-law, and cousins.
And there is he with his eternal puns,
Which beat the dullest brain for smiles, like duns
Thundering for money at a poet's door;
Alas! it is no use to say, "I'm poor!"—
Or oft in graver mood, when he will look
Things wiser than were ever read in book,
Except in Shakespeare's wisest tenderness.
You will see Hogg; and I cannot express
His virtues (though I know that they are great),
Because he locks, then barricades, the gate
Within which they inhabit. Of his wit
And wisdom, you'll cry out when you are bit.
He is a pearl within an oyster-shell,
One of the richest of the deep. And there
Is English Peacock, with his mountain fair,—
Turned into a Flamingo, that shy bird
That gleams i' the Indian air. Have you not heard,
When a man marries, dies, or turns Hindoo,
His best friends hear no more of him? But you
Will see him, and will like him too, I hope,
With the milk-white Snowdonian antelope
Matched with this camelopard. His fine wit
Makes such a wound the knife is lost in it;

A strain too learnèd for a shallow age,
Too wise for selfish bigots;—let his page,
Which charms the chosen spirits of the time,
Fold itself up for a serener clime
Of years to come, and find its recompense
In that just expectation. Wit and sense,
Virtue and human knowledge, all that might
Make this dull world a business of delight,
Are all combined in Horace Smith.—And these,
With some exceptions, which I need not tease
Your patience by descanting on,—are all
You and I know in London.
                                    I recall
My thoughts, and bid you look upon the night.
As water does a sponge, so the moonlight
Fills the void, hollow, universal air.
What see you?—Unpavilioned Heaven is fair;
Whether the Moon, into her chamber gone,
Leaves midnight to the golden stars, or wan
Climbs with diminished beams the azure steep;
Or whether clouds sail o'er the inverse deep,
Piloted by the many-wandering blast,
And the rare stars rush through them, dim and fast.
All this is beautiful in every land.
But what see you beside? A shabby stand
Of hackney-coaches—a brick house or wall
Fencing some lonely court, white with the scrawl
Of our unhappy politics;—or worse—
A wretched woman reeling by, whose curse,
Mixed with the watchman's, partner of her trade,
You must accept in place of serenade—
Or yellow-haired Pollonia murmuring
To Henry some unutterable thing.
I see a chaos of green leaves and fruit
Built round dark caverns, even to the root
Of the living stems who feed them, in whose bowers
There sleep in their dark dew the folded flowers.
Beyond, the surface of the unsickled corn
Trembles not in the slumbering air; and, borne
In circles quaint and ever-changing dance,
Like wingèd stars the fireflies flash and glance,
Pale in the open moonshine, but each one
Under the dark trees seems a little sun,

A meteor tamed, a fixed star gone astray
From the silver regions of the milky way.
Afar the Contadino's song is heard,
Rude but made sweet by distance, and a bird
Which cannot be a Nightingale, and yet
I know none else that sings so sweet as it
At this late hour:—and then all is still.
Now, Italy or London, which you will!

Next winter you must pass with me. I'll have
My house by that time turned into a grave
Of dead despondence and low-thoughted care,
And all the dreams which our tormentors are.
Oh, that Hunt, Hogg, Peacock, and Smith, were there,
With everything belonging to them fair!
We will have books, Spanish, Italian, Greek;
And ask one week to make another week
As like his father as I'm unlike mine,
Which is not his fault, as you may divine.
Though we eat little flesh and drink no wine,
Yet let's be merry: we'll have tea and toast;
Custards for supper; and an endless host
Of syllabubs and jellies and mince-pies,
And other such lady-like luxuries,—
Feasting on which we will philosophize.
And we'll have fires out of the Grand Duke's wood,
To thaw the six weeks' winter in our blood.
And then we'll talk;—what shall we talk about?
Oh! there are themes enough for many a bout
Of thought-entangled descant! As to nerves—
With cones and parallelograms and curves
I've sworn to strangle them if once they dare
To bother me, when you are with me there;
And they shall never more sip laudanum
From Helicon or Himeros. Well, come,
And in despite of God and of the devil
We'll make our friendly philosophic revel
Outlast the leafless time; till buds and flowers
Warn the obscure inevitable hours
Sweet meeting by sad parting to renew:—
"To-morrow to fresh woods and pastures new."

Ode to Naples

I STOOD within the City disinterred;
  And heard the autumnal leaves like light footfalls
Of spirits passing through the streets; and heard
    The Mountain's slumberous voice at intervals
      Thrill through those roofless halls.
The oracular thunder penetrating shook
    The listening soul in my suspended blood;
I felt that Earth out of her deep heart spoke—
    I felt, but heard not. Through white columns glowed
      The isle-sustaining ocean-flood,
A plane of light between two heavens of azure.
  Around me gleamed many a bright sepulchre,
Of whose pure beauty, Time, as if his pleasure
  Were to spare Death, had never made erasure;
    But every living lineament was clear
      As in the sculptor's thought, and there
The wreaths of stony myrtle, ivy, and pine,
      Like winter leaves o'ergrown by moulded snow,
      Seemed only not to move and grow
Because the crystal silence of the air
  Weighed on their life, even as the Power divine
Which then lulled all things brooded upon mine.

      Then gentle winds arose,
      With many a mingled close
Of wild Aeolian sound and mountain odour keen.
      And where the Baian ocean
      Welters, with air-like motion,
Within, above, around its bowers of starry green,
    Moving the sea-flowers in those purple caves,
    Even as the ever stormless atmosphere
      Floats o'er the Elysian realm,
It bore me, like an angel, o'er the waves
    Of sunlight, whose swift pinnace of dewy air
      No storm can overwhelm.
      I sailed where ever flows

Under the calm Serene
A spirit of deep emotion
From the unknown graves
Of the dead Kings of Melody.
Shadowy Aornos darkened o'er the helm
The horizontal ether; Heaven stripped bare
Its depths over Elysium, where the prow
Made the invisible water white as snow;
From that Typhaean mount, Inarime,
There streamed a sunlit vapour, like the standard
Of some aethereal host;
Whilst from all the coast,
Louder and louder, gathering round, there wandered
Over the oracular woods and divine sea
Prophesyings which grew articulate—
They seize me—I must speak them;—be they fate!

STROPHE I α

NAPLES! thou Heart of men which ever pantest
Naked beneath the lidless eye of Heaven!
Elysian City, which to calm enchantest
The mutinous air and sea,—they round thee, even
As sleep round Love, are driven!
Metropolis of a ruined Paradise
Long lost, late won, and yet but half regained!
Bright Altar of the bloodless sacrifice
Which armèd Victory offers up unstained
To Love, the flower-enchained!
Thou which wert once, and then didst cease to be,
Now art, and henceforth ever shalt be, free,
If Hope and Truth and Justice can avail,—
Hail, hail, all hail!

STROPHE II β

Thou youngest giant birth
Which from the groaning earth
Leap'st, clothed in armour of impenetrable scale!
Last of the intercessors
Who 'gainst the Crowned Transgressors
Pleadest before God's love! arrayed in Wisdom's mail,
Wave thy lightning lance in mirth;
Nor let thy high heart fail,
Though from their hundred gates the leagued oppressors
With hurried legions move! Hail, hail, all hail!

ANTISTROPHE I　α

What though Cimmerian Anarchs dare blaspheme
　　Freedom and thee? Thy shield is as a mirror
To make their blind slaves see, and with fierce gleam
　　To turn his hungry sword upon the wearer;
　　　　A new Actaeon's error
Shall theirs have been—devoured by their own hounds!
　　Be thou like the imperial Basilisk,
　　Killing thy foe with unapparent wounds!
　　　　Gaze on Oppression, till, at that dread risk
　　　　Aghast, she pass from the Earth's disk;
Fear not, but gaze—for freemen mightier grow,
And slaves more feeble, gazing on their foe.
If Hope and Truth and Justice may avail,
　　　　Thou shalt be great.—All hail!

ANTISTROPHE II　β

　　　　From Freedom's form divine,
　　　　From Nature's inmost shrine,
Strip every impious gawd, rend Error veil by veil:
　　　　O'er Ruin desolate,
　　　　O'er Falsehood's fallen state,
Sit thou sublime, unawed; be the Destroyer pale!
　　　　And equal laws be thine,
　　　　And wingèd words let sail,
Freighted with truth even from the throne of God!
That wealth, surviving fate, be thine.—All hail!

STROPHE III　γ

Didst thou not start to hear Spain's thrilling paean
　　From land to land re-echoed solemnly,
Till silence became music? From the Aeaean
　　To the cold Alps, eternal Italy
　　　　Starts to hear thine! The Sea
Which paves the desert streets of Venice laughs
　　In light and music; widowed Genoa wan,
By moonlight, spells ancestral epitaphs,
　　Murmuring, "Where is Doria?" Fair Milan,
　　　　Within whose veins long ran

The viper's palsying venom, lifts her heel
To bruise his head. The signal and the seal
(If Hope and Truth and Justice can avail)
Art thou of all these hopes.—Oh hail!

STROPHE IV δ

Florence, beneath the sun,
Of cities fairest one,
Blushes within her bower for Freedom's expectation:
From eyes of quenchless hope
Rome tears the priestly cope,
As ruling once by power, so now by admiration,—
An athlete stripped to run
From a remoter station
For the high prize lost on Philippi's shore:—
As then Hope, Truth, and Justice, did avail,
So now may Fraud and Wrong! Oh hail!

EPODE I β

Hear ye the march as of the Earth-born Forms
Arrayed against the ever-living Gods?
The crash and darkness of a thousand storms
Bursting their inaccessible abodes
Of crags and thunder-clouds?
See ye the banners blazoned to the day,
Inwrought with emblems of barbaric pride?
Dissonant threats kill Silence far away;
The serene Heaven which wraps our Eden wide
With iron light is dyed.
The Anarchs of the North lead forth their legions,
Like chaos o'er creation, uncreating;
An hundred tribes nourished on strange religions
And lawless slaveries. Down the aërial regions
Of the white Alps, desolating,
Famished wolves that bide no waiting,
Blotting the glowing footsteps of old glory,
Trampling our columned cities into dust,
Their dull and savage lust
On Beauty's corse to sickness satiating—
They come! The fields they tread look black and hoary
With fire—from their red feet the streams run gory!

EPODE II β

Great Spirit, deepest Love,
Which rulest and dost move
All things which live and are within the Italian shore;
Who spreadest heaven around it,
Whose woods, rocks, waves, surround it;
Who sittest in thy star, o'er ocean's western floor!—
Spirit of beauty, at whose soft command
The sunbeams and the showers distil its foison
From the Earth's bosom chill!—
Oh bid those beams be each a blinding brand
Of lightning! bid those showers be dews of poison!
Bid the Earth's plenty kill!
Bid thy bright Heaven above,
Whilst light and darkness bound it,
Be their tomb who planned
To make it ours and thine!
Or with thine harmonizing ardours fill
And raise thy sons, as o'er the prone horizon
Thy lamp feeds every twilight wave with fire!
Be man's high hope and unextinct desire
The instrument to work thy will divine!
Then clouds from sunbeams, antelopes from leopards,
And frowns and fears from thee,
Would not more swiftly flee
Than Celtic wolves from the Ausonian shepherds.—
Whatever, Spirit, from thy starry shrine
Thou yieldest or withholdest, oh let be
This City of thy worship ever free!

1820

Lines to a Reviewer

ALAS! good friend, what profit can you see
In hating such a hateless thing as me?
There is no sport in hate, where all the rage
Is on one side. In vain would you assuage
Your frowns upon an unresisting smile,
In which not even contempt lurks, to beguile

Your heart by some faint sympathy of hate.
Oh! conquer what you cannot satiate:
For to your passion I am far more coy
Than ever yet was coldest maid or boy
In winter noon. Of your antipathy
If I am the Narcissus, you are free
To pine into a sound with hating me.

1820

Autumn

A DIRGE

THE warm sun is failing, the bleak wind is wailing,
The bare boughs are sighing, the pale flowers are dying
   And the Year
On the earth her death-bed, in a shroud of leaves dead,
   Is lying.
  Come, Months, come away,
  From November to May,
  In your saddest array;
  Follow the bier
  Of the dead cold Year,
And like dim shadows watch by her sepulchre.

The chill rain is falling, the nipped worm is crawling,
The rivers are swelling, the thunder is knelling
   For the Year;
The blithe swallows are flown, and the lizards each gone
   To his dwelling.
  Come, Months, come away;
  Put on white, black, and grey;
  Let your light sisters play—
  Ye, follow the bier
  Of the dead cold Year,
And make her grave green with tear on tear.

1820

The Tower of Famine

AMID the desolation of a city
   Which was the cradle and is now the grave
Of an extinguished people, so that Pity
   Weeps o'er the shipwrecks of oblivion's wave,
There stands the Tower of Famine. It is built
   Upon some prison-homes, whose dwellers rave
For bread and gold and blood: Pain linked to Guilt,
   Agitates the light flame of their hours,
Until its vital oil is spent or spilt.

   There stands the pile, a tower amid the towers
And sacred domes, each marble-ribbèd roof,
   The brazen-gated temples, and the bowers
Of solitary wealth. The tempest-proof
   Pavilions of the dark Italian air
Are by its presence dimmed—they stand aloof,
   And are withdrawn—so that the world is bare:—
As if a spectre, wrapped in shapeless terror,
   Amid a company of ladies fair
Should glide and glow, till it became a mirror
   Of all their beauty,—and their hair and hue,
The life of their sweet eyes with all its error,
   Should be absorbed till they to marble grew.

                                        1820

To Night

I

SWIFTLY walk o'er the western wave,
                  Spirit of Night!
Out of the misty eastern cave
Where, all the long and lone daylight,
Thou wovest dreams of joy and fear
Which make thee terrible and dear,
                  Swift be thy flight!

II

Wrap thy form in a mantle gray,
> Star-inwrought,
Blind with thine hair the eyes of Day;
Kiss her until she be wearied out.
Then wander o'er city and sea and land,
Touching all with thine opiate wand—
> Come, long-sought!

III

When I arose and saw the dawn,
> I sighed for thee;
When light rode high, and the dew was gone,
And noon lay heavy on flower and tree,
And the weary Day turned to her rest,
Lingering like an unloved guest,
> I sighed for thee.

IV

Thy brother Death came, and cried,
> Wouldst thou me?
Thy sweet child Sleep, the filmy-eyed,
> Murmured like a noontide bee,
Shall I nestle near thy side?
Wouldst thou me?—And I replied,
> No, not thee.

V

Death will come when thou art dead,
> Soon, too soon—
Sleep will come when thou art fled.
Of neither would I ask the boon
I ask of thee, belovèd Night—
Swift be thine approaching flight,
> Come soon, soon!

1821

Time

UNFATHOMABLE Sea, whose waves are years!
　　Ocean of Time, whose waters of deep woe
Are brackish with the salt of human tears!
　　Thou shoreless flood which in thy ebb and flow
Claspest the limits of mortality,
And, sick of prey yet howling on for more,
Vomitest thy wrecks on its inhospitable shore!
Treacherous in calm, and terrible in storm,
　　　　Who shall put forth on thee,
　　　　Unfathomable Sea?

　　　　　　　　　　　　　　　1821

To ——: "Music, When Soft Voices Die"

　　Music, when soft voices die,
　　Vibrates in the memory;
　　Odours, when sweet violets sicken,
　　Live within the sense they quicken;

　　Rose leaves, when the rose is dead,
　　Are heaped for the belovèd's bed;
　　And so thy thoughts, when thou art gone,
　　Love itself shall slumber on.

　　　　　　　　　　　　　　　1821

Lines

WRITTEN ON HEARING THE NEWS
OF THE DEATH OF NAPOLEON

WHAT! alive and so bold, O Earth?
　　Art thou not over-bold?
　　What! leapest thou forth as of old
In the light of thy morning mirth,

The last of the flock of the starry fold?
Ha! leapest thou forth as of old?
Are not the limbs still when the ghost is fled,
And canst thou move, Napoleon being dead?

How! is not thy quick heart cold?
What spark is alive on thy hearth?
How! is not *his* death-knell knolled,
And livest *thou* still, Mother Earth?
Thou wert warming thy fingers old
O'er the embers covered and cold
Of that most fiery spirit, when it fled—
What, Mother, dost thou laugh now he is dead?

"Who has known me of old," replied Earth,
"Or who has my story told?
It is thou who art over-bold."
And the lightning of scorn laughed forth
As she sung, "To my bosom I fold
All my sons when their knell is knolled;
And so with living motion all are fed,
And the quick spring like weeds out of the dead.

"Still alive and still bold," shouted Earth,
"I grow bolder and still more bold.
The dead fill me ten thousand fold
Fuller of speed and splendour and mirth.
I was cloudy and sullen and cold
Like a frozen chaos uprolled,
Till by the spirit of the mighty dead
My heart grew warm: I feed on whom I fed.

"Ay, alive and still bold," muttered Earth.
"Napoleon's fierce spirit rolled
In terror and blood and gold,
A torrent of ruin to death from his birth.
Leave the millions who follow to mould
The metal before it be cold;
And weave into his shame, which, like the dead
Shrouds me, the hopes that from his glory fled."
1821

Mutability

THE flower that smiles to-day
　　　To-morrow dies:
All that we wish to stay
　　　Tempts and then flies.
What is this world's delight?
Lightning that mocks the night,
　　　Brief even as bright.

Virtue how frail it is!
　　　Friendship how rare!
Love how it sells poor bliss
　　　For proud despair!
But we, though soon they fall,
Survive their joy, and all
　　　Which ours we call.

Whilst skies are blue and bright,
　　　Whilst flowers are gay,
Whilst eyes that change ere night
　　　Make glad the day,
Whilst yet the calm hours creep,
Dream thou—and from thy sleep
　　　Then wake to weep.

1821

Sonnet: Political Greatness

NOR happiness, nor majesty, nor fame,
　　Nor peace, nor strength, nor skill in arms or arts,
Shepherd those herds whom tyranny makes tame:—
　　Verse echoes not one beating of their hearts;
History is but the shadow of their shame;
　　Art veils her glass, or from the pageant starts;
As to oblivion their blind millions fleet,
　　Staining that Heaven with obscene imagery

Of their own likeness. What are numbers knit
  By force or custom? Man who man would be
Must rule the empire of himself; in it
Must be supreme, establishing his throne
  On vanquished will, quelling the anarchy
Of hopes and fears, being himself alone.

1821

Lines: "If I Walk in Autumn's Even"

If I walk in Autumn's even
    While the dead leaves pass,
If I look on Spring's soft heaven,—
Something is not there which was.
Winter's wondrous frost and snow,
Summer's clouds, where are they now?

1821

A Lament

O World! O life! O time!
    On whose last steps I climb,
Trembling at that where I stood before,—
When will return the glory of your prime
    No more—oh never more!

Out of the day and night
    A joy has taken flight:
Fresh Spring, and Summer, Autumn, and Winter hoar,
Move my faint heart with grief,—but with delight
    No more, oh never more!

1821

Remembrance

SWIFTER far than summer's flight,
Swifter far than youth's delight,
Swifter far than happy night,
    Art thou come and gone:
As the earth when leaves are dead,
As the night when sleep is sped,
As the heart when joy is fled,
        I am left lone, alone.

The swallow summer comes again,
The owlet night resumes her reign,
But the wild-swan youth is fain
To fly with thee, false as thou.
    My heart each day desires the morrow;
    Sleep itself is turned to sorrow;
    Vainly would my winter borrow
Sunny leaves from any bough.

Lilies for a bridal bed,
Roses for a matron's head,
Violets for a maiden dead;
Pansies let *my* flowers be:
    On the living grave I bear
    Scatter them without a tear,
    Let no friend, however dear,
Waste one hope, one fear, for me.

                                        1821

To ——: "One Word Is Too Often Profaned"

ONE word is too often profaned
    For me to profane it;
One feeling too falsely disdained
    For thee to disdain it;

One hope is too like despair
  For prudence to smother;
And pity from thee more dear
  Than that from another.

I can give not what men call love:
  But wilt thou accept not
The worship the heart lifts above,
  And the Heavens reject not:
The desire of the moth for the star,
  Of the night for the morrow,
The devotion to something afar
  From the sphere of our sorrow!

1821

A Dirge

ROUGH wind that moanest loud
  Grief too sad for song;
Wild wind when sullen cloud
  Knells all the night long;
Sad storm whose tears are vain,
Bare woods whose branches stain,
Deep caves and dreary main,—
  Wail, for the world's wrong!

1822

Lines: "When the Lamp Is Shattered"

WHEN the lamp is shattered,
The light in the dust lies dead;
  When the cloud is scattered,
The rainbow's glory is shed;
  When the lute is broken,
Sweet notes are remembered not;
  When the lips have spoken,
Loved accents are soon forgot.

As music and splendour
Survive not the lamp and the lute,
    The heart's echoes render
No song when the spirit is mute:—
    No song but sad dirges,
Like the wind through a ruined cell,
    Or the mournful surges
That ring the dead seaman's knell.

When hearts have once mingled,
Love first leaves the well-built nest;
    The weak one is singled
To endure what it once possessed.
    O, Love, who bewailest
The frailty of all things here,
    Why chose you the frailest
For your cradle, your home, and your bier?

Its passions will rock thee,
As the storms rock the ravens on high:
    Bright reason will mock thee,
Like the sun from a wintry sky.
    From thy nest every rafter
Will rot, and thine eagle home
    Leave thee naked to laughter
When leaves fall and cold winds come.

                                        1822

Epitaph

THESE are two friends whose lives were undivided;
So let their memory be, now they have glided
Under their grave; let not their bones be parted,
For their two hearts in life were single-hearted.

                                        1822

From

QUEEN MAB

I

How wonderful is Death—
Death and his brother Sleep!
One, pale as yonder waning moon
    With lips of lurid blue;
The other, rosy as the morn
    When throned on ocean's wave
    It blushes o'er the world:
Yet both so passing wonderful!

Hath then the gloomy Power
Whose reign is in the tainted sepulchres
    Seized on her sinless soul?
    Must then that peerless form
Which love and admiration cannot view
Without a beating heart, those azure veins
Which steal like streams along a field of snow,
That lovely outline, which is fair
    As breathing marble, perish?

*   *   *   *   *

Hark! whence that rushing sound?
    'Tis like the wondrous strain
That round a lonely ruin swells,
Which, wandering on the echoing shore,
    The enthusiast hears at evening:
'Tis softer than the west wind's sigh;

'Tis wilder than the unmeasured notes
Of that strange lyre whose strings
The genii of the breezes sweep:
   Those lines of rainbow light
Are like the moonbeams when they fall
Through some cathedral window, but the tints
   Are such as may not find
   Comparison on earth.

Behold the chariot of the Fairy Queen!
Celestial coursers paw the unyielding air;
Their filmy pennons at her word they furl,
And stop obedient to the reins of light:
These the Queen of Spells drew in,
She spread a charm around the spot,
And leaning graceful from the aethereal car,
Long did she gaze, and silently,
   Upon the slumbering maid.

Oh! not the visioned poet in his dreams,
When silvery clouds float through the 'wildered brain,
When every sight of lovely, wild and grand
Astonishes, enraptures, elevates,
   When fancy at a glance combines
   The wondrous and the beautiful,—
So bright, so fair, so wild a shape
   Hath ever yet beheld,
As that which reined the coursers of the air,
And poured the magic of her gaze
   Upon the maiden's sleep.

   The broad and yellow moon
   Shone dimly through her form—
That form of faultless symmetry;
The pearly and pellucid car
   Moved not the moonlight's line:
'Twas not an earthly pageant:
Those who had looked upon the sight,
   Passing all human glory,
   Saw not the yellow moon,
   Saw not the mortal scene,
   Heard not the night-wind's rush,

Heard not an earthly sound,
Saw but the fairy pageant,
Heard but the heavenly strains
That filled the lonely dwelling.

*   *   *   *   *

The magic car moved on.
The night was fair, and countless stars
Studded Heaven's dark blue vault,—
    Just o'er the eastern wave
Peeped the first faint smile of morn.
    The magic car moved on—
    From the celestial hoofs
The atmosphere in flaming sparkles flew,
    And where the burning wheels
Eddied above the mountain's loftiest peak,
Was traced a line of lightning.
Now it flew far above a rock,
    The utmost verge of earth,
The rival of the Andes, whose dark brow
    Lowered o'er the silver sea.

Far, far below the chariot's path,
    Calm as a slumbering babe,
    Tremendous Ocean lay.
The mirror of its stillness showed
    The pale and waning stars,
    The chariot's fiery track,
    And the gray light of morn
    Tinging those fleecy clouds
    That canopied the dawn.

Seemed it, that the chariot's way
Lay through the midst of an immense concave,
Radiant with million constellations, tinged
    With shades of infinite colour,
    And semicircled with a belt
    Flashing incessant meteors.

    The magic car moved on.
    As they approached their goal
The coursers seemed to gather speed;
The sea no longer was distinguished; earth

Appeared a vast and shadowy sphere;
　The sun's unclouded orb
　Rolled through the black concave;
　Its rays of rapid light
Parted around the chariot's swifter course,
And fell, like ocean's feathery spray
　Dashed from the boiling surge
　Before a vessel's prow.

　　The magic car moved on.
　　Earth's distant orb appeared
The smallest light that twinkles in the heaven;
　　　Whilst round the chariot's way
　　　Innumerable systems rolled,
　　　And countless spheres diffused
　　　An ever-varying glory.
　　It was a sight of wonder: some
　　Were hornèd like the crescent moon;
　　Some shed a mild and silver beam
　　Like Hesperus o'er the western sea;
　　Some dashed athwart with trains of flame,
　　Like worlds to death and ruin driven;
Some shone like suns, and, as the chariot passed,
　　　Eclipsed all other light.

　　Spirit of Nature! here!
In this interminable wilderness
Of worlds, at whose immensity
　　Even soaring fancy staggers,
　　Here is thy fitting temple.
　　Yet not the lightest leaf
That quivers to the passing breeze
　　Is less instinct with thee:
　　Yet not the meanest worm
That lurks in graves and fattens on the dead
　　Less shares thy eternal breath.
　　Spirit of Nature! thou!
　　Imperishable as this scene,
　　Here is thy fitting temple.

II

IF solitude hath ever led thy steps
  To the wild Ocean's echoing shore,
    And thou hast lingered there,
    Until the sun's broad orb
  Seemed resting on the burnished wave,
    Thou must have marked the lines
  Of purple gold, that motionless
    Hung o'er the sinking sphere:
Thou must have marked the billowy clouds
Edged with intolerable radiancy
    Towering likc rocks of jet
    Crowned with a diamond wreath.
    And yet there is a moment,
    When the sun's highest point
Peeps like a star o'er Ocean's western edge,
When those far clouds of feathery gold,
  Shaded with deepest purple, gleam
  Like islands on a dark blue sea;
Then has thy fancy soared above the earth,
    And furled its wearied wing
    Within the Fairy's fane.

    Yet not the golden islands
    Gleaming in yon flood of light,
    Nor the feathery curtains
    Stretching o'er the sun's bright couch,
    Nor the burnished Ocean waves
    Paving that gorgeous dome,
  So fair, so wonderful a sight
As Mab's aethereal palace could afford.
Yet likest evening's vault, that faery Hall!
As Heaven, low resting on the wave, it spread
    Its floors of flashing light,
    Its vast and azure dome,
    Its fertile golden islands
    Floating on a silver sea;

Whilst suns their mingling beamings darted
Through clouds of circumambient darkness,
   And pearly battlements around
   Looked o'er the immense of Heaven.

*   *   *   *   *

   The Fairy and the Spirit
Approached the overhanging battlement.—
   Below lay stretched the universe!
   There, far as the remotest line
   That bounds imagination's flight,
     Countless and unending orbs
   In mazy motion intermingled,
   Yet still fulfilled immutably
       Eternal Nature's law.
       Above, below, around,
       The circling systems formed
     A wilderness of harmony;
     Each with undeviating aim,
In eloquent silence, through the depths of space
     Pursued its wondrous way.

*   *   *   *   *

     But matter, space and time
In those aëreal mansions cease to act;
And all-prevailing wisdom, when it reaps
The harvest of its excellence, o'erbounds
Those obstacles, of which an earthly soul
     Fears to attempt the conquest.

   The Fairy pointed to the earth.
   The Spirit's intellectual eye
   Its kindred beings recognized.
The thronging thousands, to a passing view,
   Seemed like an ant-hill's citizens.
     How wonderful! that even
The passions, prejudices, interests,

That sway the meanest being, the weak touch
  That moves the finest nerve,
  And in one human brain
Causes the faintest thought, becomes a link
  In the great chain of Nature.

*   *   *   *   *

III

*   *   *   *   *

        "Where is the fame
Which the vainglorious mighty of the earth
Seek to eternize? Oh! the faintest sound
From Time's light footfall, the minutest wave
That swells the flood of ages, whelms in nothing
The unsubstantial bubble. Ay! to-day
Stern is the tyrant's mandate, red the gaze
That flashes desolation, strong the arm
That scatters multitudes. To-morrow comes!
That mandate is a thunder-peal that died
In ages past; that gaze, a transient flash
On which the midnight closed, and on that arm
The worm has made his meal."

*   *   *   *   *

"Nature rejects the monarch, not the man;
The subject, not the citizen: for kings
And subjects, mutual foes, forever play
A losing game into each other's hands,
Whose stakes are vice and misery. The man
Of virtuous soul commands not, nor obeys.
Power, like a desolating pestilence,
Pollutes whate'er it touches; and obedience,
Bane of all genius, virtue, freedom, truth,
Makes slaves of men, and, of the human frame,
A mechanized automaton."

*   *   *   *   *

"Look on yonder earth:
The golden harvests spring; the unfailing sun
Sheds light and life; the fruits, the flowers, the trees,
Arise in due succession; all things speak
Peace, harmony, and love. The universe,
In Nature's silent eloquence, declares
That all fulfil the works of love and joy,—
All but the outcast, Man. He fabricates
The sword which stabs his peace; he cherisheth
The snakes that gnaw his heart; he raiseth up
The tyrant whose delight is in his woe,
Whose sport is in his agony. Yon sun,
Lights it the great alone? Yon silver beams,
Sleep they less sweetly on the cottage thatch
Than on the dome of kings? Is mother Earth
A step-dame to her numerous sons who earn
Her unshared gifts with unremitting toil;
A mother only to those puling babes
Who, nursed in ease and luxury, make men
The playthings of their babyhood, and mar,
In self-important childishness, that peace
    Which men alone appreciate?

        "Spirit of Nature! no!
The pure diffusion of thy essence throbs
    Alike in every human heart.
        Thou aye erectest there
    Thy throne of power unappealable;
        Thou art the judge beneath whose nod
        Man's brief and frail authority
            Is powerless as the wind
            That passeth idly by;
    Thine the tribunal which surpasseth
        The show of human justice
        As God surpasses man.

        "Spirit of Nature! thou
Life of interminable multitudes;
    Soul of those mighty spheres
Whose changeless paths through Heaven's deep silence lie;
        Soul of that smallest being
        The dwelling of whose life
        Is one faint April sun-gleam;—

Man, like these passive things,
Thy will unconsciously fulfilleth;
Like theirs, his age of endless peace,
    Which time is fast maturing,
    Will swiftly, surely, come;
And the unbounded frame which thou pervadest
    Will be without a flaw
Marring its perfect symmetry."

IV

*   *   *   *   *

            "Ah! whence yon glare
That fires the arch of Heaven?—that dark red smoke
Blotting the silver moon? The stars are quenched
In darkness, and the pure and spangling snow
Gleams faintly through the gloom that gathers round.
Hark to that roar whose swift and deafening peals
In countless echoes through the mountains ring,
Startling pale Midnight on her starry throne!
Now swells the intermingling din; the jar
Frequent and frightful of the bursting bomb;
The falling beam, the shriek, the groan, the shout,
The ceaseless clangor, and the rush of men
Inebriate with rage:—loud and more loud
The discord grows; till pale Death shuts the scene,
And o'er the conqueror and the conquered draws
His cold and bloody shroud.—Of all the men
Whom day's departing beam saw blooming there
In proud and vigorous health; of all the hearts
That beat with anxious life at sunset there;
How few survive, how few are beating now!
All is deep silence, like the fearful calm
That slumbers in the storm's portentous pause;
Save when the frantic wail of widowed love
Comes shuddering on the blast, or the faint moan
With which some soul bursts from the frame of clay
Wrapped round its struggling powers."

*   *   *   *   *

"Nature!—no!
Kings, priests, and statesmen, blast the human flower,
Even in its tender bud; their influence darts
Like subtle poison through the bloodless veins
Of desolate society. The child,
Ere he can lisp his mother's sacred name,
Swells with the unnatural pride of crime, and lifts
His baby-sword even in a hero's mood.
This infant arm becomes the bloodiest scourge
Of devastated earth; whilst specious names,
Learnt in soft childhood's unsuspecting hour,
Serve as the sophisms with which manhood dims
Bright reason's ray, and sanctifies the sword
Upraised to shed a brother's innocent blood.
Let priest-led slaves cease to proclaim that man
Inherits vice and misery, when Force
And Falsehood hang even o'er the cradled babe,
Stifling with rudest grasp all natural good.

"Ah! to the stranger-soul, when first it peeps
From its new tenement, and looks abroad
For happiness and sympathy, how stern
And desolate a tract is this wide world!
How withered all the buds of natural good!
No shade, no shelter from the sweeping storms
Of pitiless power! On its wretched frame—
Poisoned, perchance, by the disease and woe
Heaped on the wretched parent whence it sprung,
By morals, law, and custom,—the pure winds
Of Heaven, that renovate the insect tribes,
May breathe not. The untainting light of day
May visit not its longings. It is bound
Ere it has life: yea, all the chains are forged
Long ere its being: all liberty and love
And peace is torn from its defencelessness;
Cursed from its birth, even from its cradle doomed
        To abjectness and bondage!

"Throughout this varied and eternal world
Soul is the only element, the block
That for uncounted ages has remained.
The moveless pillar of a mountain's weight
Is active living spirit. Every grain

Is sentient both in unity and part,
And the minutest atom comprehends
A world of loves and hatreds; These beget
Evil and good: hence truth and falsehood spring;
Hence will, and thought, and action, all the germs
Of pain or pleasure, sympathy or hate,
That variegate the eternal universe.
Soul is not more polluted than the beams
Of heaven's pure orb ere round their rapid lines
The taint of earth-born atmospheres arise.

"Man is of soul and body, formed for deeds
Of high resolve; on fancy's boldest wing
To soar unwearied, fearlessly to turn
The keenest pangs to peacefulness, and taste
The joys which mingled sense and spirit yield.
Or he is formed for abjectness and woe,
To grovel on the dunghill of his fears,
To shrink at every sound, to quench the flame
Of natural love in sensualism, to know
That hour as blessed when on his worthless days
The frozen hand of Death shall set its seal,
Yet fear the cure, though hating the disease.
The one is man that shall hereafter be;
The other, man as vice has made him now.

"War is the statesman's game, the priest's delight,
The lawyer's jest, the hired assassin's trade;
And, to those royal murderers whose mean thrones
Are bought by crimes of treachery and gore,
The bread they eat, the staff on which they lean.
Guards, garbed in blood-red livery, surround
Their palaces, participate the crimes
That force defends, and from a nation's rage
Secure the crown which all the curses reach
That famine, frenzy, woe, and penury, breathe.
These are the hired bravos who defend
The tyrant's throne—the bullies of his fear:
These are the sinks and channels of worst vice,
The refuse of society, the dregs
Of all that is most vile: their cold hearts blend
Deceit with sternness, ignorance with pride,
All that is mean and villanous with rage
Which hopelessness of good and self-contempt

Alone might kindle. They are decked in wealth,
Honour, and power; then are sent abroad
To do their work. The pestilence that stalks
In gloomy triumph through some eastern land
Is less destroying. They cajole with gold,
And promises of fame, the thoughtless youth
Already crushed with servitude; he knows
His wretchedness too late, and cherishes
Repentance for his ruin, when his doom
    Is sealed in gold and blood!
Those too the tyrant serve, who, skilled to snare
The feet of Justice in the toils of law,
Stand ready to oppress the weaker still;
And right or wrong will vindicate for gold,
Sneering at Public Virtue, which beneath
Their pitiless tread lies torn and trampled, where
Honour sits smiling at the sale of truth.

"Then grave and hoary-headed hypocrites,
Without a hope, a passion, or a love,
Who, through a life of luxury and lies,
Have crept by flattery to the seats of power,
Support the system whence their honours flow.
They have three words—well tyrants know their use,
Well pay them for the loan, with usury
Torn from a bleeding world!—God, Hell, and Heaven.
A vengeful, pitiless, and almighty fiend,
Whose mercy is a nickname for the rage
Of tameless tigers hungering for blood;
Hell, a red gulf of everlasting fire,
Where poisonous and undying worms prolong
Eternal misery to those hapless slaves
Whose life has been a penance for its crimes;
And Heaven, a meed for those who dare belie
Their human nature, quake, believe and cringe
Before the mockeries of earthly power.

"These tools the tyrant tempers to his work,
Wields in his wrath, and, as he wills, destroys,
Omnipotent in wickedness; the while
Youth springs, age moulders, manhood tamely does
His bidding, bribed by short-lived joys to lend
Force to the weakness of his trembling arm.
They rise, they fall; one generation comes,

Yielding its harvest to destruction's scythe.
It fades, another blossoms: yet behold!
Red glows the tyrant's stamp-mark on its bloom,
Withering and cankering deep its passive prime.
He has invented lying words and modes,
Empty and vain as his own coreless heart;
Evasive meanings, nothings of much sound,
To lure the heedless victim to the toils
Spread round the valley of its paradise.

"Look to thyself, priest, conqueror, or prince!
Whether thy trade is falsehood, and thy lusts
Deep wallow in the earnings of the poor,
With whom thy Master was; or thou delight'st
In numbering o'er the myriads of thy slain,
All misery weighing nothing in the scale
Against thy short-lived fame; or thou dost load
With cowardice and crime the groaning land,
A pomp-fed king. Look to thy wretched self!
Ay, art thou not the veriest slave that e'er
Crawled on the loathing earth? Are not thy days
Days of unsatisfying listlessness?
Dost thou not cry, ere night's long rack is o'er,
'When will the morning come?' Is not thy youth
A vain and feverish dream of sensualism?
Thy manhood blighted with unripe disease?
Are not thy views of unregretted death
Drear, comfortless, and horrible? Thy mind,
Is it not morbid as thy nerveless frame,
Incapable of judgment, hope, or love?
And dost thou wish the errors to survive
That bar thee from all sympathies of good,
After the miserable interest
Thou hold'st in their protraction? When the grave
Has swallowed up thy memory and thyself,
Dost thou desire the bane that poisons earth
To twine its roots around thy coffined clay,
Spring from thy bones, and blossom on thy tomb,
That of its fruit thy babes may eat and die?

V

"THus do the generations of the earth
Go to the grave, and issue from the womb,
Surviving still the imperishable change
That renovates the world. Even as the leaves
Which the keen frost-wind of the waning year
Has scattered on the forest soil, and heaped
For many seasons there, though long they choke
Loading with loathsome rottenness the land,
All germs of promise, yet, when the tall trees
From which they fell, shorn of their lovely shapes,
Lie level with the earth to moulder there,
They fertilize the land they long deformed,
Till from the breathing lawn a forest springs
Of youth, integrity, and loveliness,
Like that which gave it life, to spring and die.
Thus suicidal Selfishness, that blights
The fairest feelings of the opening heart,
Is destined to decay, whilst from the soil
Shall spring all virtue, all delight, all love,
And judgment cease to wage unnatural war
With passion's unsubduable array.
Twin-sister of Religion, Selfishness,—
Rival in crime and falsehood, aping all
The wanton horrors of her bloody play;
Yet frozen, unimpassioned, spiritless,
Shunning the light, and owning not its name;
Compelled by its deformity to screen
With flimsy veil of justice and of right
Its unattractive lineaments that scare
All save the brood of ignorance; at once
The cause and the effect of tyranny;
Unblushing, hardened, sensual, and vile;
Dead to all love but of its abjectness,
With heart impassive by more noble powers
Than unshared pleasure, sordid gain, or fame:
Despising its own miserable being,
Which still it longs, yet fears, to disenthrall.

"Hence commerce springs, the venal interchange
Of all that human art or Nature yield;

Which wealth should purchase not, but want demand,
And natural kindness hasten to supply
From the full fountain of its boundless love,
For ever stifled, drained, and tainted now.
Commerce, beneath whose poison-breathing shade
No solitary virtue dares to spring;
But Poverty and Wealth with equal hand
Scatter their withering curses, and unfold
The doors of premature and violent death
To pining famine and full-fed disease,
To all that shares the lot of human life,
Which—poisoned, body and soul—scarce drags the chain
That lengthens as it goes, and clanks behind.

"Commerce has set the mark of selfishness,
The signet of its all-enslaving power,
Upon a shining ore, and called it gold;
Before whose image bow the vulgar great,
The vainly rich, the miserable proud,
The mob of peasants, nobles, priests, and kings,
And with blind feelings reverence the power
That grinds them to the dust of misery.
But in the temple of their hireling hearts
Gold is a living god, and rules in scorn
    All earthly things but virtue."

        *   *   *   *   *

"Yet every heart contains perfection's germ:
The wisest of the sages of the earth
That ever from the stores of reason drew
Science, and truth, and virtue's dreadless tone,
Were but a weak and inexperienced boy—
Proud, sensual, unimpassioned, unimbued
With pure desire and universal love—
Compared to that high being, of cloudless brain,
Untainted passion, elevated will,
Which Death (who even would linger long in awe
Within his noble presence and beneath
His changeless eye-beam) might alone subdue.
Him, every slave now dragging through the filth
Of some corrupted city his sad life,
Pining with famine, swoln with luxury,
Blunting the keenness of his spiritual sense

With narrow schemings and unworthy cares,
Or madly rushing through all violent crime
To move the deep stagnation of his soul,
Might imitate and equal.

But mean lust
Has bound its chains so tight about the earth
That all within it but the virtuous man
Is venal. Gold or fame will surely reach
The price prefixed by Selfishness, to all
But him of resolute and unchanging will;
Whom nor the plaudits of a servile crowd,
Nor the vile joys of tainting luxury,
Can bribe to yield his elevated soul
To Tyranny or Falsehood, though they wield
With blood-red hand the sceptre of the world."

*   *   *   *   *

"But hoary-headed Selfishness has felt
Its death-blow, and is tottering to the grave.
A brighter morn awaits the human day;
When every transfer of earth's natural gifts
Shall be a commerce of good words and works,
When poverty and wealth, the thirst of fame,
The fear of infamy, disease and woe,
War with its million horrors, and fierce hell,
Shall live but in the memory of Time,
Who, like a penitent libertine, shall start,
Look back, and shudder at his younger years."

*   *   *   *   *

VII

*   *   *   *   *

"Spirit! no year of my eventful being
Has passed unstained by crime and misery
Which flows from God's own faith. I've marked his slaves,
With tongues whose lies are venomous, beguile
The insensate mob, and, whilst one hand was red
With murder, feign to stretch the other out

For brotherhood and peace. And that they now
Babble of love and mercy (whilst their deeds
Are marked with all the narrowness and crime
That Freedom's young arm dare not yet chastise)
Reason may claim our gratitude, who now,
Establishing the imperishable throne
Of truth and stubborn virtue, maketh vain
The unprevailing malice of my foe,
Whose bootless rage heaps torments for the brave,
Adds impotent eternities to pain,
Whilst keenest disappointment racks his breast
To see the smiles of peace around them play,
To frustrate or to sanctify their doom."

*   *   *   *   *

IX

"O HAPPY Earth! reality of Heaven!
To which those restless souls that ceaselessly
Throng through the human universe aspire!
Thou consummation of all mortal hope!
Thou glorious prize of blindly-working will,
Whose rays, diffused throughout all space and time,
Verge to one point, and blend for ever there!
Of purest spirits thou pure dwelling-place,
Where care and sorrow, impotence and crime,
Languor, disease, and ignorance, dare not come!
O happy Earth, reality of Heaven!

"Genius has seen thee in her passionate dreams;
And dim forebodings of thy loveliness,
Haunting the human heart, have there entwined
Those rooted hopes of some sweet place of bliss
Where friends and lovers meet to part no more.
Thou art the end of all desire and will,
The product of all action; and the souls
That by the paths of an aspiring change
Have reached thy haven of perpetual peace
There rest from the eternity of toil
That framed the fabric of thy perfectness."

*   *   *   *   *

"Life is its state of action, and the store
Of all events is aggregated there
That variegate the eternal universe;
Death is a gate of dreariness and gloom,
That leads to azure isles and beaming skies,
And happy regions of eternal hope.
Therefore, O Spirit! fearlessly bear on:
Though storms may break the primrose on its stalk,
Though frosts may blight the freshness of its bloom,
Yet Spring's awakening breath will woo the earth
To feed with kindliest dews its favourite flower,
That blooms in mossy banks and darksome glens,
Lighting the greenwood with its sunny smile."

*   *   *   *   *

1812–13

From

ALASTOR; OR, THE SPIRIT OF SOLITUDE

*   *   *   *   *

Mother of this unfathomable world!
Favour my solemn song, for I have loved
Thee ever, and thee only; I have watched
Thy shadow, and the darkness of thy steps,
And my heart ever gazes on the depth
Of thy deep mysteries. I have made my bed
In charnels and on coffins, where black Death
Keeps record of the trophies won from thee;
Hoping to still these obstinate questionings
Of thee and thine by forcing some lone ghost,
Thy messenger, to render up the tale
Of what we are. In lone and silent hours,
When night makes a weird sound of its own stillness,
Like an inspired and desperate alchemist
Staking his very life on some dark hope,
Have I mixed awful talk and asking looks
With my most innocent love; until strange tears,
Uniting with those breathless kisses, made
Such magic as compels the charmèd night
To render up thy charge. And, though ne'er yet
Thou hast unveiled thy inmost sanctuary,
Enough from incommunicable dream,
And twilight phantasms, and deep noonday thought,
Has shone within me, that serenely now
And moveless, as a long-forgotten lyre
Suspended in the solitary dome

Of some mysterious and deserted fane,
I wait thy breath, Great Parent; that my strain
May modulate with murmurs of the air,
And motions of the forests and the sea,
And voice of living beings, and woven hymns
Of night and day, and the deep heart of man.

*   *   *   *   *

The Poet, wandering on, through Arabie,
And Persia, and the wild Carmanian waste,
And o'er the aërial mountains which pour down
Indus and Oxus from their icy caves,
In joy and exultation held his way;
Till in the vale of Cashmire far within
Its loneliest dell, where odorous plants entwine
Beneath the hollow rocks a natural bower,
Beside a sparkling rivulet he stretched
His languid limbs. A vision on his sleep
There came, a dream of hopes that never yet
Had flushed his cheek. He dreamed a veilèd maid
Sate near him, talking in low solemn tones.
Her voice was like the voice of his own soul
Heard in the calm of thought; its music long,
Like woven sounds of streams and breezes, held
His inmost sense suspended in its web
Of many-coloured woof and shifting hues.
Knowledge and truth and virtue were her theme,
And lofty hopes of divine liberty,
Thoughts the most dear to him, and poesy,
Herself a poet. Soon the solemn mood
Of her pure mind kindled through all her frame
A permeating fire; wild numbers then
She raised, with voice stifled in tremulous sobs
Subdued by its own pathos; her fair hands
Were bare alone, sweeping from some strange harp
Strange symphony, and in their branching veins
The eloquent blood told an ineffable tale.
The beating of her heart was heard to fill
The pauses of her music, and her breath
Tumultuously accorded with those fits
Of intermitted song. Sudden she rose,
As if her heart impatiently endured

Its bursting burthen. At the sound he turned,
And saw, by the warm light of their own life
Her glowing limbs beneath the sinuous veil
Of woven wind; her outspread arms now bare,
Her dark locks floating in the breath of night,
Her beamy bending eyes, her parted lips
Outstretched, and pale, and quivering eagerly.
His strong heart sunk and sickened with excess
Of love. He reared his shuddering limbs, and quelled
His gasping breath, and spread his arms to meet
Her panting bosom:—she drew back awhile,
Then, yielding to the irresistible joy,
With frantic gesture and short breathless cry
Folded his frame in her dissolving arms.
Now blackness veiled his dizzy eyes, and night
Involved and swallowed up the vision; sleep,
Like a dark flood suspended in its course,
Rolled back its impulse on his vacant brain.

*   *   *   *   *

While daylight held
The sky, the Poet kept mute conference
With his still soul. At night the passion came,
Like the fierce fiend of a distempered dream,
And shook him from his rest, and led him forth
Into the darkness.—As an eagle, grasped
In folds of the green serpent, feels her breast
Burn with the poison, and precipitates,
Through night and day, tempest and calm and cloud,
Frantic with dizzying anguish, her blind flight
O'er the wide aëry wilderness: thus driven
By the bright shadow of that lovely dream,
Beneath the cold glare of the desolate night,
Through tangled swamps and deep precipitous dells,
Startling with careless step the moonlight snake,
He fled. Red morning dawned upon his flight,
Shedding the mockery of its vital hues
Upon his cheek of death. He wandered on
Till vast Aornos seen from Petra's steep
Hung o'er the low horizon like a cloud;
Through Balk, and where the desolated tombs
Of Parthian kings scatter to every wind
Their wasting dust, wildly he wandered on,

Day after day, a weary waste of hours,
Bearing within his life the brooding care
That ever fed on its decaying flame.
And now his limbs were lean; his scattered hair,
Sered by the autumn of strange suffering,
Sung dirges in the wind; his listless hand
Hung like dead bone within its withered skin;
Life, and the lustre that consumed it, shone,
As in a furnace burning secretly,
From his dark eyes alone. The cottagers,
Who ministered with human charity
His human wants, beheld with wondering awe
Their fleeting visitant. The mountaineer,
Encountering on some dizzy precipice
That spectral form, deemed that the Spirit of Wind,
With lightning eyes, and eager breath, and feet
Disturbing not the drifted snow, had paused
In his career; the infant would conceal
His troubled visage in his mother's robe
In terror at the glare of those wild eyes,
To remember their strange light in many a dream
Of after times; but youthful maidens, taught
By nature, would interpret half the woe
That wasted him, would call him with false names
Brother, and friend, would press his pallid hand
At parting, and watch, dim through tears, the path
Of his departure from their father's door.

At length upon the lone Chorasmian shore
He paused, a wide and melancholy waste
Of putrid marshes. A strong impulse urged
His steps to the sea-shore. A swan was there,
Beside a sluggish stream among the reeds.
It rose as he approached, and, with strong wings
Scaling the upward sky, bent its bright course
High over the immeasurable main.
His eyes pursued its flight:—"Thou hast a home,
Beautiful bird! thou voyagest to thine home,
Where thy sweet mate will twine her downy neck
With thine, and welcome thy return with eyes
Bright in the lustre of their own fond joy.
And what am I that I should linger here,
With voice far sweeter than thy dying notes,
Spirit more vast than thine, frame more attuned

To beauty, wasting these surpassing powers
In the deaf air, to the blind earth, and heaven
That echoes not my thoughts?" A gloomy smile
Of desperate hope wrinkled his quivering lips.
For sleep, he knew, kept most relentlessly
Its precious charge; and silent death exposed,
Faithless perhaps as sleep, a shadowy lure,
With doubtful smile mocking its own strange charms.

Startled by his own thoughts, he looked around:
There was no fair fiend near him, not a sight
Or sound of awe but in his own deep mind.
A little shallop floating near the shore
Caught the impatient wandering of his gaze.
It had been long abandoned, for its sides
Gaped wide with many a rift, and its frail joints
Swayed with the undulations of the tide.
A restless impulse urged him to embark
And meet lone Death on the drear ocean's waste;
For well he knew that mighty Shadow loves
The slimy caverns of the populous deep.

The day was fair and sunny: sea and sky
Drank its inspiring radiance, and the wind
Swept strongly from the shore, blackening the waves.
Following his eager soul, the wanderer
Leaped in the boat; he spread his cloak aloft
On the bare mast, and took his lonely seat,
And felt the boat speed o'er the tranquil sea
Like a torn cloud before the hurricane.

As one that in a silver vision floats
Obedient to the sweep of odorous winds
Upon resplendent clouds, so rapidly
Along the dark and ruffled waters fled
The straining boat. A whirlwind swept it on,
With fierce gusts and precipitating force,
Through the white ridges of the chaféd sea.
The waves arose. Higher and higher still
Their fierce necks writhed beneath the tempest's scourge,
Like serpents struggling in a vulture's grasp.
Calm and rejoicing in the fearful war
Of wave running on wave, and blast on blast
Descending, and black flood on whirlpool driven
With dark obliterating course, he sate:

As if their genii were the ministers
Appointed to conduct him to the light
Of those belovèd eyes, the Poet sate
Holding the steady helm. Evening came on;
The beams of sunset hung their rainbow hues
High 'mid the shifting domes of sheeted spray
That canopied his path o'er the waste deep;
Twilight, ascending slowly from the east,
Entwined in duskier wreaths her braided locks
O'er the fair front and radiant eyes of Day;
Night followed, clad with stars. On every side
More horribly the multitudinous streams
Of ocean's mountainous waste to mutual war
Rushed in dark tumult thundering, as to mock
The calm and spangled sky. The little boat
Still fled before the storm; still fled, like foam
Down the steep cataract of a wintry river;
Now pausing on the edge of the riven wave;
Now leaving far behind the bursting mass,
That fell, convulsing ocean: safely fled—
As if that frail and wasted human form
Had been an elemental god.

                        At midnight
The moon arose: and lo! the ethereal cliffs
Of Caucasus, whose icy summits shone
Among the stars like sunlight, and around
Whose caverned base the whirlpools and the waves,
Bursting and eddying irresistibly,
Rage and resound for ever.—Who shall save?—
The boat fled on,—the boiling torrent drove,—
The crags closed round with black and jagged arms,
The shattered mountain overhung the sea;
And faster still, beyond all human speed,
Suspended on the sweep of the smooth wave,
The little boat was driven. A cavern there
Yawned, and amid its slant and winding depths
Engulfed the rushing sea. The boat fled on
With unrelaxing speed.—"Vision and Love!"
The Poet cried aloud, "I have beheld
The path of thy departure. Sleep and Death
Shall not divide us long."

        *   *   *   *   *

Shall it sink
Down the abyss? shall the reverting stress
Of that resistless gulf embosom it?
Now shall it fall?—A wandering stream of wind,
Breathed from the west, has caught the expanded sail,
And lo! with gentle motion, between banks
Of mossy slope, and on a placid stream,
Beneath a woven grove, it sails; and, hark!
The ghastly torrent mingles its far roar
With the breeze murmuring in the musical woods.
Where the embowering trees recede, and leave
A little space of green expanse, the cove
Is closed by meeting banks, whose yellow flowers
For ever gaze on their own drooping eyes,
Reflected in the crystal calm. The wave
Of the boat's motion marred their pensive task,
Which nought but vagrant bird, or wanton wind,
Or falling spear-grass, or their own decay,
Had e'er disturbed before. The Poet longed
To deck with their bright hues his withered hair,
But on his heart its solitude returned,
And he forbore. Not the strong impulse hid
In those flushed cheeks, bent eyes, and shadowy frame,
Had yet performed its ministry: it hung
Upon his life, as lightning in a cloud
Gleams, hovering ere it vanish, ere the floods
Of night close over it.

*   *   *   *   *

More dark
And dark the shades accumulate. The oak,
Expanding its immense and knotty arms,
Embraces the light beech. The pyramids
Of the tall cedar, overarching, frame
Most solemn domes within; and far below,
Like clouds suspended in an emerald sky,
The ash and the acacia floating hang
Tremulous and pale. Like restless serpents clothed
In rainbow and in fire, the parasites,
Starred with ten thousand blossoms, flow around
The grey trunks; and, as gamesome infants' eyes,
With gentle meanings and most innocent wiles,
Fold their beams round the hearts of those that love,

These twine their tendrils with the wedded boughs,
Uniting their close union; the woven leaves
Make net-work of the dark blue light of day
And the night's noontide clearness, mutable
As shapes in the weird clouds. Soft mossy lawns
Beneath these canopies extend their swells,
Fragrant with perfumed herbs, and eyed with blooms
Minute yet beautiful. One darkest glen
Sends from its woods of musk-rose twined with jasmine
A soul-dissolving odour, to invite
To some more lovely mystery. Through the dell,
Silence and Twilight here, twin sisters, keep
Their noonday watch, and sail among the shades,
Like vaporous shapes half-seen. Beyond, a well,
Dark, gleaming, and of most translucent wave,
Images all the woven boughs above,
And each depending leaf, and every speck
Of azure sky darting between their chasms;
Nor aught else in the liquid mirror laves
Its portraiture, but some inconstant star
Between one foliaged lattice twinkling fair,
Or painted bird sleeping beneath the moon,
Or gorgeous insect floating motionless,
Unconscious of the day, ere yet his wings
Have spread their glories to the gaze of noon.

$$* \quad * \quad * \quad * \quad *$$

"O stream,
Whose source is inaccessibly profound,
Whither do thy mysterious waters tend?
Thou imagest my life. Thy darksome stillness,
Thy dazzling waves, thy loud and hollow gulfs,
Thy searchless fountain and invisible course,
Have each their type in me. And the wide sky
And measureless ocean may declare as soon
What oozy cavern or what wandering cloud
Contains thy waters as the universe
Tell where these living thoughts reside, when, stretched
Upon thy flowers, my bloodless limbs shall waste
I' the passing wind!"

$$* \quad * \quad * \quad * \quad *$$

Oh for Medea's wondrous alchemy,
Which, wheresoe'er it fell, made the earth gleam
With bright flowers, and the wintry boughs exhale
From vernal blooms fresh fragrance! Oh that God,
Profuse of poisons, would concede the chalice
Which but one living man has drained, who now,
Vessel of deathless wrath, a slave that feels
No proud exemption in the blighting curse
He bears, over the world wanders for ever,
Lone as incarnate death! Oh that the dream
Of dark magician in his visioned cave,
Raking the cinders of a crucible
For life and power even when his feeble hand
Shakes in its last decay, were the true law
Of this so lovely world!—But thou art fled,
Like some frail exhalation which the dawn
Robes in its golden beams,—ah! thou hast fled!
The brave, the gentle, and the beautiful,
The child of grace and genius!

*   *   *   *   *

1815

From

THE REVOLT OF ISLAM

TO MARY WOLLSTONECRAFT SHELLEY

1

So now my summer-task is ended, Mary,
    And I return to thee, mine own heart's home;
As to his Queen some victor Knight of Faëry,
    Earning bright spoils for her enchanted dome.
    Nor thou disdain that, ere my fame become
A star among the stars of mortal night,
    If it indeed may cleave its natal gloom,
Its doubtful promise thus I would unite
With thy belovèd name, thou Child of love and light.

2

The toil which stole from thee so many an hour
    Is ended—and the fruit is at thy feet!
No longer where the woods to frame a bower
    With interlacèd branches mix and meet,
    Or where, with sound like many voices sweet,
Waterfalls leap among wild islands green
    Which framed for my lone boat a lone retreat
Of moss-grown trees and weeds, shall I be seen:
But beside thee, where still my heart has ever been.

3

Thoughts of great deeds were mine, dear Friend, when first
   The clouds which wrap this world from youth did pass.
I do remember well the hour which burst
   My spirit's sleep. A fresh May-dawn it was,
   When I walked forth upon the glittering grass,
And wept, I knew not why: until there rose
   From the near schoolroom voices that, alas!
Were but one echo from a world of woes—
The harsh and grating strife of tyrants and of foes.

4

And then I clasped my hands, and looked around;
   But none was near to mock my streaming eyes,
Which poured their warm drops on the sunny ground.
   So, without shame, I spake:—"I will be wise,
   And just, and free, and mild, if in me lies
Such power; for I grow weary to behold
   The selfish and the strong still tyrannize
Without reproach or check." I then controlled
My tears, my heart grew calm, and I was meek and bold.

5

And from that hour did I with earnest thought
   Heap knowledge from forbidden mines of lore;
Yet nothing that my tyrants knew or taught
   I cared to learn—but from that secret store
   Wrought linkèd armour for my soul, before
It might walk forth to war among mankind.
   Thus power and hope were strengthened more and more
Within me; till there came upon my mind
A sense of loneliness, a thirst with which I pined.

6

Alas that love should be a blight and snare
   To those who seek all sympathies in one!—
Such once I sought in vain. Then black despair,
   The shadow of a starless night, was thrown
   Over the world in which I moved alone.

Yet never found I one not false to me,
  Hard hearts and cold, like weights of icy stone
Which crushed and withered mine—that could not be
Aught but a lifeless clod, until revived by thee.

7

Thou Friend, whose presence on my wintry heart
  Fell like bright Spring upon some herbless plain,
How beautiful and calm and free thou wert
  In thy young wisdom, when the mortal chain
  Of Custom thou didst burst and rend in twain,
And walk as free as light the clouds among,
  Which many an envious slave then breathed in vain
From his dim dungeon; and my spirit sprung
To meet thee from the woes which had begirt it long!

8

No more alone through the world's wilderness,
  Although I trod the paths of high intent,
I journeyed now: no more companionless,
  Where solitude is like despair, I went,—
  There is the wisdom of a stern content
When Poverty can blight the just and good,
  When Infamy dares mock the innocent,
And cherished friends turn with the multitude
To trample: this was ours, and we unshaken stood.

9

Now has descended a serener hour,
  And, with inconstant fortune, friends return;
Though suffering leaves the knowledge and the power
  Which says,—Let scorn be not repaid with scorn.
  And from thy side two gentle babes are born
To fill our home with smiles, and thus are we
  Most fortunate beneath life's beaming morn:
And these delights, and thou, have been to me
The parents of the Song I consecrate to thee.

10

Is it that now my inexperienced fingers
    But strike the prelude of a loftier strain?
Or must the lyre on which my spirit lingers
    Soon pause in silence, ne'er to sound again,
    Though it might shake the Anarch Custom's reign,
And charm the minds of men to Truth's own sway,
    Holier than was Amphion's? I would fain
Reply in hope—but I am worn away,
And Death and Love are yet contending for their prey.

11

And what art thou? I know, but dare not speak:
    Time may interpret to his silent years.
Yet in the paleness of thy thoughtful cheek,
    And in the light thine ample forehead wears,
    And in thy sweetest smiles, and in thy tears,
And in thy gentle speech, a prophecy
    Is whispered, to subdue my fondest fears:
And, through thine eyes, even in thy soul I see
A lamp of vestal fire burning internally.

12

They say that thou wert lovely from thy birth,
    Of glorious parents thou aspiring child.
I wonder not—for One then left this earth
    Whose life was like a setting planet mild,
    Which clothed thee in the radiance undefiled
Of its departing glory; still her fame
    Shines on thee, through the tempests dark and wild
Which shake these latter days; and thou canst claim
The shelter, from thy sire, of an immortal name.

13

One voice came forth from many a mighty spirit,
    Which was the echo of three thousand years;
And the tumultuous world stood mute to hear it,
    As some lone man who in a desert hears
    The music of his home:—unwonted fears

Fell on the pale oppressors of our race,
And Faith and Custom and low-thoughted cares,
Like thunder-stricken dragons, for a space
Left the torn human heart, their food and dwelling-place.

14

Truth's deathless voice pauses among mankind!
If there must be no response to my cry—
If men must rise and stamp, with fury blind,
On his pure name who loves them,—thou and I,
Sweet friend, can look from our tranquillity
Like lamps into the world's tempestuous night,—
Two tranquil stars, while clouds are passing by
Which wrap them from the foundering seaman's sight,
That burn from year to year with unextinguished light.

CANTO I

*   *   *   *   *

23

A boat of rare device, which had no sail
But its own curvèd prow of thin moonstone,
Wrought like a web of texture fine and frail,
To catch those gentlest winds which are not known
To breathe, but by the steady speed alone
With which it cleaves the sparkling sea. And now
We are embarked. The mountains hang and frown
Over the starry deep that gleams below,
A vast and dim expanse, as o'er the waves we go.

24

And, as we sailed, a strange and awful tale
That Woman told, like such mysterious dream
As makes the slumberer's cheek with wonder pale.
'Twas midnight, and around, a shoreless stream,

Wide ocean rolled, when that majestic theme
Shrined in her heart found utterance, and she bent
    Her looks on mine; those eyes a kindling beam
Of love divine into my spirit sent,
And, ere her lips could move, made the air eloquent.

25

"Speak not to me, but hear! Much shalt thou learn.
    Much must remain unthought, and more untold,
In the dark Future's ever-flowing urn.
    Know then that from the depth of ages old
    Two Powers o'er mortal things dominion hold,
Ruling the world with a divided lot,—
    Immortal, all-pervading, manifold,
Twin Genii, equal Gods—when life and thought
Sprang forth, they burst the womb of inessential nought.

26

"The earliest dweller of the world, alone,
    Stood on the verge of chaos. Lo! afar
O'er the wide wild abyss two meteors shone,
    Sprung from the depth of its tempestuous jar:
    A blood-red Comet and the Morning Star
Mingling their beams in combat. As he stood,
    All thoughts within his mind waged mutual war
In dreadful sympathy:—when to the flood
That fair Star fell, he turned and shed his brother's blood.

27

"Thus Evil triumphed, and the Spirit of Evil,
    One Power of many shapes which none may know,
One Shape of many names; the Fiend did revel
    In victory, reigning o'er a world of woe,—
    For the new race of man went to and fro,
Famished and homeless, loathed and loathing, wild,
    And hating good; for his immortal foe
He changed from starry shape, beauteous and mild,
To a dire Snake, with man and beast unreconciled.

28

"The darkness lingering o'er the dawn of things
    Was Evil's breath and life; this made him strong
To soar aloft with overshadowing wings:
    And the great Spirit of Good did creep among
    The nations of mankind, and every tongue
Cursed and blasphemed him as he passed; for none
    Knew good from evil, though their names were hung
In mockery o'er the fane where many a groan
As King and Lord and God the conquering Fiend did own,—

29

"The Fiend, whose name was legion; Death, Decay,
    Earthquake, and Blight, and Want, and Madness pale,
Wingèd and wan diseases, an array
    Numerous as leaves that strew the autumnal gale;
    Poison, a snake in flowers, beneath the veil
Of food and mirth hiding his mortal head;
    And, without whom all these might nought avail,
Fear, Hatred, Faith, and Tyranny, who spread
Those subtle nets which snare the living and the dead.

30

"His spirit is their power, and they his slaves
    In air, in light, and thought, and language, dwell;
And keep their state from palaces to graves,
    In all resorts of men; invisible,
    But when, in ebon mirror, Nightmare fell,
To tyrant or impostor bids them rise
    Black wingèd demon forms—whom, from the hell
His reign and dwelling beneath nether skies,
He loosens to their dark and blasting ministries.

31

"In the world's youth his empire was as firm
    As its foundations. Soon the Spirit of Good,
Though in the likeness of a loathsome worm,
    Sprang from the billows of the formless flood,
    Which shrank and fled,—and with that Fiend of blood

Renewed the doubtful war. Thrones then first shook;
    And earth's immense and trampled multitude
In hope on their own powers began to look;
And Fear, the demon pale, his sanguine shrine forsook.

32

"Then Greece arose, and to its bards and sages,
    In dream, the golden-pinioned Genii came,
Even where they slept amid the night of ages,
    Steeping their hearts in the divinest flame
    Which thy breath kindled, Power of holiest name!
And oft in cycles since, when darkness gave
    New weapons to thy foe, their sunlike fame
Upon the combat shone—a light to save,
Like Paradise spread forth beyond the shadowy grave.

*   *   *   *   *

39

"When first the living blood through all these veins
    Kindled a thought in sense, great France sprang forth,
And seized, as if to break, the ponderous chains
    Which bind in woe the nations of the earth.
    I saw, and started from my cottage hearth;
And to the clouds and waves in tameless gladness
    Shrieked, till they caught immeasurable mirth,
And laughed in light and music: soon sweet madness
Was poured upon my heart, a soft and thrilling sadness.

40

"Deep slumber fell on me;—my dreams were fire,
    Soft and delightful thoughts did rest and hover
Like shadows o'er my brain; and strange desire,
    The tempest of a passion raging over
    My tranquil soul, its depths with light did cover,—
Which passed; and calm and darkness, sweeter far,
    Came—then I loved; but not a human lover!
For, when I rose from sleep, the Morning Star
Shone through the woodbine wreaths which round my casement were.

41

"Twas like an eye which seemed to smile on me.
  I watched till, by the sun made pale, it sank
Under the billows of the heaving sea;
  But from its beams deep love my spirit drank,
  And to my brain the boundless world now shrank
Into one thought—one image—yes, for ever!
  Even like the dayspring poured on vapours dank,
The beams of that one Star did shoot and quiver
Through my benighted mind—and were extinguished never.

42

"The day passed thus. At night, methought in dream
  A shape of speechless beauty did appear;
It stood like light on a careering stream
  Of golden clouds which shook the atmosphere;—
  A wingèd youth. His radiant brow did wear
The Morning Star: a wild dissolving bliss
  Over my frame he breathed, approaching near,
And bent his eyes of kindling tenderness
Near mine, and on my lips impressed a lingering kiss,—

43

"And said: 'A Spirit loves thee, mortal maiden:
  How wilt thou prove thy worth?' Then joy and sleep
Together fled; my soul was deeply laden,
  And to the shore I went to muse and weep.
  But, as I moved, over my heart did creep
A joy less soft but more profound and strong
  Than my sweet dream, and it forbade to keep
The path of the sea-shore: that Spirit's tongue
Seemed whispering in my heart, and bore my steps along.

44

"How, to that vast and peopled city led
  Which was a field of holy warfare then,
I walked among the dying and the dead,
  And shared in fearless deeds with evil men,
  Calm as an angel in the dragon's den—

How I braved death for liberty and truth,
    And spurned at peace and power and fame—and, when
Those hopes had lost the glory of their youth,
How sadly I returned—might move the hearer's ruth.

45

"Warm tears throng fast! the tale may not be said.
    Know then that, when this grief had been subdued,
I was not left, like others, cold and dead.
    The Spirit whom I loved in solitude
    Sustained his child: the tempest-shaken wood,
The waves, the fountains, and the hush of night,
    These were his voice; and well I understood
His smile divine, when the calm sea was bright
With silent stars, and Heaven was breathless with delight.

46

"In lonely glens, amid the roar of rivers,
    When the dim nights were moonless, have I known
Joys which no tongue can tell; my pale lip quivers
    When thought revisits them:—know thou alone
    That, after many wondrous years were flown,
I was awakened by a shriek of woe;
    And over me a mystic robe was thrown
By viewless hands, and a bright Star did glow
Before my steps—the Snake then met his mortal foe."

47

"Thou fear'st not then the Serpent on thy heart?"
    "Fear it!" she said with brief and passionate cry,—
And spake no more. That silence made me start.
    I looked, and we were sailing pleasantly,
    Swift as a cloud between the sea and sky,
Beneath the rising moon seen far away;
    Mountains of ice, like sapphire, piled on high,
Hemming the horizon round, in silence lay
On the still waters,—these we did approach alway.

48

And swift and swifter grew the vessel's motion,
　　So that a dizzy trance fell on my brain.
　Wild music woke me; we had past the ocean
　　Which girds the pole, nature's remotest reign—
　　And we glode fast o'er a pellucid plain
　Of waters, azure with the noontide day.
　　Ethereal mountains shone around—a fane
　Stood in the midst, girt by green isles which lay
On the blue sunny deep, resplendent far away.

49

It was a Temple such as mortal hand
　　Has never built, nor ecstasy nor dream
　Reared in the cities of enchanted land.
　　'Twas likest Heaven ere yet day's purple stream
　　Ebbs o'er the western forest, while the gleam
　Of the unrisen moon among the clouds
　　Is gathering—when with many a golden beam
　The thronging constellations rush in crowds,
Paving with fire the sky and the marmoreal floods.

50

Like what may be conceived of this vast dome
　　When from the depths which thought can seldom pierce
　Genius beholds it rise, his native home,
　　Girt by the deserts of the Universe;
　　Yet nor in painting's light, or mightier verse,
　Or sculpture's marble language, can invest
　　That shape to mortal sense—such glooms immerse
　That incommunicable sight, and rest
Upon the labouring brain and overburdened breast.

51

Winding among the lawny islands fair,
　　Whose blosmy forests starred the shadowy deep,
　The wingless boat paused where an ivory stair
　　Its fretwork in the crystal sea did steep,
　　Encircling that vast fane's aërial heap.

We disembarked, and through a portal wide
We passed—whose roof, of moonstone carved, did keep
A glimmering o'er the forms on every side,
Sculptures like life and thought, immovable, deep-eyed.

52

We came to a vast hall whose glorious roof
    Was diamond, which had drunk the lightning's sheen
In darkness, and now poured it through the woof
    Of spell-inwoven clouds hung there to screen
    Its blinding splendour. Through such veil was seen
That work of subtlest power, divine and rare;
    Orb above orb, with starry shapes between,
And hornèd moons, and meteors strange and fair;
On night-black columns poised—one hollow hemisphere:

53

Ten thousand columns in that quivering light
    Distinct—between whose shafts wound far away
The long and labyrinthine aisles, more bright
    With their own radiance than the Heaven of Day.
    And on the jasper walls around there lay
Paintings, the poesy of mightiest thought,
    Which did the Spirit's history display;
A tale of passionate change, divinely taught,
Which in their wingèd dance unconscious Genii wrought.

54

Beneath there sate on many a sapphire throne
    The Great who had departed from mankind,
A mighty Senate; some, whose white hair shone
    Like mountain snow, mild, beautiful, and blind;
    Some, female forms, whose gestures beamed with mind;
And ardent youths, and children bright and fair;
    And some had lyres whose strings were intertwined
With pale and clinging flames, which ever there
Waked faint yet thrilling sounds that pierced the crystal air.

55

One seat was vacant in the midst, a throne
    Reared on a pyramid like sculptured flame,
Distinct with circling steps which rested on
      Their own deep fire. Soon as the Woman came
      Into that hall, she shrieked the Spirit's name,
    And fell, and vanished slowly from the sight.
      Darkness arose from her dissolving frame,—
    Which, gathering, filled that dome of woven light,
Blotting its spherèd stars with supernatural night.

56

Then first two glittering lights were seen to glide
    In circles on the amethystine floor,
Small serpent eyes trailing from side to side,
      Like meteors on a river's grassy shore.
      They round each other rolled, dilating more
    And more—then rose, commingling into one,
      One clear and mighty planet hanging o'er
    A cloud of deepest shadow which was thrown
Athwart the glowing steps and the crystalline throne.

57

The cloud which rested on that cone of flame
    Was cloven: beneath the planet sate a Form
Fairer than tongue can speak or thought may frame,
      The radiance of whose limbs rose-like and warm
      Flowed forth, and did with softest light inform
    The shadowy dome, the sculptures and the state
      Of those assembled shapes—with clinging charm
    Sinking upon their hearts and mine. He sate
Majestic yet most mild—calm yet compassionate.

58

Wonder and joy a passing faintness threw
    Over my brow. A hand supported me,
Whose touch was magic strength: an eye of blue
      Looked into mine, like moonlight, soothingly;
      And a voice said:—"Thou must a listener be

This day. Two mighty Spirits now return,
Like birds of calm, from the world's raging sea:
They pour fresh light from Hope's immortal urn.
A tale of human power—despair not—list and learn!"

59

I looked, and lo! one stood forth eloquently,
His eyes were dark and deep, and the clear brow
Which shadowed them was like the morning's sky,
The cloudless Heaven of Spring, when in their flow
Through the bright air the soft winds as they blow
Wake the green world: his gestures did obey
The oracular mind that made his features glow;
And, where his curvèd lips half-open lay,
Passion's divinest stream had made impetuous way.

60

Beneath the darkness of his outspread hair
He stood thus beautiful. But there was One
Who sate beside him like his shadow there,
And held his hand—far lovelier. She was known
To be thus fair by the few lines alone
Which through her floating locks and gathered cloak,
Glances of soul-dissolving glory, shone.
None else beheld her eyes; in him they woke
Memories which found a tongue, as thus he silence broke.

CANTO II

1

THE starlight smile of children, the sweet looks
Of women, the fair breast from which I fed,
The murmur of the unreposing brooks,
And the green light which, shifting overhead,
Some tangled bower of vines around me shed,
The shells on the sea-sand, and the wild flowers,
The lamplight through the rafters cheerly spread,
And on the twining flax—in life's young hours
These sights and sounds did nurse my spirit's folded powers.

2

In Argolis beside the echoing sea,
　　Such impulses within my mortal frame
Arose, and they were dear to memory,
　　Like tokens of the dead:—but others came
　　Soon, in another shape: the wondrous fame
Of the past world, the vital words and deeds
　　Of minds whom neither time nor change can tame,
Traditions dark and old whence evil creeds
Start forth, and whose dim shade a stream of poison feeds.

3

I heard, as all have heard, the various story
　　Of human life, and wept unwilling tears.
Feeble historians of its shame and glory,
　　False disputants on all its hopes and fears,
　　Victims who worshipped ruin, chroniclers
Of daily scorn, and slaves who loathed their state,
　　Yet, flattering Power, had given its ministers
A throne of judgment in the grave—'twas fate
That among such as these my youth should seek its mate.

4

The land in which I lived, by a fell bane
　　Was withered up. Tyrants dwelt side by side,
And stabled in our homes—until the chain
　　Stifled the captive's cry, and to abide
　　That blasting curse men had no shame. All vied
In evil, slave and despot; fear with lust
　　Strange fellowship through mutual hate had tied,
Like two dark serpents tangled in the dust,
Which on the paths of men their mingling poison thrust.

5

Earth, our bright home, its mountains and its waters,
　　And the ethereal shapes which are suspended
Over its green expanse—and those fair daughters,
　　The Clouds, of sun and ocean, who have blended
　　The colours of the air since first extended

It cradled the young World,—none wandered forth
  To see or feel: a darkness had descended
On every heart. The light which shows its worth
Must among gentle thoughts and fearless take its birth.

*   *   *   *   *

CANTO III

*   *   *   *   *

5

The scene was changed, and away, away, away,
  Through the air and over the sea we sped,
And Cythna in my sheltering bosom lay,
  And the winds bore me;—through the darkness spread
  Around, the gaping earth then vomited
Legions of foul and ghastly shapes, which hung
Upon my flight, and ever, as we fled,
They plucked at Cythna. Soon to me then clung
A sense of actual things those monstrous dreams among.

6

And I lay struggling in the impotence
  Of sleep, while outward life had burst its bound,—
Though, still deluded, strove the tortured sense
  To its dire wanderings to adapt the sound
  Which in the light of morn was poured around
Our dwelling. Breathless, pale, and unaware,
  I rose; and all the cottage crowded found
With armèd men, whose glittering swords were bare,
And whose degraded limbs the tyrant's garb did wear.

7

And, ere with rapid lips and gathered brow
  I could demand the cause, a feeble shriek—
It was a feeble shriek, faint, far, and low—
  Arrested me. My mien grew calm and meek,

And, grasping a small knife, I went to seek
That voice among the crowd—'twas Cythna's cry!
Beneath most calm resolve did agony wreak
Its whirlwind rage:—so I passed quietly,
Till I beheld where bound that dearest child did lie.

8

I started to behold her, for delight
And exultation, and a joyance free,
Solemn, serene, and lofty, filled the light
Of the calm smile with which she looked on me:
So that I feared some brainless ecstasy,
Wrought from that bitter woe, had wildered her.
"Farewell! farewell!" she said, as I drew nigh.
"At first my peace was marred by this strange stir:
Now I am calm as truth—its chosen minister.

9

"Look not so, Laon—say farewell in hope:
These bloody men are but the slaves who bear
Their mistress to her task. It was my scope
The slavery where they drag me now to share,
And among captives willing chains to wear
Awhile—the rest thou know'st. Return, dear friend!
Let our first triumph trample the despair
Which would ensnare us now; for, in the end,
In victory or in death our hopes and fears must blend."

10

These words had fallen on my unheeding ear,
Whilst I had watched the motions of the crew
With seeming careless glance; not many were
Around her, for their comrades just withdrew
To guard some other victim—so I drew
My knife, and with one impulse, suddenly,
All unaware three of their number slew,
And grasped a fourth by the throat, and with loud cry
My countrymen invoked to death or liberty.

11

What followed then I know not—for a stroke
  On my raised arm and naked head came down,
Filling my eyes with blood.—When I awoke,
  I felt that they had bound me in my swoon,
And up a rock which overhangs the town,
  By the steep path, were bearing me: below
    The plain was filled with slaughter,—overthrown
The vineyards and the harvests, and the glow
Of blazing roofs shone far o'er the white Ocean's flow.

12

Upon that rock a mighty column stood
  Whose capital seemed sculptured in the sky,
Which to the wanderers o'er the solitude
  Of distant seas, from ages long gone by,
  Had made a landmark; o'er its height to fly
Scarcely the cloud, the vulture, or the blast,
    Has power—and, when the shades of evening lie
On Earth and Ocean, its carved summits cast
The sunken daylight far through the aërial waste.

13

They bore me to a cavern in the hill
  Beneath that column, and unbound me there.
And one did strip me stark; and one did fill
  A vessel from the putrid pool; one bare
  A lighted torch; and four with friendless care
Guided my steps the cavern-paths along.
    Then up a steep and dark and narrow stair
We wound, until the torches' fiery tongue
Amid the gushing day beamless and pallid hung.

14

They raised me to the platform of the pile,
  That column's dizzy height:—the grate of brass,
Through which they thrust me, open stood the while,
  As to its ponderous and suspended mass,

With chains which eat into the flesh, alas!
With brazen links my naked limbs they bound:
   The grate, as they departed to repass,
With horrid clangour fell, and the far sound
Of their retiring steps in the dense gloom was drowned.

15

The noon was calm and bright:—around that column
   The overhanging sky and circling sea
Spread forth, in silentness profound and solemn,
   The darkness of brief frenzy cast on me,
   So that I knew not my own misery:
The islands and the mountains in the day
   Like clouds reposed afar; and I could see
The town among the woods below that lay,
And the dark rocks which bound the bright and glassy bay.

16

It was so calm that scarce the feathery weed
   Sown by some eagle on the topmost stone
Swayed in the air:—so bright that noon did breed
   No shadow in the sky beside mine own—
   Mine, and the shadow of my chain alone.
Below, the smoke of roofs involved in flame
   Rested like night; all else was clearly shown
In the broad glare,—yet sound to me none came,
But of the living blood that ran within my frame.

17

The peace of madness fled, and ah! too soon
   A ship was lying on the sunny main;
Its sails were flagging in the breathless noon—
   Its shadow lay beyond. That sight again
   Waked with its presence in my trancèd brain
The stings of a known sorrow, keen and cold:
   I knew that ship bore Cythna o'er the plain
Of waters, to her blighting slavery sold,
And watched it with such thoughts as must remain untold.

18

I watched, until the shades of evening wrapped
    Earth like an exhalation. Then the bark
  Moved, for that calm was by the sunset snapped.
    It moved a speck upon the ocean dark:
    Soon the wan stars came forth, and I could mark
Its path no more. I sought to close mine eyes,
    But, like the balls, their lids were stiff and stark;
  I would have risen, but ere that I could rise
My parchèd skin was split with piercing agonies.

19

I gnawed my brazen chain, and sought to sever
    Its adamantine links, that I might die:
  O Liberty! forgive the base endeavour,
    Forgive me if, reserved for victory,
    The Champion of thy faith e'er sought to fly!—
That starry night, with its clear silence, sent
    Tameless resolve which laughed at misery
  Into my soul—linkèd remembrance lent
To that such power, to me such a severe content.

20

To breathe, to be, to hope—or to despair
    And die—I questioned not; nor, though the Sun,
  Its shafts of agony kindling through the air,
    Moved over me,—nor though, in evening dun,
    Or when the stars their visible courses run,
Or morning, the wide universe was spread
    In dreary calmness round me,—did I shun
  Its presence, nor seek refuge with the dead
From one faint hope whose flower a dropping poison shed.

21

Two days thus passed. I neither raved nor died.
    Thirst raged within me, like a scorpion's nest
  Built in mine entrails; I had spurned aside
    The water-vessel while despair possessed

My thoughts, and now no drop remained. The uprest
Of the third sun brought hunger—but the crust
Which had been left was to my craving breast
Fuel, not food. I chewed the bitter dust,
And bit my bloodless arm, and licked the brazen rust.

*   *   *   *   *

33

A dim and feeble joy, whose glimpses oft
Were quenched in a relapse of wildering dreams.
Yet still methought we sailed, until aloft
The stars of night grew pallid, and the beams
Of morn descended on the ocean-streams;
And still that aged man, so grand and mild,
Tended me, even as some sick mother seems
To hang in hope over a dying child,
Till in the azure east darkness again was piled.

34

And then the night-wind, steaming from the shore,
Sent odours dying sweet across the sea,
And the swift boat the little waves which bore
Were cut by its keen keel, though slantingly;
Soon I could hear the leaves sigh, and could see
The myrtle-blossoms starring the dim grove,
As past the pebbly beach the boat did flee
On sidelong wing into a silent cove,
Where ebon pines a shade under the starlight wove.

*   *   *   *   *

CANTO V

* * * * *

52

—When in the silence of all spirits there
Laone's voice was felt, and through the air
Her thrilling gestures spoke, most eloquently fair.—

"Calm art thou as yon sunset; swift and strong
As new-fledged eagles, beautiful and young,
That float among the blinding beams of morning:
    And underneath thy feet writhe Faith and Folly,
    Custom and Hell and mortal Melancholy!
Hark! the Earth starts to hear the mighty warning
    Of thy voice sublime and holy!
    Its free spirits here assembled
        See thee, feel thee, know thee now:
    To thy voice their hearts have trembled,
        Like ten thousand clouds which flow
    With one wide wind as it flies.
Wisdom! thy irresistible children rise
To hail thee; and the elements they chain,
And their own will, to swell the glory of thy train.

"O Spirit vast and deep as Night and Heaven!
    Mother and soul of all to which is given
    The light of life, the loveliness of being,
        Lo! thou dost re-ascend the human heart,
        Thy throne of power, almighty as thou wert
    In dreams of Poets old grown pale by seeing
        The shade of thee:—now millions start
        To feel thy lightnings through them burning:
            Nature, or God, or Love, or Pleasure,
        Or Sympathy, the sad tears turning
            To mutual smiles, a drainless treasure,
        Descends amidst us;—Scorn and Hate,
    Revenge and Selfishness, are desolate:—
    A hundred nations swear that there shall be
Pity and Peace and Love among the good and free!

"Eldest of things, divine Equality!
　　Wisdom and Love are but the slaves of thee,
　　The Angels of thy sway, who pour around thee
　　　　Treasures from all the cells of human thought
　　　　And from the Stars and from the Ocean brought,
　　And the last living heart whose beatings bound thee.
　　　　The powerful and the wise had sought
　　　　Thy coming; thou, in light descending
　　　　　　O'er the wide land which is thine own,
　　　　Like the Spring whose breath is blending
　　　　　　All blasts of fragrance into one,
　　　　Comest upon the paths of men!
　　Earth bares her general bosom to thy ken,
　　And all her children here in glory meet
To feed upon thy smiles, and clasp thy sacred feet.

"My brethren, we are free! The plains and mountains,
　　The grey sea-shore, the forests, and the fountains,
　　Are haunts of happiest dwellers; man and woman,
　　　　Their common bondage burst, may freely borrow
　　　　From lawless love a solace for their sorrow—
　　For oft we still must weep, since we are human.
　　　　A stormy night's serenest morrow—
　　　　Whose showers are pity's gentle tears,
　　　　　　Whose clouds are smiles of those that die
　　　　Like infants without hopes or fears,
　　　　　　And whose beams are joys that lie
　　　　In blended hearts—now holds dominion;
　　The dawn of mind, which, upwards on a pinion
　　Borne swift as sunrise, far illumines space,
And clasps this barren world in its own bright embrace!

"My brethren, we are free! The fruits are glowing
　　Beneath the stars, and the night-winds are flowing
　　O'er the ripe corn, the birds and beasts are dreaming.
　　　　Never again may blood of bird or beast
　　　　Stain with its venomous stream a human feast,
　　To the pure skies in accusation steaming;
　　　　Avenging poisons shall have ceased
　　　　To feed disease and fear and madness;
　　　　　　The dwellers of the earth and air
　　　　Shall throng around our steps in gladness,
　　　　　　Seeking their food or refuge there.

Our toil from thought all glorious forms shall cull,
To make this Earth, our home, more beautiful;
And Science, and her sister Poesy,
Shall clothe in light the fields and cities of the free!

"Victory, Victory to the prostrate nations!
    Bear witness, Night, and ye mute Constellations
    Who gaze on us from your crystalline cars!
        Thoughts have gone forth whose powers can sleep no more.
        Victory! Victory! Earth's remotest shore,
    Regions which groan beneath the antarctic stars,
        The green lands cradled in the roar
        Of western waves, and wildernesses
            Peopled and vast which skirt the oceans
            Where Morning dyes her golden tresses,
            Shall soon partake our high emotions.
        Kings shall turn pale! Almighty Fear,
        The Fiend-God, when our charmèd name he hear,
    Shall fade like shadow from his thousand fanes,
While Truth, with Joy enthroned, o'er his lost empire reigns!"

*   *   *   *   *

CANTO VI

*   *   *   *   *

9

A band of brothers gathering round me made,
    Although unarmed, a steadfast front, and, still
    Retreating, with stern looks beneath the shade
    Of gathered eyebrows, did the victors fill
    With doubt even in success; deliberate will
Inspired our growing troop; not overthrown,
    It gained the shelter of a grassy hill:—
    And ever still our comrades were hewn down,
And their defenceless limbs beneath our footsteps strown.

10

Immovably we stood.—In joy I found
    Beside me then, firm as a giant pine
Among the mountain-vapours driven around,
    The old man whom I loved. His eyes divine
    With a mild look of courage answered mine;
And my young friend was near, and ardently
    His hand grasped mine a moment. Now the line
Of war extended, to our rallying-cry
As myriads flocked in love and brotherhood to die.

11

For ever while the sun was climbing Heaven
    The horsemen hewed our unarmed myriads down
Safely; though, when by thirst of carnage driven
    Too near, those slaves were swiftly overthrown
    By hundreds leaping on them. Flesh and bone
Soon made our ghastly ramparts; then the shaft
    Of the artillery from the sea was thrown
More fast and fiery, and the conquerors laughed
In pride to hear the wind our screams of torment waft.

12

For on one side alone the hill gave shelter,
    So vast that phalanx of unconquered men,
And there the living in the blood did welter
    Of the dead and dying, which in that green glen,
    Like stifled torrents, made a plashy fen
Under the feet. Thus was the butchery waged
    While the sun clomb Heaven's eastern steep—but, when
It 'gan to sink, a fiercer combat raged,
For in more doubtful strife the armies were engaged.

13

Within a cave upon the hill were found
    A bundle of rude pikes, the instrument
Of those who war but on their native ground
    For natural rights: a shout of joyance, sent

Even from our hearts, the wide air pierced and rent,
As those few arms the bravest and the best
  Seized; and each sixth, thus armed, did now present
  A line which covered and sustained the rest,
A confident phalanx, which the foes on every side invest.

14

That onset turned the foes to flight almost.
  But soon they saw their present strength, and knew
  That coming night would to our resolute host
  Bring victory; so, dismounting, close they drew
  Their glittering files, and then the combat grew
Unequal but most horrible;—and ever
  Our myriads, whom the swift bolt overthrew,
Or the red sword, failed like a mountain river
Which rushes forth in foam to sink in sands forever.

15

Sorrow and shame to see with their own kind
  Our human brethren mix, like beasts of blood,
  To mutual ruin, armed by one behind
  Who sits and scoffs!—That friend so mild and good,
  Who like its shadow near my youth had stood,
  Was stabbed!—my old preserver's hoary hair,
  With the flesh clinging to its roots, was strewed
Under my feet! I lost all sense or care,
And like the rest I grew desperate and unaware.

16

The battle became ghastlier. In the midst
  I paused, and saw how ugly and how fell,
  O Hate! thou art, even when thy life thou shedd'st
  For love. The ground in many a little dell
  Was broken, up and down whose steeps befell
  Alternate victory and defeat; and there
  The combatants with rage most horrible
Strove, and their eyes started with cracking stare,
And impotent their tongues they lolled into the air,—

17

Flaccid and foamy, like a mad dog's hanging.
    Want, and Moon-madness, and the pest's swift Bane
When its shafts smite—while yet its bow is twanging—
    Have each their mark and sign, some ghastly stain;
    And this was thine, O War! of hate and pain
Thou loathèd slave! I saw all shapes of death,
    And ministered to many, o'er the plain
While carnage in the sunbeam's warmth did seethe,
Till Twilight o'er the east wove her serenest wreath.

*   *   *   *   *

33

The Meteor showed the leaves on which we sate;
    And Cythna's glowing arms; and the thick ties
Of her soft hair which bent with gathered weight
    My neck near hers; her dark and deepening eyes,
    Which, as twin phantoms of one star that lies
O'er a dim well move though the star reposes,
    Swam in our mute and liquid ecstasies;
    Her marble brow, and eager lips, like roses,
With their own fragrance pale, which Spring but half uncloses.

34

The Meteor to its far morass returned.
    The beating of our veins one interval
Made still; and then I felt the blood that burned
    Within her frame mingle with mine, and fall
    Around my heart like fire; and over all
A mist was spread; the sickness of a deep
    And speechless swoon of joy, as might befall
Two disunited spirits when they leap
In union from this earth's obscure and fading sleep.

35

Was it one moment that confounded thus
    All thought, all sense, all feeling, into one
Unutterable power, which shielded us
    Even from our own cold looks, when we had gone
    Into a wide and wild oblivion
Of tumult and of tenderness? or now
    Had ages, such as make the moon and sun,
The seasons and mankind, their changes know,
Left fear and time unfelt by us alone below?

36

I know not. What are kisses whose fire clasps
    The failing heart in languishment, or limb
Twined within limb? or the quick dying gasps
    Of the life meeting, when the faint eyes swim
    Through tears of a wide mist boundless and dim,
In one caress? What is the strong control
    Which leads the heart that dizzy steep to climb
Where far over the world those vapours roll
Which blend two restless frames in one reposing soul?

*   *   *   *   *

39

There we unheeding sate, in the communion
    Of interchangèd vows which, with a rite
Of faith most sweet and sacred, stamped our union.—
    Few were the living hearts which could unite
    Like ours, or celebrate a bridal night
With such close sympathies; for they had sprung
    From linkèd youth, and from the gentle might
Of earliest love, delayed and cherished long,
Which common hopes and fears made, like a tempest, strong.

40

And such is Nature's law divine that those
 Who grow together cannot choose but love,
If faith or custom do not interpose,
 Or common slavery mar what else might move
 All gentlest thoughts. As, in the sacred grove
Which shades the springs of Ethiopian Nile,
 That living tree which if the arrowy dove
Strike with her shadow shrinks in fear awhile;
But its own kindred leaves clasps while the sunbeams smile,

41

And clings to them when darkness may dissever
 The close caresses of all duller plants
Which bloom on the wide earth;—thus we for ever
 Were linked, for love had nursed us in the haunts
 Where knowledge from its secret source enchants
Young hearts with the fresh music of its springing,
 Ere yet its gathered flood feeds human wants,—
As the great Nile feeds Egypt, ever flinging
Light on the woven boughs which o'er its waves are swinging.

  * * * * *

46

There was a desolate village in a wood,
 Whose bloom-inwoven leaves now scattering fed
The hungry storm; it was a place of blood,
 A heap of heartless walls;—the flames were dead
 Within those dwellings now,—the life had fled
From all those corpses now,—but the wide sky,
 Flooded with lightning, was ribbed overhead
By the black rafters, and around did lie
Women and babes and men slaughtered confusedly.

47

Beside the fountain in the market-place
 Dismounting, I beheld those corpses stare
With horny eyes upon each other's face,
 And on the earth, and on the vacant air,

And upon me, close to the waters where
    I stooped to slake my thirst.—I shrank to taste,
For the salt bitterness of blood was there;
But tied the steed beside, and sought in haste
If any yet survived amid that ghastly waste.

48

No living thing was there beside one woman
    Whom I found wandering in the streets, and she
Was withered from a likeness of aught human
    Into a fiend, by some strange misery.
Soon as she heard my steps, she leaped on me,
And glued her burning lips to mine, and laughed
With a loud, long, and frantic laugh of glee,
And cried, "Now, mortal, thou hast deeply quaffed
The Plague's blue kisses—soon millions shall pledge the draught!

49

"My name is Pestilence. This bosom dry
    Once fed two babes—a sister and a brother.
When I came home, one in the blood did lie
    Of three death-wounds—the flames had ate the other!
Since then I have no longer been a mother,
But I am Pestilence;—hither and thither
    I flit about, that I may slay and smother:—
All lips which I have kissed must surely wither,
But Death's—if thou art he, we'll go to work together!

*   *   *   *   *

CANTO XI

*   *   *   *   *

15

"Ye Princes of the Earth, ye sit aghast
    Amid the ruin which yourselves have made;
Yes, Desolation heard your trumpet's blast,
    And sprang from sleep,—dark Terror has obeyed

Your bidding. Oh that I, whom ye have made
Your foe, could set my dearest enemy free
　　From pain and fear! but evil casts a shade
Which cannot pass so soon, and Hate must be
The nurse and parent still of an ill progeny.

16

"Ye turn to Heaven for aid in your distress.
　　Alas! that ye, the mighty and the wise,
Who, if ye dared, might not aspire to less
　　Than ye conceive of power, should fear the lies
　　Which thou, and thou, didst frame for mysteries
To blind your slaves.—Consider your own thought.
　　An empty and a cruel sacrifice
Ye now prepare for a vain idol wrought
Out of the fears and hate which vain desires have brought.

17

"Ye seek for happiness—alas the day!
　　Ye find it not in luxury nor in gold,
Nor in the fame, nor in the envied sway,
　　For which, O willing slaves to Custom old
　　Severe task-mistress, ye your hearts have sold.
Ye seek for peace, and, when ye die, to dream
　　No evil dreams. All mortal things are cold
And senseless then: if aught survive, I deem
It must be love and joy, for they immortal seem.

18

"Fear not the future, weep not for the past.
　　Oh! could I win your ears, to dare be now
Glorious, and great, and calm! that ye would cast
　　Into the dust those symbols of your woe,
　　Purple, and gold, and steel! that ye would go
Proclaiming to the nations whence ye came
　　That Want and Plague and Fear from slavery flow;
And that mankind is free, and that the shame
Of royalty and faith is lost in freedom's fame!

*　　*　　*　　*　　*

22

"There is a People mighty in its youth,
    A land beyond the Oceans of the West,
    Where, though with rudest rites, Freedom and Truth
    Are worshipped. From a glorious Mother's breast,
    Who, since high Athens fell, among the rest
Sate like the Queen of Nations, but in woe,
    By inbred monsters outraged and oppressed,
    Turns to her chainless child for succour now,
It draws the milk of Power in Wisdom's fullest flow.

23

"That land is like an Eagle whose young gaze
    Feeds on the noontide beam, whose golden plume
Floats moveless on the storm, and in the blaze
    Of sunrise gleams when Earth is wrapped in gloom;
    An epitaph of glory for the tomb
Of murdered Europe may thy fame be made,
    Great People! as the sands shalt thou become;
    Thy growth is swift as morn when night must fade;
The multitudinous Earth shall sleep beneath thy shade.

24

"Yes, in the desert there is built a home,
    For Freedom. Genius is made strong to rear
The monuments of man beneath the dome
    Of a new Heaven; myriads assemble there,
    Whom the proud lords of man, in rage or fear,
Drive from their wasted homes: the boon I pray
    Is this—that Cythna shall be convoyed there—
Nay, start not at the name—America!
And then to you this night Laon will I betray.

25

"With me do what ye will. I am your foe!"
    The light of such a joy as makes the stare
Of hungry snakes like living emeralds glow
    Shone in a hundred human eyes.—"Where, where

Is Laon? Haste! fly! drag him swiftly here!
We grant thy boon."—"I put no trust in ye;
    Swear by the Power ye dread."—"We swear, we swear!"
The Stranger threw his vest back suddenly,
And smiled in gentle pride, and said, "Lo! I am he!"

CANTO XII

*   *   *   *   *

34

A scene of joy and wonder to behold—
    That river's shapes and shadows changing ever!
Where the broad sunrise filled with deepening gold
    Its whirlpools where all hues did spread and quiver,
    And where melodious falls did burst and shiver
Among rocks clad with flowers, the foam and spray
    Sparkled like stars upon the sunny river;
Or, when the moonlight poured a holier day,
One vast and glittering lake around green islands lay.

*   *   *   *   *

39

Steady and swift,—where the waves rolled like mountains
    Within the vast ravine whose rifts did pour
Tumultuous floods from their ten thousand fountains,
    The thunder of whose earth-uplifting roar
    Made the air sweep in whirlwinds from the shore,—
Calm as a shade, the boat of that fair child
    Securely fled that rapid stress before,
Amid the topmost spray, and sunbows wild
Wreathed in the silver mist: in joy and pride we smiled.

*   *   *   *   *

41

Motionless resting on the lake awhile,
      I saw its marge of snow-bright mountains rear
   Their peaks aloft; I saw each radiant isle;
      And in the midst, afar, even like a sphere
      Hung in one hollow sky, did there appear
   The Temple of the Spirit. On the sound
      Which issued thence drawn nearer and more near,
   Like the swift moon this glorious earth around,
The charmèd boat approached, and there its haven found.

1817

From

ROSALIND AND HELEN

A MODERN ECLOGUE

*   *   *   *   *

O'er this fair fountain hung the sky,
Now spangled with rare stars. The snake,
  The pale snake, that with eager breath
Creeps here his noontide thirst to slake,
    Is beaming with many a mingled hue
    Shed from yon dome's eternal blue,
    When he floats on that dark and lucid flood
In the light of his own loveliness;
And the birds that in the fountain dip
Their plumes, with fearless fellowship,
Above and round him wheel and hover.
  The fitful wind is heard to stir
One solitary leaf on high;
  The chirping of the grasshopper
Fills every pause. There is emotion
  In all that dwells at noontide here:
Then through the intricate wild wood
  A maze of life and light and motion
Is woven. But there is stillness now;
Gloom, and the trance of Nature now.
The snake is in his cave asleep;
The birds are on the branches dreaming:
    Only the shadows creep;
Only the glow-worm is gleaming;
Only the owls and the nightingales
Wake in this dell when daylight fails,

And gray shades gather in the woods;—
And the owls have all fled far away
In a merrier glen to hoot and play,
For the moon is veiled and sleeping now.
The accustomed nightingale still broods
      On her accustomed bough;
But she is mute, for her false mate
Has fled and left her desolate.

                *   *   *   *   *

He dwelt beside me near the sea;
   And oft in evening did we meet,
When the waves, beneath the starlight, flee
O'er the yellow sands with silver feet,—
And talked. Our talk was sad and sweet,
Till slowly from his mien there passed
   The desolation which it spoke;
And smiles—as, when the lightning's blast
   Has parched some heaven-delighting oak,
The next Spring shows leaves pale and rare,
But like flowers delicate and fair,
On its rent boughs—again arrayed
   His countenance in tender light.
His words grew subtle fire, which made
   The air his hearers breathed delight:
His motions, like the winds, were free,
Which bend the bright grass gracefully,
Then fade away in circlets faint:
And wingèd Hope—on which upborne
   His soul seemed hovering in his eyes,
Like some bright spirit newly born
   Floating amid the sunny skies—
Sprang forth from his rent heart anew.
   Yet o'er his talk and looks and mien,
   Tempering their loveliness too keen,
Past woe its shadow backward threw;
   Till, like an exhalation spread
From flowers half drunk with evening dew,

They did become infectious,—sweet
　And subtle mists of sense and thought;
Which wrapped us soon, when we might meet,
　Almost from our own looks, and aught
The wide world holds. And so his mind
　Was healed, while mine grew sick with fear
For ever now his health declined,
　Like some frail bark which cannot bear
The impulse of an altered wind,
Though prosperous. And my heart grew full,
　'Mid its new joy, of a new care:
　For his cheek became, not pale, but fair,
　As rose-o'ershadowed lilies are;
　And soon his deep and sunny hair,
In this alone less beautiful,
　Like grass in tomb, grew wild and rare.
The blood in his translucent veins
　Beat, not like animal life, but love
　Seemed now its sullen springs to move,
When life had failed, and all its pains;
And sudden sleep would seize him oft,
　Like death, so calm,—but that a tear,
　　His pointed eyelashes between,
　　Would gather in the light serene
Of smiles whose lustre bright and soft
　Beneath lay undulating there.
His breath was like inconstant flame,
As eagerly it went and came;
And I hung o'er him in his sleep,
　Till, like an image in the lake
　Which rains disturb, my tears would break
The shadow of that slumber deep.
Then he would bid me not to weep,
And say, with flattery false yet sweet,
That death and he could never meet,
If I would never part with him.
And so we loved, and did unite
　All that in us was yet divided:
For—when he said that many a rite,
　By men to bind but once provided,
　Could not be shared by him and me,
　Or they would kill him in their glee—

I shuddered, and then laughing said:
  "We will have rites our faith to bind;
But our church shall be the starry night,
  Our altar the grassy earth outspread,
    And our priest the muttering wind."

*   *   *   *   *

I stilled the tingling of my blood;
  And followed him in their despite,
As a widow follows, pale and wild,
The murderers and corse of her only child.
And, when we came to the prison door,
And I prayed to share his dungeon floor
With prayers which rarely have been spurned,
  And when men drove me forth, and I
  Stared with blank frenzy on the sky,—
A farewell look of love he turned,
Half calming me; then gazed awhile,
As if through that black and massy pile,
And through the crowd around him there,
And through the dense and murky air,
And the thronged streets, he did espy
What poets know and prophesy;
And said, with voice that made them shiver,
  And clung like music in my brain,
  And which the mute walls spoke again,
  Prolonging it with deepened strain—
"Fear not the tyrants shall rule for ever,
    Or the priests of the bloody faith;
They stand on the brink of that mighty river
    Whose waves they have tainted with death
It is fed from the depths of a thousand dells,
Around them it foams and rages and swells,
And their swords and their sceptres I floating see,
Like wrecks in the surge of eternity."

*   *   *   *   *

I know not how, but we were free.
And Lionel sate alone with me,
As the carriage drove through the streets apace;
And we looked upon each other's face;
And the blood in our fingers intertwined
Ran like the thoughts of a single mind,
As the swift emotions went and came
Through the veins of each united frame.
So through the long long streets we passed
Of the million-peopled city vast;
Which is that desert where each one
Seeks his mate, yet is alone,
Beloved and sought and mourned of none;—
  Until the clear blue sky was seen,
  And the grassy meadows bright and green.
  And then I sunk in his embrace,
  Enclosing there a mighty space
Of love. And so we travelled on
By woods, and fields of yellow flowers,
And towns and villages and towers,
Day after day of happy hours.
It was the azure time of June,
When the skies are deep in the stainless noon,
  And the warm and fitful breezes shake
   The fresh green leaves of the hedge-row briar;
  And there were odours then to make
   The very breath we did respire
A liquid element, whereon
Our spirits, like delighted things
That walk the air on subtle wings,
Floated and mingled far away,
'Mid the warm winds of the sunny day.
And, when the evening star came forth
  Above the curve of the new bent moon,
And light and sound ebbed from the earth,
Like the tide of the full and weary sea
To the depths of its own tranquillity,
Our natures to its own repose
  Did the earth's breathless sleep attune.
Like flowers which on each other close
  Their languid leaves when daylight's gone,
We lay; till new emotions came

Which seemed to make each mortal frame
One soul of interwoven flame,—
A life in life, a second birth
In worlds diviner far than earth—
Which, like two strains of harmony
That mingle in the silent sky,
Then slowly disunite, passed by,
And left the tenderness of tears,
A soft oblivion of all fears,
A sweet sleep.

*   *   *   *   *

1818

From

JULIAN AND MADDALO

A CONVERSATION

*　　*　　*　　*　　*

　　　　　　　　　　　Oh!
How beautiful is sunset, when the glow
Of Heaven descends upon a land like thee,
Thou Paradise of exiles, Italy,
Thy mountains, seas, and vineyards, and the towers
Of cities they encircle!—It was ours
To stand on thee, beholding it: and then,
Just where we had dismounted, the Count's men
Were waiting for us with the gondola.
As those who pause on some delightful way,
Though bent on pleasant pilgrimage, we stood
Looking upon the evening, and the flood
Which lay between the city and the shore,
Paved with the image of the sky. The hoar
And aëry Alps, towards the North, appeared
Through mist—an heaven-sustaining bulwark reared
Between the East and West; and half the sky
Was roofed with clouds of rich emblazonry,
Dark purple at the zenith, which still grew
Down the steep West into a wondrous hue
Brighter than burning gold, even to the rent
Where the swift sun yet paused in his descent
Among the many-folded hills. They were
Those famous Euganean hills, which bear,
As seen from Lido through the harbour piles,
The likeness of a clump of peakèd isles.
And then, as if the Earth and Sea had been
Dissolved into one lake of fire, were seen

Those mountains towering, as from waves of flame,
Around the vaporous sun; from which there came
The inmost purple spirit of light, and made
Their very peaks transparent.
                                                    "Ere it fade,"
Said my companion, "I will show you soon
A better station." So, o'er the lagune
We glided; and from that funereal bark
I leaned, and saw the city, and could mark
How from their many isles, in evening's gleam,
Its temples and its palaces did seem
Like fabrics of enchantment piled to Heaven.

                        *   *   *   *   *

                        Then we lingered not,
Although our argument was quite forgot;
But, calling the attendants, went to dine
At Maddalo's. Yet neither cheer nor wine
Could give us spirits; for we talked of him,
And nothing else, till daylight made stars dim.
And we agreed it was some dreadful ill
Wrought on him boldly, yet unspeakable,
By a dear friend; some deadly change in love
Of one vowed deeply which he dreamed not of,
For whose sake he, it seemed, had fixed a blot
Of falsehood in his mind, which flourished not
But in the light of all-beholding truth;
And, having stamped this canker on his youth,
She had abandoned him. And how much more
Might be his woe we guessed not. He had store
Of friends and fortune once, as we could guess
From his nice habits and his gentleness:
These were now lost—it were a grief indeed
If he had changed one unsustaining reed
For all that such a man might else adorn.
The colours of his mind seemed yet unworn;
For the wild language of his grief was high—
Such as in measure were called poetry.
And I remember one remark which then
Maddalo made: he said—"Most wretched men
Are cradled into poetry by wrong:
They learn in suffering what they teach in song."

If I had been an unconnected man,
I, from this moment, should have formed some plan
Never to leave sweet Venice. For to me
It was delight to ride by the lone sea:
And then the town is silent—one may write
Or read in gondolas, by day or night,
Having the little brazen lamp alight,
Unseen, uninterrupted. Books are there,
Pictures, and casts from all those statues fair
Which were twin-born with poetry, and all
We seek in towns, with little to recall
Regret for the green country. I might sit
In Maddalo's great palace, and his wit
And subtle talk would cheer the winter night,
And make me know myself: and the fire-light
Would flash upon our faces, till the day
Might dawn, and make me wonder at my stay.
But I had friends in London too. The chief
Attraction here was that I sought relief
From the deep tenderness that maniac wrought
Within me. . . . 'Twas perhaps an idle thought,
But I imagined that—if day by day
I watchèd him, and seldom went away,
And studied all the beatings of his heart
With zeal, as men study some stubborn art
For their own good, and could by patience find
An entrance to the caverns of his mind—
I might reclaim him from his dark estate.
In friendships I had been most fortunate;
Yet never saw I one whom I would call
More willingly my friend.—And this was all
Accomplished not. Such dreams of baseless good
Oft come and go, in crowds or solitude,
And leave no trace: but what I now designed
Made, for long years, impression on my mind.—
The following morning, urged by my affairs,
I left bright Venice.

After many years
And many changes, I returned. The name
Of Venice, and its aspect, was the same.
But Maddalo was travelling, far away,
Among the mountains of Armenia:

His dog was dead: his child had now become
A woman, such as it has been my doom
To meet with few; a wonder of this earth,
Where there is little of transcendent worth,—
Like one of Shakespeare's women. Kindly she,
And with a manner beyond courtesy,
Received her father's friend; and, when I asked
Of the lorn maniac, she her memory tasked,
And told, as she had heard, the mournful tale
That the poor sufferer's health began to fail
Two years from my departure; but that then
The lady who had left him came again.
"Her mien had been imperious, but she now
Looked meek; perhaps remorse had brought her low.
Her coming made him better; and they stayed
Together at my father's—for I played,
As I remember, with the lady's shawl;
I might be six years old—but, after all,
She left him." "Why, her heart must have been tough!
How did it end?" "And was not this enough?
They met, they parted." "Child, is there no more?"
"Something within that interval which bore
The stamp of *why* they parted, *how* they met.—
Yet, if thine agèd eyes disdain to wet
Those wrinkled cheeks with youth's remembered tears,
Ask me no more; but let the silent years
Be closed and cered over their memory,—
As yon mute marble where their corpses lie."
I urged and questioned still. She told me how
All happened—But the cold world shall not know.

1818–19

From

PROMETHEUS UNBOUND

A LYRICAL DRAMA, IN FOUR ACTS

ACT I

* * * * *

Phantasm of Jupiter.   Why have the secret powers of this strange world
    Driven me, a frail and empty phantom, hither
    On direst storms? What unaccustomed sounds
    Are hovering on my lips, unlike the voice
    With which our pallid race hold ghastly talk
    In darkness? And, proud sufferer, who art thou?
Prometheus.   Tremendous Image! as thou art must be
    He whom thou shadowest forth. I am his foe,
    The Titan. Speak the words which I would hear,
    Although no thought inform thine empty voice.
The Earth.   Listen! and, though your echoes must be mute,
    Gray mountains, and old woods, and haunted springs,
    Prophetic caves, and isle-surrounding streams,
    Rejoice to hear what yet ye cannot speak!
Phantasm.   A spirit seizes me and speaks within:
    It tears me as fire tears a thunder-cloud.
Panthea.   See how he lifts his mighty looks! the Heaven
    Darkens above!
Ione.   He speaks! Oh shelter me!
Prometheus.   I see the curse, on gestures proud and cold,
    And looks of firm defiance and calm hate,
    And such despair as mocks itself with smiles,
    Written as on a scroll. Yet speak! Oh speak!

PHANTASM

Fiend, I defy thee! with a calm fixed mind,
All that thou canst inflict I bid thee do;
Foul Tyrant both of Gods and Humankind,
  One only being shalt thou not subdue!
    Rain then thy plagues upon me here,
    Ghastly disease and frenzying fear;
    And let alternate frost and fire
      Eat into me, and be thine ire
  Lightning, and cutting hail, and legioned forms
Of Furies driving by upon the wounding storms.

    Ay, do thy worst! Thou art omnipotent.
    O'er all things but thyself I gave thee power,
And my own will. Be thy swift mischiefs sent
  To blast mankind from yon ethereal tower.
    Let thy malignant spirit move
    In darkness over those I love:
    On me and mine I imprecate
      The utmost torture of thy hate;
  And thus devote to sleepless agony
This undeclining head while thou must reign on high.

    But thou, who art the God and Lord! Oh thou
    Who fillest with thy soul this world of woe,
To whom all things of Earth and Heaven do bow
  In fear and worship, all-prevailing foe!
    I curse thee! Let a sufferer's curse
    Clasp thee, his torturer, like remorse!
    Till thine infinity shall be
      A robe of envenomed agony;
  And thine Omnipotence a crown of pain,
To cling like burning gold round thy dissolving brain!

    Heap on thy soul, by virtue of this Curse,
    Ill deeds,—then be thou damned, beholding good:
Both infinite as is the universe,
  And thou, and thy self-torturing solitude!
    An awful image of calm Power
    Though now thou sittest, let the hour
    Come when thou must appear to be
      That which thou art internally:
  And, after many a false and fruitless crime,
Scorn track thy lagging fall through boundless space and time!

Prometheus.   Were these my words, O Parent?
The Earth.   They were thine.
Prometheus.   It doth repent me: words are quick and vain:
    Grief for awhile is blind, and so was mine.
        I wish no living thing to suffer pain.
            The Earth.   Misery, oh misery to me,
            That Jove at length should vanquish thee!
            Wail, howl aloud, Land and Sea,—
            The Earth's rent heart shall answer ye!
        Howl, Spirits of the living and the dead!
    Your refuge, your defence, lies fallen and vanquishèd!

FIRST ECHO
Lies fallen and vanquishèd?

SECOND ECHO
Fallen and vanquishèd!

IONE
Fear not: 'tis but some passing spasm,—
    The Titan is unvanquished still.—
But see where through the azure chasm
    Of yon forked and snowy hill,
Trampling the slant winds on high
    With golden-sandalled feet that glow
Under plumes of purple dye
Like rose-ensanguined ivory,
        A Shape comes now,
    Stretching on high from his right hand
        A serpent-cinctured wand.

Panthea.   'Tis Jove's world-wandering herald, Mercury.

IONE
And who are those with hydra tresses
    And iron wings that climb the wind,
Whom the frowning God represses,—
    Like vapours steaming up behind,
Clanging loud, an endless crowd?

PANTHEA

These are Jove's tempest-walking hounds,
Whom he gluts with groans and blood
When, charioted on sulphurous cloud,
He bursts Heaven's bounds.

IONE

Are they now led from the thin dead,
On new pangs to be fed?

Panthea. The Titan looks, as ever, firm, not proud.
First Fury. Ha! I scent life!
Second Fury. Let me but look into his eyes!
Third Fury. The hope of torturing him smells like a heap
Of corpses to a death-bird after battle!
First Fury. Darest thou delay, O Herald! Take cheer, Hounds
Of Hell! What if the Son of Maia soon
Should make us food and sport?—Who can please long
The Omnipotent?
Mercury. Back to your towers of iron,
And gnash, beside the streams of fire and wail,
Your foodless teeth!—Geryon, arise! and Gorgon,
Chimaera, and thou Sphinx, subtlest of fiends,
Who ministered to Thebes Heaven's poisoned wine—
Unnatural love, and more unnatural hate!—
These shall perform your task.
First Fury. Oh! mercy! mercy!
We die with our desire: drive us not back!
Mercury. Crouch then in silence.
Awful Sufferer!
To thee unwilling, most unwillingly
I come, by the great Father's will driven down,
To execute a doom of new revenge.
Alas! I pity thee, and hate myself
That I can do no more. Aye from thy sight
Returning, for a season Heaven seems Hell,
So thy worn form pursues me night and day,
Smiling reproach. Wise art thou, firm, and good,
But vainly wouldst stand forth alone in strife
Against the Omnipotent; as yon clear lamps
That measure and divide the weary years,
From which there is no refuge, long have taught,
And long must teach. Even now thy Torturer arms

With the strange might of unimagined pains
The powers who scheme slow agonies in Hell;
And my commission is to lead them here,
Or what more subtle, foul, or savage fiends
People the abyss, and leave them to their task.
Be it not so! There is a secret known
To thee, and to none else of living things,
Which may transfer the sceptre of wide Heaven,
The fear of which perplexes the Supreme;—
Clothe it in words, and bid it clasp his throne
In intercession; bend thy soul in prayer,
And, like a suppliant in some gorgeous fane,
Let the will kneel within thy haughty heart:
For benefits and meek submission tame
The fiercest and the mightiest.

Prometheus.   Evil minds
Change good to their own nature. I gave all
He has; and in return he chains me here,
Years, ages, night and day; whether the sun
Split my parched skin, or in the moony night
The crystal-wingèd snow cling round my hair;
Whilst my belovèd race is trampled down
By his thought-executing ministers.
Such is the tyrant's recompense. 'Tis just:
He who is evil can receive no good
And for a world bestowed or a friend lost
He can feel hate, fear, shame; not gratitude.
He but requites me for his own misdeed.
Kindness to such is keen reproach, which breaks
With bitter stings the light sleep of Revenge.
Submission thou dost know I cannot try;
For what submission but that fatal word,
The death-seal of mankind's captivity,
Like the Sicilian's hair-suspended sword
Which trembles o'er his crown, would he accept,
Or could I yield? Which yet I will not yield.
Let others flatter Crime where it sits throned
In brief Omnipotence! Secure are they:
For Justice, when triumphant, will weep down
Pity, not punishment, on her own wrongs,
Too much avenged by those who err. I wait,
Enduring thus, the retributive hour
Which since we spake is even nearer now.

But hark, the hell-hounds clamour. Fear delay!
Behold! Heaven lowers under thy Father's frown!
Mercury.   Oh that we might be spared—I to inflict,
And thou to suffer! Once more answer me:
Thou knowest not the period of Jove's power?
Prometheus.   I know but this, that it must come.
Mercury.   Alas!
Thou canst not count thy years to come of pain!
Prometheus.   They last while Jove must reign; nor more nor less
Do I desire or fear.
Mercury.   Yet pause, and plunge
Into Eternity, where recorded time—
Even all that we imagine, age on age—
Seems but a point, and the reluctant mind
Flags wearily in its unending flight,
Till it sink, dizzy, blind, lost, shelterless.
Perchance it has not numbered the slow years
Which thou must spend in torture, unreprieved?
Prometheus.   Perchance no thought can count them. Yet they pass.
Mercury.   If thou mightst dwell among the Gods the while,
Lapped in voluptuous joy?
Prometheus.   I would not quit
This bleak ravine, these unrepentant pains.
Mercury.   Alas! I wonder at, yet pity thee.
Prometheus.   Pity the self-despising slaves of Heaven,—
Not me, within whose mind sits peace serene,
As light in the sun, throned. How vain is talk!
Call up the fiends.
Ione.   O sister, look! White fire
Has cloven to the roots yon huge snow-loaded cedar!
How fearfully God's thunder howls behind!
Mercury.   I must obey his words and thine: alas!
Most heavily remorse hangs at my heart!
Panthea.   See where the child of Heaven, with wingèd feet,
Runs down the slanted sunlight of the dawn.

* * * * *

SEMICHORUS I

Drops of bloody agony flow
From his white and quivering brow.
Grant a little respite now.
See! a disenchanted nation
Springs like day from desolation;

To Truth its state is dedicate,
And Freedom leads it forth, her mate;—
A legioned band of linkèd brothers,
Whom Love calls children—

SEMICHORUS II

       'Tis another's!
See how kindred murder kin!
'Tis the vintage-time for Death and Sin.
Blood, like new wine, bubbles within:
  Till Despair smothers
The struggling world, which slaves and tyrants win.

Ione. Hark, sister! what a low yet dreadful groan,
 Quite unsuppressed, is tearing up the heart
 Of the good Titan, as storms tear the deep,
 And beasts hear the sea moan in inland caves!
 Darest thou observe how the fiends torture him?
Panthea. Alas! I looked forth twice, but will no more.
Ione. What didst thou see?
Panthea.   A woful sight: a youth
 With patient looks nailed to a crucifix.
Ione. What next?
Panthea.   The heaven around, the earth below,
 Was peopled with thick shapes of human death,
 All horrible, and wrought by human hands:
 And some appeared the work of human hearts,
 For men were slowly killed by frowns and smiles.
 And other sights too foul to speak and live
 Were wandering by. Let us not tempt worse fear
 By looking forth: those groans are grief enough.
Fury. Behold an emblem: those who do endure
 Deep wrongs for man, and scorn, and chains, but heap
 Thousandfold torment on themselves and him.
Prometheus. Remit the anguish of that lighted stare;
 Close those wan lips; let that thorn-wounded brow
 Stream not with blood; it mingles with thy tears!
 Fix, fix those tortured orbs in peace and death,—
 So thy sick throes shake not that crucifix,
 So those pale fingers play not with thy gore!
 Oh horrible! Thy name I will not speak,
 It hath become a curse! I see, I see
 The wise, the mild, the lofty, and the just,
 Whom thy slaves hate for being like to thee,

Some hunted by foul lies from their heart's home,
An early-chosen, late-lamented home,—
As hooded ounces cling to the driven hind;
Some linked to corpses in unwholesome cells;
Some—hear I not the multitude laugh loud?—
Impaled in lingering fire: and mighty realms
Float by my feet, like sea-uprooted isles,
Whose sons are kneaded down in common blood
By the red light of their own burning homes.
Fury. Blood thou canst see, and fire: and canst hear groans:—
Worse things, unheard, unseen, remain behind.
Prometheus. Worse?
Fury.   In each human heart terror survives
The ravin it has gorged. The loftiest fear
All that they would disdain to think were true:
Hypocrisy and Custom make their minds
The fanes of many a worship now outworn.
They dare not devise good for man's estate,
And yet they know not that they do not dare.
The good want power but to weep barren tears;
The powerful goodness want,—worse need for them:
The wise want love: and those who love want wisdom:
And all best things are thus confused to ill.
Many are strong and rich, and would be just,
But live among their suffering fellow-men
As if none felt: they know not what they do.
Prometheus. Thy words are like a cloud of wingèd snakes;
And yet I pity those they torture not.
Fury. Thou pitiest them? I speak no more!   [*Vanishes.*
Prometheus.   Ah woe!
Ah woe! Alas! pain, pain, ever, for ever!
I close my tearless eyes, but see more clear
Thy works within my woe-illumèd mind,
Thou subtle tyrant! Peace is in the grave:
The grave hides all things beautiful and good.
I am a God, and cannot find it there,
Nor would I seek it: for, though dread revenge,
This is defeat, fierce king! not victory.
The sights with which thou torturest gird my soul
With new endurance, till the hour arrives
When they shall be no types of things which are.
Panthea. Alas! what sawest thou?
Prometheus.   There are two woes:
To speak, and to behold:—thou spare me one.

Names are there, Nature's sacred watchwords: they
Were borne aloft in bright emblazonry;
The nations thronged around, and cried aloud,
As with one voice, Truth, Liberty, and Love!
Suddenly fierce confusion fell from heaven
Among them: there was strife, deceit, and fear:
Tyrants rushed in, and did divide the spoil.
This was the shadow of the truth I saw.

The Earth.   I felt thy torture, son, with such mixed joy
As pain and virtue give. To cheer thy state,
I bid ascend those subtle and fair Spirits
Whose homes are the dim caves of human thought,
And who inhabit, as birds wing the wind,
Its world-surrounding ether. They behold
Beyond that twilight realm, as in a glass,
The future: may they speak comfort to thee!

* * * * *

ACT II

Scene I—*Morning. A lovely Vale in the Indian Caucasus.*

asia, *alone.*

Asia.   From all the blasts of heaven thou hast descended!
Yes, like a spirit, like a thought which makes
Unwonted tears throng to the horny eyes,
And beatings haunt the desolated heart
Which should have learnt repose, thou hast descended,
Cradled in tempests; thou dost wake, O Spring!
O child of many winds! As suddenly
Thou comest as the memory of a dream
Which now is sad because it hath been sweet;
Like genius, or like joy, which riseth up
As from the earth, clothing with golden clouds
The desert of our life.—
This is the season, this the day, the hour;
At sunrise thou shouldst come, sweet Sister mine;
Too long desired, too long delaying, come!
How like death-worms the wingless moments crawl!
The point of one white star is quivering still
Deep in the orange light of widening morn
Beyond the purple mountains: through a chasm

Of wind-divided mist the darker lake
Reflects it. Now it wanes: it gleams again
As the waves fade, and as the burning threads
Of woven cloud unravel in pale air.
'Tis lost! and through yon peaks of cloud-like snow
The roseate sunlight quivers. Hear I not
The Aeolian music of her sea-green plumes
Winnowing the crimson dawn?

Enter PANTHEA.
                        I feel, I see,
Those eyes which burn through smiles that fade in tears,
Like stars half-quenched in mists of silver dew.
Belovèd and most beautiful, who wearest
The shadow of that soul by which I live,
How late thou art! the spherèd sun had climbed
The sea; my heart was sick with hope, before
The printless air felt thy belated plumes.
Panthea.   Pardon, great Sister! but my wings were faint
With the delight of a remembered dream,
As are the noontide plumes of summer winds
Satiate with sweet flowers. I was wont to sleep
Peacefully, and awake refreshed and calm,
Before the sacred Titan's fall, and thy
Unhappy love, had made, through use and pity,
Both love and woe familiar to my heart,
As they had grown to thine. Erewhile I slept
Under the glaucous caverns of old Ocean
Within dim bowers of green and purple moss,—
Our young Ione's soft and milky arms
Locked then, as now, behind my dark moist hair,
While my shut eyes and cheek were pressed within
The folded depth of her life-breathing bosom:
But not as now,—since I am made the wind
Which fails beneath the music that I bear
Of thy most wordless converse; since, dissolved
Into the sense with which love talks, my rest
Was troubled and yet sweet, my waking hours
Too full of care and pain.
Asia.   Lift up thine eyes,
And let me read thy dream.
Panthea.   As I have said,
With our Sea-sister at his feet I slept.
The mountain mists, condensing at our voice

Under the moon, had spread their snowy flakes,
From the keen ice shielding our linkèd sleep.
Then two dreams came. One I remember not.
But in the other his pale wound-worn limbs
Fell from Prometheus; and the azure night
Grew radiant with the glory of that form
Which lives unchanged within; and his voice fell
Like music which makes giddy the dim brain,
Faint with intoxication of keen joy:
"Sister of her whose footsteps pave the world
With loveliness—more fair than aught but her,
Whose shadow thou art—lift thine eyes on me."
I lifted them. The overpowering light
Of that immortal shape was shadowed o'er
By love; which from his soft and flowing limbs,
And passion-parted lips, and keen faint eyes,
Steamed forth like vaporous fire; an atmosphere
Which wrapped me in its all-dissolving power,
As the warm ether of the morning sun
Wraps ere it drinks some cloud of wandering dew.
I saw not, heard not, moved not; only felt
His presence flow and mingle through my blood,
Till it became his life, and his grew mine.
And I was thus absorbed,—until it passed;
And, like the vapours, when the sun sinks down,
Gathering again in drops upon the pines,
And tremulous as they, in the deep night
My being was condensed; and, as the rays
Of thought were slowly gathered, I could hear
His voice, whose accents lingered ere they died
Like footsteps of weak melody. Thy name,
Among the many sounds, alone I heard,
Of what might be articulate; though still
I listened through the night when sound was none.
Ione wakened then, and said to me:
"Canst thou divine what troubles me to-night?
I always knew what I desired before,
Nor ever found delight to wish in vain.
But now I cannot tell thee what I seek:
I know not; something sweet, since it is sweet
Even to desire. It is thy sport, false sister;
Thou hast discovered some enchantment old,
Whose spells have stolen my spirit as I slept,
And mingled it with thine: for, when just now

We kissed, I felt within thy parted lips
The sweet air that sustained me, and the warmth
Of the life-blood, for loss of which I faint,
Quivered between our intertwining arms."
I answered not, for the Eastern star grew pale,
But fled to thee.
Asia.   Thou speakest, but thy words
Are as the air: I feel them not. Oh! lift
Thine eyes, that I may read his written soul!
Panthea.   I lift them, though they droop beneath the load
Of that they would express: what canst thou see
But thine own fairest shadow imaged there?
Asia.   Thine eyes are like the deep, blue, boundless heaven
Contracted to two circles underneath
Their long fine lashes; dark, far, measureless,
Orb within orb and line through line inwoven.
Panthea.   Why lookest thou as if a spirit passed?
Asia.   There is a change; beyond their inmost depth
I see a shade, a shape: 'tis He, arrayed
In the soft light of his own smiles, which spread
Like radiance from the cloud-surrounded moon!
Prometheus, it is thine! Depart not yet!
Say not those smiles that we shall meet again
Within that bright pavilion which their beams
Shall build on the waste world? The dream is told! . . .
What shape is that between us? Its rude hair
Roughens the wind that lifts it, its regard
Is wild and quick; yet 'tis a thing of air,
For through its grey robe gleams the golden dew
Whose stars the noon has quenched not.
Dream.   Follow! Follow!
Panthea.   It is mine other dream.
Asia.   It disappears.
Panthea.   It passes now into my mind. Methought,
As we sate here, the flower-enfolding buds
Burst on yon lightning-blasted almond tree,
When swift from the white Scythian wilderness
A wind swept forth wrinkling the Earth with frost.
I looked, and all the blossoms were blown down;
But on each leaf was stamped, as the blue bells
Of Hyacinth tell Apollo's written grief,
OH FOLLOW, FOLLOW!
Asia.   As you speak, your words
Fill, pause by pause, my own forgotten sleep

With shapes. Methought among the lawns together
We wandered, underneath the young grey dawn,
And multitudes of dense white fleecy clouds
Were wandering in thick flocks along the mountains,
Shepherded by the slow unwilling wind;
And the white dew on the new-bladed grass,
Just piercing the dark earth, hung silently.
And there was more which I remember not:
But on the shadows of the morning clouds,
Athwart the purple mountain slope, was written
FOLLOW, OH FOLLOW! as they vanished by;
And on each herb, from which Heaven's dew had fallen,
The like was stamped as with a withering fire;
A wind arose among the pines; it shook
The clinging music from their boughs, and then
Low, sweet, faint sounds, like the farewell of ghosts,
Were heard: OH FOLLOW, FOLLOW, FOLLOW ME!
And then I said, "Panthea, look on me."
But in the depth of those belovèd eyes
Still I saw FOLLOW, FOLLOW!

Echo.   Follow, follow!
Panthea.   The crags, this clear spring morning, mock our voices,
As they were spirit-tongued.
Asia.   It is some being
Around the crags. What fine clear sounds! Oh list!

ECHOES (*unseen*)
Echoes we! Listen!
We cannot stay:
As dew-stars glisten,
Then fade away—
Child of Ocean!

Asia.   Hark! Spirits speak! The liquid responses
Of their aërial tongues yet sound.
Panthea.   I hear.

ECHOES
Oh follow, follow!
As our voice recedeth,
Through the caverns hollow—
Where the forest spreadeth—

(*More distant.*)
Oh follow, follow,
Through the caverns hollow.
As the song floats thou pursue,
Where the wild bee never flew;
Through the noontide darkness deep,
By the odour-breathing sleep
Of faint night-flowers, and the waves
At the fountain-lighted caves;
While our music wild and sweet
Mocks thy gently falling feet,
Child of Ocean!

Asia. Shall we pursue the sound? It grows more faint
And distant.
Panthea. List! the strain floats nearer now.

ECHOES
In the world unknown
Sleeps a voice unspoken;
By thy step alone
Can its rest be broken,
Child of Ocean!

Asia. How the notes sink upon the ebbing wind!

ECHOES
Oh follow, follow,
Through the caverns hollow!
As the song floats thou pursue;
By the woodland noontide dew,
By the forests, lakes, and fountains,
Through the many-folded mountains,—
To the rents, and gulfs, and chasms,
Where the Earth reposed from spasms
On the day when He and Thou
Parted, to commingle now;
Child of Ocean!

Asia. Come, sweet Panthea, link thy hand in mine,
And follow, ere the voices fade away.

SCENE II—*A Forest, intermingled with Rocks and Caverns.* ASIA *and* PANTHEA *pass into it. Two young Fauns are sitting on a Rock, listening.*

SEMICHORUS I OF SPIRITS

The path through which that lovely twain
  Have passed, by cedar, pine, and yew,
  And each dark tree that ever grew,
  Is curtained out from Heaven's wide blue.
Nor sun nor moon nor wind nor rain
Can pierce its interwoven bowers;
    Nor aught save where some cloud of dew,
      Drifted along the earth-creeping breeze
      Between the trunks of the hoar trees,
Hangs each a pearl in the pale flowers
  Of the green laurel blown anew,
And bends, and then fades silently,
One frail and fair anemone.
Or, when some star, of many a one
  That climbs and wanders through steep night,
Has found the cleft through which alone
Beams fall from high those depths upon,—
Ere it is borne away, away,
By the swift Heavens that cannot stay,—
  It scatters drops of golden light,
  Like lines of rain that ne'er unite:
And the gloom divine is all around,
And underneath is the mossy ground.

SEMICHORUS II

There the voluptuous nightingales
  Are awake through all the broad noonday.
When one with bliss or sadness fails,
And through the windless ivy-boughs,
  Sick with sweet love, droops dying away
  On its mate's music-panting bosom;
  Another, from the swinging blossom
Watching to catch the languid close
Of the last strain, then lifts on high
The wings of the weak melody,—

Till some new strain of feeling bear
The song, and all the woods are mute;
When there is heard through the dim air
The rush of wings, and, rising there
　Like many a lake-surrounded flute,
Sounds overflow the listener's brain
So sweet that joy is almost pain.

SEMICHORUS I

There those enchanted eddies play
　Of Echoes music-tongued which draw,
　By Demogorgon's mighty law,
　With melting rapture or sweet awe,
All spirits on that secret way;
As inland boats are driven to Ocean
　Down streams made strong with mountain-thaw.
　　And first there comes a gentle sound
　　To those in talk or slumber bound,
And wakes the destined, soft emotion
　Attracts, impels them. Those who saw
Say from the breathing earth behind
There steams a plume-uplifting wind
Which drives them on their path, while they
　Believe their own swift wings and feet
The sweet desires within obey.
And so they float upon their way,
Until, still sweet but loud and strong,
The storm of sound is driven along,
　Sucked up and hurrying: as they fleet
　Behind, its gathering billows meet,
And to the fatal mountain bear
Like clouds amid the yielding air.

First Faun.　Canst thou imagine where those spirits live
　Which make such delicate music in the woods?
　We haunt within the least frequented caves
　And closest coverts, and we know these wilds,
　Yet never meet them, though we hear them oft:
　Where may they hide themselves?
Second Faun.　　　　　　　　　　　'Tis hard to tell.
　I have heard those more skilled in spirits say,
　The bubbles, which the enchantment of the sun
　Sucks from the pale faint water-flowers that pave
　The oozy bottom of clear lakes and pools,

Are the pavilions where such dwell and float
Under the green and golden atmosphere
Which noontide kindles through the woven leaves;
And, when these burst, and the thin fiery air,
The which they breathed within those lucent domes,
Ascends to flow like meteors through the night,
They ride on them, and rein their headlong speed,
And bow their burning crests, and glide in fire
Under the waters of the earth again.

First Faun.   If such live thus, have others other lives,
Under pink blossoms, or within the bells
Of meadow flowers or folded violets deep,
Or on their dying odours when they die,
Or in the sunlight of the spherèd dew?

Second Faun.   Ay, many more which we may well divine.—
But, should we stay to speak, noontide would come,
And thwart Silenus find his goats undrawn,
And grudge to sing those wise and lovely songs
Of Fate, and Chance, and God, and Chaos old,
And Love and the chained Titan's woful doom,
And how he shall be loosed, and make the earth
One brotherhood: delightful strains which cheer
Our solitary twilights, and which charm
To silence the unenvying nightingales.

*   *   *   *   *

Scene V

*   *   *   *   *

voice *in the air, singing.*
Life of Life! thy lips enkindle
    With their love the breath between them;
And thy smiles, before they dwindle,
    Make the cold air fire,—then screen them
In those looks where whoso gazes
Faints, entangled in their mazes.

Child of Light! thy limbs are burning
    Through the vest which seems to hide them,
As the radiant lines of morning

Through the clouds, ere they divide them;
And this atmosphere divinest
Shrouds thee wheresoe'er thou shinest.

Fair are others; none beholds thee.
  But thy voice sounds low and tender,
Like the fairest, for it folds thee
  From the sight, that liquid splendour,—
And all feel yet see thee never,
As I feel now, lost for ever!

Lamp of Earth! where'er thou movest,
  Its dim shapes are clad with brightness,
And the souls of whom thou lovest
  Walk upon the winds with lightness,
Till they fail, as I am failing,
Dizzy, lost, yet unbewailing!

ASIA

  My soul is an enchanted boat,
  Which, like a sleeping swan, doth float
Upon the silver waves of thy sweet singing
  And thine doth like an angel sit
  Beside the helm conducting it,
Whilst all the winds with melody are ringing.
  It seems to float ever, for ever,
  Upon that many-winding river,
  Between mountains, woods, abysses,
  A paradise of wildernesses!
  Till, like one in slumber bound
Borne to the ocean, I float down, around,
Into a sea profound of ever-spreading sound.

  Meanwhile thy spirit lifts its pinions
  In music's most serene dominions,
Catching the winds that fan that happy heaven.
  And we sail on, away, afar,
  Without a course, without a star,
But by the instinct of sweet music driven;
  Till through Elysian garden islets,
  By thee, most beautiful of pilots,
  Where never mortal pinnace glided,
  The boat of my desire is guided:

Realms where the air we breathe is love,
Which in the winds and on the waves doth move,
Harmonizing this earth with what we feel above.

We have passed Age's icy caves,
And Manhood's dark and tossing waves,
And Youth's smooth ocean, smiling to betray:
Beyond the glassy gulfs we flee
Of shadow-peopled Infancy,
Through Death and Birth, to a diviner day:—
A paradise of vaulted bowers
Lit by downward-gazing flowers,
And watery paths that wind between
Wildernesses calm and green,
Peopled by shapes too bright to see,
And rest, having beheld,—somewhat like thee,—
Which walk upon the sea, and chant melodiously!

ACT III   Scene III

*   *   *   *   *

Asia.   O mother! wherefore speak the name of death?
Cease they to love and move and breathe and speak
Who die?
The Earth.   It would avail not to reply:
Thou art immortal, and this tongue is known
But to the uncommunicating dead.
Death is the veil which those who live call life:
They sleep, and it is lifted. And meanwhile
In mild variety the seasons mild,
With rainbow-skirted showers, and odorous winds,
And long blue meteors cleansing the dull night,
And the life-kindling shafts of the keen sun's
All-piercing bow, and the dew-mingled rain
Of the calm moonbeams, a soft influence mild,
Shall clothe the forests and the fields—ay, even
The crag-built deserts of the barren deep—
With ever-living leaves and fruits and flowers.—
And thou! There is a cavern where my spirit

Was panted forth in anguish whilst thy pain
Made my heart mad. And those that did inhale it
Became mad too; and built a temple there,
And spoke, and were oracular, and lured
The erring nations round to mutual war,
And faithless faith, such as Jove kept with thee.
Which breath now rises, as amongst tall weeds
A violet's exhalation; and it fills
With a serener light and crimson air,
Intense yet soft, the rocks and woods around.
It feeds the quick growth of the serpent vine;
And the dark linkèd ivy tangling wild;
And budding, blown, or odour-faded blooms
Which star the winds with points of coloured light,
As they rain through them; and bright golden globes
Of fruit, suspended in their own green heaven;
And, through their veinèd leaves and amber stems,
The flowers whose purple and translucid bowls
Stand ever mantling with aërial dew,
The drink of spirits. And it circles round,
Like the soft waving wings of noonday dreams,
Inspiring calm and happy thoughts—like mine,
Now thou art thus restored. This cave is thine.
Arise! Appear!
                    [A SPIRIT *rises in the likeness of a winged child.*
                    This is my torch-bearer;
Who let his lamp out in old time with gazing
On eyes from which he kindled it anew
With love, which is as fire, sweet daughter mine,—
For such is that within thine own.—Run, wayward,
And guide this company beyond the peak
Of Bacchic Nysa, Maenad-haunted mountain,
And beyond Indus and its tribute rivers,
Trampling the torrent streams and glassy lakes
With feet unwet, unwearied, undelaying;
And up the green ravine, across the vale,
Beside the windless and crystalline pool
Where ever lies on unerasing waves
The image of a temple built above,
Distinct with column, arch, and architrave,
And palm-like capital, and over-wrought
And populous most with living imagery,—
Praxitelean shapes whose marble smiles
Fill the hushed air with everlasting love.

It is deserted now; but once it bore
Thy name, Prometheus. There the emulous youths
Bore to thy honour through the divine gloom
The lamp which was thine emblem; even as those
Who bear the untransmitted torch of hope
Into the grave across the night of life,—
As thou hast borne it most triumphantly
To this far goal of time. Depart, farewell.
Beside that temple is the destined cave.

*   *   *   *   *

ACT IV

*   *   *   *   *

Panthea. But see where, through two openings in the forest
    Which hanging branches overcanopy,
    And where two runnels of a rivulet
    Between the close moss, violet-inwoven,
    Have made their path of melody, like sisters
    Who part with sighs that they may meet in smiles,
    Turning their dear disunion to an isle
    Of lovely grief, a wood of sweet sad thoughts;
    Two visions of strange radiance float upon
    The ocean-like enchantment of strong sound,
    Which flows intenser, keener, deeper yet,
    Under the ground and through the windless air.
Ione. I see a chariot like that thinnest boat
    In which the Mother of the Months is borne
    By ebbing night into her western cave,
    When she upsprings from interlunar dreams;
    O'er which is curved an orblike canopy
    Of gentle darkness, and the hills and woods,
    Distinctly seen through that dusk airy veil,
    Regard like shapes in an enchanter's glass.
    Its wheels are solid clouds, azure and gold,
    Such as the genii of the thunder-storm
    Pile on the floor of the illumined sea
    When the sun rushes under it; they roll
    And move and grow as with an inward wind;
    Within it sits a wingèd infant—white

Its countenance, like the whiteness of bright snow,
Its plumes are as feathers of sunny frost,
Its limbs gleam white through the wind-flowing folds
Of its white robe, woof of ethereal pearl.
Its hair is white, the brightness of white light
Scattered in strings; yet its two eyes are heavens
Of liquid darkness, which the deity
Within seems pouring, as a storm is poured
From jagged clouds, out of their arrowy lashes,
Tempering the cold and radiant air around
With fire that is not brightness. In its hand
It sways a quivering moonbeam, from whose point
A guiding power directs the chariot's prow
Over its wheelèd clouds; which, as they roll
Over the grass and flowers and waves, wake sounds
Sweet as a singing rain of silver dew.
Panthea.   And from the other opening in the wood
Rushes, with loud and whirlwind harmony,
A sphere which is as many thousand spheres,—
Solid as crystal, yet through all its mass
Flow, as through empty space, music and light:
Ten thousand orbs involving and involved,
Purple and azure, white and green and golden,
Sphere within sphere; and every space between
Peopled with unimaginable shapes,
Such as ghosts dream dwell in the lampless deep,
Yet each inter-transpicuous. And they whirl
Over each other with a thousand motions,
Upon a thousand sightless axles spinning;
And, with the force of self-destroying swiftness,
Intensely, slowly, solemnly, roll on,
Kindling with mingled sounds and many tones
Intelligible words and music wild.
With mighty whirl the multitudinous orb
Grinds the bright brook into an azure mist
Of elemental subtlety, like light;
And the wild odour of the forest flowers,
The music of the living grass and air,
The emerald light of leaf-entangled beams,
Round its intense yet self-conflicting speed
Seem kneaded into one aërial mass
Which drowns the sense. Within the orb itself,
Pillowed upon its alabaster arms,

Like to a child o'er wearied with sweet toil,
On its own folded wings and wavy hair
The Spirit of the Earth is laid asleep;
And you can see its little lips are moving,
Amid the changing light of their own smiles,
Like one who talks of what he loves in dream.

* * * * *

DEMOGORGON

* * * * *

To suffer woes which Hope thinks infinite;
To forgive wrongs darker than death or night;
   To defy Power which seems omnipotent;
To love, and bear; to hope till Hope creates
From its own wreck the thing it contemplates;
   Neither to change, nor falter, nor repent;
This, like thy glory, Titan, is to be
Good, great, and joyous, beautiful and free;
This is alone Life, Joy, Empire, and Victory!

1818–19

From

THE WITCH OF ATLAS

*   *   *   *   *

5

A lovely Lady garmented in light
   From her own beauty: deep her eyes as are
Two openings of unfathomable night
   Seen through a tempest's cloven roof; her hair
Dark; the dim brain whirls dizzy with delight,
   Picturing her form. Her soft smiles shone afar;
And her low voice was heard like love, and drew
All living things towards this wonder new.

6

And first the spotted camelopard came;
   And then the wise and fearless elephant;
Then the sly serpent, in the golden flame
   Of his own volumes intervolved. All gaunt
And sanguine beasts her gentle looks made tame,—
   They drank before her at her sacred fount;
And every beast of beating heart grew bold,
Such gentleness and power even to behold.

7

The brinded lioness led forth her young,
   That she might teach them how they should forego

Their inborn thirst of death; the pard unstrung
  His sinews at her feet, and sought to know,
With looks whose motions spoke without a tongue,
  How he might be as gentle as the doe.
The magic circle of her voice and eyes
All savage natures did imparadise.

8

And old Silenus, shaking a green stick
  Of lilies, and the Wood-gods in a crew,
Came blithe as in the olive copses thick
  Cicadae are, drunk with the noonday dew;
And Dryope and Faunus followed quick,
  Teasing the God to sing them something new;
Till in this cave they found the Lady lone,
Sitting upon a seat of emerald stone.

9

And universal Pan, 'tis said, was there.
  And, though none saw him,—through the adamant
Of the deep mountains, through the trackless air,
  And through those living spirits, like a want,—
He passed out of his everlasting lair
  Where the quick heart of the great world doth pant,
And felt that wondrous Lady all alone,—
And she felt him upon her emerald throne.

*   *   *   *   *

14

The deep recesses of her odorous dwelling
  Were stored with magic treasures:—sounds of air
Which had the power all spirits of compelling,
  Folded in cells of crystal silence there;
Such as we hear in youth, and think the feeling
  Will never die—yet, ere we are aware,
The feeling and the sound are fled and gone,
And the regret they leave remains alone.

*   *   *   *   *

28

This Lady never slept, but lay in trance
  All night within the fountain—as in sleep.
Its emerald crags glowed in her beauty's glance:
  Through the green splendour of the water deep
She saw the constellations reel and dance
  Like fireflies—and withal did ever keep
The tenour of her contemplations calm,
With open eyes, closed feet, and folded palm.

*   *   *   *   *

39

The silver noon into that winding dell,
  With slanted gleam athwart the forest tops,
Tempered like golden evening, feebly fell;
  A green and glowing light, like that which drops
From folded lilies in which glow-worms dwell,
  When Earth over her face Night's mantle wraps;
Between the severed mountains lay on high,
Over the stream, a narrow rift of sky.

*   *   *   *   *

43

And, when the Wizard Lady would ascend
  The labyrinths of some many-winding vale
Which to the inmost mountain upward tend,
  She called "Hermaphroditus!"—and the pale
And heavy hue which slumber could extend
  Over its lips and eyes, as on the gale
A rapid shadow from a slope of grass,
Into the darkness of the stream did pass.

44

And it unfurled its heaven-coloured pinions;
   With stars of fire spotting the stream below,
And from above into the Sun's dominions
   Flinging a glory like the golden glow
In which Spring clothes her emerald-wingèd minions,
   All interwoven with fine feathery snow,
And moonlight splendour of intensest rime
With which frost paints the pines in winter time.

45

And then it winnowed the Elysian air
   Which ever hung about that Lady bright,
With its ethereal vans: and, speeding there,
   Like a star up the torrent of the night,
Or a swift eagle in the morning glare
   Breasting the whirlwind with impetuous flight,
The pinnace, oared by those enchanted wings,
Clove the fierce streams towards their upper springs.

*   *   *   *   *

54

And on a throne o'erlaid with starlight, caught
   Upon those wandering isles of aëry dew
Which highest shoals of mountain shipwreck not,
   She sate, and heard all that had happened new
Between the earth and moon since they had brought
   The last intelligence: and now she grew
Pale as that moon lost in the watery night,
And now she wept, and now she laughed outright.

55

These were tame pleasures.—She would often climb
   The steepest ladder of the crudded rack
Up to some beakèd cape of cloud sublime,
   And like Arion on the dolphin's back

Ride singing through the shoreless air. Oft-time,
    Following the serpent lightning's winding track,
She ran upon the platforms of the wind,
And laughed to hear the fireballs roar behind.

56

And sometimes to those streams of upper air
    Which whirl the earth in its diurnal round
She would ascend, and win the Spirits there
    To let her join their chorus. Mortals found
That on those days the sky was calm and fair,
    And mystic snatches of harmonious sound
Wandered upon the earth where'er she passed,
And happy thoughts of hope, too sweet to last.

57

But her choice sport was, in the hours of sleep,
    To glide adown old Nilus, where he threads
Egypt and Ethiopia from the steep
    Of utmost Axumé until he spreads,
Like a calm flock of silver-fleecèd sheep,
    His waters on the plain,—and crested heads
Of cities and proud temples gleam amid,
And many a vapour-belted pyramid:—

58

By Moeris and the Mareotid lakes,
    Strewn with faint blooms like bridal-chamber floors,
Where naked boys bridling tame water-snakes,
    Or charioteering ghastly alligators,
Had left on the sweet waters mighty wakes
    Of those huge forms;—within the brazen doors
Of the great Labyrinth slept both boy and beast,
Tired with the pomp of their Osirian feast.

59

And where within the surface of the river
    The shadows of the massy temples lie,
And never are erased, but tremble ever
    Like things which every cloud can doom to die,—

Through lotus-paven canals, and wheresoever
    The works of man pierced that serenest sky
With tombs and towers and fanes,—'twas her delight
To wander in the shadow of the night.

*   *   *   *   *

1820

From

EPIPSYCHIDION

VERSES ADDRESSED TO THE NOBLE
AND UNFORTUNATE LADY

EMILIA VIVIANI

NOW IMPRISONED IN THE CONVENT OF ST. ANNE, PISA

MY Song, I fear that thou wilt find but few
  Who fitly shall conceive thy reasoning,
    Of such hard matter dost thou entertain;
  Whence, if by misadventure chance should bring
Thee to base company (as chance may do)
    Quite unaware of what thou dost contain
    I prithee comfort thy sweet self again,
My last delight: tell them that they are dull,
And bid them own that thou art beautiful.

    *   *   *   *   *

  Spouse! Sister! Angel! Pilot of the Fate
Whose course has been so starless! O too late
Belovèd, O too soon adored, by me!
For in the fields of immortality
My spirit should at first have worshipped thine,
A divine presence in a place divine;
Or should have moved beside it on this earth,
A shadow of that substance, from its birth:
But not as now.—I love thee; yes, I feel
That on the fountain of my heart a seal

Is set, to keep its waters pure and bright
For thee, since in those tears thou hast delight.
We—are we not formed, as notes of music are,
For one another, though dissimilar?
Such difference without discord as can make
Those sweetest sounds in which all spirits shake,
As trembling leaves in a continuous air.

Thy wisdom speaks in me, and bids me dare
Beacon the rocks on which high hearts are wrecked.
I never was attached to that great sect
Whose doctrine is that each one should select
Out of the crowd a mistress or a friend,
And all the rest, though fair and wise, commend
To cold oblivion; though it is in the code
Of modern morals, and the beaten road
Which those poor slaves with weary footsteps tread
Who travel to their home among the dead
By the broad highway of the world, and so
With one chained friend, perhaps a jealous foe,
The dreariest and the longest journey go.

True Love in this differs from gold and clay,
That to divide is not to take away.
Love is like understanding, that grows bright,
Gazing on many truths; 'tis like thy light,
Imagination, which from earth and sky,
And from the depths of human fantasy,
As from a thousand prisms and mirrors, fills
The universe with glorious beams, and kills
Error the worm with many a sunlike arrow
Of its reverberated lightning. Narrow
The heart that loves, the brain that contemplates,
The life that wears, the spirit that creates,
One object and one form, and builds thereby
A sepulchre for its eternity!

Mind from its object differs most in this:
Evil from good; misery from happiness;
The baser from the nobler; the impure
And frail from what is clear and must endure.
If you divide suffering or dross, you may
Diminish till it is consumed away;

If you divide pleasure and love and thought,
Each part exceeds the whole; and we know not
How much, while any yet remains unshared,
Of pleasure may be gained, of sorrow spared.
This truth is that deep well whence sages draw
The unenvied light of hope; the eternal law
By which those live to whom this world of life
Is as a garden ravaged, and whose strife
Tills for the promise of a later birth
The wilderness of this Elysian earth.

* * * * *

In many mortal forms I rashly sought
The shadow of that idol of my thought.
And some were fair—but beauty dies away:
Others were wise—but honeyed words betray;
And one was true—oh! why not true to me?
Then, as a hunted deer that could not flee,
I turned upon my thoughts, and stood at bay,
Wounded and weak and panting; the cold day
Trembled for pity of my strife and pain,—
When, like a noonday dawn, there shone again
Deliverance. One stood on my path who seemed
As like the glorious shape which I had dreamed
As is the Moon, whose changes ever run
Into themselves, to the eternal Sun;
The cold chaste Moon, the Queen of Heaven's bright isles,
Who makes all beautiful on which she smiles—
That wandering shrine of soft yet icy flame
Which ever is transformed yet still the same,
And warms not, but illumines. Young and fair
As the descended Spirit of that sphere,
She hid me, as the Moon may hide the Night
From its own darkness, until all was bright
Between the Heaven and Earth of my calm mind;
And, as a cloud charioted by the wind,
She led me to a cave in that wild place,
And sate beside me, with her downward face
Illumining my slumbers, like the Moon
Waxing and waning o'er Endymion.
And I was laid asleep, spirit and limb,
And all my being became bright or dim
As the Moon's image in a summer sea,

According as she smiled or frowned on me;
And there I lay within a chaste cold bed.
Alas! I then was nor alive nor dead:—
For at her silver voice came Death and Life,
Unmindful each of their accustomed strife,
Masked like twin babes, a sister and a brother,
The wandering hopes of one abandoned mother;
And through the cavern without wings they flew,
And cried, "Away! he is not of our crew."
I wept; and, though it be a dream, I weep.

*   *   *   *   *

The blue Aegean girds this chosen home,
With ever-changing sound and light and foam
Kissing the sifted sands and caverns hoar;
And all the winds wandering along the shore
Undulate with the undulating tide.
There are thick woods where sylvan forms abide;
And many a fountain, rivulet, and pond,
As clear as elemental diamond,
Or serene morning air. And far beyond,
The mossy tracks made by the goats and deer
(Which the rough shepherd treads but once a year)
Pierce into glades, caverns, and bowers, and halls
Built round with ivy, which the waterfalls
Illumining, with sound that never fails,
Accompany the noonday nightingales.
And all the place is peopled with sweet airs.
The light clear element which the isle wears
Is heavy with the scent of lemon-flowers,
Which floats like mist laden with unseen showers.
And falls upon the eyelids like faint sleep;
And from the moss violets and jonquils peep,
And dart their arrowy odour through the brain,
Till you might faint with that delicious pain.
And every motion, odour, beam, and tone,
With that deep music is in unison
Which is a soul within the soul: they seem
Like echoes of an antenatal dream.
It is an isle 'twixt Heaven, Air, Earth, and Sea,
Cradled, and hung in clear tranquillity;
Bright as that wandering Eden, Lucifer,
Washed by the soft blue Oceans of young air.

It is a favoured place. Famine or Blight,
Pestilence, War, and Earthquake, never light
Upon its mountain-peaks; blind vultures, they
Sail onward far upon their fatal way.
The wingèd storms, chanting their thunder-psalm
To other lands, leave azure chasms of calm
Over this isle, or weep themselves in dew,
From which its fields and woods ever renew
Their green and golden immortality.
And from the sea there rise, and from the sky
There fall, clear exhalations, soft and bright,
Veil after veil, each hiding some delight:
Which Sun or Moon or zephyr draw aside,
Till the isle's beauty, like a naked bride
Glowing at once with love and loveliness,
Blushes and trembles at its own excess.
Yet, like a buried lamp, a Soul no less
Burns in the heart of this delicious isle,
An atom of the Eternal, whose own smile
Unfolds itself, and may be felt not seen
O'er the grey rocks, blue waves, and forests green,
Filling their bare and void interstices.

* * * * *

1821

From

THE CENCI

A TRAGEDY IN FIVE ACTS

ACT IV SCENE I

* * * * *

Cenci.   Andrea! go, call my daughter;
And, if she comes not, tell her that I come.—
What sufferings? I will drag her, step by step,
Through infamies unheard of among men;
She shall stand shelterless in the broad noon
Of public scorn, for acts blazoned abroad,
One among which shall be—what? Canst thou guess?
She shall become (for what she most abhors
Shall have a fascination to entrap
Her loathing will) to her own conscious self
All she appears to others; and, when dead,
As she shall die unshrived and unforgiven,
A rebel to her father and her God,
Her corpse shall be abandoned to the hounds;
Her name shall be the terror of the earth;
Her spirit shall approach the throne of God
Plague-spotted with my curses. I will make
Body and soul a monstrous lump of ruin.

Enter ANDREA.

Andrea.   The Lady Beatrice—
Cenci.   Speak, pale slave! What said she?
Andrea.   My lord, 'twas what she looked. She said:
"Go tell my father that I see the gulf

Of Hell between us two, which he may pass;
I will not."   [Exit ANDREA.
Cenci.   Go thou quick, Lucretia,—
Tell her to come; yet let her understand
Her coming is consent: and say moreover
That, if she come not, I will curse her.   [Exit LUCRETIA.
                                                Ha!
With what but with a father's curse doth God
Panic-strike armèd Victory, and make pale
Cities in their prosperity? The world's Father
Must grant a parent's prayer against his child,
Be he who asks even what men call me.
Will not the deaths of her rebellious brothers
Awe her before I speak? for I on them
Did imprecate quick ruin, and it came.

                          Enter LUCRETIA.
Well, what? Speak, wretch!
Lucretia.   She said, "I cannot come:
Go tell my father that I see a torrent
Of his own blood raging between us."
Cenci (kneeling).   God!
Hear me! If this most specious mass of flesh
Which thou hast made my daughter; this my blood,
This particle of my divided being;
Or rather, this my bane and my disease,
Whose sight infects and poisons me; this devil
Which sprung from me as from a hell,—was meant
To aught good use; if her bright loveliness
Was kindled to illumine this dark world;
If, nursed by thy selectest dew of love,
Such virtues blossom in her as should make
The peace of life; I pray thee for my sake,
As thou the common God and Father art
Of her and me and all, reverse that doom!
Earth, in the name of God, let her food be
Poison, until she be encrusted round
With leprous stains! Heaven, rain upon her head
The blistering drops of the Maremma's dew,
Till she be speckled like a toad; parch up
Those love-enkindled lips, warp those fine limbs
To loathèd lameness! All-beholding sun,
Strike in thine envy those life-darting eyes
With thine own blinding beams!

Lucretia.   Peace! peace!
  For thine own sake unsay those dreadful words!
  When high God grants, he punishes such prayers.
Cenci (leaping up, and throwing his right hand towards Heaven).
  He does his will, I mine! This in addition:
  That, if she have a child——
Lucretia.   Horrible thought!
Cenci.   That, if she ever have a child,—and thou,
  Quick Nature! I adjure thee by thy God
  That thou be fruitful in her, and increase
  And multiply, fulfilling his command
  And my deep imprecation,—may it be
  A hideous likeness of herself! that, as
  From a distorting mirror, she may see
  Her image mixed with what she most abhors,
  Smiling upon her from her nursing breast.
  And that the child may from its infancy
  Grow day by day more wicked and deformed,
  Turning her mother's-love to misery:
  And that both she and it may live, until
  It shall repay her care and pain with hate,
  Or what may else be more unnatural—
  So he may hunt her through the clamorous scoffs
  Of the loud world to a dishonoured grave!
  Shall I revoke this curse? Go, bid her come
  Before my words are chronicled in Heaven.   [*Exit* LUCRETIA.
  I do not feel as if I were a man,
  But like a fiend appointed to chastise
  The offences of some unremembered world.
  My blood is running up and down my veins;
  A fearful pleasure makes it prick and tingle:
  I feel a giddy sickness of strange awe;
  My heart is beating with an expectation
  Of horrid joy.

*   *   *   *   *

ACT V Scene III

*   *   *   *   *

Officer.   That is the headsman's business.

[*Exeunt all but* LUCRETIA, BEATRICE, *and* GIACOMO.

Giacomo.   Have I confessed? Is it all over now?
No hope? no refuge? O weak wicked tongue
Which hast destroyed me, would that thou hadst been
Cut out and thrown to dogs first! To have killed
My father first, and then betrayed my sister—
Ay, thee! the one thing innocent and pure
In this black guilty world—to that which I
So well deserve! My wife! my little ones!
Destitute, helpless; and I—Father! God!
Canst thou forgive even the unforgiving,
When their full hearts break thus, thus?—   [*Covers his face and weeps.*
Lucretia.   Oh my child!
To what a dreadful end are we all come!
Why did I yield? Why did I not sustain
Those torments? Oh that I were all dissolved
Into these fast and unavailing tears,
Which flow and feel not!
Beatrice.   What 'twas weak to do
'Tis weaker to lament, once being done.
Take cheer! The God who knew my wrong, and made
Our speedy act the angel of his wrath,
Seems, and but seems, to have abandoned us.
Let us not think that we shall die for this.
Brother, sit near me; give me your firm hand,
You had a manly heart. Bear up! bear up!
Oh! dearest lady, put your gentle head
Upon my lap, and try to sleep awhile:
Your eyes look pale, hollow, and overworn,
With heaviness of watching and slow grief.
Come, I will sing you some low sleepy tune,
Not cheerful nor yet sad; some dull old thing,
Some outworn and unused monotony,
Such as our country gossips sing and spin,
Till they almost forget they live. Lie down!
So; that will do. Have I forgot the words?
Faith! they are sadder than I thought they were.

"False friend, wilt thou smile or weep
When my life is laid asleep?
Little cares for a smile or a tear
The clay-cold corpse upon the bier.
　　Farewell! Heigh ho!
　　What is this whispers low?
There is a snake in thy smile, my dear,
And bitter poison within thy tear.

"Sweet sleep! were death like to thee,
Or if thou couldst mortal be,
I would close these eyes of pain,
When to wake? Never again.
　　O World! Farewell!
　　Listen to the passing bell,
Listen to the passing bell,
It says, thou and I must part,
With a light and a heavy heart."

　　　　　　　　　　　　　　　　　　　[*The scene closes.*

SCENE IV

＊　　　＊　　　＊　　　＊　　　＊

Enter LUCRETIA, BEATRICE, *and* GIACOMO, *guarded.*

Beatrice.　　　　　　I hardly dare to fear
　That thou bring'st other news than a just pardon.
Camillo.　May God in heaven be less inexorable
　To the Pope's prayers than he has been to mine!
　Here is the sentence and the warrant.
Beatrice (wildly).　　　　　　　　　　　Oh
　My God! Can it be possible I have
　To die so suddenly? so young to go
　Under the obscure, cold, rotting, wormy ground?
　To be nailed down into a narrow place;
　To see no more sweet sunshine; hear no more
　Blithe voice of living thing; muse not again
　Upon familiar thoughts,—sad, yet thus lost
　How fearful! To be nothing! or to be—
　What? Oh where am I? Let me not go mad!
　Sweet Heaven, forgive weak thoughts! If there should be
　No God, no Heaven, no Earth, in the void world,
　The wide, grey, lampless, deep, unpeopled world!
　If all things then should be my father's spirit,
　His eye, his voice, his touch, surrounding me,

The atmosphere and breath of my dead life!
If sometimes, as a shape more like himself,
Even the form which tortured me on earth,
Masked in grey hairs and wrinkles, he should come,
And wind me in his hellish arms, and fix
His eyes on mine, and drag me down, down, down!
For was he not alone omnipotent
On Earth, and ever present? Even though dead
Does not his spirit live in all that breathe,
And work for me and mine still the same ruin,
Scorn, pain, despair? Who ever yet returned
To teach the laws of Death's untrodden realm?
Unjust perhaps as those which drive us now,
Oh whither, whither?
Lucretia.   Trust in God's sweet love,
The tender promises of Christ: ere night
Think we shall be in Paradise.
Beatrice.   . . . 'Tis past!
Whatever comes, my heart shall sink no more.
And yet, I know not why, your words strike chill.
How tedious, false, and cold, seem all things! I
Have met with much injustice in this world;
No difference has been made by God or man,
Or any power moulding my wretched lot,
'Twixt good or evil, as regarded me.
I am cut off from the only world I know,
From light and life and love, in youth's sweet prime.
You do well telling me to trust in God;
I hope I do trust in him: in whom else
Can any trust? And yet my heart is cold.
    [*During the latter speeches* GIACOMO *has retired conversing with*
             CAMILLO, *who now goes out;* GIACOMO *advances.*
Giacomo. Know you not, mother—sister, know you not?
Bernardo even now is gone to implore
The Pope to grant our pardon.
Lucretia.   Child, perhaps
It will be granted! We may all then live
To make these woes a tale for distant years.
Oh what a thought! It gushes to my heart
Like the warm blood.
Beatrice.   Yet both will soon be cold.
Oh trample out that thought! Worse than despair,
Worse than the bitterness of death, is hope:
It is the only ill which can find place

Upon the giddy, sharp, and narrow hour
Tottering beneath us. Plead with the swift frost
That it should spare the eldest flower of Spring:
Plead with awakening earthquake, o'er whose couch
Even now a city stands, strong, fair, and free—
Now stench and blackness yawn, like death: oh plead
With famine or wind-walking pestilence,
Blind lightning or the deaf sea; not with man!
Cruel, cold, formal man; righteous in words,
In deeds a Cain! No, mother, we must die:
Since such is the reward of innocent lives,
Such the alleviation of worst wrongs.
And, whilst our murderers live, and hard cold men,
Smiling and slow, walk through a world of tears
To death as to life's sleep, 'twere just the grave
Were some strange joy for us. Come, obscure Death,
And wind me in thine all-embracing arms!
Like a fond mother hide me in thy bosom,
And rock me to the sleep from which none wake!
Live, ye who live, subject to one another,
As we were once, who now—

BERNARDO rushes in.

Bernardo.   Oh horrible!
That tears, that looks, that hope poured forth in prayer
Even till the heart is vacant and despairs,
Should all be vain! The ministers of death
Are waiting round the doors. I thought I saw
Blood on the face of one.—What if 'twere fancy?
Soon the heart's blood of all I love on earth
Will sprinkle him, and he will wipe it off
As if 'twere only rain. O life! O world!
Cover me! let me be no more! To see
That perfect mirror of pure innocence,
Wherein I gazed, and grew happy and good,
Shivered to dust! To see thee, Beatrice,
Who mad'st all lovely thou didst look upon—
Thee, light of life—dead, dark! while I say "Sister,"
To hear I have no sister! And thou, mother,
Whose love was as a bond to all our loves—
Dead—the sweet bond broken!

Enter CAMILLO *and Guards.*
                              They come! Let me
Kiss those warm lips before their crimson leaves
Are blighted—white—cold. Say farewell, before
Death chokes that gentle voice! Oh let me hear
You speak!
Beatrice.   Farewell, my tender brother. Think
Of our sad fate with gentleness, as now:
And let mild pitying thoughts lighten for thee
Thy sorrow's load. Err not in harsh despair,
But tears and patience. One thing more, my child:
For thine own sake be constant to the love
Thou bearest us; and to the faith that I,
Though wrapped in a strange cloud of crime and shame,
Lived ever holy and unstained. And, though
Ill tongues shall wound me, and our common name
Be as a mark stamped on thine innocent brow
For men to point at as they pass, do thou
Forbear, and never think a thought unkind
Of those who perhaps love thee in their graves.
So mayst thou die as I do, fear and pain
Being subdued. Farewell! farewell! farewell!
Bernardo.   I cannot say farewell!
Camillo.   Oh Lady Beatrice!
Beatrice.   Give yourself no unnecessary pain,
My dear Lord Cardinal.—Here, mother, tie
My girdle for me, and bind up this hair
In any simple knot: ay, that does well.
And yours, I see, is coming down. How often
Have we done this for one another! now
We shall not do it any more. My lord,
We are quite ready. Well, 'tis very well.

                                        1819

From

HELLAS

A LYRICAL DRAMA

*   *   *   *   *

Enter MAHMUD *and* AHASUERUS.

Mahmud.   Thou art a man, thou sayest, even as we—
Ahasuerus.   No more.
Mahmud.   But raised above thy fellow-men
   By thought, as I by power.
Ahasuerus.   Thou sayest so.
Mahmud.   Thou art an adept in the difficult lore
   Of Greek and Frank philosophy. Thou numberest
   The flowers, and thou measurest the stars;
   Thou severest element from element;
   Thy spirit is present in the past, and sees
   The birth of this old world through all its cycles
   Of desolation and of loveliness;
   And when man was not, and how man became
   The monarch and the slave of this low sphere,
   And all its narrow circles. It is much.
   I honour thee, and would be what thou art
   Were I am not what I am. But the unborn hour,
   Cradled in fear and hope, conflicting storms,
   Who shall unveil? Nor thou, nor I, nor any
   Mighty or wise. I apprehend not
   What thou hast taught me, but I now perceive
   That thou art no interpreter of dreams;
   Thou dost not own that art, device, or God,
   Can make the future present—let it come!
   Moreover thou disdainest us and ours.
   Thou art as God, whom thou contemplatest.
Ahasuerus.   Disdain thee?—not the worm beneath my feet!

The Fathomless has care for meaner things
Than thou canst dream, and has made pride for those
Who would be what they may not, or would seem
That which they are not. Sultan, talk no more
Of thee and me, the future and the past;
But look on that which cannot change—the One,
The unborn and the undying. Earth and Ocean,
Space, and the isles of life or light that gem
The sapphire floods of interstellar air,
This firmament pavilioned upon chaos,
With all its cressets of immortal fire,
Whose outwall, bastionèd impregnably
Against the escape of boldest thoughts, repels them
As Calpe the Atlantic clouds—this Whole
Of suns and worlds and men and beasts and flowers,
With all the silent or tempestuous workings
By which they have been, are, or cease to be,
Is but a vision;—all that it inherits
Are motes of a sick eye, bubbles and dreams.
Thought is its cradle and its grave; nor less
The future and the past are idle shadows
Of thought's eternal flight—they have no being;
Nought is but that which feels itself to be.
Mahmud. What meanest thou? thy words stream like a tempest
Of dazzling mist within my brain—they shake
The earth on which I stand, and hang like night
On Heaven above me. What can they avail?
They cast on all things surest, brightest, best,
Doubt, insecurity, astonishment.
Ahasuerus. Mistake me not. All is contained in each.
Dodona's forest to an acorn's cup
Is that which has been or will be to that
Which is—the absent to the present. Thought
Alone, and its quick elements, will, passion,
Reason, imagination, cannot die;
They are what that which they regard appears,
The stuff whence mutability can weave
All that it hath dominion o'er,—worlds, worms,
Empires, and superstitions. What has thought
To do with time or place or circumstance?
Wouldst thou behold the future? Ask and have;
Knock, and it shall be opened:—look, and lo!
The coming age is shadowed on the past,
As on a glass.

Mahmud.   Wild, wilder thoughts convulse
My spirit!—Did not Mahomet the Second
Win Stamboul?
Ahasuerus.   Thou wouldst ask that giant spirit
The written fortunes of thy house and faith.
Thou wouldst cite one out of the grave to tell
How what was born in blood must die.
Mahmud.   Thy words
Have power on me! I see——
Ahasuerus.   What hearest thou?
Mahmud.   A far whisper——
Terrible silence.
Ahasuerus.   What succeeds?
Mahmud.   The sound
As of the assault of an imperial city;
The hiss of inextinguishable fire;
The roar of giant cannon; the earthquaking
Fall of vast bastions and precipitous towers;
The shock of crags shot from strange enginery;
The clash of wheels, and clang of armèd hoofs
And crash of brazen mail, as of the wreck
Of adamantine mountains; the mad blast
Of trumpets, and the neigh of raging steeds;
And shrieks of women whose thrill jars the blood;
And one sweet laugh, most horrible to hear,
As of a joyous infant waked, and playing
With its dead mother's breast:—and now more loud
The mingled battle-cry—ha! hear I not
'Εν τούτῳ νίκη!—Allah-illa-Allah?
Ahasuerus.   The sulphurous mist is raised—thou seest—
Mahmud.   A chasm,
As of two mountains, in the wall of Stamboul;
And in that ghastly breach the Islamites,
Like giants on the ruins of a world,
Stand in the light of sunrise. In the dust
Glimmers a kingless diadem, and one
Of regal port has cast himself beneath
The stream of war. Another, proudly clad
In golden arms, spurs a Tartarian barb
Into the gap, and with his iron mace
Directs the torrent of that tide of men,—
And seems—he *is*—Mahomet!
Ahasuerus.   What thou seest
Is but the ghost of thy forgotten dream;

A dream itself,—yet less, perhaps, than that
Thou call'st reality. Thou mayst behold
How cities on which Empire sleeps enthroned
Bow their towered crests to mutability.
Poised by the flood, e'en on the height thou holdest,
Thou mayst now learn how the full tide of power
Ebbs to its depths.—Inheritor of glory,
Conceived in darkness, born in blood, and nourished
With tears and toil, thou seest the mortal throes
Of that whose birth was but the same. The Past
Now stands before thee like an Incarnation
Of the To-come. Yet, wouldst thou commune with
That portion of thyself which was ere thou
Didst start for this brief race whose crown is death,—
Dissolve, with that strong faith and fervent passion
Which called it from the uncreated deep,
Yon cloud of war with its tempestuous phantoms
Of raging death; and draw with mighty will
The Imperial Shade hither.

*   *   *   *   *

CHORUS

The world's great age begins anew,
    The golden years return,
The earth doth like a snake renew
    Her winter weeds outworn:
Heaven smiles, and faiths and empires gleam
Like wrecks of a dissolving dream.

A brighter Hellas rears its mountains
    From waves serener far;
A new Peneus rolls his fountains
    Against the morning star;
Where fairer Tempes bloom, there sleep
Young Cyclads on a sunnier deep.

A loftier Argo cleaves the main,
    Fraught with a later prize;
Another Orpheus sings again,
    And loves, and weeps, and dies;
A new Ulysses leaves once more
Calypso for his native shore.

Oh! write no more the tale of Troy,
 If earth death's scroll must be—
Nor mix with Laian rage the joy
 Which dawns upon the free,
Although a subtler Sphinx renew
Riddles of death Thebes never knew.

Another Athens shall arise,
 And to remoter time
Bequeath, like sunset to the skies,
 The splendour of its prime;
And leave, if nought so bright may live,
All earth can take or Heaven can give.

Saturn and Love their long repose
 Shall burst, more bright and good
Than all who fell, than One who rose,
 Than many unsubdued:
Not gold, not blood, their altar dowers,
But votive tears and symbol flowers.

Oh cease! must hate and death return?
 Cease! must men kill and die?
Cease! drain not to its dregs the urn
 Of bitter prophecy!
The world is weary of the past,—
Oh might it die or rest at last!

1821

FRAGMENTS

The Triumph of Life

Swift as a spirit hastening to his task
  Of glory and of good, the Sun sprang forth
Rejoicing in his splendour, and the mask

  Of darkness fell from the awakened Earth.
The smokeless altars of the mountain snows
  Flamed above crimson clouds, and at the birth

Of light the Ocean's orison arose,
  To which the birds tempered their matin lay.
All flowers in field or forest which unclose

  Their trembling eyelids to the kiss of day,
Swinging their censers in the element,
  With orient incense lit by the new ray

Burned slow and inconsumably, and sent
  Their odorous sighs up to the smiling air;
And, in succession due, did continent,

  Isle, ocean, and all things that in them wear
The form and character of mortal mould,
  Rise as the Sun their father rose, to bear

Their portion of the toil which he of old
  Took as his own, and then imposed on them.
But I, whom thoughts which must remain untold

Had kept as wakeful as the stars that gem
The cone of night, now they were laid asleep
    Stretched my faint limbs beneath the hoary stem

Which an old chestnut flung athwart the steep
    Of a green Apennine. Before me fled
The night; behind me rose the day; the deep

    Was at my feet, and heaven above my head;—
When a strange trance over my fancy grew,
    Which was not slumber, for the shade it spread

Was so transparent that the scene came through
    As clear as, when a veil of light is drawn
O'er evening hills, they glimmer; and I knew

    That I had felt the freshness of that dawn
Bathe in the same cold dew my brow and hair,
    And sate as thus upon that slope of lawn

Under the selfsame bough, and heard as there
    The birds, the fountains, and the ocean, hold
Sweet talk in music through the enamoured air.
    And then a vision on my brain was rolled.

———————

As in that trance of wondrous thought I lay,
    This was the tenour of my waking dream.—
Methought I sate beside a public way

    Thick strewn with summer dust; and a great stream
Of people there was hurrying to and fro,
    Numerous as gnats upon the evening gleam,—

All hastening onward, yet none seemed to know
    Whither he went, or whence he came, or why
He made one of the multitude, and so

    Was borne amid the crowd as through the sky
One of the million leaves of summer's bier.
    Old age and youth, manhood and infancy,

Mixed in one mighty torrent did appear:
   Some flying from the thing they feared, and some
Seeking the object of another's fear.

   And others, as with steps towards the tomb,
Pored on the trodden worms that crawled beneath;
   And others mournfully within the gloom

Of their own shadow walked, and called it death;
   And some fled from it as it were a ghost,
Half fainting in the affliction of vain breath.

   But more, with motions which each other crossed,
Pursued or shunned the shadows the clouds threw,
   Or birds within the noonday ether lost,

Upon that path where flowers never grew,—
   And, weary with vain toil and faint for thirst,
Heard not the fountains whose melodious dew

   Out of their mossy cells for ever burst,
Nor felt the breeze which from the forest told
   Of grassy paths, and wood lawns interspersed

With overarching elms, and caverns cold,
   And violet-banks where sweet dreams brood;—but they
Pursued their serious folly as of old.

   And, as I gazed, methought that in the way
The throng grew wilder, as the woods of June
   When the south wind shakes the extinguished day;

And a cold glare, intenser than the noon
   But icy cold, obscured with blinding light
The sun, as he the stars. Like the young moon—

   When on the sunlit limits of the night
Her white shell trembles amid crimson air,
   And whilst the sleeping tempest gathers might—

Doth, as the herald of its coming, bear
   The ghost of her dead mother, whose dim form
Bends in dark ether from her infant's chair:

So came a chariot on the silent storm
Of its own rushing splendour; and a Shape
   So sate within, as one whom years deform,

Beneath a dusky hood and double cape,
   Crouching within the shadow of a tomb.
And o'er what seemed the head a cloud-like crape

   Was bent, a dun and faint ethereal gloom
Tempering the light. Upon the chariot beam
   A Janus-visaged Shadow did assume

The guidance of that wonder-wingèd team.
   The shapes which drew it in thick lightnings
Were lost:—I heard alone on the air's soft stream

   The music of their ever-moving wings.
All the four faces of that Charioteer
   Had their eyes banded. Little profit brings

Speed in the van and blindness in the rear,
   Nor then avail the beams that quench the sun:
Or that with banded eyes could pierce the sphere

   Of all that is, has been, or will be, done.
So ill was the car guided—but it passed
   With solemn speed majestically on.

The crowd gave way; and I arose aghast,
   Or seemed to rise, so mighty was the trance,
And saw, like clouds upon the thunder-blast,

   The million with fierce song and maniac dance
Raging around. Such seemed the jubilee
   As when, to greet some conqueror's advance,

Imperial Rome poured forth her living sea
   From senate-house and forum and theatre,
When . . . . upon the free

   Had bound a yoke which soon they stooped to bear.
Nor wanted here the just similitude
   Of a triumphal pageant, for, where'er

The chariot rolled, a captive multitude
  Was driven:—all those who had grown old in power
Or misery; all who had their age subdued

  By action or by suffering, and whose hour
Was drained to its last sand in weal or woe,
  So that the trunk survived both fruit and flower;

All those whose fame or infamy must grow
  Till the great winter lay the form and name
Of this green earth with them for ever low;

  All but the sacred few who could not tame
Their spirits to the conquerors, but, as soon
  As they had touched the world with living flame,

Fled back like eagles to their native noon,
  Or those who put aside the diadem
Of earthly thrones or gems . . .

  Were there, of Athens or Jerusalem,
Were neither 'mid the mighty captives seen,
  Nor 'mid the ribald crowd that followed them,

Nor those who went before fierce and obscene.
  The wild dance maddens in the van; and those
Who lead it, fleet as shadows on the green,

  Outspeed the chariot, and without repose
Mix with each other in tempestuous measure
  To savage music, wilder as it grows.

They, tortured by their agonizing pleasure,
  Convulsed, and on the rapid whirlwinds spun
Of that fierce Spirit whose unholy leisure

  Was soothed by mischief since the world begun,
Throw back their heads and loose their streaming hair;
  And, in their dance round her who dims the sun,

Maidens and youths fling their wild arms in air.
  As their feet twinkle, they recede,—and now,
Bending within each other's atmosphere,

Kindle invisibly, and, as they glow,
Like moths by light attracted and repelled,
    Oft to their bright destruction come and go;

Till, like two clouds into one vale impelled,
    That shake the mountains when their lightnings mingle,
And die in rain, the fiery band which held

    Their natures snap, while the shock still may tingle.
One falls, and then another, in the path,
    Senseless—nor is the desolation single.

Yet, ere I can say *where*, the chariot hath
    Passed over them—nor other trace I find
But as of foam after the ocean's wrath

    Is spent upon the desert shore. Behind,
Old men and women, foully disarrayed,
    Shake their grey hairs in the insulting wind;

And follow in the dance with limbs decayed,
    Limping to reach the light which leaves them still
Farther behind and deeper in the shade.

    But not the less with impotence of will
They wheel, though ghastly shadows interpose
    Round them and round each other, and fulfil

Their work, and in the dust from whence they rose
    Sink, and corruption veils them as they lie,
And past in these performs what . . in those.—

    Struck to the heart by this sad pageantry,
Half to myself I said: "And what is this?
    Whose shape is that within the car?—And why"

I would have added—"is all here amiss?"—
    But a voice answered—"Life!"—I turned, and knew
(O Heaven, have mercy on such wretchedness!)

    That what I thought was an old root which grew
To strange distortion out of the hill side
    Was indeed one of that deluded crew;

And that the grass which methought hung so wide
   And white was but his thin discoloured hair;
And that the holes it vainly sought to hide

     Were or had been eyes.—"If thou canst, forbear
To join the dance, which I had well forborne,"
   Said the grim Feature (of my thought aware),

"I will unfold that which to this deep scorn
   Led me and my companions, and relate
The progress of the pageant since the morn.

     "If thirst of knowledge shall not then abate,
Follow it thou even to the night; but I
   Am weary."—Then, like one who with the weight

Of his own words is staggered, wearily
   He paused; and, ere he could resume, I cried,
"First, who art thou?"—"Before thy memory,

     "I feared, loved, hated, suffered, did, and died;
And, if the spark with which Heaven lit my spirit
   Had been with purer nutriment supplied,

"Corruption would not now thus much inherit
   Of what was once Rousseau,—nor this disguise
Stain that which ought to have disdained to wear it.

     "If I have been extinguished, yet there rise
A thousand beacons from the spark I bore."
   "And who are those chained to the car?" "The wise,

"The great, the unforgotten,—they who wore
   Mitres and helms and crowns, or wreaths of light,
Signs of thought's empire over thought. Their lore

     "Taught them not this, to know themselves; their might
Could not repress the mystery within;
   And, for the morn of truth they feigned, deep night

"Caught them ere evening." "Who is he with chin
   Upon his breast, and hands crossed on his chain?"
"The child of a fierce hour. He sought to win

"The world, and lost all that it did contain
Of greatness, in its hope destroyed; and more
    Of fame and peace than virtue's self can gain

"Without the opportunity which bore
    Him on its eagle pinions to the peak
From which a thousand climbers have before

"Fallen, as Napoleon fell." I felt my cheek
Alter to see the shadow pass away
    Whose grasp had left the giant world so weak

That every pigmy kicked it as it lay.
    And much I grieved to think how power and will
In opposition rule our mortal day,

    And why God made irreconcilable
Good and the means of good; and for despair
    I half disdained mine eyes' desire to fill

With the spent vision of the times that were,
    And scarce have ceased to be.—"Dost thou behold,"
Said my guide, "those spoilers spoiled, Voltaire,

    "Frederick and Paul, Catherine and Leopold,
And hoary anarchs, demagogues, and sage—
    —— names which the world thinks always old?

"For, in the battle Life and they did wage,
    She remained conqueror. I was overcome
By my own heart alone, which neither age

    "Nor tears nor infamy, nor now the tomb,
Could temper to its object."—"Let them pass!"
    I cried. "The world and its mysterious doom

"Is not so much more glorious than it was
    That I desire to worship those who drew
New figures on its false and fragile glass

    "As the old faded."—"Figures ever new
Rise on the bubble, paint them as you may;
    We have but thrown, as those before us threw,

"Our shadows on it as it passed away.—
   But mark how chained to the triumphal chair
The mighty phantoms of an elder day.

   "All that is mortal of great Plato there
Expiates the joy and woe his Master knew not.
   The star that ruled his doom was far too fair;

"And life, where long that flower of Heaven grew not,
   Conquered that heart, by love, which gold or pain
Or age or sloth or slavery could subdue not.

   "And near him walk the . . . twain,—
The Tutor, and his Pupil whom dominion
   Followed as tame as vulture in a chain.

"The world was darkened beneath either pinion
   Of him whom from the flock of conquerors
Fame singled out for her thunder-bearing minion:—

   "The other long outlived both woes and wars,
Throned in the thoughts of men; and still had kept
   The jealous key of truth's eternal doors

"If Bacon's eagle spirit had not leapt
   Like lightning out of darkness. He compelled
The Proteus shape of Nature, as it slept,

   "To wake, and lead him to the caves that held
The treasure of the secrets of its reign.—
   See the great Bards of elder time, who quelled

"The passions which they sung, as by their strain
   May well be known: their living melody
Tempers its own contagion to the vein

   "Of those who are infected with it. I
Have suffered what I wrote, or viler pain;
   And so my words have seeds of misery—

"Even as the deeds of others, not as theirs."
   And then he pointed to a company

'Midst whom I quickly recognized the heirs
  Of Caesar's crime, from him to Constantine;
The anarch chiefs, whose force and murderous snares

  Had founded many a sceptre-bearing line,
And spread the plague of gold and blood abroad;
  And Gregory and John, and men divine

Who rose like shadows between man and God,
  Till that eclipse, still hanging over heaven,
Was worshipped, by the world o'er which they strode,

  For the true sun it quenched. "Their power was given
But to destroy," replied the leader:—"I
  Am one of those who have created, even

"If it be but a world of agony."
  "Whence camest thou, and whither goest thou?
How did thy course begin," I said, "and why?

  "Mine eyes are sick of this perpetual flow
Of people, and my heart sick of one sad thought:—
  Speak!"—"Whence I am, I partly seem to know;

"And how and by what paths I have been brought
  To this dread pass, methinks even thou mayst guess.
Why this should be, my mind can compass not;

  "Whither the conqueror hurries me, still less.
But follow thou, and from spectator turn
  Actor or victim in this wretchedness;

"And what thou wouldst be taught I then may learn
  From thee. Now listen:—In the April prime,
When all the forest tips began to burn

  "With kindling green, touched by the azure clime
Of the young season, I was laid asleep
  Under a mountain which from unknown time

"Had yawned into a cavern high and deep.
  And from it came a gentle rivulet,
Whose water, like clear air, in its calm sweep

"Bent the soft grass, and kept forever wet
The stems of the sweet flowers, and filled the grove
    With sounds which whoso hears must needs forget

"All pleasure and all pain, all hate and love,
    Which he had known before that hour of rest.
A sleeping mother then would dream not of

"Her only child who died upon her breast
At eventide; a king would mourn no more
    The crown of which his brows were dispossessed

"When the sun lingered o'er his ocean floor
    To gild his rival's new prosperity;
Thou wouldst forget thus vainly to deplore

"Ills which, if ills, can find no cure from thee.
The thought of which no other sleep will quell,
    Nor other music blot from memory;—

"So sweet and deep is the oblivious spell.
    And whether life had been before that sleep
The heaven which I imagine, or a hell

"Like this harsh world in which I wake to weep,
I know not. I arose; and for a space
    The scene of woods and waters seemed to keep,

"Though it was now broad day, a gentle trace
    Of light diviner than the common sun
Sheds on the common earth, and all the place

"Was filled with magic sounds woven into one
Oblivious melody, confusing sense
    Amid the gliding waves and shadows dun.

"And, as I looked, the bright omnipresence
    Of morning through the orient cavern flowed
And the sun's image radiantly intense

"Burned on the waters of the well that glowed
Like gold, and threaded all the forest's maze
    With winding paths of emerald fire. There stood

"Amid the sun,—as he amid the blaze
    Of his own glory, on the vibrating
Floor of the fountain paved with flashing rays—

    "A Shape all light, which with one hand did fling
Dew on the earth, as if she were the dawn,
    And the invisible rain did ever sing

"A silver music on the mossy lawn;
    And still before me on the dusky grass
Iris her many-coloured scarf had drawn.

    "In her right hand she bore a crystal glass,
Mantling with bright nepenthe; the fierce splendour
    Fell from her as she moved under the mass

"Of the deep cavern, and, with palms so tender
    Their tread broke not the mirror of its billow,
Glided along the river, and did bend her

    "Head under the dark boughs; till, like a willow,
Her fair hair swept the bosom of the stream
    That whispered with delight to be its pillow

"As one enamoured is upborne in dream
    O'er lily-paven lakes 'mid silver mist,
To wondrous music,—so this Shape might seem

    "Partly to tread the waves with feet which kissed
The dancing foam, partly to glide along
    The air which roughened the moist amethyst,

"Or the faint morning beams that fell among
    The trees, or the soft shadows of the trees.
And her feet, ever to the ceaseless song

    "Of leaves and winds and waves and birds and bees
And falling drops, moved in a measure new,—
    Yet sweet, as on the summer evening breeze,

"Up from the lake, a shape of golden dew,
    Between two rocks, athwart the rising moon,
Dances i' the wind, where never eagle flew.

"And still her feet, no less than the sweet tune
To which they moved, seemed as they moved to blot
    The thoughts of him who gazed on them. And soon

"All that was seemed as if it had been not;
    And all the gazer's mind was strewn beneath
Her feet like embers; and she, thought by thought,

"Trampled its sparks into the dust of death,—
As Day upon the threshold of the east
    Treads out the lamps of night, until the breath

"Of darkness re-illume even the least
    Of heaven's living eyes. Like day she came,
Making the night a dream. And, ere she ceased

"To move, as one between desire and shame
Suspended, I said: 'If, as it doth seem,
    Thou comest from the realm without a name

" 'Into this valley of perpetual dream,
    Show whence I came, and where I am, and why—
Pass not away upon the passing stream.'

" 'Arise and quench thy thirst,' was her reply.
And, as a shut lily stricken by the wand
    Of dewy morning's vital alchemy,

"I rose; and, bending at her sweet command,
    Touched with faint lips the cup she raised.
And suddenly my brain became as sand

"Where the first wave had more than half erased
The track of deer on desert Labrador,
    Whilst the wolf, from which they fled amazed,

"Leaves his stamp visibly upon the shore
    Until the second bursts;—so on my sight
Burst a new vision never seen before.

"And the fair shape waned in the coming light,
As veil by veil the silent splendour drops
    From Lucifer amid the chrysolite

"Of sunrise ere it tinge the mountain tops.
  And, as the presence of that fairest planet,
Although unseen, is felt by one who hopes

"That his day's path may end, as he began it,
  In that star's smile whose light is like the scent
Of a jonquil when evening breezes fan it,

"Or the soft note in which his dear lament
  The Brescian shepherd breathes, or the caress
That turned his weary slumber to content,—

"So knew I in that light's severe excess
  The presence of that shape which on the stream
Moved, as I moved along the wilderness,

"More dimly than a day-appearing dream,
  The ghost of a forgotten form of sleep,
A light of heaven whose half-extinguished beam

"Through the sick day in which we wake to weep
  Glimmers, for ever sought, for ever lost.
So did that shape its obscure tenour keep

"Beside my path, as silent as a ghost.
  But the new Vision, and the cold bright car,
With solemn speed and stunning music, crossed

"The forest; and, as if from some dread war
  Triumphantly returning, the loud million
Fiercely extolled the fortune of her star.

"A moving arch of victory the vermilion
  And green and azure plumes of Iris had
Built high over her wind-wingèd pavilion:

"And underneath ethereal glory clad
  The wilderness; and far before her flew
The tempest of the splendour which forbade

"Shadow to fall from leaf and stone. The crew
  Seemed, in that light, like atomies to dance
Within a sunbeam. Some upon the new

"Embroidery of flowers, that did enhance
The grassy vesture of the desert, played,
Forgetful of the chariot's swift advance;

"Others stood gazing, till within the shade
Of the great mountain its light left them dim;
Others outspeeded it; and others made

"Circles around it, like the clouds that swim
Round the high moon in a bright sea of air;
And more did follow, with exulting hymn,

"The chariot and the captives fettered there.
But all, like bubbles on an eddying flood,
Fell into the same track at last, and were

"Borne onward. I among the multitude
Was swept. Me sweetest flowers delayed not long;
Me, not the shadow nor the solitude;

"Me, not that falling stream's Lethean song;
Me, not the phantom of that early form
Which moved upon its motion:—but among

"The thickest billows of that living storm
I plunged, and bared my bosom to the clime
Of that cold light whose airs too soon deform.

"Before the chariot had begun to climb
The opposing steep of that mysterious dell,
Behold a wonder worthy of the rhyme

"Of him who from the lowest depths of hell,
Through every paradise and through all glory,
Love led serene, and who returned to tell

"The words of hate and awe,—the wondrous story
How all things are transfigured except Love;
For, deaf as is a sea which wrath makes hoary,

"The world can hear not the sweet notes that move
The sphere whose light is melody to lovers.
A wonder worthy of his rhyme! The grove

"Grew dense with shadows to its inmost covers;
    The earth was grey with phantoms; and the air
Was peopled with dim forms, as when there hovers

    "A flock of vampire-bats before the glare
Of the tropic sun, bringing, ere evening,
    Strange night upon some Indian isle. Thus were

"Phantoms diffused around. And some did fling
    Shadows of shadows, yet unlike themselves,
Behind them; some like eaglets on the wing

    "Were lost in the white day; others like elves
Danced in a thousand unimagined shapes
    Upon the sunny streams and grassy shelves;

"And others sate chattering like restless apes
    On vulgar hands. . . .
Some made a cradle of the ermined capes

    "Of kingly mantles; some across the tiar
Of pontiffs sate, like vultures; others played
    Under the crown which girt with empire

"A baby's or an idiot's brow, and made
    Their nests in it. The old anatomies
Sate hatching their bare broods under the shade

    "Of demon wings; and laughed from their dead eyes
To re-assume the delegated power
    Arrayed in which those worms did monarchize

"Who made this earth their charnel. Others, more
    Humble, like falcons, sate upon the fist
Of common men, and round their heads did soar;

    "Or, like small gnats and flies as thick as mist
On evening marshes, thronged about the brow
    Of lawyers, statesmen, priest, and theorist;—

"And others, like discoloured flakes of snow,
    On fairest bosoms and the sunniest hair
Fell, and were melted by the youthful glow

"Which they extinguished; and, like tears, they were
A veil to those from whose faint lids they rained
    In drops of sorrow. I became aware

"Of whence those forms proceeded which thus stained
The track in which we moved. After brief space,
From every form the beauty slowly waned.

"From every firmest limb and fairest face
The strength and freshness fell like dust, and left
    The action and the shape without the grace

"Of life. The marble brow of youth was cleft
    With care; and, in those eyes where once hope shone,
Desire, like a lioness bereft

"Of her last cub, glared ere it died. Each one
Of that great crowd sent forth incessantly
    These shadows, numerous as the dead leaves blown

"In autumn evening from a poplar tree.
    Each like himself, and each like other, were
At first. But some distorted seemed to be,—

"Obscure clouds moulded by the casual air;
And of this stuff the car's creative ray
    Wrought all the busy phantoms that were there,

"As the sun shapes the clouds. Thus on the way
    Mask after mask fell from the countenance
And form of all. And, long before the day

"Was old, the joy which waked like heaven's glance
The sleepers in the oblivious valley died;
    And some grew weary of the ghastly dance,

"And fell, as I have fallen, by the way-side;—
    Those soonest from whose forms most shadows passed,
And least of strength and beauty did abide.

" 'Then, what is life?' I cried."—

                        1822

The Boat on the Serchio

OUR boat is asleep on Serchio's stream,
Its sails are folded like thoughts in a dream;
The helm sways idly, hither and thither.
  Dominic, the boatman, has brought the mast
  And the oars, and the sails; but 'tis sleeping fast
Like a beast, unconscious of its tether.

The stars burnt out in the pale blue air,
And the thin white moon lay withering there;
To tower, and cavern, and rift, and tree
The owl and the bat fled drowsily.
Day had kindled the dewy woods,
  And the rocks above and the stream below,
And the vapours in their multitudes,
  And the Apennines' shroud of summer snow,
And clothed with light of aëry gold
The mists in their eastern caves uprolled.

Day had awakened all things that be;—
The lark and the thrush and the swallow free,
  And the milkmaid's song, and the mower's scythe,
And the matin-bell, and the mountain bee.
Fireflies were quenched on the dewy corn;
  Glow-worms went out on the river's brim,
  Like lamps which a student forgets to trim;
    The beetle forgot to wind his horn;
    The crickets were still in the meadow and hill.
    Like a flock of rooks at a farmer's gun,
    Night's dreams and terrors, every one,
    Fled from the brains which are their prey
    From the lamp's death to the morning ray.

All rose to do the task He set to each
  Who shaped us to his ends and not our own.
The million rose to learn, and one to teach
  What none yet ever knew, nor can be known;
    And many rose
  Whose woe was such that fear became desire.
Melchior and Lionel were not among those;

They from the throng of men had stepped aside,
And made their home under the green hillside.
It was that hill whose intervening brow
   Screens Lucca from the Pisan's envious eye;
Which the circumfluous plain waving below,
    Like a wide lake of green fertility,
      With streams and fields and marshes bare,
    Divides from the far Apennines, which lie
Islanded in the immeasurable air.

"What think you, as she lies in her green cove,
Our little sleeping boat is dreaming of?"
"If morning dreams are true, why I should guess
That she was dreaming of our idleness,
    And of the miles of watery way
We should have led her by this time of day."

     "Never mind!" said Lionel.
    "Give care to the winds; they can bear it well
About yon poplar tops. And see!
The white clouds are driving merrily,
And the stars we miss this morn will light
More willingly our return to-night.
How it whistles, Dominic's long black hair;
List my dear fellow; the breeze blows fair:
Hear how it sings into the air."

    "Of us and of our lazy motions,"
      Impatiently said Melchior,
    "If I can guess a boat's emotions;
      And how we ought, two hours before,
To have been the devil knows where."
And then, in such transalpine Tuscan
As would have killed a Della-Cruscan,

       .   .   .   .   .

So, Lionel according to his art
   Weaving his idle words, Melchior said:
   "She dreams that we are not yet out of bed;
We'll put a soul into her, and a heart
Which like a dove chased by a dove shall beat."

       .   .   .   .   .

"Ay, heave the ballast overboard,
And stow the eatables in the aft locker."
"Would not this keg be best a little lowered?"
"No, now all's right." "Those bottles of warm tea—
(Give me some straw)—must be stowed tenderly;
Such as we used, in summer after six,
To cram in great-coat pockets, and to mix
Hard eggs and radishes and rolls at Eton,
And, couched on stolen hay in those green harbours
Farmers called gaps, and we schoolboys called arbours,
Would feast till eight."

    . . . . . .

With a bottle in one hand,
As if his very soul were at a stand,
Lionel stood—when Melchior brought him steady:—
"Sit at the helm—fasten this sheet—all ready!"

The chain is loosed, the sails are spread,
    The living breath is fresh behind,
As, with dews and sunrise fed,
    Comes the laughing morning wind.
The sails are full, the boat makes head
Against the Serchio's torrent fierce;
Then flags with intermitting course,
    And hangs upon the wave, and stems
    The tempest of the . . . .
Which fervid from its mountain source
Shallow, smooth, and strong, doth come.
Swift as fire, tempestuously
It sweeps into the affrighted sea.
In morning's smile its eddies coil;
Its billows sparkle, toss, and boil;
Torturing all its quiet light
Into columns fierce and bright.

        The Serchio, twisting forth
Between the marble barriers which it clove
    At Ripafratta, leads through the dread chasm
The wave that died the death which lovers love,
    Living in what it sought. As if this spasm
Had not yet passed, the toppling mountains cling.
    But the clear stream in full enthusiasm

Pours itself on the plain; then, wandering
    Down one clear path of effluence crystalline,
Sends its superfluous waves that they may fling
    At Arno's feet tribute of corn and wine.
Then, through the pestilential deserts wild
    Of tangled marsh and woods of stunted pine,
It rushes to the ocean.

1821

Ginevra

WILD, pale, and wonder-stricken, even as one
Who staggers forth into the air and sun
From the dark chamber of a mortal fever,—
Bewildered, and incapable, and ever
Fancying strange comments, in her dizzy brain,
Of usual shapes, till the familiar train
Of objects and of persons passed like things
Strange as a dreamer's mad imaginings,—
Ginevra from the nuptial altar went;
The vows to which her lips had sworn assent
Rung in her brain still with a jarring din,
Deafening the lost intelligence within.

And so she moved under the bridal veil,
Which made the paleness of her cheek more pale,
And deepened the faint crimson of her mouth,
And darkened her dark locks, as moonlight doth;
And of the gold and jewels glittering there
She scarce felt conscious, but the weary glare
Lay like a chaos of unwelcome light,
Vexing the sense with gorgeous undelight,
A moonbeam in the shadow of a cloud
Were less heavenly fair. Her face was bowed;
And, as she passed, the diamonds in her hair
Were mirrored in the polished marble stair
Which led from the cathedral to the street;
And ever as she went her light fair feet
Erased these images.

The bridemaidens who round her thronging came:—
Some with a sense of self-rebuke and shame,

Envying the unenviable; and others
Making the joy which should have been another's
Their own by gentle sympathy; and some
Sighing to think of an unhappy home;
Some few admiring what can ever lure
Maidens to leave the heaven serene and pure
Of parents' smiles for life's great cheat—a thing
Bitter to taste, sweet in imagining.

But they are all dispersed—and lo! she stands
Looking in idle grief on her white hands,
Alone within the garden now her own,
And through the sunny air, with jangling tone,
The music of the merry marriage-bells,
Killing the azure silence, sinks and swells;—
Absorbed like one within a dream who dreams
That he is dreaming, until slumber seems
A mockery of itself—when suddenly
Antonio stood before her, pale as she.
With agony, with sorrow, and with pride,
He lifted his wan eyes upon the bride,
And said—"Is this thy faith?" And then, as one
Whose sleeping face is stricken by the sun
With light like a harsh voice, which bids him rise
And look upon his day of life with eyes
Which weep in vain that they can dream no more,
Ginevra saw her lover; and forbore
To shriek or faint, and checked the stifling blood
Rushing upon her heart, and unsubdued
Said: "Friend, if earthly violence or ill,
Suspicion, doubt, or the tyrannic will
Of parents, chance or custom, time or change,
Or circumstance or terror or revenge,
Or wildered looks or words, or evil speech,
With all their stings and venom, can impeach
Our love,—we love not. If the grave, which hides
The victim from the tyrant, and divides
The cheek that whitens from the eyes that dart
Imperious inquisition to the heart
That is another's, could dissever ours,
We love not."—"What! do not the silent hours
Beckon thee to Gherardi's bridal bed?
Is not that ring"——a pledge, he would have said,
Of broken vows. But she with patient look

The golden circle from her finger took,
And said: "Accept this token of my faith,
The pledge of vows to be absolved by death.
And I am dead, or shall be soon—my knell
Will mix its music with that merry bell;
Does it not sound as if they sweetly said
'We toll a corpse out of the marriage bed?'
The flowers upon my bridal chamber strewn
Will serve unfaded for my bier—so soon
That even the dying violet will not die
Before Ginevra." The strong fantasy
Had made her accents weaker and more weak,
And quenched the crimson life upon her cheek,
And glazed her eyes, and spread an atmosphere
Round her which chilled the burning noon with fear,
Making her but an image of the thought
Which, like a prophet or a shadow, brought
News of the terrors of the coming time.
Like an accuser branded with the crime
He would have cast on a belovèd friend,
Whose dying eyes reproach not to the end
The pale betrayer—he then with vain repentance
Would share, he cannot now avert, the sentence—
Antonio stood, and would have spoken; when
The compound voice of women and of men
Was heard approaching. He retired; while she
Was led amid the admiring company
Back to the palace,—and her maidens soon
Changed her attire for the afternoon,
And left her at her own request to keep
An hour of quiet and rest. Like one asleep
With open eyes and folded hands she lay,
Pale in the light of the declining day.

  Meanwhile the day sinks fast, the sun is set,
And in the lighted hall the guests are met.
The beautiful looked lovelier in the light
Of love and admiration and delight
Reflected from a thousand hearts and eyes,
Kindling a momentary paradise.
This crowd is safer than the silent wood,
Where love's own doubts disturb the solitude.
On frozen hearts the fiery rain of wine
Falls, and the dew of music more divine

Tempers the deep emotions of the time
To spirits cradled in a sunny clime.
IIow many meet who never yet have met,
To part too soon, but never to forget!
How many saw the beauty, power, and wit,
Of looks and words which ne'er enchanted yet!
But life's familiar veil was now withdrawn.
As the world leaps before an earthquake's dawn,
And, unprophetic of the coming hours,
The matin winds from the expanded flowers
Scatter their hoarded incense, and awaken
The earth, until the dewy sleep is shaken
From every living heart which it possesses,
Through seas and winds, cities and wildernesses,—
As if the future and the past were all
Treasured i' the instant; so Gherardi's hall
Laughed in the mirth of its lord's festival;—
Till some one asked "Where is the Bride?" And then
A bridesmaid went; and ere she came again
A silence fell upon the guests—a pause
Of expectation, as when beauty awes
All hearts with its approach, though unbeheld;
Then wonder; and then fear that wonder quelled:—
For whispers passed from mouth to ear which drew
The colour from the hearer's cheeks, and flew
Louder and swifter round the company.
And then Gherardi entered with an eye
Of ostentatious trouble, and a crowd
Surrounded him, and some were weeping loud.

They found Ginevra dead: if it be death
To lie without motion or pulse or breath,
With waxen cheeks, and limbs cold, stiff, and white,
And open eyes whose fixed and glassy light
Mocked at the speculation they had owned;
If it be death when there is felt around
A smell of clay, a pale and icy glare,
And silence, and a sense that lifts the hair
From the scalp to the ankles, as it were
Corruption from the spirit passing forth,
And giving all it shrouded to the earth,
And leaving, as swift lightning in its flight,
Ashes and smoke and darkness. In our night
Of thought, we know thus much of death,—no more

Than the unborn dream of *our* life, before
Their barks are wrecked on its inhospitable shore.

The marriage-feast and its solemnity
Was turned to funeral pomp. The company,
With heavy hearts and looks, broke up. Nor they
Who loved the dead went weeping on their way
Alone; but sorrow mixed with sad surprise
Loosened the springs of pity in all eyes,
In which that form whose fate they weep in vain
Will never, thought they, kindle smiles again.
The lamps, which, half extinguished in their haste,
Gleamed few and faint o'er the abandoned feast,
Showed as it were within the vaulted room
A cloud of sorrow hanging, as if gloom
Had passed out of men's minds into the air.
Some few yet stood around Gherardi there,
Friends and relations of the dead;—and he,
A loveless man, accepted torpidly
The consolation that he wanted not;
Awe in the place of grief within him wrought.
Their whispers made the solemn silence seem
More still. Some wept;
Some melted into tears without a sob;
And some, with hearts that might be heard to throb,
Leant on the table, and at intervals
Shuddered to hear through the deserted halls
And corridors the thrilling shrieks which came
Upon the breeze of night, that shook the flame
Of every torch and taper as it swept
From out the chamber where the women kept.
Their tears fell on the dear companion cold
Of pleasures now departed. Then was knolled
The bell of death; and soon the priests arrived,—
And, finding Death their penitent had shrived,
Returned, like ravens from a corse whereon
A vulture has just feasted to the bone.
And then the mourning women came.

.   .   .   .   .

1821

The Dirge

OLD Winter was gone
In his weakness back to the mountains hoar;
And the Spring came down
From the planet that hovers upon the shore
Where the sea of sunlight encroaches
On the limits of wintry night.
If the land and the air and the sea
Rejoice not when Spring approaches,
We did not rejoice in thee,
Ginevra!

She is still, she is cold,
On the bridal couch!
One step to the white death-bed,
And one to the bier,
And one to the charnel, and one—oh where?
The dark arrow fled
In the noon.
Ere the sun through heaven once more has rolled,
The rats in her heart
Will have made their nest,
And the worms be alive in her golden hair.
While the Spirit that guides the sun
Sits throned in his flaming chair,
She shall sleep.

1821

To Byron

O MIGHTY mind, in whose deep stream this age
Shakes like a reed in the unheeding storm,
Why dost thou curb not thine own sacred rage?

1818

The Lake's Margin

THE fierce beasts of the woods and wildernesses
Track not the steps of him who drinks of it;
For the light breezes, which for ever fleet
Around its margin, heap the sand thereon.

1818

The Vine-Shroud

FLOURISHING vine, whose kindling clusters glow
    Beneath the autumnal sun, none taste of thee;
For thou dost shroud a ruin, and below
    The rotting bones of dead antiquity.

1818

Torpor

MY head is heavy, my limbs are weary,
And it is not life that makes me move.

1820

From

PROLOGUE TO HELLAS

*   *   *   *   *

CHRIST
                Almighty Father!
Low-kneeling at the feet of Destiny

. . . .

There are two fountains in which spirits weep
When mortals err, Discord and Slavery named,
And with their bitter dew two Destinies
Filled each their irrevocable urns. The third,
Fiercest and mightiest, mingled both, and added
Chaos and Death, and slow Oblivion's lymph,
And hate and terror, and the poisoned rain

. . . .

The Aurora of the nations. By this brow
Whose pores wept tears of blood; by these wide wounds;
By this imperial crown of agony;
By infamy and solitude and death,
For this I underwent; and by the pain
Of pity for those who would . . for me
The unremembered joy of a revenge,
For this I felt; by Plato's sacred light,
Of which my spirit was a burning morrow;
By Greece, and all she cannot cease to be,
Her quenchless words, sparks of immortal truth,
Stars of all night—her harmonies and forms,

Echoes and shadows of what Love adores
In thee; I do compel thee, send forth Fate,
Thy irrevocable child! Let her descend,
A seraph-wingèd Victory [arrayed]
In tempest of the omnipotence of God
Which sweeps through all things.
From hollow leagues, from Tyranny which arms
Adverse miscreeds and emulous anarchies
To stamp, as on a wingèd serpent's seed,
Upon the name of Freedom; from the storm
Of faction, which like earthquake shakes and sickens
The solid heart of enterprise; from all
By which the holiest dreams of highest spirits
Are stars beneath the dawn . . .
. . . . She shall arise
Victorious as the world arose from Chaos!
And, as the Heavens and the Earth arrayed
Their presence in the beauty and the light
Of thy first smile, O Father; as they gather
The spirit of thy love, which paves for them
Their path o'er the abyss, till every sphere
Shall be one living Spirit; so shall Greece—

SATAN

Be as all things beneath the empyrean,
Mine! Art thou eyeless like old Destiny,
Thou mockery-king, crowned with a wreath of thorns—
Whose sceptre is a reed, the broken reed
Which pierces thee, whose throne a chair of scorn?
For seest thou not beneath this crystal floor
The innumerable worlds of golden light
Which are my empire, and the least of them
. . . which thou wouldst redeem from me?
Know'st thou not them my portion?
Or wouldst rekindle the . . strife
Which our great Father then did arbitrate
When he assigned to his competing sons
Each his apportioned realm?
                              Thou Destiny,
Thou who art mailed in the omnipotence
Of Him who sends thee forth, whate'er thy task,
Speed, spare not to accomplish! and be mine
Thy trophies, whether Greece again become
The fountain in the desert whence the earth

Shall drink of freedom, which shall give it strength
To suffer, or a gulf of hollow death
To swallow all delight, all life, all hope.
Go, thou Vicegerent of my will, no less
Than of the Father's. But, lest thou shouldst faint,
The wingèd hounds Famine and Pestilence
Shall wait on thee; the hundred-forkèd snake
Insatiate Superstition still shall . . .
The earth behind thy steps; and War shall hover
Above, and Fraud shall gape below, and Change
Shall flit before thee on her dragon wings,
Convulsing and consuming. And I add
Three vials of the tears which demons weep
When virtuous spirits through the gate of Death
Pass triumphing over the thorns of life,—
Sceptres and crowns, mitres and swords and snares,
Trampling in scorn, like Him and Socrates.
The first is Anarchy; when Power and Pleasure,
Glory and science and security,
On Freedom hang like fruit on the green tree,
Then pour it forth, and men shall gather ashes.
The second Tyranny—

CHRIST

Obdurate spirit!
Thou seest but the past in the To-come.
Pride is thy error and thy punishment.
Boast not thine empire, dream not that thy worlds
Are more than furnace-sparks or rainbow-drops
Before the Power that wields and kindles them.
True greatness asks not space; true excellence
Lives in the Spirit of all things that live,
Which lends it to the worlds thou callest thine.

.   .   .   .   .

MAHOMET

Haste thou, and fill the waning crescent
With beams as keen as those which pierced the shadow
Of Christian night rolled back upon the West
When the orient moon of Islam rode in triumph
From Tmolus to the Acroceraunian snow.

.   .   .   .   .

                                   Wake, thou Word
Of God, and from the throne of Destiny
Even to the utmost limit of thy way
May Triumph

                    .   .   .   .   .

         Be thou a curse on them whose creed
Divides and multiplies the most high God!

                                        1821

SONNET TO BYRON

[I AM afraid these verses will not please you, but]
If I esteemed you less, Envy would kill
   Pleasure, and leave to Wonder and Despair
The ministration of the thoughts that fill
   The mind which, like a worm whose life may share
A portion of the unapproachable,
   Marks your creations rise as fast and fair
As perfect worlds at the Creator's will.
But such is my regard that nor your power
   To soar above the heights where others [climb],
Nor fame, that shadow of the unborn hour
   Cast from the envious future on the time,
   Move one regret for his unhonoured name
Who dares these words:—the worm beneath the sod
May lift itself in homage of the God.

               1821

INDEX OF FIRST LINES

(Reference to abridged poems is by first line of excerpt.)